SALES PROGRAM MANAGEMENT: FORMULATION AND IMPLEMENTATION

McGRAW-HILL SERIES IN MARKETING

Consulting Editor
Charles Schewe
University of Massachusetts

Benson P. Shapiro

Graduate School of Business Administration
Harvard University

SALES PROGRAM MANAGEMENT: FORMULATION AND IMPLEMENTATION

McGRAW-HILL BOOK COMPANY

New York   St. Louis   San Francisco   Auckland   Bogota
Düsseldorf   Johannesburg   London   Madrid   Mexico
Montreal   New Delhi   Panama   Paris   São Paulo
Singapore   Sydney   Tokyo   Toronto

SALES PROGRAM MANAGEMENT:
FORMULATION AND IMPLEMENTATION

67890DODO 8321

This book was set in Optima by Black Dot, Inc. The editors
were William J. Kane and Matthew Cahill; the designer was
Joseph Gillians; the production supervisor was Charles Hess.
The section illustrations were done by Cheryl Cooper; new
drawings were done by J & R Services, Inc.
R. R. Donnelley & Sons Company was printer and binder.

Library of Congress Cataloging in Publication Data

Shapiro, Benson P
Sales program management.

Includes bibliographies and index.
1. Sales management. I. Title.
HF5438.4.S48   658.8'1   76-14792
ISBN 0-07-056413-2

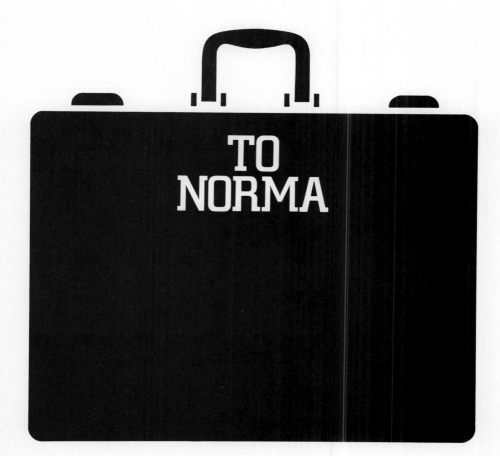

CONTENTS

SECTION FOUR
ACCOUNT MANAGEMENT

SECTION FIVE
SALES COSTS AND BUDGETS

SECTION SIX
IMPLEMENTING THE SALES PROGRAM

SECTION SEVEN
FIELD SALES MANAGEMENT

SECTION EIGHT
COMPENSATION, EVALUATION, AND MOTIVATION

SECTION NINE
ORGANIZING THE SALES EFFORT

SECTION TEN
RECRUITING AND SELECTION

ix

SECTION ELEVEN
TRAINING

SECTION TWELVE
LEGAL AND ETHICAL CONSIDERATIONS

SECTION THIRTEEN
REVIEW

PREFACE

This book is intended to provide the student with a comprehensive, in-depth view of sales management in a broad sense. Sales management has traditionally focused upon the management of the sales force. While this is an important function, it occupies only one-half of this book. The other half is devoted to defining the role of personal selling as an element of the marketing mix. This is where the book begins.

The first five sections of the text are concerned with the formulation of the sales program. Section One places the field of sales management in perspective and provides an overview of careers in sales management. Section Two introduces the concept of the sales program and considers personal selling as a part of the marketing mix. Here, the emphasis is on the efficient and effective use of personal selling as a marketing tool.

The following three sections are designed to provide the student with a more detailed view of sales program formulation. Section Three is devoted to the efficient allocation of the personal selling effort across geography, products, and customers. It also includes textual notes on determining the size of the sales force and on forecasting sales. The Honeywell Information Systems case enables the student to relate marketing strategy to deployment in a most exciting situation.

Then, the focus moves to account management—all of the activities involved in building account relationships and generating sales volume. Selling and sales promotion receive special treatment. The student has the chance to role-play in order to gain an understanding of the selling process.

The final section concerning sales program formulation deals with sales costs and budgets. Until this point, the primary emphasis has been on setting objectives—the benefits side of the analysis. Here, the emphasis is on the cost side. One major decision which receives special attention is the choice between a company sales force and independent representatives. The development and use of the sales information system is also the subject of a separate textual note.

When the student completes Section Five, he or she has had exposure to all aspects of the formulation of the sales program. The focus then shifts from formulation to implementation. Section Six is a short overview of the implementation process.

Section Seven discusses field sales management. Because of the face-to-face nature of the decisions and the realism of the material, the student gains a "hands-on" exposure to activities in field sales management. He or she learns the complexities of field sales management and the importance of strong, direct supervision.

Sections Eight and Nine focus on other aspects of sales force management. Section Eight is devoted to compensation, evaluation, and motivation. Of importance in this section is the opportunity to study the Fieldcrest Division sales force in depth so that the student learns how to relate the compensation system to the total set of motivational programs and the marketing strategy of the company.

Section Nine, which is devoted to sales organization, is perhaps the most challenging section of the book. Among the highlights in this section are the Heinz, U.S.A., and General Foods Corporation cases. General Foods, in particular, challenges even the most capable student.

Once the student has learned how to manage an ongoing sales force, he or she is ready to confront the building of the sales force—recruiting and selection, and training. While recruiting and selection come before sales force management chronologically, the subject is introduced after sales force management because the student needs to become familiar with existing problems before he or she can learn how to avoid them through astute hiring decisions. Section Ten considers recruiting and selection, and Section Eleven is concerned with training.

Section Twelve introduces the important legal and ethical concerns which face sales managers. The material enables these issues to be confronted openly and honestly in the classroom. Finally, Section Thirteen is an integrative review of all that has gone before.

The book is clearly concerned with the total management of the personal selling effort. It consists of both cases and textual notes. Each section tends to begin with simpler cases which demonstrate basic sales management principles. Then, more complex cases are presented to provide the student with a broader and deeper educational experience.

The cases and textual notes cover companies ranging from a few million dollars in annual sales to a few billion dollars. Manufacturers, wholesalers, and independent representatives are considered. Several of the cases focus on situations in which services and not physical products are sold. A wide variety of consumer and industrial goods are also discussed.

The book is not generally concerned with sales forces which sell to the ultimate consumer. Thus, door-to-door and retail floor selling are not emphasized. On the other hand, much of the material in this text is relevant to such situations.

The textual material is not intended to be a complete exposition of each subject. Instead its purpose is to ground the student in basic principles as well as to offer a broad exposure to business practice. In addition, the textual material introduces the student to a rich set of conceptual frameworks which can be used in a wide variety of situations. The bibliographies at the end of each textual note enable the student to pursue each subject in greater depth.

The book was written for the graduate student and upper-level undergraduate student who has been exposed to basic marketing and control or accounting courses. The material in the book provides the student with selling experience and the analytical tools that he or she will need to confront the cases. The prime objectives of this text have been to provide the student with a broad exposure to all aspects of sales management, an in-depth understanding of key principles and major issues, and a pragmatic point of view about the field. The book strives for realism throughout.

xiii

ACKNOWLEDGMENTS

Just as "no man is an island, entire of itself," no author can claim self-sufficiency in writing a book. Many people have contributed to this one. While it is possible to thank only a relative few, the help of all is greatly appreciated.

Several of the cases began as student reports authored by Edward Bullard, F. Paul Clipp, Robert Ihrie, Jr., Warren Nelson, Gene Payne, and Dirck Schou. Many people at the Harvard Business School labored long and hard so that the material that make up the cases and notes are managed well. I owe special appreciation to those who have kindly and competently supported my efforts. Sam Zanghi and his fine audiovisual crew made possible the videotape techniques used in some of the cases presented here and in others used in the sales management course at the Harvard Business School.

Many of my colleagues provided assistance in developing the material in the book and the course upon which it is based. Milt Brown, Ted Levitt, and Ralph Sorenson helped teach me about the organization of a course. Among those who helped to develop the outline of the course and book were Milt Brown, Bob Buzzell, Ted Levitt, and Walt Salmon. Harvard Business School and its marketing area were most kind in providing support for the developmental work necessary for the course. For this I thank Deans Fouraker, Lombard, Salmon, McArthur, and Skinner, as well as Area Chairman Bob Buzzell.

Special thanks are extended to the companies and their management who cooperated in my case development activities. The kindness of the companies, both anonymous and identified, makes the case method possible. Deep appreciation must also be given to the many sales management students in the Master of Business Administration program who cooperated in our joint learning. I am sure that I learned more than any *other* student in the class from the active, enthusiastic discussions they provided. Many executives contributed personally to the development of the thinking underlying the book. My consulting clients were especially kind in providing experience for me and adding practical insight to conceptual frameworks. Of special note among these is Mel Margolin, who provided much implicit encouragement and explicit wisdom. Another executive who contributed greatly to several of the cases and some of the notes is Russell Taylor of Taylor Associates.

A word of thanks is due to Professor Roy A. Klages of the State University of New York at Albany, Professor James E. Littlefield of the University of North Carolina, and Professor Thomas F. Stroh of Florida Atlantic University for their reviews of the manuscript and suggestions.

Finally, I must express great appreciation and gratitude to Nancy Davis, associate in research. Nancy capably wrote many of the cases and some of the notes, unsplit the infinitives, and performed yeoman editorial work on other material. Bonnie Greene patiently and graciously provided strong secretarial support, including the typing of the many drafts of the manuscript. My loving wife, Norma, and our three children, Mary Ann, Joseph, and Paul, made this book possible by sharing the time I owed to them and also made it worthwhile.

Benson P. Shapiro

An Introduction to the Case Method

The case method of management instruction is based on the belief that management is a skill more than it is a collection of techniques or concepts. The best way to learn a skill is to practice in simulated situations. Thus, the swimmer swims, the pianist plays the piano, etc. Because it is impractical for the student manager to manage a company, the case method provides a vehicle for simulation.

While there is no "one ideal way to approach a case," some generalities can be drawn. Students gain the most by immersing themselves in the case and actively playing the role of protagonist. The protagonist is usually one manager, but is sometimes a group. By actively studying the case, students begin to learn how to analyze a management situation and develop a plan of action. By participating in an involved manner in the case discussion, students learn to commit themselves to a position easily, and to express that position articulately. Management decision making consists, at the very core, of the processes of analysis, choice, and persuasion.

The case method is demanding of both teachers and students. Students who are involved in each case analysis and discussion, and who attempt to generalize their learning across cases, gain the most from the process. Each student should strive to develop the ability to ask "the right questions about each case." The instructor may provide specific questions for each case. The following questions are among those which are generally relevant to all cases:

Who is the protagonist?

What are his or her objectives (implicit or explicit)?

What decisions (implicit or explicit) must I make?

What problems, opportunities, and risks do I, as the protagonist, face?

What evidence do I have to help me make the decision? Is the evidence reliable and unbiased? Can I improve it?

What alternative courses of action are open to me?

What criteria should I use to judge the alternatives?

What action should I take?

How should I convince others that my approach is best?

What did I learn from this case?

How does it relate to past cases?

Section
ONE
Introduction

ONE   A Concept of Sales Management

Sales management can be thought of as consisting of three processes: (1) formulation of a sales program; (2) development of systems, policies, and procedures to implement the sales program; and (3) actual implementation at the field sales management level. These processes are closely related both in concept and practice. In a large organization, the formulation of the program is generally the responsibility of the highest sales and marketing executives, usually holding the titles of national sales manager (or sales vice president) and marketing vice president. The next step, development of the methods of implementing the program, is generally the responsibility of top-level sales management, often supported by staff executives. The actual implementation is handled by field sales managers with titles such as district or regional sales manager. In a smaller company, all of these functions might be performed by one or a few people.

If the total process is to succeed, each of the three parts must function well individually and must be coordinated into a unified whole. The program must be sound and implementable. The systems, policies, and procedures must support the program while being reasonable in terms of the realities in the field. Even if the program and its support systems, policies, and procedures are well constructed and appropriate, they will not succeed if field implementation is weak.

One major problem in approaching sales management is that the three processes cannot be considered separately. On the other hand, without concentrated emphasis on each part of the total process, we will be unable to understand the segments of the process. Thus, we will constantly be walking a tightrope between too narrow a view (learning much about one element of sales management and little about how it relates to the rest of the process) and too broad a perspective (concerning ourselves with the generalities of integration without confronting any specific issue in enough depth to understand it).

The course is divided into two parts. The first is the formulation of the sales program. The second is implementation of the program—managing the sales force. It includes both the development of management systems, policies, and procedures and their use in the field. The actual implementation is concentrated in the section on field sales management. After the section on formulation of the sales program, we consider management of an existing sales force. This is followed by discussion of the process of building a sales force. Since the process of building comes chronologically before the process of managing, it is reasonable to ask why they are reversed in the course. The answer is that it is easier to understand the key issues involved in the building of the sales force after one has been exposed in depth to the problems of managing the sales force. Without exposure to typical management problems, one cannot know the situations to be avoided in recruiting, selecting, and training.

TWO   Sales Management Career Paths

6

This note provides the student with a perspective on the nature of sales management positions and career paths.

CAREER PATHS

Exhibit 1 lists the typical job titles in a sales force. Small companies or divisions will, of course, not have all of the titles shown.

Young people usually enter a sales job for one of three reasons: (1) for a permanent career, (2) for entry into sales management, or (3) for entry into marketing management. The subject of sales as a career is beyond the scope of this note.

A sales job is often the only way to enter a sales management career. Most sales managers would doubt the credibility of sales managers who have not "carried the bag" or "pounded the pavement" themselves. Salespeople also expect to report to a sales manager with some experience. The concern of the sales managers and salespeople seems to be a valid one. It is important for the sales manager to be experienced in dealing with prospects and customers from a salesperson's position. Exposure to problems of dealing with one's own company is also valuable. In addition, it is useful for the new sales manager to have experienced the feelings and concerns of a salesperson in a very intimate way. That is likely to come only from actual experience.

Many companies expect young people who desire to enter marketing management to spend some time in the field as salespersons. A

Exhibit 1 TYPICAL JOB TITLES

Top-level marketing management

Marketing vice president Typically the top marketing executive in the company or division.

Sales vice president Sometimes another title for marketing vice president but sometimes the top sales executive who will report to either the president or the marketing vice president.

Top-level line sales management

National sales manager The top sales executive responsible for all sales force–related activities.

General sales manager Another title for national sales manager.

Middle-level line sales management

National account sales manager Usually responsible for a separate, high-quality sales force which calls on national accounts. Often the only person in the national account sales force and responsible for actual selling, but the accounts are so large that the position needs a relatively high-level manager.

Regional, divisional, or zone sales manager These are titles for high-level field sales managers to whom other field sales managers report. Occasionally, the titles are used for first-level sales management jobs in which salespeople are managed.

Market sales manager A sales manager responsible for salespeople calling on a specific group of accounts. Often this position has marketing responsibility in addition to sales management and perhaps sales responsibility. A company which specializes its sales force by market will have one market sales manager to head each separate sales force.

Product sales manager The same as market sales manager except that the job is organized around a product line instead of a customer category. Both positions are more likely to occur in industrial companies than in consumer-goods companies. The product sales managers are usually more involved with product-oriented decisions than are market managers.

7

Lower-level line sales management

District or field sales manager The first line sales manager to whom the salespeople report.

Upper-level sales positions

Account executive, key account salesperson, national account salesperson, major account salesperson These people are responsible for selling to major accounts. In the consumer-goods field, the title sometimes involves chain stores, meaning usually the three large national general merchandise chains (Sears, Penney, Montgomery Ward), food chains, or mass merchandisers such as discount department stores.

Typical sales positions

Salesperson, field salesperson, territory manager, account representative, sales representative All are typical titles for the salesperson responsible for selling and servicing a variety of accounts.

Staff sales management

These positions are usually functionally oriented and include titles such as manager of sales training, sales analyst, etc. The typical staff responsibilities include training, recruiting, and sales analysis. More general staff positions include the title assistant to the national sales manager. Assistant national sales managers may be either line or staff managers. Staff positions may occur at any level in the organization. Some companies with divisional sales forces, for example, have a job of corporate vice president of sales who has no line sales management responsibility. Other companies have regional or area sales vice presidents responsible for aiding salespeople from various divisions with major account sales. This is found, for example, in some weapons marketers where various product-oriented divisions call upon the same buying organization.

Note: The titles and descriptions above are generalities. Different industries and different companies in many cases use different titles for the same job and organize job content differently.

typical initial program for someone entering product management in a large consumer package-goods firm might include 6 months in a product management training position followed by 6 to 18 months of selling in the field. Each company, of course, has its own program, but most include some field exposure.

Marketing managers tend to believe that field exposure is useful because it provides knowledge about sales force attitudes and activities, as well as customer and prospect behavior. In addition, many people view it as a maturing or seasoning process for the young marketing manager.

In smaller companies the field sales job is often the only one available at the entry level. This is also true in some large companies. Firms which use a relatively short-term exposure (2 years or less) as field sales training usually do *not* expect the young salesperson to do a phenomenal job of increasing territory sales. Instead, they expect solid performance and professional behavior. Clearly, a sales disaster bodes ill for a budding marketing career, but often, average sales performance is adequate.

The typical progression through a larger sales force would include line and staff jobs and sometimes exposure to related marketing (for example, advertising, market research) and nonmarketing (for example, physical distribution, field repair and maintenance) jobs.

Those with broader career interests sometimes periodically hold a sales management position. For example, it is not unusual for a product manager in an industrial company to become a regional sales manager before moving to a higher headquarters marketing position. Although such short terms of duty in sales management are most common for managers progressing through marketing, they are also often used for managers being groomed for top-level general management. It is not unusual in such a situation for the manager *not* to have field selling experience.

Many companies use the sales force as a source of general management talent. Management skills and customer knowledge are viewed as distinct assets for a division manager or company president.

THE POSITIONS

This section will provide a brief discussion of the various types of positions in the sales management hierarchy.

The role of the salesperson depends upon the nature of the product, customer, marketing strategy of the company, and the buying process. The notes "The Role of Personal Selling in the Marketing Mix," "Account Management," and especially "Sales Costs and Budgets" explain some of these differences. The compensation of salespeople reflects the difficulty of the job and the necessary capabilities. Some industries, such as envelopes and maintenance products for factories, tend to pay relatively low wages (for example, in the $10,000 – $15,000 range) while others, such as apparel, furniture, advertising space and time, and complex industrial equipment, pay considerably more (for example, $20,000–$80,000 or more). In most sales situations, compensation of salespeople in a given company or industry varies more than the compensation for other workers.

Selling jobs vary greatly in the kind of product sold, the number of customers each salesperson is responsible for, and in the ancillary demands of the job. For example, travel varies from very little for an inside salesperson (one working in a showroom, office, or over the telephone) to a great deal for other salespeople. If the company is a regional one (for example, a wholesaler or independent representative), or if the territory is compact, the salesperson will travel little and will be home every night. On the other hand, some salespeople cover a state or several states, travel several hundred miles by car each day, and are expected to be away from home for several days each week. Other salespeople, for example, those selling specialized equipment or services, might cover a broad territory and travel by air with 3 or 4 nights away from home each week.

Selling is a lonely and demanding task. Much time is spent in going to customers and prospects and waiting to be seen. Correspondingly, most salespeople have a good deal of independence in their activities. They are not under minute-by-minute supervision.

Most sales jobs require some "cold" calls—that is, calling on prospects who do not know the salespeople. This is an onerous, psychologically taxing task which almost all salespeople dislike. Some sales jobs require a considerable number of cold calls. On the other hand, many industrial and commercial salespeople tend to deal with the same buying people for long periods of time. Cold calls are most prevalent in industries and companies where the customer base is growing rapidly and in one-shot sales of, for example, construction services.

Many young people are unsure of whether or not they have the qualifications to be a salesperson. As the note on recruiting and selection explains, the prime requirements are empathy, ego drive, and enough intelligence to understand the product and deal with the customer. Thus, intelligence requirements vary a good deal. The most successful salespeople are not necessarily of the hale-fellow, well-met stereotype, with a good story, a loud voice, and a pat on the back. To sell well, one does not have to "like people." Selling is a demanding job but a great personality is not one of the demands.

Many young people without technical education (science or engineering) assume that they cannot join an industrial sales force. This is not true. Many industrial sales forces are *not* technical in nature. Furthermore, the technical content in the job in many sales forces that deal with technical products is limited. A medical instrument company with a sales force made up of people trained in engineering, for example, found that, when it hired and trained two nontechnical people for sales, the salespeople with the highest volume by a substantial margin were the nontechnical people. Other companies have had similar experiences.

As an entry position to management, selling offers some good benefits. Management requires the ability to analyze situations, understand people, communicate well, and work independently but function as a team member. A sales position is an excellent place to learn to understand people, communicate well, and work independently. It also provides an outstanding opportunity to show results. Few jobs offer the visible, tangible results of selling. This is important feedback for the aspiring manager and important information for the person making promotion decisions.

Sales management jobs vary as much as sales jobs. The note "Field Sales Management" describes some of these differences. Usually, the more professional the salespeople, the more professional their management. Field sales management jobs require the ability to manage people in a face-to-face setting. Much time is spent in the field. Many sales management jobs require a good deal of travel.

10

As sales managers advance in an organization, responsibilities and activities become broader. They manage programs and other managers, not salespeople. It is likely that there will be some high-level executive selling with important accounts even if there is no specific sales responsibility. Top-level sales managers usually travel further but less often as their geographical interest widens but their field responsibilities lessen.

In large companies it is often necessary for a person to move geographically as they move up in the organization. This would be in marked contrast to financial and nonsales marketing personnel. The sales force is geographically dispersed, and therefore its management must be dispersed. Smaller sales forces often have their management in one location. This decreases the necessity to move, but may increase travel demands. Local or regional firms obviously do not require mobility.

Small company management positions tend to offer more breadth of authority and responsibility, but less training and staff support. This is also true at the sales level. The number two person in the sales force in a small company might have a great deal of nonsales force responsibility and would be involved directly in all sales force related activities. In the large company, the dollar involvement might be greater, but the breadth would be less. In addition, staff and line subordinates would take over more of the direct activity of sales management.

Sales management, like selling, provides an opportunity for visible performance results. This has its good and bad sides. When sales are up,

Exhibit 2 MEDIAN TOTAL EARNINGS OF SALES MANAGERS, 1971

Position	Consumer goods companies	Industrial goods companies	Total
Vice president	$44,125	$40,000	$42,798
General manager	32,105	29,000	30,000
Regional manager	27,650	27,240	27,480
District manager	22,847	27,500	24,000
Field sales manager	19,500	20,210	20,000
Field salesperson	14,138	15,864	15,000

Note: The titles used here are slightly different than those used in the previous discussion. District manager is a mid-level field manager as used here. The term "field sales manager" is used for the first line sales manager.

Source: David A. Weeks, *Compensating Salesmen and Sales Executives,* New York: The Conference Board, 1972.

sales managers are heroes. When they are down, the opposite is true. I believe that, because of this, there is generally more movement of sales managers among companies, and sales managers (and marketing managers) are typically paid more than their functional counterparts. Thus, the jobs offer greater risk and greater rewards.

Exhibit 2 provides some typical compensation ranges for sales management positions in 1971.

11

Section
TWO
Formulating the Sales Program

THREE   Formulating the Sales Program

The formulation of the sales program is the detailed definition of the tasks and objectives of the personal selling effort. Major topics included in the process are:

1 Personal selling in the marketing mix
2 Deployment
3 Account management
4 Costs and budgets

Other less important topics will be mentioned below.

Personal selling is one part of promotion or communication, one of the four elements of the marketing mix. The first part of sales program formulation is to assign to the personal selling effort those tasks which it can perform more efficiently or more effectively, or both, than any other part of the marketing mix. This is indeed a strategic process. Some companies, for example, are best defined by their sales program. As a case in point, Avon Products is most strongly differentiated from other large cosmetics manufacturers by its method of sales and distribution. Whereas its primary competitors sell through wholesalers and retailers, Avon has a sales force of hundreds of thousands of people who sell directly to the ultimate consumer.

Usually the definition of the role of the sales force in the marketing mix is not so dramatic. It is, however, always a prime marketing decision warranting careful analysis and decision making.

Next comes the decisions involving "sell what to whom, where?" This is deployment or the assignment of the selling effort to particular customers, products, and geographic territories. Deployment can be a key to the efficient, effective use of personal selling. The salesperson who calls on an unsellable customer, or on a customer whose business is unprofitable for the selling company, is being poorly managed. The same is true of the salesperson who is busy selling the wrong product, for example, a salesperson who attempts to sell a prospect a product which is maintained in the line "solely for the convenience of old customers." Astute territorial assignments can also have a great impact on the amount of sales potential converted to actual sales.

The third major phase of sales program formulation involves account management, that is, determining how each account should be approached. It concerns the interaction between the firm and its prospective and current accounts. All the rest of sales management exists solely to make this interaction result in profitable sales. It is the very core of sales management.

Account management includes selling, but it also includes a great deal more. Any program, system, policy, or procedure designed to make initial sales or to ensure that existing customers are satisfied and thus continue to buy the company's products or services is a part of account management.

The fourth major aspect of the sales program is cost. A prime consideration in sales costs is the size of the sales force. Another is the choice between a company sales force and independent representatives, that is, firms or persons who do not take possession of or title to merchandise but who sell it on a straight commission basis. A few years ago there appeared to be a trend toward independent representatives being used by smaller firms and company sales forces being used by large firms. This trend may be reversing itself. In the food industry, for example, both Kool-Aid and Skippy peanut butter are sold by brokers. There are many other examples in that industry and in others of large firms using independent representatives.

The issue of costs and budgets is at the base of all areas of sales management. In allocating funds to personal selling in the marketing mix the crucial question is marginal return versus marginal cost or investment. The same is true of all aspects of the management of the sales force. A dollar should be invested in training, for example, only if the investment will return a dollar or more of profit and only if the dollar will produce more profit by being allocated to training than to, say, recruiting or supervision.

In addition to the four prime areas of sales program formulation described above, there are several areas of lesser importance, including (1) sales forecasting, (2) sales information systems, and (3) sales promotion.

Sales forecasting is both an important task of the sales force and a useful tool. The sales force usually is responsible for developing sales forecasts for use by other marketing personnel and by other functional areas of the company such as control and production scheduling. In addition, sales forecasts are used by the sales force for deployment decisions, quota setting, and other purposes.

In almost all firms the sales force has a much more intimate view of the marketplace than anyone else in the firm, including market research-ers. The salespeople and managers usually do not have a broad perspec-tive of the market. Instead, each knows the reactions of his customers in his territory to his approaches and products. Despite the lack of perspec-tive and the replete biases of the sales force, the data they have are very useful. They are often the first to sense shifts in consumer needs, in channel attitudes, or in competitive activities. Few companies have developed effective ways to tap this rich source of data. Large companies, in particular, find it difficult to gather the data and to put them into a useful framework. In most smaller companies where the sales force is smaller and the organizational distance from marketing vice president to salesperson much shorter, the problem tends to be less serious. The better flow of information between marketing executive and salesperson is one source of the small firm's usually greater flexibility and shorter response time.

Sales promotion consists of a wide range of promotional tools whose purpose is either to increase distribution or to increase short-term sales. Sales promotion programs may be directed at the consumer (for exam-ple, cents-off deals, contests, premiums, coupons), the trade (special discounts, premiums, contests), or the sales force (contests, special commissions). Sometimes a promotion will be directed at all three groups. Because sales promotion traditionally falls explicitly in neither sales management nor advertising, it is often neglected by both. It is an important part of the marketing mix, however, and must be integrated into the sales program. For some firms promotions in the form of contests become a standard way of motivating and compensating sales-people.

15

Throughout our study of the formulation of the sales program, we will stress three themes:

1 Each aspect of the program must be understood in detail.

2 Each aspect of the program must be integrated into a coherent, focused program.

3 The total program must be coordinated with the marketing strategy as well as with its implementation systems, policies, procedures, and activities.

All of these themes are important.

BIBLIOGRAPHY

Ames, B. Charles: "Build Marketing Strength into Industrial Selling," *Harvard Business Review*, vol. 50, no. 1, January-February 1972.

Business Week: "The New Supersalesman Wired for Success," January 6, 1973, pp. 40–44.

Newton, Derek A.: "Get the Most Out of Your Sales Force," *Harvard Business Review*, vol. 47, no. 5, September-October 1969, pp. 130–143; reprinted in Thomas R. Wotruba and Robert Olsen (eds.), *Readings in Sales Management*, New York: Holt, Rinehart and Winston, 1971, pp. 301–324.

FOUR Personal Selling in the Marketing Mix

When a company reevaluates its existing personal selling effort or when it formulates a new sales program or marketing strategy, one of the first issues which must be confronted is, "What is the appropriate role for personal selling in the marketing strategy?" If the role is not correctly defined, all of the remaining formulation and implementation will be wasted.

16

Marketing management is the orchestration of the four elements of the marketing mix—product policy, pricing, channels of distribution, and communication—with the ultimate objective of ethically creating long-term profits for the firm. Communication includes advertising, personal selling, and all types of promotional activities.

Sales management is both the detailed definition of the role of personal selling in the marketing mix, which is also part of the marketing management, and the orchestration of the various approaches available in managing the sales force.

In a sense, the other issues in formulating the sales program—deployment, account management, and costs and budgets—are actually part of an exceedingly detailed definition of the role of personal selling. Operationally, however, these subjects involve issues which can be separated from the general definition of that role. The stress here is on the importance of defining the role of personal selling in the marketing mix. In addition, some insight into the process required is provided.

In defining the role of personal selling in the marketing mix, it is necessary to consider four participants in the marketing process: (1) consumers (or customers), (2) channels of distribution, (3) competitors, and (4) the company itself.

A good marketing strategy is built around:

1 Satisfying consumers so that they purchase the product or service and continue to purchase it

2 Utilizing channels of distribution in an effective and efficient manner so that they accomplish their task at minimum cost to the firm

3 Bettering competitors by avoiding their primary strengths and doing important things better than they can

4 Building upon the firm's own strengths and leaning away from its weaknesses

A good personal selling strategy contributes to these goals by assigning to personal selling those tasks or functions which it can best (most efficiently and most effectively) carry out. Many of the crucial issues in sales management focus on the relationships between personal selling and other elements of the marketing mix. One classic issue, for example, is the personal selling and channels of distribution "push" versus advertising "pull." Another is the choice between using channels of distribution to sell the product and using one's own sales force. Both of these are clearly strategic decisions in a marketing and corporate sense, as well as key sales management issues.

Consider, for example, an apparel manufacturer whose marketing strategy includes highly selective distribution of a high-fashion, high-styled product in a highly competitive industry. The company, furthermore, is currently selling to the most important retailers. In this situation it is clear that the sales force must be capable of providing each customer with heavy merchandising and service support. The salesperson does not need to be able to identify and open new accounts. Instead, he needs to be capable of keeping each account satisfied. Note that the marketing strategy has defined the role of the salesperson and that this role has defined a good deal about the appropriate recruiting, selection, training, and supervision programs for the sales force. In addition, the strategy of selective distribution and the amount of service which must be provided to each account have to a great extent determined the size of the necessary sales force.

The same process can be repeated in every company. An industrial company which supplies maintenance items (fasteners, welding supplies, etc.) should have a different sales force if it decides to go through distributors than if it decides to service customers itself. In addition, a strategy calling for coverage of all accounts, large and small, will require a different sales force than a strategy concentrating on large accounts. Furthermore, the company which sells to all accounts directly can vary the emphasis placed on low price, advertising, and the sales force.

Not only is it important for the personal selling effort to be used where it is the most efficient and effective marketing tool, but it is also important to make the selling effort consistent with the rest of the marketing mix. The salesperson must project the same image as the product, pricing, distribution channels, and advertising. The salesperson must provide the kind of service required by the rest of the marketing mix. The firm which uses a price-oriented salesperson to sell high-fashion products is wasting resources, and so too is the firm which uses a salesperson whose prime talent is selling quality and function for the purpose of selling a lower-quality, lower-priced line. In both cases the salesperson's approach and choice of accounts or distributors, or both, will be dysfunctional.

If we were able to gather perfect data and manipulate them perfectly, we could apply marginal analyses as developed by economists to assign the personal selling function tasks within the marketing mix. In that framework we would invest an additional dollar in personal selling only if two conditions were met:

1 If we received more profit return from a dollar invested in personal selling than in any other part of the marketing program (or any other phase of company activity for that matter).

2 If we received at least one dollar in marginal income for each dollar we spent (marginal income being corrected for the time value of money, of course).

The reasons for imposing these conditions should be obvious. It should also be obvious that it is impossible for a marketing manager to perform an *explicit* marginal calculation as suggested above. Uncertainties in costs and, especially, returns preclude it. The conceptual structure is, nevertheless, valid. It must, however, be applied qualitatively rather than quantitatively.

Approaches to these optimizations or tradeoffs will be discussed in somewhat more detail in later notes.

It will be important to remember that the focus is on the management of the *personal selling effort*, a much broader topic than the management of the sales force.

BIBLIOGRAPHY

Rieser, Carl: "The Salesman Isn't Dead—He's Different," *Fortune*, vol. 66, November 1962, pp. 124–127, 248, 252, 254, 259.

Warner, Jack: "The New Marketing," *Madison Avenue*, November 1972, pp. 46–49, 69.

FIVE Cole National Corporation (A)

In spring 1975, Boake Sells, the executive vice president of Cole National Corporation responsible for the Consumer Products Division, was troubled by what he termed an "excessively high turnover" among field salespeople. Despite several reorganizations of the field sales force, Mr. Sells believed that either he would have to succeed in reducing turnover, or else he would have to alter substantially the role of the field sales force in the division's marketing program.[1]   *objectives*

COLE NATIONAL AND THE CONSUMER PRODUCTS DIVISION

Cole National sales had grown from $65 million in 1970 to almost $111 million in 1974. During the same period, net income had grown from $1.2 million to $4.4 million. Exhibit 1 contains the corporate financial data.

The corporation had three major operations: specialty retailing, visual merchandising, and Consumer Products Division. The specialty retailing operation ran 266 optical departments in Sears, Roebuck and Montgomery Ward stores, 539 key departments in major retail chain stores, and several hundred gift and personalizing, and craft shops in shopping centers (not within other stores). The Susan Crane operation sold custom gift wrapping to stores for use in the stores' own gift-wrap operation and supplied retailers with a variety of display "props."

The Consumer Products Division sold keys, knives, and letters, numbers, and signs (LNS) to 56,000 retail stores through 90 sales representatives. This field force also provided the retailer with in-store services designed to improve the saleability of Cole products. Services included the training of store personnel in the use of key-duplicating equipment installed by the company, maintenance of displays, and introduction of new products suitable to a particular store.

In addition, the division created occasional national advertising programs. In 1972, cooperative advertising for one-cent key sales[2] was arranged with a number of large variety chains such as Woolworth's. Full-page color ads extolling the qualities of the "Kabar" line of hunting knives (Cole's best quality line) appeared in *Field and Stream*, *Sports Afield*, and other outdoor recreation magazines. For 1973, there was a national consumer sweepstakes planned to promote colored keys. This sweepstakes would include advertising in major "shelter" magazines[3]

[1]The field sales effort is described in "Cole National Corporation (B)."

[2]In these sales, a consumer was offered two keys for the price of one, plus one cent. Cole adjusted its prices to make such sales profitable for both the store and itself.

[3]Shelter magazines were those devoted to articles on the home, such as *House and Garden*, *Better Homes and Gardens*, and *House Beautiful*.

19

Exhibit 1   CORPORATE FINANCIAL DATA

Statement of income	Year ended October 26, 1974	Year ended October 27, 1973
Net sales	$110,729,000	$96,161,000
Costs and expenses		
Cost of goods sold	42,033,000	36,997,000
Operating expenses	56,395,000	48,001,000
Depreciation and amortization	2,679,000	2,309,000
Interest expense, net	1,146,000	829,000
Other income, net	(156,000)	(166,000)
Total costs and expenses	$102,097,000	$87,970,000
Income before income taxes	$ 8,632,000	$ 8,191,000
Provision for income taxes	4,241,000	4,112,000
Net income	$ 4,391,000	$ 4,079,000
Earnings per share	$ 2.12	$ 1.95

	($000 omitted)				
Five-year review[a]	1974	1973	1972	1971	1970
Net sales	$110,729	$96,161	$83,562	$70,100	$65,145
Income before income taxes	8,632	8,191	6,662	4,622	2,403
Income taxes	4,241	4,112	3,237	2,249	1,215
Income before extraordinary items	4,391	4,079	3,425	2,373	1,188
Extraordinary items	—	—	109	(1,555)	—
Net income	4,391	4,079	3,534	818	1,188
Earnings per share[b]					
Income before extraordinary items	2.12	1.95	1.65	1.14	.56
Extraordinary items	—	—	.05	(.79)	—
Net income	2.12	1.95	1.70	.35	.56
Dividends per common share	.52	.47	.445	.44	.44
Working capital	20,375	18,690	14,212	12,715	10,099
Current ratio	2.51	2.51	2.23	2.01	1.73
Shareholders' equity	26,653	23,281	20,226	17,527	17,753
Total assets	$ 55,090	$49,832	$40,785	$39,454	$42,213

[a]The above financial information includes, for all periods presented, businesses acquired in pooling of interests transactions.

[b]The earnings per share data are based upon the weighted average of common shares outstanding and common share equivalents.

and point-of-purchase materials which would be placed in the stores by the field sales forces.

Segments of the product line could be found in a number of different departments in a large store—hardware, sporting goods, housewares, notions, and jewelry. The one feature common to all products, according to management, was their need for fairly frequent servicing and reordering. This implied a high degree of personal contact between the field sales force and the store management.

Sales by product line were:

	1973	1974
Keys and key accessories	$10,538,000	$11,154,000
Pocket and hunting knives	4,820,000	6,000,000
Letters, numbers, and signs	5,679,000	6,787,000
Total	$21,037,000	$23,941,000

Average gross margins for the product lines were:

Keys, 70 percent
Knives, 40 percent
Letters, numbers, and signs (LNS), 50 percent

Exhibit 2 contains a division income statement for 1974.

Mr. Sells was responsible for the activities of three headquarters departments and the chain and field sales forces (see Exhibit 3, p. 22). One other headquarters department, marketing research, had been authorized but not yet staffed.

For each of its product lines, the division's basic merchandising and service program consisted of an initial assortment of merchandise arranged on a display fixture, in-store promotional materials, training retail clerks in how to sell the products and reorder them by mail, and periodic checking of individual store displays to provide additional assurance of balanced inventories.

The objective of the display as well as the entire merchandising and service program was, as one executive put it, to establish a retailer in a particular line of business and then to do almost everything to run that business, except taking cash from the ultimate consumer. Because of its emphasis on in-store service, the division shipped all of its merchandise direct to individual stores, bypassing entirely wholesalers and chain store warehouses.

21

The Key Product Line

The division's key program involved more in-store service than either the knife or LNS programs. The division provided, at no charge to the

Exhibit 2 1974 INCOME STATEMENT
(IN THOUSANDS OF DOLLARS)

Sales	$23,941
Cost of goods sold[a]	10,217
Gross margin	13,724
Expenses	
Field sales expenses[b]	3,807
H.Q. sales administration	709
Advertising and sales promotion[c]	646
Chain store sales	192
Division general overhead	2,921
Total expenses	**$ 8,275**
Division contribution to corporate overhead and profit	5,449

[a]Includes total manufacturing costs and outbound freight charges.
[b]Detail in Exhibit 1, "Cole National Corporation (B)."
[c]Detail on page 29.
Source: Cole National Corporation records.

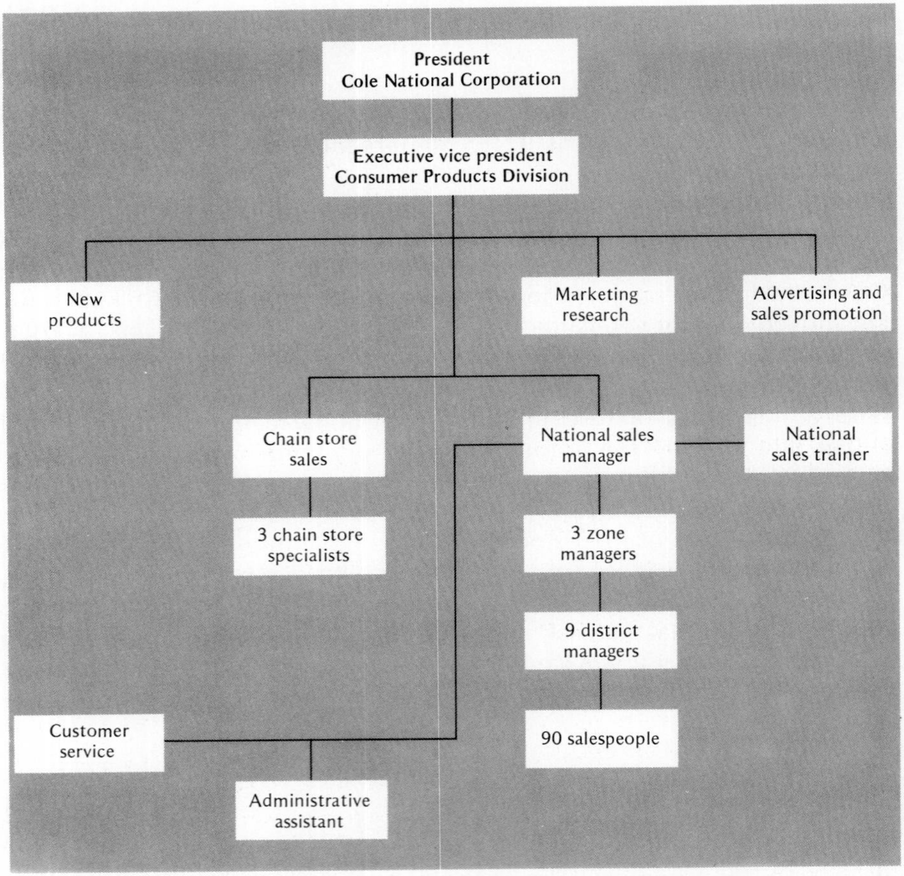

Exhibit 3   Condensed organization chart of the Consumer Products Division.

retailer, a key-duplicating machine similar to those sold by other manufacturers for prices between $100 and $200. In addition, the division's
field salespeople trained retail clerks to select the correct key blanks from
the assortment it provided of different blanks and to cut keys on the
machine. Division salespeople also periodically adjusted and maintained
the key machines.

The division's program enabled a retail clerk with very little training
to produce an exact copy of almost any key brought in by a customer.
Once an operator had learned how to select key blanks quickly and to
operate the machine, duplicate keys typically could be produced in less
than a minute.[4]

In most stores, only the one or two clerks who serviced the hardware
counters typically were trained to operate the key-duplicating machine. If

---

[4]The key-duplicating machine could not produce original keys. If a customer had no key at
all for a particular lock, he had to seek assistance from a locksmith.

these clerks resigned or were transferred to other departments, new clerks had to be trained.

To eliminate retailer loss from miscut keys, the division exchanged miscut keys for new key blanks. This policy, management believed, was highly instrumental in the success of the key product line. In 1974, the division issued credit or exchanged over $740,000 (at division selling price) of miscut keys.

The suggested retail selling price (which most stores followed) was 69 cents for a brass key and 69 cents for a colored aluminum key. Since retailers paid 26 cents each for brass key blanks and 26 cents each for aluminum key blanks, the division stressed that retailers' gross margin was 62 percent on key sales, whereas it was seldom more than 30 to 40 percent on most hardware items which were priced below $1.00. In addition, on other items, part of the gross margin defrayed the expense of damaged merchandise, display maintenance, and warehouse distribution which the division's key program covered at no charge.

The division offered programs for both brass and aluminum keys in four bright colors. A popular initial assortment consisted of 40 dozen brass and 36 dozen color fast-selling key blanks. The cost to the retailer of this assortment was $237 ($0.26 × 76 × 12). Sales of brass keys had been increasing more rapidly than color keys, a situation the reverse of that which had occurred in the mid-1960s when the color keys had been introduced. The division prepaid freight charges on keys as well as on all other product lines.

Sales of initial assortments of keys accounted for 2 to 4 percent of total key sales. This figure had been stable for many years and was expected to remain so. All other key sales were reorders. About one-third of the reorders, according to management estimates, were mailed in directly by individual stores rather than submitted by field sales personnel.

In discussing the reorder business, one division executive described a situation which arose in a territory consisting of a large metropolitan area. The territory was over quota because of a high volume of mail reorders even though there was no one in the field for several weeks. "Nevertheless," this executive commented, "even though a high percentage of our sales come from mail orders, it's the salesperson who generates those orders. We can't do without him."

Management believed that Cole's program emphasized an entirely different philosophy of selling from that of competitors. Division executives estimated that Cole's service program was more aggressive and comprehensive and that Cole's sales in total were considerably higher than competitors' sales. Only one major competitor offered a similar service program. This company sold key blanks direct to chain and independent retailers for 24 cents each.

Most other manufacturers of key blanks provided no service program along with their products. They sold key blanks to retailers either

23

directly or through hardware jobbers. Blanks sold in this manner custom-arily cost the jobber 4 to 8 cents apiece. Retailers paid 6 to 11 cents for them and sold duplicate keys for 25 to 50 cents. Most of the retailers who purchased key blanks from jobbers and owned their own key-duplicating machines were locksmiths, repair shops, and small hardware stores. A typical display of Cole keys and accessories is shown in Exhibit 4.

The Knife Product Line

The division's knife program was similar to the key program. The division offered eight different assortments of knives. Each assortment was available in a display case. The display case contained reserve stock of the displayed items behind the front display. Display cases, as well as monthly mailings of promotional, display, and training material, were free to the retailer.

The division's field sales force was supposed to check the knife inventory in each store regularly and to make up reorders for the approval of the store manager. Between salesperson's visits, however, store managers were encouraged to mail reorders directly to the division. Mail orders accounted for approximately one-third of the total sales of knives. They seldom, however, were orders for initial assortments, which accounted for an estimated 15 to 20 percent of all knife sales.

The most popular assortment contained 15 different types of import-ed pocket and hunting knives, ranging in price from $1.99 to $10.95. The total retail value of this assortment was $283. On individual items, the division offered discounts of 40 percent off retail list price to independent stores and 50 percent off to chain stores.

Although there were literally hundreds of jobbers and importers that offered popular-priced knives, the division was the only supplier which provided a complete service program. Competitors, however, sometimes offered discounts of 50 and 10 percent to jobbers and large chain accounts. Jobbers usually priced knives to retailers at 40 percent off list price. According to management estimates, the division accounted for a much smaller share of the popular-priced knife market than did the key market.

Letters, Numbers, and Signs

As a result of the acquisition of the Gene Upton Company in 1966, the division offered a line of letters, numbers, and signs (LNS). Like the key and knife programs, the LNS program provided an initial assortment, display fixtures, promotional materials, a mail order program for reor-ders, and service by the division's field sales force.

The most popular assortment of plastic, adhesive-backed letters, numbers, and small signs contained more than 100 individual items which

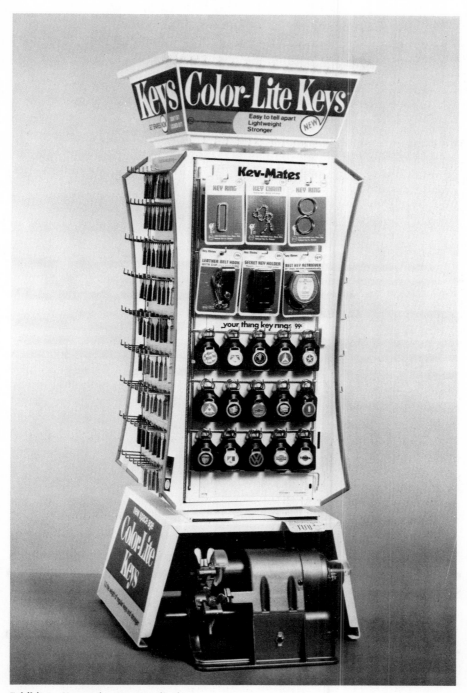

Exhibit 4 Key and accessory display.

were housed in a revolving floor rack. The retail value of the assortment was $165. Small letters and numbers were priced at 35 cents each at retail; large numbers at 69 cents apiece; and signs at $1.29 each. The division offered discounts of 40 percent off retail list price to independent stores and 50 percent to chains. Competitors, on the other hand, regularly offered discounts of 50 percent off list price to independents and 50 to 10 percent to chains.

During 1974, between 35 and 40 percent of the sales of LNS were of initial assortments. Management regarded this percentage as high. It attributed it to the placement, since the acquisition of the Gene Upton Company, of a large number of initial assortments in accounts which already carried one or more of the division's other product lines. An analysis of LNS showed that sales were concentrated among relatively few standard items in the line. One division executive estimated that volume was also concentrated among relatively few items in the division's key and knife lines.

Management estimated that approximately 40 percent of all sales of LNS came through mail orders. These mail orders seldom included initial assortments.The remaining 60 percent of sales came through orders obtained from field salespeople.

Division executives estimated that LNS sales of the Consumer Products Division accounted for more than 50 percent of the total market for plastic and metal LNS. They estimated that the division's sales of LNS were more than twice those of the nearest competitor. Although this firm also offered a service program, management did not believe that it was competitive with that offered by the division, since its products were sold through manufacturers' representatives who carried several lines in addition to the competitor's LNS line. The third largest firm in the industry, which accounted for an estimated 10 percent of the market, sold through wholesalers and offered no service program. The remainder of the market was served by a large number of small regional companies. Exhibit 5 shows a LNS display.

Channels of Distribution

The Consumer Products Division sold its products through 56,000 stores composed primarily of hardware, automobile supply, variety, drug, and discount stores. The division's customers included both independent stores and chain organizations such as Western Auto, F. W. Woolworth, and Sears. Chain organizations differed from independent stores in that part or all of the buying and general management functions in a chain were performed by a headquarters staff, whereas the owner or manager of an independent store typically made all the buying and management decisions at the store level.

Chain organizations could generally be classified into one of two categories: corporate chains (that is, chains which owned or leased their

Exhibit 5 Letters, numbers, and signs display.

retail stores and employed their own store managers and personnel), or franchise chains (that is, locally owned stores which were franchised by the payment of an annual fee or percentage of profit to use a name and to receive management, buying, and promotional services from a head quarters organization). Chain headquarters typically approved particular items of purchase for member stores and typically approved only one supplier's line of keys, knives, or LNS. Although owners of franchised stores had almost complete freedom to refuse "approved" items, whereas managers of corporate chain stores were less independent, most followed the "approved" list fairly carefully, as did managers of corporate chain stores.

The retail outlets of 1,100 chains (both corporate and franchise) accounted for approximately 60 percent of the stores serviced and 80 percent of sales during fiscal 1974. According to one executive, 15 large chain accounts accounted for one-half of the chain store sales. Sales to independent stores accounted for approximately 20 percent of sales, 80 percent of which was obtained from 50 percent of the independent accounts.

Of all the retail outlets which the division served, some 31,000 carried only one of the division's four product lines: brass keys, keys in color, knives, and LNS. (For this purpose, brass and colored aluminum keys were considered separate product lines.) About 14,700 carried two lines, some 8,200 carried three, and fewer than 2,100 carried all four product lines. Generally speaking, retail outlets of chain stores were more likely to carry several of the division's product lines than were independent stores.

Of the stores which carried only one line, 13,400 carried standard brass keys, 9,800 carried LNS, and 7,800 carried knives. Among the stores which carried two lines, the most common combinations were both standard and colored keys and standard keys plus knives. The most common three-line combination was standard keys, colored keys, and knives.

According to one division executive, prior to the acquisition of the Gene Upton Company, the division had few customers among the stores which carried the Gene Upton line. Similarly, the Gene Upton line had been poorly represented in most of the stores to which the division sold keys or knives. Since the acquisition in 1966, however, the division's field salespeople had begun to place the Upton line in existing accounts and had also introduced the key and knife lines to stores which had been Upton customers. Division executives expected to continue this cross-selling process.

According to management, sales were distributed by channel as follows:

Discount and variety stores	33%
Automotive and hardware stores	26
General merchandise and department stores	13
Drugstores	7
Wholesalers and distributors	4
Other	17
	100%

Variety stores were losing market share to large discount stores, home centers, and various types of specialty stores.

Advertising and Sales Promotion

The division's advertising and sales promotion budget of $646,000 focused on materials directed to the trade. The estimated expenditures for 1974 were:

	(000 omitted)
Direct mail to stores (including postage)	$226
In-store display materials	53
Catalog sheets	31
Trade advertising	61
Consumer adverstising	161
Agency fees, administration, and miscellaneous	114
Total	**$646**

The division mailed out at least one piece of promotional literature on each product line every month. Direct mail material typically provided display and selling suggestions. In addition, the division sent dealers point-of-purchase display materials. Management believed that the division's promotional program was the strongest in the industry and that dealers welcomed the support which the program provided.

The division had not generally advertised its products directly to consumers, except for an occasional advertisement whose purpose was to build trade acceptance of the division's products rather than consumer demand.

Chain Store Sales

The chain sales group consisted of a director of chain store sales and three assistants. This group, headquartered in Cleveland, called on the headquarters buying offices of chain stores throughout the country. They maintained regular personal contact with the buying offices in 75 percent of the division's chain accounts. Contact with buying offices in the remaining 25 percent were handled by the national sales manager and field sales managers, and in some cases, by field salespeople. In addition, Mr. Sells and the president of Cole National Corporation would occasionally call on chains when particular problems arose.

Only the chain accounts that agreed to increase the number of the division's lines they carried, or that were dealing with the division for the first time, would purchase initial assortments outright for some or all of their stores.

When a chain headquarters placed a definite order, each field salesperson received notification of items purchased, date shipped, and the address of every store affiliated with that chain within his territory. Each field salesperson received credit for all such sales within the territory and was expected to call on each store to set up displays and train store personnel.

On the other hand, when a chain headquarters "listed" a division product as "approved for purchase," the task of selling individual stores then fell to the field sales force.

The chain sales specialist at Cole often suggested a test to convince a chain's buyer that the division's program was superior to the present purchase arrangements. The specialist typically proposed a test in two to six stores within the chain. The sales which would have to be attained within a specified time period were designated in advance. Should the test be unsuccessful, the division agreed to take back unsold merchandise. Management estimated that the vast majority of such tests was successful and resulted in a chain ordering or approving for purchase one or more of the division's programs.

The chain store sales group continued to call on chain headquarters even after consummation of the initial sale. The purpose was to ensure that all retail outlets had ordered the division's product if the initial "sale" to chain headquarters had been an "approval" and to ensure that each store was producing as high a volume of sales as possible. To support these service calls, the chain sales group received a computer-generated quarterly report, which summarized sales by product line to each store in every chain, so that chain store sales specialists could identify stores whose sales of the division's products were low.

30

SIX Cole National Corporation (B)

ORGANIZATION OF THE FIELD SALES FORCE[1]

The field sales force was responsible for calling on the individual stores in chains which had listed[2] the division's products and for contacting independent stores. Field sales expenses were $3,807,000 and are detailed in Exhibit 1. The field sales effort was directed by George McGonagle, who had been national sales manager (NSM) since early 1972. The NSM's headquarters staff in Cleveland consisted of:

[1]For background data on the concerns of management and the Consumer Products Division's marketing strategy, see "Cole National Corporation (A)."

[2]The term "listed" meant that the chain headquarters personnel had approved the product for sale in the stores if the store manager concurred. For some chains a listing almost required that the store manager carry the line. In other situations, listing was little more than a "hunting license" for the salesperson.

Exhibit 1   FIELD SALES EXPENSES, 1974

	($1,000)	Percent
Compensation: territory salespeople	$1,333	35.0
Compensation: field management	362	9.5
Fringe benefits	190	5.0
Auto expense	453	11.9
Travel expense	403	10.6
Other	1,066	28.0
Total	**$3,807**	**100.0**

1 An administrative assistant responsible for the preparation, development, and monitoring of all necessary reports. The administrative assistant also resolved all problems with regard to salesperson's bonuses and quotas and conducted any necessary research for Mr. McGonagle.

2 A customer service department responsible for resolving all customer complaints, from credit problems to defective key machines. If at all possible, the customer service department attempted to handle all problems without contacting the salesperson. Each salesperson was required to call customer services at least once a week to report weekly activities and all problems not related to compensation. The customer service department was regarded very highly by the salespersons because it made their jobs easier.

3 A national sales trainer position, which was vacant.

Reporting directly to the NSM were three zone managers, a relatively new position which had been created when the increasing number of districts had become impossible for one person to manage. Each zone manager was responsible for supervising three district managers who in turn supervised between 9 and 11 salespersons, referred to as territory managers.

The district manager's supervision included motivating and training present salespeople to perform their selling, servicing, and order-processing activities. Hirings and terminations were also handled by the district manager with the approval of the zone manager. District managers were expected to spend as much time as possible in the field calling on accounts with their salespeople and talking by telephone with each salesperson in the district every week to discuss progress and/or any problems that may have been encountered. The district manager also conducted quarterly district sales meetings to review the district's performance against plan and to discuss operating procedures for the next quarter. Bonus checks were distributed by the district managers at these meetings.

The number of salespersons had gradually risen from 50 in 1964 to approximately 118 in 1970. Straight growth of the sales force as the primary means of growth fell out of favor in 1970 and was replaced by the strategy of stabilized territories which would become increasingly more profitable through increased efficiency of salespeople and wider product lines offered. With this in mind, the number of territories was reduced to 90 in 1970 and was maintained at that level.

Compensation of district managers included both salary and a bonus. Salaries ranged from $10,000 to $18,000. Bonuses, which were based on district contribution (the gross margin on shipments made into the region minus district expenses), ranged from 15 percent to as high as 25 percent of salary.

In performing their supervisory duties, district managers relied upon personal observations of field salespeople's activities and the weekly district representative's performance evaluation (DRPE), which indicated, according to one division executive, what a salesperson had done. A sample, DRPE is included in Exhibit 2. Copies of the DRPE for each person were available to home office personnel, field managers, and the salesperson.

The Salesperson

Salespersons were accountable for producing profitable sales within their geographic territory equal to, or in excess of, the quotas assigned to them for each of the three main product lines. The salesperson had approximately 600 accounts, 450 to 500 of which were active at any given time. They called on major accounts (those with a volume in excess of $1,000 per year) once every 6 weeks, and made six to eight calls per day. They were required to establish a call schedule designed to ensure that they were obtaining maximum exposure to major accounts while minimizing sales expense.

On each call, the salesperson took an inventory of all merchandise on hand, ensured that it was properly displayed, serviced the key machine, trained new personnel operating the key machines, and wrote an order for the needed merchandise in quantities that would provide the store with a balanced inventory and prevent overstocking. The salesperson also attempted to meet with the store management personnel accountable for their product lines to discuss and resolve any problems that may have existed and, where possible, to sell additional merchandise. Management believed that it was imperative that the salespeople concentrate on selling all product lines to ensure the profitability of their territory.

Chain accounts carried only those products which were approved in their listings. (A separate chain headquarters sales force was responsible for obtaining listings with the chain buying group.)[3] The procedures for

---

[3]See "Cole National Corporation (A)."

Exhibit 2 DISTRICT REPRESENTATIVES PERFORMANCE EVALUATION (DRPE) FOR WILLIAM BONNIE

DIST. NO. 101	REP. NAME William Bonnie	CUMULATIVE MONTH TO DATE SALES THROUGH	Mo. 10	Day 31	Yr. 74

PRODUCT LINES	MAIL ORDERS NO.	AMOUNT	WRITTEN REORDERS NO.	AMOUNT	WRITTEN NEW ORDERS NO.	AMOUNT	TOTAL ORDERS NO.	AMOUNT
NATIONAL KEY	210	13,887	31	5,600	9	1,725	250	21,212
LETTERS NUMBERS SIGNS	32	1,655	16	1,927	6	1,665	54	5,247
AMERICAN KNIFE	14	2,740	23	3,867	4	1,430	46	8,037
TOTALS	261	18,282	70	11,394	19	4,820	350	34,496

TO DATE

	NK	LNS	AK	TOTAL	
	19,296	3,232	5,566	28,094	QUOTA
	21,212	5,247	8,037	34,496	ACTUAL
	1,916	2,015	2,471	6,402	DIFFERENCE (−UNDER)
	109.93	162.34	144.40	122.79	PERCENT REALIZATION ACTUAL/QUOTA

YEAR TO DATE

	NK	LNS	AK	TOTAL	
	60,054	12,499	15,993	88,546	QUOTA
	66,413	21,331	21,784	109,528	ACTUAL
	6,359	8,832	5,791	20,982	DIFFERENCE (−UNDER)
	110.59	170.66	136.20	123.70	PERCENT REALIZATION ACTUAL/QUOTA

COMMENTS:

STORE CALL ANALYSIS

NUMBER OF CALLS CHAINS	INDEPT.	TOTAL	DAYS WORKED	SATURDAYS WORKED	CALLS PER DAY	WRITTEN $ PER CALL	WRITTEN ORDERS PER CALL	DAYS OFF	CALLS LOST	DOLLARS LOST	TOTAL ORDERS PER CALL	TOTAL SALES PER CALL
136	71	207	23	4	9.00		.34				1.69	166.64

PERCENT MAIL TO TOTAL BUSINESS

NK	LNS	AK	TOTAL
65.5	31.5	34.1	53.0

PERCENT NEW BUSINESS TO TOTAL BUSINESS

NK	LNS	AK	TOTAL
8.1	31.8	17.8	14.0

AVERAGE ORDER

	MAIL	REORDER WRITTEN	TOTAL
NK	66.12	180.63	
LNS	51.72	120.38	
AK	144.24	168.12	

33

individual chains were presented in a procedures manual and the field salesperson was required to adhere to it strictly. Although the salesperson was limited in what could be sold to a chain account, an attempt was made to convince each store manager to carry all the types of merchandise approved in the listing. The salesperson also sold special deals or promotions that had been approved by chain store management, such as one-cent key sales. Salespeople continually attempted to obtain business from independent accounts not previously serviced and to expand the lines carried by existing independents. They developed mailing lists from the Yellow Pages and their own knowledge of the territory and sent brochures to prospective accounts in hopes of creating interest in their lines.

The salesperson was responsible for responding to and promptly resolving customer's complaints to their satisfaction and within the best interest of the division. Most frequently, customers would contact salespeople at their homes. However, some complaints were relayed through the home office or field management. The salesperson evaluated each request and determined whether to drop what he was doing and respond immediately or whether to fit the call into the existing schedule. The type of problem and the volume of the account determined the course of action. To minimize service requests and customer complaints, the salesperson attempted to ensure that each account was properly serviced on the scheduled call, and all orders were placed in accordance with established procedures.

The manager of customer services was the salesperson's principal contact with the home office. Through the manager, salespeople resolved customer complaints regarding credit or billing problems, incomplete or delayed orders, or order processing. Salespeople also ordered their supplies through the customer services manager, mailed their daily call reports to him, and received their reports from him.

The salesperson was accountable for completing and submitting a variety of reports including the daily call report, automotive report, expense report, and monthly summary report, copies of which were mailed to the district manager and the home office. Salespeople had weekly telephone contact with their district manager regarding service requests, questions relative to information reflected in the various reports, and negative trends or complaints which might have occurred.

Sales Calls

On the average, field salespeople were expected to make about 8 calls per day. This average varied, however, from 5 calls per day in some territories to 16 calls per day in others.

To service existing accounts properly, management thought each salesperson should call on the average store four to six times per year. It was recognized, however, that some stores—usually, but not always the larger ones—needed monthly service calls.

In addition to servicing existing accounts, management believed that "prospecting" for new accounts was an essential part of each salesperson's job; two out of every ten calls, it was asserted, should be "prospecting" calls. A salesperson could search for new customers both among the chain stores where approvals but not purchases had been obtained and among independent stores or small, locally headquartered chains. New business was expected to represent 10 percent of a person's sales, but in fact, sales to new accounts averaged 3 percent of sales.

Once a person sold an initial order to an independent account or to the headquarters of a chain which operated solely within the assigned territory, one could elect to call back personally for "fill-in" orders, or to have the customer mail in the orders. The latter course was often taken with smaller stores. Management did not disapprove of this practice if additional personal visits would not adequately stimulate a store's sales of the division's products, and if key machines and displays were kept in serviceable order. Management expected each salesperson, however, to write personally about twice as many orders as came in by mail.

Sales Force Composition

35

An analysis of the division's employment records showed that almost all field salespeople had at least one full-time job before joining Cole National, but fewer than 20 percent had worked longer than 7 years for any nongovernment employer.

With a few exceptions all the field salespeople had had previous selling experience, although the products they had sold varied from window shades to life insurance. A few had, in addition, either technical, clerical, or supervisory experience.

All the field salespeople had at least a high school education. In addition, about 10 percent had attended trade schools, and more than 40 percent had some college experience. Nearly half were 30 years old or younger, and more than three-fourths were 40 or under.

Recruiting and Selection

The recruiting and selection process had changed only marginally since the mid-1960s. Recruiting decisions were made by the district manager with the approval of the zone manager.

The recruiting process began as soon as a salesperson gave notice or was given notice by a district manager. Salespeople who intended to leave the division typically gave notice 1 week (that is, one pay period) before their intended departure.

As soon as district managers became aware of an impending vacancy, they advertised in one or more Sunday newspapers within the open territory and contacted a local employment agencies, usually those with which the company had previously dealt. The Sunday newspaper ads included a telephone number at which either the district manager or a secretary could be reached on Sunday. When prospective candidates telephoned, they were asked several specific questions relating to family status, income, etc. Answers deemed inappropriate would disqualify a person from further interviewing, unless the person administering the "knockout" questions thought the candidate nevertheless possessed unusual qualities.

The telephone interview and the employment agency screening usually reduced the number of applicants from 15 to 25 to 10 or 12. These people would be scheduled for interviews by the district manager on Monday and Tuesday.

In the first personal interview, district managers asked about educational background and work experience and attempted to evaluate appearance, poise, and manner. The division wanted people experienced in dealing with customers and programs similar to its own. People with experience in the hardware, tobacco, and food business often met this standard.

36

After the first personal interview, the district manager hoped to have three or four candidates left for another similar interview within a day or two.

Whenever possible, if the prospective salesperson were male this second interview was supplemented by having dinner with the prospect and his wife. When practicable, the interviewer also visited the prospect's home. One division executive said that he had found that meeting a man's wife and visiting his home provided one of the best single indicators of his potential success with the division sales force. "It's important that she provide a stable home life for him," this executive stated, "and it's essential that she be willing to let him travel. In six out of seven of our territories a man must be 'on the road' at least one day, and often up to five days a week. If he can't travel, or if he tries to cover too much ground in too little time, our customers don't receive proper service—and service is what we sell."

Within 5 to 6 days after the appearance of a Sunday newspaper ad, the district manager had usually selected a person, checked his references, and arranged for him to begin training immediately.

Training [4]

Regardless of their previous experience, all new salespeople, after spending a week or 10 days in the field with an experienced salesperson, were sent to Cleveland for a week of training. New people generally

[4]"Cole National Corporation (C)" describes the training program in detail.

went through the Cleveland training program in groups of two to eight.

The training program included instruction in the operation and maintenance of a key machine, as well as lectures on the division's and customers' policies and procedures. Management considered it essential that each salesperson be familiar with the merchandise-ordering procedures of the chain accounts to be serviced, and that those procedures be followed exactly. Each salesperson was given a manual which described each chain's procedures in detail. Salespeople were expected to follow these procedures to the letter.

Upon completion of the week of training, the new salesperson began to work his territory. For the first week, the district manager worked with him, typically in a major metropolitan area so as to minimize travel time. District managers often suggested that the new salesperson concentrate upon large, high-volume accounts with which the division had good working relationships. Selection of these accounts hopefully built the confidence of new salespeople by enabling them to generate a large volume of sales in their first week. District managers were expected to spend another week with new salespeople after they had been "on their own" for 2 to 4 weeks. In practice, however, district managers often could not return to work with their new salespeople for several weeks.

Compensation

Under the present compensation plan, salespeople received biweekly salaries, quarterly bonus payments, and occasionally, prize money won in a divisional or district sales contest. In addition, the division provided field salespeople with cars which they were free to use for their own activities on evenings and weekends. Field salespeople were given an expense allowance of $23 for every night their work required them to spend away from home.

In 1975, new salespeople typically started at $200 per week. The median salary for the sales force was $210. In general, weekly salaries of $210 or more were paid to field salespeople who had been with the division more than a year. As a rule, the higher salaries tended to go to the older people. Half the people with 3 or more months' service who earned more than the median salary of $210 per week were over 40 years old. Two-thirds of those earning the median salary were in their thirties. Finally, over 70 percent of the people who earned less than $210 per week were 30 or younger.

Each field salesperson's bonus depended partly upon the amount by which sales in his territory exceeded the quota established by the national sales manager's office. Until 1966 annual sales quotas for each territory had been established "largely by 'feel,'" according to one division executive.

A new plan was introduced in 1967. Since the final 3 months of the fiscal year customarily accounted for 30 percent of the total sales in each territory, the sales for those months were to be multiplied by $3\frac{1}{3}$ to determine the sales quota for the coming fiscal year. For example, if total sales in a particular territory from August 1 to October 31, 1974, were $36,000, the sales quota for the period November 1, 1974, to October 31, 1975, would be $3\frac{1}{3}$ × $36,000 or $120,000. Quarterly sales quotas were computed by seasonally adjusting the annual sales quota. Quotas were not set for any territory until the salesperson had at least 3 months' experience in that territory.

According to one division executive, this new system of setting quotas generally increased quotas. He added that reports from field salespeople indicated that more than 90 percent regarded the quotas as fair.

The bonus plan related each salesperson's personal bonus to (1) the amount, in dollars, by which his sales in each product line exceeded quota, (2) the particular product lines on which he exceeded or fell short of quota, and (3) the number of product lines on which he exceeded his quota. For every dollar of sales over each line's quota, a salesperson received points. For each dollar of sales over quota in standard and colored keys and LNS, a salesperson received three points. For every dollar of sales over quota in knives, he received two points. This differential in points had been included because the gross margin on keys and LNS was substantially greater than gross margin earned on knife sales. Management believed, however, that salespeople who did a particularly good business in knives relative to other products would not be adversely affected by the differential because the average reorder for knives was about twice as large as that for the other products.

Each point was worth 1, 2, or 4 cents, depending upon the number of product lines in which the salesperson had exceeded quota. If a salesperson exceeded quota in all three product lines (standard and colored keys, knives, LNS), each point was worth 4 cents. If he exceeded total quota through sales in excess of quota on two out of the three lines, each point was worth 2 cents. If a salesperson was over total quota because of sales in excess of quota in only one product line, each point was worth 1 cent. No bonuses were paid, however, unless a salesperson exceeded total quota. The purpose of valuing points differently, depending on the number of lines over quota, was to encourage a balance of sales among all three product lines. A sample calculation of a salesperson's personal bonus appears below:

Product line	Quota	Actual sales	Sales over quota	Bonus points per dollar of sales over quota		Total points earned	Bonus point value	Total personal bonus
							Sales over quota in	
Keys: standard and colored	$ 70,000	$ 90,000	$20,000	× 3	=	60,000	1 line − 1¢	
Knives	90,000	94,000	4,000	× 2	=	80,000	2 lines − 2¢	
LNS	60,000	86,000	26,000	× 3	=	78,000	3 lines − 4¢	
Total	$220,000	$270,000	$50,000			146,000	@$.04	= $5,840

Bonuses averaged slightly over $4,000 in 1974, with salespeople with at least 5 years' experience receiving almost $5,400 on average and people with less than 1 year's experience about $1,800 on average.

Although management reserved the right to retain any portion of a salesperson's personal bonus until the end of the division's fiscal year, payments were usually made quarterly. Furthermore, if a salesperson earned and was paid a personal bonus in one quarter and fell below quota in succeeding quarters, he was not expected to return money to the company.

Previously, salespeople had also been eligible for a district bonus if sales exceeded quota in the district of which their territory was a part. The district bonus amounted to 25 percent of the salesperson's personal bonus if the district exceeded quota in all three product lines. If the district exceeded quota in only two product lines, the salesperson's district bonus was 20 percent of the personal bonus, and if district sales exceeded quota in only one line, the district bonus was dropped to 10 percent of the personal bonus. District bonuses had been paid only at the end of the division's fiscal year. They were discontinued in 1971.

In addition to salary and bonus, a salesperson could earn prize money from divisional sales contests. In 1974, the division spent approximately $10,000 on contests.

To qualify for prizes in one contest which ran for 8 weeks in the fall of 1973, salespersons had to exceed their individual quotas for orders written per call and calls made per day. Average goals were 0.75 orders per call, and 11 calls per day. According to management, these goals ranged from 100 to 115 percent of a particular salesperson's recent performance.

If a salesperson exceeded both of the individual contest quotas, he could win up to $100 in each of 8 weeks. Management estimated that more than 30 percent of the salespeople had won at least one prize in the contest.

In order to compare the compensation plan with plans used in other companies, division executives had obtained a published research report which contained information on compensation in companies in a wide variety of consumer industries. The report indicated that for inexperienced sales trainees, the median starting salary was $9,000.

Turnover

Exhibits 3 and 4 show the relatively high rate of turnover in the sales force. This turnover was, however, substantially lower than in the 1960s.

Division executives cited two major reasons for the high rate of turnover among the field sales force: management limitations and a generally tight labor market. In the opinion of one executive, the lack of management attention had resulted in a failure to detect problems and an

Exhibit 3 SALES FORCE COMPOSITION

Year hired	Before 1968	1968	1969	1970	1971	1972	1973
Western zone	7[a]	4	5	2	2	7	2
Central zone	8	2	0	2	7	8	3
Eastern zone	7	2	2	2	3	9	5
Total[b]	22	8	7	6	12	24	10

[a]To be read "7 salespeople of those now in the Western zone were hired before 1968."
[b]The total number of salespeople for each zone was:

Western	29
Central	30
Eastern	30
Total	**89**

inability to take corrective action once a problem had been discovered. This executive believed that the division was beginning to "manage" rather than "fight fires."

Management was disturbed by the lost sales which resulted from high salesperson turnover. Executives estimated that a new salesperson had to be with the division for more than 6 months before becoming a "productive salesperson." Management estimated that out-of-pocket expenses were approximately $1,000 for each new salesperson hired. More disturbing to management, however, was the time which the selection and training process required of division executives.

To obtain first-hand information on the activities and attitudes of field salespeople, the casewriter spent a day with a field salesperson. This information is presented in the Appendix.

40

THE FUTURE

The president of Cole National and Mr. Sells had similar views on the division's major problems and objectives. Mr. Sells summed up these views as follows:

> Our future lies in *servicing* independent stores, franchised stores, and chain operations with a growing variety of products. We offer not a product but a complete merchandising and field service program. This program is our strongest competitive advantage.
>
> Our unique program has helped us to establish good relations with the chains at two levels. At headquarters they like us because of the profit we produce and the store services we perform for them. In the stores, the managers welcome our complete ready-to-display assortments and our training of store personnel to operate a key, knife, or sign department.
>
> As I see it, the chains we're in—variety, automotive, drug, hardware, discount—as well as most of our independent outlets will continue to grow and prosper. So far, no competitor has been able to hurt us seriously either

Exhibit 4 TRAINING PROGRAM—NEW HIRES, TERMINATIONS, AND RESIGNATIONS, 1969–1973

Month	Number of terri-tories	New hires	Termina-tions	Resig-nations
Nov. 1969	116	n.a.	14[a]	
Dec.	116	10	7[a]	
Jan. 1970	117	7	5[a]	
Feb.	n.a.	n.a.	6[a]	
March	n.a.	n.a.	10[a]	
April	116	7	14[a]	
May	115	9	8[a]	
June	114	9	7[a]	
July	112	8	5	11
Aug.	112	9	5	7
Sept.	111	8	1	10
Oct.	94	1	17	5
Nov.	89	3	1	4
Dec.	82	2	—	1
Jan. 1971	82	5	—	7
Feb.	90	6	1	5
March	89	5	4	5
April	89	5	2	3
May	89	5	5	1
June	89	5	1	5
July	89	5	2	2
Aug.	89	1	—	—
Sept.	89	1	6	—
Oct.	89	6	—	1
Nov.	90	7	1	3
Dec.	90	—	1	2
Jan. 1972	90	5	1	3
Feb.	90	5	1	2
March	90	3	2	4
April	90	4	1	1
May	90	1	1	2
June	90	5	3	2
July	90	4	2	1
Aug.	90	2	—	—
Sept.	90	4	1	5
Oct.	90	6	2	1
Nov.	90	2	2	4
Dec.	90	3	—	1
Jan. 1973	90	6	1	3
Feb.	90	2	1	4

[a]Breakdown of terminations and resignations not collected before July 1970 or after February 1973.

Note: n.a. = not available.

41

by taking accounts away from us or preventing us from taking some accounts away from him. Our customer relations are very good, and we should be able to find additional products to keep us growing.

The division's immediate problem is to solidify the organization and to improve our effectiveness as executives. Being executives is something new to many of the top people in the division. Most of our sales managers, for example, have excellent field sales records, but little experience as executives. Even now, they often have to act as salespeople in "problem" territories. But as our field salespeople become more experienced, these managers will become executives.

Ninety percent of our problems revolve around the field sales personnel. We must be able to attract, train and keep the kind of people we need if we're to continue to offer the unique field service program on which our continued success depends.

APPENDIX: COLE NATIONAL CORPORATION (D)

On November 14, 1974, a casewriter visited with William Bonnie, a district sales representative, and accompanied him on his calls. This appendix describes Mr. Bonnie's background and his reactions to his job. The appendix also includes a description of Mr. Bonnie's activities on November 14, together with excerpts from two sales calls.

During the 8 years before he joined Cole National Corporation, Mr. Bonnie had attended college on a part-time basis. He estimated that he needed one more year on a full-time basis in order to graduate.

While in college Mr. Bonnie had held a variety of jobs, including one as a hospital orderly from June 1972 to June 1974. His wife, a registered nurse, had also worked since their marriage, but was planning to stop work after the birth of their third child in early 1975.

Mr. Bonnie joined Cole National Corporation in July 1974. After completing the division's week-long training course, Mr. Bonnie began to work his territory on July 8, 1974. Although the district manager had been unable to accompany him during his first week in the field, the national sales trainer traveled with Mr. Bonnie during that week.

According to Mr. Bonnie, the district manager telephoned him weekly for the first 10 weeks after he began to work his territory. At the end of September the district manager spent a week making calls with Mr. Bonnie.

"Frankly, I like the freedom this job allows," Mr. Bonnie stated. "I don't impose any rigid structure on my daily activities, nor do I do things 'by the book.' Management looks at the figures, not the methods you use."

"I like to treat my customers as individuals, not just account numbers. This takes time and may mean that I'll have to call back two or three times to get an order that a higher-pressure salesperson might close the first time. But I think my method builds better customer relations."

Mr. Bonnie's territory included Maine, Vermont, New Hampshire, and portions of northern Massachusetts (not including Boston). He serviced this territory from his home in Portsmouth, New Hampshire. Mr. Bonnie estimated that, on the average, he did not have to remain away from home for more than one night a week.

Mr. Bonnie stated, "I have between 700 and 800 stores, spread throughout four states. My largest concentration of stores is in Portland, Maine, where I have 18 stores. On most days, however, I drive more than 200 miles from the time I leave home in the morning until I return at night."

Mr. Bonnie estimated that he made, on the average, 8 or 9 calls in a day. According to Mr. Bonnie, his district manager continually encouraged him to raise his average to 15 calls per day. "I'd rather get more sales from each store by selling in additional product lines," Mr. Bonnie stated, "but my boss thinks it's more important to 'get our foot in the door' in a larger number of stores." Mr. Bonnie estimated that fewer than 10 percent of his calls were made on stores which did not carry the division's products.

Mr. Bonnie continued, "I try to cover the really high-volume stores once every 5 weeks. That way they never have to mail in an order. Although I haven't yet been around my territory to all the medium-volume stores, I hope to call on them once every 3 to 4 months. As for the small outlets, I'll be lucky to get around to them once or twice a year. Right now I call on them only when they need service or want a salesperson to call."

Although Mr. Bonnie had been among the top 25 percent of the people in his district in terms of bonus payments received for exceeding sales quotas, he had not been able to meet his quotas for the sales contest in the fall of 1974. Mr. Bonnie's quotas for this sales contest, as distinct from the annual sales quota, were 10.5 calls per day in September and 9.1 calls per day in October. His quotas for orders per call were 0.45 in September and 0.41 in October.

Mr. Bonnie believed that a number of people had met their quotas for calls per day and orders per call simply by paying courtesy calls on particular stores and writing up small token orders. In contrast, Mr. Bonnie preferred to spend more time with each store manager and to write fewer, large orders. Mr. Bonnie recalled one instance in which he had met a chain buyer at the opening of a new store in that chain and had sold $1,600 worth of assortments of colored keys, one assortment for each store in that chain. In another instance, Mr. Bonnie had sold a large order to each of several stores in a chain whose headquarters buyer had approved the division's programs for purchase. In Mr. Bonnie's words, "Sandy Feder [a chain store specialist] opened the door, and I walked in." He recalled another case in which he called on a store manager whom no field salesperson from the division had visited for over a year. Mr. Bonnie recalled that he had persuaded the store manager to reinstate the division lines and obtained an order in excess of $1,200.

Between 10:00 A.M. and 4:30 P.M. on November 14, Mr. Bonnie made six calls. On a typical day, when not accompanied by a visitor, Mr. Bonnie made his first call before 10:00 A.M. and continued to work until

5:00 P.M. or later. A schedule of Mr. Bonnie's activities between 10:00 A.M. and 4:30 P.M. on November 14 appears in Exhibit A-1; Exhibit A-2 contains a summary of the data in Exhibit A-1; Exhibit A-3 contains an analysis of sales by product line for each store called on. A copy of Mr. Bonnie's DRPE is included in the text, as Exhibit 2.

Mr. Bonnie's first call was a service station affiliated with a major oil company.[5] The station, which had three gasoline pumps and two bays for mechanical work, was located on a main road about 5 minutes from the center of a northern suburb of Boston. On the door of the service station was a "Keys Made" sign furnished by the division. The key machine and attached displays of standard and colored keys were clearly visible through the service station window.

[5]Oil companies allowed their lessees complete freedom in purchasing items such as keys.

Exhibit A-1   MR. BONNIE'S SCHEDULE, 10:00 A.M. −4:30 P.M., NOVEMBER 14, 1974

10:00–10:20	Drove to first call, a gasoline station which had requested service on a key machine
10:20–11:00	First call
11:00–11:05	Wrote report[a] on first call
11:05–11:10	Drove to second call, a nearby gas station
11:10–11:25	Second call
11:25–11:30	Wrote report on second call and walked to third call, a national chain variety store
11:30–11:45	Third call
11:45–11:50	Wrote report on third call
11:50–12:05	Planned route for remainder of day[b]
12:05–12:35	Drove to fourth call, a large leased hardware department located in a discount department store
12:35– 1:55	Fourth call
1:55– 2:00	Wrote report on fourth call
2:00– 2:15	Drove to restaurant (located on direct route between fourth and fifth calls)
2:15– 2:55	Lunch[c]
2:55– 3:10	Drove to fifth call, a large variety store operated by a regional chain
3:10– 3:25	Fifth call
3:25– 3:30	Wrote report on fifth call
3:30– 3:45	Drove to sixth call, a large self-service department store
3:45– 4:25	Sixth call
4:25– 4:30	Wrote report on sixth call

[a]Making out the complete daily report typically took Mr. Bonnie an additional hour after he returned home in the evening.
[b]On days when he was not accompanied by a visitor, Mr. Bonnie planned his route before leaving for his first call.
[c]Mr. Bonnie estimated that lunch typically took no more than 15 to 20 minutes. The presence of the casewriter, however, prolonged lunch on this particular day. The presence of the casewriter did not, however, noticeably affect the remainder of the schedule.

Exhibit A-2 SUMMARY OF SALESPERSON'S
ACTIVITIES ON NOVEMBER 14, 1974

Time spent in stores	3 hours, 25 minutes
Time spent writing call reports	30 minutes
Time spent planning calls and driving between stores	1 hour, 55 minutes
Lunch	40 minutes
Total time: 10:00 A.M. –4:30 P.M.	**6 hours, 30 minutes**

Exhibit A-3 SALES BY STORE AND PRODUCT

	Brass keys	Colored keys	Knives	LNS	Total
First call	$ 44	$ 23	Not carried	Not carried	$ 67
Second call	51	161	Not carried	Not carried	212
Third call	119	Nil	Not carried	Not carried	119[a]
Fourth call	91	26	$70	$158	345
Fifth call	Nil[a]	Nil[a]	Not carried	Not carried	Nil
Sixth call	161	65	Nil	Nil[b]	226
Total	**$466**	**$275**	**$70**	**$158**	**$969**

[a]Store had recently sent in an order by mail.
[b]Sign assortment had been on display less than a week.

The service station owner had mailed a request to Cleveland for a service call on his key machine, which had not been cutting properly. When Mr. Bonnie arrived, the owner asked him to give him credit for miscut keys. Mr. Bonnie explained that he could not do so. He told the owner to accumulate miscuts until he had about 100, and then ship them to Cleveland where credit would be issued.

Mr. Bonnie then adjusted the key machine and showed the service station owner how to make minor adjustments, if they were needed. At the owner's request Mr. Bonnie cut a key for the station's rest room to demonstrate that the machine was functioning properly. He also left the owner some spare parts for the machine. The entire procedure took about 25 minutes. The station owner and Mr. Bonnie then engaged in the following conversation:

Owner I received this machine in February and figured out how to use it. The salesperson (Mr. Bonnie's predecessor) didn't come back 'til April. You know, every dealer in town who has your machines is always running out of key blanks. We have to get them locally. If it's profitable you ought to put on more salespeople. Of course, I don't have to see you too often—every 2 months ought to do it.

Mr. Bonnie I'll try to make it every 3 months. Here's my home phone if you have any problems.

Have you thought about adding our house keys in color to your car keys in color? It's the same deal, an initial assortment of 12 dozen keys . . . how about putting it on?

Owner	No, not now. Better wait and see how things go now that the machine's in order.
Mr. Bonnie	OK, maybe after you see that service has improved you'll be interested. By the way, your key blank inventory is low.
Owner	Go ahead and figure out your order. Be sure to add some L4's [a specific key blank]. They're big sellers around here. Don't make the order too big—just include the popular ones. Don't give me any slow sellers.
Mr. Bonnie	OK, low inventory, more frequent reorder. That's fine with us.

Mr. Bonnie spent the next 5 to 10 minutes taking inventory of the key blanks and making up an order. The owner signed the order, and Mr. Bonnie said goodbye and left.

Mr. Bonnie's fourth call was the hardware, housewares, and toy department of a discount department store. The store covered about 18,000 square feet and was located in a small shopping center off of a major highway. A "Keys Made" sign was on the door. The department itself was operated by a firm which leased space in which to operate such departments from several stores throughout Mr. Bonnie's territory. The hardware and housewares sections occupied about 1,500 square feet. Merchandise was piled on some counters to a height of more than 10 feet. The aisles were narrow and crowded with cartons and merchandise. Displays of brass and colored keys, knives, and LNS shared a booth with the department's cash register.

After exchanging greetings with the department manager and the clerk, Mr. Bonnie discovered that almost 90 keys had been miscut since his last visit.

Mr. Bonnie	You've got too many miscuts for 2 months.
Clerk	So we've got too many miscuts. I can't help it. (Clerk looks on while Mr. Bonnie adjusts key machine.) Sometimes it's hard to find the right key blank for a customer.
Mr. Bonnie	If it gets to take too long to look for it, tell them you don't have it. It's a high-profit but low-dollar sale.
Clerk	It's not just the odd ones I have trouble with.
Mr. Bonnie	If it takes too long, don't bother.
Clerk	We've got about 80 miscuts.
Mr. Bonnie	Who trained you? I didn't.
Clerk	The manager did.
Mr. Bonnie	Who has more miscuts?
Clerk	He does.

Need customer service reps.

Mr. Bonnie   Show me how you cut a key.

The clerk cut a key while Mr. Bonnie watched and made suggestions. Mr. Bonnie discovered that the key machine needed additional adjustment, performed the required adjustment, and showed the clerk how to adjust the machine. The clerk then cut a key while Mr. Bonnie explained why the machine might need adjustment from time to time. The entire key-machine servicing procedure had consumed about 35 minutes. Mr. Bonnie spent an additional 10 minutes inventorying the key blank stock and made out an order for $117, while exchanging banter with the department manager.

Manager   How come it takes you so long to make out an order?

Mr. Bonnie   If I made it out fast, without a careful inventory, you'd be over-stocked, and that's no good for you or me.

Manager   How about my letters? They're stealing them at a good clip.

Mr. Bonnie   How're your knives? Would you open the case? (Knife cabinets were kept locked to avoid pilferage.)

Manager   I don't know about knife sales. I don't have time to check.

Mr. Bonnie   Not even on a high-profit item? (While he checked the knife inventory and put in order, Mr. Bonnie and the department manager exchanged jokes.)
Do you sell many linoleum knives? Guess I'd better get you some more. You've sold half your assortment.

While he made up a knife order which totaled $70, Mr. Bonnie chatted with the department manager about personal matters. Servicing the knife cabinet and making up the order required about 15 minutes.

Mr. Bonnie then checked the LNS display and told the manager that he would make up an order for 3 dozen each of the letters that had sold best.

Mr. Bonnie   I won't get you many of these larger letters. You don't need many. OK?

Manager   If you say so.

Mr. Bonnie   Do you have to keep these plastic signs down so low? Can't you put them where people can see them?

Manager   Not a chance 'til after Christmas. Need everything I have right now for toys. When are you coming down to get the kids' presents?

Mr. Bonnie   We'll probably be down next week or the week after.

Mr. Bonnie then made up an order for $158 worth of LNS. The department manager signed the order and then insisted that Mr. Bonnie

47

inspect the department's new stockroom. After a 5-minute tour, Mr. Bonnie excused himself and left.

SEVEN   DiMedici

In the summer of 1973, top management of diMedici, the world's largest manufacturer of branded hosiery for men and boys, secured approval to incorporate sportswear into the diMedici product line. By February 1974, company executives had selected the initial sportswear product line, redrawn 37 sales territories, hired 6 new salespeople, and selected 43 of the company's 105 salespeople to participate in a 1-year test to see if they could sell sportswear successfully without decreasing their effectiveness in selling hosiery. By July 1974, the first half of the test, the spring selling season, had been completed. During this time, diMedici's hosiery sales had actually increased in most areas where sportswear was sold, but sportswear sales were considerably below target. Bruce Masser, diMedici's vice president of sales, was now considering whether he should make any changes before the fall selling season began or maintain the status quo at least until all the information for the year-long test was in.

COMPANY HISTORY

DiMedici was the men's and boys' branded hosiery division of VanDer-Koff Corporation, the world's largest manufacturer of apparel. In fiscal 1974 (July 1, 1973–June 30, 1974), the corporation's 22 autonomous divisions generated net sales of $571,820,000 and net earnings after taxes of $10,079,000.

Founded in 1904, diMedici rapidly gained a reputation for high quality men's and boys' hosiery and excellent service to retailers. A pioneer in advertising and in-store display and fixturing, it soon had a sufficiently strong position with retailers to set retail prices by printing the price on its products' labels. Its sales force, one of the largest in the clothing industry, sold directly to department stores and men's specialty shops which catered to a middle- and an upper-income clientele.

DiMedici was acquired by VanDer-Koff in 1961. In 1972 an arrangement was made with Hotowko, Inc., whereby diMedici would distribute and sell Hotowko toiletries for men to department stores and men's specialty shops, outlets not then covered by Hotowko's sales organization. In December 1973 the sportswear line was added. By the end of fiscal 1974, diMedici's annual net sales had reached $35 million, with net earnings of $3.5 million. (See Exhibit 1 for divisional organization chart and Exhibit 2 for operating statements.)

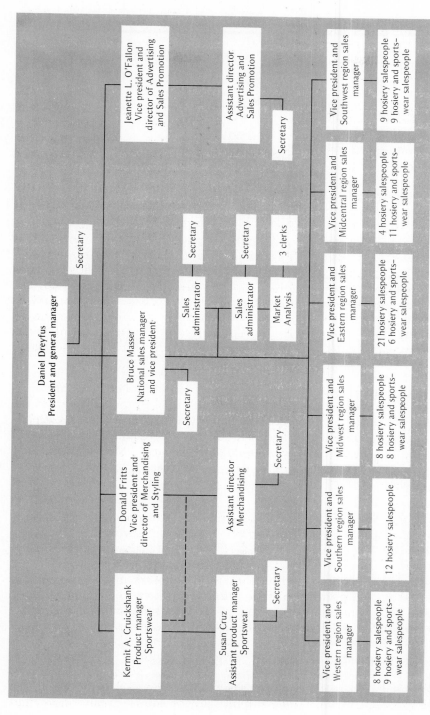

Exhibit 1   DiMedici organization chart.

Exhibit 2 OPERATING STATEMENTS (1973 and 1974)

	Fiscal 1973 (July 1, 1972 – June 30, 1973)		Fiscal 1974 (July 1, 1973 – June 30, 1974)	
Net sales	$30,896,000	100.0%	$34,865,000	100.0%
Gross profit: standard	12,490,000	40.4	14,538,700	41.7
Adjustments for markdowns and manufacturing variations	619,000	2.0	1,011,800	2.9
Gross profit: actual	11,871,000	38.4	13,526,900	38.8
Direct expenses				
Direct selling (salespeople's commissions, and regional manager salary and expenses)	2,051,000	6.6	2,283,650	6.5
Indirect selling[a]	1,437,000	4.7	1,680,000	4.8
Total selling	3,488,000	11.3	3,963,650	11.3
Advertising	1,850,000	6.0	2,170,000	6.2
Warehouse and shipping	1,190,000	3.9	1,411,000	4.0
Office and administrative	865,000	2.8	1,061,000	3.0
Total direct expenses	7,393,000	24.0	8,605,650	24.5
Headquarters allocated administrative costs	1,035,000	3.4	1,429,465	4.1
Total expenses	8,428,000	27.4	10,035,115	28.6
Net profit	**$ 3,443,000**	**11.0%**	**$ 3,491,785**	**10.2%**

[a]Included sales and marketing executives' salaries and expenses, secretaries, non-New York sales offices, sales conventions, public relations, special salespeople's contests, and several miscellaneous items.

50

DiMEDICI'S OPERATIONS BEFORE SPORTSWEAR WAS ADDED

Until February 1974, diMedici's product line consisted of about 150 styles of socks, two styles of Supp-hose support stockings, 15 styles of casual house slippers known as "Softies" and about 30 Hotowko toiletries for men. Boys' stretch socks were available in two sizes and men's stretch socks came in sizes 10 to 13 and 14 to 16. There were nine sizes of "sized" socks. Softies had five sizes. Beginning in February, diMedici also started selling sportswear. In fiscal 1974, its sales were as follows:

Hosiery	$24,560,000
Softies	4,000,000
Hotowko men's toiletries	2,000,000
Sportswear	440,000
Military[1]	3,000,000
Export[1]	1,000,000
Total	**$35,000,000**

Of its hosiery business, 20 percent was in athletic socks, 20 percent in leisure socks, 35 percent in basic dress socks, and 25 percent in fancy dress socks. From season to season, about 35 percent of the product line changed, and about 45 percent changed from year to year. The average

[1]DiMedici's military sales were handled by 12 salespeople who sold products for all VanDer-Koff divisions to military exchanges. Export sales were handled by a similar international division. Military and international salespeople are not shown on diMedici's organization chart, though their sales are included in diMedici's sales figures.

wholesale unit price for socks was about $.80, while the average retail price was about $1.50. DiMedici's average gross margin on hosiery was about 37.5 percent.

DiMedici's domestic nonmilitary sales were made to about 11,000 customers who had about 13,000 retail outlets. About 85 percent of these accounts were men's specialty stores and about 15 percent were department stores. The men's specialty stores accounted for about 75 percent of diMedici's sales volume. DiMedici sold some products to about 85 percent of all major U.S. department stores, but only 10 percent of those were considered "truly major accounts." According to Mr. Dreyfus, president of diMedici, a major reason for retailers to carry diMedici products was the services the company provided:

> We offer a wide variety of fixtures, displays, and sales aids to help a retailer set up the most profitable sock department possible. Moreover, our sales-people have small enough territories so they can check stores as often as necessary to make sure they are never stocked out or overstocked, and they equip retail salespeople with as much know-how as possible to sell socks to consumers.

DiMedici directed its advertising toward upper- and middle-income consumers who shopped in retail stores that featured nationally adver-tised brand name merchandise. While it did most of its national advertis-ing in male-oriented magazines, it used television advertising during peak holiday selling seasons. It offered cooperative advertising and back-up material, such as display cards, statement enclosures, and posters, to its customers. It also advertised heavily in trade publications and did frequent direct mailings to its customers. Its advertising often featured well-known sports figures, such as baseball star Willie Mays and tennis champion John Newcombe.

51

The Sales Organization

Bruce L. Masser, vice president of sales, presided over diMedici's sales organization. Under him were two sales administrators, a market analyst, and six regional managers. The sales administrators handled a wide variety of administrative tasks, including customer and salesperson requests and complaints. The market analyst compiled information about individual salespeople's performance with various accounts to determine where diMedici's major opportunities and problems lay.

All except one of the regional managers had come up through diMedici or other VanDer-Koff divisions. Their chief tasks included motivating and training salespeople and establishing rapport with major accounts. They were not held responsible for the profitability of their regions. Rather, each received a base salary plus a bonus based on the territory's increase in sales volume over the previous year. The average annual salary and bonus for a regional manager was about $33,000, plus expenses of $15,000 to $18,000.

DiMedici's 105 salespeople (average age 35) were all high school graduates, and most had some college training. They received 7 percent commission on hosiery sales. Their gross incomes ranged from $13,000 to $45,000, with the average being about $18,500. The average income had grown by about 15 percent during the last 2 years. While competitive hosiery manufacturers generally paid commission rates comparable to diMedici's (6 to 8 percent), diMedici salespeople had a much higher average income because they sold substantially larger volumes. Salespeople paid all their own expenses.

DiMedici's sales territories were organized geographically, and salespeople covered both department stores and specialty shops. The larger accounts, especially those with several retail outlets, often had two or three sock suppliers, while the smaller ones usually had only one. With multi-outlet accounts, diMedici salespeople sold merchandise at headquarters and serviced all the accounts' retail outlets. With many accounts, both selling and servicing were done in retail outlets. The number of accounts and retail outlets which salespeople were responsible for varied from 10 accounts with 60 outlets to 200 accounts with 220 outlets.

Sales meetings were held before each of the two hosiery selling seasons. Sometimes national meetings were held, which generally lasted 2 working days, plus the weekend, and at other times, 2-day regional meetings were held. At the national meetings, one day was devoted to merchandise presentations, another to advertising presentations, a third to techniques of selling, and the fourth to general procedures. Meetings usually broke up by 2:00 P.M., and afternoons and evenings were recreation periods. At regional meetings, the recreation periods were shortened considerably, and the same topics were covered in only 2 days. The major selling season for the spring hosiery line was January, February, and the first 2 weeks in March. The spring line accounted for about 35 percent of a salesperson's annual hosiery volume. The bulk of the fall line was sold in July and August for back-to-school purchases, and in September and October for the Christmas selling season. October was diMedici's single biggest month for bookings. Fill-in selling was done throughout the year, and orders were shipped immediately. The average initial order size for hosiery was about $400, and the average fill-in order size was about $200.

At small department stores and specialty shops, the salesperson usually contacted the owner or manager. At larger accounts, the men's hosiery buyer was always visited. In some cases, the salesperson also visited the sporting goods department buyer, the young men's department buyer, and the boys' department buyer. He usually visited buyers once every 4 to 6 weeks, depending on the size of the account and the territory to be covered. The time spent with a buyer varied from about 30

minutes for normal fill-in sales to a whole morning for major presentations of new lines. Salespeople were expected to service retail outlets
every 3 to 6 weeks. This involved counting inventory, stocking display
racks, writing normal fill-in orders, making sure inventories for Christmas, Father's Day, and back-to-school periods were adequate, and
keeping retailers well informed about market conditions, diMedici's
products, and their movement. Retail visits could last from 30 minutes to
3 hours.

Mr. Masser commented on the hosiery selling task as follows:

> One advantage our salespeople have is that they're selling a brand product
> that already has a certain amount of acceptance. However, though our
> competitors don't have lines as extensive as ours, they do have well-
> respected brand names and quality products priced comparable to ours.
> Therefore, our salespeople have to work hard to maintain rapport with the
> customers, keep their trust, and continually provide consistent, top-notch
> service. It's impossible to overrate the importance of service in this business.
> If our people don't take inventory regularly, a customer will become stocked
> out of a popular product, and he'll soon start looking for another supplier.

DiMEDICI'S DECISION TO GO INTO SPORTSWEAR

Since the late 1960s, VanDer-Koff and diMedici management had discussed the possibility of adding sportswear to diMedici's line. While the
sock business had been increasing steadily, the increments were relatively small. "We convinced corporate management that life's too short to
wait around for our sock business to grow significantly," said Mr.
Dreyfus. "We already sell twice the volume of our nearest competitor.
Now we want to seize the opportunities in the sportswear business while
the field is still hot."

DiMedici's managers stated that they chose sportswear rather than
another field of apparel partly because it was the fastest-growing area of
men's clothing. They felt the growth would continue as consumers
enjoyed a more casual life-style; had more leisure time; and with
year-round daylight saving time, spent more time outdoors. They
suspected the fuel shortage would prevent people from traveling as
much as in the past and would result in their spending more time at
tennis courts or golf courses in their own communities.

Another factor that influenced the decision was that, while there
were several well-known sportswear manufacturers, none dominated the
market. Retail buyers usually purchased items they thought would sell
well from several different manufacturers, rather than carrying the whole
product line of a single manufacturer. Still another point was that,
because of the extensive "housekeeping" (for example, taking inventory)
services necessary in the hosiery business, diMedici had probably the
largest sales force in men's wear in the United States, certainly a larger

one than any other hosiery or sportswear manufacturer. This force serviced accounts in both major metropolitan areas and more remote areas. DiMedici management was sure its force could service sportswear customers better than any other sportswear manufacturer. It pointed out that, since the salespeople would have to spend more time at each stop, their territories and account loads would have to be reduced. However, the reduction would be compensated for by more sales per stop and the reduction of traveling time and costs.

Still other arguments in favor of diMedici's getting into sportswear were that its brand name was recognized and respected and that it already had numerous well-established accounts. With many customers, especially independent specialty shops, sportswear and hosiery were purchased by the same buyers. Even if they were bought by different buyers, management thought the hosiery buyers would provide favorable introductions to the sportswear buyers. Management stressed, however, that men's hosiery would still be the company's primary business. Mr. Dreyfus commented as follows:

> The important growth in the sock business in the last two years gave us the means to expand into other areas. We're not about to let our sportswear business be a success at the expense of our sock business. We'll have a problem if our salespeople think there's greater opportunity in sportswear and neglect hosiery sales as a result.

By the beginning of 1974, Kermit A. Cruickshank, formerly of a large manufacturer of men's wear, had been named product manager of diMedici sportswear. Production facilities had been expanded somewhat to manufacture a few sportswear items, but management planned to contract most of the production to other manufacturers until the company was established in the sportswear field. Plans were also under way to strengthen the diMedici name by increasing the consumer advertising budget from $1,600,000 for fiscal 1974 to $1,850,000 for fiscal 1975.

In choosing the product line, management was careful to avoid duplicating items produced by other VanDer-Koff divisions. The first sportswear line consisted of sweaters and sweater shirts which retailed for $12 to $28 and knit shirts which retailed for $12 to $20. The average retail price was $14. Many of the items were patterned coordinates. In all, the line included 60 styles, 5 colors to the style, with 4 sizes to each color. For the spring of 1975, diMedici planned to add tennis and golf wear.

DiMedici's goals for sportswear sales in the United States were $800,000 (114,500 units) for the 1974 spring selling season and $1.2 million (171,500 units) for the 1974 fall selling season. It was thought that the military would account for another $300,000, but that sportswear would not initially be given to the export salespeople. The average opening order per customer was expected to be about $500 (70 units). DiMedici's average gross margin on sportswear was expected to be about 30 percent.[2] Company management estimated that by fiscal 1977, the diMedici sales force would be increased to 165 salespeople plus 16 sales managers. The major selling seasons for sportswear would be the last week in February, March, and April for the fall line and late August, September, and October for the spring line. The fall line would then be delivered from July through December and the spring line from January through June. (See Exhibit 3 for sportswear budget for calendar year 1974 and for results for the first 6 months.)

In March 1974, in a test designed to see whether the sock salespeople could in fact sell sportswear without interfering with sock sales, diMedici introduced sportswear in six states—California, Illinois, Michigan, Ohio, Texas, and New Jersey. In order for the salespeople to complete their first round of selling hosiery in time to begin selling sportswear by the last week in February, their territories had to be decreased. In deciding which of diMedici's 99 territories to change initially, Mr. Masser identified 37 where diMedici had good distribution; which had a good mix of large and small accounts; and whose size, volume, and potential were large enough to accommodate two salespeople. Out of these, Mr. Masser created six new territories and hired six new salespeople. On the average, the account load of the 37 salespeople whose territories were redrawn was decreased from 160 to 130. (For an example of how the territories were redrawn, see Exhibit 4.) These 37, plus the 6 new salespeople, were given both sportswear and socks to sell. Their commission on sportswear would be 5 percent of sales. Targeted sportswear sales were $50,000 per salesperson during the 1974 calendar year. While other sportswear manufacturers were thought to pay lower commissions,

55

[2]This margin was not expected in the first year (see Exhibit 3).

Exhibit 3 OPERATING STATEMENTS FOR SPORTSWEAR

	Planned calendar 1974				Actual January 1– June 30, 1974
	U.S.	Military	Total	%	
Net sales	$2,000,000	$300,000	$2,300,000	100.0	$440,000
Gross profit (standard)	600,000	90,000	690,000	30.0	
Adjustments for markdowns and manufacturing variations	100,000	12,000	112,000	4.9	
Gross profit (actual)	$ 500,000	$ 78,000	$ 578,000	25.1	
Direct expenses					
Direct selling (salespeople's commission, regular salary and managers' salary	$ 100,000	$ 21,000	$ 121,000	5.3	
Indirect selling	100,000		100,000	4.4	
Total selling	200,000	21,000	221,000	9.7	
Advertising	100,000	3,000	103,000	4.5	
Warehouse and shipping	80,000	12,000	92,000	4.0	
Office and administrative	20,000	3,000	23,000	1.0	
Total direct expenses	400,000	39,000	439,000	19.2	
New York allocated administrative costs	37,500	5,550	43,050	1.9	
Total expenses	$ 437,500	$ 44,550	$ 482,050	21.1	
Net profit	$ 62,500	$ 33,450	$ 95,950	4.0	

Exhibit 4 (a) Sales territories in New Jersey before the introduction of sportswear; (b) sales territories in New Jersey after the introduction of sportswear; (c) sales territories in Ohio before the introduction of sportswear; (d) sales territories in Ohio after introduction of sportswear.

their sales volumes were known to be substantially higher. The average annual income for a good sportswear salesperson was thought to be about $25,000.

Since decreasing their territories obviously meant that the 37 salespeople would lose some hosiery volume and therefore some commissions, Mr. Masser guaranteed that their incomes for the first year would not fall below those of previous years if they made up only half of the volume they lost. He explained the new compensation system for these 37 salespeople as follows:

To illustrate how the plan will work, let's make these assumptions:

1973	Territory hosiery volume	$300,000
1973	Commission (7 percent)	21,000
1974	Territory hosiery volume ($40,000 taken to make part of new salesperson's territory)	260,000

This loss of $40,000 will represent an income loss of $2,800. It establishes the salesperson's territory volume at $260,000 and his income at $18,200. Now let's look at what his income would be under a variety of circumstances.

Example 1 *Salesperson makes up half the hosiery volume lost and reaches targeted sportswear volume.*

If during 1974 the salesperson brings back his loss of volume 50 percent (in this case $20,000), he will automatically get $21,000, his 1973 income. On any hosiery volume above that, he will receive 7 percent commission. Also, whatever he sells in sportswear will be additional income dollars. His income would be calculated as follows:

	Salesperson's income
1974 Hosiery sales:	
7 percent commission on $260,000	$ 18,200
Commission on additional $20,000	2,800
1974 Sportswear sales:	
5 percent commission on $50,000	2,500
	$ 23,500

Example 2 *Salesperson makes up part but less than half of the hosiery volume lost and reaches targeted sportswear volume.*

Suppose this salesperson increases hosiery volume by only $19,000, less than 50 percent of his $45,000 loss. He would then receive 7 percent of his total hosiery sales plus 5 percent of his sportswear sales:

	Salesperson's income
1974 Hosiery sales:	
7 percent commission on $279,000	$ 19,530
1974 Sportswear sales:	
5 percent on $50,000	2,500
	$ 22,030

Example 3 *Salesperson makes up none of hosiery volume lost but reaches targeted sportswear volume.*

	Salesperson's income
1974 Hosiery sales:	
7 percent commission on $260,000	$ 18,200
1974 Sportswear sales	
5 percent commission on $50,000	2,500
	$ 20,700

Example 4 *Salesperson makes up half the hosiery volume lost but sells no sportswear.*

Salesperson's income

1974	Hosiery sales:	
	7 percent commission on $260,000	$ 18,200
	Commission on additional $20,000	2,800
1974	Sportswear sales	0
		$ 21,000

Example 5 *Salesperson makes up none of hosiery volume lost and sells no sportswear.*

Salesperson's income

1974	Hosiery sales:	
	7 percent commission on $260,000	$ 18,200
1974	Sportswear sales	0
		$ 18,200

This $2,800 loss in income indicates that we have a problem. Unless there are extenuating circumstances, the salesperson should be terminated.

58

Toward the end of February 1974, diMedici management held three regional meetings, each of which lasted one day, for the salespeople who were to sell both socks and sportswear. Mr. Dreyfus attended two of the meetings, and Mr. Masser and Mr. Cruickshank attended all three.

By July 1974, Mr. Masser had determined that, at least during the spring selling season, sportswear had not hurt hosiery sales. In fact, most of the salespeople who sold both hosiery and sportswear had sold more hosiery than those who sold only hosiery. He thought this was the result of the former salespeople's visiting customers more frequently and writing more fill-in orders. Sportswear sales, however, had reached only $440,000. Mr. Masser attributed this poor performance to five problems.

The first problem, Mr. Masser thought, was that, while customers readily perceived diMedici as a fine hosiery manufacturer, they did not yet think of it as a sportswear manufacturer. He suspected that, as a consequence, their initial orders were very small, and some of them were probably token orders placed out of allegiance to diMedici salespeople. This "image" problem was compounded by the fact that diMedici's first sportswear line was not as strong as management had expected, largely because it contained numerous patterned sweaters which were to be coordinated with patterned sweater shirts. Not only did these items prove to be unpopular industry-wide, but they also required a good deal of explanation by the salesperson. The introduction would have been better, Mr. Masser thought, if it had started during a fall selling season when the line consisted primarily of ordinary sports shirts which were easier to sell than sweater coordinates.

A second problem, Mr. Masser thought, was that selling socks required very different skills than did selling sportswear. While the former depended heavily on the manufacturer's regularly providing retail merchandising services, such as inventory checks, to customers, these services were not so important to sportswear selling. To sell sportswear well, Mr. Masser thought, the salesperson needed more flair and creativity than was needed to sell socks. He commented as follows:

> All our salespeople who sell sportswear well seem to have some psychological tie to youth. They're lively and energetic and would feel perfectly at ease wearing our sports clothes. I don't necessarily mean, however, that age should be the most important criterion in choosing salespeople now. We have one 68-year-old salesperson who ran circles around two of our new 25-year-old salespeople!

Mr. Masser thought that a third reason sportswear sales had not reached target was that the training program had been inadequate. The February meetings had dealt only with the products. Mr. Masser now felt they had not been long enough to teach the salespeople all they needed to know about a completely different line, much less to teach them fundamental techniques of presenting sportswear to customers. To cover both product and selling techniques well would require that the sports-wear sales meetings he was planning for August be substantially longer than those he had held in February. However, because the cost of sales meetings was skyrocketing, top management was urging him to limit sales meetings whenever possible. A recent memorandum from Mr. Dreyfus had stated:

59

> It could very well be that, in the interest of economy and in an effort to gain efficiency, we must compromise and eliminate the four times a year sales meeting direction toward which we are heading. I see no way for us to go on a four times a year basis—December and June for socks and February and August for sportswear.

Mr. Dreyfus attached the following data on recent diMedici sales meetings:

Date	Type of meeting(s)	No. of days	Approximate no. of people attending	Total out-of-pocket cost
December 1973	1 national meeting held for introduction of spring line of socks	4	105 salespersons and 6 regional managers	$75,000
February 1974	3 regional meetings held for introduction of fall line of sportswear[3]	1 day per meeting	43 salespersons, 6 regional managers, Mr. Dreyfus, Mr. Masser, Mr. Cruickshank	$10,000
June 1974	3 regional meetings held for introduction of fall line of socks[3]	2 days per meeting	105 salespersons, 6 regional managers, Mr. Dreyfus, Mr. Masser, Mr. Fritts	$35,000

[3]Two regions were combined for each of these meetings.

A fourth problem, Mr. Masser felt, was that giving both sportswear and socks to the new salespeople had been a mistake. "Most of our problems have been with our newer people," he said. "We threw them in too soon. Not only was their knowledge about sportswear inadequate, but they didn't know the hosiery line either, and they hadn't yet built rapport with their accounts. They certainly needed a stronger training program, but more important, they needed time to establish good relationships with their customers." (See Exhibit 5 for sportswear and hosiery sales by salesperson.)

The fifth problem Mr. Masser identified was the state of the economy. Competitors, he noted, had not had an exceptionally good season either.

> Retail buyers have limited budgets, and since all manufacturers' prices have gone up, the buyers simply can't buy as many units and offer the selection they would like to. This problem could be even worse during our fall selling season if inflation keeps growing. Of course, buyers could probably get more money if they convince management they could sell additional merchandise. But several buyers I've talked to aren't very optimistic about selling seasons in the immediate future.

Mr. Masser felt strongly that these problems should be solved as completely as possible before the fall selling season, because he expected the fall to present entirely new challenges. First, there would be more overlap in selling seasons. The bulk of the fall hosiery line, which accounted for twice the sales of the spring line, was sold from July through October, while initial spring sportswear sales were made from late August through October. DiMedici was running a contest to encourage salespeople to get hosiery bookings done during July and August, but Mr. Masser doubted the salespeople would be able to get retailers to make Christmas purchases as early as August.

A second potential area of difficulty was that diMedici management had decided that, for the fall selling season, all salespeople would sell a new line of tennis sportswear in addition to their regular sock or sock and sportswear lines. This line had been endorsed by John Newcombe and management planned to give it substantial advertising support. Delivery of tennis wear to retailers was scheduled to begin during November 1974.

Finally, Mr. Masser was concerned that his salespeople were going to run into a more serious time problem in the fall selling season than they had in the spring. "I'm not really sure they'll have time to go after both socks and sportswear aggressively," he commented. "They may spend too much time on sportswear because it's new and challenging and they've been disappointed in their performance thus far. If they do that and neglect socks, we could have real problems."

Exhibit 5 HOSIERY AND SPORTSWEAR VOLUME BY SALES-PERSON, JANUARY 1–JUNE 30, 1974

Salesperson	Annual hosiery volume lost by territorial reorganization (based on fiscal 1972 sales)	Hosiery sales volume	Increase in hosiery volume	Sports-wear sales volume
New Jersey				
Fredrick	$ 3,700	$111,300	$19,800	$ 3,400
Peter	15,800	99,900	14,000	2,800
Banks	21,200	94,900	16,800	8,900
Brakebill	66,400	175,300	19,300	24,900
George	14,600	73,300	1,400	9,600
Kreyling[a]	—	24,800	—	5,100
Ohio				
Dance	$23,700	$113,400	$12,900	$14,800
Terry[b]	3,900	85,900	19,900	16,500
Saunders	43,600	116,100	25,200	6,200
Kerry	10,400	107,500	23,000	5,900
Karnes[a]	—	12,200	—	3,900
Illinois				
Butters	$33,600	$148,100	$19,300	$23,300
Hall	31,600	156,600	17,200	—
Eldridge	5,000	134,700	20,100	6,900
Henson	20,900	76,000	6,700	2,800
Schuller	4,600	64,700	3,300	10,200
Francis	40,000			
Wheeler	—			
Curtis[a]	—	10,000	—	3,200
Michigan				
Barnes	$35,700	$125,000	$16,700	$ 8,300
Darling	50,500	159,500	11,700	19,500
Ellis	28,200	257,500	8,400	18,200
Clem	6,800	89,800	8,400	9,000
Belcher	26,200	84,000	7,200	—
Thomas[a]	—	19,900	—	6,900
Texas				
Andrews	$19,100	$143,300	$13,300	$37,100
Bull				
Evans	20,800	108,100	13,400	1,200
Hollis				
Zimny	61,900	133,000	49,600	16,300
Albert				
Cane				
Yeats[a]	—	13,355	—	7,100
California				
Cullen				
Vance				
Keane	$20,400	$95,244	$ 500	$7,200
Fence				
Harrow	10,500	85,200	25,700	—
France	64,700	53,800	900	
Jones	—			
Rogers	—			
Klee[a]	—	(5,129)[c]	—	3,375

[a]New salespeople.

[b]Also had part of Michigan.

[c]Indicates deficit—can occur when returns exceed shipments.

Note: Missing data were not available in company records.

61

EIGHT   Allied Chemical Corporation: Industrial Chemicals Division

In the spring 1973, Dr. H. W. Schultze, president of the Industrial Chemicals Division of Allied Chemical Corporation was reviewing the division's programs and organization for marketing and selling sulfuric acid. He was concerned about the lack of apparent organizational structure in two of the sulfuric acid selling programs and wondered if the organization could be streamlined in some way.

ALLIED CHEMICAL CORPORATION

Allied Chemical Corporation, with 1972 sales of $1,500,977,000 and profits of $66,037,000, was among the nation's major industrial firms. It had operations in energy, fibers and fabricated products, and chemicals. In 1972 the chemical operation accounted for 54 percent of the sales and 41 percent of profits. It sold chemicals through the Industrial Chemicals Division, the Specialty Chemicals Division, the Plastics Division, and the Agricultural Chemicals Division.

62

INDUSTRIAL CHEMICALS DIVISION

The Industrial Chemicals Division had been organized in 1966 when it took over the operations of three predecessor divisions, which much earlier had been three separate firms brought together through a series of mergers to form Allied Chemical Corporation. In 1968, the Specialty Chemicals Division was separated from the Industrial Chemicals Division. It was responsible for the sale of low volume products with a relatively high value per pound, such as dyes. The Industrial Chemicals Division maintained responsibility for high volume products with a low value per pound, including sulfuric acid, soda ash (sodium carbonate), chlorine, caustic soda (sodium hydroxide), and calcium chloride. They were used in tonnage quantities by a variety of industries.

Dr. Schultze became president of the division in late 1968. The division was organized on a functional basis and had a marketing director for each major product or product category. Each market director was responsible for the profits generated by his products. The division had a sales force of 60 salespeople, reporting to seven regional sales managers who reported to the director of sales. Exhibit 1 is a division organization chart, and Exhibit 2 provides position descriptions of a marketing director, sales managers, and a salesperson.

Division sales in 1972 were approximately $300 million. The division

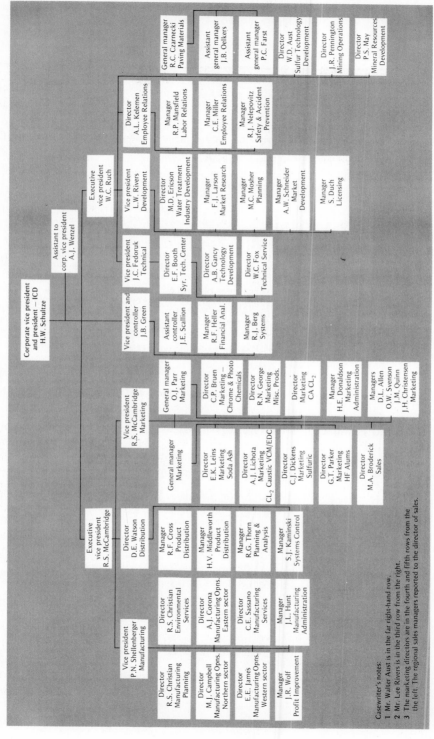

Casewriter's notes:
1 Mr. Walter Aust is in the far right-hand row.
2 Mr. Lee Rivers is in the third row from the right.
3 The marketing directors are in the fourth and fifth rows from the left. The regional sales managers reported to the director of sales.

Exhibit 1 Organization chart of the Industrial Chemicals Division.

63

Exhibit 2   POSITION DESCRIPTIONS (PRINCIPAL FUNCTIONS OF POSITION ONLY)

Marketing director (sulfuric acid)

1   Directs development of policy and coordination of strategies, objectives, and action plans for assigned business areas into a cohesive, unified plan, resulting in optimum divisional profit

2   Provides to management and to operating departments total market and product expertise and guidance in assigned area. Constantly reviews performance against plans, and initiates corrective action when plan fails to reach objectives, when manufacturing operations are interrupted, or when market conditions shift

3   Directs exchange of current and timely information on developments related to the product area, and provides guidance and recommends action plans to properly cope with threats or take advantage of opportunities as they develop

4   Directs the initiation of price changes and establishes, within delegated authority, price changes, price schedules, price exceptions, and product quality

Director of sales

1   Plans, controls, and directs activities of the sales force to obtain maximum sales volume to yield optimum profits, at a prudent selling-expense level, from all domestic markets for the division's products

2   Develops and secures approval of sales objectives, policies, and programs, and periodically evaluates and reports results. Directs the preparation of consolidated sales forecasts; recommends short- and long-term goals. Identifies and reports on problems and opportunities in the market place; recommends strategies and action plans to meet or counter problems or utilize opportunities to best advantage

3   Directs and plans changes in the sales organization required for achievement of sales objectives

4   Counsels regional sales managers in the preparation and negotiation of complex major sales proposals. Maintains contacts with major customers, reviews analysis of sales trends, and takes appropriate action to correct indicated deviations from forecasts

64

Regional sales manager

1   Directs sales of all divisional products in assigned geographic area in accordance with established marketing policies

2   Reviews expenses, itineraries, summary of calls reports and records of salespeople

3   Assumes personal responsibility for servicing some major accounts and obtaining new business from major accounts

4   Reviews sales performance of major customers in line with contractual commitments bringing to attention of proper persons deviations from stated objectives

5   Communicates with management with respect to changes in market trends, including competitive activity, market demand, and price stability

6   Plans and executes special sales programs and efforts in accordance with overall marketing emphasis

7   Initiates and conducts periodic sales meetings with salespeople to inform them of changes in sales strategy and product information, including availability, quality, and packaging. Reviews plans for increasing sales volume and profitability. Prepares sales operating budget for the regional office. Forecasts sales of products for which the particular sales office is responsible

Assistant regional sales manager

1   Performs functions of regional sales manager in the latter's absence, with certain limitations on confidential matters

2   Supervises salespeople in effective coverage and sales penetration of assigned territories and accounts

3   Conducts training program for new salespeople assigned to his office

Exhibit 2 *(Continued)*

4 Assists salespeople and account executives in servicing major accounts and obtaining new business from major accounts

5 Assists in preparation of sales forecasts and operating-expense budget for regional sales office

6 Attends and participates in area trade associations and meetings

7 Supervises and guides every salesperson in the preparation of their operational plans, based on the management-by-objectives philosophy

8 Assists in the preparation and execution of the regional operational plan, based on the management-by-objectives philosophy

Sales representative

1 Responsible for the sale and promotion of ICD products within assigned territory

2 Handles assigned major account responsibility and works with regional management and marketing on negotiating major contracts

3 Responsible for gathering and reporting market intelligence and maintaining an accurate survey of ICD and competitive product sales within assigned territory

4 Responsible for profitability of sales transactions and the control of budgeted selling expenses of assigned territory

5 Responsible for all service and administration connected with sales to customers

[a]*Casewriter's note:* This particular description was for sales representative III who had responsibility for "special major accounts" in a large metropolitan area. He thus was an unusually experienced and capable salesperson. Sales representatives I and II would be responsible for smaller accounts or a mixture of small and major accounts.

65

had almost 9,000 customer accounts.[1] Direct selling expenses averaged about 2 percent of sales. The total sales operation, including salespeople, clerical support in the regional offices, and regional managers and their assistants, consisted of about 180 people.

THE SULFURIC ACID INDUSTRY

In the early 1970s total demand for sulfuric acid was about 30 million tons, making sulfuric acid the highest tonnage volume chemical in the country. Allied executives estimated that 18 million tons of annual production were accounted for by captive producers, that is, firms which produced sulfuric acid for their own needs only. Of the remaining 12 million tons, they estimated that 8 million were sold on long-term (more than 1-year) contracts. The remaining 4 million were sold on the short-term market. Most of the captive production was performed by fertilizer manufacturers who had large plants, primarily in Florida, at the source of their most important raw material. Because captive production was growing at a

[1]Each plant of a customer company which had separate purchasing responsibility was considered a customer account.

faster rate than total consumption, the merchant market was growing slower than total consumption. Industry experts expected the disparity in growth rate between captive production and merchant production to disappear in a few years. Industry sources estimated that there were 220 sulfuric acid plants in the United States.

Sulfuric acid was usually produced by the contact process which had been developed and commercialized by a predecessor of the division. In this process, sulfur was converted to sulfur dioxide which, in turn, was converted to sulfur trioxide in the presence of a catalyst. The trioxide was then reacted with water to produce acid of any desired concentration. Sulfur-bearing ores could also be used as raw materials, as could sulfur dioxide-containing fumes from smelters, refineries, and power plants. In addition, the acid could be recovered from mixtures of material containing used acid.

Over 50 percent of sulfuric acid demand came from fertilizer production. About 15 percent of the acid produced was used in the production of other chemicals such as aluminum sulfate, titanium dioxide, and hydrofluoric acid. Another 8 percent of demand was accounted for by petroleum refining. Here it was used primarily as an alkylation catalyst and in the refining of lubricating oil. Alkylation was a process by which the octane rating of gasoline was improved. Other uses included the production of synthetic detergents, organic chemicals, steel and other metals, and synthetic fibers.

The market for sulfuric acid was undergoing some changes in the early 1970s. One major use in the steel industry was being converted to hydrochloric acid. The growth of the nylon market, on the other hand, was contributing to the growth of sulfuric acid, because one form of nylon required large amounts of the acid in its production. Sulfuric acid was also a primary raw material in the production of hydrofluoric acid which was used in the manufacture of fluorocarbons (for example, aerosol propellants, refrigerants, and nonstick coatings for cookware) and aluminum.

Because sulfuric acid was used in so many customer industries, its demand was highly cyclical. Both volume and price fluctuated over the business cycle. Price also varied with the price of raw sulfur. In general, higher sulfur prices led to higher dollar gross margins for sulfuric acid producers. In 1973, the price of sulfuric acid was about $34 per ton, but long-term contract prices were reported to be 20 to 25 percent lower.

Sulfuric acid consumption was growing slightly faster than the gross national product or industrial production indices. In 1967, 3 million tons per year of additional capacity were added by the industry. The equivalent figures for 1968, 1969, 1970, and 1971 were 0.8 million tons, 2.4 million, almost 3 million, and slightly over 4 million. Substantial amounts of this capacity were for replacement of older facilities.

Because sulfuric acid had such a low value per pound, it was not

Exhibit 3   ALLIED CHEMICAL SULFURIC ACID PLANTS

Plant	Size in thousands of tons per year	Date built	Regeneration available
Anacortes, Wash.	78	1958	Yes
Baton Rouge, La.	100	1954	Yes
Buffalo, N.Y.	195	1906	Yes
Chicago, Ill.	160	1906	Yes
Cleveland, Ohio	130	1909	No
East St. Louis, Ill.	190	1928	Yes
Elizabeth, N.J.	200	1957	Yes
Fort Royal, Va.	160	1945	No
Geismar, La.	500	1967	No
Hopewell, Va.	200	1966	No
Newell, Pa.	250	1911	Yes
Nitro, W. Va.	140	1948	No
North Claymont, Del.	350	1913	Yes
Richmond, Calif.	220	1943	Yes
San Francisco, Calif.	140	1910	Yes
The following plants had been closed in 1971 or 1972:			
Denver, Colo.	50	1921	Yes
Detroit, Mich.	200	1941	Yes
El Segundo, Calif.	180	1921	Yes

shipped very far. One Industrial Chemicals Division (ICD) executive described the domestic market for it as being "a collection of regional markets." Prices and supply-demand relationships differed by region.

ICD was the largest producer of sulfuric acid in the country and had 18 plants. Approximately 20 percent of the division's dollar sales was accounted for by the product. Most of its plants were located in the Northeast quadrant of the nation, although in 1967 it had built a large plant in Louisiana to supply its own needs as well as for outside sales. ICD had approximately 15 percent of the noncaptive market.

Other major factors in the business were Stauffer Chemical (total corporate sales of $542 million in 1972), with sulfuric acid sales almost as great as ICD; Du Pont; Monsanto; and American Cyanamid. It was estimated that there were probably 2 dozen competitors in the market. Exhibit 3 is a list of ICD sulfuric acid plants.

ICD produced substantial amounts of sulfuric acid for captive use by it and other Allied Divisions and purchased relatively large amounts of sulfuric acid from other producers to balance its captive and marketing requirements.

ICD's Approach to the Sulfuric Acid Market

ICD divided its sulfuric acid sales operation into three parts. First was the sale of sulfuric acid produced from sulfur. The field sales force and its management had primary responsibility for this function. Second was the development of long-term contracts for the recovery and production of sulfuric acid from used acid sludges. Much of this operation focused on the regeneration of alkylation ("alky") sludges from refineries. The regenerated acid was sold back to the refinery. This selling operation involved primarily headquarters marketing people and plant personnel. Finally, there was the sale of sulfur recovery and sulfuric acid production services to smelters and power plants. In such a situation ICD would process sulfur dioxide from waste gases into either elemental sulfur or sulfuric acid. Such agreements would typically call for ICD to dispose of the sulfur or sulfuric acid. Sale of these services was a time-consuming process which involved a special marketing staff.

Selling Sulfuric Acid

The sales force was divided into seven regions, each with a regional manager. Each region typically had two assistant regional sales managers, with several salespeople reporting to each. In addition, each office had order-processing and clerical support. The Atlanta regional office with six salespeople did not sell sulfuric acid because ICD had no sulfuric acid plants in the Southeast.

Of the division's sulfuric acid sales, 80 percent was accounted for by about 60 major accounts. A large but not unusual account could buy $3 million worth of acid in one year. Some customers were substantially larger than this. Each of these 60 accounts was assigned to a division executive for "executive attention." Typically, the executive personally contacted his accounts twice each year for the purposes of "planning and problem solving." Because many of these accounts had long-term contracts, it was important for ICD to be aware of plans which would affect the account's use of sulfuric acid.

Most of the selling, however, was performed by the field salespeople. They had a total of about 3,500 sulfuric acid accounts. Each salesperson was assigned a geographic territory and was responsible for the sales of all of ICD's products.[2] While some salespeople were based at the regional offices, many were "resident salespeople" in regions removed from the regional office. New Orleans, for example, was covered by a resident salesperson because it was quite far from the regional office in Houston.

Although the salespeople did not specialize by product or customer type, the geographic concentrations of certain industries led to some specialization. Salespeople in the Pittsburgh and Chicago areas, for example, had a higher percentage of steel companies among their accounts than salespeople in other areas. Some senior salespeople specialized in selling to larger accounts (see Exhibit 2).

The salespeople usually had technical educations. They were paid straight salary, with starting salaries of about $11,000. Average compensa-

68

---

[2]There were exceptions to this when a salesperson worked in a region in which ICD did not supply a particular product. The Atlanta sulfuric acid situation described above was one of those.

tion was in the $15,000 to $17,000 range, with the highest-paid salesperson making in excess of $20,000. Some salespeople received cars or country club memberships, or both. The firm also paid the salesperson's expenses. It was expected that the salesperson would take a customer to lunch each day. One long-term salesperson said, "If he doesn't, it's a wasted 2 hours." When salespeople were away from home, they usually took customers to dinner. The expense accounts were described as "adequate but not lavish, especially compared to other industries."

The product offered by different competitors was essentially the same. Price changes by one competitor in a region were usually quickly met by other competitors. Sometimes, freight absorption could be used as a competitive pricing weapon but this typically was not effective unless a firm had a transportation or location advantage. Because price and product were usually equal, the salesperson attempted to sell on the basis of service. Two important forms of service were customer engineering and technical service.

Customer engineering included the analysis and design of sulfuric acid storage and handling equipment. Because the acid was exceedingly dangerous, this was very important to a customer. ICD also provided information on materials resistant to different dilutions of sulfuric acid.

To provide technical service, ICD had a technical center in Syracuse, New York. Laboratories at the various plants also assisted customers on a part-time basis. Technical service included the supplying of technical data on sulfuric acid and its uses and the provision of some laboratory testing. ICD made information on standard laboratory techniques available to its customers. Because sulfuric acid was an established product in heavy use for many years, new problems or situations did not often present themselves. Larger, older customers, in particular, were familiar with its properties and uses and knew how to handle it.

Another form of service was on-time delivery, which was crucial according to ICD management. Because of its low value and bulk, customers did not tend to store large supplies relative to their usage. ICD maintained a large fleet of company-owned and company-operated tank trucks, tank cars, and tank barges, supplemented by leased and common-carrier equipment. Large customer plants were often situated next to ICD (or competitor) plants so that they could be supplied by pipeline.

ICD management believed that it had an excellent record for on-time delivery. One executive, in describing the importance of delivery, mentioned that a competitor had had trouble because of plant problems. He went on to say that ICD gained considerable business from its competitor's misfortune. "Sulfuric acid is so crucial to many customer processes that they *must* have uninterrupted supply."

Major accounts usually had more than one supplier unless there was some "compelling reason" for relying on only one resource. One ICD executive stated that geography (a supplier plant considerably closer to the customer than competitors' plants) and pipeline supply arrangements were the usual compelling reasons. ICD management believed that its multiplant operation was an important selling advantage. "If one plant had a production problem we could supply the account from another."

There was not much turnover of accounts in the industry. When a new plant was constructed by a supplier or a customer, there was usually some displacement of accounts. According to one experienced executive, existing accounts changed suppliers primarily because of delivery problems such as those described earlier. Much of the salesperson's job revolved around maintaining current business and attempting to obtain a larger portion of the sales to an account who purchased from more than one supplier.

One reason for the relative stability in the market was the size of the orders. Large accounts could not typically shift suppliers without making plans with the proposed supplier. The orders were so large that the plants had to be adjusted to the new business. This was, of course, much less true in times of industry overcapacity.

Another reason for the stability was the negotiated contracts. These were usually for the largest accounts who had predictable needs. Both prices and terms were negotiated. The regional manager had the authority to negotiate contracts for as long as one year at list price. Longer-term or very large contracts were negotiated by the division's headquarters marketing personnel. These contracts had to be approved by corporate top management and the office of the general counsel to ensure that Robinson-Patman Act[3] requirements were met.

The regional manager's job was to assist and train salespeople and to call upon the higher-level purchasing personnel at customer firms. "The regional manager deals with the director of purchases and the salesperson deals with the purchasing agent," according to one ICD marketing executive.

One important phase of competition was the captive supplier. If a customer had requirements for more than 100,000 tons of sulfuric acid per year, it became economical for it to make its own. The technology was standard and easily available in the form of completely designed and constructed plants. Several established engineering construction firms offered such "turnkey" installations. Some large users also had the capability to design and build their own plants. According to ICD management, captive plants were most prevalent in the fertilizer business where customer plants were large and sulfuric acid was a primary raw material.

Dr. Schultze had changed the selling philosophy of the division when he had joined it. According to ICD management, he emphasized

[3]The Robinson-Patman Act was a federal law requiring equal treatment for competing customers by a supplier.

the generation of profits and not sales volume. Regional managers received data on product margin and each salesperson had a management-by-objectives program for each of his major accounts, which stressed the generation of profits.

Headquarters marketing personnel were critical of the low amount of prospecting for new accounts done by each salesperson. ICD management generally believed that the situation had improved, but was still not good. One executive stated, "It depends upon the individual, so that it ends up that only the exceptional salesperson prospects. Most salespeople only prospect with specific direction and that direction usually comes from Morristown [headquarters]." Each salesperson had between 90 and 120 accounts to service.

ICD had several forms of sales training. Newly hired salespeople typically spent some time working in the laboratory to become familiar with ICD products. Occasionally, experienced salespeople were brought into headquarters for a full week of exposure to "every department in the corporation." This program which was provided to three salespersons at a time sometimes included some time to be spent in the technical service laboratory in Syracuse. The corporation also had a training program administered in the field, which stressed management and communication abilities.

Regional sales meetings were held about three times per year at a resort type of area in the region. ICD management explained that national sales meetings were not appropriate because the problems of each region were unique.

Turnover in the sales force was low and was primarily through promotion. All regional managers and most headquarters marketing personnel had been salespeople. The sales force had undergone radical change during the 1966 consolidation and during the reorganization of 1968. But recently, its structure and organization had been quite stable.

Used-Acid Regeneration Contracts

A substantial portion of the sulfuric acid produced was through the regeneration of used or spent acids. In such a situation the used acid in the form of a sludge (a viscous, thick liquid) was returned to the plant and reprocessed into acid. Three industries provided almost all of the sludge: petroleum refineries, detergent manufacturers, and organic chemical producers. The alkylation process in refineries was the largest generator of spent acid. A typical sludge would contain 90 percent acid, 4 percent carbon, and 6 percent water. The sludge was not useful as an alkylation catalyst despite its high acid content. Sludge from other industrial processes typically contained between 70 and 90 percent acid. The sludge would be delivered to the plant by pipeline, barge, tank car, or tank truck. Quantities were often substantial. Close to 90 percent of the acid shipped to a petroleum refinery by a sulfuric acid plant would be returned to the plant as sludge.

The plant typically burned the sludge so that the used acid was converted to sulfur dioxide which was then processed into new acid. A regeneration plant had to be considerably larger than a plant that used elemental sulfur as its raw material, because it had to have space to process the waste products out of the sulfur dioxide. The cost of processing sludge was a function of its acid strength and the amount of fuel needed to burn it.

In the early 1970s the market for used-acid regeneration services was growing. Petroleum refineries were expanding their alkylation capacity. If government regulations forced large sales of low-lead or no-lead gasoline, alkylation capacity might grow very quickly, because alkylation increased the octane rating of gasoline without the addition of lead. Sulfuric acid had competition as an alkylation catalyst. The choice between it and its primary competitor was based on the location and size of the refinery, as well as on the nature of the raw petroleum processed. In addition, those refiners usually using sulfuric acid tended to design newer installations to use it. The spent-acid market was growing at 6 to 7 percent per year, slightly faster than the gasoline market.

While the regeneration of sulfuric acid was not a technologically complex operation it did require "some degree of know-how," particularly in the blending, pumping, and burning of the sludge. ICD management estimated that, although completely designed and constructed regeneration plants were available from engineering firms, only six had been installed by U.S. refiners. One marketing executive went on to state that "it's easiest to deal with those prospects who own a plant in one of their refineries. They understand all of the costs and difficulties."

Because of the impurity of the used acid, a regeneration plant had to be about twice as large in terms of capital investment as an elemental sulfur plant of the same capacity. There were limited economies of scale to be had from increasing the size of the regeneration plants, according to ICD executives.

Contracts for used-acid recovery tended to be large and long term. An ICD executive estimated that 30 to 40 percent of the contracts involved pipeline return of sludge to the processing plant. Prices were usually based primarily on the purity of the incoming sludge and its average volume. The contracts usually set a maximum amount of sludge which could be reprocessed in one month—typically 10 percent of the annual estimated volume. Sludge which was especially difficult to process was priced at a premium.

Competition was oriented regionally because of the cost of shipping the sludge. ICD executives thought that Stauffer Chemical had the largest share of the regeneration business, with about 50 percent of the business. Stauffer's primary strength was west of the Mississippi and along the Gulf Coast. ICD and Stauffer competed in the Chicago and San Francisco areas, where both had regeneration facilities. ICD had about 25 percent of the regeneration business, according to ICD estimates. ICD had more regeneration plants, but Stauffer had larger ones.

Selling the regeneration services was a complex process. The salesperson's role was described primarily as that of "bird dog" by one of the ICD marketing executives. The major influence in the buying decision varied from company to company, according to ICD management. "In some petroleum firms the decision is made at the refinery level with assistance from headquarters refinery department[4] people such as the general manager, the assistant general manager, and staff personnel. In other firms it is primarily the purchasing department. In general, the longer the term the contract is to run, the higher up in the organization the decision is made."

Leads came either through industry announcement of an increase in alkylation capacity or by requests to "come to talk about added capacity." Current suppliers were usually contacted first. Often, according to one executive, the current supplier was almost assured of the business if his price was at all close to that offered by other suppliers. "A long relationship and a good performance history count a great deal. The alkylation process is central to the refinery operation and is run on a continuous basis. The investment is huge and no one wants to risk an interruption of its production."

73

On the ICD end, the selling process varied. The first company contact was usually with the local salesperson. He usually received a sample of the sludge. If it were a relatively standard formulation, it was sent to the plant which would be required to reprocess it. If it were unusual, it would be sent to the technical center for evaluation. Sometimes it was sent to both. The marketing director then developed a price for the reprocessing, depending upon the plant or technical evaluation of the sludge, or both. Every reprocessing agreement required the approval of the marketing director. On smaller or 1-year contracts, the marketing director usually drew up the contract, but on sizeable or long-term contracts, other headquarters managers became involved.

The selling began in earnest after the price had been developed. The salesperson was accompanied by marketing personnel if the contract was sizeable. The local plant manager often became involved. Sometimes technical and engineering personnel joined the selling team. One executive described a recent, very large negotiation in which the ICD president and controller called on the customer. He went on to say that it usually depended upon who in the division had the best contacts at the prospective firm.

[4]Most petroleum firms separated the production function (getting the oil from the ground), the refinery function (producing saleable products from the oil), and the marketing function.

By and large the industry is quite stable. Most reprocessors have dedicated a substantial amount of their plant capacity to specific customers. It isn't easy to change suppliers or customers. The pipeline contracts scare away competitors. Regeneration capacity is added slowly because suppliers tend to build only for specific customer needs.

Right now the virgin acid business is in balance and capacity in reprocessing is snug so prices are firm. But when overcapacity does hit as it has in every recession, prices are cut.

The selling process for regenerated acid was based on much more complex data than that for virgin acid and took much longer. Large contracts were in the $1 million to $2 million range. When spare capacity was available, the negotiation typically took 1 to 6 months. Large contracts which involved capital expansion took 3 to 12 months normally and sometimes up to 36 months.

Sulfur and Sulfuric Acid Generation for Pollution Control

By the late 1960s Allied Chemical Corporation had invested over $15 million in research and development related to sulfur and its uses. An important result of this expenditure was the development of a process for the conversion of sulfur dioxide to sulfur. While competitors were working on similar processes, none, according to ICD management, was close to practical commercialization.

ICD executives viewed this technology as very valuable. Sulfur dioxide was created by the combustion of sulfur-bearing fuels or the refining of sulfur-bearing minerals and petroleum. Coal mined in the eastern United States, for example, contained between 2 to 5 percent sulfur. When the coal was burned to generate heat and power, the sulfur was converted to sulfur dioxide which was released to the atmosphere through tall stacks which dispersed it well above the plant.

Industry sources estimated that total U.S. sulfur dioxide emissions to the atmosphere in 1968 contained 15 million tons of sulfur, enough to produce 45 million tons of sulfuric acid. Electric power generation was thought to be responsible for 45 percent of the emission; industrial and commercial fuel uses, for about 30 percent; and the smelting of ores, for 12 percent. Smelter emissions were, however, much more concentrated in composition (more sulfur dioxide per cubic foot of exhaust fumes) and were discharged at fewer locations (less than 40) than power plant emissions (about 950). ICD executives believed that total emissions had grown slightly since 1968 and knew that substantial amounts of by-product sulfur products were already being produced in smelters and refineries. Sulfur dioxide emissions differed by region, because coal mined in the East was high in sulfur content, whereas coal mined in the West was almost sulfur free, and because the large smelters were primarily located in the Rocky Mountains.

In the late 1960s, public and government pressure against air pollution in general had grown strong. Power plants, smelters, and other sources of emission were under pressure to drastically reduce the emissions.

Before the ICD sulfur dioxide reduction process to convert sulfur dioxide to sulfur was developed, there were two ways to remove sulfur dioxide from stack gases. One was the conversion of sulfur dioxide to sulfuric acid, the last part of the traditional route to produce sulfuric acid from sulfur. The other was to treat the stack gas with lime, a relatively cheap mineral, to produce gypsum, a relatively cheap chemical. The sulfur dioxide in smelter gases could be directly processed into sulfuric acid because of its high concentration. The sulfur dioxide in power-plant stack gases, on the other hand, had to be concentrated before processing into sulfuric acid. Power-plant stack gas could be treated with lime without concentration. The primary problem with lime treatment was the disposal of the gypsum.

Both of these processes were fairly well developed technologically, according to ICD executives. A considerable number of large smelters already were producing sulfuric acid from their waste gases. These usually used part of the acid they produced for their own processing needs and sold the rest, often through a chemical firm experienced in sulfuric acid marketing. ICD, in fact, purchased most of its outside sulfuric acid from smelters. Power plants were not yet using the sulfuric acid route, but a few had used the lime process.

ICD executives believed that the sulfur dioxide reduction technology had a great deal of market promise, primarily because the end product was easier to ship and store than sulfuric acid, and because they could now offer a complete pollution abatement service. They believed that they would sell their technology, operating skill, and marketing expertise. Under the proposed program, ICD would license its technology to a utility or smelter. The utility or smelter would hire an engineering construction firm to design and build a sulfur dioxide concentration plant (usually for a utility), if necessary, and to build the sulfur dioxide reduction plant. ICD would then operate the plant for a fee consisting of all direct expenses, an overhead charge calculated as a percentage of direct wages, and a management fee of 5 percent of the original (undepreciated) capital assets. ICD management expected that the management fees for large plants would range from $300,000 to $1,000,000 and that total labor and overhead would be in the $500,000 range. The utility itself could either market the sulfur or could sell it to ICD at market value and ICD would dispose of it. ICD also had the capability to offer a sulfuric acid plant on the same basis to a smelter or utility. An acid plant would involve revenues in the same size range as a sulfur plant. Traditionally, smelters had operated their own sulfuric acid plants because they had substantial chemical manufacturing know-how, but had sold the excess sulfuric acid to chemical firms. Utilities, on the other hand, did not have chemical plant operating experience.

ICD executives were confident of their process and their ability to sell it. Walter Aust, the manager in charge of selling the process, stated, "We know more about the technology of sulfur dioxide reduction than our competitors. We are experienced in sulfur chemistry." The ICD process was quite simple in concept in that it reacted the sulfur dioxide with natural gas, producing sulfur, water, and inert carbon dioxide, but quite complex in operation because its economics depended upon an unusual catalytic system, careful use of waste heat, and meticulous control of the whole process. ICD had patents covering the catalytic system, the heat regeneration equipment, and the valve system, as well as the whole process.

Mr. Aust went on to describe his view of ICD's approach to utility customers. "We can offer a utility advice on which process, sulfuric acid production, sulfur production, or lime treatment, is best. Although we aren't in the lime business, it is a simple business and we are in some allied activities. We can offer the prospective customer credibility and an honestly unbiased view."

ICD management believed that the choice between their proprietary sulfur process and a sulfuric acid process would depend upon local market conditions. If there were a market for sulfuric acid near enough to be serviced economically, the utility or smelter would opt for acid production. If nearby markets were either not large, as was the case in New England which did not use much acid, or near smelters which were located in remote places, the sulfur process would be more economical. A given amount of sulfur weighed only one-third as much pure as it did as sulfuric acid. In addition sulfur was noncorrosive, inert, and solid, but sulfuric acid was liquid, highly reactive, and difficult to store and ship.

ICD executives believed that their position in selling the sulfur and sulfuric acid production systems to utilities in the Northeast was especially strong. One executive stated, "We will be able to sell the by-product sulfuric acid because we can assure customers of a reliable supply from our extensive network of plants in the area."

Despite the political and governmental emphasis on pollution abatement, ICD executives believed that selling the sulfur or sulfuric acid processes would not be easy. Mr. Aust estimated that either process would increase power plant operating costs and investment by about 40 percent. The sulfur dioxide control equipment for a 1,600-megawatt power plant (large but not unusual for new plants) would raise the initial investment from $100 million to $145 million. The Allied process would be an investment of only $5 million dollars with the other $40 million going for the equipment to capture and concentrate the sulfur dioxide. Utilities in the Northeast, however, would have little choice but to install some sulfur dioxide abatement equipment, according to ICD executives, because it was uneconomical to ship low sulfur coal east of Chicago. Mr. Aust believed that the small power plants would probably find it most economical to use the lime process, but that larger ones would find the sulfur or sulfuric acid process better.

ICD had established a special organization to pursue the utility and smelter markets. Walter Aust, who was director of marketing of the Sulfuric Acid Division, was chosen to head it in 1971.[5] Mr. Aust had previously been director of sales and still earlier had been a salesperson and regional sales manager. By early 1973, he had a staff which included a financial specialist, the technical specialist who was most experienced in the sulfur dioxide reduction process, an operations expert, and three engineers. These six people were responsible for providing detailed studies and data to support Mr. Aust in his negotiations and to help him develop an approach to the marketplace. Lee Rivers, vice president of development of ICD, was responsible for licensing the technology to firms which would not require ICD to operate the sulfur reduction plant. He expected that most of these would be smelters. Mr. Rivers and Mr. Aust worked closely on the development of a sales approach.

By 1973, ICD had had two successes in the marketplace with its sulfur production process. One was licensing of the process to Falconbridge Nickel Mines Ltd., in Sudbury, Ontario, Canada, where it was used to remove sulfur at a rate equivalent to about $\frac{1}{2}$ million tons of sulfuric acid per year from smelter gases. Although the ICD process had worked well since the plant had opened in 1970, the total plant was shut down in 1972 because of problems with other manufacturing processes. Its future was uncertain.

Mr. Aust and his team had also successfully sold the process to Northern Indiana Public Service (NIPSCO) for a power plant in Gary, Indiana. Here, the process was to be installed on an existing boiler in the medium-sized range. ICD executives considered this demonstration unit to be of great importance because it could help them to understand better the selling process and could be used to show utilities the value of the process.

The NIPSCO negotiations had evolved out of Mr. Aust's first attempt to introduce the process to the utility industry. Because of ICD's situation and the type of coal available to utilities in the Northeast, it was decided that the initial attempts to sell the sulfur and sulfuric acid producing processes should be in the Northeast. It was further decided to limit initial discussions to the largest utilities in the major metropolitan areas. It was felt that these were the ones under greatest pressure to abate pollution and that their large power plants were most appropriate to the process. These restrictions left ten prospects. Before visiting them, Mr.

[5]See Exhibit 1 for an organization chart.

Aust had gathered trade data concerning plans for abatement at each prospect's major generating plants. He was particularly interested in those which had abatement schedules requiring early commitments to particular processes. He furthermore knew that Illinois, Indiana, and Maryland were particularly stringent in their regulation of pollution. Mr. Aust also maintained a close watch on the sulfuric acid markets surrounding each utility, because conversion of a single very large power plant could generate as much as 1 million tons of sulfuric acid.

Mr. Aust and the technical specialist visited each of the chosen utilities to discuss abatement plans and to offer assistance. In each firm they called on either the vice president of engineering or the environmental engineering director, or someone of comparable position and responsibility. They attempted to ascertain the abatement plans for each location; general plans to expand generating capacity; alternatives available to the firm; physical characteristics, including site and transportation availability; and previous experience in abatement. They also discussed their two processes, expecting to generate more interest in the sulfuric acid process because there was room in most local markets for more by-product acid capacity to be added. Mr. Aust expected that, as the best sites for acid production began producing acid, other sites in the area would be forced to produce sulfur.

In those utilities where the response was less than warm, Mr. Aust and his technical specialist made plans to update the information every 3 to 6 months and to monitor the utilities' general situation so that, if it were changed by, for example, a court ruling, they would be aware.

Where they were greeted more warmly, they began discussions of alternative approaches, including studies of marketing and economic feasibility. The staff prepared most of these studies while Mr. Aust and the technical specialist made the calls and planned future calls.

Mr. Aust found that some utilities had agreed to abatement schedules, while others were still unsure of what action, if any, to take. Those with established schedules appeared to make better prospects. Some utilities were resistant to the idea that they would have to pay money to have their emissions controlled. One ICD executive attributed this to the "euphoria of the late 60s when people talked about making money from the reclaimed pollutants." He went on to state that it was not possible to recover the sulfur at a profit, or even at break-even.

Mr. Aust found out during his calls at NIPSCO that the vice president in charge of environmental affairs was receptive to doing something innovative which also made "good economic sense." Mr. Aust also was aware of the willingness of the Environmental Protection Agency (EPA, a federal government agency) to invest in a demonstration plant which had a good chance to succeed.

Sales negotiations soon started in earnest among the four parties likely to be involved: EPA, NIPSCO, ICD, and Wellman-Power Gas Inc.

Wellman was an experienced engineering contractor which had proprietary rights to the Wellman-Lord sulfur dioxide concentration technology. As soon as the negotiations began, Mr. Aust requested and received the assistance of a lawyer from Allied's corporate counsel office. Mr. Aust believed that "it was easier to get the lawyer in on the negotiations than to try to convey the agreement to him so that he can draw it up after it has been negotiated." Because some of the discussion involved the patented sulfur generation process, a patent attorney was often involved in the negotiations. As the negotiation got more involved, Mr. Aust called on other specialists, including those concerned with marketing, planning, manufacturing, employee relations, and finance. The employee relations experts were needed because the agreement would call for ICD personnel to work on the premises of NIPSCO. The financial specialists had to develop integrated billing and accounting procedures because of the complexity of the agreement.

All of the discussions included all four parties although some of the subjects related to only two or three. The EPA wanted to ensure that its standards would be met and that its $4.5 million would be well spent. NIPSCO wanted to be sure that the plants and processes would operate continuously and economically. Wellman, the engineering contractor, needed guarantees that the Allied process would meet EPA standards. ICD was anxious to protect its proprietary patent rights from loss, and data from the demonstration from dissemination because of the EPA funding. The licenses for the process, in fact, were a separate set of agreements which accompanied the contract. The negotiating sessions usually had no more than ten people present.

The contract was important to all parties because of its size and innovative nature. The EPA considered it important enough for the administrator of the Agency to personally report the contract to the public. Each of the final contracts was between 30 and 50 pages long.

Negotiations had begun in early 1972. The final primary agreement was drafted in June 1972. After some minor changes, it was signed in early October 1972. In late October 1972, the vice president of NIPSCO resigned and was replaced by one new to the negotiations. He needed several months to familiarize himself with the situation. By February 1973, ICD's operating contract had not been signed. The plant would not go into operation until mid-1974.

Between the time the agreement had been signed and early 1973, ICD had made a concerted effort to bring people who would later be operating the plant into the relationship with NIPSCO. According to Mr. Aust, they had to be made aware of contract limitations so that they could effectively deal with their counterparts. Throughout this time, the emphasis was on developing and maintaining an intimate working relationship. The top personnel from each party maintained close involvement.

As Mr. Aust reviewed the NIPSCO situation, he commented on its difference from other ICD selling situations. "The field sales people have reacted to this type of selling in an interesting manner. They continually try to orient the negotiation to traditional sales calls. But it just doesn't work that way. We didn't even talk to the purchasing agent. As we have become a service-oriented business selling a complex operation, the mode of selling has changed."

Mr. Aust considered this form of selling somewhat similar to selling long-term sulfuric acid regeneration contracts, but even more complex. "In some of these situations we may need to bring in Dr. Schultze or the President or Chairman of Allied itself. As you get closer to the decision, it moves up in the organization and we need someone of equal status and responsibility to meet their decision makers."

As Mr. Aust looked at the market, he saw a difficult selling job but great market potential. "NIPSCO was probably easier than most sales will be because the EPA put up half of the money. But even if the selling is hard, the market is big. Just the new boilers being installed in the future make a good market. Of course, if the potential situation forces older boilers to be fitted with pollution control equipment, the market is even bigger."

Mr. Aust and Mr. Rivers (responsible for licensing) were impressed with the worldwide possibilities for their technologies. They exhibited at trade shows in Europe and had developed a short slide-and-sound presentation for use at the shows. Even Communist countries had shown interest in the sulfur generating process.

DR. SCHULTZE'S CONCERN

As Dr. Schultze reviewed his division's approach to the sulfur and sulfuric acid market, he was impressed by the changes which had taken place in the market and in the firm. He was concerned about having three different selling approaches and organizations for the same product categories. Although results were about up to budgeted projections, he wondered if there were a more efficient way to sell or to organize the sales effort.

Section

THREE

Deployment and Account Coverage

NINE   Deploying the Sales Effort

Deployment is the assignment of the sales effort to territories, customers, products, and functions. Discussions about deployment have traditionally focused on the efficient assignment of salespeople to territories and on the efficient allocation of a salesperson's selling time among accounts in the territory. Recently, however, more attention has been given to the allocation of the selling effort of multiproduct salespeople to the various products. An even newer issue involves deployment by function (for example, opening new accounts and servicing existing accounts).

This note provides a conceptual structure for considering deployment situations and shows some of the practical problems in applying the structure.

A CONCEPTUAL BASIS

An earlier note proposed that sales management be viewed as a series of optimizations or tradeoffs. This approach will be used in discussing deployment. To simplify the discussion, first we will focus only on deploying sales effort among customers. Later the analogues to territories, products, and functions will be developed.

A salesperson should make a particular call on a particular customer only if (1) the marginal profit returned to the firm will be greater than the marginal cost expended, and (2) the marginal profit from this call will be greater than that of competing uses of the time, such as calling on other prospects or customers.

These two conditions imply concern for a ratio which is the marginal profit from a call divided by the marginal cost of the call. If we use the following nomenclature,

ΔP is the marginal or incremental *profit* from a call
ΔC is the marginal or incremental *cost* of a call

we can write the ratio of the marginal profit from a call divided by the marginal cost of a call as:

$$\frac{\Delta P}{\Delta C}$$

The two conditions presented above then become

1 $\Delta P/\Delta C$ must be greater than or equal to one.

2 $\Delta P/\Delta C$ for this particular call must be greater than or equal to the ratio for other calls which the salesperson might make.

Sophisticated sales managers often use this ratio as the return per dollar of sales expense or return per hour of selling time. The idea is to maximize return on a scarce resource—dollars or sales time.
Intuitively the two constraints are clear:

84

1 Do not spend money on a call unless the return is greater than the cost.

2 Do not make a call if there is a more profitable one to make.

Conceptually, the salesperson would calculate this ratio for each potential call and make those calls with the highest ratio until either time ran out or all possible calls with ratios of one or above were exhausted. There are, however, a variety of practical problems involved in actually applying this conceptual scheme.[1]

The Practical Problems

The practical problems associated with the above framework include:

1 Estimating the cost of a call or series of calls on a particular customer
2 Estimating the sales which would result from those calls
3 Estimating the profits which would result from the sale
4 Estimating these three parameters for the relevant alternative calls

The fourth item listed is just a repetition of the other three, so that it can be dispensed with if we assume that a salesperson can identify the

[1]See Leonard M. Lodish, "'Vaguely Right' Approach to Sales Force Allocation," *Harvard Business Review*, January-February 1974, for a computerized application of a similar conceptual scheme.

relevant alternatives. Often he cannot without doing some prospecting to find out who in his territory might be interested in his firm and products.

Estimating the cost of a call in itself is probably not too hard if the salesperson knows the location of the call and has a good idea of the cost of such extras as a lunch or dinner for the prospective buyer. The problem is that a call usually cannot be viewed as a single entity, but must be considered a part of a selling program. Therefore, the difficulty arises in estimating the number of calls which might be needed.

If one could estimate the dollar amount of sales, it would not be too difficult to estimate profit from the sale. Factors, such as product mix and special services (for example, design or unusually rapid delivery), would complicate the profit estimate, but it nonetheless can be made with a fair degree of accuracy if the sales can be estimated.

Estimating sales is usually the largest problem of those stated above. It must be solved by a *sales response function* which relates the dollar amount of sales generated to the amount or cost of sales effort expended. These are exceedingly difficult to develop. Davis and Webster, *Sales Force Management*, Ronald Press, 1968, pp. 338–339, give some examples. *Operations Research* published two articles in 1956 which showed different approaches to the problem.[2]

85

Because the selling process is so complex, often involves people whom the salesperson does not see or in some cases even know about, and is usually tied to a variety of organizational and personal considerations, the estimating job is horrendous. Sometimes it can be argued that, at certain points in the selling process, there is actually a negative relationship between the amount of selling effort and the likelihood of a sale; the salesperson's attention is viewed as undesirable by the purchaser. Furthermore, the situation is complicated by the number of accounts and prospective accounts salespeople handle. It is not unusual for a salesperson to have a territory with 100 accounts and 200 prospects. Obviously, the data manipulation problems are not inconsequential, especially given most salespeople's hesitancy to make sales forecasts and their frequently negative attitudes toward quantitative methods.

There are a variety of ways to forecast the sales to an individual account. It helps if the selling process is viewed as having two steps: (1) persuading a prospective account to buy an opening order and thus become a customer, and (2) increasing the sales to the current customer.

In many product lines, it is also useful to separate prospects into those not using the generic product at all and those using the product of

[2]"Allocation of Sales Effort in the Lamp Division of the General Electric Company," by Waid, Clark, and Ackoff, pp. 629–647, and "A Study of Sales Operations," by Brown, Hulswit, and Kettelle, pp. 296–308, both in *Operations Research*, vol. 4, December 1956. (The Penstock Press case in Newton, *Cases in Sales Force Management*, Homewood, Ill., Irwin, 1970, pp. 264–276, is based on the second article.)

a competitor, because this difference can greatly influence the likelihood of making a sale and its probable size if made.

But even if all of the forecasting problems could be overcome, there is still another one—the salesperson. He often has definite call preferences. For example, most salespeople enjoy calling on customers, especially established customers providing relatively large sales, more than calling on prospects, because (1) the salesperson knows the customer better, often on a close social basis; (2) he is more likely to obtain an order; (3) he knows what to expect; and (4) the customer and the salesperson are more congenial about a variety of things (for example, more alike in age, social class, values, views of the industry) which is the reason the sale was made in the first place.[3] These four factors mean that the salesperson is more likely to obtain reinforcement and acceptance in both a personal and a business sense from the customer than from the prospect. For many sales managers, it is a major problem to get the salespeople to prospect.

Another idiosyncrasy among salespeople involves their interest in calling on certain categories of accounts. Some salespeople, for example, are called "plate-glass shy," or hesitant to call on major department stores, because the selling process is more complex and buyers are more sophisticated in both social and business matters than in smaller stores. Salespeople who sell to several industries (for example, printing, advertising specialties) sometimes begin to concentrate on one particular industry because they learn the language and the approach necessary to sell to that industry. This has an important advantage for the selling firm because the salesperson concentrates on prospects and customers who are likely to buy. On the other hand, it often leads to an unbalanced, incomplete sales effort because the salesperson neglects accounts in other categories.[4]

It should be understood that these situations sometimes occur despite the loss of compensation to the salesperson. Familiarity, congeniality, and ease are often more important motivations than compensation.

In spite of all of these problems the deployment issue must be confronted. Effective resolution requires two things: (1) determining an optimum allocation of the selling effort, and (2) implementating the allocation—that is, getting the salespeople to perform as desired. Motivation will be considered in more depth later in this book, but it must not be neglected when one develops a program for optimum allocation. An unimplementable program is not of much use.

[3]See M. S. Gadel, "Concentration by Salesmen on Congenial Prospects," *Journal of Marketing*, vol. 28, April 1964, pp. 64–66, for more on this phenomenon.

[4]The organizational implications of such specializations are discussed in the note "Organizing the Sales Effort."

There are three approaches to determining the optimum deployment of the sales effort. At one extreme are the expensive and comprehensive quantitative approaches such as those described in the *Operations Research* articles[2] or "Call Plan"[5] which is a more modern interactive approach. At the other extreme is the concept of assigning salespeople a territory and letting them decide how to allocate their efforts. Between are various programs which often include customer-by-customer sales forecasts and much interaction between the field sales managers and the salespeople. The structure of the specific industry helps determine which approach is best. The fewer the accounts and prospects located in a territory, the easier it is to do detailed planning. The higher paid the salesperson, the greater his expenses, and the larger his impact upon the profits of the firm, the more important it is to deploy him effectively, and the greater the expense justified in improving deployment.

One aspect of the deployment problem which deserves special attention is the deployment of salespeople to national or key accounts.[6] Some firms handle these accounts with a separate sales force to ensure careful, competent attention. It can, however, create some very sticky problems, especially when the sales force is on commission and the buying authority is divided among national, regional, and local influences. Consider, for example, a large ink company that sells to packaging firms such as American Can or Continental Can which operate many plants. The national account salesperson who calls on headquarters does much of the selling. But the territory salesperson who calls on individual plants also makes important contributions. If both are on commission, it is difficult to divide the commission between them and expensive to pay double commissions.

DEPLOYMENT ACROSS PRODUCT LINES

Up to this time we have focused on deployment among customers. Deployment also involves allocation of sales effort among territories and products.[7] The product deployment situation is analogous to the customer deployment situation. Here, the desire is to allocate the salesperson's time optimally among products. This becomes exceedingly complex when one salesperson calls on heterogeneous customers who buy different mixes of a diverse line of products. The sales manager then needs a sales response function for each product at each customer or prospect.

[5]See Leonard Lodish, "Call Plan: An Interactive Salesman's Call Planning System," *Management Science*, vol. 18, no. 4, part II, December 1971, pp. P25–P40.

[6]The note "Organizing the Sales Effort" provides more information on this important issue.

[7]See Montgomery, Silk, and Zaragoza in the bibliography at the end of this note.

87

As in the case with customer deployment, product deployment can present difficult implementation problems. Often salespeople are anxious to second-guess the product policy decision makers and choose the products to present to their accounts and prospects. This has its positive side because the salespeople can often choose those items which most appeal to their customers or potential customers. They are, in effect, segmenting the market and tailoring the firm's offering to each individual segment. There is a negative side, too. The salesperson will sometimes choose items to present on personal taste, bias, or poor judgment. In the women's shoe trade, for example, there is a phrase "garage shoes" to describe those shoes which do not create enthusiasm among the salespeople. Instead, the samples remain in the salesperson's garage, never receiving customer exposure.

Such situations lead to a multistage concept of sales. Marketing management has to sell the salespeople, the salespeople sell the retailers, and the retailers sell the customers. Failure at any stage precludes success at the following stages. This view explains the interest which product managers and others responsible for product policy decisions have for sales meetings.

88 TERRITORIAL DEPLOYMENT

The territory allocation problem is a bit different. The territory can, of course, be viewed as a collection of prospects and customers. One way, then, to develop a territory would be to determine the optimum amount of effort needed for accounts and to allocate accounts to the salespeople until they have a full workload. Then, another territory would be established. This process could be continued until all of the areas to be covered were taken care of. It would be a monumental job in most companies, and it ignores the existing situation, including current salesperson-customer relationships, and established compensation standards.

Most territory allocation problems involve realignments of existing territories or additions of territories rather than setting up a whole new territory system. Usually, territories are developed on the basis of three criteria: (1) workload, (2) potential, and (3) current sales.

The usual desire is that all salespeople have equal workloads, potential, and current sales. But workload, usually measured by a combination of the number of accounts and the travel time, is often not related to either potential or current sales. Sparsely populated areas tend to have smaller accounts spaced further apart than the larger accounts in more densely populated areas. Contrast, for example, an apparel salesperson in Manhattan versus one in the Rocky Mountain and Great Plains area. Industry locational patterns influence territories, too. The Gulf

Coast salesperson for the manufacturer of heavy chemical pumps has a different kind of territory than the company's New England salesperson because of the different density and size of customer plants.

Even potential and current sales are not too closely related in many situations. Most companies are stronger relative to competition in some areas than others because of differing product mix desires among customers, shipping cost structures, or salesperson history (for example, a good salesperson who built the territory).

Salespeople paid on commission are especially sensitive to differences in potential, current sales, and workload among territories. A traditional problem is the salesperson who has a territory of greater-than-justified potential. When the sales manager attempts to divide the territory, the salesperson may complain bitterly—not because of the loss of potential but because of the loss of current sales and thus commissions. Sometimes these situations work out for the best, however, because the salesperson is forced to cover a smaller territory in more depth. A salesperson can be strangled by too much potential and too many accounts because he puts too little effort into each of his prospects and accounts. This can be very expensive from the firm's point of view.[8]

Territorial assignments are made more complex by two other factors: (1) traditional boundaries and (2) topography. If territories do not follow traditional boundaries (often political boundaries, such as state lines), several problems can arise. First, outside data are often gathered on the basis of these boundaries, and these data often provide the most useful information on potential and, hence, penetration. The data come from government agencies such as *Census of Business* or *Census of Manufacturers*, trade associations, and other sources such as *Sales Management* magazine's "Survey of Buying Power." When territories do not follow the traditional boundaries, management is sometimes forced to interpolate questionable data—a hazardous process.

89

Second, customers tend to follow those boundaries in setting up their organizations. Thus, the salesperson who calls on a chain of stores can call on both the buying office and the stores themselves, if the chain follows the boundaries of his territory. Companies selling to state and local governments are prime examples. Sometimes, the best territorial boundaries follow those of Standard Metropolitan Sales Areas (SMSA) as established by the Bureau of the Census. Many retailers spread according to SMSA's and print and broadcast media boundaries. Unfortunately, many of the most important SMSA's overlap state boundaries (for example, New York, Chicago, and Kansas City).

The third problem with nontraditional boundaries involves the hiring of salespeople, especially independent representatives carrying more

[8]A good technique for relating potential to sales coverage is presented in Walter J. Semlow, "How Many Salesmen Do You Need," *Harvard Business Review*, May-June 1959, pp. 126–132.

than one line. If the representatives in an industry tend to cover certain territories, a firm using them will have to concur on whether or not they are appropriate for its other territories. If, for example, industry tradition dictates Kansas-Nebraska representatives, one firm would find it exceedingly difficult, if not impossible, to arrange a Kansas-Missouri territory and an Iowa-Nebraska one. The same problem occurs to a lesser degree when companies hire salespeople from competitors. If a salesperson is given a territory different from the one before, the hiring firm loses some of that person's value in the form of established account relationships.

Topography becomes important because the road system and the sites of cities and major accounts often determine the viability and ease of making calls in specific areas. Most salespeople, for example, have greater sales effectiveness nearer their homes, probably because coverage is easier for the salesperson and possibly because customers feel they will receive attention whenever they need it. Remote accounts are often not serviced because of the cost or effort required.[9] Considerations such as these are often important in companies with very large territories. For example, in some companies one salesperson will cover the entire East Coast from New York City. In such cases, New York customers probably feel more at ease about sales attention (either perceived or actual, or both) than Richmond, Virginia, customers.

90

DEPLOYMENT ACROSS FUNCTIONS

Each salesperson is called upon to perform a variety of functions such as prospecting for new accounts, making presentations to existing accounts, setting up displays, controlling customer inventory, training customer employees, adjusting and/or repairing machinery, and doing missionary selling either to customer organizations or among end users. The list varies with the industry, the company, and often, the time of the year. The important point is that most salespeople perform several functions.

The marketing strategy and sales program usually put varying emphasis on these tasks. Some companies might emphasize extensive inventory and display aid as part of a strong service orientation. Others might emphasize long-detailed, information-filled presentations.

Deployment across function, like deployment across customers, products, and territories, is a two-part process. The policy must be developed, and then it must be implemented. Both parts have long been neglected with regard to function because of three reasons. First, the area is less obvious than territories, customers, or products. Second, it is easier to keep records on sales by product line, territory, or customer

[9] As the note "Sales Costs and Budgets" describes, some of the remote areas are best covered by telephone or mail.

than on time spent on each function. Third, there has not been a great deal of advocacy for different functions. In many companies, on the other hand, product and/or market managers have constantly attempted to ensure that their products or market segments, or both, receive at least their "fair share" of sales attention.

EFFECTS ON OTHER ASPECTS OF SALES MANAGEMENT

Deployment cannot be considered as an area separate from other key sales management concerns. Deployment decisions have a major effect on the size and organization of the sales force. One common way to implement deployment decisions regarding key or national accounts, as well as allocation of the sales effort by customers and products, is to organize the sales force around these issues. Thus, each market segment or product line might receive its own sales force.

Implementation of deployment decisions often involves various motivation approaches. Compensation can be adjusted to improve implementation. For example, salespeople can be paid commissions which vary by product line, with larger commissions for lines with higher gross margins or for lines requiring and justifying special attention, such as new products. Some companies stress sale of the full line, with special bonuses for salespeople meeting quotas in every product line. Others have contests which relate to the size of individual sales or to opening new accounts.

Salespeople must be trained to consider their deployment decisions. Every time salespeople choose a prospect or customer, a product to push at the expense of another, and a function to perform, they are making a deployment decision. Thus, they must be sensitized to the importance and impact of these decisions and trained in how to effectively make them.

The sales information system has a critical function in deployment. It must provide data which enable sales management to develop deployment policies. Thus, sales must be reported by customer segment and product line when these variables are important. These types of data also enable management to assess the impact of various deployment policies and implementation programs. While data regarding the actual allocation of sales effort and time are very valuable, they are hard to gather because of most salespeople's negative attitudes toward "paper work."

There are other relationships between deployment and other aspects of sales management. Account management policies to a great extent determine the desired emphasis on various functions of salespeople. Recruiting and selection decisions are sometimes made on the basis of deployment decisions. Functional or customer specialists, for example, might be hired to implement policies.

91

EFFECTS BEYOND SALES MANAGEMENT

Deployment policies can have effects beyond sales management. The company, on the basis of a cost analysis, may choose not to accept orders below a certain amount or call on accounts which provide less than a certain minimum volume. This is usually because the cost of processing small orders is sometimes as great as the cost of processing larger orders and because the cost of a sales call sometimes does not vary with the size of the account. Of course, the higher the gross margin and the greater the open capacity of the sales force, the less need there is for these policies.

Product policy can be affected by deployment. It may be necessary to introduce new products to appeal to a desired customer group or to provide a large enough line to justify a separate sales force for a particular category of customer. Emphasis on large customers may necessitate the provision of special or private brands or of specially designed products. Companies that sell to the three large general merchandise chains or to large supermarkets often face this situation. Different brands must sometimes be developed for separate sales organizations. Advertising and sales promotion programs must be coordinated with such activities.

92

Deployment can also be related to other aspects of product policy and pricing (for example, volume discounts). All policies in these areas must be both ethical and legal. In particular, the Robinson-Patman Act makes illegal certain policies regarding special pricing and provision of extra, nonequal services to competing customers.

A TOTAL DEPLOYMENT PROGRAM

A total deployment program includes policies, procedures for setting these policies, and systems for implementing the policies. The relationship between policies and procedures is very close. In some companies, policies are made at the top level. In others, each salesperson decides which products to sell, customers or prospects to approach, and functions to perform. If there is no procedure by which executives develop policies, the sales force will make ad hoc policies in the field. Often such field sales procedures are in reality abdication of a key responsibility of sales management—assigning the sales effort in the most effective and efficient manner.

BIBLIOGRAPHY

Brice, M.A.: "The Art of Dividing Sales Territories," *Dun's Review*, vol. 85, no. 5, May 1967, pp. 47, 93–98; reprinted in Thomas R. Wotruba and

Robert Olsen (eds.), *Readings in Sales Management*, New York: Holt, Rinehart and Winston, 1971, pp. 61–68.

Davis, Otto A., and John V. Farley: "Allocating Sales Force Effort with Commissions and Quotas," *Management Science*, vol. 18, no. 4, part II, December 1971, pp. P55–P63.

Fogg, C. Davis, and Josef W. Rokus: "A Quantitative Method for Structuring a Profitable Sales Force," *Journal of Marketing*, vol. 37, July 1973, pp. 8–17.

Hess, Sidney W., and Stuart A. Samuels: "Experiences with a Sales Districting Model: Criteria and Implementation," *Management Science*, vol. 18, no. 4, part II, December 1971, pp. P41–P54.

Lodish, Leonard M.: "Sales Territory Alignment to Maximize Profit," *Journal of Marketing Research*, vol. 12, February 1975, pp. 30–36.

Montgomery, David B., Alvin J. Silk, and Carlos E. Zaragoza: "A Multiple-Product Sales Force Allocation Model," *Management Science*, vol. 18, no. 4, part II, December 1971, pp. 3–24.

Talley, Walter J., Jr.: "How to Design Sales Territories," *Journal of Marketing*, vol. 25, no. 3, January 1961, pp. 7–13; reprinted in Robert F. Gwinner and Edward M. Smith, *Sales Strategy*, New York: Appleton Century Crofts, 1969, pp. 500–510.

Wedemeyer, Henry: "Planning and Organizing Territorial Coverage," in Albert Newgarden (ed.), *The Field Sales Manager: A Manual of Practice*, New York: American Management Association, 1960, pp. 95–111.

Wolfe, Harry Deane, and Gerald Albaum: "Inequality in Products, Orders, Customers, Salesmen, and Sales Territories," *Journal of Business*, vol. 35, no. 3, July 1962, pp. 298–301; reprinted in Thomas R. Wotruba and Robert Olsen (eds.), *Readings in Sales Management*, New York: Holt, Rinehart and Winston, 1971, pp. 345–351.

93

TEN Grafton Industries (A)

On Friday, September 12, 1975, Harrison ("Harry") Oates, assistant product manager at Grafton Industries in Chicago, Illinois, was promoted to district sales manager for the capital district which included Delaware, Maryland, the District of Columbia, Virginia, and West Virginia. Samuel Goldberg, the previous district sales manager, had died suddenly earlier that week.

Jack Falzarano, Eastern regional sales manager, was slated to leave the following week to become marketing vice president of Grafton's United Kingdom subsidiary. The new regional sales manager, Ted Newbury, who had previously been a district sales manager on the West Coast, had learned of his new assignment only 2 weeks earlier and had returned to his San Francisco office after spending a week with Mr. Falzarano visiting each district in the region.

The national commercial sales manager had stressed the importance of getting the capital district "back on the move," apparently implying that the district had been a problem in recent years. He indicated that it was a great opportunity for Harry to prove himself as an operating manager.

Mr. Falzarano, in a brief meeting alone with Mr. Oates later in the day, had explained that because of personal commitments related to his move to Europe he could not meet with Harry over the weekend or on Monday. They scheduled a Tuesday morning meeting to discuss the district. Mr. Falzarano went on to explain that he would prepare a brief description of each of the eight salespeople in the district for Mr. Oates and would have it available by early afternoon on Monday. Mr. Falzarano also mentioned that the district's monthly sales meeting was scheduled for Friday, September 19th.

> I wish I could be with you at the meeting but I must be on a plane to London at 3:00 P.M. on Tuesday afternoon. You might consider spending next Wednesday and Thursday meeting the salespeople in the field and having the sales meeting as an introductory session. On the other hand you might want to postpone the September 19th meeting until you have traveled with each salesperson and assessed the situation. You might want to discuss the matter with Ted Newbury before you make a decision.

Mr. Falzarano and Mr. Oates agreed to meet at 9:00 A.M. on Tuesday. Mr. Falzarano then gave Mr. Oates a collection of material on the district. He again mentioned that he would have his own brief assessment of each salesperson available Monday and that Mr. Oates would find the detailed personnel files for each person at the district office in Baltimore. He cautioned him against asking for the district office files to be sent to Chicago, since Mr. Falzarano felt that it might unduly concern the office and sales personnel.

Harry Oates

Harry Oates had turned 29 in August 1975. He had grown up in Cleveland and attended Morgan State College in Baltimore, where he majored in economics. He had been active in student government and varsity sports, as well as maintaining an enviable academic record. After graduating from college in 1967, he joined the Navy as a line officer. He served aboard destroyers operating off Asia and in the Mediterranean and had a successful tenure in the Navy. He then attended the Graduate School of

Business, Columbia University, and graduated in 1972. Among his honors were several scholarships and consistent recognition on the dean's list.

Upon graduation, he joined Grafton Industries as a salesman in a territory including part of Chicago and the suburban and exurban areas north and west of the city. He was a successful salesman. By the end of his tour of duty he had won several sales contests and was viewed as a "comer." In April 1974 he became assistant product manager responsible for part of the Measuring Instrument business. Again he was successful.

Mr. Oates had been married since he had entered Columbia and had two children, a boy of 3 years and a girl of 2 months.

GRAFTON INDUSTRIES

Grafton Industries was one of the largest manufacturers of tools and accessories in the world. It sold hand and power tools to industrial concerns and consumers through three different sales forces. The industrial sales force called on large end users, industrial distributors, and mill supply houses.[1] The private-label sales organization dealt with a few large retail organizations such as Sears, Montgomery Ward, Penney, and K-Mart. The commercial sales force called on all other retailers, including department, hardware, and discount stores and other outlets.

Grafton had total domestic U.S. sales of $270 million in 1973. The product line was divided as follows:

Stationary metalworking power tools
Stationary woodworking power tools
Portable power tools
Hand tools—general shop
Masons, plasterers, and bricklayers tools
Measuring instruments

Industrial sales were $117 million, commercial sales $105 million, and private label sales $48 million. Management estimated that Grafton had a market share of about 21 percent in commercial sales in the product categories in which it competed.

The Commercial Product Line

Exhibit 1 provides sales data by product line. There were substantial differences among these lines:

1 *Stationary metalworking power tools* This line was divided into two distinct groups. Better than half of the sales were of bench grinders

---

[1] A mill supply house played the role of "hardware store" to factories and other industrial users. They typically offered a wide range of products from paint to tools to maintenance supplies.

95

Exhibit 1 COMMERCIAL SALES BY PRODUCT LINE AND OTHER DATA (IN MILLIONS)

	1974 sales		1975 budget	
	Dollars	**Percent of total**	**Dollars**	**Percent of total**
Stationary metal- working power tools	6.0	5.7	7.0	6.0
Stationary wood- working power tools	17.0	16.2	19.0	16.2
Portable power tools	32.0	30.5	36.0	30.8
Hand tools— general shop	36.0	34.3	38.0	32.5
Mason, plasterer, and bricklayer tools	5.0	4.8	6.0	5.1
Measuring instruments	9.0	8.6	11.0	9.4
Total or average[a]	**105.0**	**100.0**	**117.0**	**100.0**

[a]Percentage totals do not add to exactly 100 percent because of rounding.
Source: Grafton Industries records.

96

used to grind and sharpen tools, etc. These retailed from about $30 to about $110. The remainder of the sales were for metalworking lathes and electric hacksaws which retailed for between $150 (simple hacksaw) to $1,000 (lathe). Items in this category tended to be for the very serious home craftsperson or the small commercial concern. These items were viewed by the firm as not gift oriented and not very promotable.

2 *Stationary woodworking power tools* These included stationary circular saws, bandsaws, lathes, drill presses, shapers, and planers. They retailed for between about $150 and $400 and were used by avid home craftspersons. Some of these tools were promotable as gift items, primarily for Christmas, Chanukah, and Father's Day.

3 *Portable power tools* These tools (sanders, saber saws, drills, and routers) were highly promotable, especially as gift items. They retailed for between $10 and $60 and were often sold as gifts.

4 *Hand tools—general shop* These included a wide variety of tools, ranging from hammers and screwdrivers through saws. They retailed for between $1 and $50 and were purchased by users and as gifts by a wide range of individuals. Some were promotable.

5 *Mason, plasterer, and bricklayer tools* These had developed from a line acquired in 1965. The tools were specialized and used by professionals and home craftspersons. Most of the professional sales came through the industrial sales force and are not counted in the figures in Exhibit 1. The items included various types of trowels, hammers, etc., and retailed in the $2 to $10 range. Sales were concentrated in the spring.

6 *Measuring instruments* These included tape measures, replacement

Exhibit 1   COMMERCIAL SALES BY PRODUCT LINE AND OTHER
DATA (IN MILLIONS)   *(Continued)*

First half 1975 budget		First half 1975 sales		1974 gross margin		
Dollars	Percent of total	Dollars	Percent of total	Percent	Dollars	Percent of total
3.4	6.6	3.5	6.6	40	2.4	6.7
8.0	15.4	7.8	14.7	36	6.1	16.9
14.0	27.0	16.0	30.2	33	10.6	29.4
17.0	32.8	16.0	30.2	30	10.8	30.0
4.5	8.7	4.4	8.3	50	2.5	6.9
5.0	9.6	5.2	9.8	40	3.6	10.0
51.9	**100.0**	**52.9**	**100.0**	**34.3**	**36.0**	**100.0**

tapes, levels, calipers, micrometers, combination squares, protrac-
tors, yardsticks, and gauges of various types. Prices at retail varied
from less than $1 to more than $30. Some of the tools were highly
specialized, but a few, such as tape measures, were promotable.

The Commercial Sales Force

The national commercial sales manager had three regional managers
reporting to him. These supervised 12 district managers who were
responsible for the 103 salespeople.

The regional managers had three prime tasks: (1) to participate in the
making of sales management and marketing policies, (2) to call on major
accounts within the region, and (3) to supervise the district sales
managers. They operated from offices in Chicago and spent much of their
time on policy matters involved with pricing, promotions, incentive
programs, and product planning. They also assisted district sales managers in recruiting and selection. This was not a large part of the job since
turnover was low.

The district sales managers were responsible for recruiting and
selection, training, evaluation, and supervision of the sales force. Each
also made calls on major accounts within the district, although the district
managers did not have actual sales responsibility.

The sales force was felt to have good morale and was experienced.
Ages ranged from the mid-twenties to sixty-five, the company's mandato-
ry retirement age. Most were college educated, especially the younger
ones. Each salesperson covered a specific territory and called upon
department, discount, and hardware stores, as well as home centers[2] and
lumberyards. In multiunit operations where the functions of buying and

[2]Home centers were large retail units which sold lumber, tools, electrical, heating, and
plumbing supplies, and other things for the do-it-yourself market. They were growing
rapidly in the mid-1970s.

store operations were separate, the salespeople were expected to call upon each store to arrange for display and placement. It was generally believed that better salespeople conducted in-store training sessions for retail sales personnel. These sessions were deemed especially important for new products.

Salespeople were paid by a combination of salary and commission. The salary was negotiated by the district manager and salesperson, and usually was based on experience, tenure with the company, account service, performance in special programs such as promotions or new product introductions, and general effort. Commission was 2 percent of sales.

The company paid all justified business expenses, including a mileage allowance for automobiles. The district managers were responsible for expense control.

District managers were paid a base salary, plus a small override on district sales.

Each salesperson was expected to make from five to six calls per day. Brief reports were required for each call. Grafton management believed the call reports to be relatively accurate because of a stringent company policy requiring dismissal for falsifying records.

The Capital District

In the Friday meeting alone with Mr. Oates, Mr. Falzarano had provided a brief introduction to the capital district:

> Sam Goldberg's district was a problem. It wasn't living up to its potential. I have been concerned with the problem for quite some time. We had plenty of data showing that we weren't getting the sales we should there. It's a great area—vibrant and growing. It seemed like Sam wasn't managing the eight salesmen very well. There have been some indications that morale was lower than it should be and turnover higher. The salesmen are a mixed bag as you will see. From your point of view it is a real turn-around situation.
>
> If Sam hadn't been so old we probably would have taken some action one way or the other. But he was close to retirement, and the problems weren't urgent. It seemed wrong to replace Sam since he was not anxious to take early retirement. He seemed healthy and really enjoyed working with the men and the customers. But he was clearly not as effective as he should have been.
>
> We began to analyze the district in depth about a year ago and have gathered considerable data. I have copies of the material for you. By next Monday afternoon I'll have my comments on each salesman. Remember, however, that I was only in the position three years and that as a regional manager it wasn't my business to second guess a district manager. So, my comments may be of limited value. Sam's own files on the salesmen will be of additional help.

The material Mr. Oates was given is reproduced in Exhibits 2 to 7.

EXHIBIT 2
Memo on Capital District

February 7, 1975

To: Ben Donovan, National Commercial Sales Manager
From: Jack Falzarano, Eastern Regional Manager
Subject: Capital District

As we decided at our meeting last week, I have attempted to pull together some material on the Capital District. Everything that I can see shows clearly that we have a problem there. I looked at three areas: (1) potential of the district versus our penetration, (2) sales growth of the district versus the region and the country, and (3) profit delivery and growth versus the region and the country.

Potential
According to the July 8, 1974, *Sales Management Survey of Buying Power,* the district has 5.7 percent of the potential sales in the nation:

	Buying power index	Percent of U.S. retail sales
Delaware	.2924	.2971
Maryland	2.0203	1.9776
District of Columbia	.4345	.3999
Virginia	2.2016	2.1827
West Virginia	.7159	.6860
Total	**5.6647**	**5.5433**

Our sales in the district in 1973 were only $5,040,000, or 4.8 percent of our sales. This would certainly be cause for concern alone, but to make matters worse, our primary competitive strength in commercial sales has always been in the Boston-Washington-Chicago triangle where the private-label sales have been relatively lower and the commercial sales relatively higher. Thus, we are led to expect below-average performance in the Southwest, Mountains, and Plains, but must make up for it in the East.

As another way of looking at the situation, our average sales per salesperson in the United States is $105 million per 103 territories or $1,020,000. The average in the district is $5,040,000 per 8 territories or $630,000, only 62 percent of the average.

Sales Growth
All sales figures are in millions in the following table.

	U.S.	Region	Capital district
1974	$105.000	$49.500	$5.040
1973	93.460	44.400	4.760
Growth, $	$ 11.540	$ 5.100	$ .280
Growth, %	12.3%	11.5%	5.9%
1973	$ 93.460	$44.400	$4.760

1972		85.100	39.500	4.450
Growth, $	$	8.360	$ 4.900	$ .310
Growth, %		9.8%	12.4%	7.0%
Average growth, %		11.1%	12.0%	6.5%

Thus, the sales growth in the district is about one-half of that of the region and only slightly better than one-half of that for the country.

Profitability

	U.S.	Region	Capital district
Gross profit, %			
1974	34.3%	34.6%	34.0%
1973	34.8	35.1	34.5

The profitability figures are below par when compared with both the nation and the region.

Exhibit 3 SALES PERFORMANCE: CAPITAL DISTRICT (in order of decreasing 1974 sales)

Salesperson	1974 sales ($000)	% of district	First half 1975 sales ($000)	% of district	1974 active accounts	1974 calls per year
1 Eaton	920	18.3	414	17.2	205	1,120
2 Burke	800	15.9	376	15.6	310	1,350
3 Durfee	750	14.9	390	16.2	160	1,470
4 Harlow	650	12.9	319	13.2	120	1,525
5 Furness	610	12.1	244	10.1	220	1,075
6 Gibson	560	11.1	252	10.4	130	940
7 Caplan	440	8.7	238	9.9	307	1,210
8 Alderson	310	6.2	180	7.5	458	1,640
Total	5,040	100.0	2,413	100.0	1,910	10,330

Source: Grafton Industries records, including call reports for data on the number of calls. Active accounts were those which had placed an order in the past year.

Exhibit 4 COMPENSATION AND EXPENSES: CAPITAL DISTRICT, 1974 (in order of decreasing sales performance)

Salesperson	Salary	Commissions	Total compensation	Expenses	Total
1 Eaton	$20,000	$18,400	$38,400	$4,100	$42,500
2 Burke	16,000	16,000	32,000	6,800	38,800
3 Durfee	11,000	15,000	26,000	4,300	30,300
4 Harlow	14,000	13,000	27,000	3,900	30,900
5 Furness	13,000	12,200	25,200	7,400	32,600
6 Gibson	15,000	11,200	26,200	3,500	29,700
7 Caplan	9,500	8,800	18,300	8,900	27,200
8 Alderson	7,000	6,200	13,200	7,300	20,500
Total	$105,500	$100,800	$206,300	$46,200	$252,500
Average	$ 13,188	$ 12,600	$ 25,788	$ 5,775	$ 31,563

Source: Grafton Industries records.

Exhibit 5 TERRITORY DATA: CAPITAL DISTRICT (in order of decreasing sales performance)

Salesperson	Territory	Number of potential accounts	Buying power index	Percentage of total U.S. retail sales	Population	Land area in square miles
1 Eaton	Metropolitan Baltimore, except for Harford County	504	.9407	0.9548	2,003,000	1,806
2 Burke	Eastern part of Virginia, including Richmond, Norfolk, and Newport News but not Delmarva Peninsula or suburban Washington, D.C.	525	.8142	0.8256	1,839,000	9,045
3 Durfee	Virginia suburbs of Washington, D.C.	185	.5790	0.6638	989,000	1,301
4 Harlow	District of Columbia	139	.4345	0.3999	743,000	61
5 Furness	Maryland except for Delmarva Peninsula and metropolitan Baltimore	358	.9061	0.8410	1,717,000	4,239
6 Gibson	Delmarva Peninsula and Harford County, Maryland	427	.4798	0.4931	1,019,000	6,524
7 Caplan	West Virginia	883	.7159	0.6860	1,794,000	24,070
8 Alderson	Western part of Virginia	933	.7945	0.6791	1,962,000	28,738
Total		**3,954**	**5.6647**	**5.5433**	**12,066,000**	**75,784**
Average		**494**	**.7081**	**0.6929**	**1,508,000**	**9,473**

Source: Number of potential accounts was estimated from data in the *1968 Census of Business.* Potential accounts included all hardware, building material, and department stores and 30 percent of other general merchandise stores. Each store, not each company, was counted as one potential account. The buying power index, retail sales, and population data were from the *1974 Sales Management Survey of Buying Power,* copyright 1974, *Sales Management,* reprinted by permission. The data on land area are drawn from *1975 Commercial Atlas & Marketing Guide,* Rand McNally & Company.

101

Exhibit 6　1974 SALES BY PRODUCT LINE

Dollar sales ($000)

	Eaton	Burke	Durfee	Harlow	Furness	Gibson	Caplan	Alderson	Total
Stationary metalworking	28	8	53	52	43	17	—	9	210
Stationary woodworking	147	32	150	117	104	67	44	43	704
Portable power	267	360	248	182	207	190	141	109	1,704
Hand tools	358	360	150	207	189	207	176	127	1,774
Mason, etc.	28	—	74	33	18	34	35	6	228
Measuring instruments	92	40	75	59	49	45	44	16	420
Total	**920**	**800**	**750**	**650**	**610**	**560**	**440**	**310**	**5,040**

Percentage of dollar sales

	Eaton	Burke	Durfee	Harlow	Furness	Gibson	Caplan	Alderson	Total
Stationary metalworking	3	1	7	8	7	3	—	3	4
Stationary woodworking	16	4	20	18	17	12	10	14	14
Portable power	29	45	33	28	34	34	32	35	34
Hand tools	39	45	20	32	31	37	40	41	35
Mason, etc.	3	—	10	5	3	6	8	2	5
Measuring instruments	10	5	10	9	8	8	10	5	8
Total	**100**	**100**	**100**	**100**	**100**	**100**	**100**	**100**	**100**

Source: Grafton Industries records.

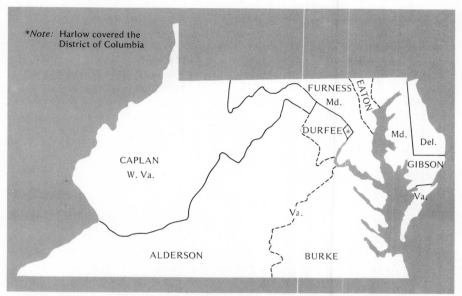

Note: Harlow covered the District of Columbia

FURNESS
Md.

EATON

DURFEE(*)

Md.

Del.

CAPLAN
W. Va.

GIBSON

Va.

Va.

ALDERSON

BURKE

Exhibit 7 Grafton Industries. Map of the capital district. State boundaries are denoted by solid lines, territory boundaries by broken lines.

103

ELEVEN   Honeywell Information Systems (A)

On April 23, 1974, Honeywell Information Systems announced a new product line—the Series 60 family of computers. (See the Appendix for a description of the introduction.) Following the introduction, Chris Lynch, marketing vice president of HIS for North America, was reviewing the deployment of his sales force.

He was particularly concerned about the tendency of the sales force to concentrate on the sale of very large systems, defined as computer systems with a shipment value of $1.5 million or larger.

> In a sense, it's not a problem. The profit margin on the very large units is higher than on smaller units. The sales dollars generated per hour of selling time is also greater at the large end since our very large systems, the current 6000 line, average $2.5 million per installation. Our 58 line of small computers averages about $60 thousand per installation.
>
> But, this situation is not all to the good. First, Clancy Spangle [the executive vice president of Honeywell directly responsible for the HIS division] has made it clear that overemphasis on very large systems is playing havoc with our world-wide production facilities. The medium sized units are

produced in France and that factory needs production to maintain its workforce and to keep costs reasonable. Second, the smaller systems provide an entry level for new customers.[1] And, in this business existing customers are usually your best prospects. Finally, we fear that if we let this thing get out of hand, we will lose our position as a full line company.

The irony of the situation is that a few years ago we had the opposite problem. We were "nobody" in the very large systems market. But, the 6000 product line, combined with a charged-up sales force really established our position.

HONEYWELL INFORMATION SYSTEMS

Honeywell Information Systems (HIS) was the largest division of Honeywell, Inc. In 1973 it had sales of $1,177 billion, 49 percent of Honeywell; and earnings (before interest and taxes) of $93 billion, 41 percent of the corporation. In 1972 the respective figures were $1,061 billion and $73 million. Corporate gross margins averaged about 37 percent.

HIS was the direct responsibility of one of the two corporate executive vice presidents. It was divided geographically with slightly more than one half of its sales and profits in the North American operation.[2]

104

Background

Honeywell Information Systems had been formed in 1970 when Honeywell acquired General Electric's computer operations and merged it with its own. At that time General Electric (GE) was considered to have an operation which was strong technologically but weak in marketing and sales. Its strongest product offerings were in the large and very large systems. Honeywell, on the other hand, was viewed as having more marketing strength than technical strength, and as being most effective in the small to medium-sized computers.

During the period between 1970 and 1974, Honeywell concentrated on several activities. The major one was to build a functioning organization out of the merged operations. Industry experts viewed Honeywell as successful in developing an effective organization. Some even expressed surprise at Honeywell's apparently successful performance in the industry. The Appendix provides some insight into these issues.

During the postmerger period, HIS invested over $100 million per year in research and development of new hardware and software. The

---

[1] Almost three-quarters of HIS's new customers purchased small systems.

[2] This case is concerned only with the North American operation. HIS as used hereinafter will mean the North American part of HIS.

new product line, Series 60, alone accounted for over $300 million in development cost. Industry experts viewed such expenditures as essential to success because of the rapid change and complexity of computer technology.

Following the merger there was a strong emphasis on profit generation. This created a desire to emphasize the large units, as well as to make outright sales or third-party leases[3] instead of rentals. Before the merger, in fact, GE had attempted to convert previously written rental agreements into sales. This endeavor continued after the merger.

Organization

Exhibit 1 shows the sales and marketing organization for HIS.[4] The line sales organization had four vice presidents, each responsible for marketing operations in a part of the country. Each vice president had a staff as well as two or three regional marketing directors. The 11 regional

[3]Third party leases are explained below.

[4]Federal government sales were not the responsibility of Mr. Lynch or the organization described here.

105

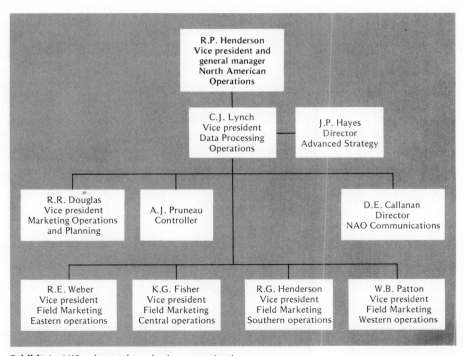

Exhibit 1 HIS sales and marketing organization.

marketing directors[5] supervised the field sales force through 41 branch managers to whom reported 129 marketing managers. The marketing managers actually supervised the 605 salespeople.

The branch managers had considerable freedom in organizing their sales offices. Some, particularly those in the larger metropolitan areas, were organized by broad customer industry. Others were organized geographically. The Boston branch, for example, had four marketing managers. The three who operated within the Boston metropolitan area were organized by customer industry: financial and banking, manufacturing and distribution, and government, education, and medical. The fourth marketing manager supervised salespeople in the Worcester area. Some salespeople there concentrated by customer type while others covered a territory with a variety of industries.

The marketing effort (see Exhibit 2) was organized by function, product, and industry. There were separate managers for large systems, small and medium systems, and minicomputer and communication systems. The industry group contained three subgroups. The industry strategy personnel provided intensive sales support for the field sales force when it approached particular customers, attended customer

[5]There was a twelfth regional marketing director who was responsible for national accounts and stationed in New York.

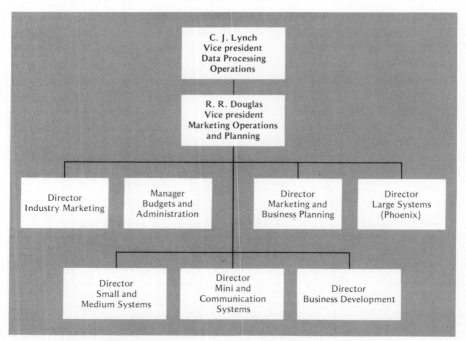

Exhibit 2   Marketing organization.

industry trade shows and meetings (for example, a convention of hospital administrators), and developed industry sales programs. The industry programs group was responsible for acquisition of industry-oriented software and computer programs developed by users and organizations such as trade associations and universities. The industry planning and development group was responsible for the development of proprietary Honeywell software for specific industry application. The staffs of the regional vice presidents also included industry experts.

Profit Planning

Late in each year, headquarters personnel developed a profit plan for the next year. Dollar profit and sales goals were established for each of the four operations areas. Personnel in the offices of the operating vice presidents, field sales management, and headquarters personnel divided the plan into goals for each region, branch, and salesperson. The data upon which the plans were developed were gathered from industry sources, marketing research personnel, field sales management, and salespeople by the headquarters marketing staff. Profit and sales goals were developed for each month. Product-line sales goals were developed for each branch. The product line goals, according to one field sales manager, had been more strongly communicated in the past. "Now, the emphasis is on profit generation. I am judged on my ability to meet my profit goals."

107

Headquarters did not develop definitive sales quotas by industry. Product-line sales information was gathered during the year, but industry sales data were not gathered until the end of the year.

One branch manager stated, "The company makes an effort to control goals by product line but no one at HIS will turn away business. If my people do well and I do well in terms of profit generation we are heroes regardless of the mix of business. When you are number two to IBM with seventy percent of the business, you have to let business come from where it may."

According to one marketing executive, the competitive computer companies did not give field sales management profit goals. "They give each selling unit a sales goal by product line as well as a rental goal and a purchase goal. There the philosophy is 'you get the sales, we'll turn it into profits.'"

One area of discussion concerned the amount of direction to come from headquarters. One senior marketing manager stated, "There is no way that we can make the decisions for the salespeople and the field managers. They have the incentive[6] and they are closest to the market so they can best decide whom to call on and how to sell."

[6]Salespeople were paid on commission using a complex scheme which considered both rental and sale revenue.

Another headquarters manager believed, "The sales force has too much autonomy. It is difficult to coordinate or control the sales force when it has so much freedom. We must provide strong direction so that the sales force approaches the market in a strong coherent fashion consistent with the products (hardware and software) developed at headquarters and with available industry specialists. The sales force can only operate in areas in which we provide support. By the same token, we waste valuable effort when they don't use what we develop."

THE COMPUTER INDUSTRY

The history of the computer business had been an unusual combination of rapid growth in demand and intense competitive activity. Several major firms had dropped out, including GE, RCA, and Westinghouse.

The nature of the industry had changed radically during its relatively short history. The first uses of computers were in scientific applications, where they were used for massive, often repetitive calculating tasks. The commercial applications grew rapidly, however, as computers replaced manual processing of data. Technological change led to increasing capacities and faster speeds at lower cost. As the industry developed, the emphasis shifted to more complex systems. Programs and software became increasingly important as computers were used in more difficult, management-oriented applications.

Almost all companies except the very small ones were potential customers. Large firms usually either purchased, leased, or rented their equipment. The leases had often been third-party arrangements in which a leasing company purchased the machine from the manufacturer and leased it to a customer. Smaller companies could also purchase, lease, or rent their own computers, or they could have their computing done by a service company, either on their premises or at the service company's facility.

The 1960s had seen perhaps the most rapid changes in technology. By the mid-1970s, product introductions had become less frequent. New products, however, were still being introduced at a rate faster than in many other industries. Many of the products were peripheral accessories other than the main computer processing unit.

Large computers[7] were purchased only by large organizations. Large organizations might also purchase small and medium-sized computers for specific purposes or remote locations. Small firms, however, were unlikely to purchase a large unit unless it was central to their operation, as in the case of a computer service bureau which sold computing services.

[7]Large computers were those with a purchase value of above $1,500,000. Small computers had a purchase value between $40,000 and $200,000.

According to one HIS executive the large sales were slow,[8] involved matters. Top management was almost always involved, and meticulous financial justification was necessary. Medium-sized units were usually purchased as part of upgrading programs by growing organizations. The purchasers were experienced and sophisticated.

When small units were purchased by a larger user, the responsibility often lay with the top data-processing executive who was a sophisticated buyer. In a small organization, however, the situation was quite different. The purchase decision generally involved top management which was not sophisticated in computers. Often, it was the initial computer purchase, and a substantial commitment from the buying company's point of view. In such a situation, the salesperson had to be able to communicate well and to understand the process by which the computer would be installed and used. He thus had to understand the customer's business. On the other hand, the small size of the sale did not justify the long selling time and high-level effort utilized in the larger sales. Instead, according to another HIS executive, "The salesperson has to be aggressive to find the potential customer and aggressive to close the sale in a reasonable period of time. He must make cold calls to find good prospects." An IBM sales manager confirmed that "it takes a different type of salesperson to sell the small user."

The large sales often involved the computer company's sales management and industry sales specialists. The larger the sale, generally, the higher the level of personnel brought into the selling process and the more people involved. "Honeywell Information Systems (B)" presents an example which was not atypical, according to industry experts.

One executive believed that the toughest competition and the best competitive talent were in the large computer end of the business. He went on to state that the large systems were often purchased, but the smaller ones were usually rented. There were, according to him, many situations in which this general rule was not true.

The sales emphasis throughout all sizes of computers was increasingly away from the physical capacity of the hardware (referred to as "feed, read, and speed" in the industry) to the usefulness of the unit and its supporting systems as a business tool.

Customers tended to be loyal to suppliers because there was not a general compatibility among different manufacturers' hardware and software. Thus, it was a major job for a customer to convert from one manufacturer's hardware and systems to another. There were some instances where certain competitors had developed new systems which were compatible with competitors' (usually IBM because of the large number of units it had installed) or which could be compatible when equipped with certain software systems.

---

[8]Large sales were expected to take between 6 and 12 months to consummate while small sales took 1 to 2 months.

IBM

IBM was the largest industry competitor. It had an estimated 6,000 salespeople who were organized primarily by customer industry. The firm had a reputation for developing outstanding marketing personnel. Some of HIS's top marketing and general management personnel, including Mr. Lynch, had entered the computer industry with IBM. This was also true of most other competitors.

IBM was strong in all parts of the computer market. Some industry experts considered its greatest competitive strength to be in the medium-sized part of the market. Its domestic market share (dollar basis) was estimated at about 70 percent. In 1973-1974, it had made a strong effort in the small computer area. It had, in fact, divided its data processing operations into two parts—one division for the medium and large systems and one for the small systems. This change was accompanied by increased advertising in the general (as opposed to business) media, including radio.

Other Competitors

Honeywell was generally considered to be the second largest domestic supplier of computers, with a market share of about 8 percent. This had been increasing slowly and was thus higher than its share of the installed base—that is, the number of its computers in use. One HIS executive described the company as especially strong in tailoring proposals to a customer's specific hardware and software needs and in pricing its proposals aggressively. By late 1973 HIS had more than 16,000 systems installed world-wide.

There were two other competitors who made a wide range of computers: Sperry-Rand/Univac and Burroughs. Sperry-Rand had a market share of 7 to 8 percent, which was less than its share of the installed base. Its large-computer product line was generally considered the most successful part of its line. It also had a strong base in the medium-sized machines and appeared to be beginning a rebirth in this area.

Burroughs had strength in both the large and small ends of the market. Many of its small users had been converted from its very strong line of accounting machines—semiautomated, electromechanical machines for routine bookkeeping chores. Burroughs was relatively weak in foreign markets but had shown increasing strength domestically. Its domestic market share was estimated to be about 4 to 6 percent. Burroughs tended to concentrate on selected markets in which it had strength, such as banking and retailing. Its smaller computers were sold by its accounting machine sales force. There were industry rumors that it would cut the price of its medium-sized units substantially in the near future.

Control Data had been very active in the very large computers where it had enjoyed an early technological advantage. Many of its major installations were special-purpose scientific and governmental units. Its share was 2 to 3 percent.

National Cash Register (NCR) had suffered reverses in the early 1970s, culminating with a $60 million loss (corporate-wide) in 1972. By 1973 it had reversed this situation and brought its computer operation into profitability for the first time. In late 1973 it separated its sales and marketing forces along industry lines: retail, financial, commercial and industrial, and medical, educational, and governmental. Each sales force sold all relevant NCR products, including cash registers and accounting machines. Its primary strength had been in retailing, banking, hotels, and hospitals. It had a domestic market share of 2 to 3 percent.

Digital Equipment Corporation (DEC) had entered the computer market from its strong position in minicomputers. Most of its minicomputers were sold to other manufacturers to be incorporated into their products. DEC sold small computer systems for scientific and general purpose use. It had been more profitable in the very small end of the market than many industry experts had thought possible. Its market share, however, was low on a dollar basis, perhaps 2 to 3 percent, because of the low price of its units.

THE DEPLOYMENT SITUATION

Honeywell executives viewed deployment as a key sales management issue because HIS had only 10 percent as many salespeople as its largest competitor.

According to one field sales manager, IBM's strength was primarily in the metropolitan areas.

> Out in the rural areas, we are relatively better off than in the cities. We have been quite successful in these areas because our sales force does not meet the 10+:1 ratio it hits in the cities where IBM concentrates its people. In the city we must pick our targets carefully. They [IBM] can play the numbers game and overwhelm any prospect or customer. They can use two or three people for each one we have calling on a prospect or servicing an account. They have size and depth. Thus, ours must be a concentration game. We have come to realize that we can compete in every product line but not on every account. The salespeople want to sell everything to everybody, but field sales management must provide the focus.

HIS expected to get 80 percent of its sales from existing customers. These would be upgrades to larger or newer systems, sale of additional software, or sale of peripheral equipment such as printers, terminals, etc. One HIS executive stated, "It costs much less to sell existing customers.

Finding worthwhile prospects among noncomputer users or competitive customers is a time-consuming process. Teaching them how to use a computer for the first time is particularly time consuming." This 80 to 20 percent division was almost universally accepted among Honeywell management.

A field executive stated,

> We devote our time to three types of sales. First is the prospect who does not presently have a Honeywell unit. Here the emphasis is on the qualification process—we want to separate the "prospects from the suspects." The second type of sale involves an upgrade of an existing system. Here we try to recognize the potential quickly and to understand the customer's needs well. Finally is the existing customer who is under competitive attack. We emphasize a three phase process of "sell, install, protect." Because the customer base is a valuable competitive asset, we work hard to protect it. The successful salesperson is constantly on the alert for competitive activity among his customers.

Before the merger, Honeywell had been strongly oriented to manufacturing and was beginning to make some moves into distribution and finance. GE was primarily committed to finance and manufacturing. After the merger, HIS continued to develop toward manufacturing and finance. In addition, the health-care industries and government received additional emphasis.

One marketing executive declared,

> It is expensive to be involved with an industry. We sell five things: (1) hardware (the central processing unit), (2) operating software (the internal computer operating system), (3) peripherals, (4) applications software, and (5) terminals. The first two are generally not industry specific, although the operating software may vary with application. The same basic system, for example, can be used for on-line updating and interrogation of record files whether they are wholesaler inventory or hospital patient records. The last

Exhibit 3 THE COMPUTER MARKET BY SIZE

Size	Number of systems installed	Percentage of total	Estimated value ($000)	Percentage of total	Projected dollar growth rate 1974–1979
Very small ⎫ Small ⎭	39,300	71	6,250	25	18 8
Medium	10,200	18	7,000	28	5
Medium-large	3,270	6	4,500	18	9
Large	1,970	4	5,250	21	8
Very large	390	1	2,000	8	13
Total	55,130	100	25,000	100	9

Notes: Medium and medium-large units would be grouped as medium in the more crude delineation used in other parts of the data. Large and very large would be grouped as large.

The data in this exhibit were derived from generally available industry data and, although useful for discussion purposes, do not necessarily reflect the actual situation.

Exhibit 4   ESTIMATED DOLLAR SHARE OF INSTALLED BASE (computers in service)

Size	IBM	HIS	Univac/ Sperry	Burroughs	NCR	Control Data	Other	Total
Small	16.3	2.8	1.7	1.7	2.3	0.1	0.1	25.0
Medium	21.9	3.2	1.0	1.3	0.2	0.1	0.2	27.9
Medium-large	12.1	1.2	2.2	1.1	0.0	0.5	0.6	17.7
Large	17.5	.5	2.1	0.5	0.0	0.9	0.1	21.6
Very large	6.0	.8	0.0	0.0	0.0	1.0	0.0	7.8
Total	73.8	8.5	7.0	4.6	2.5	2.6	1.1	100.0

Notes: Medium and medium-large units would be grouped as medium in the more crude delineation used in other parts of the data. Large and very large would be grouped as large.

The data in this exhibit were derived from generally available industry data and, although useful for discussion purposes, do not necessarily reflect the actual situation.

three items are to a great extent industry specific. In addition, the salespeople must be trained for the customer industry, and you need headquarters industry specialists. Once you begin to sell to customers in a specific industry, of course, you gain momentum. You develop knowledge of the industry and buying patterns, and the industry starts to know you. Purchasers talk to each other and your reputation grows.

One headquarters executive who worked on an industry team stated that the sales force tended to gravitate toward areas which they knew. "This means that a company becomes increasingly strong in its existing strength but does not grow into new areas." He suggested two approaches to ameliorate this tendency: First: provide headquarters and field industry specialists to work with the sales force by (1) educating the force, and (2) helping with the actual calls. (He described the HIS approach to

Exhibit 5   INSTALLED VALUE OF COMPUTERS BY INDUSTRY AND SIZE

Industry	Small	Medium	Large	Total
Manufacturing (assembly)	3.8[b]	6.3	5.4	15.5
Manufacturing (process)	4.8	6.2	3.1	14.1
Retail and wholesale	3.0	3.2	1.1	7.3
Financial	3.1	9.6	5.3	18.0
Education	1.4	2.2	2.6	6.2
Medical	0.8	0.9	0.1	1.8
Services	2.3	5.7	6.0	14.0
Service bureau	1.6	3.7	1.8	7.1
Government[a]	2.6	6.3	5.7	14.6
Other	0.6	0.5	0.3	1.4
	24.0	44.6	31.4	100.0

[a]Includes federal, state, and local.

[b]To be read "3.8% of the total installed value of computers is represented by small computers installed in assembly manufacturing companies."

Note: The data in this exhibit were derived from generally available industry data and, although useful for discussion purposes, do not necessarily reflect the actual situation.

Exhibit 6   HONEYWELL MARKET SHARE BY INDUSTRY

Industry	HIS market share-dollar basis	Percentage of HIS total-dollar basis	HIS market share-unit basis	Percentage of HIS total-unit basis
Manufacturing (assembly)	12.7	25.4	12.3	23.3
Manufacturing (process)	8.3	15.2	7.7	16.8
Retail and wholesale	8.5	8.2	8.6	12.2
Financial	7.8	18.5	8.9	14.2
Education	5.5	4.1	5.3	3.6
Medical	10.6	2.5	10.2	3.6
Services	6.7	12.1	8.3	10.7
Service bureau	9.3	8.5	11.1	9.2
Government[a]	5.0	4.2	7.7	4.7
Other	6.9	1.3	5.4	1.8
Total	8.5	100.0	9.0	100.0

[a]Includes state and local government, not federal.
Note: The data in this exhibit were derived from generally available industry data and, although useful for discussion purposes, do not necessarily reflect the actual situation.

banking as an example in which this had worked.) Second: provide strong direction from top management, including sales goals by product and industry. "If we remove the profit goals, we can exert more control over the sales effort. That way we can develop and implement a strategy."

He went on to say that he would prefer to see a sales force which was organized by customer industry and product. The rural areas would continue to receive general coverage.

> NCR has organized by industry and Control Data has organized by product. It makes sense. It's the only way to show commitment to customers as well as to create the necessary sales force training. Each customer industry requires special knowledge especially in a business in which you are so intimately involved with the customer's needs and operations.
>
> There are problems with this approach of course. Everyone wants to sell the large systems because of their glamour so it's hard to get people to stay with the small systems. Another problem is that industry specialization can lead to a feast-or-famine business. A salesperson responsible, for example, for stock brokerage and investment banking firms would starve today because that whole industry is doing poorly.

Mr. Lynch and his management team were concerned about the total deployment area. He stated: "There are good reasons to put more emphasis on certain industries, but we can't run away from IBM and the other competitors who are strong. The only way to compete with IBM is head-on. IBM is so big, so good, and so pervasive that there is no decent market where they are not strong. If a competitor of IBM can make money in a market whether it's defined by geography, product, or industry, IBM can also make money there."

Control Data and Burroughs, on the other hand, apparently attempted to avoid head-on competition. Control Data, for example, had concentrated upon giant special-purpose computers and was now apparently tending toward providing computer services.

He went on to say, "IBM is so big, however, that it works to our advantage. Some of their customers have to be dissatisfied. And our salespeople have a big, visible target. We get tremendous sales force excitement when we gain a former IBM customer."

Mr. Lynch had data available on the sales of computers by size, company, and customer industry (see Exhibits 3 to 6).

APPENDIX: HONEYWELL UNSCRAMBLES ITS COMPUTER MIX[1]

A Whole New Line Leaves the Company No Choice But to Meet Competitors Head-on

For Honeywell, Inc., competing in the computer industry has been something like having a bear by the tail. Admits Stephen F. Keating, president and chief executive: "We began with a relatively modest joint venture with Raytheon, but computers really burst on our consciousness with the success of the Honeywell 200 in the 1960s. Then it became apparent that it was a hell of a challenge that couldn't be treated as just another business venture."

This week, Keating and Honeywell's top computer boss, executive vice president C. W. (Clancy) Spangle, spent several days at a sprawling Honeywell plant in Billerica, Mass., to preside at the official uncaging of a whole new line of computers that the company has developed during the last three or four years at a cost, according to Keating, "well in excess of $300 million." The new computer systems, characterized in the company's promotion by a pride of lions sculptured from wires and electronic components, puts Honeywell in the worldwide data processing arena with no possibility of graceful exit. From now on, Honeywell's future will depend on how aggressively the company can scratch in across-the-board competition with IBM and the others in the industry.

115

Of all the survivors in the so-called main-frame, or full systems, part of the computer industry, Honeywell has been the most changed and perhaps the most challenged. Its competitors, beginning with IBM and continuing down the ranks through Burroughs, NCR, Sperry Rand, Control Data, and Xerox, all had the roots that most survivors consider essential: experience in the office equipment market or, in the case of Control Data, an initial dedication to pure computer technology.

By contrast, Honeywell was more like the companies that dropped out of the mainstream of computers—Westinghouse, RCA, Raytheon, Philco-Ford, and General Electric. All had solid positions in other industries, somewhat like Honeywell's strong base in industrial and heat controls, but they all proved unwilling to meet the huge capital demands and constant drain of executive energy that the blistering pace of computer technology, marketing strategy, and financing required.

Honeywell's financial statements show what happens when a manufacturing company moves heavily into computers. In 10 years:

[1]Reprinted by permission of *Business Week*, April 27, 1974.

Revenues increased 2.7 times—from $667 million to $2.4 billion—of which about half now come from data processing equipment sales and rental.

Rental and service revenue from computers jumped 27.6 times, reaching a level of $663 million, nearly equaling Honeywell's total sales in 1964. This income from installed equipment provides the well-known "flywheel" effect of continuous revenues even during business downturns.

Short- and long-term debt, needed largely to finance leased computers, increased $6\frac{1}{2}$ fold to $585 million.

Research and development costs for computers and software have been running over $100 million a year.

But with all the increased revenues and investment in computers, profits have lagged. Last year, Honeywell earned 7.9% before taxes and interest on revenues from its Information Systems group, while its other divisions turned in an 11% profit. But if the $40-million interest burden on Honeywell's debt were allocated to the computer group, it would have cut the company's computer profit to about 4%. And the quality of Honeywell's earnings in computers is criticized by analysts because the company still defers some research expenditures and, unlike some other companies, uses straight-line rather than accelerated depreciation for its rental equipment.

116

But that could be nitpicking at this time. Honeywell is now plowing back into the business more than $200 million a year in depreciation expenses. More important, the company's computer group has just come through an extraordinary three years. Since 1970, Honeywell has managed to digest the largest merger in the history of the computer industry: the acquisition of GE's computer group. It has reorganized its entire operation along international lines and developed a single new line of computers out of the welter of plans and products that faced it at the time of the merger.

Both Keating and Spangle still discuss the GE takeover as the most momentous in their careers. Says Keating: "The earlier decision to go into computers with Raytheon was easy. Then the decision was relatively small. Later, with the development of the Honeywell 200, the stakes got higher."

A Bigger Share

The 200 line of computers might well have worked into a mousetrap play for Honeywell. The machines went after the then-aging small to medium-sized IBM machines of the middle 1960s. Touted as "liberators" from IBM, the 200s were sold on the basis that they would run programs written for IBM equipment. But the cost of converting some programs ran Honeywell's expenses sky-high. Still, the machines were largely responsible for winning Honeywell about 5% of the market by the end of the 1960s.

The Honeywell 200 brought some hard lessons. It proved that getting a narrow market share away from the competition was simply too expensive. It also showed that a limited product line offered no way to grow with a customer, or to capture first-time customers who began with smaller machines.

"We were into computers so far that we never thought of selling out, and we couldn't abandon it," says Keating. The problem was to get a bigger market share in a hurry, and GE's decision to get out of the business provided the opportunity. "We faced ourselves, realized we had to be bigger, and made the biggest decision since the company decided to go into heat control," says Keating.

The acquisition of GE's computer operations in 1970 virtually doubled Honeywell's share of the market, but at the cost of more than doubling its management problems. It had its own computers, GE's large and medium domestic line, and a family of small machines acquired through a troubled French connection in GE-Machines Bull. On top of that, there was a recession in the computer industry.

The Basic Plan

The recession may well have provided the breather that Honeywell needed. The fundamental problem the company faced was to plan and build one coordinated product line that would compete across the board from small to very large systems. "It had to be new and different," says Spangle, "but not so different that it scared our present customers away from growing into it. In this business, new products always have that paradox."

The first contact between the GE and Honeywell new-product teams took place in 1969 during early discussions of the acquisition. Honeywell executives call it the "Shangri-La" meeting. GE's plans were for a full-line series of computers, and the initial description filled a 3-inch-thick binder titled NPL, for new product line. Honeywell's plans also filled a 3-inch binder and outlined a full product line, but they were titled ACS, for advanced computer system.

Spangle set up task teams to go over the GE plans and to reappraise Honeywell's. By May 20, the day the acquisition was announced, the task forces decided that the two plans made a reasonably good fit. Both had envisioned a five-level product line ranging from small terminal processors to very large computers, with heavy emphasis on communications for data networks.

The technical teams came up with a full product line plan by November, 1970, a month after the Honeywell-GE agreement was formally completed. By late December, Honeywell had developed full business plans, including pricing strategies, and final engineering got under way.

Once it had the basic system plan, Honeywell doled out "mission assignments" to its operations in five countries for 23 major product development projects ranging from printers to the large central processors that make up the new Series 60 line. Its French operation, Compagnie Honeywell Bull, has full responsibility for the smallest of the five computers in the line. Honeywell Italia has the next larger machine, and the French and American operations share responsibility for the critical middle-sized Model 64. The two largest models in the line are the responsibility of Honeywell's Phoenix (Ariz.) operation, which was GE's major computer manufacturing facility. Even programming languages and software systems—now the most crucial part of computer projects—are shared between Honeywell's British and U.S. operations.

Product Changes

As complex as the allocation of resources may seem, it represents a vast simplification of the Honeywell-GE combination when it was first put together.

Spangle points out that after the merger, there were 10 product lines with 20 central processors, and 12 separate software, or programming, systems. On top of that, the merged operations had 33 different design families turning out 157 peripheral equipment products.

While the design and engineering work on the new system was under way, Honeywell consolidated the existing GE and Honeywell line through evolutionary product changes from 10 to 4 computer families and narrowed down its accessory lines to 15 groups containing 54 products. Some of the work on new peripheral products, such as disk storage and tapes, will meld into the new Series 60 family of computers.

More significant than hardware consolidation in the Series 60 line is a comprehensive programming system that provides a common thread from the smallest through the largest machines. Much of it is based on the very successful operating system programs known as GCOS, which are used in the larger computers of Honeywell's current line. To add further spice to the high end of the new Series 60 computers, Honeywell will provide support for a massive system called MULTICS, which incorporates some of the most advanced concepts in large, shared computer networks developed over the years at Massachusetts Institute of Technology. This, Honeywell executives believe, provides the new line with a unique, open-ended development path toward the big, integrated computer networks of the future.

118

TWELVE Ivan IV

In January 1974, Ralph Wyzanski, vice president of sales for Ivan IV, a division of Waverley Clothiers, Inc., was considering what changes should be made in the division's target market program. The program included 169 stores which Mr. Wyzanski had identified as prime candidates for increased Ivan IV sales. One of seven executives, as well as a regular salesperson, was responsible for each target store. After the 1973 fall selling season—the first on the target market program—Mr. Wyzanski labeled the program "extremely successful." Unit sales increased 68 percent over the 1972 fall selling season, and 25 new accounts had been opened. However, executive staff cutbacks threatened to weaken the program for 1974, and Mr. Wyzanski had to restructure the program with these changes in mind.

DIVISION HISTORY

Waverley Clothiers, one of the largest and most respected companies in the clothing industry, manufactured and marketed a wide variety of apparel—dresses, suits, pants, jackets, raincoats, heavy winter coats, and sportswear—for women, men, and children. In the 1960s, Waverley acquired Ivan IV, manufacturer of high-quality outerwear for men,[1] and Eaton Hall, manufacturer of high-quality outerwear for young men (ages 16 to 22). Ivan IV's and Eaton Hall's product lines consisted primarily of winter coats and raincoats. While both companies historically had strong sales and profits, they began to have problems in the late 1960s.

In March 1972, Barry Allison became president of Ivan IV. He assembled a new management team and made many other changes. The results were dramatic. Whereas in 1972 Ivan IV sustained a $380,000 loss, in 1973 it showed a $306,000 operating profit.

From 1969 through 1972, Eaton Hall showed modest though declining profits. Early in 1973, Waverley management combined the Eaton Hall and Ivan IV sales forces as a first step toward consolidating the two companies into the Ivan IV Division. By late 1973, Eaton Hall's total management operations had been placed under Mr. Allison. However, the changes were too late to reverse the downward spiral. In 1973, Eaton Hall registered a $133,000 loss.

In 1973, the total Ivan IV Division had gross sales of $12,033,000 with before-tax profits of $173,000. The division's goals were to increase sales annually at 25 percent per year and to improve before-tax profits to 5 percent in 1974, $7\frac{1}{2}$ percent in 1975, and 10 percent in 1976. (See Exhibit 1 for an organization chart and Exhibit 2 for an income statement.)

INDUSTRY BACKGROUND

In 1974 numerous companies manufactured some high-quality outerwear for men. Only about ten, however, focused solely on this product line. The lowest-priced garments in this segment generally retailed for about $60. There was no real leader in this market except in the rainwear, where the dominant force by far was Endicott, developers of the classically styled raincoat with a zip-in lining, which was merchandised as an "all purpose" coat. Endicott's estimated annual sales of men's coats were $20 million. Mr. Wyzanski commented on Endicott's position as follows:

> Endicott sets the raincoat market by working closely with key stores and carefully testing ideas. It keeps customers happy by giving excellent service and consistently high quality. The only way other manufacturers can compete is by continually updating their lines with new fabrics and new styles.

In the outerwear market for young men (ages 16 to 22), only Eaton Hall and one other manufacturer targeted their efforts solely at the very top of the market. Retail prices of their garments began at about $50. Six other

---

[1]Outerwear included jackets and coats designed to be worn outdoors. It did not include suit coats or sport coats designed to be worn inside.

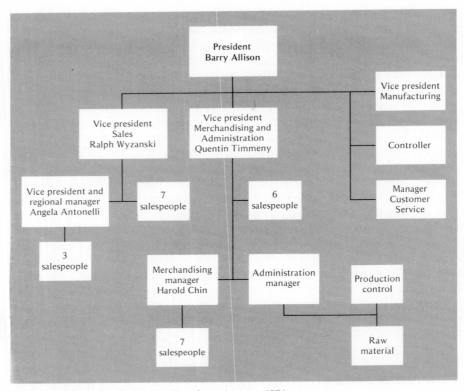

Exhibit 1 Abbreviated organization chart, January 1974.

Exhibit 2 1973 DIVISION INCOME
STATEMENT (000 OMITTED)

Gross sales (less discounts)	$12,033
Less returns and allowances	573
Net sales	$11,460
Cost of sales	9,241
Gross profit	**$ 2,219**
Advertising expense	185
Distribution expense[a]	286
Salespeople's commissions[b]	522
Finished stock and shipping expense[c]	249
Administrative expense	804
Total expense	**$ 2,046**
Operating income	**$ 173**

[a]Included are some executive selling salaries, payroll taxes, travel and entertainment, rent, and miscellaneous expenses for three branch sales offices, depreciation on office equipment, conventions, sales meetings, and swatches.
[b]Included are commissions for 23 salespeople plus commissions and expenses for Ms. Antonelli.
[c]Included are warehouse labor and supervision, shipping supplies, and some freight.

major manufacturers produced young men's outerwear, but their lines usually contained only a few high-priced, high-quality items.

During the economically unsettled late 1960s and early 1970s, the men's and young men's quality outerwear business, like the rest of the apparel industry, experienced a major decline. Many department stores which over the years had traded up in price and quality began to carry some lower-priced merchandise. At the same time, a merchandising revolution brought styling into the essentially staple men's clothing market, so that it suddenly became much like the women's clothing market. Manufacturers of men's clothing had to alter their operations considerably. Retailers demanded more styles, smaller initial purchases in each style, and quick replenishment of styles which sold well. Manufacturers were forced to take greater inventory risks and make smaller, less efficient cutting and sewing runs.

While manufacturers had always made decisions regarding styles and fabrics on the basis of very rough sales estimates, the proliferation of styles greatly complicated this task. The development of their fall lines normally began the previous November. From current best-selling items, fashion advice of store buyers, and trends in European design, the merchandising managers[2] sketched potential styles. The designers then made patterns for sample coats, and the fabric buyers shopped for suitable fabrics. Because delivery time on fabric could range anywhere from 4 weeks to 5 months, about half of the fabric orders had to be placed in December for factories to begin production in mid-February. Therefore, by December, a tentative line and pricing structure and a rough sales estimate had to be completed. "We constantly walk a tightrope," commented one manager. "If we delay in order to be right about styles, we risk not getting fabric in time. If we order fabric early enough to ensure adequate delivery, we risk being wrong about styles."

121

On the average, in department stores with sales over $1 million, men's clothing accounted for 3.9 percent of total store net sales, and men's outerwear accounted for 1.2 percent.[3]

IVAN IV OPERATIONS, JANUARY 1974

The Ivan IV Division marketed outerwear for middle-aged consumers under the Ivan IV label and classically styled outerwear for young men under the Eaton Hall label. The average size of an opening order was 184

[2]In a typical apparel firm the merchandising functions included all or most nonsales marketing functions with special emphasis on product policy, design, and pricing.
[3]*Department Store and Specialty Store Merchandising and Operating Results of 1972*, Financial Executive Division, National Retail Merchants Association. Men's clothing included overcoats, raincoats, dual purpose coats, suits, formal wear, casual jackets and slacks, and uniforms. It did not include shirts, sweaters, hosiery, sleepwear, underwear, hats, accessories, sportswear, and footwear.

units; the average price per unit was $33; and the average gross margin was 30 percent. The 1973 fall line, which accounted for 70 percent of annual unit sales, contained 100 different items, and the 1974 spring line had 60. The spring line was extremely important in testing new fabrics and styles which, if successful, were incorporated into the next fall line. About 40 percent of the line remained the same from one fall to the next, and about 50 percent from one spring to the next. In 1973, for the first time, the division also offered a supplementary line for delivery just before the Christmas selling season. These garments were used to test ideas and to pick up true incremental sales, as opposed to simply decreasing the advance order for the next season. Merchandised only to larger accounts, they netted about 5,000 units.

Ivan IV sold regular branded merchandise to about 1,300 high-quality department stores and specialty shops. In 1973 the top 50 accounts generated sales of $4,933,500, while the top 100 produced $6,016,500. About 500 accounts carried both the spring and fall lines. Many accounts in the South bought only the fall line. About 850 purchased both the Ivan IV and the Eaton Hall lines. Mr. Wyzanski estimated that the division could profitably serve "at least 2,000 customers." Even though almost 700 new accounts had been opened since Mr. Allison became division president, distribution was still spotty, especially in big department stores in leading metropolitan areas. In the top 22 markets in the United States, Ivan IV had only 70 accounts out of a potential of at least 200. Mr. Wyzanski stated that Ivan IV's number one goal was to establish nation-wide distribution. He continued as follows:

> We've got to build volume quickly by opening new accounts. We want to be in *every* major marketplace, with 1,500 accounts throughout the United States. Right now, we're just too under-represented, particularly in the major stores. Last year we opened 25 majors and we expect to open 25 more during each of the next two seasons. If we succeed with that, and if we do well with the rest of our accounts, we can then start worrying about building volume within accounts and decreasing turnover.

Mr. Allison said that the division had experienced relatively little trouble opening accounts, but repeatedly had been unable to keep those accounts, usually because of inadequate delivery and/or follow-ups by salespeople. He commented as follows:

> To adequately service customers, our salespeople have to see that goods are delivered as promised, that buyers place reorders when inventories get low, and that special orders are filled accurately. Our salespeople are not doing that very well now. From one fall selling season to the next, we lose about 20% of our accounts.

Mr. Allison thought the division might institute a telephone-selling program under which all accounts would be called every 7 to 10 days to obtain fill-in orders and to handle any problems the customer was having with Ivan IV merchandise. (See Exhibit 3 for record of Ivan IV's advance orders and fill-in orders, Exhibit 4 for customer data, and Exhibit 5 for sales data.)

In addition to regular merchandise sold under Ivan IV and Eaton Hall labels, the division did a substantial volume of promotional, private-label, and off-price business. Promotional merchandise was regular branded top-quality garments offered to customers at a reduced profit margin. It consisted of both merchandise which was originally manufactured for promotional purposes and regular merchandise which was left over at the end of a selling season. In 1973 the division's promotional sales were $2,406,000. Private-label business consisted of garments manufactured for and carrying the label of a particular retailer. An Ivan IV executive negotiated style, fabric, price, and all other specifications with the customer. The division's ten private-label accounts generated $1,205,000 sales in 1973. The largest customer purchased about $300,000. Off-price business consisted of irregular garments without labels which were sold to discount retail outlets, many of which were budget or basement stores of large department stores. Off-price business generated by 20 customers accounted for $600,000 in 1973.

Exhibit 3 REGULAR-PRICE UNIT SALES, ADVANCE, AND FILL-IN

Year	Spring advance (sold preceding fall)	Fill-in or reorder	Percent fill-in	Fall advance (sold preceding spring)	Fill-in or reorder	Percent fill-in
Ivan IV label						
1974	42,124					
1973	31,981	20,155	63.0	86,461	39,013	45.2
1972	24,070	15,455	64.1	66,120	27,424	41.4
1971	33,895	22,468	65.7	83,463	33,783	40.4
Eaton Hall label						
1974	87,383					
1973	54,045	10,349	19.1	113,416	14,974	13.2
1972	43,794	6,608	15.1	121,422	14,573	12.0

Exhibit 4 ACCOUNT ANALYSIS BY CUSTOMER STATUS

	1973, spring	1974, spring	1972, fall	1973, fall
Accounts purchasing; Ivan IV label only				
Old customers	390	323	688	577
Reactivated	191	243	97	258
New	115	186	122	259
Total	**696**	**752**	**907**	**1094**
Accounts purchasing; Eaton Hall label only				
Total accounts[a]				965

[a]Further history for Eaton Hall was not available due to lack of information prior to company consolidation. About 850 accounts bought both Eaton Hall and Ivan IV products.

Exhibit 5 ADVANCE SALES OF 1973 FALL LINES AND GOALS FOR 1974 FALL LINES

Salesperson	Ivan IV label[a]		Target market accounts[b]		Regular accounts[b]		Eaton Hall label[a]		Target market accounts[b]		Regular accounts[b]		Territory
	Fall 1973 units	Fall 1974 unit goal	Accounts	Units	Accounts	Units	Fall 1973 units	Fall 1974 unit goal	Accounts	Units	Accounts	Units	
Anderson	5,573	7,524	7	2,408	66	3,165	2,498	12,490	2	242	47	2,256	Md., Washington, D.C., W. Va., Va.
Bledsow	2,314	2,777	4	902	34	1,420	1,769	2,476	2	790	22	979	Tex., Okla.
Blount	3,606	5,439	4	1,204	44	2,422	1,752	6,710	3	1,031	14	721	Fla., Ga., Ala.
Danforth[c]	4,681	5,617	—	—	80	4,681	5,122	7,426	—	—	55	5,122	Mich.
Donnell and Turner[d]	10,592	12,710	7	4,033	94	5,559	24,691	29,567	9	11,243	160	13,398	Ill., Wis. (part)
Everett	4,185	n.a.	2	60	87	4,185	2,876	—	2	523	58	2,876	Mass., R.I., Conn.
Greeb	1,252	1,753	3	511	29	741	574	2,296	1	181	7	393	Ark., La., Miss., Tenn. (part)
Grant	3,229	3,874	3	1,169	75	2,061	7,889	8,007	4	541	119	7,348	Iowa, Nebr., N. Dak., S. Dak.
Hamill[c]	980	5,880	—	—	29	980	618	1,082	—	—	12	618	Ohio
Jeffrey	2,504	5,008	4	893	35	1,581	2,190	6,570	3	823	21	1,367	Kans., Mo.
Jones and Maynard[d]	10,080	12,600	8	7,698	58	2,382	17,000	21,259	6	3,871	91	13,136	North N.J., N.Y. (part)
Lancaster[c]	1,404	3,408	5	510	26	894	1,380	2,778	2	740	24	649	Ind., Ky.
Long	4,920	7,380	3	2,319	42	2,601	4,463	8,926	3	3,335	24	1,128	N.Y. State (part)
Loomis and Friedheim[d]	2,765	11,060	3	2,187	26	2,837	1,530	6,120	3	1,070	4	1,762	Cal., Ariz., Nev.
Lucas	3,933	6,293	5	1,902	50	2,031	2,371	4,386	4	1,327	27	1,044	Wash., Oreg., Idaho (part)
Marshall	2,605	3,256	—	—	84	2,605	1,721	2,289	—	—	33	1,721	N.C., S.C., Tenn. (part)
O'Riely	3,421	5,132	1	739	43	2,682	5,512	8,268	1	1,671	54	3,841	Md., Del., N.J., Pa. (part)
Trevelian	2,900	4,930	2	723	44	2,177	13,116	15,739	3	2,728	98	10,388	Minn.
Vincent	1,978	3,186	3	554	50	1,425	2,038	3,357	2	260	54	1,825	Colo., Wyo., Utah, Mont., N. Mex.
Antonelli (regional manager)	5,969	n.a.	12	3,277	26	2,692	4,038		6	1,670	10	2,368	Mich., Ohio, Ind., Ky.
Unfilled territory	1,232	n.a.	—	—	62	1,232	4,447		—	—	60	4,447	Wis. (part), Mich. (part), Minn. (part)

[a] To project units on a full-year basis, multiply by 2.0 for Ivan IV, 1.6 for Eaton Hall.

[b] These were actual accounts and actual units sold, not goals.

[c] Salesmen under Angela Antonelli.

[d] These two salespersons worked together as a team.

Note: n.a. = not available.

The Annual Selling Cycle

The selling cycle for the fall line began early every February, when Ivan IV management showed the tentative fall line to some retail buyers. The process of selecting new models continued to mid-February when the selling season formally began with a national sales meeting in New York. The initial selling season for the fall line ran from February 15 through June 30, with peak booking between March 1 and May 15. Given the fixed amount of piece goods for certain delivery dates, salespeople were constantly pressured to get larger accounts booked before smaller accounts had been assigned all the fabric. As sales feedback was obtained, colors and entire models were dropped if performance was poor.

Ivan IV shipped original orders of fall merchandise from June 1 through September 15. In late August, it began receiving reorders. If an item were selling well, the buyer would want to replenish the stock immediately. If Ivan IV could not fill the reorder within a few weeks, the buyer often tried to purchase comparable merchandise from another manufacturer. To keep salespeople and buyers informed of available merchandise, Ivan IV sent them a monthly "in-stock booklet" detailing items which could be shipped immediately. The "fill-in season" ran until December 31. Management felt it was extremely important to get the salespeople into the stores as often as possible because most stores operated on a monthly open-to-buy system, and salespeople should be there when the buyer had extra money to commit. This was especially true if the salespeople had a few new items to show.

125

The spring line had a similar cycle. Salespeople were selling initial orders from September 15 through November 15, and factory production began October 1. Initial orders were delivered from December 15 through February 15, and fill-ins from February 15 through June 30. The overlap in seasons allowed salespeople to solicit fill-in orders at the same time they showed the next season's line.

During the two heavy initial selling periods, salespeople were constantly on the road showing the line, often working 6 or 7 days a week. Visits made at other times were mainly to solicit reorders, transmit product and industry data, and take inventory. They were relatively inactive in July and August and from January to mid-February, except to ensure that the factory shipped their orders.

Sales Organization

Shortly after becoming Ivan IV's vice president of sales in January 1973, Mr. Wyzanski began combining the Ivan IV and Eaton Hall sales forces into a single force. He first reduced the number of salespeople from 29 to 24, all of whom reported directly to him. He also reorganized sales territories, altering the existing geographic areas according to potential volume and a salesperson's ability to cover a given area.

Mr. Wyzanski said that by mid-1973, he was forced to spend so much time on contacts with major customers, advertising programs, and marketing plans that he was unable to supervise his salespeople adequately. He decided, therefore, to create four regional manager positions. However, adequate managerial personnel were not available to fill these positions. Mr. Wyzanski himself served as regional manager for the Southern and Western states and Chicago. Quentin Timmeny, vice president of merchandising and administration, and Harold Chin, merchandising manager, reluctantly agreed to be regional managers for the New England and California regions and the Baltimore-Washington and North Central regions, respectively. As they had anticipated, prior commitments prevented their devoting the necessary time to supervision. "The system collapsed in two weeks," Mr. Wyzanski said. "For the spring of 1974, it just isn't feasible to have top executives acting as regional managers."

By January 1974, Mr. Wyzanski still had not found full-time regional managers. Mr. Timmeny and Mr. Chin were once again acting as part-time regional managers. "This time Quentin and Harold weren't coerced as they were before," said Mr. Wyzanski. "Moreover, Barry Allison and I clearly spelled out that sales force supervision is one of their most important responsibilities. I'm going to get on their tails immediately if they start to fall down." Mr. Chin commented as follows on his position as regional manager:

> I'll do my best because there's no one else available, but there are major barriers to success. In the first place, the job requires a full-time person, and I've already got a full-time job shopping the piece goods market and merchandising the lines. Furthermore, the salespeople are accustomed to getting directions regarding sales from the vice president of sales, and they just are not as effective coming from me.

The only region that was successful under the regional manager structure was the Ohio and Michigan area which was supervised by Ms. Angela Antonelli, one of Ivan IV's best salespeople. Ms. Antonelli supervised two other salespeople and had full responsibility for most of the major accounts in the region. Her region's fall advance season sales increased from $740,000 in 1972 to $2,960,000 in 1973. One salesperson who had been assigned to cover small accounts opened 100 new ones. For the 1974 spring season, Ms. Antonelli's region was expanded to include Indiana and Kentucky, and she was assigned an additional salesperson. Ms. Antonelli received a salary, expenses, and a bonus based on total regional volume. Mr. Chin, Mr. Timmeny, and Mr. Wyzanski did not receive additional compensation for serving as regional managers. Like other Ivan IV executives, they were paid a base salary, expenses, and a bonus based on division profitability.

Ivan IV had 24 salespersons (including Ms. Antonelli), each of whom was responsible for selling and servicing about 55 established accounts and for opening about 30 more. A salesperson's call frequency varied according to the size, importance, service requirements, and location of the account. While some of the largest accounts required two to four visits each selling season before a decision was made plus six to eight follow-up visits, on the average, a salesperson visited most established customers only about four times a year. In addition, salespeople were expected to maintain "regular" telephone contact with buyers. In larger department stores, there were separate buyers for the men's and young men's departments. Both buyers usually reported to the same merchandise manager[4] whom they often brought in to make decisions on major purchases. It was very difficult, and often not advisable, for a salesperson initially to contact the merchandise manager. Doing so meant "going over the buyer's head" and usually alienating him.

Salespeople received a weekly delivery schedule listing models, units, and delivery dates for each of their accounts. They were expected to average three visits per week to potential customers. The company benchmark was that, during selling seasons, a salesperson should make 12 to 15 showings per week. To show both complete lines required $3\frac{1}{2}$ to 4 hours.

Except for a 3-day sales meeting which began each selling season, a salesperson's training was entirely on the job. Either Mr. Wyzanski or a "regional manager" would travel with the salesperson for a week at a time, analyze the strengths and weaknesses of each call, and discuss possible actions for the next visit to that customer. When salespersons were out alone, they transmitted oral reports on each day's activities to their regional managers every 2 or 3 days.

Salespeople were paid a straight 4.3 percent commission on net sales. The average gross income was about $18,000. Three were in the $40,000 range, and one made about $60,000. (The industry average for a company the size of Ivan IV was $23,000.) The division offered health and disability insurance and a retirement plan, but the salespeople (except for Ms. Antonelli) themselves paid all business expenses. Mr. Wyzanski stated that he had not yet had time to organize special incentive programs but that he hoped to do so in the future. He thought a contest for opening new accounts would be especially useful.

Salespeople ranged in age from 28 to 60. About 75 percent were college graduates. Before joining Ivan IV, most had worked for other apparel companies or for retail stores. It was common practice for salespeople, once they sensed their companies going downhill, to

[4]In a typical large department store, merchandise managers were responsible for merchandising policies and decisions and for supervising several buyers. They reported to a general merchandise manager, the top-level executive in charge of all merchandising policies and decisions. In smaller department stores, the merchandise-manager link was usually eliminated, and buyers reported directly to a top executive.

switch to another manufacturer and take their accounts with them. This had apparently taken place with both sales forces before 1970. Of the 24 salespeople, 14 had joined the division since 1971. Mr. Wyzanski thought that the turnover problem was over now, because they were getting larger commissions. Mr. Wyzanski recruited and hired all salespeople.

TARGET MARKET PROGRAM

In mid-1973, in an attempt to increase Ivan IV's representation in major markets, Mr. Wyzanski instituted a special target market program. He first selected specific stores in 32 cities on the basis of estimated potential volume. (Target stores which were already Ivan IV customers each purchased between $75,000 and $100,000 annually.) He then designated each city as either a primary or secondary market and assigned it to one of seven top executives: Barbara Veronna, Waverley vice president who oversaw the operations of several Waverley divisions, including Ivan IV; Milton Friedman, executive vice president of Ivan IV, formerly in charge of Eaton Hall; Mr. Timmeny; Mr. Chin; Paul Shapp, vice president of marketing and advertising; Mr. Allison; and Mr. Wyzanski. The executives were responsible for working with regular salespeople in selling and servicing target stores. Assignments were made primarily on the basis of the personal contacts that the different executives had. Mr. Wyzanski explained his rationale for using executives in selling as follows:

128

> First, our executives are some of our best sales talent, and it is useful training for our newer people to observe a top-flight salesperson in action. Second, the selling situation is an excellent way to keep executives in touch with what is happening in the marketplace. A third factor is that all the accounts we are trying to open are major ones that often require on-the-spot decisions about special advertising money and promotional goods. My people aren't authorized to make these decisions, but an executive can do so immediately. Finally, the most important reason for using executives is that it allows us to open lines of communication within the store. In addition to our regular salesperson-buyer contacts, we can establish an executive-president or an executive-general merchandise manager link. It is extremely difficult for a salesperson to establish contact with these top level retail people. Executive selling is not a general trend in the industry, so if a store executive knows he can contact one of our executives whenever he has problems, it will help us establish an atmosphere that shows we care.

During the fall of 1973, in addition to offering the target accounts no-match[5] advertising funds equal to $7\frac{1}{2}$ percent of net shipped volume,

[5]Under no-match advertising plans, retailers were not required to put any of their own money into advertising the manufacturer's line. Ivan IV's basic plan to stores other than target stores was $2\frac{1}{2}$ percent of net sales which then had to be matched by the retailer.

Ivan IV made a special effort to channel promotional goods to them and to ensure early delivery. Mr. Wyzanski considered the program "extremely successful"; 25 new accounts had been opened, and his goal for 1974 was 25 more during each selling season. (See Exhibit 6 for sales data on specific stores.)

Mr. Chin said he enjoyed his target market activities very much and thought the program was useful in establishing a foundation on which good selling could be done. Mr. Allison stated that executive selling improved Ivan IV's competitive position, but that he had trouble trying to see so many customers because of his other responsibilities. Ivan IV's major competitors used regional managers to cover their major accounts.

For the 1974 spring selling season, Mr. Wyzanski was considering making some changes in the program. His most serious problem was that Mr. Shapp, Ms. Veronna, and Mr. Friedman had recently been transferred to other Waverley divisions, and he had failed to get other executives to assume their target market responsibilities. Therefore, he had only four executives to handle the program.

One problem precipitated by the departure of the three executives was that careful records on each account had not always been kept. Whoever took over would have to depend on the salesperson who had been visiting the account for information regarding it. Mr. Wyzanski felt that a central master file should be set up at company headquarters to handle all target market account information. Copies of correspondence and activity reports would be kept in the file. In addition to keeping headquarters executives up to date on the target accounts, the file would give them data to analyze and to see where they had succeeded or failed and perhaps why.

A second decision Mr. Wyzanski had to make was whether to continue with the present target market stores or work with fewer stores. He also had to determine which executives would handle which target accounts. He thought he might cut back the number of stores and assign the executives supervisory responsibility for salespeople within their target market areas.

A third issue which had come up frequently was how and by whom the first contact should be made. Some argued that the salesperson should feel out the situation, set up the initial appointment, and perhaps even show the line before the executive got involved, in order not to waste the valuable and limited executive time. Others felt, however, that Ivan IV would be much more likely to get a receptive audience if an executive made the first contact. Mr. Wyzanski also wondered if, once the line was shown, the executive should take over completely or if he should continue to work with the regular salesperson. He estimated that, in most cases now, an executive visited a target market account with a salesperson three or four times a year and the salesperson visited the account alone about six to eight more times.

Exhibit 6 TARGET MARKET SUMMARY: IVAN IV'S SALES (in units)

Executives, cities, and accounts	1973[b] account's total sales (000 omitted)	1973 spring line (sold in fall 1972)	1973 fall line (sold in spring 1973)	1974 spring line (sold in fall 1973)
Paul Shapp				
New York				
Bloomingdale's	$223,000	—	—	—
Macy's	456,000	—	—	—
Gimbel's	215,000	—	—	—
Abraham & Straus	406,000	90	—	—
Wallach's	n.a.	4,844	4,401	6,374
B. Altman	145,000	—	—	—
Brownings	n.a.	—	—	—
Field Bros.	n.a.	602	150	529
Rogers Peet	n.a.	200	—	201
F. R. Tripler	n.a.	245	415	214
Barney's	30,000	305	668	1
Lord & Taylor	125,000	—	—	—
Total		6,286	5,634	7,319
Philadelphia[a]				
Wanamakers	$181,500	—	—	—
Strawbridge's	169,200	—	—	—
Gimbel's	129,400	—	—	—
Jacob Reed	n.a.	791	2,410	857
Total		791	2,410	857
Boston[a]				
Kennedy's	n.a.	—	—	
Filene's	$155,000	120	95	—
Jordan Marsh	272,500	—	—	—
Total		120	95	—
Hartford				
G. Fox	$102,000	—	15	—
Sage-Allen	28,100	—	—	—
Total		—	15	—
Providence				
The Outlet	$82,400	206	356	—
Shepard	n.a.	50	—	—
Total		256	356	—
Shapp total		**7,453**	**8,510**	**8,176**
Harold Chin				
Syracuse				
Wells & Coverly	n.a.	71	525	749
Dey Bros.	n.a.	—	—	—
Total		71	525	749
Rochester				
Sibley Lindsey	$88,000	—	—	821
McCurdy	37,000	93	—	315
National Clothing	n.a.	890	1,727	1,631
Total		983	1,726	2,767
Charleston				
Frankenberger's	n.a.	212	559	184
Total		212	559	184

Exhibit 6 *(Continued)*

Executives, cities, and accounts	1973[b] account's total sales (000 omitted)	1973 spring line (sold in fall 1972)	1973 fall line (sold in spring 1973)	1974 spring line (sold in fall 1973)
Buffalo				
Wm. Hengerer	n.a.	104	—	570
Kleinhan's	n.a.	1,656	3,510	2,329
Adam Meldrun & And.	$55,500	—	—	—
Total		1,760	3,510	2,899
Louisville				
Levy Bros.	$7,000	—	46	—
Rodes-Rapier	n.a.	—	504	—
Total		—	550	—
Indianapolis[a]				
L. S. Ayres	$213,110	—	441	274
W. H. Block	69,000	—	—	—
Strauss & Company	n.a.	—	98	100
Total		—	539	374
Richmond				
Miller & Rhoads	$73,575	—	—	—
Thalhimer Bros.	74,024	—	—	—
Total		—	—	—
Baltimore				
Hecht Company	$63,700	—	—	—
Stewarts	n.a.	—	—	624
Hamburgers	n.a.	899	977	19
Hutzler's	77,000	47	25	98
Total		946	1,002	741
Washington[a]				
Hecht Company	$146,000	—	—	—
Raleigh's	n.a.	—	604	183
Kann Sons	22,000	—	—	—
Garfinckel's	45,000	55	260	754
Landsburgh's	28,000	—	—	—
Woodward & Lothrop	169,000		103	—
Total		55	967	937
New York City				
Saks	$120,000	500	899	1,137
Browning	n.a.	563	1,194	922
Brooks	n.a.	1,000	—	2,000
Total		2,063	2,183	4,059
Philadelphia				
Mooreville	n.a.	—	—	—
Total		—	—	—
Chin total		**5,878**	**11,562**	**12,710**
Quentin Timmeny				
Cincinnati[a]				
John Shillitos	$133,000	—	—	387
H & S Pogue	51,450	317	468	277
Mabley & Carew	27,250	166	161	15
Burkhart's	n.a.	—	—	—
Dunlaps	n.a.	16	67	—
Total		499	696	679

131

Exhibit 6 TARGET MARKET SUMMARY: IVAN IV'S SALES (in units) *(Continued)*

Executives, cities, and accounts	1973[b] account's total sales (000 omitted)	1973 spring line (sold in fall 1972)	1973 fall line (sold in spring 1973)	1974 spring line (sold in fall 1973)
Pittsburgh				
Joseph Horne	$129,700	114	—	124
Kaufmann's	142,245	125	—	—
Gimbel Bros.	125,000	—	—	—
Hughes & Hatcher	n.a.	—	—	—
Total		239	—	124
Timmeny total		**738**	**696**	**803**
Barbara Veronna				
Chicago				
Carson, Pirie, & Scott	$164,900	1,602	4,530	3,743
Marshall Field	374,500	272	3,231	2,531
Lytton's	n.a.	1,084	200	293
Karoll's	n.a.	—		
Baskin's	n.a.	3,832	6,116	5,319
Capper & Capper	n.a.	405	305	647
Total		7,195	14,382	12,533
Omaha				
Brandeis	$75,100	171	250	200
Nebraska Clothing	n.a.	21	677	187
Kilpatrick's	n.a.	—	—	—
Total		192	927	387
Los Angeles[a]				
Desmonds	n.a.	—	—	—
Broadway	$306,000	—	—	—
May Company	278,800	—	—	—
J. W. Robinson	135,000	—	—	—
Harris & Frank	n.a.	—	—	—
Foreman & Clark	n.a.	—	—	—
Bullock's	208,000	—	—	—
Silverwood's	n.a.	2,327	836	1,791
Total		2,327	836	1,791
San Francisco[a]				
Rhodes Liberty	n.a.	—	—	—
Smith's	n.a.	—	—	—
Grodin's	n.a.	—	—	—
Macy's	$204,000	—	—	—
Bullock's	208,000	—	—	—
Roos & Atkins	52,000	—	—	—
Emporium	241,500	—	—	—
Hastings	n.a.	873	1,700	773
Total		873	1,700	773
Tampa[a]				
Maas Bros.	$140,000	—	61	—
Wolf Bros.	n.a.	—	90	1
Total		—	151	1
Veronna total		**10,587**	**17,996**	**15,485**

Exhibit 6 *(Continued)*

Executives, cities, and accounts	1973[b] account's total sales (000 omitted)	1973 spring line (sold in fall 1972)	1973 fall line (sold in spring 1973)	1974 spring line (sold in fall 1973)
Milton Friedman				
Cleveland				
May Company	$154,800	215	321	259
Higbee Company	149,472	116	447	1,410
Halle Bros.	64,000	60	—	604
Baker Company	n.a.	436	1,196	1,010
Total		827	1,964	3,283
Dayton[a]				
Lazarus	n.a.	—	—	—
Rike's	$110,900	—	—	—
Metropolitan	n.a.	—	—	—
Dunhill's	n.a.	—	—	—
Total		—	—	—
Milwaukee[a]				
Boston Store	$ 80,000	—	—	—
Gimbels-Schusters	149,800	—	685	869
T. A. Chapman	10,000	—	—	—
Schmitt-Orlow	n.a.	81	225	—
Total		81	910	860
Minneapolis				
Dayton's	$205,216	920	1,304	398
Donaldson's	56,680	—	967	516
Powers	27,000	—	314	—
Justers	n.a.	85	—	—
Young-Quinnlan	n.a.	—	—	—
Liemandt's	n.a.	470	1,180	603
Total		1,475	3,765	1,517
New York				
Bonds	n.a.	—	3,000	—
Total		—	3,000	—
Des Moines				
Younker Bros.	$90,766	209	—	—
Frankels	n.a.	36	150	130
Kucharo's	n.a.	210	622	475
Total		455	772	605
Seattle[a]				
Bon Marche	$119,100	66	—	—
Nordstrom	88,300	—	—	326
Frederick T. Nelson	52,500	—	—	171
Klopfenstein's	n.a.	740	1,838	650
Littler's	n.a.	125	188	21
Total		931	2,026	1,168
Spokane[a]				
Bon Marche	n.a.	—	—	—
Crescent	n.a.	—	—	—
Total		—	—	—
Portland				
Meier & Frank	$87,200	—	—	—
Lipman Wolf Co.	63,666	—	214	—
Rosenblatt's	n.a.	270	804	524
Total		270	1,018	524

Exhibit 6 TARGET MARKET SUMMARY: IVAN IV'S SALES (in units) *(Continued)*

Executives, cities, and accounts	1973[b] account's total sales (000 omitted)	1973 spring line (sold in fall 1972)	1973 fall line (sold in spring 1973)	1974 spring line (sold in fall 1973)
Columbus[a]				
The Union	n.a.	37	75	118
F & R Lazarus	$185,000	—	71	—
Walkers	n.a.	911	1,584	1,175
Denver				
K & G Stores	n.a.	—	—	—
Total		—	—	—
Friedman total		**4,987**	**15,185**	**9,250**
Barry Allison				
Atlanta				
Rich's	$260,670	—	328	—
Muse's	n.a.	—	—	42
Hirsch's	n.a.	62	—	—
Davison's	58,800	—	—	30
Parkes-Chambers	n.a.	54	120	61
Zachry's	n.a.	520	1,563	304
Total		636	2,011	437
Detroit[a]				
J. L. Hudson Co.	$421,200	731	—	3,509
Hughes & Hatcher	57,000	335	173	1
Capper & Capper	n.a.	165	242	378
Total		1,231	415	3,888
Miami[a]				
Burdine's	$141,700	—	—	—
Jordan Marsh	93,740	—	—	—
Wallachs	n.a.	387	147	558
Total		387	147	558
Allison total		**2,254**	**2,573**	**4,883**
Ralph Wyzanski				
St. Louis[a]				
Stix Baer & Fuller	$107,900	—	—	—
Famous-Barr	203,800	—	—	—
Boyd's	n.a.	—	—	—
Wolff's Clothiers	n.a.	310	447	1,018
Total		310	447	1,018
Kansas City				
Macy's	$60,000	—	400	—
Rothschild's	n.a.	250	356	—
Jones Stores	60,000	—	52	45
Wolff Bros.	n.a.	—	447	—
Henry's	n.a.	421	870	963
Total		671	2,125	1,008
Denver[a]				
Fashion Bar	$35,000	—	—	—
Cottrell's	n.a.	28	263	133
Denver Dry Goods	64,000	—	—	1,472
Gano-Downs	n.a.	104	—	100
May D & F	65,000	39	—	—
Total		171	263	1,705

Exhibit 6 *(Continued)*

Executives, cities, and accounts	1973[b] account's total sales (000 omitted)	1973 spring line (sold in fall 1972)	1973 fall line (sold in spring 1973)	1974 spring line (sold in fall 1973)
Houston[a]				
Foley's	$142,000	—	214	—
Leopold Price & Rolle	n.a.	88	460	460
Battlesteins	n.a.	—	—	—
Sakowitz	25,000	—	—	35
Total		88	674	495
New Orleans[a]				
Rubenstein Bros.	n.a.	—	45	—
D. H. Holmes	$69,400	—	—	—
Maison Blanche	63,770	—	—	—
Godchaux's	12,000	—	—	—
Porter-Stevens	n.a.	15	338	300
Total		15	383	300
Memphis				
J. Goldsmith & Sons	$51,800	—	—	—
Total		—	—	—
Nashville				
Cain Sloan	$25,000	—	250	1
Total		—	250	1
Salt Lake City				
Auerbach's	$15,000	—	—	—
Z.C.M.I.	44,000	1	—	—
Arthur Frank Clo.	n.a.	168	340	289
Total		169	340	289
Dallas[a]				
Sanger-Harris	$88,200	72	—	—
Neiman-Marcus	59,000	—	—	330
Titshe-Goettinger	48,500	—	—	—
J. K. Wilson	n.a.	370	773	363
Total		442	773	693
Wyzanski total		**1,866**	**5,255**	**5,509**
Total Target Market		**33,763**	**61,777**	**56,816**

[a]Primary target cities.

[b]These data were compiled by the casewriter from the following sources: Willard H. Campbell, "1972 Sales of 100 Top Department Stores," *Stores*, August 13, 1973, pp. 13–16; "Summary of Available Sales Figures by City/Market Area of Leading Department Stores, 1972," Fairchild Publications, Inc., Market Research Department, November 1973.

Note: n.a. means "not available."

The fourth issue was whether executives should be compensated for their role in the selling process and, if so, how. In the past, they had not received additional compensation for their target market activities.

Finally, Mr. Wyzanski wanted to plan in advance the sale of promotional goods to target market stores and to book those units at the same time that they booked regular business. Under the plan he had in mind, if an account opened with 300 regular-priced units, Ivan IV would allow it to purchase up to 100 units at 20 percent off; stores opening with 500 regular-priced units could purchase up to 250 units at 20 percent off; and stores opening with 750 regular-priced units could purchase up to 750 units at 20 percent off. He recognized that the difficulty of this plan was that it was very hard to know at the beginning of a season exactly how much promotional merchandise would be available. He thought, however, that past experience could provide adequate guidelines.

THIRTEEN   Sales Force Size

Deployment is closely related to decisions about sales coverage, call frequency, and the number of salespeople to be hired. All of these involve the deployment of sales expense dollars and selling time against accounts and prospects.

This note will look specifically at the ways in which sales force size can be determined. It will begin with simple approaches and move toward more complex ones. The techniques discussed can be used in starting a new sales force, evaluating the size of an existing one, or restructuring one or more related existing sales forces.

136

"QUICK-AND-DIRTY" APPROACHES

There are three standard, quick approaches to estimating the size of a sales force. Most industries, companies, or both have guidelines concerning three aspects of sales force size: accounts per salesperson, dollar sales per salesperson, and percentage of sales dollars to be spent on the sales force. These are easy to apply.

If sales managers have a good idea of the sales they hope to achieve and/or the number of active accounts[1] they expect their sales force to work with, they can simply divide the sales and/or number of accounts by the guidelines to develop steady-state sales forces. Clearly, the sales force is unlikely to start out that big. The subject of implementing decisions to change the size of the sales force is covered below in a separate section.

An even more common approach is to multiply expected sales by a desired sales expense ratio[2] to obtain a total sales budget. Sales managers

[1]The note "Sales Forecasting for the Sales Manager" provides sources and methods for forecasting the number of accounts and sales.

[2]The sales expense ratio is the percentage of dollar sales accounted for by direct and indirect selling costs.

then subtract an amount for fixed sales costs (for example, their own salary, order processing department, etc.) and divide the remainder by the cost (compensation or if expenses are company paid, compensation plus expenses)per salesperson to find the number of salespeople.

These approaches are useful in two ways: They are conceptually simple, requiring little thinking. Second, they are quick. On the other hand, they are likely to be somewhat inaccurate and certainly imprecise.

Their accuracy is improved if more than one of the three approaches is used, if other related ratios seem to make sense (for example, if sales per account look reasonable), and if the guidelines used are accurate. Usually a range (for example, industry salespeople who sell $600,000 to $800,000 on average) is more useful than a single figure guideline. The list which accompanies the note "Sales Costs and Budgets" provides some sources of guidelines. Others can be gained from industry-specific sources and from the cases in the course.

Given the limitations of these methods, it is useful to pursue some more sophisticated methods related to the simple ones above.

WORKLOAD MEASUREMENT

One of the most popular methods of determining the size of a sales force is based on workload measurement. The typical process would proceed as follows:

1 Determine the number of accounts which should be called upon.

2 Segment the accounts on the basis of the amount of service they need. This usually includes separation of prospects from customers and segmentation by size.

3 Assign a call frequency to each category of account. For example, large customers might be called upon twelve times per year, medium-sized prospects twice per year, and so on.

4 Multiply the number of accounts by the number of calls per account and sum for all accounts categories, coming up with the number of calls which must be made per year.

5 Estimate the number of calls which can be made per salesperson. A relatively sophisticated system would consider geographic differences and differences in call length per account among different types of accounts.

6 Divide the calls needed by the calls per salesperson to determine the number of salespeople needed.

It should be noted that this approach is actually an extension of the method based on accounts per salesperson. The logic is about the same. This more sophisticated method corrects for differences among accounts and prospects in desired call frequency.

The determination of the calls which are needed by each category of account, and the calls which can be made by a salesperson, can be based on estimates, analysis of past data (for example, call reports), or time studies. The time study could be detailed enough to account for each function which is to be performed. Clearly the large sales force can justify much more expense for increasing precision, because the dollar impact of good data will be much higher.

It is important to understand the philosophy of each of these approaches. This one is based on the belief that a sales force of a given size has a certain call capacity and that the call capacity should equal the call demand. The approach focuses upon work input, not sales output.

POTENTIAL AND PENETRATION

Another standard approach involves the allocation of potential[3] to each salesperson. In its simplest form, the sales manager estimates the market potential. Then, he has several alternatives. The easiest is to estimate penetration (share of market), multiply to obtain a sales estimate, and then divide by the sales per salesperson guidelines. Another approach is to assume that each person should have a certain amount of potential. Then, the total potential is divided by the potential per salesperson.

Walter Semlow[4] has suggested a more sophisticated method in which the generally accepted relationship that penetration goes down as potential goes up is used. His method proposes the addition of salespeople until their cost is greater than the profits they generate (marginal costs exceed marginal profit). By and large, each additional salesperson costs about the same, but the sales amount they generate is lower, because the size of the potential in their territory decreases faster than their penetration increases. This general method has been applied with good results in a variety of situations.

Researchers at Stanford University[5] have shown that the relationship between potential and penetration is not so much because sales increase in territories with smaller potential as because potential (the denominator in penetration) decreases. They also found that sales decreased as workload increased.

[3]The note "Sales Forecasting for the Sales Manager" provides ways of estimating potential.

[4]Walter J. Semlow, "How Many Salesmen Do You Need," *Harvard Business Review*, May-June 1959.

[5]Henry C. Lucas, Jr., Charles B. Weinberg, and Kenneth W. Clowes, "Sales Reponse as a Function of Territory Potential and Sales Representative Workload," *Journal of Marketing Research*, August 1975.

Leonard Lodish[6] has developed an interactive computer-based approach which can be used for decisions concerning both deployment and sales force size. It depends upon estimates of potential on an account-by-account basis and on the development of estimates of the relationship between sales calls and sales. This approach is especially useful when the sales force is an expensive one and the number of accounts relatively small.

The philosophy underlying these approaches is that the determination of the sales force size depends upon the allocation of potential. In that sense, the approach is more oriented toward sales output than the workload approach.

With both approaches, however, it is important to remember that the purpose in adding salespeople is to generate sales. The salesperson is the cause, and the sale the effect. Any relatively mechanistic approach tends to hide that relationship and focus on estimated or expected sales as the cause for future salespeople.

Assessing Risk

If the decision to be made on the size of the sales force involves the addition of salespeople, especially a small number relative to the size of the existing sales force, a useful technique is break-even analysis. Here, the question is how much sales do the new salespersons have to generate to offset the added cost they incur. The method is that of a standard break-even analysis:

1 Marginal profit is defined as minimum break-even sales (an unknown) times profit contribution (sales revenue minus variable cost).

2 Marginal cost is the out-of-pocket cost of the salesperson.

3 Marginal profit and marginal cost are equated at break-even.

4 The equation is solved.

In practice this simplifies to the following relationship:

$$\text{Break-even sales} = \frac{\text{out-of-pocket expense}}{\text{profit contribution percent}}$$

This enables the sales manager to assess the chances of making the necessary sales. Most of the time, the break-even sales are much lower than the average sales per salesperson.

In situations where training costs are high and sales low during the initial selling period, the addition of a salesperson can be thought of as an

[6]Leonard M. Lodish, "Call Plan: An Interactive Sales Call Planning System," *Management Science*, November 1971, pp. P25–P54.

investment and standard amortization, pay back, discounted cash flow, and return on investment calculations performed.

Individual Territories

Much of the material outlined above can be applied to the design of individual territories. The classic discussion in setting up territories has been on the choice between alignment based on potential, workload, and sales.

Implementing Changes

It is often easier to develop sales management policies than to implement them. Evolutionary changes are much better than revolutionary or major changes. For example, if because of growth which is expected to continue, it is decided that a sales force of 50 people should be doubled in size, it is usually wiser to do that piecemeal rather than all at once.

The evolutionary approach creates less financial risk, enables the sales force to absorb the change gradually rather than in one monumental shock, and enables the sales managers to develop systems and approaches appropriate to the larger sales force. It also provides time to test the assumption that additional salespeople are needed.

140

On the other hand, if changing the size of the sales force requires the reorganization of an existing sales force (for example, reorganizing into several product-related sales forces), it is usually preferable to make one big change. Otherwise, rumors and hints of change will cause a long period of sales force unrest which will almost undoubtedly hurt performance.

Support Burden

When the size of the sales force is changed, the support organization (line management and staff support) usually needs to be altered. As a sales force increases in size, its "fixed" costs usually go up too.

In planning sales force size changes, it is wise to consider carefully these changes, because their impact upon costs and performance can be large.

BIBLIOGRAPHY

Lambert, Zarrel V.: *Setting the Size for the Sales Force*, Center for Research of the College of Business Administration, University Park: Pennsylvania State University, 1968.

Semlow, Walter J.: "How Many Salesmen Do You Need," *Harvard Business Review*, May-June 1959, pp. 126–132.

FOURTEEN Sales Forecasting for the Sales Manager

INTRODUCTION

Sales forecasting is a complex subject, worthy of a complete book. It is included here for completeness and because certain aspects of sales forecasting are highly relevant to the sales manager. Thus, our interest in sales forecasting will be limited in scope. We will not address sales forecasting techniques and approaches which are related to market research or market planning. By and large, the focus will be on taking company sales forecasts and dividing them among salespeople and territories.

Sales forecasts can be divided into four categories, based on the intended user and the part of the company responsible for developing the data. These lead to the following framework:

141

		User	
		Sales force	Other functions
Developer	Sales force		
	Other functions		

The other functions which develop data usually include marketing management, market research, and corporate planning. The other functions which use sales forecasts include marketing management, inventory control, production scheduling, capacity planning, and finance and control.

One further dimension should be added to this framework—time. Sales forecasts can be short term (for example, several months) or long term (for example, several years), or both.

Before turning to those parts of sales forecasting of most interest in sales management, it is useful to consider briefly the other types of sales forecasting. Long-range sales forecasts are usually developed by marketing management or corporate planning for strategic activities such as capacity planning (for example, planning for new manufacturing facilities), development of capital structure (for example, long-term financing), and diversification planning.

Short- and medium-term forecasts are used for more operational purposes such as production scheduling, inventory planning, cash forecasting, etc.

There are a variety of sales management uses of sales forecasts. Long-term forecasts are useful in determining the most appropriate size of the sales force and its supporting functions such as training, management, and sales analysis. Medium-term forecasts are useful for recruiting and deployment. Short-term forecasts are useful for evaluation of sales effort by salesperson and district.

Before we can look more deeply into these uses of sales forecasting and the development of sales forecasts, it is useful to differentiate among the terms used in discussing sales forecasting as it relates to sales management.

STANDARD NOMENCLATURE

There are many terms used in sales forecasting. Although the definitions presented below are not universal, they are generally accepted.

Market potential The expected sales for an industry to a group of customers for a stated time period. When existing products are discussed, the term "market potential" is fairly straightforward. When a new product is discussed, the term usually means that amount of the product which the market would be able to absorb. In managing the sales force, concern is usually with expected total industry sales, a more limited definition than the one above associated with new products. Because the measurement of market potential is very important in several phases of sales management, we will consider it separately below.

Sales forecast The dollar or unit sales volume which a particular company *expects* to achieve in a specific market, territory, and/or product. The emphasis here is on realistic expectation.

Sales goal The dollar or unit sales volume which a particular company *hopes* to achieve in a specific market, territory, and/or product if all goes well. Sales goals are usually viewed as something high enough to strive for, but low enough to provide some reasonable chance of success. The sales goal is always at least as high as the sales forecast.

Sales budget The same as sales forecast.

Sales quota A variety of different things, all of which relate to an individual salesperson or territory. Usually the quota is an expected figure, but sometimes it is a "hoped for" figure. In the former case, sales quotas sum to the sales forecast, in the latter case to the sales goal. Quotas may be used for motivation, evaluation, compensation, and/or planning. In some cases, usually where quotas are used for compensation, they have little to do with either the forecast or the goal. In those situations the quota is part of the compensation system *not* the forecasting system. Many companies use the term "quota" very loosely and therefore develop major communication problems. Most often a sales quota is the sales volume expected of an individual salesperson.

Sales standards and sales bogies   Usually, the same as sales quotas, although particular companies may use these terms in a specific way. Some sales managers, for example, do not like to use the term "quota" because it seems too dictatorial. Some companies have a minimum sales quota (sell less and your job is in jeopardy), a sales forecast (the expected sales volume), and a sales standard (obtain this and get an extra bonus).

It is critical for marketing management, sales management, and the sales force to understand the meaning of the terms used, the method of arriving at the specific numbers, and the way in which the numbers are used.

Two other types of nomenclature should be clarified. First, in some situations "unit volume" is used and in others "dollar volume" is used. Each has its advantages. If the product line is heterogeneous or customized, it is almost impossible to develop unit sales forecasts. If the product line is narrow, homogeneous, and standardized, unit volume forecasts eliminate the need to do price forecasting and eliminate the effect of price changes. This last point was especially important during the double-digit inflation of 1973–1975. Many salespeople were able to achieve sizeable dollar sales increases—10 to 20 percent—without increasing unit sales volume. This confused evaluation.

Second, the terms "potential," "goals," "quotas," and "forecasts" can be used for any particular product category, geographic area, customer category, and time period. Thus, one may talk about the market potential for hammers sold in department stores in Washington, D.C., during March 1975, as well as the sales forecast for a particular tool company for the total United States during 1975.

DETERMINING MARKET POTENTIAL

Market potential has several important uses in sales management, including (1) determination of the appropriate sales force size; (2) deployment of the sales force, especially by geography but also by product and market; (3) development of the appropriate sales organization structure; (4) evaluation of the performance of the total sales force, regions, districts, and individual salespeople; (5) evaluation of sales programs directed toward particular markets or products, or both.

As noted above, market potential can be developed by product, product category, market, etc.

Before considering the ways of developing market potential estimates, it is useful to differentiate between total market potential and "realizable" market potential. In some situations, it is useful to differentiate between the total industry demand for a product (market potential) and a lesser figure which adjusts the market potential figure by removing clearly unattainable sales. A company may, for example, decide that, because of multisourcing by buyers,[1] it is impossible for it to obtain more than 60 percent of the market. The realizable potential then becomes 60 percent of the total market potential. Note that the realizable percentage share of the market has no relationship to the company's current market share or production capacity. The concept of realizable instead of total share is a flexible one which can be used to increase realism in deployment and evaluation.

Market potential data are usually developed in a two-step process: (1) the total market potential is determined, usually on a national, regional, or state basis, (2) the potential is apportioned among sales territories. In general, the first part of the process is a marketing research function. There are instances when this is not true. Sales management and the sales force may, for example, be asked to ascertain and/or estimate the purchases of an existing product by existing customers. A chemical company may find it useful to ask its sales force to estimate on an account-by-account basis the usage of sulfuric acid. In other situations, the sales force may be asked to present a new product to current and prospective customers so that their reaction can be gauged. In some industries which change products on a fast fashion cycle (for example, apparel, upholstered furniture) this is done informally. That is, if the sales force does not generate enough sales on its first exposure of the new product, the new style is dropped from the line. In other instances, it is done on a more irregular basis as part of a market research program. Such test exposure can be on the basis of the nation, a region, or a specific set of territories or salespeople. Thus, a consumer package-goods company might ask several especially experienced and reliable key-account salespeople to test buyer reaction to a proposed product or promotion.

Because of its intimate knowledge of and relationship with the marketplace, the sales force is used for these purposes since it comes into regular contact with customers and prospects. Such market research

---

[1]"Multisourcing" is the practice of buying the same product from several suppliers to ensure continued delivery and availability even if one supplier is crippled by a work stoppage due to accident, natural catastrophe, or labor problems.

presents several problems, however. First, in many cases, the sales force may be biased. They may consciously or unconsciously estimate customer usage of their products to be low, so that their individual market shares appear to be high. Second, they are basically sellers, not researchers. Thus, they view such a function in a "jaundiced" light and lack the appropriate analytical tools. If they are personally in favor of the product, they may attempt to sell it, whereas if they are against it, they may tend to be negligent in testing the customer's reaction. Third, it detracts from their major activity—selling.

There are many market research approaches to the determination of market potential which do not involve the sales force; they will not be discussed here.

Once the overall market potential is established, the issue becomes its allotment on a territory-by-territory basis.

As a general rule, it is somewhat easier to allot market potential for consumer goods and services than for industrial goods and services. This is because the data related to consumers are more highly developed and more generally available, and because standard population data gathered in the censuses are usually the basis for estimation. For these reasons, allotting marketing potential for consumer goods and services will be considered separately from the industrial situation.

145

Allotting Market Potential: Consumer Sales

There are three basic types of primary data used in allotting consumer market potential on a territory-by-territory basis: (1) population, (2) product category sales, and (3) numbers of stores. Before looking at the sources of these data, it is useful to consider their use. The sale of many products can be related to the territory's population. For example, a manufacturing bakery might make the assumption that the market potential for bread is directly related to the number of people in the territory. This approach has definite limitations. In this case, for example, it may be that rural residents purchase less bread than the average person because they bake their own and that poor people in the city purchase more bread than wealthier urban dwellers who eat more protein-containing foods and less bread.

Thus, the number of people in a territory is, in many cases, of limited usefulness in assessing market potential. On the other hand, population data are usually quite accurate, precise (available for very small subdivisions), up to date, and easily available. With some careful thought, it is possible to use more sophisticated data than the gross number of people in a territory. Population data are available on many bases, including age, income, education, and family situation.

Thus, a sales manager can develop market potential data by considering certain important market segments. The marketer of geriatric products, for example, is more interested in the number of older people in an area than in the total population of the area.

Management judgment can also be used to modify population data. A manufacturer of women's coats, for example, might develop a ratio of coat sales to population based on weather patterns. Thus, in colder areas, the assumption might be one-half coat per adult woman per year, in moderate areas, one-third per adult per year, and in warmer areas, zero coats.

In many situations it is possible to obtain data on sales by product category or by type of outlet. Such data usually have two limitations: (1) the product categories tend to be relatively broad, and (2) the geographic divisions are often large. Thus, a manufacturer of men's socks who desires over-the-calf sock sales by territory might find that the best data he can obtain are men's apparel—underwear and socks by state and Standard Metropolitan Statistical Area (SMSA).[2] If the proportion of the large product category accounted for by the more narrowly defined product of interest remains constant over different areas, then the problem is solved. While this sometimes occurs, differences based on local tradition and taste (for example, corn meal consumption in the South versus New England), income distribution, weather, etc., cause problems.

146

Another approach is based on the number of stores in a territory. This is most useful in developing an estimate of the number of potential accounts, but also can be used in some cases to determine market potential. For example, a supplier of paper products to fast-food outlets could develop an estimate of the market potential in a territory by multiplying the number of outlets by the estimated amount of paper products used per unit.

All of these approaches have their limitations. The best way to develop market potential data by territory is to use several of them. If the results replicate each other, the sales manager can be confident of them. If they do not, he can review them to determine the problem.

Data on population, product category sales, and number of stores are available from many sources. The most accessible source of population and category sales data for most managers is the "Survey of Buying Power," published by *Sales Management* magazine in two parts. Part I, which appears in July, contains the following information by state and SMSA:

Population
Total
Percent of U.S.

---

[2]SMSA is the designation used by the Bureau of the Census for larger (specifically defined) metropolitan areas. The area boundaries are set by county, not by state, so that some SMSAs include parts of more than one state.

Median age
Population by age group
Number of households
Households by age of household head

Income

Effective buying income (EBI)[3]
Percentage of U.S. EBI
Per capita EBI
Median household EBI
Average household EBI
Households by EBI
Buying power index (BPI)[4]
Three graduated buying power indices
    (EPP, MPP, and PPP)[4]

Store group sales

Total retail sales
Percentage of U.S. retail sales
Food store sales
Supermarket sales
Eating and drinking place sales
General merchandise store sales
Department store sales
Apparel store sales
Furniture, home furnishings, and appliance store sales
Furniture and home furnishings store sales
Automotive store sales
Gas station sales
Lumber, building material, and hardware dealer sales
Drugstore sales

Merchandise line sales[5]

Groceries and other foods sales
Groceries and other foods in supermarket sales
Cosmetics sales

[3]EBI—Effective Buying Income is personal income (wages, salaries, interest, dividends, etc.) minus federal, state, and local taxes and, thus, generally equivalent to disposable personal income.

[4]BPI—Buying Power Index is "a weighted index that converts three basic elements—population, Effective Buying Income, and retail sales—into a measurement of a market's ability to buy, and expresses it as a percentage of the U.S. potential. The graduated buying power indices are weighted by household income and are EPP for economy-priced products, MPP for moderate-priced products, and PPP for premium-priced products.

[5]Merchandise line sales provide data on sales by product line for all types of retail outlets. The store group sales, on the other hand, provide sales by store type, regardless of the product category sold.

Cosmetics in drugstore sales
Women's and girls' clothing sales
Department store sales of women's and girls' clothing
Men's and boys' clothing sales
Apparel store sales of men's and boys' clothing
Footwear sales
Apparel store footwear sales
Major appliance sales
Appliance store major appliance sales
Furniture sales
Furniture sales in furniture and home furnishing stores

Part I also includes data for each county although not in the detail provided by state and SMSA. In addition, it provides data on Canada and on specific demographic market segments, such as on-base military spending, the black middle-class, and rural markets. The data are also available on computer tape.

Part II, published in October, provides material such as projections of metropolitan markets to 1978 and media-related market data (for example, survey of television markets).

Detailed data on population are available in the *Census of Population* which is prepared in its complete version every 10 years and includes data such as the number of people in each political unit, employment, occupation, income, age, race, nationality, birth place, family composition, material status, etc. It is a very complete document with a great deal of data which are useful to sales and marketing executives. Much of the data are available on computer tapes. Special studies on population segments are prepared at irregular intervals.

The *Census of Business* provides a great deal of data on retailing, wholesaling, and some consumer services. The most complete data are available by state and SMSA. Somewhat fewer data are available for larger cities and counties, and some data are available for even relatively small counties. The type of data available includes the number of outlets in each store category, the sales and payroll for these stores, and in some cases the sales of specific merchandise lines through those stores. Some of the data are divided by store size or company size, or both (for example, multiunit companies versus single units). While the merchandise categories are broad the data are quite useful, especially if the assumption can be made that the ratio of the sales of the particular product of interest to the broad product category sales remains constant.

Trade associations and journals are another rich source of data. *The Discount Merchandiser*, for example, publishes "The True Look of the Discount Industry" every June. It includes store sales and square footage by state, as well as a good deal of data on each department. One important piece of information is the monthly sales pattern of various departments—very useful for allotting annual market potential and sales quotas by month or quarter. It also includes financial data on various major chain operations.

The National Retail Merchants Association (NRMA) publishes *Merchandise and Operating Results for Department and Specialty Stores* annually. It breaks product category sales into tightly defined product lines (for example, housedresses, aprons, and uniforms, pianos and organs) and separates larger from smaller stores. It also includes data on retail markups useful for translating retail sales figures into manufacturers' sales and vice versa.

There are many other useful sources of data, including *Progressive Grocer's Marketing Guidebooks; Hardware Age, Directory of Hardlines Distributors;* and *Chain Store Age "Super Markets."* Some provide sales data, others operating data, and still others provide lists of stores, addresses, and merchandising personnel by name and title. Credit rating organizations, such as Lyon's, which is used in the furniture trade, or Dun & Bradstreet, are useful for developing lists of prospective accounts.

There are also many market research services that provide data on sales by product category. Many offer data at regular intervals on a subscription plan. Some of those and others do special studies. Most of this information is concerned with consumer package-goods sales.

149

Allotting Market Potential: Industrial Sales

Because industrial market potential is not as homogeneously spread or as closely related to population, the data tend to be harder to gather. The task of allotting industrial market potential is not impossible, however.

The basic source of data is the *Census of Manufacturers*. It provides data on sales and payrolls and the number of plants on an industry and geographic basis. *Sales Management* began to publish in 1974 a *Survey of Industrial Buying Power*, which updates and improves the availability of data like that in the *Census of Manufacturers*. Dun & Bradstreet and other market information firms also publish data such as directories of factories and companies. Listings are usually divided by industry or geography, or both. Many trade journals publish annual directory issues or can supply market information through their advertising sales departments. Finally, the *Thomas Register* is often a useful source of lists of companies engaged in specific manufacturing operations.

There are other sources related to specific industries. These include government organizations (for example, the Tariff Commission's material on organic chemicals), trade associations, and trade journals.

Some of these data must be manipulated to be made useful. If a steel wholesaler, for example, wants to determine sales potential by county, one way to do it is to develop indices of steel usage per employee for various types of manufacturing operations. Then, using employment data from the *Census of Manufacturers*, he can derive an estimate of steel usage. Complete process knowledge and/or the cooperation of some customers with whom a manufacturer has good relations can enable the manufacturer to develop indices relating the use of his products to customer sales or value added, or both.

Because some industrial markets are highly concentrated in both geographic and company terms, it is often possible to develop market potential estimates on an account-by-account basis. Thus, an oil-well equipment manufacturer is likely to be intimately aware, through the sales force, of almost every well being drilled. With this type of information, it is easy to develop market potential estimates.

SALES FORECASTS

One major use of market potential data is the development of sales forecasts and quotas. Remembering that the sales forecast is an expectation, let us look at the development of sales forecasts on a territory-by-territory or salesperson-by-salesperson[6] basis.

The most often used methods of sales forecasting on a salesperson-by-salesperson basis follow:

1 Add a fixed percentage (10 percent is a typical number) to each salesperson's previous sales.

2 Develop a forecast based on some expected penetration level times the market potential.

3 Build up a forecast for each salesperson by adding account-by-account forecasts for each account.

4 Develop a total sales forecast (usually done by marketing management and/or market researchers) and allocate a portion to each salesperson based on previous sales, market potential, or some combination of the two.[7]

5 Use some mixture of approaches. Often, for example, approaches 1 and 2 are combined, and sometimes all 4 general approaches are used together.

The process of adding a fixed percentage to each salesperson's previous performance has one major advantage: It is simple—simple to

---

[6]It is necessary to differentiate, because in many businesses (for example, printing and insurance) the salespeople are not assigned specific geographic territories.

[7]We shall be concerned only with the allotment of the national or total forecast, not its development.

perform, simple to communicate, and simple to administer. Its primary drawback is that it is not accurate. Some people (for example, new hirees who have completed training), some territories (for example, those exhibiting growth in market potential or low penetration), and those in which the seller is particularly interested (for example, near a new plant) can be expected to increase in sales faster than the average. Others can be expected to increase more slowly.

Developing a forecast based on potential depends upon accurate estimates of (1) market potential and (2) expected penetration. The difficulty of gathering market potential data has already been described. The expected penetration can be estimated from past performance of the territory or by varying company averages based upon such factors as territory size, salesperson experience, etc. This whole approach, incidentally, falls down when salespeople are not assigned specific territories and/or accounts. The market penetration method is a bit more sophisticated than the straight percentage increase approach and a bit more difficult.

Most companies which do territory-by-territory forecasting use some combination of these two approaches. It can be formalized by formulas, but more likely it is based on using past sales to estimate the expected market penetration or using market potential and penetration to vary the expected percentage sales increase. With good judgment, this approach can work well.

151

When the territory includes a small number of large accounts, it is possible to forecast their sales on an account-by-account basis. This can be very accurate. In addition, it forces the salesperson and salesmanager (1) to review each account situation, (2) to gather data on the account's own plans, and (3) to plan a specific approach to the account for the next time period. When a territory includes both a few large accounts and many small ones, it is typical to forecast the large accounts' sales on an account-by-account basis and to estimate the remainder of the sales by starting with past sales or market potential. Fieldcrest uses this approach for their sales quotas.

The final method, allotment of a total market forecast, involves two issues. The first is the classic top-down versus bottom-up discussion. The other involves the best way to allocate the total forecast. The forecast is allocated on the basis of past sales plus a percentage increase, expected penetration times market potential, account-by-account analysis, or a combination of two or three approaches.

Without getting into a long discussion of the top-down versus bottom-up issue, it can be clearly stated that, since each has its disadvantages, the best approach is probably to combine the two. This forces sales management and salespeople to analyze territories and accounts and marketing personnel to analyze products and markets. The process is valuable—it leads to the review, analysis, and planning processes which are the core of management. The time is well spent if only to force that process. An additional benefit is greater accuracy. The merged forecast tends to be better than either alone. The process of merging encourages communication in specific terms between sales and nonsales marketing personnel—an important benefit.

The best sales forecasting systems use several approaches to improve accuracy. After a few annual iterations, the various methods can be calibrated against each other and actual performance to improve accuracy.

Before considering the uses and abuses of sales forecasts it is useful to discuss quotas.

SALES QUOTAS

Sales quotas are different from sales forecasts because they serve very different functions. Forecasts are the best estimates of what will happen—a planning function.

Quotas, on the other hand, are used for three sales management functions: evaluation, motivation, and compensation. To be used for evaluation, a quota does *not* need to be communicated to the salesperson of concern. The sales manager might have an implicit target for one of his salespeople, such as "If Charlie doesn't sell 500 tons this year he has got to go."

When quotas are used for motivation they must be communicated. Here they are set up as goals. Of course, to work they must be attainable. They can be formal, developed as part of a companywide program, or informal, such as "Jane, I think that you should plan on selling at least $100,000 worth of product line 3 this year."

Finally, they can be used as part of the compensation system. Many plans pay a bonus for reaching quota or a commission on all sales past it.

Quotas are developed in a variety of ways, usually similar to the ways forecasts are developed. Because they are a management tool and not a planning device, they often should be different from the forecast. In addition, if they are to be used for motivation, the prime concern should not be their accuracy or precision, but their effect on performance. The note "Compensation, Evaluation, and Motivation" discusses their use in greater depth.

USES AND ABUSES OF SALES FORECASTS AND QUOTAS

The sales forecasting and quota-making mechanisms are replete with opportunities for gamesmanship. For example, when quotas are set from the top down through a negotiation process, the conventional wisdom has said that subordinates will try to negotiate a lower goal so that they can easily surpass it. Fieldcrest and many other companies, on the other hand, have not found this to be true with their salespeople. Instead, the optimism and exuberance of the salespeople led to unrealistically high goals and forecasts. At the management level, the "low-balling" of goals seems more prevalent.

Part of the gamesmanship comes from continuing confusion over the difference between quotas and forecasts (the reason the distinction has been made so strongly here).

This gamesmanship can be kept to a minimum by the following approaches:

1 Clearly define the function of the number being generated. Is it a forecast or quota? If a quota, is it for evaluation, compensation, or motivation?

2 If the quota and forecast are the same, confusion is always going to occur.

3 Have a rational basis for setting the number—one which is explicit and clear to all concerned.

4 If the numbers being set are forecasts, be sure that accuracy is the quality rewarded. For example, it is wrong to praise someone for selling more than his forecast. The ideal forecast is correct. On the other hand, it is most appropriate to reward someone for surpassing his quota.

5 The quota-setting and forecasting function in a company with open communication will be much less political than in one in which information is used as a political weapon.

6 Quotas which involve compensation are especially liable to gamesmanship. Thus, they must be separated as far as possible from forecasting.

7 Understand the problems involved in the quota-setting process. For example, if quotas are automatically set at 90 percent of the past year's sales, the salesperson who has constant sales will always make 111 percent of quota, while the person who doubles sales will have to maintain almost that whole gain to make quota the second year. Formulas are especially dangerous although easy to communicate.

8 Handle the process with openness and candor.

It is important to realize that perfection will not be achieved in forecasting or quota setting. No approach is perfect, even for a specific situation, but if the process is managed with care, it will minimize ill will and disruption.

BIBLIOGRAPHY

Bolt, Gordon J.: *Market and Sales Forecasting—A Total Approach*, New York: Wiley, 1972.

Chambers, John C., Satinder K. Mullick, and Donald D. Smith: "How to Choose the Right Forecasting Technique," *Harvard Business Review*, vol. 49, no. 4, July–August 1971.

Copulsky, William: *Practical Sales Forecasting*, New York: American Management Association, 1970.

Hellquist, George A.: "Why Sales Forecasts Fail," *Industrial Marketing*, vol. 54, December 1969, pp. 46–49.

Keay, Frederick: *Marketing and Sales Forecasting*, Elmsford, N.Y.: Pergamon Press, 1971.

Lippitt, Vernon G.: *Statistical Sales Forecasting*, New York: Financial Executives Research Foundation, 1969.

National Industrial Conference Board: *Forecasting Sales*, New York, 1964.

PoKempner, Stanley J., and Earl L. Bailey: *Sales Forecasting Practices*, New York: The Conference Board, 1970.

Staelin, Richard, and Ronald E. Turner: "Error in Judgmental Sales Forecasts: Theory and Results," *Journal of Marketing Research*, vol. 10, February 1973, pp. 10–16.

Section
FOUR
Account Management

FIFTEEN   Selling

One of the major tasks of the sales manager is to manage a pool of prospective or current accounts, or both. All sales management activities should be focused on the generation and maintenance of profitable accounts. That is the very core of our concern.

While our prime orientation is not selling, it would be hard to discuss sales management and account management without at least a brief discussion of selling. The objective is not to make everyone a supersalesperson, but rather to introduce enough material about selling so that the general process is understood and can be managed by those active in it. While our prime interest will be on commercial and industrial selling—one company selling to another—many of the subjects discussed can be applied to consumer selling. The family, in fact, can be looked upon as an organizational buying unit with several participants, each with different needs. Consider, for example, the purchase of an automobile in a one-car family, consisting of a husband, a wife, a 16-year-old son, and an 8-year-old daughter, or a vacation decision for the same family. Each person will have differing needs and a different power position from which to present those needs.

ORGANIZATIONAL INTERACTION

Because we are primarily involved with commercial or industrial selling it should be clear that an account must be defined in terms of both the organization and the individuals within the organization. Exhibit 1 provides abbreviated organization charts for a relatively typical selling firm and two types of buying firms: a retailer (in this case, a department store or discount store) and a manufacturer.

Selling to an organization is much more complex than selling to an

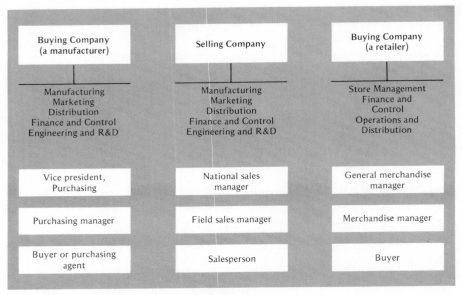

Exhibit 1 Typical buying and selling organizations.

individual. There are two reasons for this: (1) an organization is made up of different individuals with different needs, and (2) these individuals interact with each other in complex ways. While it is impossible to consider organizational buying and selling in depth here, some of the more important points will be considered.[1]

Consider first the different explicit needs of various participants in a purchase decision. When a firm buys a large piece of equipment, the manufacturing managers may desire an efficient machine which will require little repair and which is technically advanced; the treasurer's department will be interested in financing terms; while the purchasing department's primary interest may be both total cost of the manufacturing system (raw materials, depreciation, installation, etc.) and outright cost of the machine. The selling company must take account of these various needs and of the importance and power of the persons possessing the needs. That, however, is only the first part. Not only does everyone in the firm have explicit needs based on his position and professional interests, but everyone also has personal needs. Buying decisions, because they involve authority and responsibility, represent a primary focus for the satisfaction of personal needs in the organizational setting. The young treasurer, for example, might be trying to consolidate his newly won power by showing how well he can do the job. The

[1]One of the best books on the subject is *Organizational Buying Behavior*, by Frederick E. Webster and Yoram Wind, Englewood Cliffs, N.J.: Prentice-Hall, 1972, which does an excellent and concise (128 pages) job of covering the subject.

manufacturing people, on the other hand, might be smarting over a recent loss to the engineering people and be anxious for revenge.

The astute firm, sales manager, and salesperson, of course, work very hard to gather information such as that mentioned above. It is a good deal of what both selling and account management are about.

As the size of the buying and selling companies has increased, and as the importance of major sales—those involving large sums of money—has grown, the selling process has become more complex. More people are involved in the purchase decision, and more needs have to be satisfied. The industrial salesperson, who previously sold capital equipment to engineers and supplies to the purchasing agent, must now sell systems to a buying committee including manufacturing, engineering, financial, and purchasing personnel. The apparel salesperson who sold items to Macy's Herald Square store and its two small branches in 1950 now sells programs to Macy's New York, with almost 2 dozen stores.

THE SELLING PROCESS

Exhibit 2 provides a diagram of a typical selling situation involving reselling. The process consists of five steps: opening the relationship, qualifying the prospect, presenting the message, closing the sale, and servicing the account—with assorted feedback loops.

Opening

The opening has two purposes: (1) to determine the right person in the organization to approach initially and (2) to generate enough interest so that it is possible to obtain the information necessary for qualification. The end result of the good opening should be an appointment with an appropriate and enthusiastic person. Given the complexity of many organizational buying situations, it is crucial to identify the key buying influences and their desires, the important interactions among buying influences, and the allocation of power among the influences. Typically, the salesperson should try to enter the situation with the most powerful buying influence on his side. It is even better, of course, if all of the people involved are in favor of the seller's position. If the buying decision is a contested one, the salespersons who ally themselves with the weaker buying influences will, of course, be at a great disadvantage. Sometimes, the opening must be made through a particular participant in the decision. Often, the purchasing agent plays this role. In such situations, tradition and policy dictate that the salesperson contact the purchasing department before being allowed to contact other company personnel. In these situations, the purchasing agent can veto a salesperson's proposal but cannot ensure acceptance.

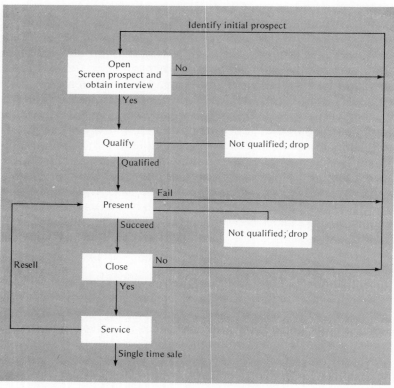

Exhibit 2 Account building process.

Qualifying

Qualifying is the process in which a salesperson determines whether or not the prospect is worth the effort of a sales presentation. The key questions are:

1 Does this company have a need for my product or service?

2 Can I make the people responsible for buying so aware of that need that I can make a sale?

3 Will the sale be profitable to my company?

The qualification is a very complex process because the answers to these three general questions are really dependent upon the answers to a much longer set of specific questions including:

1 Will I be allowed access to enough information to assess the need?

2 Is the risk of changing current suppliers so high that the company will not make the change?

3 Does the current supplier have a special relationship, such as family or close personal friendship, which cannot be broken?

4 Can I identify and satisfy the personal and organizational needs of each major buying influence?

5 Will the sales time be such that the process is not justified by the size of the sale?

The qualification is a difficult activity because it requires the salesperson to be disciplined and objective about the chance to make a profitable sale. Although scholars of selling and sales management tend to gloss over the qualifying process, salespeople and sales managers constantly discuss it. The executives of one sales training firm, who are all ex-salespeople, have developed a cassette sales training program which devotes a whole cassette to this single subject. Two leading salesmanship books, on the other hand, cover the subject only briefly. If the prospect does not qualify, then the salesperson can spend the time better somewhere else.

Presenting

The presentation is the core of the selling process and requires astute management on the part of the salesperson. It is the "pitch," the actual attempt at persuasion. There are a great many issues concerned with the presentation, including:

161

1 Location

2 Attendees
   (a) Who should represent the selling company?
   (b) Of the selling company's participants, who should play which role?
   (c) Who should the selling company want to represent the buying company?
   (d) Should it be a group presentation or a series of one-to-one presentations?

3 Content and order of presentation
   (a) Should material, both positive and negative to the selling company's position, be presented?
   (b) How long and detailed should it be?
   (c) Should it be informal or formal?

Closing

The presentation sooner or later culminates in an attempt to close the sale. Closing is obtaining the final agreement to purchase. This is the

Achilles' heel of many would-be-successful salespeople. "Poor old Charlie, he's got a great personality, people like him, and he makes a great presentation but he just can't ask for the order—he can't close." The close is almost always performed with a question such as "When do you want it delivered?" or "Do you want the red one or the green one?"

It is not only important to close the sale, but it is important to close it quickly. The salesperson who can close the sale quickly can then be off to make another call. The profit per sale goes down as the amount of time necessary to close goes up. In addition, the risk of losing the sale increases. Until it is closed, it is not a sale, nor is it safe from competitors or from a decision not to buy a product in that generic category.

Servicing

After the actual sale comes the service aspect. Often the salespeople will be responsible for managing installations, training, maintenance support, etc. In addition, they frequently sell supplies, take repeat orders as well as additional and/or larger orders, and perform services. These service functions are important for two reasons. First, they lead to additional sales. Second, they generate sales. In some capital equipment lines, for example, service contracts, supplies, and replacement parts account for greater dollar sales revenue than the initial order. Often, such business also carries very high margins.

TEAM AND MULTILEVEL SELLING

Two lively issues in selling are multilevel selling and team selling. Multilevel selling is the process by which several authority levels are called upon. The salesperson selling to a retailer, for example, may attempt to contact the buyer and merchandise manager, so that when the buyer takes the salesperson's proposal to the merchandise manager for approval, the merchandise manager is presold, or at least receptive. Multilevel selling is, in a sense, a product of system selling, because the chief buying influence in the firm resides at a higher level in the organization than traditional buyers, and because that person is responsible for the total system instead of individual components. Consider, for example, the firm that has a manufacturing system for which one buyer purchases raw material and another machinery. If a selling firm wants to sell a system involving both, it is almost required to move up the purchasing organization to one person in charge of both raw materials and machinery. The sheer dollar size of some commitments or major changes in supplier relationships also forces the buying authority in some organizations to move upward in the organization.

Multilevel selling not only involves selling to different people in the buying firm, but it also often involves people at different levels in the selling firm. This generally occurs when the size of the sale justifies the cost, and the complexity of the buying process necessitates the approach. In a multilevel team sales approach, each level of the selling organization calls upon his counterpart in the buying organization. One reason for this is etiquette—it is more appropriate for the national sales manager to call on the general merchandise manager than for him to climb beyond his own level or to deal with someone beneath his own level. Another reason is that it demonstrates appropriate interest on the part of the management of the selling firm. Still a third reason is that an exchange of power is involved. The two top managers can make arrangements (for example, private branding, special products) that their subordinates cannot.

Team selling does not necessarily have to involve different levels in the organization. It can involve members of different functional areas in the selling organization. If members of different functional areas in the buying organization have different needs and viewpoints, it is reasonable that those needs can best be met and those viewpoints best understood by the functional equivalents in the selling organization. For example, if the treasurer of the buying firm is concerned about financial arrangements, then the treasurer of the selling firm is probably better suited to deal with him than the salesperson whose primary job is to deal with manufacturing and purchasing personnel.

Three things should be clear about team selling. First, it is not always appropriate, since sometimes the sale is simple, repetitive, or small. Team selling is most appropriate for the selling of heavy capital equipment or long-term supply relationships, in the form of either formal contracts of informal commitments. These involve enough dollars and enough different functions in the buying organization to justify the high expenditure of time involved in team selling. Second, team selling is complex and difficult to manage. It is possible for the sales team to spend more time getting coordinated than selling. Or, even worse, it can spend too little time getting coordinated and end up presenting contradictory impressions to the buying influences. Third, team selling is, in a sense, an extension of the marketing concept which stresses the importance of having all parts of the firm directed toward satisfying the customer needs.

Although team selling is usually thought of as involving relatively high-level personnel and of being used primarily to "open" an account instead of to provide continuing maintenance selling, it can also be used with lower-level personnel and for maintenance selling. A soft drink bottler may, for example, primarily use a route delivery salesperson for selling, but may supplement his efforts with an in-store display and merchandising expert. In other situations, inside sales liaison personnel, expediters, or even shipping personnel may join the sales team in keeping the account satisfied.

SELLING IN NONSELLING SITUATIONS

In many industries, selling has not been performed in a formal sense. Usually this is because of tradition or "professional ethics." Nonetheless, for example, lawyers and accountants both, who are prohibited from selling by "professional ethics," sell. It may be a very "soft," informal selling process, but it is selling.

The typical approach in such industries is to develop informal contact either through personal social relationships or by referral. The opening and the qualification are handled informally. After that, a more formal presentation may be made, or the presentation may also be informal. Finally, the close is executed. Throughout the process, the lack of explicit selling does not diminish the amount of strong persuasion brought to bear. Recently, "selling" has become more accepted in these situations. This is actually an explicit realization of a situation which has existed for many years. Whether it is called selling or not, it is selling.

THE SALES MANAGER'S ROLE

164

In some situations, sales managers sell. In all situations, they are responsible for generating profitable sales. Thus, they must constantly focus on the salesperson-customer interaction. All of sales management are devoted to making profitable sales through astute formulation of the sales program and effective management of the sales force.

Personal selling allows the company to segment the market at its lowest level of disaggregation, the individual customer, and to respond to the unique needs of that market segment. The sales manager must ensure that the appropriate prospects are approached and that their needs, both personal and organizational, and the needs of existing customers are met by the sales effort.

BIBLIOGRAPHY

Brand, Gordon T.: *The Industrial Buying Decision*, New York: Wiley, 1973.

Cardozo, Richard N., and James Cagley: "Experimental Study of Industrial Buyer Behavior," *Journal of Marketing Research*, vol. 8, August 1971, pp. 329–334.

Cyert, Richard M., Herbert A. Simon, and Donald B. Trow: "Observation of a Business Decision," *Journal of Business*, vol. 29, October 1956, pp. 237–248; reprinted in Kenneth R. Davis and Frederick E. Webster, Jr. (eds.), *Readings in Sales Force Management*, New York: Ronald Press, 1968.

Davis, Harry L., and Alvin J. Silk: "Interaction and Influence Processes in Personal Selling," *Sloan Management Review*, Winter 1972, pp. 59–76.

Faris, Charles W.: "Market Segmentation and Industrial Buying Behavior," in M.S. Mayer and R.E. Vosburgh (eds.), *Marketing for Tomorrow . . . Today*, American Marketing Association, June 1967, pp. 108–110; reprinted in Robert F. Gurnner and Edward M. Smith (eds.), *Sales Strategy: Cases and Readings*, New York: Appleton Century Crofts, 1969, pp. 220–226.

Gwinner, Robert F.: "Base Theory in the Formulation of Sales Strategy," *MSU Business Topics*, vol. 16, no. 4, Autumn 1968, pp. 37–44; reprinted in Thomas R. Wotruba and Robert Olsen (eds.), *Readings in Sales Management*, New York: Holt, Rinehart and Winston, 1971, pp. 158–169.

Harding, Murray: "Who Really Makes the Purchasing Decision," *Industrial Marketing*, September 1966, pp. 76–81.

"How Systems Selling Is Revolutionizing Marketing," *Business Management*, vol. 32, no. 3, June 1967, pp. 60–86; reprinted in Harper W. Boyd and Robert T. Davis (eds.), *Readings in Sales Management*, Homewood, Ill.: Richard D. Irwin, 1970, pp. 124–142.

Howard, William C.: "Reassuring the Industrial Buyer," *Marketing Times*, July-August 1974, pp. 20–23.

Levitt, Theodore: "Communications and Industrial Selling," *Journal of Marketing*, April 1967, pp. 15–21.

McMurray, Robert N.: "The Mystique of Super-Salesmanship," *Harvard Business Review*, March-April 1961, pp. 113–122.

Robinson, Patrick J., and Bent Stidsen: *Personal Selling in a Modern Prospective*, Boston: Allyn and Bacon, 1967.

Sales Management: "Closing the Sale," June 1, 1971, reprint series.

————: "Opening the Sale," October 30, 1972 (entire issue).

Sheth, Jagdish N.: "A Model of Industrial Buyer Behavior," *Journal of Marketing*, vol. 37, October 1973, pp. 50–56.

Webster, Frederick E., Jr., and Yoram Wind: "A General Model for Understanding Organizational Buyer Behavior," *Journal of Marketing*, vol. 36, April 1972, pp. 12–19.

Wilson, David T.: "Industrial Buyers' Decision-Making Styles," *Journal of Marketing Research*, vol. 8, November 1971, pp. 433–436.

SIXTEEN Caine and Callahan, Incorporated (Selling Role)

Casewriter's note: This case was designed to be used in conjunction with Tight Grip Fastener Corporation. The two cases are used in a two-person, role-playing experience, with one person taking the role of Joseph Caine of Caine and Callahan, Inc., and the other of Edward DeRucco of Tight Grip Fastener Corporation. Each participant should read *only* the case on the firm he represents before the session. He should *not* read his partner's case until the role-playing session is over.

Joseph Caine had been born of a wealthy family in 1950. He attended an Ivy League college and graduated in 1972. He went directly to a well-known business school from which he graduated in 1974. During the summers while still a student, he either traveled or gave tennis lessons at a prestigious country club. He was reputed to be an excellent tennis player and had been a standout on his college's varsity team. Upon receiving his M.B.A. he formed a consulting company, called Caine and Callahan, Inc., with his classmate John Callahan.

Mr. Caine majored in marketing while in graduate business school. During the summer between his two graduate years, Mr. Caine had worked in product management for a large consumer package-goods manufacturer. In the spring of 1974, Messrs. Caine and Callahan decided to go into the consulting business. They believed that there was a great need for good rational analysis among small businesses. They were sure that they could provide it. Mr. Callahan had been a dean's list scholar at business school and was among the top finance students in his class of 800. Mr. Caine had received honors. Messrs. Caine and Callahan were convinced that their educational background, outstanding academic credentials, and great ability to articulate their points of view, as well as Mr. Caine's contacts, would make them successful. They had agreed that wherever possible and advisable they would accept payment in stock from their clients. Mr. Callahan commented, "That's the way that we can make big money and be paid on a incentive basis. It's good for a small cash-hungry firm which wants to pay us based on our ability and it has great potential for us."

The firm did well during the summer of 1974. Mr. Caine's father had introduced the new firm to some of his acquaintances, and the initial months went about as expected. The fall was lean, and the winter was leaner. Part of this, Messrs. Caine and Callahan thought, was due to an unsettled economy. Revenues were considerably below budget for spring 1975. The two partners hoped that as economic activity increased and as their reputation grew they would attract more business. Their clients seemed happy with their work although average billings per client had been lower than expected. Exhibit 1 is a list of services provided their clients.

On May 10, 1975, Mr. Caine had attended a cocktail party at the home of the father of a friend of his, Philip Fortunato, Jr. He had met young Mr. Fortunato in college.

At the party he met Edward DeRucco, president of Tight Grip Fastener Corporation. Mr. DeRucco had been a long time client of the senior Mr. Fortunato's law firm and had obviously known the young Mr. Fortunato since childhood.

Mr. Caine talked about Mr. DeRucco and his business.

DeRucco has built a good small business in the fastener and fastening machinery business. I'd guess that its sales are $4 to 5 million per year and that its profits are pretty good. But, it looks like DeRucco has outgrown his ability to manage the firm. He's really just a clever machinist. He doesn't understand marketing strategy or finance. He has had little formal schooling—I doubt if he finished high school—and he speaks with a definite accent. He certainly doesn't have the polish to call on large potential customers like the auto companies. I really think that he needs our help worse than we need him as a client. Philly Fortunato told me that the business hasn't been growing for the past few years, and DeRucco told me that he had a sales force problem. Those are symptoms of a company out of control. He probably runs it by the seat of his pants with our plans, controls, or reports. We could combine his knowledge of machinery without knowledge of business and really make that company grow. It's a great opportunity for both of us."

167

Mr. Caine had arranged to discuss his firm's capabilities with Mr. DeRucco and had a 10:00 A.M. appointment at the latter's office on May 12th, the Monday after the cocktail party. He arrived slightly early and announced his arrival to Mr. DeRucco's secretary just before 10:00 A.M. She said that Mr. DeRucco would be with him shortly.

The outer office smelled of the same little cigars Mr. DeRucco had smoked at the party. Mr. Caine hoped that Mr. DeRucco would not be smoking one at their meeting.

Shortly after 10:00 A.M. he was ushered into Mr. DeRucco's office.

Exhibit 1   LIST OF CONSULTING SERVICES FOR CLIENTS

1 Review of drug legislation suggested to medium-sized, specialized drug company in Boston by local law firm.
2 Retail bank marketing study with emphasis on sales promotion for large local bank.
3 Sales training study for local firm specializing in textile machinery.
4 Funds-flow analysis for small real estate firm.
5 General financial consulting for client of local venture-capital firm.
6 Study on ways and means of going public for small conglomerate.
7 Study of financial needs of local electronics firm.

SEVENTEEN Tight Grip Fastener Corporation (Buying Role)

Casewriter's note: This case was designed to be used in conjunction with Caine and Callahan, Inc. The two cases are used in a two-person, role-playing experience, with one person taking the role of Edward DeRucco of Tight Grip Fastener Corporation, and the other of Joseph Caine of Caine and Callahan, Inc. Each participant should read *only* the case on the firm he represents before the session. He should *not* read his partner's case until the role playing session is over. The role of Edward DeRucco is especially appropriate for one who enjoys smoking cigars.

Tight Grip Fastener Corporation had been founded in 1948 by Edward DeRucco. At the time of its founding, Mr. DeRucco was 34 years old. He had been born in Italy but had come to the United States with his parents and seven older brothers and sisters when he was 10 years old. He still spoke English with a pronounced accent. He had quit school in the eighth grade and gone to work in a machine shop. Because he was mechanically inclined and worked hard, he had become a foreperson by the time he was 23. At age 30, he had been made shop superintendent, with responsibility for a total work force of 70 persons.

Mr. DeRucco had always dreamed of owning his own business and of being wealthy. He and his wife carefully saved to accumulate the $2,000 he used to start Tight Grip Fastener Corporation.

The business orginally supplied special-sized nuts, bolts, and screws in small quantities to firms in the Boston area. Often the items were specially coated by other firms. In the early days, Mr. DeRucco was the firm's only employee, selling during the day and producing the product on the firm's one machine in the evening. His wife kept the books and performed all of the office work.

The firm prospered during the 1950s, after a halting start. In 1951 it moved to larger quarters and by 1953 employed 15 persons. The recession after the Korean war (1950–1953) stopped the growth of the company and convinced Mr. DeRucco that a proprietary line of fastening machinery and fasteners was a necessity. Mr. DeRucco personally developed such a system and, after a poor experience with patent attorneys who, he believed, were attempting to steal the idea, patented the system. The system worked very well, and sales grew.

By 1960 the firm had grown to over $2 million in sales. It progressively brought in more outside contracting, such as the coating operations, so that its value added increased faster than sales. The product line was broadened and machinery became an increasingly important source of revenue.

By 1975 the firm's net sales were $7.5 million, with after-tax profits of almost $500,000. The firm had an enviable balance sheet, with little debt and much liquidity. It had recently enlarged the Everett, Mass., plant it had built in 1965. The plant was divided into two sections—one for machinery manufacturing and one for fastener manufacturing. Exhibit 1 is an organization chart. Machinery accounted for one-third of sales and profits.

The firm's products were sold through independent representatives paid on straight commission (4 percent of net sales). In New England, however, the firm employed two salespersons. They were paid a base salary of $1,500 per month, plus 1 percent of net sales, and together generated almost $3 million in sales.

Mr. DeRucco was concerned about sales growth. The firm had grown rapidly through the late 1960s but sales had reached $7 million in 1969 and had grown very slowly since then. He suspected that one problem was the sales force. He was not sure that he should have independent representatives who also carried other lines. On the other hand, he did not know what type of sales force was appropriate.

Mr. DeRucco talked about the way in which he thought about the problem and his business.

This is a large problem for me. I want this company to grow big. Probably I will sell it sometime, and I want my children and wife to be very rich. The business wasn't right for my two boys—one is studying to be a doctor and the other one teaches philosophy at Yale. They're bright and they are good boys but they couldn't run a business. I didn't let them learn the business the hard way. They went to school—that's no way to learn a business.

169

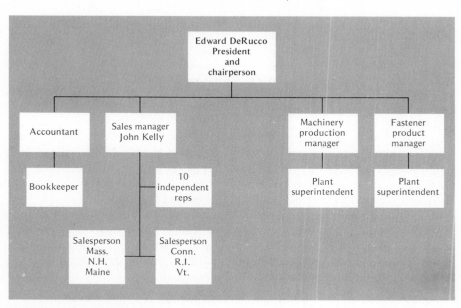

Exhibit 1 Organization chart.

The salespeople don't seem to be selling enough, and I don't know what's wrong. I'd talk to John Kelly about it, but he really doesn't know a damn thing about how to run a sales force. He's a great salesman—he knows how to drink and throw around the baloney. But he doesn't know what the reps or the salesmen are doing.

We had an advertising agency in here a while ago, but they know even less than Kelly. They're all pony and dog circuses. They talk well but don't really deliver.

I built this business by paying very careful attention to detail. I get so many reports on costs that it takes me 2 hours every day to go through them. And, I'm not about to blow a bundle on a pile of baloney generated by an agency.

On May 10, 1975, Mr. DeRucco had attended a cocktail party at the home of his attorney Philip Fortunato. Mr. Fortunato was the senior partner in a small law firm which his son had recently joined. The senior Fortunato had invited some old friends and the son had also invited a few friends to the party.

Among the people Mr. DeRucco met was Joseph Caine, a recent M.B.A. graduate. Mr. Caine had formed a consulting business upon graduation.

Mr. DeRucco described the meeting.

Young Philly Fortunato introduced me to this kid. Philly is a nice boy but not as smart as his father. He needs to get a lot of experience. He thinks he knows everything but he's still wet behind the ears.

Anyway, Young Philly introduced me to this Caine kid. Caine has put together his own consulting company, and he moved in fast when Philly mentioned my sales problem.

Anyway, he started telling me about how he might be able to help me—like it's some favor he's going to do for me to allow me to pay him! He wanted to get together to talk about the situation. Now, I wasn't born yesterday but who knows, maybe I can learn something by listening to this guy's pitch. It never hurts to listen.

On May 12, the Monday after the cocktail party, Mr. DeRucco was expecting Joseph Caine in his office at 10:00 A.M. Mr. DeRucco was busy reviewing cost reports for the last week as he sat behind a massive mahogany desk in the Federal style. His office was very large and had been decorated to provide a plush and elegant air.

Just a few minutes before 10:00 A.M. Mr. DeRucco was interrupted by his secretary who announced that Mr. Caine had arrived. Mr. DeRucco told her that he would be with Mr. Caine as soon as he finished looking at the important cost reviews. At about 10:05, Mr. DeRucco lit up a Parodi cigar and told his secretary to send in Mr. Caine.

EIGHTEEN Honeywell Information Systems (B)

AIMING HIGH

At the age of 29, Kim Kelley is already something of a legend around Honeywell Inc. "He's the one who cried when he made his sale, isn't he?" a fellow Honeywell salesman asks with a chuckle.

Indeed he is. Kim stood there in his customer's office last June and bawled like a baby. And for good reason. Kim had just shaken hands on an $8.1 million computer sale to the state of Illinois. He had gambled his whole career on making that sale. He had spent three years laying the groundwork for it, and for three solid months he had been working six days a week, often 14 hours a day, competing against salesmen from four other computer companies.

It was a make-or-break situation for Kim Kelley, and, standing there with tears of joy and relief streaming down his cheeks, he knew he had it made. A bright future with Honeywell was assured, and he had just made an $80,000 commission—more money than he had earned in all four of his previous years with the company.

Looking back on it now, Kim says: "It was pure hell." And his wife, Sandy, agrees emphatically: "I'd never want to go through it again." Such is the life of the "big-ticket" salesman who pursues multimillion-dollar contracts while others sell in bits and drabs. Lured by fat commissions (1 percent of the equipment's total value in Honeywell's case), they devote months to delicate planning and months more to the heat of battle, all to make one big sale.

GAMBLING A PIECE OF YOUR LIFE

"You're playing for big stakes, and what you ante is your life," says Dick Kuszyk, a Honeywell computer salesman in Pittsburgh. He just "gambled three years" of his life, he says, to sell a $4.5 million computer to Jones & Laughlin Steel Corp. Before he finally clinched the deal, his home life got so hectic that his wife packed up and went home to her mother for seven weeks.

A Honeywell salesman in Denver, Don Sather, was so wrapped up in trying to sell a $250,000 prototype computer system to Mountain States Telephone that he barely found time to slip away when his wife gave birth

171

at 1:08 A.M. last Aug. 15. "I stayed through labor and delivery, and then went back to the office," he says. He made the sale.

Kim Kelley thrives on such high-stakes action and always has, according to his mother in Davenport, Iowa, Mrs. Dorothy Rynott. He was aggressive even as a paper boy; he pulled in $150 in Christmas tips one year. After a year at the University of Iowa he spent a year in California cooking pizza, selling shoes and hustling at pool. He returned to Iowa, married his high school sweetheart in 1965 and prepared to follow the career of his late father, who had been a tire salesman. For four years he wandered from one retail sales job to another. Finally, in 1969, he landed at a Honeywell sales office in Peoria, Ill.

VISITING THE LEGION HALL

He was sent to Springfield in 1970 and told to keep four or five big sales simmering but to put only one at a time "on the front burner." Kim wasted little time picking his target, the state government, the biggest potential customer in his region. His long-range strategy was to devote at least half his time to pursuing the state, and to use the balance to scratch out small sales elsewhere to meet his annual quota of $500,000 worth of new equipment.

172

For three years, he patiently made daily rounds of key state offices, pausing a few minutes in each one to drop off technical documents or just to chat. He pursued the bureaucrats further at after-hours hangouts like the American Legion Hall.

"People don't buy products, they buy relationships," Kim believes. To that end, he even molded his personal life to suit his customer's preferences. He bought a big Buick and expensive suits, even though he could barely afford them. "People like to deal with a winner," Kim reasons. "They don't buy $8 million products from some guy who's worrying can he pay his rent." On the other hand, he says, it doesn't pay to appear *too* prosperous; for that reason, he quit his country club when he sensed that state employees resented his being able to afford it.

Thanks to a succession of nonstate sales, Kim's income was steadily, if unspectacularly, expanding, from $18,000 in 1970 to $22,000 in 1971 and $25,000 in 1972. The state bought hardly anything. In those three years, Kim made less than $3,000 in commissions on sales to the government.

THREE-MONTH SCRAMBLE

But when the break finally came, Kim was ready. Toward the end of 1972, the Illinois secretary of state asked for bids for a massive new computer system. Five manufacturers responded: Honeywell, Burroughs, Univac division of Sperry Rand, Control Data and International Business Machines.

In the ensuing three-month scramble, Control Data was eliminated because of "high cost," according to Noel Sexton, head of a technical commitee assigned by the state to evaluate the bids. IBM was never in strong contention, says Hank Malkus, who was then division administrator in the secretary's office. "IBM doesn't tailor its equipment to a customer's need. They just say, 'Here's our equipment, you make your system fit it,'" Mr. Malkus contends. (An IBM spokesman, asked to comment, says: "IBM feels it offers an extremely broad range of products. . . . We strive to combine all these products in each proposal to provide a prospect the best possible solution to his data-processing requirements.")

That made the contest a three-horse race between Honeywell, Burroughs and Univac. "The equipment was close," says Patrick Halperin, executive assistant to the secretary of state. "But the staff felt far more comfortable with Honeywell because they felt Kim had been more thorough in his marketing."

Indeed he was. Kim dealt solely with the committee. "Some of the other vendors put more emphasis on selling to the front office and tried to play on previous friendships," Mr. Sexton recalls.

Kim fed the committee information, not persuasion. "When we asked to see customers, says Mr. Malkus, "Kim just gave us a list of Honeywell users and said, choose." Univac, on the other hand, annoyed committee members by discouraging them from interviewing users.

Kim flew in Honeywell experts and top marketing officials from Boston, Minneapolis, Phoenix and Chicago to answer technical questions on engineering, financing, installation and service. "He showed the ability of his firm to cooperate," says Mr. Halperin.

"Incredible attention to detail" helped, too, Kim thinks. The committee was asking for new bits of information daily—things like how much air conditioning his equipment would need. Kim answered every question within two days, always hand-delivering replies to each committee member. "That gave me five minutes more selling time with each one," he explains.

A SLOW PLANE RIDE

Kim hates to fly, but he flew the six committee members and their bosses to Atlanta to meet Honeywell users, to Phoenix twice to see performance tests at a Honeywell facility there, and to Houston to interview another user. When he could, he used Honeywell's "slow propeller plane," carefully chosen, Kim says, to allow more selling time in the air. Kim and his secretary arranged everything—hotel and plane reservations, rental cars, meals, meetings, even the committee's spare time.

For the Houston trip Kim even made a dry run by himself before-hand, so he'd know the best flights, how to find the Hertz counter, good restaurants and ways to avoid rush-hour traffic. The committee had picked up a rumor that Tenneco Inc., in Houston, was dissatisfied with its Honeywell computer. Kim knew the rumor to be false, but wanted to let Tenneco itself tell that to the committee. He persuaded Tenneco to give the committee a bargain rate at a hotel it owns, and while scouting Houston, he learned that two companies there were having trouble with a competitor's equipment. He dropped hints about them to Pat Halperin, who took the bait and spent his time in Houston talking with a disgruntled customer of another vendor. "I left nothing to chance," Kim says. "Detail is what sells computers."

Kim's hot pursuit of the sale, meanwhile, was taking a toll in his family. Sandy Kelley says the "tension" was dreadful. Kim "snapped" at their three-year-old daughter, Brook, and had only a few hours on Sundays to spend with her. "Every morning she asked if Daddy would be home tonight," Sandy says.

"I'd keep lists of things I wanted to talk to Kim about," Sandy says. She resented having to manage the family alone, even the new house they were building. "When Kim walked into the new house for the first time, he was like a stranger." Had this happened earlier in their marriage, she says, "it might have reached the point of breaking up." As it was, what she did most was worry. "I'd wake up in the middle of the night and wonder what I'd do if Kim didn't get the order. I knew he'd be crushed, and I didn't know how it would affect our lives."

174

A GRIN, A HUG AND TEARS

Kim was worried sick himself. When Hank Malkus gruffly ordered him down to the state capitol last June, Kim knew it was "decision day," but he didn't know who had won. He paused only long enough to vomit into a wastebasket before hurrying to Mr. Malkus's office. Minutes later, Mr. Malkus was grinning, his secretary was hugging Kim, and Kim was crying.

By now, Kim has recovered his poise and made his peace with Sandy and Brook. He's busy supervising installation of the equipment, a chore that will take him until next September to complete. How well he handles this job and how smoothly the equipment performs later are important in keeping his new customer happy and in paving the way for future sales to the state.

And Kim is also stalking other big game. He put the finishing touches on a campaign with A. E. Staley Manufacturing Co. in December and expects to close the $1.8 million deal in February. It was a relatively easy sale to a long-time Honeywell customer that Kim had worked diligently to provide with special service. Now the Illinois Department of Revenue is "going on the front burner," Kim says. His goal: an $8-million to $10-million sale of dual computers sometime in 1974.

Meanwhile, Kim is still a bit astonished when he thinks back on what he endured to make his first big sale and when he looks at his current bank balance. He got 40% of his commission, or about $32,000, when he signed the contract in August. He'll get the rest when it's all installed next September.

Kim traded in his 1972 Chrysler (which he bought after driving the Buick awhile) for a new $9,250 Lincoln Continental (paying the $5,430 balance in cash), turned Sandy's old Ford in for a $2,200 used Volkswagen and paid cash for a $2,000 dining-room set. But the Kelleys have no plans to continue their spending spree. "A year from now our lives will be the same, except that I'll have $60,000 more in cash," Kim says.

And he likes that just fine. In fact, when Honeywell recently rewarded Kim by promoting him to sales manager, he requested "demotion" in order to avoid going on straight salary. Honeywell refused but did allow Kim a special status where he runs a 18-person sales office but stays on commission. His salary is $12,600 a year; he expects more than three times that much in commissions next year. Kim says he expects to move high in management eventually, but right now, "I can't afford the pay cut."

175

NINETEEN Paper Distributors, Incorporated (A)

Paper Distributors, Inc., was one of eight major printing paper merchants in Pittsburgh. Firms such as PDI acted as wholesale distributors of paper products for many paper mills (manufacturers). Some paper merchants carried both industrial paper [that is, paper towels for commercial (nonresale) use, wrapping papers, and other generally inexpensive paper products] and fine or printing paper. Others, like PDI, specialized.

Business

Paper merchants performed three functions for the mills: selling, inventorying, and credit extension and management. Most mills had more than one merchant in each major city. Some merchants were parts of chains, some of which in turn were owned by paper mills.

Paper merchants sold to four types of customers: publishers, in-house printing operations owned by organizations whose primary business was not printing (for example, banks, manufacturers, nonprofit organizations, etc.), commercial printers, and specifiers. Specifiers included company purchasing agents, design departments, advertising agencies, and other people who chose the paper to be used in a printing

Target Customers

job not done on their facilities. For example, when a company had its annual report printed, it was typical for the financial and communications personnel of the company to choose the paper as well as the printer. In most printing situations, however, the printer chose the paper in conjunction with the purchaser. Industry sources estimated that 15 percent of the Pittsburgh paper merchant volume (dollar basis) was sold to publishers, 25 percent to in-house printing operations, and 60 percent to commercial printers (50 percent not specified by the purchaser, 10 percent specified by the purchaser). The in-house printing market was the only market exhibiting substantial growth. Other markets were static, with publishing possibly decreasing in size in the area.

PDI, which competed with seven other paper houses in the Pittsburgh area, had sales of $9.9 million and was an old, well-established house. Two-thirds of its sales volume was direct, that is, orders shipped directly from paper mill to customer, and the remainder was sold from warehoused stock. The direct orders were usually large or highly specialized, or both.

Although the market was static, PDI's stated growth goal was 15 percent per year in gross trading margin.[1] Current sales were divided as follows:

Publishing	15%	
In-house printers	30%	
Commercial	55%	12% specified 43% nonspecified

Management estimated PDI's market share at between 14 and 15 percent.

PDI carried a large inventory of paper (2,700 different sizes, colors, and types) and offered the products of about 12 different paper mills. It represented two mills exclusively in the Pittsburgh area. These were Quality Coated Papers, Inc., and Gondola Company, which offered a high-quality uncoated line of papers.

In addition to its general growth goal, PDI wanted to increase sales of Quality Coated and Gondola products so that it could maintain its exclusive representation. These papers tended to be used on commercial printing jobs. For this reason, as well as for the higher margins and often larger order size, PDI especially wanted to increase its sales to commercial printers.

PDI was known in the industry as being particularly anxious to maintain list prices. Some other companies were quite price aggressive, especially under the generally soft economic conditions of early 1975. PDI put great emphasis on high margin, "profitable" business.

Industry experts rated the PDI sales force as generally good, with a reputation for strong service. It had about 485 active accounts. The area had about 260 commercial printers.

[1]Gross trading margin was defined as sales revenue minus cost of goods sold (including the mill or purchase cost and inbound freight).

Exhibit 1   FINANCIAL DATA

Income statement

Net sales	$9,942,000
Cost of sales and operating expenses	9,408,000
Income from operations	$ 534,000
Other expense	60,000
Income before taxes	$ 474,000
Provision for taxes	228,000
Net income	$ 246,000

Balance sheet

Assets		Liabilities	
Cash	$ 298	Accounts payable	$ 464
Accounts receivable	965	Accrued taxes	204
Inventories	493	Other liabilities	161
Other current	17	Total current	$ 829
Total current	$1,773	Long-term debt	14
Plant and equipment	265	Stockholders equity	1,195
Total	**$2,038**		**$2,038**

How sales were made.

In 1974, PDI had processed 18,500 warehouse orders and 2,000 direct orders. About 80 percent of the orders came by telephone and 10 percent by mail. The remainder was received personally by the salespeople on their calls. Exhibit 1 provides an income statement and balance sheet.

177

THE PDI SALES FORCE

PDI employed 14 salespeople. Exhibit 2 provides data on experience, age, sales, commissions, and expense. The president, Dean Hogarth, and his brother Bill, the sales manager, were both active in the sales function.

Salespeople who operated within the metropolitan area were assigned specific accounts, not geographic territories, although there was a general tendency to group accounts geographically.

The sales force was stable. Only two people had left in the past 4 years. New recruits were usually hired from among relatively young people who had some selling experience. The company had not usually hired salespeople from competitors. Bill Hogarth stated, "The good ones are too expensive, and we don't want the poor ones. In addition, when an average grade salesperson is hired from a competitor, he typically cannot hold onto his old accounts."

Generally younger recruits — with exp.

Sales trainees went through the following training program:

Training Program

1   Three to four months in the sample department learning the vast array of papers, the company, and the sample process

2   Three weeks on the incoming order desk to learn its function and gain some experience with customers

Exhibit 2 DATA ON THE SALES FORCE

Person	Years with PDI	Age	1974 actual sales ($1,000)	1974 actual margin	1974 budget margin	1974 commission	1974 expenses
Banks[a]	16	46	$ 264	$ 37,475	$ 36,874	$ 18,414	$ 3,522
Collins	28	59	$ 557	$ 94,806	87,150	24,027	2,456
Dow[b]	1/2	30	139	15,373			
Edmunds	12	47	818	122,443	185,473	35,701	1,904
Harvey	23	57	614	123,978	133,509	31,121	2,066
Hatch	23	50	604	111,452	130,965	27,998	2,128
Long	5	32	233	47,717	83,162	12,826	2,952
Moore	16	41	372	106,915	85,011	28,038	1,831
Needham	5	52	327	71,913	78,879	18,571	1,775
Phillip	12	47	332	59,348	38,433	17,764	3,544
Rice[b]	1	23	306	43,527	41,434		2,181
Serino	31	48	404	36,058	23,898	11,153	1,836
Thompson	11	43	590	105,464	138,622	27,990	1,949
Young	34	56	1,557	133,362	148,792	28,407	3,450
Total without Dow and Rice			$6,672	$1,047,931	$1,170,768	$282,010	$29,413
Total with Dow and Rice			$7,117	$1,106,831	$1,212,202	$282,010	$31,594

[a]Banks worked on a special commission arrangement because of special situations existing with some of his accounts.
[b]Dow and Rice were new salespeople and were paid a training salary, not a commission. In addition, some of the data for their performance were attributable to salespeople who were no longer with the company.
Note: The remainder of sales and margin was accounted for by house accounts serviced by PDI management. Expense data include auto allowance and reimbursable entertainment expenses.

3   Three weeks in the mill department, which ordered paper from the mills for inventory and direct shipments, arranged for technical support when necessary, and managed the PDI inventory

4   A few days watching an experienced salesperson make calls

5   Assignment of some smaller and inactive accounts as well as some better customers

During the period as a sales trainee each new trainee attended one or two mill-sponsored programs for paper salespeople. Each program lasted 1 week and was attended by sales trainees from paper merchants who represented the mill. In addition, each trainee was given several paper- and/or sales-related books to read.

Between 2 and 6 months after the salespersons received their accounts, they attended the Xerox Professional Selling Skills training program. The use of this program had begun in 1974.

Salespeople other than trainees were compensated by commission. The commission[2] on items shipped from inventory was 25 percent of the gross trading margin (GTM) after the GTM was reduced for the direct cost of order processing and delivery. The commission rate on direct shipments was 30 percent on the same basis. City salespeople received an auto allowance of $125 per month and the company paid 50 percent of all other business-related expenses (motel, entertainment, etc.). Country

[2]Some salespeople had special commission arrangements for some of their accounts.

salespeople worked on the same basis, but received $145 per month for auto expense.

Salespeople worked independently and were not visited by the sales manager or other managers. Every quarter the sales manager reviewed the performance of each salesperson on an account-by-account basis and discussed results with the person.

Sales meetings were held each Monday to discuss such new developments as price changes, special sales on excess inventory, and new products. At some meetings, mill sales representatives, who were sometimes not highly respected either by merchant or by printer personnel, spoke about their lines.

One salesperson specialized in selling to specifiers. On such sales he received 50 percent of the commission and the printer salesperson received 50 percent. Specifications customers and their orders tended to be large and for high-priced paper.

THE ROLE OF THE SALESPERSON

Bill Hogarth, the sales manager, described the job of a salesperson as being a mix of service and selling. "Among other things, he is responsible for his three prime sales aids: the price book, samples and dummies, and printed pieces." The price book was a loose-leaf book containing the current list prices. It had 227 pages, 4 by 8 inches in size, plus 24 pages of index. During the inflation of 1974, these books had to have new pages inserted about once each month. Each customer received a price book from each paper merchant who served him.

179

In addition, each printer had a collection of paper samples from each merchant. The samples, usually kept in a one-drawer metal file cabinet supplied by the merchant, included small sheets of each type, weight, and color of paper carried by the merchant. The mills supplied the samples in the form of small brochures for each line. Sometimes printers or specifiers asked for full-sized sheets of paper to show customers or to examine. In some other situations, such as more complicated jobs, they asked for dummies—unprinted but bound sets of sample paper in the size and configuration to be actually used. Thus, an annual report dummy might have two cover sheets and a dozen text sheets. The merchant's sample department maintained samples and prepared dummies.

Each mill also supplied printed matter to show the paper in use. Sometimes these were samples of pieces printed by a commercial printer for an actual customer. At other times, the mill had special pieces printed. These would typically have material of business interest (for example, a primer on direct mail marketing), of personal interest (for example, a description of woods for the amateur cabinetmaker), or of technical interest (for example, a variety of unusual printing techniques on a particular type of paper).

The young aggressive president of one printing company listed his requirements for a paper merchant in the following order: (1) price, (2) product lines carried and inventory stocked, and (3) salesperson. In talking about the salesperson he stated:

Requirements of a good paper merch.

I need someone who can keep me up to date on new developments For example, I want to know which paper will be in short supply, etc. I also need to know of new ideas and to see new samples that I can show to my customers. The salesperson must be able to obtain answers to my technical questions. I don't care whether he knows the answer himself but he must be able to get the answer for me. Some people like to be entertained. I don't. My dinners and evenings are for myself. On the other hand, I enjoy lunches and breakfasts with supplier salespeople. I like to see a supplier salesperson once a week if he has something to tell me or show me. Otherwise, I don't need to see him much.

I also like a salesperson who understands my customers' needs and where necessary can call on my customer to arrange the proper specifications.

180

Ideal Sales Person

Dean Hogarth described the ideal sales person as "hungry for the order and willing to provide the service necessary to get it." He went on to say, "On the other hand, he must be sincere and willing to say when his product won't do the job. He also must be prudent in making delivery promises."

Most commercial printers were small companies [for example, a $5-million (sales) company was a large printer]. In all, including the largest, top management was involved in selling. Most jobs were small (for example, a $10,000 sale was large), and quite different. Almost every printer purchased paper from several paper merchants.

Printers/ Buying Characteristics

Printers tended either to be general commercial printers or to specialize in a product line such as letterheads and business cards, checks, forms, etc. Larger ones often emphasized multicolor work, while smaller ones concentrated on 1-color jobs. Equipment cost had a great deal to do with such specialization. Small companies could not justify purchase of the large, fast 4-color presses and their supporting equipment.

In-house printing operations tended to perform relatively simple printing operations, ranging from one and two copy reproduction (for example, Xerox) to the production of simple brochures. Few had multicolor printing capability. Most tended to concentrate their purchases with one, or perhaps two, paper merchants. They tended to purchase standard grades and sizes of paper, ranging from inexpensive grades to very high-quality bond paper with high margins for the merchant.

TWENTY   Paper Distributors, Incorporated (B)

On Tuesday, January 28, 1975, and Wednesday, January 29, 1975, Frank Hatch, a salesperson for Paper Distributors, Inc., was accompanied by a casewriter while he covered his territory.

FRANK HATCH AND HIS TERRITORY

Frank Hatch had joined PDI in 1952, after graduating from the University of Pittsburgh, working as a salesperson for a tobacco manufacturer, and as an office manager of the local branch of an equipment supplier. He was 50 years old, married, and had two sons, one in graduate school and one in college.

PDI management described Hatch as family oriented, very ethical, and well respected among his customers. He was seen as methodical in his approach and not particularly amenable to being managed. One manager stated: "He isn't money motivated, and he will not sacrifice his free time for sales. On the other hand, he puts in a full day and provides a great deal of service."

PDI management had received numerous unsolicited compliments about Mr. Hatch from his customers. When management had attempted to move some of his larger accounts to Bill Hogarth, the sales manager, the customers had objected and were returned to Mr. Hatch. The company's concern at the time had been Mr. Hatch's apparent inability to gain as much volume as PDI desired from larger accounts.

Mr. Hatch described his approach as one of service, frequent calls, and honesty. He usually spent one lunch time per week with a customer. Major customers were entertained one or two evenings each per year at his home, if he felt compatible with them. Such activities took one or two evenings per month. He also took customers to about six football games per year. And he provided baseball and hockey tickets to customers desiring them, but did not accompany them to these games.

He covered about 70 accounts of a mixed variety. About half were in the city and half on the outskirts. His accounts included two large 4-color printers, one large forms printer, several medium-large color printers, no specifiers, and no publishers. He had about 12 in-house printing operations.

Exhibit 1 provides a list of accounts and their volume and Exhibit 2 a commission and expense history. Exhibit 3 is a log of Mr. Hatch's activities on the afternoon of Tuesday, January 28, and Wednesday, January 29, 1975.

Exhibit 1 ACCOUNT LIST—FRANK HATCH

Account	1974 budget margin	1974 actual margin	1974 actual sales
Budget margin of $10,000 and over			
Major Printing Company[a]	$ 14,850	$ 16,753	$ 90,660
Piawarski Business Forms	10.740	7,672	73,419
Slater Printing Company[a]	10,000	7,154	42,620
Hillside Printing Company[a]	10,000	8,061	30,880
Subtotal	$ 45,590	$ 39,640	$237,579
Budget margin of $1,000–$9,999			
Donovan Printing Company[a]	$ 8,400	$ 8,905	$ 33,062
Grossman Business Forms	6,955	4,409	132,890
Rosenfeld Printing Company	6,140	3,635	13,231
Color Printing Company	5,940	3,272	10,571
Jupiter Lithography	5,330	3,937	19,270
Allied Equipment	5,000	2,040	5,584
Mutual of Pittsburgh	4,620	2,916	8,980
Meddletown Engraving	4,380	3,577	11,979
Horatio Truck Company	3,370	2,320	6,241
Simon Printing Company[a]	3,260	2,581	9,537
Northeast Airlines	2,250	2,593	9,254
Better Business Bureau	2,060	3,199	13,381
United Brotherhood Insurance[a]	2,035	978	2,674
Hudson Printing Company[a]	1,900	1,039	4,087
Mohawk Associates[a]	1,700	2,125	5,964
Bennett Manufacturing	1,665	2,304	7,775
XYZ Litho	1,630	3,524	10,507
Busby Berkley Manufacturing	1,560	1,227	4,104
Midwest Art	1,200	2,370	6,610
Boggs Business Equipment	1,125	822	7,559
Stiffler Printing Company[a]	1,100	793	1,983
Jevelekian Press	1,050	1,026	2,596
Smith Company[a]	1,035	1,051	3,548
Eagle Heights Hotel	1,000	775	2,131
Subtotal	$ 74,705	$ 61,148	$333,518
Budget margin below $1,000			
38 accounts	$ 10,670	$ 10,394	$ 32,767
Total	**$130,965**	**$111,452**	**$603,864**

[a]Accounts visited during the time covered by Exhibit 3.
Notes: These data were gathered from a quarterly report which presented the accounts in alphabetical order.

The 38 accounts with a budgeted margin below $1,000 include the following, which were visited during the time covered by Exhibit 3:

Account	1974 budget margin	1974 actual margin	1974 actual sales
Kaufman Printing Company	$ 420	$ 226	$ 740
Loeb Printing Company	725	1,091	3,022
Nelson Printing Company	520	386	934
O'Hara Business Service	600	419	1,486
Parkway Printers	240	291	655
Shea Printing Company	430	454	1,172
Stahler Printing Company	400	298	734
Total	**$3,335**	**$3,165**	**$8,743**

Exhibit 2 SALES, COMMISSION, AND EXPENSE HISTORY—
FRANK HATCH

	1972	1973	1974
Commissions	$22,403	$24,746	$ 27,998
Auto allowance	1,500	1,500	1,500
Entertainment expense[a]	511	587	628
Total	**$24,414**	**$26,833**	**$ 30,126**
Actual sales			$603,864
Actual margin			$111,452
Budget margin			$130,965

[a]The entertainment expense is the amount which is reimbursed. The actual expenditures were twice that amount, with Mr. Hatch paying one-half and PDI paying one-half.

Exhibit 3
Log of Mr. Hatch's Activities

On Tuesday, January 28, 1975, the following activities took place.

1:05 P.M. Left office and drove to call 1 on edge of downtown Pittsburgh.

Call 1 Arrived at Stahler Printing, a two-man printing company, the majority of
1:20 P.M. whose work was with one stationer located in the same building. Total
paper purchases were estimated at $10,000, of which $700 came from
PDI. Mr. Hatch expected this to be a "short call," primarily to update the
price book and to show Mr. Stahler a new brochure on pressure-sensitive
labels.

183

When he arrived, the owner was on the telephone. Mr. Hatch said
hello to the other printer who greeted him sourly, and waved to the owner
who smiled warmly. Mr. Hatch waited for a few minutes and then mo-
tioned to Mr. Stahler that he would go and change the price book. Mr.
Hatch rummaged through the group of price books in a desk drawer,
found the PDI book, took out the obsolete pages and replaced each with a
new page. He then replaced the book toward the bottom of the drawer. He
returned to Mr. Stahler who at 1:23 was off the telephone.

They discussed Mr. Stahler's new granddaughter after Mr. Hatch had
mistakenly asked about his new grandson. After seeing the baby's picture,
Mr. Hatch discussed its effect on Mr. Stahler's family.

Before leaving, Mr. Hatch showed the label brochure and sample and
described its advantages for Mr. Stahler's customers as well as its ease in
printing. After a brief discussion of label printing with Mr. Stahler, Mr.
Hatch left.

1:30 P.M. Walked to call 2.

Call 2 Arrived at Shea Printing, a somewhat larger company which purchased an
1:35 P.M. estimated $20,000 per year in paper ($1,200 from PDI), most of it in high
margin, pressure-sensitive labels, and specialty papers. Mr. Hatch expected to gain little additional business because the major portion of
Shea's purchases were from a competitor who had Shea do much of its

printing. Mr. Hatch was greeted in the office by Mr. Shea's two daughters. He spent 10 minutes chatting with them about the weather, the economy, and the printing business. He heard from them that Mr. Shea had been concerned about the color of his last shipment of safety paper[a]—it had been orangeish rather than the standard pink. He explained in detail that color consistency in safety paper was poor because of the manufacturing process. He left the young women two copies of an artistic calendar manufactured each month by one of the paper companies. He also updated the price book.

Mr. Hatch then visited with Mr. Shea and discussed his business. He asked Mr. Shea about the safety paper problem, and they both looked at the paper together. Mr. Hatch explained the color consistency situation in technical detail and agreed with Mr. Shea that "this is the worst discrepancy I've seen." Mr. Shea stated that he did not think it would bother the customer.

Mr. Hatch discussed the price changes and explained that one change was a decrease in material Mr. Shea used regularly. He presented the pressure-sensitive label material, and then left.

2:00 P.M. Drove to call 3.

Call 3 Arrived at Stiffler Printing which, he estimated, purchased $18,000 per
2:10 P.M. year in high margin, primarily high-quality and specialty papers ($2,000 from PDI). Mr. Stiffler operated an artist's studio in conjunction with his printing operation. The receptionist-secretary explained to Mr. Hatch that he was at home working on a rush job for a major customer. Mr. Hatch greeted the printers in the shop and the owner's son. He changed the price book and listened to the secretary describe a problem she had in working with a specialized paper. He discussed the technique she had used and said it seemed correct. He suggested that she call him the next time she was to work with the stock so that he could see the problem firsthand. He showed her the new pressure-sensitive label brochure and sample.

Call 4 Walked down two flights of stairs to next call.
2:20 P.M.   At Hudson Printing, a specialist in letterheads and business cards who purchased an estimated $20,000 of high-quality paper ($4,000 from PDI), he greeted three generations of Hudsons (grandfather, father, and son) and printers. He changed the price book and chatted and teased the owners. The eldest Hudson discussed the changes he had seen in 55 years as a printer.

Call 5 Walked across the hall to a one-man shop. Mr. Hatch said he called here
2:35 P.M. only because it was so accessible. He estimated Parkway's purchases at $5,000 per year ($700 from PDI). He quickly revised the price book and then explained the pressure-sensitive label material. The owner asked Mr. Hatch about some paper, and Mr. Hatch responded in hurried but polite fashion.

2:45 P.M. Drove to call 6.

184

[a]Safety paper is the paper on which checks are printed.

Call 6 Arrived at United Brotherhood Insurance Company whose paper pur-
2:55 P.M. purchases he estimated at $6,000 ($2,700 from PDI). This was a complete
in-house printing operation which tended to purchase inexpensive papers.
Mr. Hatch stated to the casewriter that he expected to receive no higher
percentage of the business because a competitor's vice president was on
the company's board of directors. The presses were not running. Mr. Hatch
was greeted warmly by the manager and press operator. He changed the
price book, but he did not attempt to sell the labels. (He explained later
to the casewriter that the company had no need for the product.) The press
operators chatted with Mr. Hatch who extricated himself as soon as
possible.

Not Aggressive Assumed he Couldn't get more biz.

3:10 P.M. Returned to car, explained to casewriter that he would skip two calls to
save time,[b] and drove to call 7.

Call 7 Arrived at Major Printing Company, one of the largest printers in Pitts-
3:20 P.M. burgh with an estimated paper purchase of $1 million ($90,700 from PDI).
Mr. Hatch explained to the casewriter that most of the paper, about
$700,000, was purchased at cut prices from a highly aggressive competi-
tor. The other 20 percent went to another competitor whose sales manager
was a close friend of Charles Harrison, the president of Major. Mr. Harrison
and the competitive sales manager had recently been on a joint vacation
with their wives in the West Indies. Mr. Hatch also explained that he
(Mr. Hatch) and Mr. Harrison had been fraternity brothers in college.

Losing out on biz?

185

In this plant, the factory was quite distinct from the office in contrast
to the smaller shops. The estimators and salespeople had desks in one
large area.

Mr. Hatch began with an estimator, Abe, and thanked him for a
previous order. He discussed another large order which would require
PDI to carry a special 5,000-pound inventory. Mr. Hatch gave Abe a
sample of the paper he was suggesting for the job, indicated PDI's willingness to keep the backup inventory, and described his interest in getting the
business. He then showed the pressure-sensitive label brochure.

Next he saw Bill, another estimator. He described the label and, as
he had in most calls, asked if "there is anything on the hook" which he
could help with.

He then went to Carl, a salesperson. He gave Carl a dummy of an
annual report he had requested. He also described and showed a sample
of a new color recently introduced by Quality Coated Papers. Carl was
interested so Mr. Hatch called his sample department and asked them to
prepare a sample for him immediately. He also promised to find out the
amount and location of the mill inventories of the item.

Mr. Hatch then presented a set of samples of a less-expensive coated
paper supplied by another mill. He explained that it was a relatively cheap
way to obtain color paper instead of stark white.

The discussion focused almost solely on business. Mr. Hatch told

---

[b]It was apparent to the casewriter that his presence slowed Mr. Hatch down because he was an
object of curiosity and interest. Customers wanted to know his function and discussed travel and
business with him.

Carl that he would deliver the paper sample he was having prepared early the following morning.

3:40 P.M. In car to make call 8.

Call 8 Arrived at Donovan Printing, with estimated paper purchases of $50,000
3:50 P.M. ($33,000 from PDI). The major purchasing influence, the production manager, was ill at home, so Mr. Hatch chatted with several people, primarily with Mr. Donovan. During this time, Mr. Hatch called his office, learned of a customer wanting to speak to him, called the customer, and got a $200 order.

4:10 P.M. In car to return to office.

4:15 P.M. Back at office to return other calls, obtain the sample for Major Printing (call 7), and complete any paperwork. Since most printers left the office by 4:15, he could not call many back.

4:45 P.M. Left for home.

The following activities took place on Wednesday, January 29, 1975.

7:40 A.M. Left home.

Call 9 Arrived at Major Printing Company to deliver the sample requested by
8:20 A.M. Carl. Mr. Hatch also informed Carl of the schedule of a delivery he had been expecting. He also said good morning to all of the office.

8:23 A.M. In car to office.

8:32 A.M. Arrived in office to pick up messages, gather samples and literature. He called a customer to tell when an expected order would be delivered. He also received a telephone order for $250. He received a request from a customer for a quote on some printing supplies. He checked inventory, delivery, price, and a change of name in the product with the order department and then called the customer to provide the information. He received a $70 order from the customer. He called another customer to provide data that had been requested. He gathered data from another customer to help the order department develop a price quotation. He gave the order department copies of orders and arranged for a customer to take photographs of PDI's warehouse for a promotional brochure he was making. Finally, he prepared an itinerary so that the PDI receptionist could contact him.

9:20 A.M. Left office for call 10.

Call 10 Arrived at Nelson Printers which, he estimated, purchased $15,000 in
9:40 A.M. paper ($900 from PDI). He showed a printed brochure on the new Quality Coated Papers color. He also completed arrangements for a mill visit for the owner's son. Then he showed Mr. Nelson a list of sale products being closed out of inventory. He described those he thought would be of greatest interest to Mr. Nelson and indicated the price savings. He left a list with Mr. Nelson. He also reiterated the usefulness of the new Quality Control color and pushed the usefulness of the same inexpensive coated color paper as he had at Major. Here he emphasized readability, looks, ink

hold, and usefulness for certain printing operations. He also presented his pressure-sensitive labels.

He spent some time comforting the secretary and wife of the owner who had recently lost her mother.

Call 11
10:00 A.M.   Walked to call 11. Chatted with the three people at Loeb Printers (estimated paper purchases of $8,000 with $3,000 from PDI). Mr. Hatch explained to Mr. Loeb that he had arranged to obtain some paper from another printer's inventory until one of Mr. Loeb's shipments arrived. Mr. Hatch stated that he would not lie to Mr. Loeb about the delivery date.

Call 12
10:10 A.M.   Walked to call 12. Arrived at Kaufman Printing which purchased about $5,000 worth of paper, including $700 from PDI. It specialized in unusual printing operations and used high margin paper as well as a great deal of customer-supplied paper. Mr. Hatch talked to the president about a technical problem at some length. He offered to obtain some particular samples and work with the company in their use. As was his usual practice, he distributed his calendars to the people, especially office personnel, and greeted all press operators.

10:30 A.M.   In car to call 13.

Call 13
10:40 A.M.   Arrived at Simon Company, with estimated paper purchase of $75,000 ($9,500 from PDI). On his way from his car to the office, he met the vice president and a salesperson who were leaving to make calls. They exchanged pleasantries and discussed some pending business. Mr. Hatch asked if he could help them with anything at that time, and the vice president said that he would telephone him later in the day.

Mr. Hatch went into the office and waited while the bookkeeper-receptionist and office manager discussed a bookkeeping discrepancy. After 10 minutes of waiting, he talked to the production manager about some technical considerations and explained to the office manager the benefits of the new Quality Coated color and the pressure-sensitive labels.

10:55 A.M.   In car for call 14.

Call 14
11:05 A.M.   Arrived at Slater Brothers with estimated purchases of $1 million in paper ($42,600 from PDI). Mr. Hatch explained that Slater purchased large amounts of inexpensive paper in rolls. PDI was not traditionally in this business and could not supply it during the 1973–1974 paper shortage. Slater had a long-standing relationship with one paper merchant. Mr. Hatch called on Arthur Carr, the purchasing agent. He delivered some full-year calendars Mr. Carr had requested, as well as several of the one-month calendars. Mr. Hatch invited Mr. Carr to lunch, but he declined, saying that he had other plans.

They talked about business conditions, and then Mr. Hatch showed Mr. Carr a very high-quality brochure prepared by another printer on one of PDI's Quality Coated paper lines. Mr. Carr examined it under a magnifying glass, and they discussed the paper and its printing. Mr. Hatch used this discussion to lead to a presentation of his new Quality Coated color. He also presented his pressure-sensitive label line.

187

They discussed competitive activities. Mr. Hatch offered to supply some samples for special applications. He also asked for orders for jobs currently pending. Before leaving Mr. Hatch again asked Mr. Carr about lunch and was again turned down.

Perceived
Lack of Confidence? During the exchange the casewriter noted a lack of confidence in Mr. Hatch and some amount of discomfort between both parties. In the car after leaving Slater, Mr. Hatch denied that the casewriter had interpreted the situation correctly. He described Mr. Carr as easy going and easy to do business with.

11:30 A.M. In car to return to office.

11:45 A.M. Arrived at office. At the office he did the following: returned a telephone call and gathered the information for a bid on $160,000 worth of paper. This would be very price sensitive. Received a telephone order for $70.

1. Personable
2. Detail-Oriented Returned a telephone call and received an order from United Brotherhood Insurance (call 6) for $250. Returned a telephone call to Parkway Printers
3. Good Follow-up (call 5) and arranged to send a sample on an order for $250. Choosing the right sample with the sample department took a good deal of time. Returned a telephone call and explained to a customer the status of an inquiry. Received a call requesting a quotation. Returned a telephone call and received a request for several quotations on different alternatives.

188

1:00 P.M. Left office.

The following is a synopsis of the afternoon's calls in suburban Pittsburgh.

1:10 P.M. Arrived at restaurant for lunch.

1:45 P.M. In car to call 15.

Call 15 Arrived at Smith Company, with estimated purchases of $35,000 ($3,500
2:00 P.M. from PDI).

2:10 P.M. In car to call 16.

Call 16 Arrived at O'Hara Business Service, with estimated purchases of $30,000
2:20 P.M. of mostly inexpensive paper ($1,500 from PDI).

2:55 P.M. In car to call 17.

Call 17 Arrived at Hillside Press, with estimated purchase of $90,000 ($30,900
3:15 P.M. from PDI).

3:35 P.M. In car to call 18.

Call 18 Arrived at Mohawk Printing, with estimated purchases of $50,000 ($6,000
3:55 P.M. from PDI).

4:15 P.M. Left for office.

4:30 P.M. Arrived back at office, found a $1,500 order.

General comments: Mr. Hatch was almost universally warmly greeted by office personnel and press people. He knew almost everyone by name and gave calendars to almost all customers. He also asked almost all customers if there was "something on the hook" he could help them with.

TWENTY-ONE Account Management

Account management is the process of turning prospects into accounts and of servicing existing accounts in such a manner that they remain long-term, loyal accounts, continually buying more from the selling company. Selling is a part of account management. But account management is much more than selling. Some of the aspects beyond selling are the responsibility of the salesperson in his normal servicing of the account. Others are beyond the typical scope of the salesperson.

Account management is especially important in business selling— one firm selling to another—because, in almost all instances, the selling process is a continuing one. A supplier will sell the same type of merchandise to a buyer over and over again. Since the market for most products is quite finite, each seller must constantly face the same buyers. This is less true for the consumer market where there are many more buying units and where the "rebuy" process is infrequent for many products, such as houses, televisions, etc. Many of the subjects to be discussed here, however, are applicable to consumer selling.

189

THE RELATIONSHIP BETWEEN SALES AND ACCOUNT MANAGEMENT

The truly astute firm is not interested in only making sales; it wants to build account relationships. Account relationships are a major asset of the successful firm. Although account relationships are not a tangible asset which accountants record on a financial statement, they are valuable to the company because they represent the ability to sell merchandise and services in the future relatively easily. If the company does a decent, not necessarily outstanding, job of servicing the customer, the customer is likely to continue to purchase from the seller unless a product or service with a demonstrably clear advantage is offered. In high risk situations and in major sales, the customers are especially hesitant to change suppliers. Thus, the established firm must protect its customer base, and the new growing firm, in addition to attracting new customers, must maintain its position with established customers.

The account relationships, of course, must result in sales sooner or later. The tradeoff between immediate sales and long-term account relationships leads to a phenomenon called the *Pyrrhic sale*. The term is borrowed from military strategy in which a Pyrrhic victory is one so costly to the protagonist that although he wins the battle, he "loses" the war.

There can be a definite tradeoff between "forcing" a customer to buy something and developing a long-term relationship with that customer. Because the customer is in the position of repeatedly being able to purchase the product, the salesperson must show discipline. He must be willing to forego a sale that is not in the best long-term interest of the account and therefore of his relationship with the account. In forcing a marginal sale, the salesperson often destroys credibility and the opportunity for future sales. The salesperson who can control the desire for the sale in favor of a desire to help the account builds a relationship. For example, the apparel salesperson who is willing to tell a customer that some items in her line do not sell well at retail, in spite of their apparent appeal, is helping the customer and herself over the long run. Or, picture the response to the pump salesperson who says, "Yes, we offer the best pumps for your needs a, b, and c, but unfortunately our pumps are not as good in application d as those offered by competitors x and y." The Pyrrhic sale, on the other hand, is one in which the salesperson gets the sale and loses the account.

190

THE SALESPERSON'S ROLE

Account relationships depend upon more than the salesperson's prudence in pushing for orders. The salesperson can perform functions for the customer which make the salesperson a valuable adjunct to the customer's organization.

One of the most important roles of a salesperson is that of ombudsman. In that role the salesperson is the *customer's representative* to the selling company, and the job is to ensure that the firm is meeting the needs of the buyer. For example, the salesperson is responsible for arranging for the return, repair, or replacement of damaged merchandise and for expediting shipments which are either late or needed quickly. Often, the salesperson is the customer's representative to the credit and billing departments. Obviously, the more effective the salesperson is in dealing with his or her own company the more effective he or she can be in helping customers.

Many salespeople make it a specific duty to get to know order entry, credit, expediting, and shipping personnel. They attempt to involve these people in the customer's concerns and to alert them to the customer's needs.

The salespeople's roles go beyond the function of ombudsmen. Consumer goods salespeople can be responsible for providing advice or services, or both. It is typical for the better apparel and furniture salespeople to help buyers choose those items which will sell best in their stores. In addition, they will provide advertising and display counseling.

Their purpose becomes selling *through* the store, not *to* the store, and they do those things which enhance the store's ability to successfully sell their products. Another assistance provided in many situations is careful choice of outlets. Salespeople who place their lines in stores of all types (good and bad, high quality and low quality, etc.) often find their best potential customers unhappy because of the poor image the products gain from poor stores.

Some consumer goods salespeople also perform more physically oriented services, usually including display setup and inventory control. Cole National salespeople, for example, are expected to service the Cole key-making machine, inventory keys, and other Cole products, and to maintain displays.

Some companies build their marketing strategy around strong sales force service. L'eggs stockings and hosiery strategy, for example, depends upon heavy sales force service.

Industrial salespeople are also responsible for both advisory and service functions. Many provide applications engineering support, helping customers design their products around the selling company's product. Some salespeople supervise applications engineers. This is typical in the minicomputer industry. Capital goods salespeople provide advice on the use of their product and sometimes provide actual supervision during start-up. Some capital goods salespeople provide maintenance services and others arrange for it. Industrial salespeople are often responsible for maintaining inventory control. Parts suppliers often must check supply room stock and write orders for approval of customers. Again, the importance of the services varies with the situation and the company's marketing strategy.

191

It is typical for salespeople, both industrial and consumer, to provide training to customers. Industrial salespeople often train machine operators while consumer goods salespeople train retail clerks in how to sell their merchandise. Salespeople who call on distributors often provide management advice and assistance.

BEYOND THE SALESPERSON

The salesperson should not be the only important aspect of the firm's account management procedures and policies. Many marketers develop special programs to help their customers. Some wholesalers, for example, provide such things as site-selection advice and store-layout help to their retailers. Many firms that sell through distributors provide sales training programs to those distributors.[1] Other firms attempt to help their

[1]For a brief description of an excellent example, see "Sales Training: Down to Basics with Retail Clerks," *Sales Management*, July 9, 1973.

dealers manage inventories. Special packaging may help some accounts. A producer of materials such as nuts and bolts may be willing to package his wares in containers capable of fitting specially designed machinery which uses the products.

Delivery and credit are two other important account management techniques. Fast delivery or emergency backup of spare-parts inventories can cut down the dealer and/or user inventory carrying costs. Special credit arrangements can help customers with their businesses. One important credit arrangement is "dating." Datings are credit extensions provided to highly seasonal industries, such as toys, to encourage dealers to accept early delivery.

Some of these programs may be companywide, while others may be directed toward special categories of distributors or even toward particular accounts. It is important to bear in mind that all customers who compete with each other must be treated equally under the Robinson-Patman Act.

It is also important to realize that most of these programs cost money. Sales managers must make careful tradeoffs between their costs and the benefits to their customers. The analytical, creative, and flexible sales manager can probably find a large number of approaches which in fact meet these criteria.

The nonselling parts of the firm have an important role to play in account management. The rude receptionist and the truculent delivery person have probably lost as many accounts as the insensitive salesperson.

PERSONAL VERSUS ORGANIZATIONAL NEEDS

The people who make purchase decisions are indeed people and as such they have personal needs. An important part of the salesperson's task is to fill those needs. Different industries have different traditions, but almost all salespeople use personal interest, lunches, and industry "gossip" as appeals to specific customers. In some industries, entertainment is also important. After a point, of course, such expenditures can get beyond the bounds of propriety and eventually become illegal. Bribing a buyer is called *commercial bribery* and is illegal.[2] There is often a delicate line between treating buyers well and bribing them. Lately the trend has generally been away from lavish entertainment and personal attention.

For most buyers, their greatest personal needs are to do a good job for the organization. Thus, the salespersons often do the best job of serving buyers' personal needs by serving those of their organizations.

[2]See the note "Legal and Ethical Considerations."

CONCLUDING NOTE

Account management is the very essence of the concern of sales managers. All sales management policies should focus on account management. The ultimate success or failure of the sales force is judged primarily upon its ability to manage account relationships.

BIBLIOGRAPHY

Andelson, R. P.: "Harnessing Engineers and Scientists to the Sales Effort," from *New Ideas for Successful Marketing*, American Marketing Association, June 1966, pp. 204–215; reprinted in John M. Rathmell (ed.), *Salesmanship: Selected Readings*, Homewood, Ill.: Irwin, 1969, pp. 129–140.

Belasco, James A.: "The Salesman's Role Revisited," *Journal of Marketing*, vol. 30, no. 2, April 1966, pp. 608; reprinted in Kenneth R. Davis and Frederick E. Webster, Jr. (eds.), *Readings in Sales Force Management*, New York: Ronald Press, 1968, pp. 41–46.

Cascino, A. E.: "Continuous Innovation in Customer Service," in Proceedings of 1963 Summer Conference, American Marketing Association, pp. 673–683.

Howard, William C.: "Generating Stronger Distributor Support for the Product," presented at the 1973 Conference Board Meeting Conference, *Giving an Extra Boost to the Sales Effort*, New York, October 17, 1973.

Kelley, Eugene J., and William Legea: "Basic Duties of the Modern Sales Department," *Industrial Marketing*, vol. 45, no. 4, April 1960, pp. 68–74, 78; reprinted in Harper W. Boyd and Robert T. Davis (eds.), *Readings in Sales Management*, Homewood, Ill.: Irwin, 1970, pp. 234–239.

Pegram, Roger M.: *Selling and Servicing the National Account*, New York: The Conference Board, 1972.

Pruden, Henry O.: "The Outside Salesman: Inorganizational Link," *California Management Review*, vol. 12, no. 2, Winter 1969, pp. 57–66.

193

TWENTY-TWO   Sales Promotion

The term "sales promotion" is not always clear. Some companies use it in a general sense to include personal selling, advertising, and supplementary selling activities *other than* personal selling and advertising.

Probably the most generally accepted definition is that (1) it consists of communication and promotional activities outside of personal selling and advertising, and (2) its primary objective is a *short-term* increase in sales or distribution.

Sales promotion activities take place both in consumer goods markets and in industrial goods markets. The consumer goods promotions are usually more complex and sophisticated. They will be discussed first.

CONSUMER GOODS PROMOTION

Sales promotion activities for consumer goods are usually classified as consumer, trade, or sales force promotions. Some promotions, especially those aimed at salespeople and the trade, are usually designed to "sell in" merchandise so as to increase distribution. Others, especially those aimed at consumers and occasionally some aimed at the trade, are designed to "sell out" merchandise, that is, to create consumer level sales. Often companies will coordinate sell in and sell out programs. For example, a company might run a "Hawaiian Holiday" promotion which includes trips to Hawaii for its salespeople who achieve certain sales goals and similar trips for winners of a consumer sweepstakes or contest. Moreover, an off-invoice merchandise allowance might be offered to wholesalers or retailers to get them to purchase large quantities of the product, and display allowances and special point-of-purchase materials might be provided for the retailers to encourage consumer purchases and participation.

194

Consumer Promotions

Although, in a sense, all sales promotion devices are aimed at ultimately increasing consumer sales, nevertheless, certain devices are designed more specifically than others to attract the consumer to a particular product. The choice of a consumer sales promotion device varies with the nature of the product, its market, and the competitive situation it faces. Three devices—samples, price-off coupons, and refund offers— are most frequently used to generate *trials* for new or existing products, while price-off deals, premiums, and contests or sweepstakes are most frequently employed to generate *repeat purchases* and therefore increase the use of a product.

Free samples might be mailed, delivered door to door, placed in bins in retail stores, or attached to or inserted in another package. While sampling is one of the most effective devices for getting consumers to try a product, it usually requires a long lead time to develop programs and is very expensive.

Coupons are certificates which, when presented for redemption at a retail store, entitle the bearer to a stated savings on the purchase of a specific product. Coupons may be issued by either manufacturers or retailers. If the coupon is issued by a manufacturer, the retailer, after taking the coupon in part payment for a purchase, sends it to the manufacturer for reimbursement plus handling fee (usually about 5 cents for each redeemed coupon). If the coupon is issued by a retailer, it is often issued for a kind of product rather than for a specific brand. Coupons can be quickly activated, and their cost is very low. While samples usually produce a higher degree of trial, coupons generally create more triers per dollar spent.[1] The negative side of coupons includes long lapses in redemption time, susceptibility to counterfeit coupon rings, and misredemption (retailers applying them against the wrong product or redeeming them for cash). Furthermore, they are, in a sense, little more than price reductions, and price-cutting in any form tends to be rejected by some marketers.

Money-refund offers are propositions in which a sum of money (occasionally the full purchase price) is returned by mail to participants who mail in proof of purchase, such as a box top. Money-refund offers when used alone generate few redemptions and are thought to have little pulling power. Their chief attribute is their low cost to manufacturers.

195

Price-off deals offer consumers a certain amount of money off the regular price of a product and state the amount on the product's label. These devices are often called *cents-off deals* or *price packs*. Price-off deals are the most controversial of all consumer sale promotions. They are strong trial-gaining devices, encourage quantity purchasing by the trade, earn special display locations in stores, and are highly controllable by the manufacturer. On the other hand, frequent price-off promotions tend to cheapen a product's image, are self-defeating in as much as they offer price reductions to regular customers (many of whom would otherwise purchase the product at the normal price), create only short-lived sales increases, and create additional handling problems for retailers. Furthermore, price-off deals are frequently the object of deceptive practices in that retailers merely raise the supposed "regular" price of the product. Federal Trade Commission regulations now require that the sale price of a product must indeed be different from the established price. However, policing the large number of price-off deals is a difficult task, and additional problems arise with new products that do not have established prices. Usually, price-off deals cannot be offered until 60 or 90 days after a product's introduction.

Premiums are items of merchandise offered free or at a low cost as a bonus to purchasers of a particular product. The most effective premiums are those which offer an obvious, easily understood, and immediately available bonus. Reusable containers, for example, have proved to be

[1]See Luick and Ziegler, p. 48, in the Bibliography at the end of this note.

extremely strong premiums as have so-called in-pack, on-pack, and near-pack premiums. As their names suggest, these are gifts placed within, attached to, or located near the product being sold. Because visibility tends to increase the impact of the premiums, plastic packages known as "blister packs" (clear plastic over an item attached to cardboard) and "shrink wraps" (clear plastic wrapped around two items to hold them together) are frequently used for on-pack premiums. Because near-pack premiums require a retailer to allot special space for them and his salespeople to handle the premiums, they are recommended only for products whose volume and profit are of significant importance to the retailer.

Free-in-the-mail premiums are gifts sent by return mail to consumers who send in a request for them and include a proof of purchase. *Self-liquidating premiums* are items offered at well below their normal retail price but at a price high enough to cover the wholesale cost of the merchandise to the manufacturer who runs the promotion. Other costs, such as displays, application blank pads, promotion design, etc., are typically borne by the manufacturer running the promotion as part of its sales promotion budget. In some promotions, the manufacturer and the consumer share the cost of the item. Self-liquidating premiums are by far the most frequently used, even though a redemption rate of 2 percent is usually the maximum that can be expected.[2]

Contests and sweepstakes are also major consumer-oriented promotion devices. These differ in that in a contest the participants compete for a prize or prizes on the basis of their skill in fulfilling a certain requirement, usually analytical or creative. In a sweepstakes, participants merely submit their names to have them included in a drawing of prizewinners. Sweepstakes cannot legally require purchase or other significant expenditure of time or effort because to do so puts them in the category of a lottery which is, in general, a form of illegal gambling. The contest avoids this problem because the winner is not chosen by chance but on the basis of demonstrated skill. Many contests require purchase of the product.

Industry experts tend to believe that contests stimulate purchases, since that is usually a requirement of entry, and because entering the contest usually involves significant thought and effort. A contestant, for example, must spend time thinking of an answer "in 25 words or less." Contests, however, typically receive less than 10 percent of the response of sweepstakes.

In the past, legal problems with contests and sweepstakes arose when promoters overstated the value of the prizes, misstated the rules and requirements or presented them in opaque language, or overstated the opportunities for winning.

196

[2]*Ibid.*, p. 75.

Another common consumer promotion device is the *demonstration*, that is, actually showing products in use. As with any promotion that uses direct labor, the cost of demonstrations is quite high. However, for some products, they are one of the most efficient means of promotion. Other very frequently used devices are *point-of-purchase* (POP), often called *point-of-sale* (POS), displays. These include outside signs, window displays, all kinds of counter pieces, display racks, self-service cartons, shelf strips, and overhead banners. Similar to these are catalogs, various consumer literature, and price lists.

TRADE PROMOTIONS

Trade promotions are devices designed to obtain special short-term merchandising support from retailers or wholesalers. While some people consider trade deals to be little less than bribery, others feel they are highly acceptable and productive merchandising incentives. Trade promotions generally fall into three categories, according to their objectives.

The first category consists of deals or merchandising devices designed to encourage a wholesaler or retailer to carry a particular product. One such deal is the *buying allowance* (often called *off-invoice allowance*), a short-term offer of a stated reduction in price for a certain quantity of a product purchased. Sometimes buying allowances are escalated—a manufacturer might offer 25 cents off each case if a retailer purchases one size of a brand, 50 cents per case if he buys two sizes, and so on. This is more controversial than the simple buying allowance, however, because many feel that it constitutes unusual and unwarranted pressure from a supplier. Another merchandise deal is the *count and recount*, an offer of a certain amount of money for each unit of merchandise moved out of a wholesaler's or retailer's warehouse in a specified period of time. It involves a salesperson's taking inventory at the beginning and again at the end of a sale. Yet another merchandise deal is the *buy-back allowance*, an event which immediately follows another trade deal and offers a certain reduction in price for new purchases based on (but not exceeding) the quantity of purchases made on the first deal. This device is not used very often. The fourth merchandise deal is the *free-goods* deal, an offer of a certain amount of a product to wholesalers or retailers at no cost to them, but dependent on the purchase of a stated amount of the same or another product. This differs from the previous three deals only in that goods, rather than money, are given.

The second category of trade promotions consists of deals used to induce retailers to promote a product through advertising and display. The first of these is the *merchandise allowance*, a short-term, contractual agreement through which a manufacturer compensates wholesalers or

197

retailers for "features"—for example, advertising or in-store displays of the products. Proof of performance is an essential factor in merchandise allowances. If it is an advertising allowance, for instance, this proof usually takes the form of a "tear sheet" of the advertisement showing the manufacturer's product or a radio or television affidavit of broadcasting with the invoice. On display features, retailers furnish written certification or pictures showing compliance with the terms of the agreement.The second device in this category is *cooperative advertising*, a long-term contract in which a manufacturer pays an allowance based on the quantity of merchandise a retailer orders, and the retailer runs advertisements for both his store and the manufacturer's product with the allowance. In practice, retailers are not paid until the ads are run and they submit proof of performance. This is one of the most widely used of all trade promotions. The final device in this category is *dealer-listing promotions*. These are advertisements placed by a manufacturer, carrying a message on a particular product, and announcing the names and sometimes the addresses of retailers who stock the product. Retailers receive no payment of money or goods in this promotion. In fact, sometimes they contribute funds to help pay for the listings.

198

Cooperative advertising and merchandising allowance programs are difficult to control and police. It is a legal necessity as well as good business to ensure that retailers are paid only for services performed. Sometimes, manufacturers who are zealous in their control find themselves in adversary relationships with customers. Several service companies whose primary business is policing cooperaive advertising and merchandising allowances have developed. They take care of the meticulous detail of these programs and deal with the channels of distribution on disputes over reimbursement, thus protecting the manufacturer's relationship with his accounts while ensuring compliance with the program's rules.

The final category of trade promotions is aimed at stimulating retailers and their sales clerks to "push" a certain manufacturer's product rather than that of a competitor. The first of these is *PM* or *push money* (so-called premium money or spiffs). It consists of money given to a sales clerk in addition to the normal compensation as a reward for selling a particular product. Push money is widely criticized by consumer-advocate groups and by many retailers because it encourages sales clerks to emphasize only one line of merchandise rather than showing the variety of merchandise the retailer offers and helping customers select the merchandise that is right for them. A second device is the *sales contest*. This cannot be a lottery, but has to be based solely on the amount of goods sold by each participant. In an effort to allow all participants to have an equal chance in winning, the goal of many contests is a percentage increase over quota rather than the highest total amount sold. The last device in this category is the *dealer loader*, a premium presented to retailers for the purchase of certain quantities of merchandise. Dealer loaders are of two kinds—buying loaders, or gifts given in return for an order, and display loaders, a premium which is a part of a special display piece. The purpose of dealer loaders is to gain new distribution or to sell an unusually large quantity of goods. Some manufacturers avoid dealer loaders because of the aura of price-cutting. The premium-oriented programs are typically used in industries in which a large amount of sales moves through small owner-operated retailers.

PROMOTION TO SALESPEOPLE[3]

Promotional devices aimed at motivating a manufacturer's salespeople consist of rewards that supplement their regular sales compensation plans. While direct sales personnel are the main recipients of sales incentives, many plans include nonselling personnel. There are four basic types of promotional devices aimed at salespeople—sales incentive plans, sales contests, sweepstakes, and recognition programs. In addition, most companies provide a wide range of so-called sales aids for their salespeople.

199

Sales incentive plans bestow on all participants who achieve certain sales performance goals rewards over and above their regular compensation. The three most common rewards are cash, merchandise, and trips.

In *sales contests*, prizes are set up for the salespeople who achieve the best performance as spelled out by the contest's rules. Since top performers generally win these contests, average or below average salespeople often acknowledge early that they will not win and therefore do not put forth any extra effort.

Sweepstakes are occasionally used as supplementary activities in a sales-incentive program. They are not considered powerful motivators because rewards are granted not on the basis of an accomplished goal but merely by chance.

Recognition programs usually take the form of titles (for example, salesperson of the year), trophies, lapel pins, plaques, certificates, etc. They are generally bestowed at sales meetings and again acknowledged in company newsletters, so that the salesperson's accomplishments are known to his fellow salespeople and to company management.

Sales aids include a very wide range of devices and activities designed not to motivate salespeople but to assist them in the actual selling situation. They include such presentation devices as flip charts, price lists, specification data sheets, product bulletins, movies, and things to be left with the customer such as catalogs, advertising specialties which are relatively inexpensive items imprinted with the name of the

[3]These are considered again in the note "Compensation, Evaluation, and Motivation."

selling firm, and business gifts which are more expensive items given to special customers and executives. Some companies consider direct mail which supplements or sometimes even replaces a salesperson's visit as a part of their sales promotion activities.

INDUSTRIAL GOODS PROMOTION

Sales promotion is generally somewhat different in industrially oriented companies. Those companies, however, which sell to many industrial or commercial customers sometimes use consumer-type promotions. Pen companies which sell pens to office managers are typical of this type of operation.

Most industrial companies who sell through distributors or wholesalers use promotions similar to those used for the trade in the consumer-goods area. Industrial companies also use promotions oriented toward salespeople.

Sales aids tend to be more sophisticated and complex in the industrial field. Technically oriented companies often offer design guides, or user brochures, which provide a great deal of information. Some offer special calculation aids (for example, specialized slide rules) or small pieces of equipment particularly suited to the industry (for example, tape measures, magnifying glasses, magnets to detect iron and steel, etc.). Business gifts are perhaps more prevalent in the industrial area where buyer-seller relationships seem more permanent and closer because of intimate design and production scheduling activities.

200

GENERAL COMMENTS

The best promotions are those which are well integrated and coordinated with other marketing activities. One reason that it is difficult to develop successful promotions is that success depends upon cooperation from manufacturer salespeople, wholesalers, and retailers. Few promotions generate the enthusiastic cooperation necessary.

Promotions are heavily regulated by the Federal Trade Commission (FTC). The basis of FTC guidelines is the Robinson-Patman Act which provides that, if a seller offers advertising, promotion, or merchandise allowances; payments; or services to one customer, he has to offer them to all his competing customers on proportionally equal terms. "Competing customers" are wholesalers or retailers who sell or attempt to sell to the same buyers. The law further stipulates that allowances, payments, or services must be of equal quality as well as quantity, and sellers must make a "reasonable effort" to inform all their customers of an offer. If the offer can be used by only one buyer or a small group of buyers, then it probably will not be allowed. These are only a few of the many stipulations of what is considered to be an extremely complex and ambiguous law.

The whole area of trade premiums and business gifts is an especially difficult one. Premiums and gifts beyond "ordinary tokens traditionally used in the industry" are clearly not appropriate because they place the buyer or purchasing agent in a conflict of interest situation. On the other hand, the run-of-the-mill calendars and imprinted pens are often viewed as ineffective. This difficult area is treated in the note "Legal and Ethical Considerations."

BIBLIOGRAPHY

Aspley, John Cameron, and Ovid Riso: *Sales Promotion Handbook*, Chicago: Dartnell Press, 1966.

Engle, James F., Hugh G. Wales, and Martin R. Warshaw: *Promotional Strategy*, Homewood, Ill.: Irwin, 1971.

Luick, John F., and William Lee Ziegler: *Sales Promotion and Modern Marketing*, New York: McGraw-Hill, 1968.

Margolis, Milton J.: "How to Evaluate Field Sales Promotion," in James U. McNeal (ed.), *Readings in Promotion Management*, New York: Appleton Century Crofts, 1966.

Scanlon, Sally: "Onward and Upward with Mr. Average," *Sales Management*, September 3, 1973, pp. 35–42.

Tillman, Rollie, and C. A. Kirkpatrick: *Promotion: Persuasive Communication in Marketing*, Homewood, Ill.: Irwin, 1968 (see especially part V, pp. 282–370).

Turner, Howard M., Jr.: *The People Motivators*, New York: McGraw-Hill, 1973.

Wolfe, Harry Deane, and Dik Warren Twedt: *Essentials of the Promotional Mix*, New York: Appleton Century Crofts, 1970.

Section
FIVE
Sales Costs
and Budgets

TWENTY-THREE   Sales Costs and Budgets

A sales manager is responsible for two sets of optimizations: (1) optimizing the use of the personal selling effort in the marketing mix, and (2) optimizing the accomplishment of personal selling objectives through the use of various sales management techniques. Optimization implies concern for (1) the return in terms of sales, profits, and account relationships from each program and activity, and (2) the cost of each program.

It is usually more difficult to analyze the impact on return than on cost for each program and activity. The cost portion is, however, as important and is certainly not simple. This note is devoted to the cost portion of the analysis.

Three topics will be considered here. The first involves the general structure of costs related to the personal selling effort. The three sections devoted to that subject discuss the economics of personal selling as part of the marketing mix, the impact of the nature of the personal selling effort, and the important differences between fixed and variable costs.

The second general topic involves the use of ratios and other quantitative devices in managing the sales force. The final topic considered is sales budgets and the budgeting process.

THE ROLE OF PERSONAL SELLING

One classic tradeoff within the marketing mix is that between advertising and personal selling. This is closely related to choice of advertising "pull" and channels of distribution "push." Much of the choice between advertising and personal selling as the prime method of communication or promotion depends upon the way in which consumers and channel members make decisions and upon the influence different communications approaches have upon them. Another major consideration is the relative cost of the different approaches. Advertising is inexpensive in terms of cost per person reached, but its impact is relatively low. In addition, the message is standardized, at least for each advertisement, and the flow of communication is totally one way.

On the other hand, personal selling is expensive but has high impact. The salesperson can segment the market at its most disaggregate level, the individual consumer. The message can be tailored to that customer, and communication can flow in both directions. Intermediate points on the scale include direct mail advertising, which can be more tailored than media advertising but is still a one-way communication flow, and telephone selling, which is more expensive than direct mail but has greater impact, more flexibility, and is a two-way flow. It is cheaper than personal face-to-face selling, but has less impact. Exhibit 1 shows the differences.

Thus personal selling should be used only in situations where (1) the high impact, flexibility, and two-way communication flow are needed, and (2) the high cost is justified.

204

The first condition typically depends upon the complexity of the selling task, including such things as the amount of information to be transmitted, its subtlety and nature, the customer's perception of risk which needs to be alleviated, and the number of people involved. The varying appropriateness of personal selling is apparent even in consumer purchases. Furniture, for example, is viewed as a shopping good requiring intensive personal selling, but flour is a convenience item appropriate for advertising. The second condition depends upon the profit impact of a sale which is a function of the size of the sale and its gross margin percentage. Sales with low profit impact do not justify the cost of personal selling.

Often, marketing and sales managers fail to consider the flexibility possible with a combination of approaches. It might be wise for a particular firm to use outside salespeople to call on large or otherwise important accounts, inside telephone salespeople to call on smaller accounts which are near the office but which do not justify the cost of face-to-face calls, and catalogs or direct mail to sell small accounts in remote areas. A more complex scheme might utilize salespeople to make

Exhibit 1 THE ADVERTISING–PERSONAL SELLING CONTINUUM

	Media advertising	Direct mail advertising	Telephone selling	Face-to-face personal selling
Impact	Low	Medium low	Medium high	High
Cost per message	Low	Medium low	Medium high	High
Flexibility in tailoring message	Low	Medium low	Medium high	High
Flow of communication	One-way	One-way	Two-way	Two-way

occasional calls on customers who are regularly serviced by other means.

There are, of course, other tradeoffs within the marketing mix which involve personal selling. A firm may choose, for example, to provide limited sales service while giving the customer a lower price in return. Discount stores use this approach in retailing. Cash-and-carry wholesalers also use it. Another tradeoff is that between using the firm's own personal selling effort and using a distribuion channel. Most consumer-goods manufacturers use retailers, but some, such as Avon and Fuller Brush, use personal selling to communicate with the consumer. The costs of the distribution channel, in terms of its discount or commission, must be measured against added benefits to the customer, such as greater service or more intensive selling effort. Still other tradeoffs involving product policy also exist.

NATURE OF THE PERSONAL SELLING EFFORT

The conceptual structure presented earlier can also be used to analyze the nature of the personal selling effort. The core of the structure is that two factors are the primary determinants of the nature of the sales force. These are (1) the complexity of the selling task and (2) the profit implication of the work done by one salesperson. The more complex the selling task the more reason or need there is to have a high-powered sales force. The higher the profit created by a single salesperson, the greater is the firm's ability to pay for a high-powered sales force.

205

The term "high powered" should not in any way be viewed as synonymous with high-pressure selling. High powered means capable of performing a complex selling task—a creative, intellectually demanding job. The task demands capabilities and performance which are vastly different from those of the stereotypical fast-talking, high-pressure salesperson.

When the selling task is complex, the salesperson is called upon to "design the product" for the customer. Apparel salespeople, for example, select items in their lines most appropriate for their customers. They remerchandise their company's offerings to meet a particular customer's needs. The industrial equipment salesperson is often called upon to tailor equipment to a particular customer's needs. In each of the above situations the salesperson is developing an individual "product policy" for the smallest customer segment—one buyer. To accomplish this difficult task, the salesperson operates in a customer-oriented, client-centered, problem-solving mode and must transmit a great deal of complex intellectual information while providing reassurance in answer to psychological needs.

At the other extreme is the salesperson with the simple product, whose function is to "go out and sell it." The mode is typically either persuasion or merely making the product available (for example, the milkman). Little information needs to be transmitted. Often the task is merely to be "likable," or at least "not unlikable," and to deliver the goods physically. This type of selling demands only a "low-powered" sales force, while the complex task needs a high-powered one.

A high-powered sales force is expensive. Salespersons must be carefully selected, often receiving substantial training before joining the firm (for example, the engineers who sell complex equipment). More training after joining the firm is standard. The only way to attract such intelligent, trained, and trainable individuals is to compensate them well. Usually such salespersons thrive on independence. A "programmed pitch" does not work. Geographically, territories are often large, but the number of customers serviced small. Because each customer requires individualized service, the salesperson cannot visit many customers.

Obviously, such an expensive sales force can be justified only when the profit impact of each salesperson is high. If the profit impact is not high, the industry tends toward higher prices to support high compensation and costs for the sales force. On the other hand, if the profit impact is high but the selling task is simple, a downward price pressure develops and prices are lowered by cutting commissions and expenses. Such changes, however, like most macroindustry changes, occur slowly.

206

Other parts of the marketing mix affect the nature of the personal selling effort, too. The more the firm relies on sales service, the better the selling effort needed. On the other hand, if the firm relies on an established reputation, innovative products, meticulous delivery, low price, or other attractions, the importance of the personal selling effort and the money available to pay for it are reduced.[1]

Exhibit 2 is a diagram of much of the above conceptual structure.

VARIABLE VERSUS FIXED COSTS

The amount is not the only important aspect of costs. Often their nature—that is, their relationship to volume—is as important. Media advertising costs are fixed; they do not vary with the unit sales volume. Sales costs, on the other hand, may be either fixed or variable.

Sales overhead costs, such as the salaries of sales managers, are usually fixed. Sometimes, however, they include a bonus portion which varies with unit or dollar sales volume. Order processing costs are usually semivariable, with costs going up in a partially stepwise manner.

The major costs of the sales force itself may be either fixed or variable. A commission sales force, whether independent reps or compa-

[1]For some evidence of the effect of company reputation on salesperson compensation, see Richard C. Smythe, "Financial Incentives for Salesmen," *Harvard Business Review*, January–February 1968, pp. 109–117.

Exhibit 2 THE NATURE OF THE SELLING EFFORT

	Intricacy of sales task			
	Simple	Moderately simple	Moderately complex	Complex
Aspects of the task				
Mode	Persuasion or delivery			Problem solving
Importance of information transmittal	Low			High
Needs served	Personal and physical			Intellectual and psychological
Where prevalent	Consumer and retail			Industrial and commercial
Profit impact	Low			High
Management of the sales force				
Training	Less			More
Compensation	Low			High
Independence	Low			High
Number of customers	High			Low
Typical examples				
Consumer selling	Milk	Clothing	Real estate insurance	Stocks and bonds
Industrial and commercial selling	Simple industrial supplies		Industrial equipment	High-volume OEM components
			Fashion at wholesale	Large private-label sales

ny salespeople, is a variable cost except for fixed salary guarantees, fringe benefits, and expenses. A salaried sales force is primarily a fixed cost. Usually, however, as sales volume per salesperson increases, there is a tendency to increase salaries. This reflects the previous conceptual structure and shows the importance of the profit impact per salesperson.

The cost for a particular company of a straight-salaried sales force can be viewed as being directly related to the number of calls it makes. If the number of calls a salesperson can make in a given period of time is relatively fixed, the total number of calls which the sales force can make in a given period of time will depend upon the number of salespeople. The cost of the sales force will also depend upon the number of salespeople.

Theoretically, travel and entertainment expenses are fixed costs. In practice, however, most companies are more liberal with expense money in times of high sales than in times of low sales. One could argue that this is contrary to the way it should be. When business is dismal, perhaps all possible action should be taken to increase it. This reasoning is usually not followed, however, because the emphasis on cost control increases in poor times, especially among publicly held companies.

208

Sales promotion occupies an important point in the continuum between personal selling and advertising. A few forms of promotion, such as some contests, presentation aids, and sales or distributor meetings, are fixed costs. However, price-off deals, special packages, some contests, and most other types of promotions are purely variable costs.

Each type of cost has its own advantage. Variable costs are more conservative in that they protect the company in times of poor sales—costs automatically decrease as volume does. Thus, they lessen the profit impact of poor sales. They also help the firm with the small market share. The largest competitor in the market can spread its fixed costs over the largest volume, thus resulting in a low communication cost per unit sold. The smaller competitor does not have that advantage. If it spends as much per unit, its fixed costs of advertising or personal selling will be much smaller, but its program probably will not have as much impact. If the small competitor has as large a program, its costs per unit, and thus its percentage of sales spent on advertising or a salaried sales force, will be much higher, and its profits, all other things about equal, will be much lower. Competition on the basis of variable costs such as sales promotion, however, gives it a better chance. It can spend as much per unit as its larger competitor while getting equal impact.

Fixed costs have their advantages, too; they offer great upside opportunity. As sales grow, costs grow more slowly and profits more rapidly. They also provide the large competitor an advantage over smaller ones.

Regardless of the situation, it is important for sales and marketing management to understand the relationship between costs and sales volume and to build a program which provides the cost structure they desire.

USE OF RATIOS AND SIMPLE CALCULATIONS

The sales manager uses ratios for a portion of his analysis just as the financial analyst does. This discussion is not meant to be exhaustive. Instead, it provides some thoughts on useful ratios and simple calculations. It should also be clear that ratios should be only a part of the analysis. They mean little without consideration of the market context from which they are developed.

One of the basic ratios in sales management is the sales expense ratio—sales cost divided by dollar sales volume, usually expressed as a percentage. Often, industry data can be used for comparison. The last part of this note provides some sources for such data.

It is often useful to compare the sales cost to the cost of other parts of the marketing mix, especially advertising. This is by far the quickest way to learn the firm's communications strategy, and the precise quantitative impact of the strategy.

It is also useful to divide the sales expense ratio into its components so that one can focus on the most relevant parts of the sales program. For example, if one is interested in cost cutting and field supervision accounts for only 5 percent of total sales cost, field supervision is not a good candidate for cuts with large impact.

A wide range of other ratios and calculations does not involve dollars only. One of the most basic is the calculation of the call capacity of the sales force and of individual salespeople. This involves multiplying the number of calls a salesperson can make in a day by the number of days in a year by the number of salespeople available. Call capacity should be compared with the number of calls needed, which comes from estimates of (1) the number of calls needed to service an account or various types or sizes of accounts, and (2) the number of accounts to be serviced and the number of prospects to be approached. Estimates of call capacity needed improve dramatically when prospects and customers are carefully divided into different categories, depending upon the number of calls needed to service them. Sometimes the sales manager who complains about the small amount of prospecting calls his sales force makes is surprised to find that the sales force needs all of its available call capacity for servicing existing accounts.

It is often useful to work this calculation in the other direction to find the number of calls being made on existing accounts. Experience and discussion will give a good idea of whether it is sufficient, too little, or even too much. These same numbers can be used to find out the number of calls salespeople have to make in a day. If they are supposed to do extensive in-store service, visit several departments (for example, purchasing, engineering, and manufacturing), or make extensive presentations, their call capacities per day are limited. Long travel time between accounts also cuts severely into call capacity.

The number of active accounts and prospective accounts per salesperson provides some feel for the equity of territorial assignments. Sales and potential per salesperson are also useful, as is market penetration by salesperson. Again, the market context is crucial. The ratio of a salesperson's expenses to compensation can be a useful control and can explain her way of selling. Expenses which are too low can be a problem because they may indicate a lack of travel or entertaining when necessary. Obviously, expenses which are more than they should be can be a problem.

There are several other ways to measure the nature and quality of the selling job. The ratio of accounts sold to total available accounts is important as is average volume per sale and per account. Some salespeople try to cover a small percentage of their prospective accounts in depth, while others do a more cursory job of selling more accounts. The firm's marketing and sales strategies should include explicit statements on the correct way to cover accounts. If a company desires both intensive coverage of each account and a high ratio of active to potential accounts, it must provide the necessary call capacity. The number of previously active accounts no longer buying is of great importance.

Many companies attempt to measure the profitability of each account and/or of each salesperson. When an account purchases a variety of goods and services (for example, a banking customer), it may be difficult to do this; however, in most situations, it is quite possible. Sales managers often attempt to train salespeople to trade the profit impact of an account, usually in terms of gross margin, against the cost of the call. Sometimes, even a rough cut can be useful. For example, if the toal cost of the personal selling effort is divided by the total number of calls the sales force makes, one obtains the cost per call. In one *limited* sense, the amount of sales necessary to justify the call is the cost divided by the gross margin percentage. This is misleading in a way because it does not consider alternative uses of the call time nor the development of an account relationship. Nonetheless, it can sometimes provide a *minimum* viable order size.[2]

It is often useful to consider the gross margin per sale, per call, per salesperson. Comparisons can be meaningful when taken in context.

Several kinds of comparisons can be made using the above figures. One is among salespeople or groups of salespeople such as districts or regions. Another is between the company and other companies either in

[2]For more on this aspect of deployment see the note "Deploying the Sales Effort."

the same industry or in general. Sill another is between different sales approaches (for example, telephone selling versus face-to-face selling). Always, the comparison should be the beginning of the analysis, not the conclusion.

Two additional approaches should be mentioned here: leverage and "quick-and-dirty" break-even analysis. Leverage is the idea of investing dollars where they will have the most impact. Getting back to the advertising-personal selling issue, the question is often phrased, "Are we likely to get more return from $100,000 in advertising or from four additional salespeople at $25,000 each?"

"Rough cut" numbers and "quick-and-dirty" break-even analysis can be useful. For example, if a salesperson's salary is $15,000 and his expenses are $10,000, and if gross margin is 33 percent, an additional salesperson breaks even in a limited sense at $75,000 in sales. The questions then become, "Can an additional salesperson sell $75,000 of our products? If it is possible, how long will it take her to attain that rate of sales?"

One place in which a sales or marketing manager might want to use such thinking would be, "Given the increasing cost of having a salesperson make a sales call, can we substitute telephone or mail order selling for the field salesperson?" One could estimate the costs of each method of selling and then could estimate the revenue likely to be generated by each approach.

211

SALES BUDGETS AND THE BUDGETING PROCESS

Much of the thinking behind standard budgeting, control, and reporting procedures is relevant to managing the sales force. Plans should be made, programs developed, and budgets established. Generally speaking, the more specific the plans, programs, and budgets, the more likely they are to succeed.

Before confronting the budgeting process directly, it is useful to note the relationship between it and several other aspects of sales management. Sales forecasting, discussed in the note "Sales Forecasting for the Sales Manager," and quota setting, discussed in the note "Compensation, Evaluation, and Motivation," are closely related to the budgeting process. Cost control in general is a function of effective deployment (see the note "Deploying the Sales Effort"). Budgets are meaningless unless they are compared with actual results as supplied by a sales information system as discussed in the note "Sales Information Systems." Finally, a crucial cost-related issue is that between independent representatives and a company sales force, considered in the note "Company Sales Force or Independent Representatives?"

A good budgeting process will consider both revenue generation and costs. Estimating sales revenues is a most difficult task but a very necessary one. The projection of sales costs is not easy, although careful application of the ratios noted earlier and of the difference between fixed and variable costs makes the task much easier.

The best budget processes tend to involve the individual salespeople who will be required to implement the programs developed and meet the goals chosen. Sales forces which call on few accounts often plan their approaches and forecast their accomplishments on an account-by-account basis. Where that is not possible, it is useful to combine accounts or activities, or both, into categories for planning purposes. Thus, a salesperson might be budgeted to open a certain number of accounts of a specific type with average sales of some budget figure.

The specific technique used in the budgeting process is perhaps of less importance than the care and attention the process receives. As a crucial function of sales management it requires meticulous care and careful attention.

SOURCES OF SALES COSTS

The Conference Board: *Compensating Salesmen and Sales Executives*, Conference Board Report no. 579, 1972.

Dartnell Corporation: *Compensation of Salesmen*, Chicago. (This is a serial publication which is updated regularly.)

McGraw-Hill Publications Company: "Cost of an Industrial Salesman's Call in 1969." (Note an updated version of this study was issued as a press release in 1972.)

Sales Management: "Compensating the Field Sales Manager," February 19, 1973, pp. 21–24.

————: "New Approaches in Compensating the Field Sales Manager," March 5, 1973, pp. 35–37.

————: "1975 Survey of Selling Costs," complete issue. (This appears annually in January.)

————: "What Top Sales and Marketing Executives Earn," October 2, 1972, pp. 27–30.

BIBLIOGRAPHY

Beik, Leland L., and Stephen L. Buzby: "Profitability Analysis by Market Segment," *Journal of Marketing*, vol. 37, July 1973, pp. 48–53.

Chaplick, John P.: "Take Your Accountant to Lunch," *Sales Management*, February 5, 1973, pp. 32–35.

Dowd, James: "Analyzing Selling—Expense Data for More Profitable Sales," in Albert Newgarden (ed.), *The Field Sales Manager: A Manual of Practice*, American Management Association, 1960, pp. 126–140.

Fogg, C. Davis, and Josef W. Rokus: "A Quantitative Method for Structuring a Profitable Sales Force," *Journal of Marketing*, vol. 37, July 1973, pp. 8–17.

Henry, J. Porter: "Failing at the Controls," *Sales Management*, June 11, 1973, pp. 25–29.

Levin, Richard I.: "Who's on First," *Sales Management*, July 17, 1964, pp. 53–56; reprinted in Thomas R. Wotruba and Robert Olsen (eds.), *Readings in Sales Management*, New York: Holt, Rinehart and Winston, 1971.

Minkin, Jerome M., James K. Brown, and Earl L. Bailey: *Sales Analysis*, National Industrial Conference Board, 1965.

Reynolds, Edward B.: "The Field Sales Manager's Responsibility for Planning, Organization, and Control," in Albert Newgarden (ed.), *The Field Sales Manager: A Manual of Practice*, American Management Association, 1960, pp. 45–75.

Schiff, J. S., and Michael Schiff: "New Sales Management Tool: ROAM," *Harvard Business Review*, vol. 54, July–August 1976, pp. 59–66.

213

TWENTY-FOUR   The Smithville Company

In March 1973 Katherine O'Brien, vice president of marketing, was attempting to decide whether or not the Smithville Company should discontinue the use of manufacturers' representatives[1] in favor of a company-owned sales force. The president of the firm, James Petroskey, had expressed great interest in the idea. It was clear, however, that the primary input into the decision would be Ms. O'Brien's.

The Smithville Company had been founded just before World War I and had remained a modest, family-run operation, producing crocks, pots, and miscellaneous garden and kitchen ceramic articles until the late 1950s. At that time, Mr. Petroskey assumed the responsibilities of chief

[1]Manufacturers' representatives or reps were independent selling organizations which sold lines of complementary but noncompetitive items of different manufacturers. The representatives usually were compensated with a commission on merchandise shipped and paid their own expenses. They did not take possession of the merchandise. Commission rates and standard policies differed by industry.

executive officer and put the company on a course of developing and selling complete lines of stoneware,[2] dinnerware, and related kitchen and table accessory items. The projected sales of $6.7 million for 1973 represented a doubling in volume since 1970. Mr. Petroskey desired to maintain a growth rate of at least 20 percent per year in both sales and profits for the foreseeable future. Exhibit 1 provides recent income statement information.

In 1973 the company was producing and selling three lines of dinnerware and an assortment of mugs and was devoting approximately 18 percent of its production to contract work for other manufacturers. Its oldest line of dinnerware, the Greenwich line, was begun in the late 1950s and contained approximately 70 separate items. Its newest line, Saratoga, was developed in the late 1960s and comprised approximately 40 items. Exhibit 2 lists the items in the Greenwich line, and Exhibit 3 shows several of the items. Exhibit 4 provides item sales. Smithville distributed its branded lines through an estimated 12,000 active accounts. Although

[2]Stoneware is a form of pottery which is considerably cheaper than china. It is also considered to be less fragile.

Exhibit 1 STATEMENTS OF INCOME (in $1,000)

	1970	1971	1972	1973 (projected)
Net sales	3,500	4,142	5,611	6,712
Cost of sales	2,484	2,868	3,866	4,365
Gross profit	1,016	1,274	1,745	2,347
Selling expenses	500	621	703	936
G&A expenses	195	213	232	262
Total	695	834	935	1,198
Net profit (loss) before other income and expense	321	440	810	1,150
Other income (expense) net	(73)	(27)	(14)	(50)
Net profit before tax	248	413	796	1,100

Breakdown of selling expenses

		1971	1972	1973
Salaries		95	79	132
Commissions		353	403	490
Advertising and promotion		84	118	166
Travel and entertainment		6	4	12
Office expense		33	42	53
Shows (primarily china and glass show in Atlantic City)		12	14	22
Royalties (paid for the design of one of the lines)		38	43	54
Training and meetings				7
		621	703	936

Breakdown of net sales

	1972
Sales by representative	4,025
Sales by sales manager	99
Sales to jobbers	300
Other house accounts	222
Total captive line sales	4,646
Contract sales	965
Net sales	5,611

THE SMITHVILLE COMPANY

WHOLESALE PRICE LIST

TERMS: 1%   15 DAYS, NET 30
F.O.B.   FACTORY

Sold to: _____   Ship to: _____

_____   _____

Zip Code _____   Zip Code _____

Order No. _____ 14-23	Direct/Indirect _____ 36	Common Code _____	53 54
Order Date _____ 24-29	Ship Date _____ 37-42		
Dept. _____ 30-34	Cancel Date _____ 43-48 49-50 51-52	Ship Via _____ 55-68	
Pricing Code _____ 35	Salesman _____ #1 #2	New Cust. Code _____ 69	

CREDIT INFORMATION: ☐ OLD ACCOUNT   ☐ D&B RATING   ☐ CREDIT REFERENCES ON REVERSE SIDE   H.F.C. ☐ YES ☐ NO   BUYER _____

GREENWICH STONEWARE

QTY	ITEM NO.	DESCRIPTION	STD. PACK	PRICE	EXT. AMT.	CODE	QTY.	ITEM NO.	DESCRIPTION	STD. PACK	PRICE	EXT. AMT.	CODE
	1G	CUP, 9 OZ.	24	.60 EA.		001-01311		249G	OVAL ROASTER, 16"	3	3.50 EA.		249-01316
	2G	SAUCER	24	.50 EA.		002-01319		250G	OVAL ROASTER, 16" ON WARMER	1	5.50 EA.		250-01314
	3G	SALAD PLATE, 7"	24	.50 EA.		003-01317		265G	OVAL RAREBIT, 9½"	6	1.00 EA.		265-01312
	4G	DINNER PLATE, 10"	24	.85 EA.		004-01315		270G	OVAL RAREBIT, 11"	6	1.50 EA.		270-01312
	5G	LUNCHEON PLATE, 8½"	24	.60 EA.		005-01312		282G	MUG, 12 OZ.	24	.55 EA.		282-01317
	6G	BARBEQUE PLATE, 11"	6	1.25 EA.		006-01310		286G	MUG, 16 OZ.	12	.75 EA.		286-01318
	7G	STEAK PLATE	12	1.25 EA.		007-01318		288G	4 PC. MUG SET, 8 OZ.	6 SETS	2.00 SET		288-01314
	8G	FRUIT, 4½"	24	.40 EA.		008-01316		300G	4 PC. IND. CASSEROLE SET	6 SETS	3.00 SET		300-01317
	9G	4 PC. BOWL SET, 5½"	6 SETS	2.00 SET		009-01314		305G	CASSEROLE, 12 OZ.	12	1.00 EA.		305-01316
	10G	BOWL, 7"	12	.65 EA.		010-01312		310G	CASSEROLE, 1 QT.	6	2.00 EA.		310-01316
	11G	ROUND VEGETABLE, 9"	6	1.25 EA.		011-01310		315G	CASSEROLE, 2 QT.	1	2.50 EA.		315-01315
	12G	FLANGED SOUP BOWL	12	1.00 EA.		012-01318		316G	CASSEROLE, 2 QT. ON WARMER	1	3.50 EA.		316-01313
	14G	DIVIDED VEGETABLE	4	2.25 EA.		014-01314		325G	CASSEROLE, 3 QT.	1	3.50 EA.		325-01314
	16G	PLATTER, 14"	6	2.25 EA.		016-01319		326G	CASSEROLE, 3 QT. ON WARMER	1	4.50 EA.		326-01312
	17G	PLATTER, 16"	4	3.00 EA.		017-01317		330G	CASSEROLE, 4 QT.	1	5.00 EA.		330-01314
	20G	SUGAR & CREAMER SET	6 SETS	2.25 SET		020-01311		335G	CASSEROLE, 2QT. ROUND ON WARMER	1	3.00 EA.		335-01313
	25G	SALT & PEPPER SET	6 SETS	1.75 SET		025-01310		340G	TWIN CASSEROLE SET, 2 QT. ON WARMER	1 SET	7.00 SET		340-01313
	28G	COVERED BUTTER DISH	6	1.75 EA.		028-01314		405G	INDIVIDUAL SOUFFLE/RAMEKIN	12	.50 EA.		405-01314
	34G	16 PC. SET SERVICE FOR 4	1 SET	6.00 SET		034-01312		406G	SOUFFLE, 1 QT.	6	1.25 EA.		406-01312
	36G	45 PC. SET SERVICE FOR 8	1 SET	17.50 SET		036-01317		408G	SOUFFLE, 2 QT.	6	1.75 EA.		408-01318
	39G	SERVER, 3 COMPARTMENT, 11"	1	2.50 EA.		039-01311		415G	PITCHER, 1½ QT.	6	1.50 EA.		415-01313
	40G	CHEESE & RELISH DISH, 15"	4	2.50 EA.		040-01319		416G	PITCHER, 2 QT.	4	2.00 EA.		416-01312
	43G	JAM & RELISH SERVER	1	2.50 EA.		043-01313		433G	GRAVY BOAT ON SAUCER	4	1.75 EA.		433-01316
	44G	DEVILED EGG DISH	1	2.50 EA.		044-01311		434G	GRAVY BOAT/BUTTER MELTER ON WARMER	6	1.75 EA.		434-01314
	46G	4 PC. CORN DISH SET	6 SETS	2.50 SET		046-01316		453G	3 PC. MIXING BOWL SET, 6", 8", 10"	1 SET	2.50 SET		453-01314
	70G	BEAN POT, 2½ QT.	6	2.50 EA.		070-01316		495G	COFFEE CARAFE ON WARMER	1	3.50 EA.		495-01315
	80G	BEAN POT, 3½ QT.	6	3.00 EA.		080-01315		500G	4 PC. SUGAR & CREAMER SET	1 SET	3.00 SET		500-01312
	81G	BEAN POT, 3½ QT. ON WARMER	1	4.00 EA.		081-01313		511G	SPOON REST	6	1.00 EA.		511-01319
	120G	TIER TRAY	4	2.50 EA.		120-01319		520G	4 PC. CANISTER SET	1 SET	7.00 SET		520-01310
	130G	LAZY SUSAN, 14"	1	4.00 EA.		130-01318		540G	COOKIE JAR	1	2.50 EA.		540-01318
	140G	LAZY SUSAN WITH CASSEROLE, 16"	1	6.50 EA.		140-01317		550G	TEA POT, 6 CUP	4	2.50 EA.		550-01317
	150G	SOUP TUREEN, 2½ QT.	1	4.00 EA.		150-01316		551G	TEA POT, 6 CUP ON WARMER	1	3.50 EA.		551-01315
	170G	SOUP TUREEN, 8"	1	5.00 EA.		170-01314		574G	CHAMBERSTICK	6	1.50 EA.		574-01317
	180G	CHIP AND DIP ON STAND	1	3.00 EA.		180-01313		578G	6 PC. CUSTARD CUP SET	6 SETS	1.50 SET		578-01318
	200G	SAMOVAR, 20 CUP	1	7.50 EA.		200-01319							
	220G	3 PC. SALAD SET	1 SET	3.00 SET		220-01317							
	221G	4 PC. SALAD SET ON STAND	1 SET	3.00 SET		221-01315							
	225G	7 PC. SALAD SET	1 SET	4.50 SET		225-01316							
	230G	SPAGHETTI DISH, 14"	4	2.50 EA.		230-01316							
	231G	SHIRRED EGG DISH, 6"	12	.75 EA.		231-01314							
	240G	OVAL BAKER, 7"	6	.75 EA.		240-01315							
	241G	OVAL BAKER, 9½"	6	1.00 EA.		241-01313							
	247G	OVAL ROASTER, 14"	3	2.75 EA.		247-01310							

YOU MUST ORDER IN STD. PACK QUANTITIES   TOTAL

Exhibit 2   Greenwich stoneware order form.

department stores, chain stores, and mail-order catalog outlets were becoming increasingly important, it was estimated that as of the end of 1972, over 60 percent of sales revenue (exclusive of contract work) came from small gift shops.

Ms. O'Brien believed that Smithville products were purchased as

Exhibit 3   The Greenwich line.

Exhibit 4   SALES OF THE GREENWICH LINE

Item number	Description	Unit sales	Dollar sales
Primary items	**(Dinnerware)**		
1G	Cup, 9 oz.	21,288	$11,883
2G	Saucer	13,145	6,025
3G	Salad plate, 7 in.	29,328	13,107
4G	Dinner plate, 10 in.	33,226	26,006
5G	Luncheon plate, $8\frac{1}{2}$ in.	17,415	10,209
6G	Barbeque plate, 11 in.	3,552	4,296
7G	Steak plate	7,307	8,681
8G	Fruit, $4\frac{1}{2}$ in.	30,557	11,937
9G	4 pc. bowl set, $5\frac{1}{2}$ in.	13,359	24,974
10G	Bowl, 7 in.	17,796	11,377
11G	Round vegetable, 9 in.	11,042	13,154
12G	Flanged soup bowl	10,246	9,900
14G	Divided vegetable	7,324	16,182
16G	Platter, 14 in.	8,720	19,203
17G	Platter, 16 in.	4,366	12,506
20G	Sugar & creamer set	11,336	25,299
25G	Salt & pepper set	12,533	21,813
28G	Covered butter dish	9,741	16,938
34G	16 pc. set (service for 4)	9,662	55,481
36G	45 pc. set (service for 8)	6,661	114,669
39G	Server, 3 compartment, 11 in.	2,260	5,509
	Total primary	**280,864**	**$439,149**

Exhibit 4 *(Continued)*

Item number	Description	Unit sales	Dollar sales
Secondary items	***(Related accessory)***		
40G	Cheese & relish dish, 15 in.	2,316	$ 5,610
43G	Jam & relish server	6,739	15,084
44G	Deviled-egg dish	2,364	5,749
46G	4 pc. corn dish set	2,889	7,013
70G	Bean pot, $2\frac{1}{2}$ qt.	5,118	12,069
80G	Bean pot, $3\frac{1}{2}$ qt.	2,889	8,100
81G	Bean pot, $3\frac{1}{2}$ qt. on warmer	1,453	5,620
120G	Tier tray	2,360	5,881
130G	Lazy Susan, 14 in.	3,645	14,041
140G	Lazy Susan with casserole, 16 in.	9,799	58,107
150G	Soup tureen, $2\frac{1}{2}$ qt.	4,210	16,348
170G	Soup tureen, 5 qt.	4,941	24,143
180G	Chip and dip on stand	3,019	8,699
220G	3 pc. salad set	3,085	8,903
225G	7 pc. salad set	978	4,295
230G	Spaghetti dish, 14 in.	4,877	11,660
231G	Shirred-egg dish, 6 in.	4,464	3,039
240G	Oval baker, 7 in.	7,470	5,680
241G	Oval baker, $9\frac{1}{2}$ in.	10,040	10,054
247G	Oval roaster, 14 in.	3,949	10,298
249G	Oval roaster, 16 in.	3,782	11,982
250G	Oval roaster, 16 in. on warmer	2,009	$10,702
265G	Oval rarebit, $9\frac{1}{2}$ in.	8,778	8,970
270G	Oval rarebit, 11 in.	5,988	8,717
282G	Mug, 12 oz.	33,702	18,235
286G	Mug, 16 oz.	10,742	8,179
288G	4 pc. mug set, 8 oz.	18,409	35,439
300G	4 pc. individual casserole set	5,136	15,004
305G	Casserole, 12 oz.	14,477	14,716
310G	Casserole, 1 qt.	5,408	10,441
315G	Casserole, 2 qt.	7,665	18,431
316G	Casserole, 2 qt. on warmer	4,703	16,113
325G	Casserole, 3 qt.	3,822	12,592
326G	Casserole, 3 qt. on warmer	2,198	9,789
330G	Casserole, 4 qt.	2,081	9,883
335G	Casserole, 2 qt. round on warmer	7,824	22,454
340G	Twin casserole set, 2 qt. on warmer	5,805	37,094
405G	Individual souffle/ramekin	4,617	2,264
406G	Souffle, 1 qt.	4,717	5,769
408G	Souffle, 2 qt.	7,135	12,296
415G	Pitcher, $1\frac{1}{2}$ qt.	3,101	4,601
416G	Pitcher, 2 qt.	3,974	7,907
433G	Gravy boat on saucer	7,441	12,564
434G	Gravy boat/butter melter on warmer	4,497	7,586
453G	3 pc. mixing bowl set, 6 in., 8 in., 10 in.	6,268	15,045
495G	Coffee carafe on warmer	4,323	14,505
500G	4 pc. sugar & creamer set	1,356	3,978
511G	Spoon rest	11,449	11,102
520G	4 pc. canister set	3,158	21,205
540G	Cookie jar	4,299	10,517
550G	Tea pot, 6 cup	5,344	12,778
551G	Tea pot, 6 cup on warmer	2,875	9,812
574G	Chamberstick	4,176	6,035
578G	6 pc. custard cup set	15,391	20,346
	Total secondary	**323,255**	**$ 687,445**
	Grand total	**604,119**	**$1,126,594**

217

gifts as often as they were purchased for personal use and that most of the purchases resulted from in-store displays. Some unsophisticated market research conducted by the company through the use of warranty cards seemed to verify this assumption. (Exhibit 5 describes the results of this survey.) The larger dollar volume in all lines came from the related items rather than the dinnerware sets. She attributed this to three factors. First, once a consumer had either purchased or received as a gift a 45-piece set (eight 5-piece place settings and five serving dishes), she would add, or receive as a gift, pieces related to her original set on a continuing basis. Second, the related items were sufficiently attractive and functional in their own right to serve as welcome additions to any home, whether the core dinnerware set was possessed or not. Finally, most of the articles were moderately priced and widely distributed. This thinking led Ms. O'Brien to conclude that the relevant definition of the Smithville market was the entire gift and decorative accessory market, as well as the dinnerware market.

Exhibit 5 STONEWARE MARKETING SURVEY

	Saratoga amount, %		Greenwich amount, %		Columbia amount, %		Total amount, %	
Received as a gift	601	56	340	65	244	56	1185	58
Purchased for own use	471	44	182	35	190	44	843	42
Where purchased								
Department store	377	39	239	54	162	43	778	43
Gift shop	370	38	82	18	119	31	571	32
Stamp plan	4	1	8	2	0	0	12	1
Other	217	22	116	26	98	26	431	24
Newly wed								
Yes	237	21	76	17	51	12	364	18
No	868	79	360	83	382	88	1610	82
First Smithville								
Yes	741	76	352	69	339	83	1432	76
No	235	24	160	31	67	17	462	24
Cause to purchase								
Magazine ad	71	8	23	8	29	11	123	9
Newspaper ad	11	1	4	1	3	1	18	1
TV	0	0	0	0	1	0	1	0
Sales clerk	21	2	2	1	17	6	40	3
Store display	749	88	260	90	214	81	1223	87
Live in								
City	397	37	174	34	155	38	726	36
Suburbia	672	63	338	66	257	62	1267	64
Income								
Under $8,000	281	27	111	22	78	15	470	23
$8,000–$12,000	336	33	200	39	143	28	679	33
Over $12,000	411	40	199	39	287	56	897	44
Age								
18–25	397	36	128	26	99	23	624	21
26–35	298	27	166	34	115	26	579	29
36 and over	403	37	191	39	220	51	814	40

Ms. O'Brien was optimistic about the future for stoneware articles in the United States. For one thing, the clearly recognized trend toward casual and convenient living remained strong. And, it was reasoned, as Americans spent more leisure time in their homes, they would seek both artistic and functional ware to fill their environment. Stoneware was more craft oriented than traditional fine china, and its low price and rugged nature (it could be placed in the oven directly from the refrigerator) made it particularly well suited to take advantage of these trends. Americans were also building more second homes, which would mean an increase in the need for inexpensive furnishings. In addition to these considerations, the more general economic developments, such as the devaluation of the dollar, the increasing amounts of import taxes being placed on foreign goods, and the rapidly increasing wages in both Europe and Japan, all contributed to the increasing competitiveness of American-made stoneware, which had suffered considerably at the hands of foreign imports in the late 1950s and early 1960s.

The Smithville lines were sold primarily by a nationwide system of manufacturers' representatives. The manufacturers' representatives varied widely in their method of operation. Some were one-man operations. Others were members of small organizations, composed either of unrelated representatives or family members. These organizations generally comprised one or more principals and several subrepresentatives and/or detail personnel. The subreps and detail personnel differed from the reps in that they normally received half of the manufacturer's commission on all the merchandise they sold, with the other half going to the rep organization that employed them. Detail personnel were sometimes compensated by salary. Subreps were usually given a territory within which they would sell and service accounts. Detail personnel would often only service[3] large, established accounts. A list of the reps, the territory they covered, and brief sketches of their principal characteristics is given in Exhibit 6. Smithville's reps accounted for approximately 87 percent of the branded line sales. Exhibit 7 is a breakdown of the sales and commissions of the reps. The remaining 13 percent of captive line sales were accounted for by the following sources: James Fletcher—the company sales manager who also covered all the territory within a 50-mile radius of company headquarters, 2 percent; jobbers, 6 percent; and house accounts, 5 percent. The appendix contains a review of the casewriter's travel with two salesmen.

219

Should it be decided to start a direct force, not all the reps would probably be replaced. The decision on whether to replace a person or organization depended upon such things as the size of the territory

---

[3] In this context servicing means the maintenance of displays, taking of inventories, and other such tasks. It did not include the actual selling.

versus the present and potential sales from that territory, the nature of the outlets the person was serving, and the geographical location of the territory. Ms. O'Brien had tentatively selected those reps whom she would replace and those whom she would keep, based upon her personal knowledge of their volume, territories, and outlets. That list is reproduced below:

	To be replaced		Replacements	
Name	Number of reps	Number of showroom personnel	Direct salesperson	Showroom personnel
Austin	7	3	6	2
Blumberg	2	2	3	1.5
Pote	1	0	2	0
Shutzer	2	2	0	0
Kammer	1	0	1	1.5
Blinn	1	0	1	0
Whitwer	1	0	1	0
Norton	1	0	1	0
Martin	4	0	2	0
Riggs	7	2	3	2
	27	9	20	7

Reps to continue with company

Flinton	Alaska and Pacific Northwest
Miller	Rocky Mountain states
Fries	Hawaii
Orlinoff	Military exchanges
Gerard	Caribbean countries

In order to calculate the monetary effects of the potential change in the sales force, the following data were collected:[4]

Average cost to locate and train salespeople	$ 6,073
Average annual compensation of highest paid housewares salespeople	$ 20,550
Average annual expenses as percentages of gross pay	42.7%
Average annual turnover	10%
Average training time	7 months
Average annual volume per salesperson (hardware, tools, and housewares)	$501,000

Ms. O'Brien's tentative plan called for hiring 20 field salespersons. Of these 20, she estimated that approximately 3 would come from the existing reps or their subreps, leaving 17 people to be recruited and trained. To allow for possible dropouts and for some rejection discretion, she assumed that she would initially hire and train 4 more people than would be ultimately needed. All the people hired would have to have at least one year of successful experience selling housewares. This was because Ms. O'Brien believed that in order to achieve the transition with a minimum disruption in sales volume, all territories must be switched

[4]*Source: Compensation of Salesmen*, A Dartnell Management Guide, The Dartnell Corporation, Chicago, Illinois.

simultaneously. If the switch were to take place one territory at a time, over a period of 6 months to a year or longer, she knew that the reps in those territories which had not yet been converted would be devoting their time to increasing the volume of their other lines and looking for new lines, at the expense of Smithville. Therefore, the people who replaced the reps would have to be qualified to service existing accounts without much assistance from the home office initially.

Whereas it would be more expensive to hire experienced people, it was assumed that it would be less expensive to train them and that the initial turnover rate would be much lower. It was estimated that one month of training would be sufficient to acquaint the people with the product line, familiarize them with the marketing program and the sales administrative system, and give them refresher training in selling technique. The three persons who were to come from the existing rep force would not go through this program, since it was planned that they be recruited during the wekks immediately preceding the switch. They would receive individual attention from the sales manager after they had joined Smithville.

Ms. O'Brien estimated the costs of recruiting and training the field salespeople as follows:

Recruiting and training $\quad \frac{1}{7} \times \$6,000 \times 21 \quad = \$18,000$

Salary while training $\quad \frac{1}{12} \times \$15,000 \times 21 = \dfrac{\$26,250}{\$44,250}$

This was developed as follows: The Dartnell data mentioned previously suggested that $6,000 was the cost of a 7-month recruiting and training period. Ms. O'Brien estimated that it would take her only one month to recruit and train a new salesperson. There would be 21 people recruited and trained. The $15,000 salary during training was estimated.

In addition to recruiting and training the field salespeople, four of the showroom personnel would be recruited and trained at the same time. These four would then train the additional showroom personnel once they had begun working. These people would also have to have at least one year's selling experience in housewares. Their responsibilities would include supervising the operation of the showroom, servicing the key accounts in their area, and some actual field selling.

The costs of recruiting and training these people were estimated to be:

Recruiting and training $\quad \frac{1}{7} \times \$6,000 \times 4 \quad = \$3,429$

Salary while training $\quad \frac{1}{12} \times \$15,000 \times 4 = \dfrac{\$5,000}{\$8,429}$

On a continuing basis, the following additional overhead and per person costs were anticipated if a direct force were started:

Overhead (per annum)	
1 field sales manager at 133% of estimated salesman compensation[5]	$ 27,000
Recruiting and training 3 people per year to allow for turnover	
$7,000 × 3	21,000
Salaries of recruits while training $\frac{7}{12}$ × $9,000 × 3	15,750
Showroom expense[6]	
Rent and maintenance 4 × $7,000	28,000
Salaries for personnel (4 at $20,000 and 3 at $7,500)	102,500
	$194,250
Salespeople (per person, per year)	
Pay (base and incentive)	$20,000
Expenses (42.7% of pay based on Dartnell data)	8,540
Benefits	2,000
	$30,540

The analysis below compared the costs of a rep force with the estimated costs of a company-owned sales force over the next 5 years:

	Projected, in 000's				
	1974	1975	1976	1977	1978
Branded line sales (20% per annum growth)	$6,766	$8,215	$9,858	$11,830	$14,196
Reps					
Sales by reps (87% of total)	5,886	7,147	8,576	10,292	12,351
Rep's commissions (assume 12%)[7]	706	858	1,029	1,235	1,482
Company-owned sales force					
Retained reps (5% of sales at 12%)	35	43	51	62	74
Direct people					
Number of people	20	20	22	22	24
Overhead	194	194	194	194	194
Salespersons' pay	612	612	672	672	763
Total direct force costs	$ 841	$ 849	$ 917	$ 928	$ 1,031
Savings (cost) of direct versus reps	(135)	9	112	307	451
Start-up costs (recruiting and training) = $52,679					

In addition to and perhaps more important than the economic side of the analysis, according to Ms. O'Brien, were many qualitative factors that had to be considered before making a switch. For example, she believed that by and large, a company-owned sales force would make it easier for the retailers to buy Smithville products. The company salespeople would

[5]The assumption that the field sales manager's salary would be 133 percent of salesperson's compensation was an industry rule of thumb.

[6]The $7,000 estimate of showroom rent and maintenance came from company experience. It was at present maintaining a showroom in New York.

[7]The standard industry commission rate was 12 percent; Smithville had been paying 10 percent.

be spending less time with each account, and the time saved would allow them to get in at least one and possibly more calls per year per account. Retailers would appreciate this, since they would then be able to order (and inventory) smaller amounts of merchandise and yet not have to worry about missing sales because of being out of stock. During the time that salespeople did spend with each account, they could spend time maintaining the displays, educating the retail clerks, backing up national ads with better in-store merchandising, and educating the buyers. Negative attitudes caused by problems in delivery, back orders, cancellations, and quality could be, she thought, more credibly countered on the spot by a company person.

A company sales force, Ms. O'Brien expected, could be directed and managed so that Smithville could receive broader placement in department stores. Very few reps, in her experience, were good at or liked servicing the larger department stores. One of the reasons for this was that it took a long time for an order placed by the department store buyer to receive funding. A rep, she reasoned, could not be bothered to follow up with the store as necessary to ensure that funding was obtained. She also thought that reps wanted orders that were sent to the factory immediately, so that they could get their commissions quickly. Furthermore, it was more expensive to visit the downtown areas where the department store buyers were usually located; reps' expenses came right out of their pockets. Finally, the buyers in department stores expected salespeople to take stock, arrange displays, and educate retail clerks at the main store and at all the branches. She believed that reps avoided these duties whenever possible.

Placement with department stores was important to Ms. O'Brien for several reasons in addition to the increased sales revenue to be obtained from a new account. The department stores typically ordered in larger quantities and were thus able to receive and use cooperative advertising allowances from Smithville. Ms. O'Brien thought that local advertising not only helped sell more at the department store, but had a spill-over effect on the outlying gift shops. Also, a consumer who might purchase a 45-piece set at a department store would be likely to purchase accessory pieces when visiting a local gift shop.

Ms. O'Brien hoped that in addition to broadening placement with department stores, the company sales force would be able to gain additional placement in the smaller outlets as a result of additional cold calls made at the suggestion of the home office. She had found it extremely difficult to make some reps perform missionary selling work. Many reps appeared to believe that, once they had established themselves in an area, they could either write more business than they could handle or that they could add another line more easily than they could open new accounts.

She hoped that company salespeople would be able to obtain

223

broader product coverage with the existing accounts. Since they would be selling fewer products than the reps, they could concentrate their selling efforts. This was particularly important to Smithville, since much of the projected growth was to come from new lines and new products within existing lines.

In Ms. O'Brien's mind, one of the most important reasons for having a company sales force was the fact that a direct force could provide the company with much more information about the marketplace than could the reps. Actions of competitors, new product ideas, and new styling and color trends would all flow back to the marketing office much more frequently, given a good communications system.

Ms. O'Brien believed that the advantages of a company sales force revolved around the greater control which was possible in dealing with it. With the reps, the company did have the option of replacing someone who was not performing adequately. However, this was a complicated process. For one thing, most of the individual reps with whom the company dealt were members of an organization of more than one rep. Therefore, if the company was displeased with the conduct of one of the reps, it had to take into consideration what relationships the person might have with the rest of his organization before recommending his removal. Even in cases where Smithville was an organization's major source of income, this was a problem. And when a rep was removed, it was not an easy task to find a replacement who had the right product mix to enable that person to continue serving his existing accounts as well as Smithville's.

Perhaps the most concern to Ms. O'Brien relative to the switch was the question of initiative in the company sales force. Would a direct sales force have the requisite initiative and resourcefulness to sell new accounts, educate the retail clerks and buyers, develop creative in-store displays, and work with the department stores? Furthermore, what would prevent the more creative salespeople from becoming manufacturers' representatives themselves? This concern tended to force Ms. O'Brien to focus on the question of size. Perhaps, she reasoned, a sales force is appropriate only when a company is large enough to have either a strong consumer or retail franchise, so that it can affort to turn its selling function over to its own salespeople who would then be required to do little more than detail work. She was not sure that the company salespeople could "sell" as well as the better reps.

She also wondered about the nature of the administrative system needed to properly utilize and control a direct sales force. For example, how fast could the recently hired marketing administrative manager develop the needed tools to process and present the added information the sales force could generate? He appeared to have a good working knowledge of electronic data processing, and Ms. O'Brien was confident that together with the electronic data processing department manager he could eventually develop the appropriate tools. However, both executives had a great many everyday responsibilities that would limit their ability to devote maximum effort to the development of a more complete sales information system.

Ms. O'Brien also wondered how many accounts would discontinue carrying Smithville because of their loyalty to the reps. While she did not feel that this would be a major factor, when coupled with the fact that a company salesperson would mean one more person for the buyer to see, she estimated that a few marginal accounts would be lost.

Finally, Ms. O'Brien knew that she must factor expansion plans into her thinking. In addition to the 20 percent growth planned, the company was presently investigating the possibility of acquiring a small pewter operation for the production of a full line of serving and decorative accessories. Furthermore, a small German pottery which Smithville owned had just recently begun exporting a limited line of earthenware, and while its volume was very small at present (estimated to be $300,000 in 1973), it would hopefully grow and perhaps more lines would be imported in the future. Finally, a new pottery was to be built in the near future which would greatly increase capacity. Ms. O'Brien wondered if it might not be wise to let the existing rep organization develop the sales to support this plant and then make the switch.

Exhibit 6
Smithville's Manufacturers' Representatives: Opinions from James Fletcher, Sales Manager
Austin Company

Territory: Connecticut, New Jersey, Delaware, New York, District of Columbia, Rhode Island, New Hampshire, Vermont, Massachusetts, Maine, Maryland, Pennsylvania

Jim Henderson (manager)   Jim is a shrewd manipulator. He comes across as a crass blowhard, but there is a lot behind the huff-'n-puff exterior. Henderson now has the power as well as the know-how to get the Austin reps up out of the trenches.

Louise Boyer (rep for District of Columbia, Maryland, Delaware, Pennsylvania). Louise does a good job with the major department stores and larger independents. Doesn't want to be bothered with small accounts. Louise is one of the people who feel that she and the other Austin reps shouldn't go out opening up a flock of new accounts because her various manufacturers can't produce enough to keep their existing accounts well stocked.

Bob Spoerri (rep for Connecticut, New Jersey, New York)   Bob is a more quiet type. He is well liked and respected by his customers. He is thorough and works to a plan. Bob projects a very professional image.

Doug Burns (rep for New Hampshire, Vermont, Rhode Island, Maine)   One of the

Exhibit 6 *(Continued)*

Smithville's Manufacturers' Representatives: Opinions from James Fletcher, Sales Manager

Austin Company

newer Austin reps, he's been with them for 2 or 3 years. Prior to that he had worked for NCR. Doug is a young and aggressive rep and does a fine job opening up new accounts. He is too customer oriented.

Joe Schotz (rep for New York, Pennsylvania.)   Another newcomer to the Austin ranks, Joe is an ex-machinery salesman and a personal friend of Jim Henderson. Joe is a professional BS artist and a detail nut. He is very thorough and believes in working to a plan. Unfortunately, sometimes his plans aren't too well laid.

Sandy Boothby (rep for Massachusetts)   This will probably be his last year as a rep. He'll be handling only the state of Massachusetts for '73. Sandy is an old timer who is not willing to put up with the frustrations involved in dealing with major department stores. He is not willing to get involved in detail work. (See Appendix A for a description of a day with Sandy Boothby.)

Bernard Metnik (rep for New York)   Buddy does a reasonably good job with the Mom & Pop type stores, but has done a deplorable job with Manhattan department stores. Buddy simply isn't of high enough caliber to sell to major accounts. He's the kind of salesman buyers love: a pushover.

Gary Blinn, Independent

Territory: North Carolina, South Carolina, Virginia. Gary is an old timer. His arrival is a big event for his customers. He is very well liked, understands the importance of co-operative advertising, and has pretty good control of his territory. Blinn has substantial outside income and doesn't have to work. The thought that he may actually be working on a semi-retired basis has crossed my mind. I feel we could get more out of him.

Blumberg & Associates, Inc.

Territory: Alabama, Florida, Georgia, Tennessee.

Mitch Blumberg (manager)   Mitch is the son of an old timer in the gift field. He's a reasonably good rep, but a poor manager. He has little if any control over his subreps. He carries too many lines. He carries lots of lines to guard against losing Normandy which is his biggest source of income. He is the only rep that Normandy now uses.

Harold Pote, Independent

Territory: Indiana, Kentucky, Ohio, West Virginia. A genuine smile-and-shoe-shine type. Hal *sells,* but is terrible on detail work. Despite his allergy to paper work he is a sales manager's joy. Aim him at a target and most of the time he'll hit it.

William Shutzer Associates, Inc.

Territory: Michigan

William Shutzer (manager)   Another smile-and-shoe-shine type. Bill has good lines, owns a portion of the major exhibit building in Detroit, and knows everybody in the

Exhibit 6 *(Continued)*

Smithville's Manufacturers' Representatives: Opinions from James Fletcher, Sales Manager

William Shutzer Associates, Inc.

industry. He also runs a small but very profitable import operation. Bill is a stickler for detail.

Gerry Kammer, Independent

Territory: Illinois, Wisconsin, Indiana. Gerry believes in loving his customers to death. Any one of his customers' problems must be taken care of at once or he'll have a nervous breakdown. He is thorough to a fault and does a fine job selling to all classes of customers. Kammer worries too much. I'm sure he goes to bed every night worrying he's going to lose one of his lines.

Lonnie Martin and Associates

Territory: Iowa, Minnesota, South Dakota, North Dakota, Nebraska, Wisconsin
Lonnie Martin (manager)   *Territory:* Minnesota. Lonnie is a pain. He expects lots of cooperation from the home office but isn't willing to reciprocate. It's a constant prod, prod, nudge, nudge, with him. He is a nitpicker and loses sight of major objectives. He requires constant supervision. Though he's done a reasonably good job in his territory, I feel that there is much room for improvement.

227

Riggs & Fields

Territory: Mississippi, Kansas, Oklahoma, Arkansas, Missouri, Louisiana, Texas

Mike Riggs (manager)   I'm very impressed with Riggs. I feel that he is probably one of the most professional reps we have. His major difficulty has been attracting and holding on to good subreps. Mike is hungry, aggressive, and doesn't let too many things stand in his way.

The Millers

Territory: Arizona, Colorado, North Dakota, South Dakota, Montana, Nebraska, New Mexico, Wyoming

Ed Miller (manager)   Miller and his subrep, Don Tiner, are coming through with substantial increases in their sparsely populated territory. Miller has a tendency to be just a little bit on the nitpicky side. He is the son of an old time gift and glassware rep. He comes across as being a bit introverted.

V. A. Demery, Independent

Territory: Arizona, New Mexico, Utah, Montana, Colorado, Idaho, Wyoming.

Jack Fries, Independent

Territory: Hawaii

Exhibit 6 *(Continued)*

Smithville's Manufacturers' Representatives: Opinions from James Fletcher, Sales Manager

Jennifer Flinton, Independent

Territory: Alaska, Oregon, Idaho, Washington. Jennifer is full of ideas, which she presents in a very logical and convincing manner. The problem is that the ideas when implemented turned into nightmares because she didn't know what she was talking about. She is a very strong willed, good basic salesperson. Jennifer would do a better job if she simply worked harder and concentrated on selling rather than getting into areas that aren't her bag.

Glenn Whitwer, Independent

Territory: Southern California, Nevada. Glenn is now producing several times his predecessor's volume. He requires a lot of reassurance and coddling. However, the extra effort that he requires is worthwhile since he usually achieve his objectives. Glenn is a nervous, sensitive guy who isn't allergic to pounding the pavement.

Hughes Norton, Independent

Territory: Northern California. Norton does a reasonably good job with major department stores in northern California; he does a poor job with independent gift shops. He has fallen into a rut and wants to keep calling on the same familiar faces. He is probably our poorest rep when it comes to pioneering. He is lazy and lethargic.

Carl, Inc.

Territory: military exchanges

Dave Orlinoff (rep)   Orlinoff heads up Carl, Inc. They handle our military representation. Orlinoff has some good high-volume electronics lines and handles our line as a side line. Constant pressure is required to keep him on the ball. He is thorough and perceptive. If we can provide the motivation we can get a lot better results.

APPENDIX: TRAVELS WITH TWO SALESMEN

The casewriter accompanied two salesmen, Sandy Boothby and Doug Burns. The following is a brief diary of their activities. The trips were made in April 1973.

A Day with Sandy Boothby

Sandy Boothby was one of the original members of the Austin Company, Smithville's largest and most important representative organization. He was 64 years old, had 2 years of college, had been an insurance and pickle

Exhibit 7 SALES AND COMMISSION DATA FOR MANUFACTURERS' REPRESENTATIVES

| Name | No. of salespeople | Sales | | | Commissions | | | Smithville CPS[b] | Total CPS | % of commission by Smithville[c] |
		Smithville	Other[a]	Total	Smithville	Other	Total			
Austin Co.	10	$1746	$1229	$2975	$174	$195K	$369K	$17.4K	$36.9K	47
Gary Blinn	1	170	152	322	16	15	31	16.0	31.0	52
Blumberg Assoc.	4	225	n.a.	n.a.	17	n.a.	n.a.	4.2	n.a.	n.a.
Pote	1	360	218	578	37	29	66	37.0	66.0	56
Shutzer	3	204	1,300	1,504	19	196	215	6.3	72.0	9
Gerry Kammer	1	315	153	468	25	16	41	25.0	41.0	61
Martin Assoc.	4	278	430	708	27	63	100	6.7	25.0	27
Riggs & Fields	9	240	n.a.	n.a.	23	n.a.	n.a.	2.6	n.a.	n.a.
The Millers	4	122	250	372	16	33	49	4.0	12.2	33
Jack Fries	1	2	n.a.	n.a.	0.4	n.a.	n.a.	0.4	n.a.	n.a.
Jennifer Flinton	2	60	709	769	8	63	71	4.0	35.5	11
Glenn Whitwer	1	86	212	298	11	26	37	11.0	37.0	30
Hughes Norton	1	114	318	432	12	40	52	12.0	52.0	23
Dave Orlinoff	8	93	3,000	3,093	11	287	398	1.4	50.0	3
Gerard and Son	n.a.	10	n.a.	n.a.	2	n.a.	n.a.	n.a.	n.a.	n.a.

[a]Estimates of a reps sales and commissions in other lines were made from information furnished by the reps, and hence is highly suspicious.

[b]CPS is commission per salesperson and is arrived at by dividing the commissions by the number of persons listed in the second column.

[c]This figure is the percentage of a rep's total income that comes from Smithville.

Note: n.a. = not available

salesman before becoming a giftware manufacturers' representative, chain smoked, drove a Cadillac, and had 11 grandchildren. Sandy's son was also a giftware rep.

Half of the commission paid by the manufacturers of the lines he sold for the Austin Company was paid directly to him, the other half was paid to the Austin Company.

First Call: Arbor Gift Shop (10:15 A.M.–12:30 P.M.)

The store was a family-owned and operated gift store located in a mall south of Providence, Rhode Island. It was an account which Sandy opened 6 years ago when he was still covering Rhode Island and which he had kept even though he now only covers Massachusetts.

The store carried a large variety of gifts ranging from plastic flowers to lead crystal. The most important lines in the store were lamps (115 styles ranging in price from $30 to $115), casual wood furniture, wooden accessories, pottery (stoneware dinnerware), glassware, metalware (wrought iron, brass, copper, pewter, and aluminum), clocks, and framed pictures. The store owner estimated his inventory at $50,000 and, together with a second store he had some 30 miles away, he got approximately nine turns per year. The store this meeting took place in had 1,900 square feet. The second store had 1,100 square feet. As the buying-selling session began, the owner pulled up a stool for Sandy, remarking that he was the only salesman that gets to sit down while working in this shop.

230

After first asking what Sandy had on special (promotion), the owner and Sandy began to systematically thumb through the catalogs of the lines Sandy carried, selecting the items to be ordered. In determining what to order, the store owner referred to the very limited stock he had in the room, an order form on which he kept a record of the inventory he had in a nearby warehouse, and scurried back and forth from the shop floor. At the end of this 2-hour session, Sandy casually mentioned the new product line Smithville had introduced. Sandy did no merchandising of the store displays. The total order taken was $3,100.

Second Call: Peach Tree (2:00–2:15)

No sale. Owner did not want to reorder before paying his outstanding bills with Sandy's companies. Sandy left a promotion flyer with the owner.

Third Call: Revolutionary Shop (3:00–3:45)

This store was owned by a husband and wife and was a separate operation (in back of their house) in the middle of nowhere. The woman ran the gift shop while the husband operated a small lamp assembly shop upstairs. The lines carried were essentially the same as those in the first store. Again, the owner offered Sandy a small stool and took physical inventory as she ordered.

When asked if she had a fixed dollar amount she would order from a given salesman, she replied no, that she ordered whatever she needed. However, even though she had recently sold out of one of Sandy's lines, she did not reorder it. Her order amounted to $475.

Fourth and Final Call: The Carriage (4:00–4:15)

This shop was not more than 3 miles from the previous shop. It was by far the most professionally merchandized store. The store had approximately 4,000 square feet and carried essentially the same lines as the preceding store, with a very large selection of casual furniture and earthenware.

As Sandy walked in, the manager, who was very busy, told Sandy to write up a well-rounded $250 order of Sandy's metalware line.

As we departed, the owner remarked about how well his club plans had been doing, accounting for as much as 50 percent of his sales in recent days. (Club plans are arrangements whereby a group of women make periodic visits to the gift shop and purchase gifts over time, depositing the money with the gift shop until the selected item is payed for. The organizer of the plan periodically receives free gifts, as do the club members upon making X amount of purchases.) Sandy remarked that approximately 25 percent of his customers had club plans.

231

Two Days with Doug Burns: First Day

Doug was a man in his early thirties, with 3 years of gift-selling experience, all of it with the Austin Company. He had worked for a small computer software company before joining Austin. Doug had also worked for IBM and the Bank of America. Doug lived in Concord, New Hampshire, centrally located to service Maine, New Hampshire, Vermont, and Rhode Island, his assigned territory. Since joining the Austin Company, he had more than doubled the volume Austin had done in his territory.

The territory covered on this trip was Rhode Island, primarily around the city of Providence. This territory was given to Doug on January 1, 1973. Prior to January, the territory was nominally assigned to Sandy

Casewriter's notes: Sandy serviced about 300 accounts, calling on each account once every 40 days or so. He stated that it took him from 6 months to a year to gain the confidence of a new account.

Sandy planned his day so that he was virtually assured of placing at least one major order for his two largest lines. He would always order his best lines first, leaving little time for pushing new products. By the time he would get to the new products, the buyer was tired of talking, taking inventory, and spending money.

The buyers estimated that they saw an average of two salesmen a day, every day.

Boothby. However, Boothby had done very little selling in Rhode Island for the past 5 years, and many of the accounts we called on had not seen a salesman in at least 5 years.

First Call: Woodlawn Drug and Gift (10:00–10:20 A.M.)

This combination drugstore and gift shop was owned by a pharmacist and his wife. The wife did the giftware buying and merchandising. She had recently ordered one of Doug's lines for the first time at a trade show, and Doug was interested primarily in seeing that it was properly displayed.

The wife was not in and the line was not displayed. Doug spent some time talking with the husband. However, he would not let Doug arrange a display of the line since his wife was not there.

Second Call: Arlington Country Store (10:45–11:45)

This was a retail outlet associated with a manufacturer of decorated linens. It carried a full line of gifts and casual furniture and it served as a seconds outlet for the linen company. The store was a freestanding operation in the middle of the country with no other commercial buildings within at least one mile. It had approximately 6,000 square feet of usable floor space and was very professionally merchandised.

The buyer for this store had never seen a Smithville salesman or anyone connected with the company and yet carried every product made by the company. She stated that Smithville products were one of her five largest volume lines.

Doug spent most of his time listening to her complaints about breakage and suggested methods for her to expedite claim settlements with the trucking companies.

Third Call: Cassis's Hardware (12:15–12:45 P.M.)

As the name implied, this store was primarily a hardware store. The owner-buyer was making out a Smithville order and writing a letter to the company concerning an inaccurate dunning notice he had received when Doug arrived. Doug promised to settle the dunning mix-up. He also attempted to get the buyer to let him write up the order that the buyer had been working on when we arrived but was not successful. (Doug received credit for all sales in his territory, whether or not he wrote the order.)

Fourth Call: Belmont Jewelry and Gifts (1:00–1:30)

This store carried a very small assortment of cheap jewelry and gifts. They did very well with Doug's metalware line. They had not seen a salesper-

232

son for this line in about 9 years. They ordered approximately $500 of the metalware line.

When asked (after departing the store) how he ensured an account was credit worthy, Doug stated that since they were being shipped the line, they were OK.

Fifth Call: Oak Lane Gift Shop (2:30–2:35)

The buyer was out and the clerk who was minding the store knew very little.

Sixth Call: Kewish's Gifts, Furniture, and Housewares (2:50–3:00)

The buyer was out and the store attendant was unwilling to discuss Doug's lines with him.

Seventh Call: Jacque's Gifts and Interiors (3:15–3:45)

The owner was in, but not in a buying mood. He spent considerable time complaining about the damage done to the Smithville products in transit and talking about how slow things were.

Eighth Call: Morse's Jewelry Store (4:00–4:10)

This jewelry store, located in a new shopping center, did not carry any of Doug's lines. It carried several china patterns and several ironstone patterns of dinnerware, in addition to moderately priced jewelry. Doug spoke to the store manager, suggesting that the Smithville line of casual dinnerware would serve to round out the store's selection of dinnerware. While the store manager did not buy, stating that this was a recently opened store and hence was proving to be a cash drain on the original store (located downtown in a nearby village), he did take a catalog, customer brochures, and several promotion fliers from Doug. The store manager was concerned about where the nearest outlet offering Smithville was located. Doug told him, adding that as he drove by that particular outlet today he saw a "for sale" sign posted on it. (It was this "for sale" sign and the knowledge that the amount had traditionally been a small volume account that led Doug to make this cold call in the first place.)

Second Day

The territory covered on this trip was southern New Hampshire. This territory had been Doug's territory since he joined the Austin Company. The nature of these calls was completely different from those made in Rhode Island a month earlier. All the buyers knew Doug very well.

First Call: Free Spirits (10:40–11:00 A.M.)

Free Spirits was a freestanding furniture and gift store with furniture becoming more and more the primary business. The owner's brother was a furniture sales representative. The owner and his wife both did the buying.

The owner's wife stated that she had just sent in an order for some of Doug's products and was not interested in buying any more at this time.

Second Call: Archer's Department Store (11:15 A.M.–12:15 P.M.)

This store was one of many stores making up Baltimore, Inc., a chain of department stores in the Northeast. Each store did its own buying. All orders were approved at headquarters located in Boston. Doug has been working for some time on getting the headquarters to allow him to write orders for each store, as Doug deemed necessary within an assigned budget. In order to get them to approve this method of buying, Doug kept his own inventory report on his items carried by the store. He then attempted to show the individual store buyers and the approving authorities that his items turned over rapidly. He reasoned that their buyers could not keep as close a watch on his products as he could and often ordered less than the optimal product mix and insufficient quantities of the faster selling items. He also noted that during the particularly busy season before Christmas, when the buyers and other seasoned store personnel were busy with part-time, inexperienced help, and with in-store selling, he could order on his own without taking up their time. Doug reminded them that he would do all of their inventorying, would maintain their in-store displays, and would educate the retail clerks when he came in.

On this particular stop, recent store actions played directly into his hands. A newly assigned buyer had not ordered sufficient quantities of two of Doug's lines in February because of a tight budget and poor planning and hence was completely out of stock of many of the items. This buyer had recently made out an order on his own to fill in the gaps he was now suffering, but because the items needed were so many, the buyer again had bought short for fear of spending too much money. After taking inventory (at which time Doug discovered that several of the items the buyer had thought he was out of were in the storeroom), Doug was able to convince the buyer to let him make out a more complete order.

Following lunch, Doug returned to the store to talk to the assistant manager about this situation. The recounting of the above described chain of events to the assistant manager fell on fertile soil, and he urged Doug to get approval from the central office as quickly as possible and assured Doug that he would also contact headquarters on Doug's behalf.

Third Call : Olde Taverne Gift Shop (1:30–1:40)

This shop was a freestanding building in a small village that houses three shops: a toy shop, a gift and candle shop, and a dress shop.

Doug was very well known by all personnel at this establishment, but since the buyer (who had returned from Europe the night before) was out, no business was done.

Fourth Call: Monroe Trading Post (2:00–2:20)

This store did not carry any of Doug's lines. Its owner, however, was the sister of a representative who was a good friend of Doug's and who had suggested to Doug that he try to get his lines into the store. Doug had become increasingly concerned over the deterioration he had been witnessing in the management of a nearby store that presently carried his lines. Doug, therefore, hoped to get this store to carry his lines.

The store owner, Mrs. Monroe, liked the Smithville products very much, and considerable time was spent talking about how well they had served several of her relatives. However, she felt that her store was presently too crowded to be able to allow her to carry Smithville and do it justice. She said she was planning to build an addition and would like to carry Smithville when the addition was finished.

Fifth Call: Bonnie's (2:30–2:50)

This was another freestanding, husband-and-wife gift shop at which Doug stopped mostly because he happened to be in the area. Since the owner was collecting items for a Rotary auction, Doug reluctantly donated a sample he had in the car. No order was taken, but arrangements were made for a buying session for the middle of June.

Sixth Call: Harris' Department Store (3:00–3:10)

The owners of this store had declared bankruptcy on May 1 and were not interested in talking with Doug.

Seventh Call: Concord Gift and Candle (4:00–4:30)

This store adjoined an animal hospital where the owner's husband practiced. The owner had approximately two to three times as much inventory as she needed in all items. Doug had recently sold her a starter assortment of one of his lines she had not previously carried and was interested in finding out how well the line was moving. The order had just arrived that day and stood crated on the receiving dock. After helping the owner find space to store some other recently received merchandise,

Doug attempted to assist the owner in selecting an appropriate display location for the new line. This attempt was only moderately successful as the conversation kept drifting to a discussion of the store's cash and tax problems.

Casewriter's notes: One of the more subtle problems Doug found he had in dealing with his customers was ensuring that they keep an adequate supply of merchandise on hand at all times. Without statistical tabulations to keep precise track of a line's performance, buyers would often not buy the amount needed to support the display necessary to properly merchandise the line. Buyers were more likely to buy based on their subjective experiences at the time they decided to buy, experiences which were often not related to the line's performance. Occasionally, when this behavior caused the whole line to go unordered for an order cycle, buyers would find themselves completely out of a line and yet unwilling to make the larger-than-normal expenditure to "buy back into the line."

Hence, once Doug had achieved placement of a line, he saw his primary responsibility as ensuring that the line never became so depleted that it would be necessary to get the buyer to "buy back into the line."

TWENTY-FIVE Newport Instrument Division

236

In June 1975, Eric May, division president, Stu Tucker, marketing manager, and Harvey Lester, sales manager, all of the Newport Instrument Division (NID), were reviewing the sales-distribution strategy for NID's medical instrument line. As a relatively young division, NID had grown rapidly but erratically. (See Exhibits 1 and 2 for sales data and organization chart.)

Newport management believed that the medical instrument industry was still young and in the process of "rationalizing" its distribution system. While they appreciated the role NID's distributors had played in the past, they wondered whether the distributors would be able to provide the support needed in the future, especially in view of (1) the expected frequent introduction of new products, and (2) the increasingly rapid rate of technological and environmental change.

COMPANY BACKGROUND

Newport Chemicals was a well-established supplier of industrial and specialty chemicals which had diversified into the laboratory reagent business in the 1920s. Laboratory reagents were chemicals of high purity used in analytical and research laboratories. Because of their unusual purity they were high priced relative to production-grade chemicals. In the late 1950s, Newport management instituted a program to enter the

Exhibit 1 INCOME STATEMENTS

	1974		1973		1972	
	($1,000)	%	($1,000)	%	($1,000)	%
Sales	12,350	100	11,050	100	8,970	100
Cost of goods	7,904	64	7,183	65	6,010	67
Gross margin	4,446	36	3,867	35	2,960	33
Operating expense	2,470	20	2,431	22	2,422	27
Operating margin	1,976	16	1,436	13	538	6
Corporate expense	618	5	332	3	179	2
Net income	1,358	11	1,104	10	359	4

Note: Includes United States and Canadian results only. Does not include inter-divisional sales transferred at standard cost.
Source: Newport Instrument Division records.

instrument market since many of the tests previously performed with laboratory-grade reagents were beginning to be performed by instruments.

In 1963, NID introduced its first product, a conductivity meter to measure the electrical resistance of liquids. Since then, NID had defined its market as medical laboratory instrumentation.

237

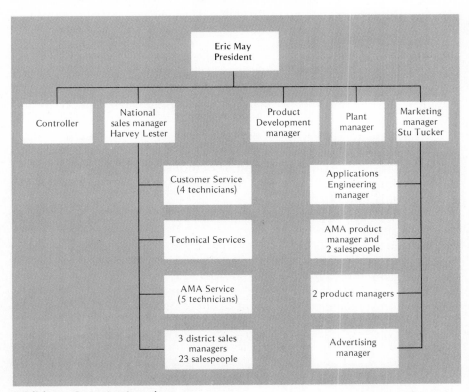

Exhibit 2 Organization chart.

NID employed 650 people and had domestic (U.S. and Canadian) sales of $12.4 million in 1974. It employed 23 sales representatives who called upon end users and the division's distributors, and 4 field service (repair and maintenance) personnel who worked with NID's dealers to improve the service that the dealers provided for the division.

PRODUCT LINE
Conductivity Meters

The conductivity meter had a variety of medical and nonmedical uses. Because physicians had found blood conductivity to be an important patient variable, the test was performed on almost every patient in a hospital. There were many industrial applications, and any research laboratory interested in chemical relationships would be expected to have at least one meter.

Newport had a full line of conductivity meters ranging in price from a $100 student model to $1,300 for the most sophisticated. Conductivity measurement capability was also built into some models of other NID instruments. Management thought of the conductivity meter as a commodity. The product was sold through NID's 6 national dealers as well as through some 32 regional and local outlets who had been selling the product since its introduction.

238

The division also sold meter electrodes which wore out in proportion to the meter's use. A large customer might use eight to ten per instrument per year at an average price of $45 each. Since many industrial installations had 50 or more instruments, supply sales were viewed as important.

Conductivity meters were thought to be relatively easy to sell for several reasons. First, the test performed was widely understood. Second, a salesperson could be taught to demonstrate the instrument in 10 to 15 minutes. Third, there was substantial brand acceptance for the Newport instrument.

The line had several competitors. The oldest, which was viewed as having a product of equal quality, was Eigner Instruments. Eigner sold its instrumentation directly to end users through its own sales force and manufacturers' representatives.[1] In 1973 Eigner created a special hospital sales force of about 80 salespersons trained in a full range of products for hospital and clinical laboratories. Its hospital and clinical sales were estimated at 30 percent of the company's $220 million sales in 1974.

A relatively new competitor was Gemini. Gemini had done substan-

---

[1]Manufacturers' representatives were commission sales agents who represented several noncompeting manufacturers. They did not provide inventory service or extend credit to their customers.

tial advertising recently (Newport had done none) and was forwarding leads generated to its distributors, some of whom were also distributors of Newport's products.[2]

Management believed that users of Newport meters tended to repurchase Newport and that this phenomenon applied to Eigner. Brand loyalty was considered to be important in all aspects of medical instrumentation. New customers for conductivity meters were believed to be influenced by advertising, a sales presentation, or by the mere existence of a conductivity meter in a local distributor's catalog. There was thought to be little difference in performance between a "major" brand (Newport, Eigner, or Gemini) and a private-label instrument.[3]

Newport had found that when improved products were introduced in the conductivity meter line it was fairly easy for a technical support person to explain the new features to the end user or distributor sales force.

For further information on prices of NID products, dealer discounts, sales by product line, and competitive discounts, see Exhibit 3.

Medical Electronics Instruments

Newport used only its six national distributors in selling the medical electronics product line, which in 1975 consisted of four types of

[2]Newport did not, as a rule, attempt to obtain "exclusive" agreements with dealers. Newport also did not supersede the distributor relationship by shipping directly to any class of customer in any product line.

[3]Private-label instruments were manufactured by one company and labeled with the name of a distributor or another manufacturer who did not manufacture such a product itself.

Exhibit 3   PRODUCT LINE DATA

Product	% of NID sales	Typical price range	Dealer discount, %	Competitive discount, %
Conductivity meter	28			
Meter		$100–$1,300	36.5	33.5[a]
Electrodes		30–60	36.5	35.0[a]
Medical electronics	65			
Single function instruments		$1,200–$1,600	35	n.a.
Protein analyzers		4,000–4,800	35	25[b]
Blood chemistry		4,300–7,000	35	25[b]
Calibrator kit-blood chemistry		450	40	40[b]
Supplies			40	40[b]
Immunologic supplies	7			
Equipment		$350	35	c
Diagnostic kit		150	35	c
AMA	0	$100,000	18	c

[a]Gemini.
[b]Midwood Corporation.
[c]No competitor sold through a distributor. In many situations dealers did not maintain list price.
Note: n.a. = not available.

instruments. The division had plans to add instruments in the next 1 to 3 years which would reflect state-of-the-art advanced technology.

The division was spending the least amount of its marketing resources on two single function instruments. Because they involved only one test, demonstration and training were relatively simple. The market for these instruments was not viewed as rapidly growing, however, since the tests performed were not of high volume. Once a laboratory had procured one instrument, it was unlikely to need a replacement for many years.

The major part of the medical electronics product line—protein analyzers and blood chemistry analyzers—met important and direct competition from Midwood Corporation.

Midwood sold its products exclusively through Medical Supply (M/S), a major distributor of NID products, as well. Midwood was well respected in the industry and had experienced rapid growth during the preceding 10 years. Newport management estimated that Midwood had some 70 field sales and service technicians assisting M/S in selling the two medical electronics instruments and selling the rest of the Midwood line. Midwood's total sales were estimated at $40 million.

The protein analyzer was not an especially difficult instrument to demonstrate. Its use in hospital and clinical laboratories was quite common and understood, and NID management estimated that a Newport salesperson was needed to assist the dealer salesperson in only about half the sales.

Blood chemistry instrumentation was viewed as one of the division's strongest product areas. The major difference from products described thus far was in the relative complexity and difficult demonstration requirements of the instruments. Once sold, a Newport sales representative might spend a full day "installing" the instrument. Installation included unpacking the instrument from its crate, performing sample tests to ensure that nothing had been damaged in shipment, and training lab technicians in the proper use of the device. This installation was not required in the rare instances when the instrument was the second to be purchased, and lab personnel were already familiar with its use. A blood chemistry analyzer sold for $5,000 or more. Some models could also be used for testing blood conductivity.

In late 1974 and 1975, there had been no advertising of the blood chemistry instrument line. Management expected that lead generation (customer inquiries) for new sales would come as a result of distributor contacts and mail promotions, in which NID supplied material suitable for direct mailing to its distributors, who would send such material to their mailing list. This both promoted products and kept customers abreast of current developments. In addition to mailings, each distributor devoted space (one or two pages) to the Newport blood chemistry line in its catalog. The M/S catalog, for example, was over 1000 pages long, illustrated, and cloth (hard) bound. Over 100 major suppliers were featured as well as many smaller manufacturers. The index alone was over 40 pages long, cataloging items from acid bottles to wire squares.

Once interest was generated in the product, Newport sales representatives were to assist the distributor salesperson in demonstrating and selling the somewhat technical instrument. Warranty cards returned to NID indicated that, in the case of blood chemistry instrumentation, 90 percent of all sales were preceded by at least one call from an NID salesperson. In some cases, distributor personnel would make several calls prior to getting a blood chemistry order. Often the final sale came only after the customer had advertised for competitive bids for the instrument, at which time competitive instruments might also be considered by the customer.

NID management believed that one stumbling block to the effective sale of a blood chemistry instrument was that the sales force tended to rely upon the distributor salesperson to "close" the sale. Harvey Lester expressed dismay over this attitude, since it was his opinion that the distributor salesperson was often an "order taker."

The blood chemistry instrument was thought to be very important in a hospital, since almost every patient underwent blood chemistry testing. The instrument appeared to require reliable and swift service support. As of 1975, service was provided through NID's six national distributors.

NID expected to introduce a new instrument within the year. It was hoped that it would revolutionize the blood chemistry instrument market. Certain hospital laboratories were being given an opportunity to test it, and distributor interest was thought to be keen. The instrument was expected to sell for more than $15,000.

Immunology

NID acquired a small manufacturer of immunology equipment in 1971. This segment of the product line was sold to hospitals for analytical use. It consisted of fairly straightforward equipment, but the application for the product was new and extremely technical. Sales were through the six national distributors, but only in limited geographic areas. The diagnostic kits of supplies required special refrigeration facilities for storage and had a limited shelf life. The test equipment costs were incidental in comparison with the monthly requirements of supplies. Typical costs were $350 for equipment and $150 per month for diagnostic kits.

Newport's product development had uncovered a new application for immunology equipment. It was believed that pathologists could now determine whether or not an individual had certain disease resistance.

In 1975, this development showed so much potential that Mr. Lester dedicated two NID salespeople to the line. The salespeople were to contact pathologists and explain the latest developments in immunology.

Once the pathologists convinced the hospitals that there was a need for the test equipment, the hospitals would usually issue a standing order for diagnostic kits from its NID dealer. The dealer would then automatically ship a certain amount of merchandise each month to the hospital, with little need to make further calls on the hospital or the pathologist.

Management characterized the immunology market as generally mature, but believed that NID had an application advantage. The difficulty was in explaining the sophisticated basis for the test's success to physicians. In early 1975 Newport noted that the older, more established competitors were becoming involved in this new applications area. Newport was the only major manufacturer to sell immunologic equipment through a distributor network.

Automatic Microbiology Analyzer

In 1974, the division introduced a new machine capable of classifying and counting bacteria and other microorganisms. It was called the *automatic microbiology analyzer* (AMA).

The AMA was designed in response to a request from Medical Supply (M/S). M/S wanted an instrument that would allow it to gain ground in the high-priced, highly technical segment of medical instrumentation, which was becoming a field dominated by direct selling manufacturers. As a result, AMA was made available to M/S on an exclusive basis. It was sold for over $100,000, including the required minicomputer and television equipment. A training program for the buyer's personnel was given at NID's factory. Management described the AMA as a new breakthrough in analysis, since it would perform lab tests which were among the last to be automated. Prior to AMA's introduction, lab technicians were highly valued when they possessed skill in performing microbiological analyses. Management claimed that the AMA enabled technicians to obtain much more accurate test results than with manual methods.

Sale of the AMA was viewed as extraordinarily complex. The instrument required that laboratory technicians utilize special new equipment to prepare the media plate (slide) for interpretation by the computer. The plate preparation was totally different from the techniques for manual analysis.

In order to best communicate the concepts behind AMA, NID management believed that specially trained sales personnel were required. NID had two sales and five service people dedicated to the AMA. As only a few machines had been installed, management expected that these staffs would have to be increased markedly to allow total coverage in the future. It was estimated that one service person would service ten to fifteen AMAs. NID was to perform all service work.

When AMA was first introduced, M/S assigned its sale to its general sales force of 350 people. This arrangement was not satisfactory to NID, since it was felt the sales force was ill-equipped to sell such a product. NID insisted, instead, that M/S form a dedicated sales force to handle the AMA.

M/S had already formed, some years before, a special field applications engineering group that was designed to aid general sales force personnel in demonstrating and selling high-technology medical instrumentation. M/S management agreed that these specialists should be trained to sell AMA. As of June 1975, the 40 specialists were undergoing AMA training by NID personnel.

NID's management, at the same time, decided that M/S needed even greater incentive to prove that the specialists could learn AMA's concepts and begin to meet NID growth projections. Thus, management made it clear that NID would review the situation and consider taking over more marketing functions itself if performance did not improve after training had been completed.[4]

In the high-technology microbiological analysis field, there were two notable competitors either in the market or about to enter it. Frick-Farrand Instruments, a division of a large pharmaceutical house, introduced its instrument within months after Newport, and NID management considered it to be an adequate entry into the market. Frick-Farrand sold all of its instruments direct and was believed to have six salespeople engaged full time on this product. Like Newport, Frick-Farrand would also have its own service facilities for the instrument.

Wellsley Instruments, a relatively young instrumentation company with a fine reputation, had announced plans to enter the market in 1976 with a very highly sophisticated system. Wellsley sold its instruments direct, and through Dubroff-Funari-Hall (DFH), a national distributorship which it had purchased in 1974. DFH was one of NID's six national distributors.

THE MARKET FOR NID PRODUCTS

Newport's entry into the instrument business came about as a result of major breakthroughs during World War II. The company had historically supplied chemical reagents to hospital laboratories. The reagent division continued to serve this market, but it became clear that electronic instrumentation would be the source of future growth, reducing much of the reagent demand. Since reagents had been sold historically through major supply houses, it seemed natural to use this distribution channel for the instruments. As manufacturers became larger and more adept at the high-technology end of the business, however, they tended to move

[4]As NID continued to offer more support to M/S, the discount was lowered by mutual agreement.

toward direct sales forces to improve margins, better control the marketing effort, and ensure the proper level of service for their product lines.

The largest market for NID products was hospital laboratories.[5] Of the 7,000 hospitals in the United States, it was estimated that the 1,800 with 200 or more hospital beds accounted for 50 percent of the medical equipment market (dollar basis). These hospitals were serviced by manufacturers through a number of channels. The various means through which health care institutions purchased their total equipment and supply needs (including disposables, syringes, etc.) are shown in Exhibit 4.

Within the hospital environment, it was often difficult to determine who made the purchase decision. Especially where large dollars were involved, there was an increasingly more complicated decision-making process involving several or even several dozen people.

Because new purchased equipment often did not result in a significant savings to the patient, hospitals were being criticized for not being as cost conscious as they might be. Thus, the medical equipment salesperson had to be adept at learning of a need and demonstrating the advantages of his particular product in order to be assured the chance of a sale.

The doctor, nurse, technician, or pathologist was the salesperson's

244

[5]NID conductivity meters and some other equipment were sold to industrial users through another Newport division, Industrial Instrumentation Division. In such sales, NID acted as a manufacturing unit only. This sales volume is not included in the NID sales figures.

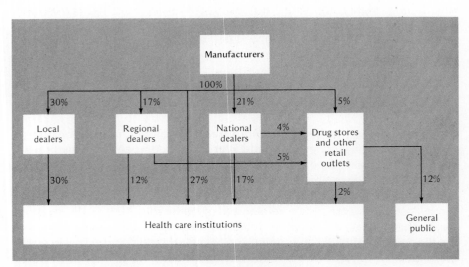

Exhibit 4 Primary distribution channels for medical supplies and equipment, 1972 (percent is of total manufacturers' sales).

primary contact who would identify the need for and type of equipment required. This person, however, could not always place the order for NID products, since in many cases the price of instrumentation required budgetary approval by the hospital administrator.

The administrator would often call upon advice from department heads and/or an equipment purchase committee who might ask to evaluate a product prior to approving it. If the product were very expensive, the hospital's board and various government agencies might become involved as well. Governmental forces were playing increasingly important roles in the process, since certain pieces of equipment were so expensive that a regional hospital planning agency had to approve purchase. The agency was interested in minimizing overcapacity of high-technology medical equipment within the hospital service area.

The procedure would culminate in the purchasing department of the hospital requesting quotations from several sources in addition to the initial one. The process was at times frustrating to the salesperson since it meant that people with no understanding of sophisticated products were actively involved in the purchase and selection of such products.

The distributor had historically performed an important function in making supply contracts with hospitals for the full range of their needs (disposables, syringes, etc.). This practice essentially "locked in" a distributor with an account for periods of up to a year. The successful distributor salesperson had to know his customers intimately in order to offer the best supply contracts, as well as to be available to quote upon noncontract items. While the contract supplier was often in the best position to learn of such items since he would be at the hospital regularly, competitive salespeople were also eager to demonstrate their firm's ability to service an account.

245

The average distributor of hospital equipment emphasized service and the ability to handle the customer's needs for thousands of small items. In the instrument market, however, the process and people were more sophisticated. Thus, the distributor was forced to move quickly to remain a factor in this market.

Most affected by the changing market conditions were the smaller, nonnational distributors who lacked the capital, personnel, or both to gain expertise in rapidly forming new technologies. The national distributors had adapted better, and it was for this reason that Newport had relied upon them.

NID management was concerned about the distributor salespeople's ability to sell complex medical instruments on their own. New equipment was constantly introduced by many suppliers and training distributor sales personnel required substantial time. A study commissioned by Newport showed that some 75 percent of medical instrumentation sold in the United States was being sold direct in 1974. Management also felt that with the exception of the AMA (automatic microbiology analyzer), no medical instrumentation was being sold at prices higher than $10,000 through distributors.

NID'S DISTRIBUTORS

Newport was primarily represented by six major distributors of scientific and hospital equipment in the United States and Canada. Of these six, only four were of any notable consequence. The other two sold only small amounts of NID products. The distributors had various regional strengths, but were all considered nationwide in scope. Over 80 of their offices served as Newport's sales and service centers.

Distributor salespeople were paid on a straight commission or on a salary plus incentive basis. The average salesperson would be expected to earn $15,000 to $20,000 per year, including any bonus or commission but not expenses. Distributor management attempted to turn their instrument inventories four times per year, their supplies five or six times. Accounts receivable might represent 45 to 60 days of sales. Exhibit 5 shows pertinent information about NID distributors.

Medical Supply Corporation

Medical Supply Corporation was the largest single force in the U.S. hospital supply business. 1974 sales were in excess of $1 billion. An estimated 40 percent of sales was from products manufactured by the company. Sales had been growing at over 12 percent per year. It was viewed as a service-oriented commodity supply house.

The M/S Division was formed in 1948 to handle equipment sales and had grown from 18 representatives to 350 in 1975 and had 24 distribution centers in the United States. Salespeople were paid a straight commission based upon gross margin. Many of the older salespeople were making as much as $60,000–$80,000 per year, including expenses under this system, but newer salespeople, viewed as "young trainee types" were thought to

Exhibit 5 DISTRIBUTOR SALES INFORMATION

Distributor name	Sales ($ million) (estimated)	% of NID sales sold in:			
		Conductivity meters	Medical electronics	Immunologics	AMA[a]
M/S Division	$330	8	29	n.a.	
Dubroff-Funari-Hall	$170	4	20	n.a.	
Franklin Company	$160	3	13	n.a.	
The Josephson Company	$130	4	4	n.a.	
Others	Not applicable	9	—	—	
Total: (represent % of NID sales in each product line)		**28**	**65**	**7**	**0**

[a]No significant AMA sales to date. M/S had exclusive.

Note: n.a. = not available.

be earning $15,000–$20,000 annually, excluding expenses, due to greatly reduced territories. Industry sources claimed that the older salespeople were a small minority of the total M/S force in 1975.

It was believed that, due to the compensation system and size of M/S, top M/S management had limited control over its sales force. NID had found that it was difficult for M/S to execute in the field programs which had been developed at a higher level.

M/S desired exclusive distributorships. Once secured, the sales force was often found to favor selling these exclusively distributed products over similar products in the M/S line. For example, in 1973 M/S had been made the exclusive distributor of the Midwood line including its medical electronic instruments. When this happened NID management noted a lack of support from M/S for its medical electronics product line.

M/S also carried many items bearing its own brand. These items were either private label or manufactured in its own factories. M/S-branded products were generally considered to be of no better quality than brand name products, but could sometimes be purchased at a lower price.

Some industry sources thought that M/S wanted to prevent a single manufacturer from dominating a market segment, since that could threaten the success of other firms represented by M/S. Other industry experts believed that M/S would try to prevent a single manufacturer from growing large enough in a variety of products to be able to justify a direct sales force. This concern was not to discredit M/S's intent, for the company had, according to the study made for NID, performed a genuine service for small instrumentation companies. Its marketing strengths had allowed young, high-technology companies time to work on product development and manufacturing problems.

247

NID management estimated that M/S had a 50 percent share of the medical instrument sales volume sold through distributors, although it carried products accounting for only 75 percent of the distributor sales volume.

NID management was also quick to recognize that M/S was NID's largest and most successful distributor. It represented almost half of the division's domestic sales volume in 1974. As NID products moved away from areas where M/S had exclusive distributorships, it was felt that the relationship could improve in the future.

Dubroff-Funari-Hall Company

DFH was characterized by management as doing a good job for NID, although not at M/S's level. The company was especially successful with protein analyzers. It carried no competing lines.

In 1974, DFH was acquired by Wellsley Instruments, a competitor of NID in the microbiological analyzer market. Wellsley's management was described as "super goal-oriented." DFH, which prior to the merger had tried and failed to become a major force for NID products, was seen as moving ahead under the new management. The past problem of cash shortages was expected to be alleviated under the new ownership.

Industry sources claimed that the major problem in the change of ownership resulted from the substantially different management styles of the old DFH and Wellsley. Turnover had become somewhat of a problem at the higher levels of management.

DFH had 22 offices in the United States and 180 to 200 salespeople. The sales force was compensated through a commission system. The firm was viewed as an "instrument-oriented house."

Franklin Company

The Franklin Company was viewed as an unaggressive marketer of items it sold under the manufacturers' brands. On the other hand, it did a capable job of marketing products which bore its own brand and which had been produced exclusively for its sale by other manufacturers.

Mr. Lester believed that Franklin did not maintain a high market share in specific product segments because it maintained list price in the face of competitive price-cutting.

248

The company had 18 outlets in the United States and 8 across Canada, representing the sole outlets in the latter country for NID. Franklin had about 220 salespeople who were compensated with a salary and a commission.

The Josephson Company

Josephson was a southeast-based firm that Mr. Lester characterized as "industrially oriented except in specific locations." Mr. Lester maintained that he spent essentially no time on the account. He believed that Josephson was not sincerely interested in the medical instrument business, since they showed no desire to become a force in the total market. Josephson was thought of as number 4 of NID's national distributors, althouth it accounted for 16 to 20 percent of NID's conductivity business. Josephson's prime business was the distribution of industrial instruments and as such was a major distributor of Newport's industrial instruments line, including the conductivity meters.

The firm had 15 offices in the United States and 160 salespeople, compensated with salaries plus commission.

THE CURRENT SITUATION

NID management realized that it had limited resources and that it could ill afford to lose any of its present market position. NID's present sales

Exhibit 6   SELLING EXPENSE INFORMATION

Selling expenses as % of sales	1974	1973
Ethical pharmaceutical industry (includes surgical supplies and equipment)	13.2%	11.2%
Instruments (includes sales personnel compensation, sales management expense, travel lodging, meals, entertainment, and sales promotion)	10.3%	16.7%

Sales force selling expenses as % of sales

	Compensation		Travel and entertainment		Total	
	1974	1973	1974	1973	1974	1973
Ethical pharmaceuticals	5.7	3.5	3.4	3.0	9.1	6.5
Instruments	3.5	4.4	1.0	1.4	4.5	5.8

Sales personnel compensation (annual)

1974	$13,300 to $17,680
1973	$12,540 to $15,950

(Average, nationwide including both straight salary and salary and commission plans)

Source: Sales Management, January 6, 1975.

force could not be expected to service all customers for Newport products. Salespeople were paid between $16,000 and $22,000 in base salaries, plus an average of $3,000 in bonuses per year. This did not include fringe benefits, expenses, and the use of a company car which added another 25 percent of salary and bonus to compensation. NID management believed that their sales force was in the top 10 percent of the industry in terms of compensation. They were also aware of a recent survey of sales costs (Exhibit 6).

NID management wondered if perhaps distributor discounts were at the proper level. One option was to lower them to competitive levels and reinvest the difference in the sales budget. While they felt that they were providing adequate support to their dealers, management wondered if increased support were warranted. Management felt that a direct sales force would also require a direct service capability. Presently customers could use the distributor's service capabilities in major U.S. markets. Service personnel might earn $13,000 –$16,000 plus fringe benefits and expenses.

Future products from the division were expected to continue the tradition of product excellence and state-of-the-art technology. Management expected that larger firms in the industry would continue to introduce new products and that the industry would become increasingly complex and technical. They were unsure as to how many sales personnel would be needed to service all customers.

It was also difficult to estimate sales growth over the next year, since no new products were expected until the end of the year, and the economic situation in June 1975 was at best foggy.

Industry experts expected competition to grow because many pharmaceutical manufacturers were beginning to enter the market. They had large resources and knew the drug market although not, in general, the hospital equipment market.

NID management was reluctant to ask for further funds directly from the corporate treasury, as it was felt that NID should begin to support its own growth plans.

TWENTY-SIX Company Sales Force or Independent Representatives?

One of the major decisions facing a manufacturer's sales management is that between using independent representatives and a company sales force to accomplish the personal selling task.

THE NATURE OF THE DECISION

It is important to differentiate between the situation in which the issues involve only personal selling and those in which other functions are also involved. In the first case, the choice is between independent represen-tatives and a company sales force. In the second, it is between a company distribution system and independent wholesalers. Before considering these two decisions, it is necessary to define some terms.

1 *Independent representative* A sales agent or sales agency firm that is paid a commission for selling a company's product to an end user, wholesaler, or retailer. Independent representatives, or reps as they are often called, vary from one-person firms to large companies with sales forces of several hundred people. Most reps carry several noncompeting lines which they sell to one or more categories of customers. Independent representatives are sometimes called by different names in different trades. For example, food brokers and manufacturers' representatives are both forms of independent repre-sentatives. Reps do *not* take physical possession or legal title to the merchandise. They act only as sales agents. Some also offer services such as applications engineering, maintenance and repair, or in-store (display and stocking) support.

2 *Wholesalers* A person or firm that takes title and possession (in general) to merchandise which is bought from manufacturers (or importers) and sold to retailers or in some cases end users. Wholesal-ers are responsible for the selling function, physical distribution, and

credit operations. They have their own sales force, warehouse, and credit manager. They are paid by the margin between the cost of the merchandise to them (manufacturer's price) and the price at which they sell the merchandise. Wholesalers are often called distributors, and in some trades are called by special names. A paper merchant, for example, is a paper wholesaler. In some industries, distributors provide sales support such as applications engineering and repair and maintenance.

3 *Retailers* Purchasers of merchandise from manufacturers, wholesalers, and importers for sale to consumers. In some industries they are called dealers.

It is not unusual for a manufacturer or importer to have manufacturers' representatives calling upon distributors (wholesalers) who sell to dealers (retailers). It is important to remember that three functions are involved: (1) selling,[1] (2) physical distribution, and (3) credit extension. An independent representative only sells and does not take title or possession of the merchandise. The wholesaler or distributor does all three functions. In some industries certain specialized firms may perform one or more of these functions. Some warehouses, for example, may receive, store, and deliver merchandise for manufacturers while doing no selling or credit extension, and without taking possession of the merchandise.

251

It is also important to differentiate between a company sales force which calls its salespeople *sales representatives* or *territory representatives*, and one which actually uses independent representatives. Some company salespeople are employed as "outside contractors," a legal term which offers certain legal benefits, although they represent only one company. For sales management purposes, such a person is a company salesperson, not an independent representative.

A company which sells to consumers must choose between independent representatives and a company sales force and, in some industries, between a company-owned distribution operation and independent distributors. In the latter case, physical distribution and credit costs (including cost of capital tied up in accounts receivable, credit administration and collection, and bad debts) are of great importance. Because of that, we will not consider that decision here. On the other hand, in the comparison between the selling function in a company-owned distribution operation and one in independent distribution the comments below are relevant.

The "Old" View

In the past, the typical view of the choice between reps and a company sales force was that reps were good for a "small" company, but that as

[1] In this context selling includes sales support functions such as those described above.

soon as a company became "large enough" it should develop its own sales force.

Much of this approach was predicated upon the concept that reps were a variable cost and that a company sales force, even when paid on commission, was at least partially a fixed cost. Thus, the small company, with limited resources and low sales over which to spread fixed costs, went to the rep organization. As the company grew, the reasoning went, it had more resources with which to build a sales force and it had enough sales to absorb the fixed costs of its own sales force.

As an example, if reps received a commission of 6 percent and company sales people only 4 percent, and if the fixed cost of a sales force were $200,000, it was easy to calculate that, below $10,000,000 in sales, the rep force was cheaper, and above that, the company force was cheaper.

In the past few years, however, the situation has been viewed in a much more sophisticated manner.

The "Current" View

The generally held current view considers the following aspects: (1) costs, (2) results, (3) control, (4) flexibility, and (5) availability.

Part of the cost situation looks much the same as it did in the past. Independent representatives are still a totally variable cost and a company-owned sales force a mixture of fixed and variable costs. Thus, the general tendency would still be for the larger companies to have their own sales force and the smaller ones to use independent representatives.

Some large companies believe, however, that they obtain better sales results, that is, more sales per dollar of sales expense, with independent representatives than with a company-owned sales force. In the food industry, for example, General Foods uses food brokers for some of its product lines and Skippy peanut butter is also sold by reps. This is not just the result of tradition—Heinz U.S.A. went from a company sales force in New England to a food broker in late 1974.

The key to the reason that some large companies prefer representatives appears to be control and flexibility. In the past, the general assumption was that a company-owned sales force was more amenable to control than a representative organization. With the reps, a company took on a group of rep organizations, each of which had its own recruiting, training, supervision, and compensation policies. Thus, control of the actual sales representative resided with the management and/or ownership of the rep organization. It would be almost impossible for a manufacturer to bring about the discharge of one sales representative from a rep organization. Of course, a manufacturer which accounted for a substantial share of a rep organization's sales was more powerful than one whose product line produced a small proportion. Small companies thus viewed themselves as at the mercy of their reps. As soon as possible they built a company sales force.

It appears, however, that as a sales force gets large it becomes very difficult to manage. The large sales force becomes cumbersome, and field management loses the tight cost consciousness and disciplined approach which many top managers desire. Thus, as the large sales force grows larger, it becomes less controllable and responsive and more bureaucratic. The switch back to representatives, on the other hand, introduces an aggressive level of management in the field—the rep organization management and ownership. They tend to be well-paid entrepreneurs who manage their organizations tightly.

Thus, one is left with a conceptual structure in which small companies use reps out of economic necessity, switch to a company sales force for reasons of economics and control as they grow, and finally, when large, switch back to reps because of greater responsiveness and effectiveness.

Some managers claim, furthermore, that independent representatives have three other benefits in some industries. First, the management of rep organizations tend to be highly motivated salespeople of great skill. Thus, they are excellent at dealing with major accounts. Second, because reps are calling on the accounts for other manufacturers, they can call on customers more economically than a company sales force. In essence, travel and waiting time is minimized and selling time is maximized because the rep presents several lines in succession. The argument here is that it is actually cheaper for a representative than for a company salesperson to make the call and that the companies which use the representative share in the cost savings. These savings would be especially important in high-service industries where frequent calls are a necessity, and in sparsely populated parts of the country.

253

The third reason given involves flexibility, especially seasonal flexibility. Some argue that an independent rep who represents many products with different selling seasons can more efficiently service a product with a highly seasonal cycle than can a company sales force which carries only a few products. Some see this as the reason that Kool-Aid is handled by reps. This drink mix is summer oriented and requires a great in-store sales push in late spring when displays are set up and stocked. The thought is that a company sales force could not absorb that high once-a-year work load as well as reps.

A final consideration involves the availability of independent representative organizations. Some industries have strong organizations available. On the other hand, in industries where that is not true, a firm is strongly pushed toward a company-owned sales force.

Implementing the Decision to Change

If a company decides to move from independent representatives to a company sales force or vice versa it is a difficult decision to implement. In one case, it involves creating a new sales force and sales management team where none existed; people must be hired and trained; policies must be established; and procedures must be developed, tested, and disseminated.

It is difficult for a company to find a "good time" to go through such a change. In good economic times, a manager fears that his company will be badly hurt by the change at a time when sales are without doubt available. In a recession, he is often too hungry for sales to risk the upset, including the fear that competitors will make arrangements with his better independent representatives and threaten his established accounts. Small companies fear the change, but the change is, in absolute terms, even bigger for larger companies.

Meticulous planning and careful implementation are needed to minimize the shock of change. The shock is great because it is generally believed that it is impossible to make the change piecemeal; once it is done in one part of the country, the remaining reps fear the same treatment and neglect the line.

Going from a company sales force to independent representatives is not easy either. The sales personnel must be either relocated inside the company, a hard task with even a small sales force, or helped to find employment elsewhere. Sometimes the rep organizations can absorb some of the people and others can be retired early or transferred. Sometimes this change can be made in one region or in one region at a time. That lessens the implementation problem.

254

Managing Independent Representatives

Often one option open to a company considering replacement of independent representatives with a company sales force is improved management of the reps.

A group of independent reps needs management just as a sales force does. The techniques and problems are somewhat different, but the need is as crucial. Because the sales manager cannot choose each individual sales representative, he must carefully select each representative organization. In a sense, it is like recruiting and selecting a whole regional sales force in one motion.

Independent rep organizations tend to do well for those companies which enable them to make money. Thus, the rep organization wants a margin which is appropriate by industry standards, saleable products, attractive price, and adequate quality and delivery, as well as effective sales aids, training, and advertising support. The sales reps working for the rep organizations need training in product knowledge and company procedures and capabilities, although it is reasonable to expect that the rep organization provides training in selling and market-customer knowledge. Independent reps like to receive advertising-generated leads just as company salespeople do.

In a sense each principal, that is, each manufacturer represented by a rep organization, competes with the others for the rep's effort and time. The rep organization management will spend that limited time and effort where it will generate the most profit. Sometimes the rep organization management is too shortsighted, but nonetheless the principal must respond to the perceived need.

A good rep organization-manufacturer relationship leads to long-term profits for both' parties. Both parties must work to make that relationships mutually profitable.

Another Option

Some companies choose to use neither independent representatives nor a company sales force. Instead, they "piggyback" their products through the sales force of another manufacturer which is already selling noncompeting products to the markets of interest. The company without the sales force gains nationwide or regional distribution without having to select a group of independent reps or having to build a sales force and management. Often the company gains credibility from having an established sales force carrying its line. On the other hand, such arrangements are expensive and offer little control to the company acting as principal. In addition, it loses contact with the marketplace and often tends to neglect development of an in-house marketing and sales staff. In many situations, furthermore, there is no company available which is both able and willing to act as a sales agent.

255

BIBLIOGRAPHY

Berry, Dick: "Motivating the Manufacturer's Agent," *Sales Agency Magazine*, I, January 1973; II, February 1973, pp. 8–11.

Grocery Manufacturers of America, Inc., and National Food Brokers Association: *Professional Working Relations between Manufacturers and Food Brokers*, Washington, D.C., undated.

McLaughlin, Richard: "The Case for Using Manufacturers' Agents," *Industrial Marketing*, November 1966, pp. 82–85.

TWENTY-SEVEN Sales Information Systems

The sales information system has typically been thought of as providing sales management and other parts of the company with important data for decision making. Most of these data concern sales performance. This note provides an introduction to some of the basic issues involved in the development and use of the traditional sales information systems, considers the use of the sales force as information gatherers, and the dissemination of information to salespeople.

THE USE OF THE SALES INFORMATION SYSTEM
WITHIN THE SALES FORCE

The major decisions facing sales managers involve people, programs, and territories. The sales information system provides some of the data upon which these decisions can be made.

Territorial decisions are primarily related to deployment. Typical of these are questions such as:

1 How many salespeople do we need to cover the Western states?
2 Is Sarah Stahler's territory so large that it should be broken up?
3 Can a salesperson survive economically in the Dakotas?
4 Should we split the sales force by product, market, or geography?

To make these decisions, the sales manager needs data on actual sales, active accounts, sales potential, and potential accounts by geographic division (for example, states, counties, Standard Metropolitan Statistical Area), customer type, and product type.

The program decisions usually involve the efficiency and effectiveness of current or proposed sales force management or selling programs related to, for example, training, recruiting, compensation, account management, sales approaches, etc. Here data must consider the cost of the program as well as its effect versus the effect of relevant alternatives. Data on program effectiveness are often very difficult to develop.

People-oriented decisions involve the selection, training, evaluation, compensation, and other supervision programs aimed at analyzing and improving a salesperson's performance. These decisions require information such as actual sales and sales potential, and active and prospective accounts under the salesperson's responsibility. Effective diagnosis and improvement depends, however, on going considerably deeper into the way in which the person sells and manages his accounts, the manner in which he implements company programs, etc.

It should be clear from the above that a wide variety of data is needed by sales management. It is useful to divide the data needed into three categories:

1 Regularly gathered and reported data, such as sales by territory, potential per account, etc.

2 Data gathered for special decision making, such as that needed in a sales reorganization study. For that purpose, it may be necessary to do an in-depth study of how salespeople spend their time.

3 Nonquantitative data which can, in general, be gathered only by personal observation.

The acquisition of the data will be discussed below.

Sales managers, by and large, tend to be action oriented and to shy away from the analysis of data. This is clearly less true, and perhaps not true at all, for sales managers whose backgrounds are strongly quantitative (for example, engineers). But for most sales managers to make effective use of a sales information system, they must receive understandable, usable data in a form which they perceive to be understandable and usable. Lengthy reports and confusing forms tend to be neglected. Exception reports, as well as those information systems which are structured around the sales manager's own view of his decision alternatives and responsibilities, tend to be received best and used most. Simplicity is very important.

257

THE MORE GENERAL USE OF SALES INFORMATION SYSTEMS

The sales force does not operate in an organizational vacuum. It is a part of the marketing mix and a part of the total corporation. Other marketing and nonmarketing functions rely upon the sales information system for important data.

Marketing management is interested in the sales effectiveness and efficiency of marketing programs. For example, it might be interested in customer reaction to a new product, customer needs which are not being addressed by the company, sales and sales potential by product line or customer category, and new competitive moves. It also might be interested in more elusive data, such as why a customer bought a product or why a prospective customer did not purchase.

The operations and service organizations might be interested in product performance in the field and specific performance problems. In addition, operating personnel may need to know the impact of programs such as expedited delivery or field inventories.

Credit personnel are interested in the credit worthiness of specific customers as well as general credit trends in the industry.

Marketing, operations, and finance people need sales forecasts as described in the note "Sales Forecasting for the Sales Manager."

As in the case of data needed by sales management, these data tend to divide into three categories: (1) regular needs, (2) special needs, and (3) nonquantitative information. This is one good conceptual framework for looking at data gathering.

Gathering the Data

The basic part of the sales information system is the data which are gathered and reported regularly. There are usually two prime sources of these data—the order and the salesperson. By its nature the order is a very important source of data. It has the customer and the product purchased. In addition, it often has other information such as products purchased with each other, the size of the total order, etc. It has another definite advantage—it is generated automatically. Few salespeople object to writing orders.

If the customer is coded into a market or customer category (for example, banks, variety stores) and into a territory designation, the order alone can be the basis for reports on sales by product, territory, customer, order size, etc. Simple computer processing also allows analysis, for example, of sales by product and by territory. Thus, the sales manager can see which salespeople are selling a particular product line and the marketing manager can attempt to identify regional buying patterns by product.

The other regular source of data, the salesperson, is sometimes less reliable than the order, and usually less happy about supplying the data. Many salespeople abhor reports and reporting can be perceived as taking so much time that it detracts from the selling effort. Sometimes this is in fact true. It should be understood, however, that outstanding salespersons maintain a variety of files for themselves, ranging from company data, order status, and call history to personal restaurant preferences of the prime buying influences.

In some industries and companies, the salespeople do no regular reporting. In those that do have salespersons reporting, the reports are usually call reports—a report on the activity and results involving each call—daily activity reports which typically include the number of calls made, sales made, etc., or call exception reports—call reports providing unusually pertinent data.

Call reports are among the most controversial aspects of sales management although their use appears to be growing. They range from short daily postcards, reporting a series of calls, to long detailed reports on every call. Many sales managers have strong feelings about whether or not to use call reports. Often the basis for their attitudes is industry tradition. Here, as in all other areas of sales management, one must consider the benefits and costs (financial and nonfinancial) before adopting a stance. One good rule of thumb is that if the data are of no readily apparent use to sales management, they are not worth gathering. Salespeople rightfully object to making reports which serve no purpose.

One of the paradoxes of call reports is that they tend to be of real value only when they are detailed and explain why the customer did or did not buy. Usually, shorter reports are useful only to determine whether or not a salesperson has made the call. Occasionally, the reports can be used to develop relationships between call frequency and sales.

The same comments can be made about daily activity reports and exceptional call reports. They should be used only when they are going to result in some impact upon decision making, and they are most useful when they are hardest to do, that is, when they are complex and rich. One of the most useful of the exception reports is the "lost order report" which is required for each sale not made. Of course, it can be used with ease only to track sales which come to a definite choice among competitors. Such a situation exists, for example, where bids are used. On the other hand, many orders are lost long before a definite choice point on the part of the seller is apparent to the buyer.

From management's point of view, one problem with call reports is that even a medium-sized sales force makes a lot of calls. For example, a sales force of 50 people, making an average of 5 calls per day, will generate 1,250 call reports per week.

Salesperson-generated data are also subject to questions of reliability and honesty. If a strong emphasis is not placed upon reliability and honesty, the data become suspect.

Some of the better sales information systems contain data beyond those usually generated from orders and/or salespeople. Some of this may be from external, market research-related sources such as credit ratings and customer size. Others may include data infrequently gathered from the sales force such as sales potential, end use, etc. Once these data are in the information system, they can be very useful.

Other regularly input data may include budgets, forecasts, and/or quotas. These data are necessary if the information system is to measure performance against plan.

When an unusual decision is to be made, it is often necessary to gather special data. For example, a company which is considering establishing a minimum order or customer size might need detailed data on sales costs per call, or data on travel times and call patterns might be needed in a sales reorganization study. Such data are usually gathered by surveying the sales force and/or sending market researchers or data gatherers into the field. The surveys may be by mail, telephone, or interview and may include the complete sales force or a sample selected either randomly or on some specific basis. All of the general concerns about surveys regarding clarity, ease of completion, and lack of ambiguity apply.

Some data can be gathered only by firsthand management exposure.

This topic is considered after the discussion on the use of the information system.

Working with the Information System

The preceding discussion has provided examples of the types of uses of sales information systems. The system works only if the sales manager and other involved managers use the data. Sometimes sales managers get relatively few reports, some of which are irrelevant. This is partially the result of a traditional animosity and misunderstanding between data-processing specialists and managers and between salespeople and sales managers. The situation is improving, and much of this traditional problem has been eliminated in technical companies where the salespeople are quantitatively oriented. Apparel and furniture sales forces, on the other hand, are among those that still suffer from this problem.

It is important for each manager to receive reports that are most meaningful to him. Thus, first-level sales managers should receive relatively detailed reports on each of their salespeople. The national sales manager of a large sales force, on the other hand, should receive broader, less detailed data on the sales force and its activity.

Good sales information is crucial to good sales management. Many decisions ranging from the evaluation of an individual salesperson to the total reorganization of a sales force are made primarily on the basis of the information provided by the system. It is hard to believe that good decisions can be made on the basis of poor, irrelevant, or nonexistent data. The truly effective sales manager goes beyond the information system in data-gathering efforts.

Beyond the Sales Information System: Confronting Reality

The sales information system provides quantitative data which are necessary in the sales management process, but sales managers need more.

They must go into the field to gain a complete understanding of the performance and activities of the sales force, customers, and competitors. It is important for the first-line sales managers regularly to be in the field with their salespeople. The sales information system may report lagging performance, but it seldom provides a complete picture of the causes of the poor performance or of the likely effects of alternative approaches to curing the ailment.

The national sales manager and other top-level sales executives must also be in the field with salespeople and customers on a regular basis; otherwise, an executive becomes insulated from the realities of the situation and responds to problems, risks, and opportunities in a limited way.

It is also important for marketing people, especially inexperienced people, to learn the nature of the sales force, customers, and competitors, and their relationships. In addition, it is important for marketing managers and top-level sales managers to be in regular contact with the sales force through sales meetings or headquarters visits by salespeople.

Regular involvement also pays substantial dividends in sales force motivation. Selling is a lonely task, and salespeople very much want to have their ideas and thoughts heard and to be given attention.

Salespeople as Information Gatherers

Most of the material considered so far looked at the information system as supplying information on sales performance and activities. The sales force can be an excellent source of market intelligence. Of particular importance are unmet customer needs and competitive activities.

Such data can be gathered on a regular basis. The problem with such a system is that the truly exceptional information becomes buried in routine data. It can also be gathered on an exception basis through written reports from salespeople, field sales management contact, or oral reports from the salespeople to marketing and marketing research managers. While each salesperson is subject to personal biases and is knowledgeable primarily about his or her particular situation, territory, and customers, the total knowledge of the sales force is vast. Salespeople are closest to the marketplace and usually the first to hear of new developments.

Data will tend to flow from the salespeople only if they perceive that the information is appreciated and acted upon. The sales manager or marketing manager who treats the receipt of an important piece of marketing intelligence as important in accomplishing a sales-related task will receive more information.

Large sales forces have found it especially difficult to encourage market intelligence to flow upward. In the small one, the short distance between the salesperson and the president makes data acquisition seem more important and data transmission easier. This is perhaps one reason for the greater responsiveness of small companies.

Salespeople as Information Users

It is easy when considering sales information systems to neglect the flow of information to the salespeople. While much of their information comes from the field sales manager, a great deal should come through the sales information system. All salespeople need data concerning the following:

1 Their own performance

2 The performance of the sales force, division, and company in general

3 New products and programs

4 Competitive activity

5 Important changes in the organizations they deal with (for example, a new shipping or credit manager)

6 News and gossip about sales personnel and other company people

A good sales information system helps each salesperson evaluate and improve performance. The best and least-expensive management is self-management. Because selling is a lonely task and because salespeople often have high security and social needs, they like to feel they are part of an organization or team. They need hard data on company performance as well as personal information on the other team members.

Many companies use a combination of regular newsletters and special bulletins to supplement the field sales manager in communicating with salespeople. Each has its own purpose, and used together they can improve morale and build camaraderie.

BIBLIOGRAPHY

Deboer, Lloyd M., and Ward William H.: "Integration of the Computer into Salesman Reporting," *Journal of Marketing*, vol. 35, January 1971, pp. 41–47.

PoKempner, Stanley J.: *Information Systems for Sales and Marketing Management*, New York: The Conference Board, 1973.

Robinson, Sumner J.: "Fact-Finding for Improved Sales Performance," in Albert Newgarden (ed.), *The Field Sales Manager: A Manual of Practice*, New York: American Management Association, 1960, pp. 112–125.

Stephens, H. V.: "A Profit-oriented Marketing Information System," *Management Accounting*, September 1972, pp. 37–42.

Turner, Ronald E.: "Market Measures from Salesmen: A Multidimensional Scaling Approach," *Journal of Marketing Research*, vol. 8, May 1971, pp. 165–172.

Webster, Frederick E., Jr.: "The Industrial Salesman as a Source of Market Information," *Business Horizons*, vol. 8, no. 1, Spring 1965, pp. 77–82.

Section
SIX
Implementing
the Sales Program

Once the sales program, the detailed statement of objectives for the personal selling effort, has been formulated, the focus shifts to implementing the program—the actual management of the sales force.

Sales force management will be discussed in five separate textual notes. The first three involve the management of the ongoing force and cover (1) field sales management; (2) compensation, motivation, and evaluation; and (3) organizing the sales effort. The last two involve the building and improvement of a sales force and cover (4) recruiting and selection and (5) training.

SALES FORCE MANAGEMENT AS A SYSTEM

It is important for the sales manager to combine each of the five elements of sales force management into an integrated program. None of the elements can be totally neglected, but much of sales force management consists of trading off one of the elements against another. For example, in building a sales force some companies emphasize the hiring of capable, experienced salespeople who are expensive in terms of starting compensation and difficulty in recruiting and selecting. Other companies hire young, inexperienced trainees and devote their resources to the training function.

The same form of tradeoff exists between field sales management and compensation systems. Some companies with strong, independent salespeople who require high pay and justify autonomy in their work can afford to have a larger span of control at the field sales manager–salesperson interface. In essence they pay more for salesperson compensation and less for field sales managers.

The tradeoffs among the elements of sales force management involve three aspects: (1) feasibility, (2) costs, and (3) results. Feasibility is important because it defines the available options. For example, because it may be impossible for a small or newly organized firm to put together an adequate training program for salespeople, it is forced to hire experienced salespeople.

Once feasibility is established, the main issue involves the projection of costs and results and their comparison for various alternatives. The projection of results is especially difficult. It becomes impossible without the careful specification of objectives and criteria for measuring accomplishment of objectives. Thus, if opening new, large accounts is an objective, the sales manager can build a sales force management system to accomplish that.

The outstanding sales manager has the ability to orchestrate the elements of sales force management so that each element is used in a way which maximizes impact and minimizes cost. Elements are combined in synergistic ways instead of in ways which create conflict. The evaluation scheme, for example, supports the sales force organization, and both build toward the same goals.

MONITORING RESULTS

When a new system is installed, it is important for top-level sales management to moniter the results. The importance of monitoring results does not disappear once the system is operating smoothly. Changes in the marketplace, such as shifts in customer buying processes or competitive approaches, as well as changes in the company's position, resources, and goals, necessitate constant review and change. While a sales force cannot accept constant reorganization or continual change in basic policies, regular review of the situation and regular changes must be made. Because too frequent change is so upsetting, each major change must be carefully formulated and implemented. If the new compensation system does not work, a rapid change to another one is not likely to produce outstanding results.

BIBLIOGRAPHY

Katzenbach, Jon R., and R. R. Champion: "Linking Top-level Planning to Salesman Performance," *Business Horizons*, vol. 9, no. 3, Fall 1966, pp. 91–100.

Newton, Derek A.: *Sales Force Performance and Turnover*, Cambridge, Mass.: Marketing Science Institute, 1973.

Section
SEVEN
Field Sales Management

TWENTY-EIGHT   Field Sales Management

The field sales manager as described in this note is the first-level sales manager. Typical titles include branch sales manager, district sales manager, and occasionally area sales manager. In some organizations it is difficult to define which level has the first real sales management responsibility. The large insurance companies, for example, usually have a unit or staff manager below the district sales manager. The comments in this note would probably apply more to district sales managers in such a situation than to the unit or staff managers because their management responsibilities and authority are very limited.

The typical field sales manager is responsible for a group of between 3 and 20 salespeople. Often, the field sales manager has the authority to hire and fire subordinates. He or she is usually located "out in the field" (that is, in office which is not at headquarters) with the exception of the field sales manager whose subordinates cover the territories surrounding headquarters.

Small sales forces may not include field sales managers. In such situations, the salespeople report to the president, marketing vice president, or sales manager. Large sales forces often have several levels of field sales management, with the ones above the first often designated regional sales manager, divisional sales manager, or zone sales manager. A later part of this note, as well as the note "Organizing the Sales Effort," discusses some of the vertical relationships.

THE ROLE OF THE FIELD SALES MANAGER

One of the basic decisions a company must make is the importance of the field sales manager in the management of salespeople. On the one hand, a company may place heavy emphasis on other elements of sales force management such as formal compensation, evaluation, and motivation systems. On the other hand, it may emphasize the role of the field sales manager. This choice is shown in Exhibit 1. There are, of course, infinite combinations of these two approaches and infinite variations involving the other four elements of sales force management.

Because the field sales manager is the only personal, day-to-day link between the company and the salespeople, the field sales manager plays a crucial role in managing the sales force and is responsible for communicating and interpreting company policies and procedures to subordinates, as well as to customers in certain situations. On the other hand, the field sales managers are supposed to transmit the concerns and views of the salespeople to their superiors in policy-making positions. They walk a tight rope, with conflicting demands often limiting the ability to maintain balance.

The field sales manager usually has two distinct responsibilities: selling and managing. Selling will be considered first.

Selling Responsibilities

In most sales forces the field managers retain some selling duties. Sometimes they have direct sales responsibilities, usually for the larger and/or more important prospects and accounts. In some situations, however, the field manager has a territory similar to but smaller than that of the other salespeople. This is usually a transition organization, used before a company believes it can justify full-time field sales management. Selling to larger and/or more important accounts is more likely to be a permanent situation. Such accounts often need and justify the greater authority of field sales managers. In addition, since they are likely to have

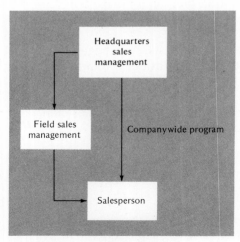

Exhibit 1 Companywide programs.

been capable, and often outstanding salespersons, they are likely to have substantial selling talents which can be utilized with the more important accounts.

In other sales forces, the field managers will assist the salesperson with selling rather than maintain direct sales responsibility. They usually become involved in matters such as closing large sales, negotiating contracts, and handling major complaints when their greater authority or experience is necessary.

One of the key issues concerning field sales management is the relative importance of selling versus managing. Field sales managers have traditionally overemphasized their selling responsibilities to the detriment of their managerial ones. This is understandable. Many have achieved their positions through their selling skills. They are more familiar and more at ease in the selling role than in the management role. Because they often have been ill-prepared for managing, they take the course of least resistance and sell. Sometimes a compensation scheme compounds the problem. Of course, a compensation scheme which encourages them to manage and not to sell improves the situation. Some companies, for example, limit the amount of commission sales managers can receive on their own sales, but do not limit their compensation based on the sales of subordinates.

It is important to carefully determine and explicitly state the selling responsibilities of the sales manager. Such a statement makes it more likely that the field sales manager will understand and follow policies limiting selling activities, and it will also help to ensure that the field sales manager maintains selling responsibility where appropriate. The latter is not often a problem.

It is also important for management to realize that a field sales manager cannot spend three-fourths of his time selling and three-fourths managing. Realism in job design at this point can prevent an unfortunate situation.

Management Responsibilities

The field sales manager's typical management duties include training, motivation or supervision, and evaluation. Some field sales managers have complete authority for hiring and firing, others only assist in the process, and some have virtually no involvement. The same is true of compensation decisions. Regardless of who hires the field salespeople, they quickly become the responsibility of the field sales manager.

Hiring and Firing

The note "Recruiting and Selection" covers the subject of hiring. It should be noted here, however, that it is one of the prime responsibilities of the field sales manager. Poor recruiting and selection is usually one of the prime causes of problem salespeople.

Firing often falls to the field sales manager whether he made the decision to dismiss the salesperson or not. Since it is an unpleasant job, it is often forced as far down in the organization as possible.

Firing is a difficult task and little has been written about it. One of the most frequent mistakes involving firing is not doing it soon enough. Often, in an effort to be equitable or nice or to avoid an unpleasant task, the unsuccessful salesperson is maintained on the job despite little objective hope for improvement. This is a favor to no one—the salesperson, the customer, the company, or the field sales manager. Almost no one likes to do a marginal or unacceptable job. The salesperson who is kept on with no hope of recovery loses confidence and gains nothing. During this grace period, the salesperson could be building a career and making headway elsewhere; customers receive less than acceptable service; the company loses sales, damages existing account relationships, and has no chance of creating new account relationships. The sales manager suffers because the customers and company are not satisfied, a problem is not faced, and sales force morale is weakened because the other salespeople must work with a poor performer.

Even worse than neglect is the "ship-out or shape-up" approach, which rarely succeeds. It removes the last of the failing salesperson's self-respect and self-confidence. It is a rare individual who can respond positively to such a thoroughly debilitating approach.

Thus, when an unsatisfactory performer with no real expectation (note that a "hope" is not enough) of improvement is found, the humane approach is the direct one—immediate transfer to an unrelated position or discharge.

When the day of reckoning comes, it is important to keep in mind that only a limited amount of help can be provided at that time to the employee about to be discharged. It is a mistake for the sales manager to assume that substantial helpful advice can be provided during the termination. The objective is to fire the employee with the least harm to the person involved, as well as to the firm. Terminated salespeople are, of course, in almost all cases inappropriate to call on customers after discharge.

Training

Training is a much more pleasant subject than termination. The emphasis here, as it should be throughout the field sales manager's role, is on growth and development.

There are many different approaches to training. Some firms rely primarily upon centralized and specialized training programs, while others rely more on field sales managers. Exhibit 1 can be considered as showing the two options.

Centralized and specialized training programs are discussed in the note "Training for Selling and Sales Management." It is important for the company to determine carefully what mix of centralized and in-the-field training to use and to coordinate these two approaches.

If a centralized program is used, the field sales manager usually is responsible for direct coaching and follow-up. The field sales manager will often be required to help the salesperson tailor general techniques and approaches to the particular territory, customers, and prospects. The field sales manager might, for example, help the salesperson plan calls in accordance with a procedure that the manager learned in a central training program. Since few firms have training programs for experienced salespeople, their training usually falls entirely to the field sales manager.

Training can involve four aspects: (1) the product, (2) the company (including such things as how to expedite an order, credit policies, etc.), (3) the selling process (including servicing of a current account), and (4) the customer. Product training is usually the most centralized portion of the training function. Training in company procedures is usually a mixture of straightforward material handled centrally and more subtle or complex issues confronted in the field during the normal course of business. The field sales manager usually is more concerned with the nature and techniques of selling and the complexities and subtleties of customer and prospect behavior.

273

The field sales manager usually trains by a mixture of four techniques: (1) demonstration, (2) individual coaching, (3) individual counseling, and (4) sales meetings. Demonstration is the simplest and, in many cases, not the best approach, especially for sales situations demanding high-quality selling. In the demonstration, the salesperson accompanies the sales manager and watches the selling technique. Often these demonstrations are just shams so that field managers can do more selling while claiming that they are managing. To be effective, the demonstration should be preceded and followed by an open discussion of the approach. Low-level salespeople who use a memorized or semimemorized approach can be taught more by a demonstration than can high-level salespeople who must go through a complex process. For low-level personnel the demonstration shows the supposedly "one way to sell." In the high-level situation it should be clear that the demonstration shows one approach among several.

In the coaching session, the field sales manager accompanies the salesperson, watches him, and then discusses the performance. This approach, often called *curbside coaching*, is most useful if the visit is preceded by a discussion in which the salesperson explains the purpose of the call and the approach used. Questioning and enlightened probing can help the manager facilitate the salesperson's learning. The postsales discussion must be frank and open to be worthwhile. Again, questioning is a very useful technique because it forces the salesperson to think and learn. Many sales managers are too anxious to "push" their own approach and do not let the salesperson develop individual thinking and style.

Field sales managers counsel the salespeople when problems are brought to them or when they raise issues such as, "Why are sales down in the XYZ account?" or "Why did we lose the ABC bid?" Salespeople will raise problems only if they find that the sales manager is (1) receptive, (2) supportive, and (3) helpful. The field sales manager who is too busy for such discussion or who uses them as a way to pressure salespeople will only find out about problems at his own initiative. Effective salespeople will also stop coming in to talk if they do not gain helpful advice.

Finally, most sales forces encourage regular district sales meetings to discuss new approaches, products, policies, and procedures. Such meetings are usually held weekly, biweekly, monthly, or quarterly. The meetings can also be for general discussions of matters such as deployment (which customers to call upon and which products or services to sell), call planning, and working with other departments within the salesperson's own company. The same issues can, of course, be handled on an individual basis.

Usually, the best field sales managers are those who employ all these approaches, carefully relating one to another, and coordinating their efforts with the centralized activities of the firm.

274

Evaluation

Evaluation is for many field sales managers the most difficult part of their job. It consists of four parts: (1) assessing the salesperson's performance, (2) assessing the salesperson's potential, (3) communicating these assessments to the person involved, and (4) developing a plan of improvement.

The assessment is a difficult task. Often companies have formal rating programs utilizing numerical or qualitative rating forms. Such systems are discussed in the note "Compensation, Evaluation, and Motivation." Most field sales managers also like to supplement these systems with their own assessments. The notes "Sales Costs and Budgets," and "Deploying the Sales Effort" provide some insight into likely measures of performance.

It is important to differentiate between performance and behavior. In the past much effort was placed on a salesperson's behavior: "Shine your shoes, comb your hair, and give the spiel in this order." This is not appropriate to most business selling situations. The salesperson must tailor the approach to himself, the prospect or customer, the product, and the history of the interaction among them. Behavior becomes difficult to evaluate when there are several right approaches. Performance becomes a more clear-cut indicator of success.

In many situations performance, too, is hard to judge. For some major industrial sales, the purchase cycle time may be many months or even a few years. Then, performance cannot be used as a criterion. Behavior must be used. In addition, sales performance is usually easier to evaluate than service performance.

The performance assessment is actually, however, the easiest part of the task. Assessing potential is more difficult. There are two reasons to assess potential. One is relevant to a poor performer. If the person does not have the "realizable" potential to improve, then as mentioned earlier, termination is probably the best approach. The second is relevant to all salespeople.

It is not humane to ask or expect people to perform beyond their potential. Thus, if a salesperson is operating at potential, little more can realistically be expected. If a salesperson is operating below potential, it is a waste of a resource for the individual and the company, and every effort should be made to improve performance. Communicating the assessment is most difficult; few managers do it well. The same is true of the mutual development of a plan for improvement.

The performance appraisal may be part of a companywide evaluation program, or it may be an informal part of training. It should, in any case, happen at regular intervals, perhaps no more often than four times a year or less often than once a year except in unusual circumstances.

275

The *Harvard Business Review* reprint series on performance appraisals provides an interesting perspective on the whole appraisal area. Two articles, "An Uneasy Look at Performance Appraisal," by Douglas McGregor, and "Reappraisal of Appraisals," by Philip R. Kelly, appeared in 1957 and 1958. They warned of the negative consequences of poorly done appraisals. In 1960, "In Defense of Performance Appraisal," by Harold Mayfield, presented some of the opportunities for appraisal as well as some proposals for taking advantage of the opportunities. Ten years later in "Performance Appraisal: Managers Beware," Paul H. Thompson and Gene W. Dalton again raised concerns about the negative consequences.

The performance appraisal should be viewed with caution. Regardless of these concerns, however, it is a necessity. Evaluation and communication of the evaluation can be done either in a haphazard, random fashion or in a reasoned, coherent way. It is done regardless of whether or not a manager likes doing it. Subtle and often nonverbal communication does it, even if the intent is to avoid it.

Performance appraisals can be useful, and what is more important they must focus on improving performance. To successfully generate improvement, it must provide three things: (1) the realization that change is necessary (if indeed it is), (2) the belief that change is possible (if indeed it is), and (3) a program to accomplish the change. Thus, the overconfident salesperson must be made to see that change is necessary and the underconfident that change is possible. People can be persuaded to take action only when they are moderately self-confident. Those who are high in self-confidence are not persuadable—they "can figure it out for themselves." Those low in self-confidence are too afraid to take action.[1]

The emphasis throughout should be on the future—what can occur—not on the past—what did occur. Mutual trust and honesty are important. Tact is appropriate, but it is important that the message not be hidden for the sake of diplomacy.

A good deal of the performance appraisal involves the manager's management of the salesperson's level of aspiration. If the salesperson's level of aspiration is too high, the salesperson will not meet preconceived aspirations and will lose the self-confidence necessary for improvement and selling. If the level of aspiration is too low, the salesperson's output will be below the firm's expectations and his own capabilities. Because selling is an emotionally taxing job, the management of the level of aspiration is indeed difficult.

Motivation

Motivation is directly related to training and evaluation. Both training and evaluation, in fact, are important methods of motivation. The well-trained salesperson is confident and capable. Confidence and capability breed success, and success begins to be its own motivator.

There are some parts of motivation which go beyond training and evaluation. They are necessary because selling is a difficult job. The best salespeople have high ego drives[2] and need to win. Yet, if each sale is contested by four potential sellers, there will be one winning salesperson and three losers. While quality control managers talk in terms of being on target better than 95 percent of the time, salespeople are probably good if they make the sale 60 percent of the time. Thus, the "no sales" can lead to a lack of confidence and poor motivation.

In addition, selling is often a lonely task with much time used for driving and waiting. Travel often appears glamorous to the uninitiated; to the veteran salesperson (or "commercial traveler" as they used to be called), it is often tedious and uncomfortable. These difficulties make it very important for salespeople to receive reassurance. Most have high security needs, although sometimes the needs are hidden by bravado.

The field sales manager must maintain confidence and motivation by thoughtful counseling, stimulating (if not inspiring) meetings, and constant assistance. As the primary link to the firm, the field sales manager can attempt to make the salesperson's work easier and more effective. The field sales manager can communicate needs for changes in policies

---

[1]This concept was originally developed for purchase behavior, but it is apparently applicable to management. The original research by Donald Cox and Raymond Bauer, "Self Confidence and Persuasibility in Women," appeared in the *Public Opinion Quarterly*, Fall 1964.

[2]See the note "Recruiting and Selection."

such as a new product or better quality for an existing product, more intelligent credit procedures, or more supportive sales promotion programs. The field sales manager can assist the salesperson in dealing with the company, for instance, in obtaining more expeditious processing of orders or shipping of merchandise.

The sales manager must provide both inspiration and substance. In fact, the dull delivery of substance is almost always more effective than the inspired delivery of nothing. The salespeople quickly lose confidence in a field manager who provides nothing bur forceful oratory.

One of the strongest motivators for salespeople is faith in the competence and integrity of the company and its management. Because the field sales manager is top management's ambassador or representative, and because he is the only manager seen on a regular basis, the competence and integrity of the company and its management are judged by the evaluation of the field sales manager.

Managing Independent Representatives

Many firms sell through independent representatives who carry several product lines rather than through their own sales force.[3] Many use field sales managers to supervise the work of the independent representative organizations. These field sales managers are not very different from those supervising regular sales forces, except that they have less leverage over an independent agent who obtains much of his income from his other product lines.

Managing the Field Sales Manager
Selection

The field sales manager should be selected on the basis of management potential, not selling ability. Thus, the best salesperson does not necessarily make the best manager, and a moderately successful salesperson can often make a highly successful field sales manager. Among the specific characteristics which might be considered are:

1 Ability to move beyond field sales management into policy making jobs
2 The ability to organize his work and that of his subordinates
3 A willingness to delegate authority and responsibility
4 Intelligence
5 The ability to teach
6 The ability to communicate
7 The capability to recruit and select
8 A willingness to work as part of a team

---

[3]See the note "Company Sales Force or Independent Representatives?" for more information on independent representatives and their use.

The big differences between the sales manager and a salesperson are:

1 The salesperson does the job personally; the sales manager accomplishes things through others.

2 The salesperson can have a relatively limited perspective of time and people. The sales manager must be able to plan significantly into the future and to plan for several people.

Obviously good field sales managers are more likely to be found in sales jobs which are complex and high level than in repetitive, low-level selling situations. In fact, the very high ego drive of many salespeople literally prevents them from operating effectively as sales managers.

Training

Field sales managers must be trained to manage themselves and their subordinates. Few receive any really effective training, especially in firms with fewer than 50 first-level managers. The task is complex and training absolutely necessary if the sales manager is to live up to his potential.

The field sales manager must be trained, for example, in performance appraisal and in selection techniques. Here videotaped role playing might be appropriate. Training cannot be done casually. It needs all the preparation and thought which sales training requires, as described in the note "Training for Selling and Sales Management."

Supervision

Supervision is also necessary. The field sales manager needs coaching, counseling, evaluation, and motivation just as other managers do. Sales performance alone does not tell the story. The responsibilities are much broader, and the problems are much more difficult to identify and define.

Career Paths

Most companies obtain their field sales managers from among their salespeople. Some use temporary staff positions, such as training, analysis, or recruiting, to develop candidates before or after their initial management assignment. Such policies can provide good experience for the candidate, a useful basis for evaluation by one's superiors, and useful work output. Too often, however, such positions do none of these. Instead, they are a boring way station on the career path up, with little useful output. Such assignments must be challenging and rewarding.

Exhibit 2   ONE-PAGE JOB DESCRIPTION

General responsibility

1   To maximize long-term profit generation within his district by the effective management of the assets directly under his control, including district potential, account relationships, market intelligence, and the district sales force

2   To contribute to the profitability of the total firm by assisting other organizational units, including product development, advertising, and other sales districts

Specific responsibilities and activities

1   At a minimum, to meet assigned district sales, gross margin, and expense quotas

2   To develop and maintain a sales organization capable of continuing to achieve district sales and profit objectives and whose major activities include recruiting and selection; training; evaluation, coaching, and development; and administration of compensation

3   To contribute to the development of corporate, territorial, and account sales plans, including the assessment of potential, development of sales quotas, establishment of expense budgets, and development of selling programs

4   To communicate and interpret corporate policies and sales policies to salespeople and other district personnel

5   To communicate and interpret district marketing intelligence and salespeople's concerns to national sales and marketing management

6   Where necessary and appropriate, to assist salespeople in selling and handling account problems

7   To contribute to the development of oneself and one's subordinates so that all can attain higher positions

279

The Field Sales Manager in the Sales Organization

The field sales manager should be viewed in the perspective of the total sales organization.

Job Description

The field sales manager is responsible for relation with accounts and prospects as well as for sales. In addition, the field sales manager is responsible for the development and welfare of his sales force. A proposed job description based on this view is shown in Exhibit 2.

The role of the field sales manager is not determined by the job description; it provides a set of guidelines. It must be backed up by an appropriate organizational structure, compensation policies, and relationship to the management style of the organization.

Span of Control

At the beginning of this note, the importance of carefully choosing between dependence on the sales manager and other formal sales force management systems was discussed. This decision must not only be stated, it must be acted upon.

One important decision is the span of control. Clearly, the sales manager who supervises 15 salespeople can do less with them than one who supervises 5. A large span will lower both the *direct* cost of field supervision and the amount of supervision provided. By and large, the more complex selling tasks requiring higher level salespeople also require a shorter span.

Closely related to span of control is the level of staff support. The manager who receives staff support (for example, training and analysis specialists) can either supervise more people or supervise them better. Most first-level field sales managers receive no staff support. At higher levels, however, the staff support can be substantial, sometimes amounting to more than 24 people at the regional manager level.

Compensation

Some field sales managers are paid a salary and a commission (called *overrides*) on the sales from their areas. Most are paid a combination of salary and incentive compensation. Some earn commission on their own sales, and some do not.

Obviously, compensation is a strong communicator of the wishes of top management. The field sales manager who receives commissions on his own sales will see it as a monetary incentive, as well as a strong communication. The field sales manager is likely to sell to the detriment of his management activities. This may sometimes be appropriate and sometimes inappropriate, but it should always be understood.

Field sales manager compensation plans should be carefully developed.

Management Style

The field sales manager's style should be an amalgam of personal predispositions, the style of the organization, and the needs of the situation. In all situations, the field sales manager will be in good stead if he views himself as a developer and educator of people. The field sales manager cannot watch over subordinates in the same manner as a manager of people in an office or factory. Therefore, the field sales manager must help them to manage themselves. This is difficult to learn and requires that the company provide the field sales manager with effective training and continuing management.

BIBLIOGRAPHY

Austin, Barry: "Selecting a Sales Manager," *Marketing*, November 1973.

Davis, Robert T.: "A Sales Manager in Action," in Harper W. Boyd and

Robert T. Davis (eds.), *Readings in Sales Management*, Homewood, Ill.: Irwin, 1970.

————: *Performance and Development of Field Sales Managers*, Cambridge, Mass.: Harvard University Press, 1957.

————: "Sales Management in the Field," *Harvard Business Review*, vol. 36, no. 1, January–February 1958, pp. 91–98.

Harvard Business Review: "Performance Appraisal Series," 1955–1970, including Philip R. Kelly, "Reappraisal of Appraisals," vol. 36, May–June 1958; Harold Mayfield, "In Defense of Performance Appraisal," vol. 38, March-April 1960; Douglas McGregor, "An Uneasy Look at Performance Appraisal," vol. 35, May–June 1957; Paul H. Thompson and Gene W. Dalton, "Performance Appraisal: Managers Beware," vol. 48, January-February 1970.

Leon, Raymond O.: "Sales Managers Must Manage," *Harvard Business Review*, vol. 42, no. 3, May-June 1964, pp. 107–114.

Livingston, J. Sterling: "Pygmalion in Management," *Harvard Business Review*, vol. 47, July-August 1969.

Newgarden, Albert (ed.): *The Field Sales Manager*, New York: American Management Association, 1960.

Sales Management: "Compensating the Field Sales Manager," February 19, 1973, pp. 21–24.

Sales Management: "New Approaches in Compensating the Field Sales Manager," March 5, 1973, pp. 25–27.

TWENTY-NINE   Grafton Industries (B)

Early on Monday afternoon, September 15, 1975, Harry Oates, newly appointed manager of Grafton Industries' capital district, received a brief description of the salespeople in the district from Jack Falzarano, outgoing Eastern regional manager. This report is reproduced below:

> *Alderson*   Bill Alderson joined the sales force in July 1974. He is 25 years old and had been a food company salesman. Before his arrival, the territory had been a problem. He seems eager to learn and hard working if not exceptionally bright. I'm not sure that he is the best person to turn the territory around because he seems too unaggressive in his sales approach. On the other hand, he has opened and reopened quite a few new accounts, although most are small.

Burke Ernie Burke is a solid performer who refuses to sell based on our merchandising programs and to push our most profitable items. He has been with us and in the same territory for 15 years and is in his early forties. He has a classic sales personality but is a bit lazy.

Caplan Sonny Caplan is 31 and has had the territory for 2 years. He seems unwilling to really work hard. He has concentrated on opening the larger accounts without too much success. This is definitely one of your more serious problems.

Durfee Gene Durfee is developing into a solid performer. He is in his early forties and has been with us for 5 years. He joined us from a smaller competitor. His major problem is that he's in all of the smaller stores but not active enough in the large ones.

Eaton Doug Eaton is one of the long-term strong performers in our sales organization. Although he's 62 and has been with us for over 30 years, he is able to adapt to new merchandising programs. There is no doubt, however, that he is slowing down because of age and health. When we talked to him about decreasing his territory 2 years ago, he reacted violently. He is very popular with the customers and the sales force.

Furness At one time Tom Furness was a good salesman. But he is having some severe problems. He is in the process of getting a divorce and he seems to be drinking to excess. He has 8 years experience with us and is in his early thirties. It would be a shame to lose him now.

Gibson Zeke Gibson has been successfully investing in real estate and seems to be losing his interest in Grafton. His real estate investments apparently provide enough income to insulate him from financial pressure. He is in his early fifties and has been a good performer for at least 20 years.

Harlow Ed Harlow is a plugger—an average guy who seems OK. He is in his late thirties and has been with us for 12 years.

282

THIRTY Grafton Industries (C)

Harry Oates, the new manager of the capital district for Grafton Industries, met with Jack Falzarano, the Eastern regional manager who was being transferred to Europe, for about an hour on Tuesday morning, September 16, 1975.

In general, Mr. Oates found the meeting disappointing. It seemed to him that Mr. Falzarano was preoccupied with his move to Europe, both in a professional and personal sense. The meeting turned out to be a general reiteration of (1) the meeting on the previous Friday afternoon [see Grafton Industries (A)], (2) the data presented to Mr. Oates at the meeting, and (3) a brief memo describing each of the capital district's salespeople [see Grafton Industries (B)].

As Mr. Oates reviewed the Tuesday afternoon meeting mentally, three things stood out. First, Mr. Falzarano had stressed the poor performance of the district relative to both the region and the nation. He had emphasized "the lack of control and discipline" which Samuel Goldberg, the previous district manager, had allowed to exist.

Second, he expressed specific concern about some of the salespeople. "Even Doug Eaton, the highest volume salesman in the district, is below our national average. And the immediate problems are pretty bad. Something had to be done about Eaton, but that can wait a bit. The really pressing problems include Furness, Gibson, and Caplan."

Third, he reiterated the need to make some decisions about the upcoming Friday sales meeting.

Following the meeting, Mr. Oates called Ted Newbury, the new regional manager who was preparing to leave his current district manager's assignment in Los Angeles. Mr. Newbury sympathized with Mr. Oates's predicament but provided no concrete help. To Mr. Oates, the summary seemed to be, "You'll have to run things on your own for the next two weeks, then I'll be working as Eastern regional manager and we can move along together." Mr. Oates was pleased with the rapport he had developed with Mr. Newbury, and with Mr. Newbury's apparent willingness to let him run the district on his own. Still, he was concerned about his lack of concrete advice as to how to proceed.

283

The one piece of advice which stood out was that Mr. Oates would have to decide how to handle the Friday sales meeting before he arrived in Baltimore on Wednesday morning.

THIRTY-ONE Grafton Industries (D)

On Friday, October 24, 1975, Harry Oates, newly appointed manager of the Capital district for Grafton Industries, made a commitment to himself to make some important decisions over the upcoming Veterans Day 3-day weekend. The decisions concerned the four salespeople he viewed as his most pressing problems: Sonny Caplan, Doug Eaton, Tom Furness, and Zeke Gibson.

MR. OATES'S PROBLEMS

Mr. Oates had been appointed district sales manager on September 12, 1975. He arrived on the job on Wednesday, September 17. During September and October he spent at least one day traveling with each of the eight salespeople in the district. He also made it a point to meet with each major account, as well as to review each salesperson's file.

He also had several discussions with his newly appointed regional manager, Ted Newbury. Together they decided that the other four salespeople were not perfect but that they did not present the types of immediate problems presented by Messrs. Caplan, Eaton, Furness, and Gibson.

Mr. Newbury, however, made it clear that he considered the district to be under Mr. Oates's control and he gave him a great deal of latitude. Mr. Oates believed that part of this freedom was a function of Mr. Newbury's management philosophy, and part was due to Mr. Newbury's newness on the job.

Sonny Caplan

Mr. Caplan had joined Grafton in October 1973 and covered West Virginia. This had been a good territory for the previous salesperson who had resigned to start his own retail hardware business in another state. Mr. Caplan was a college graduate and had previous experience as a toy salesman in Georgia. Preemployment tests indicated that he was very bright and possessed "the general attributes of a successful salesman."

His performance during 1974 was not particularly good and 1975 to date was not very good either.

The previous district manager, Sam Goldberg, had been concerned about Mr. Caplan's performance. The following abstracts represent the gist of the comments he had placed in Mr. Caplan's file.

October 1973 Sonny Caplan seems like a capable young man who can handle West Virginia. He is bright and personable and has sales experience. I expect that it will take him some time to learn the Grafton line, the hardware industry, and the territory. He seems aggressive and well able to implement Grafton's major account programs.

November 1973 Caplan seemed to impress headquarters personnel with his ability to understand our programs and products. I traveled with him for a couple of days after he returned from the training program, and he seemed to be doing well. On one occasion we visited several major outlets in Charleston. He seemed able to develop rapport with the younger buyers but seemed a bit ill at ease with the older ones. He is very personable and did well in informal settings.

April 1974 I traveled with Sonny Caplan for the first time this year. He had made progress learning the line and seems to understand our programs and procedures well. On the other hand, he doesn't seem to be making as many calls as he should on existing customers. He says that he is making a real effort to break into the larger accounts.

June 1974 After spending another day with Sonny Caplan I have some concerns about his willingness to work. He seemed a bit lackadaisical and not as familiar with the territory as he should be.

August 1974 I met Charlie Harrison of ABC Home Centers of Wheeling for dinner in Baltimore. Among other things we discussed the service he was receiving from Sonny Caplan. He seems pleased with Caplan's headquarters attention but complained that his follow-up with branch stores and factory problems was slow and generally lackluster. I mentioned this to Sonny and he said that he would improve this performance.

October 1974 I made a 2-day pre-Christmas swing with Sonny Caplan through the populous Huntington-Charleston areas. His rapport with buyers seemed OK but the in-store displays and shelf position seemed inadequate. When I asked him about this he claimed to be spending his time with the "big guns"—larger stores and more important merchandising personnel. Of course, if he can gain a couple of big accounts it is worth more than smaller ones. However, he does seem to neglect some routine servicing of even the large stores.

June 1975 (Mr. Goldberg had been sick for about two months during early 1975.) I have been disappointed by Caplan's performance. We had a talk today and he assured me that several large accounts were looking good. He also complained about the factory service he was receiving. I'm concerned about his attitude.

Mr. Oates spent 2 days traveling with Mr. Caplan in early October. He, too, became concerned about the low level of store service, as well as the lack of attention devoted to smaller existing accounts. Mr. Caplan seemed to resent the intrusion into his activities and seemed reluctant to discuss his activities on an account-by-account basis. His call planning seemed weak to Mr. Oates.

285

Doug Eaton

Doug Eaton was the largest producer in the district. He was 62 years old and had been with the company over 30 years. In spite of his age and a relatively severe case of osteoarthritis (noncrippling), he was robust and full of good cheer. He was well known and respected by the Grafton sales force and was active in a variety of industry and general sales organizations.

Mr. Goldberg had made no significant entry in his file for the 5 years before Mr. Oates became district manager. He and Jack Falzarano, the previous regional manager, had discussed Mr. Eaton's situation because they were concerned about the size of his territory and his ability to handle it. In 1973 the issue had been broached with Mr. Eaton who had reacted violently. It was not raised again.

Mr. Eaton had greeted Mr. Oates with a kind of reserved warmth. He had made a comment about his willingness to help Mr. Oates "learn the ropes." The comment appeared to have been made in a combination of condescension and sincerity. The day they traveled together was uneventful.

Over the month, he and Mr. Oates had dealt with each other on a relatively friendly basis but had little contact. Mr. Oates had made a conscious policy of avoiding Mr. Eaton until the situation had settled down and he knew the district better.

Tom Furness

Tom Furness had been a fairly good performer during his first 6 years on the sales force. He was physically attractive and a "smooth talker." It was common knowledge among the sales force that he was a heavy drinker and an accomplished "ladies" man. He also tended to be a loud but fashionable dresser.

Sam Goldberg's philosophy about Mr. Furness had been that "as long as he gets the job done, I don't care what he does on his own time." Some prospects and customers seemed "turned off' by his activities while others shared his interests. The district sales force seemed pretty much to accept Mr. Furness's activities. Some had shown concern that "he talked too much when he drank," and others expressed concern for his wife who was described as "very sweet and very patient."

Over the past 5 years, Mr. Goldberg had not made many entries in Mr. Furness's record until late 1973. At that time he noted that Mr. Furness's after-hour activities had become more frequent and that his service to his customers appeared to be decreasing. Mr. Furness also often seemed tired and "out of sorts" at the monthly district office meetings.

Mr. Goldberg traveled with Mr. Furness three times during 1974. Each time Mr. Goldberg noted that the days were uneventful. Mr. Furness seemed to know his customers and they seemed well serviced. He did not drink during lunch or dinner. The conversation in the car was a bit strained but not unfriendly.

Soon after he became manager of the district, Mr. Oates took one 2-day trip with Mr. Furness to western Maryland. They covered a variety of small towns and rural areas, as well as Hagerstown with a population in excess of 100,000. Mr. Furness seemed friendly but reserved.

Some of the customers greeted Mr. Furness warmly, but others clearly were not friendly toward him. Many of the accounts seemed to be understocked and displays seemed haphazard. The retail-store clerks greeted Mr. Furness warmly in general, but seemed surprised to see him. From the routing pattern, Mr. Oates suspected that some fairly large prospects and accounts had been skipped during their time together. When he raised this possibility, Mr. Furness responded that they had covered those accounts which he thought would most interest Mr. Oates.

In reviewing Mr. Furness's performance, Mr. Oates became further concerned because he had opened no new accounts, and some larger accounts had been lost or had decreased purchases substantially. When Mr. Oates raised this issue at a meeting in the office between the two on October 16, the previous Thursday, Mr. Furness became visibly upset.

He said that he and his wife were in the process of attempting to work out some problems. In June 1975 she had asked for a divorce, and Mr. Furness had become involved with another woman on a continuing basis. During September, the Furnesses had begun an attempt to reconcile their differences. Mr. Furness asked Mr. Oates for a few more months to "pull his life together." The meeting ended without resolution. It had taken Mr. Furness quite some time to regain composure at the end of the encounter.

Zeke Gibson

Zeke Gibson had been with Grafton for over 20 years. Both he and his wife were from comfortable if not wealthy families. He lived in a large house in suburban Wilmington.

Mr. Oates spent one day traveling with Mr. Gibson. The day started at about 9:30 A.M. and ended at 4:30 P.M., and included a long lunch with the owner of a large Wilmington-based hardware store chain. Mr. Gibson was clearly close socially to the customer, and Mr. Oates gathered from the conversation that Mr. Gibson and the other man had some real estate investments in common.

287

Mr. Gibson knew the line, the territory, and the customers. When they passed a new, large home center without making a call, Mr. Oates asked Mr. Gibson why he did not stop. The answer was, "It wouldn't be good for my customers, Grafton, or myself. My customers would be pretty mad if I sold to such a promotionally oriented upstart. They are very aggressive price cutters. That would hurt Grafton and me. In addition, it's not really worth the effort to try to break into such a store. I've got enough customers to keep Grafton and me happy."

Mr. Goldberg had not made any comments in Mr. Gibson's file over the past 5 years.

The other salespeople seemed to respect Mr. Gibson for his professional manner and to envy his successful outside investments. It was well known that he worked a 4-day week and vacationed for long periods of time during the early summer and mid-winter. Some of the vacations included old friends who were customers.

MR. OATES'S OPTIONS

Mr. Oates had a variety of options open to him, including firing and probation. Although he would need Mr. Newbury's approval if he were to fire someone, he knew that company policy and tradition gave the

Exhibit 1 DATA ON SALESPERSONS CAPLAN, EATON, FURNESS, AND GIBSON

	1974 sales ($ 000)	First half 1975 sales ($ 000)	July-Sept. 1975 sales ($ 000)	Active accounts, July 1 – Sept. 30, 1975	Calls, first half 1975	Calls, July 1 – Sept. 30, 1975	Salary, first 9 months 1975	Commission, first 9 months 1975	Total compensation	Expenses, 9 months 1975	Total
Caplan	$ 440	$ 238	$ 140	250	575	325	$ 7,125	$ 7,560	$ 14,685	$ 7,500	$ 22,185
Eaton	920	414	290	201	515	280	15,000	14,080	29,080	3,300	32,380
Furness	610	244	102	175	480	210	9,750	6,920	16,670	5,900	22,570
Gibson	560	252	165	130	410	225	11,250	8,340	19,590	2,800	22,390
Other district sales-people	2,510	1,265	822	1,020	2,840	1,520	36,000	41,740	77,740	18,300	96,040
Total district	$5,040	$2,413	$1,519	1,776	4,820	2,560	$79,125	$78,640	$157,765	$37,800	$195,565

Source: Grafton Industries records including call reports for data on the number of calls.

district manager a relatively free hand in such matters. This would also be in agreement with Mr. Newbury's apparent management philosophy.

Probation was essentially a 90-day written warning. If at the end of that period the salesperson had not brought his performance up to a satisfactory level, he was discharged.

Mr. Oates also had other less formal options open to him. In addition, salary reviews were made in early February after the year-end results were available. The district managers had some latitude in the amount of salary increase which could be granted. Salary decreases had not been used at Grafton to the best of Mr. Oates's knowledge.

Exhibit 1 provides data on the four salesmen and the district. Exhibit 6 of "Grafton Industries (A)" provides product-line sales data by salesperson for 1974. Exhibits 5 and 7 of "Grafton Industries (A)" provide information on the sales territories. "Grafton Industries (B)" provides descriptions of the salespeople. Sales by product line for each salesperson had not changed appreciably from 1974 to 1975.

THIRTY-TWO Grafton Industries (E)

On Friday, February 6, 1976, Harry Oates left his office just after lunch so that he could spend the afternoon at home reviewing several important situations.

Each February the Grafton Industries district sales managers were required to submit salary recommendations for each of their salespeople to top-level sales management. When the salaries were finally agreed upon, each district sales manager was required to conduct a performance appraisal with each of his salespeople. This appraisal was to include an explanation of the new salary.

Mr. Oates had decided that by Monday, February 9, he would have his salary recommendations completed for four of his salespeople: Messrs. Alderson, Burke, Durfee, and Harlow. In addition, he wanted to have a set of notes prepared for his performance appraisal of each.

This year he also had two other tasks which had not been performed by district managers in the past. First, he was required to develop a sales quota for each of his salespeople for calendar 1976. He wanted to finish his quota setting for the four salespeople by February 9.

In addition, he had been asked to participate in a special project. Ben Donovan, national commercial sales manager, had asked several district managers, including Mr. Oates, to develop a format for performance appraisals for salespeople. Mr. Donovan had specifically asked for recommendations on both a process of appraisal and an evaluation form. He had suggested that quantitative ratings might be considered as

Exhibit 1 1975 DATA ON SALESPERSONS ALDERSON, BURKE, DURFEE, and HARLOW

	Sales ($000)	Active accounts	Calls	Salary	Commissions	Total compensation	Expenses	Total
Alderson	420	445	1,670	$ 7,000	$ 8,400	$ 15,400	$ 7,700	$ 23,100
Burke	840	295	1,250	16,000	16,800	32,800	7,600	40,400
Durfee	860	175	1,450	11,000	17,200	28,200	4,900	33,100
Harlow	725	130	1,520	14,000	14,500	28,500	4,600	33,100
Total	$2,845	1,045	5,890	$48,000	$56,900	$104,900	$24,800	$129,700

Source: Grafton Industries records.

part of the form. In addition, he mentioned that he would like the form to indicate those attributes and performance measures which would be most important to the salesperson's job.

Mr. Oates viewed this fourfold task—salary recommendations, appraisal notes, quotas, and appraisal format—as both an opportunity and a risk. While he liked the fact that Mr. Donovan had singled him out for the evaluation form project, he would have liked to have more appraisal experience before he developed such a form. He was also particularly concerned about the salary recommendations, because in 1975 his predecessor, Samuel Goldberg, did not recommend any salary changes.

Exhibit 1 provides data on the four salespersons for 1975. Exhibits 3, 4, and 6 of "Grafton Industries (A)" provide information on the salespeople's 1974 performances. And Exhibits 5 and 7 of "Grafton Industries (A)" provide data on their territories. Product-line sales percentages had not changed appreciably in 1975 from 1974. "Grafton Industries (B)" provides descriptions of the salespeople.

290

THIRTY-THREE Metropolitan Life Insurance Company (A)[1]

This case can be used in conjunction with "Metropolitan Life Insurance Company (B)," which contains detailed material on the district sales manager.

Objectives of the Appraisal Process

Three objectives are sought through this process: (1) to improve the individual's performance on his present job; (2) to develop the individual for future assumption of greater responsibility; and (3) to facilitate planning for necessary personnel changes, including orderly succession in both regional sales manager and agency vice president positions.

[1]Excerpts from the manual entitled, *Evaluating the District Manager's Performance*.

Executive management views the district sales manager as the key element in attaining the company's objectives at the district level. It recognizes that inadequate performance may not be wholly the responsibility of the district manager. It charges the regional manager, therefore, to provide to the district manager those tools he needs to deliver the results expected. It charges him as well to provide the necessary coaching and directional guidance and to engender the proper management climate conducive to growth and progress. This appraisal process is intended to help serve those purposes.

Operating Principles

Adherence to the following principles is basic to the successful operation of this performance appraisal program:

1 Performance is the payoff area and should be the major focus of this review. However, a key consideration is the manner in which results were obtained, especially in terms of their consistency with company policy and good management practice.

2 Total results since appointment as manager in his present district should be encompassed in the review. Short-term considerations may be very significant, but should not be inflated out of proportion.

3 This is a *qualitative* appraisal designed to supplement the quantitative facts in the record. Use the review form to interpret the record so that its significance is understood today and in the future when others may have to make placement decisions on the basis of *this* appraisal.

When Performance Is Appraised

The most important performance appraisal is the continuing one that the manager makes of his own performance. He knows when his performance is "on time" and how good a job he is doing in discharging his other basic responsibilities. In addition, almost every contact between him and his regional sales manager involves some degree of appraisal of performance. This kind of appraisal would be ongoing.

Annually, after the prior year's results are in, a formal all-inclusive performance review should be held by the regional sales manager with the district sales manager. At this time every facet of performance would be reviewed, discussed, and evaluated.

In preparation for this review, the regional sales manager is requested to have the district sales manager appraise himself. This can be accomplished by sending the district sales manager a copy of the appraisal form and guide at least 2 weeks in advance of the date scheduled for the joint appraisal discussion. Prior to the appraisal discussion the regional sales manager should complete his own copy of the appraisal review, except for Part V.

When the formal review is completed, the district sales manager should know exactly how his performance is viewed by the regional sales manager. He will be in a position to take corrective action to strengthen any of his methods which may not be up to maximum proficiency. At the same time the regional sales manager will be in a position to recommend such action as may be appropriate.

Following this review the regional sales manager should complete Part V, file the completed appraisal review in accordance with the instructions thereon, and schedule a discussion of the review with the agency vice president. An appraisal will be completed more frequently than annually when justified by performance factors, and wherever promotion, repositioning, or termination is recommended.

PART I: APPRAISAL OF PERFORMANCE

This part of the review suggests guidelines for appraisal of *performance*. Here the regional sales manager should consider the actual results which were achieved versus the objectives, plans, and requirements expected of this particular district manager. The appraisal should measure *what* he accomplished, *how much* he did, and *how well* he did it. Later parts of the procedure request comparison of his results with those achieved by the other district sales managers in the region.

Basis for Appraisal

The district sales manager's job has two dimensions. One is his responsibility for obtaining the results set forth in the district's annual marketing plan. These short-term results are sought through others—the unit sales managers and sales representatives—but the district sales manager remains accountable for them.

The second dimension concerns the basic management responsibilities involved in the district sales manager position. Here he stands on his own, to be appraised in terms of what he accomplished versus what he was expected to do. This dimension of his position is described in "The Metropolitan Manager."

Results versus Marketing Plan Objectives

Four areas of district performance are to be appraised: first-year commissions, premium growth, personnel growth, and other pertinent subobjectives—all of which should be set forth in the annual marketing plan. In completing these entries consider both the results of the current year and the district's record since this manager's appointment to the position.

"Absolute" levels of performance, performance in terms of percentage of objectives achieved, and per person results are significant and useful yardsticks. Simply reporting these as achievement measures is inadequate evaluation, since each has well-known limitations as a complete performance measure.

Develop and Maintain a Sales Program

A sound sales program hinges directly on the district sales manager's ability to accurately assess the market potential in his area, to develop a sales organization capable of capturing an increasingly larger share of the market, and to prepare a district marketing plan that can be used as a "road map" in capturing that share.

1 What specific evidence is there that this manager knows his markets and properly matches available personnel with them?

2 The extent to which the district's sales activity demonstrates penetration of all reasonably productive markets and shows relations to market potential.

3 Specific progress being made in refocusing marketing efforts on higher income markets.

4 The extent to which the district is moving successfully into specialized situations, such as variable annuity sales, brokerage, group sales, etc.

5 Specific indications of support for companywide sales programs, such as "Policyholder Month."

6 Evidence of progress in achieving higher business quality objectives, including results in stimulating sales of larger size policies, Keogh plans, tax-sheltered annuity cases, pension plans, etc.

7 To what extent does the district's sales program emphasize and actually realize balanced sales throughout the year?

8 Adequacy and realism of objectives he proposes during the planning process.

9 The extent to which he effects timely modification of district objectives to meet change during the year; realism in responding to unsatisfactory situations.

10 Evidence of progress in developing new markets, promoting new policies or service.

Casewriter's note: The other five areas previously discussed were covered here.

PART II: HOW THE DISTRICT SALES MANAGER'S ACCOMPLISHMENTS WERE ACHIEVED

We have long since passed the day when record is the sole consideration. The manner in which results were achieved is an important criterion of executive success.

One reason for this is that use of the best methods should lead to continuing improvement in operating results, increased district manager job satisfaction, enhanced potential for advancement, and increased earnings. A second reason is that poor methods or immature management behavior can produce excess costs and harmful by-products. These are demonstrated by such examples as negative premium growth; unacceptable personnel turnover rates; and poor management, public, and employee relations.

294

The regional sales manager has a clear responsibility to diagnose the problems and weaknesses in the management methods and approaches of his district managers. In which are they highly proficient; in which is their function acceptable; where do they need improvement, what can be done about it; when are they going to do it; and what role does the regional sales manager have in securing these ends? These questions are intended to be explored by the regional sales manager as he evaluates the management methods of his district managers.

Use specific examples to the maximum possible extent in making the following evaluations. *Again, employ the exception principle—deal with those matters which require comment because they are either good or poor.*

Management Functions and Skills

This section is intended to deal with the basic tools used in the performance of the management job. These include but are not limited to such functions as planning and organizing, directing and administering, appraisal and measurement of results, and communication. These are, of course, simply means to ends and are not necessarily ends in themselves. Thus, while we consider them in order to help the district sales manager do a better job, they are less important than his performance in determining his effectiveness as a manager.

Some of the questions which should be considered are:

1 Does he use the priority approach? Does he think it and practice it as well? Does he make a work plan and follow it?

2 Consider the accuracy and realism of the objectives he sets for his district; how adequate is his longer-range planning? How effectively does he help his unit managers develop action plans? To what extent does he follow them up?

3 Examine the allocation of his time between routine administrative duties and key management functions.

4 Consider his delegation practices and the extent to which he encourages his unit sales managers to function independently and to be accountable.

5 Describe his ability to appraise and evaluate results, to identify and analyze variances and to initiate corrective actions. How effectively does he probe behind superficialities to get to the heart of the matter? Having done so, do the facts disclosed have real meaning to him?

6 Consider his effectiveness—both orally and in writing—in getting over his ideas. Does he encourage communication from others and solicit their ideas and opinions? How does he handle written communication, particularly in terms of letters, bulletins, notes to leaders, dissemination of worthwhile sales hints, and operating guidelines?

Casewriters note: Other sections involved *relationships, personal operations,* and *overall approach to the job.*

PART III: ACTION PLANS FOR PERFORMANCE IMPROVEMENT

While the implications of this part of the appraisal are clear, a few suggestions may be helpful:

1 Only in rare cases should these action plans be formulated by the regional manager. Unless they are fully those of the district manager, he cannot really be held accountable for their fulfillment.

2 The regional manager's role in helping the district sales manager fulfill these plans should be clearly specified.

3 Objectives, target dates, priority activities, and progress review points should be spelled out.

4 Generalizations will not suffice: show what specific action is proposed, what is to be accomplished, and when it is to be completed.

Exhibit 1

Part I: Appraisal of Performance

A. Results versus marketing plan objectives. (In evaluating the district's record, consider both current year results and performance since the manager's appointment.)

    1. First-year commissions: _____

    2. Premium growth: _____

    3. Personnel growth: _____

    4. Pertinent subobjectives: _____

B. Performance as to basic management responsibilities

    1. Develop and maintain a sales program: _____

    2. Recruit and select district personnel: _____

    3. Train and develop district personnel: _____

    4. Motivate district personnel: _____

    5. Direct administrative activities: _____

    6. Develop and maintain good public relations: _____

296

Part II: How the District Manager's Accomplishments Were Achieved

Evaluate the manager's methods and their effects:

A. Management functions and skills: _____

B. Relationships: _____

C. Personal operations: _____

D. Overall approach to the job: _____

Part III: Action Plans for Performance Improvement

Describe what the manager plans to do to improve present performance; describe what you plan to do to help the manager.

Actions	Objectives and target dates

Part IV: Performance Rating

A. Performance versus objectives

Annual performance ratings   197___ _____   197___ _____   197___ _____
5 prior years   197___ _____   197___ _____

Current year's performance: Outstanding _____   Superior _____
Acceptable _____   Marginal _____   Unsatisfactory _____

B. Performance versus that of other district managers

	Year	Region	Territory	Company
Annual leadership standing 5 prior years:				
Current year's standing:				

C. Current direction of trends in performance and methods: _____
_____
Is the manager equal to the task of achieving the district's long-term goals? _____

297

D. Extenuating circumstances which should be considered in interpreting the ratings entered above.
_____
_____

Part V: Confidential Information

Note: Complete this part *after* discussion of the performance review with the district manager and *before* discussing the review with the agency vice president. Do not discuss your entries on this page with the district manager and do not ask the manager to complete this page as a part of the self-appraisal process.

A. Ranking

Based on leadership standing, overall performance and my evaluation of the individual as a sales manager. I rank him #_____ out of my _____ district managers.

B. Advancement potential

Next position possibility _____ Date ready _____
Training or experience needed to qualify _____

C. Recommendations on position

Position recommendation _____

Section
EIGHT
Compensation, Evaluation, and Motivation

THIRTY-FOUR   Compensation, Evaluation, and Motivation

These three topics must be considered together, because the primary purpose of compensation and evaluation is motivation. Sales managers, in fact, often talk of financial and nonfinancial motivation. Financial motivation is compensation. Evaluation is a primary part of nonfinancial motivation.

Employees are compensated for past performance and in expectation of future performance. They perform among other reasons in expectation of future compensation. This is especially true of salespeople, because their compensation is often directly based on performance through commissions or bonuses.

The primary purpose of evaluation is to develop improved performance.

This note is concerned with compensation, evaluation, and motivation systems which are companywide.[1] The alternative to these systems is to put added emphasis on the field sales manager.[2] These approaches are not conflicting; to the contrary, they can usefully complement each other. The field sales manager can be used to apply the system in a "customized" manner for each salesperson and situation. The system can provide important support and a useful framework for the field sales manager.

This note is divided into four further sections, covering compensation, evaluation, motivation, and quotas and contests.

[1] In this sense companywide means used throughout one particular sales force.

[2] See the note "Field Sales Management" for more on this approach.

COMPENSATION

Compensation is the most discussed but not the most important aspect of sales force management. Because the literature is so complete this note will attempt to highlight only the most important thoughts and then to provide a review of the available literature.

There are two cardinal rules in developing compensation systems:

1 Assess the objectives carefully and be sure that the system meets the objectives.

2 Meticulously cover all of the details and investigate all of the possible questions of interpretation so that unnecessary and damaging conflicts are avoided.

Compensation is primarily a motivational tool. Thus, the key question in developing a compensation system is, "What behavior and performance are to be encouraged and what is to be discouraged?" Some of the typical objectives to be encouraged are:

1 Development of long-term account relationships

2 Sales

3 Sales to particular categories of customers or even to specific customers

4 Sales of particular products or product lines or, on the other hand, a uniform rate of sales of all products

5 Sales in a particular way (for example, outright sale versus rental)

6 Particular types of servicing (for example, shelf location, display)

7 Creation of new customers as opposed to greater sales to existing customers

8 The attraction of a particular type of salesperson

If the objectives are many and complex it is most difficult to develop a compensation system which will engender their accomplishment. Compensation systems which are complex tend to (1) confuse the sales force, causing substantial frustration; and (2) encourage some dysfunctional behavior because of unforeseen consequences.

Thus, it is usually best to develop a compensation system which will motivate the accomplishment of a limited set of objectives and which will clearly *not* motivate dysfunctional behavior. The compensation system is a communication which enables policy-making management to explain to salespeople what is important. If the policymakers have not decided what is important, they obviously cannot communicate it. And, if the communication is complicated, or very subtle, it is not likely to be clearly received. The message should be loud and clear. Long and complex messages are usually neither.

The prime decisions which must be made regarding compensation are:

1 The gross level of compensation

2 The amount of "incentive" compensation

3 The form of the incentive compensation, usually a choice between commissions and bonuses

4 The role of a sales quota and the nature of the quota

5 The role of contests (short-term incentive awards)

Usually the higher the gross level of compensation, the better the salesperson. "You get what you pay for." In fact, the best quick indication of the overall quality of a sales force is the level of compensation of the salespeople.

301

The major traditional discussion in compensation has concerned the amount of incentive compensation, including commissions, bonuses, etc. Some sales forces are straight salary and some straight commission. Others use a combination. Two things tend toward straight salary: (1) the inability to measure the sales impact of the salesperson in a reasonable period of time; and (2) policy-making management's desire to emphasize objectives other than immediate sales. Sometimes it is difficult to identify and measure the salesperson's impact on sales. This is typically true where (1) the sale is long and complex, such as in the selling of atomic reactors, weapons systems, etc.; (2) other parts of the marketing program are the primary determinants of sales success, such as in some phases of consumer package goods; and (3) sales are generated indirectly by the salesperson, such as in a pharmaceutical detailing situation.

If too strong an emphasis on sales is dangerous, straight salary or a high percentage of salary is called for. In banking, for example, it is important for loan officers (salespersons) to be careful about the ability of their customers to pay back their loans. Thus, too much emphasis on sales (making loans) would be dysfunctional. In other situations, top management may be more concerned with the development of long-term account relationships than with short-term sales. Straight salary is, of course, also much easier to administer and is thus often the choice of companies weak in management talent or information-processing skills.

There is a myriad of different forms of incentive compensation. The simplest is one commission rate which applies to all sales. Some companies vary the commission rate by product, to reflect profitability to the company or the difficulty of selling the product. Others do the same thing by category of customer or type of sale. Sometimes commissions are paid only when sales are above quota, or different commission rates are used for sales above and below quota.

Bonuses are sometimes used. These are lump sums paid for the attainment of specific objectives. Sometimes they are based on a formula, while at other times they are at the discretion of a particular manager.

The incentive systems can get very complex. For example, some companies will not pay a commission on an established product until the salesperson has attained the quota on a new product. Some companies pay a bonus or commissions only when sales of all product lines or sales to all customer categories are above quota. The most complex systems tend to use points which are later converted to dollars in some fashion. Some computer firms, with long and complex product lines and differing types of sales, have compensation plans that take as many as 10 to 12 pages to explain. Quotas and contests are discussed later in this note.

As mentioned before, meticulous attention to detail is an absolute necessity in planning compensation systems. Apparently minor details, such as "Are commissions paid when sales are booked, shipment made, or payment received?" are crucial. Systems with complex formulas are particularly prone to problems. It is important to apply the formula to the best and worst performers in the sales force, on a paper-and-pencil basis, before the plan is announced. Many plans instituted on the basis of a quick look at the "average territory" have led to disasters and near disasters because they were inequitable or foolish at the top and bottom of the sales force. Careful testing and algebraic manipulation of formula systems is an absolute necessity.

Careful analysis of objectives and meticulous attention to detail will lead to a system which motivates appropriate behavior and fits well with the philosophy of the firm and other aspects of sales force management.

The bibliography following this case provides many references on compensation. The work by Tosdal, including the two articles and the books by Tosdal and Carson, are old but by no means outdated. The books, in fact, are the most complete analysis of sales compensation ever published. The article by Richard Smyth is also very useful. Quotas are well covered by Risley's article.

Several sources provide data on average level of compensation, including:

1 Dartnell, *Compensation of Salesmen*. This is a serial publication which is updated annually.

2 The Conference Board, *Compensating Salesmen and Sales Executives*, 1972.

3 *Sales Management*, "1975 Survey of Selling Costs," 1975. This publication appears in January of each year.

EVALUATION

There are a variety of approaches to salesperson evaluation, which appear to be divisible into three major categories: (1) systems based solely on sales results, (2) complex systems using extensive numerical ratings, and (3) no system.

The last type is perhaps the worst. Evaluation takes place whether it is formally recognized or not. People are fired, promoted, transferred, and rewarded whether there is a system or not. If there is no system, such activities are likely to be haphazard and inequitable. At best such an approach results in a great many missed opportunities—poor performers are retained, average performers wallow in mediocrity, and star performers leave. At worst, it leads to a loss of morale and great unrest throughout the sales force.

303

Systems based solely on sales results are simple to administer, but they neglect a large part of most salespeople's jobs. The better ones do not just look at total dollar sales; they consider sales by category of account and product line.

The complex systems often are applied in a perfunctory manner. The boxes are filled in, but the total performance is not considered in relation to the person or the situation. It is most difficult to develop a numerically based system which provides uniformity and general applicability without sacrificing flexibility. In addition, in almost all cases, most salespeople end up being rated "above average."

The best approach seems to be a formalized system which provides some flexibility for the field sales manager to take into account his own style, the person being evaluated, and the situation. More important than the system, however, is the training of the person administering it. As the note "Field Sales Management" pointed out, performance appraisals are perhaps the most difficult task a field sales manager faces, yet few receive any training in appraisal. The poorest system can operate satisfactorily with well-trained people. These people, in fact, will then improve the system. The best system will, on the other hand, be a failure without well-trained field management.

The ideal system will provide a framework and guidelines for the well-trained manager. It will ensure that performance appraisals are made on a regular basis. It will allow flexibility while providing some standardized basis for comparisons among salespeople.

MOTIVATION

There are five parts to strong motivation:

1 Careful selection of appropriate salespeople (covered in the note "Recruiting and Selection")

2 Relevant, continuing, and effective training (covered in the note "Training for Selling and Sales Management")

3 A clear and equitable compensation system which rewards people for appropriate performance

4 A well-designed evaluation system administered by well-trained field sales managers

5 A set of intelligent, well-designed motivation practices

304

It is almost impossible to motivate poorly selected people. If they are too powerful for the job, they will be bored and underpaid. If they are "underpowered," they will lack confidence, and poor performance will lead to less confidence and even poorer performance. Training contributes to motivation by providing competence and confidence. Sometimes, in fact, it is difficult to separate training from motivation. As described earlier compensation and evaluation programs are effective only if they contribute to motivation.

There are other aspects of motivation, including sales meetings, recognition programs, career paths, and management style. Before discussing these, however, one cautionary statement is appropriate. Sales force management has been replete with all sorts of "inspirational" programs. When they are pure form, not backed by substance, they are useless. Some of these techniques and approaches with even a minimal amount of substance have some value for very low-level sales forces. Professional-level sales forces, however, require a high proportion of substance to inspiration.

This is not to downgrade the importance of genuine excitement. Selling is an arduous, demanding task which is full of setbacks. Highly promotional approaches are useful, but they are not a substitute for good training, well-designed sales programs, and effective management. They are supplements—the frosting on the cake. The "inspiration" cannot stand alone without the substance of sales force management.

Sales Meetings

Sales meetings may be national or local. National meetings are likely to generate more excitement and enthusiasm because of the size of the audience and the distance traveled. In addition, they justify a more complete and professional approach. It is possible, for example, for all of top management to attend one national meeting, but impossible for the total group to attend several regional meetings.

Local meetings may be held at the district (first) level, or at the regional (second or higher) level. District meetings were covered in the note "Field Sales Management." Regional meetings are cheaper than national meetings because of lower travel costs. In addition, they can be tailored to special regional situations, such as unusual customer needs or competitive situations.

Sometimes meetings are open to all salespeople. At other meetings, only those who attain quotas or meet some other requirement are eligible to attend. Meetings with attendance requirements should really be viewed as recognition programs. They are, in fact, often held in the more glamorous locations with spouses frequently invited.

Sometimes meetings are held primarily as a tradition, with no real objective other than "to get the troops together" or "to show them we care about them." Such meetings may derive some benefit from the attention and camaraderie, but these benefits are less than those achieved through careful planning.

Sales meetings can have a variety of objectives, including the following:

305

1 To introduce a redesigned or restyled product line (for example, fashion goods marketers, such as apparel and furniture firms, who usually have meetings at the beginning of each selling season for this purpose)

2 To introduce a new product line to the sales force

3 To explain new plans, policies, and procedures

4 To provide training

5 To introduce new headquarters personnel, including policy-making executives as well as operating executives (for example, credit manager, shipping manager, product manager, etc.)

6 To develop motivation through camaraderie, executive attention, and the general excitement of a well-executed meeting

Some sales meetings are elaborate and expensive. They are not necessarily the most effective. Usually, the ones with well-developed objectives and careful attention to detail come out the best.

Sales meetings can also be dangerous forums for complaints and gossip. These problems are usually spawned by sales management's refusal to confront problems in the open. The best sales meetings provide time for the salespeople to air their concerns in a constructive fashion. This is more likely to be constructive if the sales force as a whole has open two-way communication.

Since national sales meetings are the only time that all the salespeople are gathered together, they present an excellent opportunity for continuing training.

Recognition Programs

A recognition program provides salespeople with nonmonetary awards for performance. Many contests are of this nature, but they will be discussed below separately.

Recognition is usually provided for sales performance but sometimes for longevity. Thus, a salesperson might be given a pin for 10 years' service, a plaque for 20 years, and a watch for 25. These are usually companywide programs, including nonsales employees as well.

Performance awards can include pictures in the company newspaper or at headquarters, local or national announcement of the award, a special desk in the office, a bigger automobile, a special place of honor at the sales meeting, and other visible recognition.

Usually, only the good performers receive recognition. Sometimes, however, the poor performers receive negative recognition, either through having sales results posted or published or by being singled out. One well-known company, for example, lets the leading salespeople sit in the president's chair and places "crying towels" over the back of the chairs of poor performers. Such ridicule usually has negative consequences. The whole sales force feels discomfort. Those barely above the poor performers suffer great fear, and the poor performers typically gain nothing from the humiliation. Termination seems more humane.

Recognition programs have proved effective, especially when they are equitably designed and administered. To motivate everyone, they must be designed so that everyone has an equal chance of winning. If the program is based on sales, the salesperson with the greatest sales during the previous period has a substantial advantage. If it is based on penetration (market share), the salesperson with the smallest territory has an advantage. Many of the better programs have several winners, for example, those with the highest sales, the biggest percentage increase, the biggest dollar increase, the highest penetration, or the largest sales per account.

It is important not only for the program to be equitable, but for it to appear to be equitable.

Some companies have meetings for the best performers. This provides recognition as well as some of the standard benefits of sales meetings. It also provides a chance for the top performers to discuss advanced approaches and techniques, to learn from each other. Sometimes they are the best able to learn and teach this material.

Other companies have a "club" for the top performers, complete with many of the other recognition awards such as special conventions, pins, special desks, bigger automobiles, etc.

Recognition programs are useful supplements to the other parts of sales force management.

Career Paths

Another method of providing recognition and motivating salespeople is through promotion. Some companies offer two career paths. One leads to management positions for promising candidates. The other leads to advanced sales positions, usually involving key-account responsibility. Often the titles include senior sales representative, major account representative, etc. Usually this cadre of advanced salespeople is drawn upon for candidates for national-account selling. The advanced salesperson typically receives appropriate perquisites, including higher compensation and a bigger automobile.

Promotion from within provides motivation because it offers rewards for performance. The advanced selling ladder is useful because it provides an alternative method of advancement for the capable salesperson who is either not suited to management or who does not want responsibility.

307

Management Style

This is a most elusive subject. Much has been written about it, including well-received works by Likert and by McGregor. Of more direct relevance is the article by Olsen.

It seems clear that any one of several management styles will work, depending upon the situation and the people. Certainly clear, open communication will be helpful in encouraging motivation. Much of this depends upon the first-level sales manager. His tone, of course, will reflect that of his superiors.

QUOTAS AND CONTESTS

Two of the most confusing parts of the compensation, evaluation, and motivation subject are quotas and contests, and since they involve all three aspects, they are treated separately here.

It is crucial that the function of the quota be made explicit. Typically, a quota can be used either for a combination of evaluation and motivation or for those two functions and compensation as well. Many quotas are used in pure commission and pure salary compensation schemes, where they do not play a role in compensation but are important in evaluation and motivation. In compensation use, they normally set a limit below which commission or bonus is *not* paid. A scheme of that nature might have compensation as salary plus a bonus of 5 percent of sales dollars between 100 and 110 percent of quota and 10 percent for all sales dollars above 110 percent of quota. A simpler system might provide a lump sum bonus for all salespeople meeting quota.

When quotas are used for evaluation and motivation, they can be used with either "strong" signals or "weak" ones. Some companies have policies by which salespeople who make quota get the opportunity to do it again next year. Those who do not make quota are fired. At the other extreme are firms which send the salesperson a quota at the beginning of the year and do not mention it until the quota for the beginning of the next year arrives without comment or with a form letter encouraging the salespeople to do better. In such a system, the quota serves little purpose other than to generate work for the quota developers.

Quotas can be expressed in a variety of ways, including dollar sales volume, unit sales volume, gross margin dollars, product-line sales volume, new accounts opened, new account sales volume, customer type sales volume, prospecting calls, bids, presentations, requests for bids, number of orders received, size of average order, etc. Combinations of these can also be used. It is important for the quota to be relevant to the company's marketing strategy and sales program. Thus, the nature of the quota can change through the life cycle of a product or company.

Quotas can be developed from existing sales (for example, quota is 10 percent above last year's actual sales), potential (for example, quota is one-third of the territory's potential), or in some other way. It is important for the quotas both to be and to appear to be equitable among salespeople and over time. Quotas can be developed at headquarters and then divided among salespeople in a "top-down" system, or they can be summed from salesperson and/or account quotas in a "bottom-up" approach. In either case, the individual territory, product, and account quotas should be consistent with the firm's marketing plan and sales program. For example, if every salesperson makes quota, the sales force as a whole should make quota.

The note "Sales Forecasting" provides additional material on quotas. The article by Risley is a most useful one. Contests are discussed in the note "Sales Promotion." For continuity and completeness, a short discussion is included here.

Contests are supposed to be short-term promotions with very specific sales objectives. Sometimes, however, they cease to be short term and do not have specific objectives. If they are used on a repetitive basis, they lose their effect which is to some extent based upon excitement and novelty.

Successful contests require the following:

1 A clear set of reasonable objectives
2 An exciting theme
3 Reasonable probability of reward for all salespeople
4 Reasonably attractive awards

Contests work best when the objective is clear and simple. It might, for example, be the opening of new accounts or the sale of a new product. Attainment of the total objective should be measurable and each salesperson's contribution should be measurable. The contest should be relatively short so that salespeople are encouraged to put forth a great effort without having to wait long to find out the results—certainly no longer than a few months. Contests longer than one month should have intermediate goals and awards.

The theme should engender excitement. The better ones are related to the objectives, the firm, the product, and the award. The theme is often tied into trade and consumer-customer promotions for added consistency and excitement.

Each salesperson should have a chance at winning. It is particularly important to make it possible for the average performers to get involved. They are the ones who produce most of the sales and who are hard to motivate, yet worth motivating. The star performers are doing well and are clearly motivated. The poor performers cannot, in general, contribute that much to the sales effort. The section above on recognition programs provides some insight into appropriate ways to put fairness into the program.

309

The awards should be attractive to the salespeople. Thus, they must be varied so that a consistent winner does not receive the same prize each time. In addition, the prizes must reflect the compensation of the salespeople. A portable television set will have less impact on a sales force with compensation of $40,000 average than on one with $15,000 average. In general, prizes should be the equivalent of at least 2 percent (one week's compensation) of the people being appealed to.

The article by Scanlon provides some useful insights into contests, as does the Haring and Morris book. Used in moderation, contests can be very effective. Used too often and without planning, they become expensive and ineffective.

BIBLIOGRAPHY

The Conference Board: *Compensating Salesmen and Sales Executives*, New York, 1972.

————: *Incentive Plans for Salesmen, Studies in Personnel Policy 217*, New York, 1970.

Dartnell Corporation: *Compensation of Salesmen* (appears annually).

Farley, John V.: "An Optimal Plan for Salesmen's Compensation," *Journal of Marketing Research*, May 1964, pp. 39–43.

Haring, Albert, and Malcolm Morris: *Contests, Prizes, Awards for Sales Motivation*, Sales and Marketing Executives—International, New York, 1968.

Herzberg, Frederick: "One More Time: How Do You Motivate Employees?" *Harvard Business Review*, vol. 46, January-February 1968.

Levin, Richard I.: "Who's on First," *Sales Management*, vol. 93, no. 2, Part I, July 17, 1964, pp. 53–56; reprinted in Thomas R. Wotruba and Robert Olsen (eds.), *Readings in Sales Management*, New York: Holt, Rinehart and Winston, 1971, pp. 368–372.

Likert, Rensis: "New Patterns in Sales Management," in Martin R. Warshaw (ed.), *Changing Perspectives in Marketing Management*, Michigan Business Papers, No. 37, Ann Arbor: University of Michigan; reprinted in Kenneth R. David and Frederick E. Webster, Jr. (eds.), *Readings in Sales Force Management*, New York: Ronald Press, 1968, pp. 419–439.

McGregor, Douglas: "An Uneasy Look at Performance Appraisal," *Harvard Business Review*, vol. 35, May-June 1957.

Myers, M. Scott: "Conditions for Manager Motivation," *Harvard Business Review*, vol. 44, January-February 1966.

Olsen, Robert M.: "The Liberating Motivational Climate—An Essential for Sales Effectiveness," in Thomas R. Wotruba and Robert Olsen (eds.), *Readings in Sales Management*, New York: Holt, Rinehart and Winston, 1971, pp. 245–257.

Pruden, Henry O., William H. Cunningham, and Wilke D. English: "Nonfinancial Incentives for Salesmen," *Journal of Marketing*, October 1972, pp. 55–59.

Risley, George: "A Basic Guide to Setting Quotas," *Industrial Marketing*, vol. 46, no. 8, July 1961, pp. 88–93; reprinted in Thomas R. Wotruba and Robert Olsen (eds.), *Readings in Sales Management*, New York: Holt, Rinehart and Winston, 1971, pp. 69–80.

Sales Management: "1975 Survey of Selling Costs," appears every January.

Scanlon, Sally: "Onward and Upward with Mr. Average," *Sales Management*, September 3, 1973, pp. 35–42.

Smyth, Richard C.: "Financial Incentives for Salesmen," *Harvard Business Review*, vol. 46, January-February 1968, pp. 109–117.

Thompson, Paul H., and Gene W. Dalton: "Performance Appraisal: Managers Beware," *Harvard Business Review*, vol. 48, January-February 1970.

Tosdal, Harry R.: "Administering Salesmen's Compensation," *Harvard Business Review*, March-April 1953, pp. 70–83.

———: "How to Design the Salesman's Compensation Plan," *Harvard Business Review*, vol. 31, September-October 1953, pp. 61–70.

———, and Waller Carson, Jr.: *Salesmen's Compensation*, Harvard Graduate School of Business Administration, 1953 (2 vols.).

THIRTY-FIVE Hero Machine Company, Incorporated

Issue — Should they change compensation method?

During the fall of 1974, executives of the Hero Machine Company, Inc., manufacturers and distributors of equipment and parts for the specialty chemical industry,[1] debated the wisdom of changing the company's method of compensating salespeople. In an attempt to obtain greater sales effort and control of the sales force, the executives considered several alternatives to the current payment system of salary and expenses.

311

Hero Machine Company, located in Providence, Rhode Island, had been in the busiess of supplying capital equipment and replacement parts for 80 years. Of the company's 1973 sales of $4,726,000, 20 percent consisted of grinding machines used in specialty chemical plants and selling for as much as $40,000 each. The remaining sales were divided among such items as replacement parts for grinding machines, rollers for grinders, and other supply items relevant to the specialty chemical industry. These items varied in price, but seldom exceeded $6,000.

The company originally manufactured replacement parts only. This was unique in an industry where each manufacturer of original equipment sold replacement parts only for machines of his own manufacture, while Hero Machine manufactured and sold replacement parts for all brands. The manufacturing of grinding machines was intended initially to be a sideline.

The market consisted of about 1,000 chemical specialty plants in the United States and Canada. The customer plants generally tended to be small. While large plants had laboratories and engineering staffs, industry

---

[1] The specialty chemical industry included producers of low-volume, high-value per pound chemicals such as perfumes and fragrances, flavorings, etc.

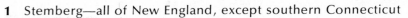

Market Competition & Share

technology was described as "more art than science." Although the company had sold to most of these accounts at one time or another, only 500 of them could be considered active as of September 1974. Hero Machine's primary competition came from three other firms, one of which was considerably larger and carried a wider line of capital goods. The other two were comparable in size. Hero had about one-third of the original grinding machine market, one-tenth of the grinder roller market, and an undetermined part of the replacement parts market. All three competitors had their own sales forces.

The capital equipment portion of the business was cyclical, although the replacement parts and supplies portion of the business tended to offset these fluctuations. In fact, industry sources hypothesized an inverse correlation between parts sales and grinder sales.

THE SALESPEOPLE

The company had eight salespeople. With the exception of one new person, Tom Temple, the Hero Machine salespeople had been with the company for at least 6 years and were considered to be an unusually loyal sales force. The salespeople were assigned territories as follows:

1 Stemberg—all of New England, except southern Connecticut

2 Brown—southern Connecticut, New Jersey, eastern Pennsylvania, Delaware, Washington, D.C., and Virginia

3 Temple—North and South Carolina to Texas

4 Reichmann—Canada east of Toronto, and New York State

5 Peters—western Pennsylvania, Ohio, Indiana, Illinois, Missouri, and Colorado

6 Bowman—Michigan, Minnesota, Wisconsin, and northern Iowa

7 Gray—California, Washington, Oregon, Idaho, and British Columbia

8 Carmody—New Jersey and southern Connecticut[2]

The product mix sold and the relative sales potentials varied substantially between territories. Thus, there might be considerable potential for capital equipment in a new growth territory, but little opportunity to sell replacement parts. Grinder rollers, a very profitable item, were sold only to certain types of customer plants. In territories where there were none of these plants, there was no potential for this product.

[2]Carmody, originally responsible for the entire Middle Atlantic teritory, was close to retirement and his accounts and territory had been largely reassigned to other salespeople. He still retained, however, a limited number of his old accounts.

Some products lasted for 30 years before requiring replacement. If a territory's potential were fixed, each new sale would decrease the area's remaining potential for that product. Thus, if sales were substantial in such a product line, the resulting decrease in sales potential would affect the future product mix.

Traditionally, Hero Machine had given its selling personnel a free hand in their territories, though this philosophy was under review in the fall of 1974. Bernard Manuel, director of market research and sales analysis, estimated that two-thirds of the person's time was spent in actual selling and one-third in building goodwill. The selling activity itself had two aspects: (1) selling equipment, parts, and supplies; and (2) servicing present equipment. The salespeople did not perform the actual service, but they often discussed semitechnical problems with plant personnel and sometimes helped to arrange for repair or installation. By building goodwill, Mr. Manuel meant the "many nonselling activities required of salespersons who would build good customer relations."

Multisell

On their calls, the sales personnel had to contact various people, including superintendents, purchasing agents, plant and production engineers, production supervisors, technicians, machine operators, master mechanics, and vice presidents. Frequently, many of these people had to be "sold" on the Hero equipment. For instance, it was not unusual in the plants for the technical people to favor experimentation while the production people were opposed. In the smaller plants, the purchasing agent was usually the key official involved in the buying decision; in the larger operations, on the other hand, the purchasing agent often played a secondary role. It was part of the salesperson's job to discover who the important contacts were at each plant.

313

Target Customer

At smaller plants, salespeople usually maintained only one contact, the purchasing agent, while several were necessary at larger installations. In some instances, a salesperson had 30 contacts at a single large plant. Mr. Manuel pointed out that the average salesperson had 688 contacts.[3] The turnover of personnel at the plants was 14 percent per year. Some employees merely moved from one company to another. When a salesperson already knew the individual, the contact problem was simplified.

# of Contacts

The average salesperson traveled extensively and was expected to call on each plant in the territory at least once a year. In New England, by way of illustration, the salesperson had 190 accounts to cover.[4] Not all plants, of course, took the same amount of time. Some calls were "hello" stops, while others might last for several days. These extended calls

---

[3]Mr. Manuel had derived this estimate from a telephone survey of the salespeople. The salesperson's estimates had varied from 437 to 894 contacts in active accounts. The 14 percent figure for turnover was derived from the same survey.

[4]This included both "active" and "inactive" accounts.

frequently resulted from the customer's request for help on a special problem.

The number of calls needed to make a sale varied with the type of product being sold and the relationship which existed between Hero Machine and the customer. Thus, a grinding-machine replacement part could frequently be sold on only one call, or the customer might even call in his order to the company. On the other hand, the sale of a new grinding machine might require repeated calls for a year or more. More time was required if the salesperson had to demonstrate a plant's need for a new grinder as well as to create a preferential desire for the product. Mr. Carson, the sales manager, said that generally more time could be justified selling a machine to a customer who already purchased accessories and parts than one who did not. Seldom did a customer require as many as six calls in a year. Accessory sales required more calls than parts sales, but less than capital equipment.

According to Mr. Carson, selling success depended upon three major ingredients: the personality of the salesperson, the quality of the product, and good delivery. Even though there was some product differentiation among the firms in the industry, the sales manager considered the relationship of the salesperson to the customer the most important selling element. The Hero salespeople were not graduate engineers, although two of the old-timers had built up enough knowledge to advise the mills on their technical problems.

[handwritten notes in margin: Selling Process; Capital Equip. — Intensive; long, intensive sell.; Replacement Parts easy sell.; 314]

[handwritten: ← Criteria for Selling Success.]

COMPENSATION PLAN

The sales personnel were all paid straight salary plus expenses. Sales volume, salaries, and expenses are shown in Exhibit 1. Although there was no exact formula, Mr. Carson said that four considerations were involved in setting salaries:

[handwritten: Salary Considerations.]

1 The sales volume and gross margin contribution of each salesperson
2 The going rate for salespersons of equal ability
3 The earnings of other employees
4 The value of the salesperson as a good will emissary

Gross margin varied for each salesperson with sales volume and product mix. For 1972, the average salesperson contributed to gross margin 12 times his salary. But the range varied among the salespeople as shown in Exhibit 2.

Regardless of the particular margin earned per salesperson, it was apparent to the executives that salary had to be commensurate with the salesperson's opportunity for earning elsewhere. Although the number of competitors was limited, many of the sales force could transfer to

[handwritten at bottom: Issue of Fair Compensation because of competition.]

Exhibit 1 SALES VOLUMES, SALARIES, AND EXPENSES

Salesperson	1972			1973		
	Sales	Salary	Expense	Sales	Salary	Expense
Peters	$ 858,000	$ 18,000	$ 13,914	$ 846,000	$ 19,000	$ 16,698
Reichmann	410,000	15,000	14,736	370,000	15,000	14,210
Gray	408,000	15,600	17,104	688,000	17,000	15,868
Stemberg	675,000	22,000	8,444	829,000	22,000	9,786
Carmody	502,000	22,000	9,338	414,000	22,000	10,674
Dennison[a]	950,000	12,000	15,736	426,000[b]	2,500	2,872
Temple					7,000	11,624
Bowman	570,000	13,500	11,132	726,000	14,000	13,206
Brown	309,000	10,000	15,160	427,000	12,000	15,804
	$4,682,000	$128,100	$105,564	$4,726,000	$130,500	$110,742

[a] Dennison was fired on March 31, 1972. Temple replaced him June 1, 1972.
[b] Some of these sales resulted from Temple's efforts.

Exhibit 2 RELATIONSHIP BETWEEN GROSS MARGIN AND SALARIES, BY SALESPERSON (1973)

Salesperson	Ratio of gross margin to salary
Peters	15.9
Reichmann	8.8
Gray	9.1
Stemberg	13.3
Carmody	6.9
Dennison } Temple	16.1
Bowman	18.5
Brown	12.7

315

another company if they were so disposed. Mr. Carson was particularly concerned about this possibility. Accordingly, salary payments tended to reflect the marketability of the individual salesperson.

Although the company had not set a rigid pattern of relative job values, there was no question among executives that the compensation of salespeople should be kept within "certain bounds of reason" to avoid companywide problems that might arise should salespeople be paid "out of proportion to other employees."

The role of the salesperson was primary in the overall sales strategy of the company. Advertising and sales promotion were used sparingly; much of the trade advertising, for example, was of the "news" variety intended to keep the company name in front of customers. Company executives placed more faith in word-of-mouth advertising, a medium which depended upon general customer goodwill. Hence, the salesperson played a major role. Furthermore, because of its general strategy of relying primarily upon personal selling, Hero Machine considered the value of the individual salesperson to be quite substantial. This consideration affected the general compensation level.

Under the straight salary plus expenses plan, the salespeople re-

Relied on personal selling.

Salespeople played major role.

ceived an annual or semiannual review of their performance. Raises in pay were given on the basis of these reviews. The company did not use definite yardsticks to determine the increases. Much of the raise was the result of a "hassle" between the employee and Mr. Carson.

There were several reasons why the executives debated the wisdom of the current compensation plan, although the plan had been used successfully for many years and seemed well suited to the nonselling aspects of the salesperson's job. In the first place, the plan called for high fixed-selling expenses, regardless of the volume of sales. Secondly, there was some question in management's mind about the subjectivity of salary increases. Finally, the question was raised as to the possible limitations that a straight salary plan might impose on selling effort. Would a person do as well with no immediate incentive as he would if he knew that his efforts would be reflected directly in his take-home pay?

In addition to increasing sales effort (primarily by increasing calls and selling time), a new compensation plan might encourage salespeople to strike a proper balance between capital equipment and other sales. Some executives believed that salespeople frequently spent more time than justified trying to sell a grinding machine when there was no certainty that an order would be forthcoming.

Product mix, according to Mr. Manuel, could be controlled by a properly weighted plan. The salespeople would become more conscious of what pays off and what does not, would make long-range territory plans, improve their routing, and generally become more efficient. Finally, a good compensation plan would provide a common yardstick for all of the territories, "so we will know if someone isn't doing a good job, where we might have kidded ourselves before."

The principal competitor paid a straight salary plus an end-of-the-year Christmas bonus. Other competitors generally paid a salary plus commission.

Alternatives Considered

The executives reviewed with care three alternative plans: a point system, a salary with commission system, and a bonus system.

Point System

The first proposal involved a system of salary and bonus-or-penalty points for various selling activities. Under this plan the salespeople would receive points for performing tasks spelled out by the sales manager. Nonselling activities accordingly would earn the salespeople direct compensation. On the other hand, penalty points would be assigned for such adverse items as customer complaints. A bonus plan of this kind promised specific control of the many facets of the salespeople's jobs.

But this proposal had weaknesses. In order to assign points, the executives would have to receive from the salespeople quite detailed activity reports. Such reports were foreign to the salespeople's job environments and would add a considerable amount to the company's overhead.[5] Furthermore, several executives argued that salespeople received a salary already, for which they were expected to perform their many nonselling duties. Why pay a bonus, they argued, for activities considered an essential part of their job?

Disadvantages

Salary and Commission

The second proposal was that of paying a salary, expenses, and a commission on sales. In their preliminary discussions, the executives thought that salary should amount to 75 percent of the salesperson's compensation, and commission 25 percent. By this ratio the executives felt that the salespeople would have security (and would therefore "buy" the plan more readily) but still have the incentive to do a better-than-average job.

Stemberg Example

It was also argued that commission rates should vary among the several products, depending upon profitability, the degree of difficulty in obtaining initial and repeat sales, and the company's desire to push certain items.

317

As a first step at testing the soundness of their rate proposals, the executives looked at the 1973 record of salesperson Stemberg. Stemberg's sales were broken down by products and gross margin, and the proposed rates were applied to each group. Assuming he had been on straight commission for the year, it was apparent that the proposed rates would compensate him in about the same amount that he received in salary. The work sheet for these computations is Exhibit 3.

The executives realized, of course, that the percentages would have to be tested against each salesperson. But most important, perhaps, they agreed that a commission plan with these general specifications would mean that most salespeople would take a cut in salary so that the incentive payment would amount to 25 percent of total compensation. Only in this way would the ratio of sales expense to sales not vary drastically.

But there were questions involved with this alternative. Would the salespeople accept the reductions? Assuming the relative efficiency of the salespeople to be the same, would differences in territory potentials affect the plan? When should the incentive be paid? Should there be an upper limit?

Questions about alternative #2.

---

[5] In 1973 the salespeople prepared call reports only on "unusually important or notable" calls and filed biweekly expense reports. These were the only reports the salespeople prepared.

Exhibit 3 EARNINGS OF SALESPERSON STEMBERG UNDER PROPOSED PLAN

Group number	Products in group	Proposed commission rate, %	1973 sales	Commission	Gross margin, %	Gross margin
I	Supplies	1.0	$ 24,292	$ 243	15	$ 3,600
II	Repair work and small parts	1.5	56,854	853	15–50 Avg. = 27.5	15,600
III	Grinding machines	2.0	(128,820)	(2,576)	20	(25,800)
	Major parts for grinding machines	2.0	(89,546)	(1,791)	30–45	(28,200)
Total		2.0	$218,366[b]	$ 4,367		$ 54,000
IV	Accessories	3.0	$123,060	3,692	30–50	$ 62,200
V	Miscellaneous	4.0	22,810	912	30	6,800
VI	Major parts[a]	3.5	341,914	11,967	30–55	131,400
VII	Grinding rollers	4.0	41,996	1,680	45	18,800
Average		2.9	$829,292	$23,714	35	$292,400

[a]Not for grinding machines but for other specialty chemical equipment.
[b]The parentheses above denote subamounts, not negative amounts. Thus, the $218,366 is the sum of $128,820 and 89,546.

Illustrative of the variations in product mix among the territories were the sales records of four people, shown in Exhibit 4.

Bonus Plan

The marketing vice president, Jerry France, questioned the advisability of a commission plan that required cutting back current base salaries. He felt that each person should receive the same salary as before but be given the opportunity of earning a bonus for sales without limit beyond a target. Such a plan, he realized, would run counter to the firm's current philosophy of maintaining a predictable ratio of sales cost to sales. But he considered that the attractions of such a plan outweighed the disadvantages. For the sake of discussion, Mr. France suggested the following plan, which he presented to his colleagues for their comments:

1 A target in dollars would be established for each territory based upon such factors as:
   (a) Past sales
   (b) Salesperson's own estimates
   (c) Analysis of individual product potentials (based upon the best available statistics and executive estimates)

2 Having established a territory target, the next step would be to provide a yardstick for product mix. To accomplish this, the company products would be grouped and each group assigned points reflecting margins, ease of selling, and so forth. Probably the points could reflect the same percentages already shown in Exhibit 3. Thus, 1 percent might be worth 1 point; 2 percent, 2 points; and so forth. Using these points, the point average per territory could be computed by analyzing last year's sales by product group. If territory A had sales of

Product 1	$100,000
Product 2	200,000
Product 3	50,000

Exhibit 4 PERCENTAGE OF DISTRIBUTION OF SALESPEOPLE'S SALES, 1973 (Selected salespeople only)

	Salespeople			
Product group	Bowman	Peters	Carmody	Reichmann
I	2	1	1	3
II	3	3	2	2
III	5	11	20	25
IV	10	8	15	22
V	10	12	5	10
VI	50	40	45	30
VII	20	25	12	8
Total	100	100	100	100

and the products had point values of 1, $1\frac{1}{2}$, and 2, respectively, then the weighted point average for that territory would be 1.43 points.[6] The *theoretical* point average, however, might be higher or lower, depending on the product potential in that territory. The theoretical point average could be computed by estimating what the sales, by product group, would have been had the salesperson received a fair portion of each product's potential. Having the actual and the theoretical point average, Mr. France proposed that the lower of the two be taken and multiplied by the territory target. This would give a *number of points* beyond which the salesperson could earn a bonus. He might exceed his point goal by selling more volume or by improving his product mix (point score).

3 The bonus would be computed as "so many cents" per point beyond the target points.

To better illustrate the mechanics of this plan, Mr. France made a hasty calculation of 1974 quota, average and theoretical point averages, and "points to break-even" for three salespersons. He used sales data for the first 6 months of 1974, as well as his intimate knowledge of the three territories. It appears in Exhibit 5.

Expense Control

Concern over expense accounts.

One of Mr. Carson's major concerns was the amount of expenses incurred by the salespeople. He wanted to give serious consideration to a plan in which each salesperson would pay his own expenses. He said that he resented the job of checking the expense statements. "I am constantly

[6]The calculation was as follows: [($100,000 × 1) + ($200,000 × $1\frac{1}{2}$) + ($50,000 × 2)] / [$100,000 + 200,000 + 50,000] = $500,000/$350,000 = 1.43.

Exhibit 5 MR. FRANCE'S EXAMPLES

Salesperson	Actual average points per $100 sale first 6 months, 1974[a]	Theoretical average points per $100 sale[b]	1974 quota[c]	Points to break-even
Peters	3.08	2.94[d]	$834,886	24,546
Gray	3.05	2.96[d]	701,296	20,758
Carmody	3.04[d]	3.15	431,944	13,132

[a]For all salespeople the minimum was 2.40 and the maximum 3.08.
[b]The theoretical average points were developed by Mr. France from estimates supplied by Messrs. Manuel and Carson.
[c]The quotas were those developed by Mr. Carson to help him manage the sales force. Little emphasis had previously been placed upon their attainment. Mr. Carson, in fact, stated that he had little faith in their validity.
[d]Denotes figure used to calculate point total in the last column.

fighting between my conscience and the salesmen." He also believed that it was very difficult to develop an equitable approach to sales expense control. "We have excellent salesmen and they should be allowed to live in a way which reflects well upon the firm and them. But putting that standard into practice is difficult. Some territories require more travel than others. Some customers want more wining and dining. Some salesmen use entertainment as a more important selling tool than others."

THIRTY-SIX Fieldcrest Division of Fieldcrest Mills, Incorporated (A)

BACKGROUND ON THE COMPANY AND THE INDUSTRY

When Fieldcrest Mills, Inc., was spun out of a parent company in 1953, its lines included domestic products such as sheets, towels, blankets, automatic blankets, and bedspreads, as well as rugs and carpets. Separate marketing divisions were maintained to handle bed and bath fashions on one hand, and rugs and carpets on the other. The two divisions operated entirely separately. (Hereafter, "Fieldcrest" will be used to refer to the Fieldcrest Marketing Division, not to the total corporation.)

321

At the beginning, the Fieldcrest line, like that of its competitors, consisted of plain white sheets, towels, blankets, automatic electric blankets, and bedspreads sold on a utilitarian basis. They were usually the least profitable items in a department store and were sold in poorly located linen and domestics departments. According to Fieldcrest management, in 1953 the firm initiated a series of design, merchandising, and marketing innovations which transformed the industry into a fashion business. After studying color and design trends in apparel and home decorating, Fieldcrest stylists created new designs and colors for all their products. Fieldcrest worked with store management to secure prominent locations and better lighting and display for domestics. They were often successful in establishing "Fieldcrest Shops" in which the total Fieldcrest line was displayed together.

In 1957 Fieldcrest acquired St. Mary's, a well-established manufacturer of quality woolen blankets. Company managers decided to use the St. Mary's name for a full line of products targeted at the rapidly expanding mass merchandiser market.[1] Doing this, they reasoned, would not

[1]The mass merchandiser market primarily consisted of discount houses, such as K-Mart and Zayre, and variety stores, such as Kress and Woolworth.

jeopardize the Fieldcrest luxury and quality image since the Fieldcrest name would be reserved for items sold to fashionable department stores and specialty shops.

During the late 1960s and early 1970s, Fieldcrest made significant product improvements by using new production processes and blends of fibers. Moreover, once again focusing on contemporary consumer interests, it brought *haute couture* personalities into the industry with the introduction of collections designed by Yves St. Laurent, Pierre Cardin, and Marimekko. For the American bicentennial, it was planning a collection of Early American designs derived from artifacts in the Smithsonian Museum, and it had recently reached an agreement whereby well-known football star Joe Namath would endorse and help advertise a "Playmaker" collection for the St. Mary's brand.

By the end of 1972,[2] Fieldcrest's annual sales had reached $167,110,000, with operating income before interest of $10,026,000. Volume was divided as follows:

Fieldcrest	40%
St. Mary's	15%
Private label	25%
Seconds and discounts	4%
Institutional and military	16%

Over the next 5 years, Fieldcrest management anticipated a 68 percent increase in total sales and a 250 percent increase in total operating income. In 1973 corporate management decided to invest $20 million in expanding production facilities for bed and bath products.

THE BED AND BATH FASHION INDUSTRY

In 1972 the total wholesale volume of the industry was over $1.5 billion. There were about 50 manufacturers, many of whom specialized in only one or two product lines. Since manufacturers increasingly targeted their efforts toward specific market segments, overall market share data were not necessarily the best indication of success. For example, while Fieldcrest ranked seventh among all sheet manufacturers, in the high-quality sheet market, it ranked first. (See Exhibit 1 for industry data.)

Since the mid-1950s, products were offered in an increasingly wide selection of colors, sizes, and textures. Bed sheets, for example, progressed from cotton to no-iron, flat to fitted, white to color to fancy, full size to queen size to king size. The proliferation of products meant that product life cycles were shortened and a constant flow of new styles was

[2]Fieldcrest's fiscal year was the same as the calendar year.

Exhibit 1 INDUSTRY DATA AND FIELDCREST'S POSITION WITHIN THE INDUSTRY (1972)

Product	Total industry sales (000 omitted)	Fieldcrest sales (000 omitted)	Fieldcrest market shares, %	Number of manufacturers in the industry	Fieldcrest's rank
Blankets	$ 125,600	$ 25,800[a]	20.5	10	2
Automatic blankets	41,500	15,700	37.8	3	2
Bedspreads	226,000	24,100	10.7	13	1
Sheets	597,000	34,700	5.8	10	7
Shower curtains	28,000	500	1.8	7	6
Towels	361,500	61,700	17.1	11	2
Bath rugs	141,000	4,000	2.8	18	16
Total	**$1,520,600**	**$166,500**	**10.9**		

[a] Included channels for automatic blankets sold to other manufacturers.
Source: Fieldcrest Division of Fieldcrest Mills, Inc., records.

essential. By 1973 at least five major manufacturers were hiring well-known designers, and styling had become an extremely important competitive area. Each brand had two major product introductions annually. The multiplicity of items made accurate forecasting both essential and extraordinarily difficult and created the need for a larger inventory investment.

By 1973 manufacturers' difficulties were compounded by raw material shortages and skyrocketing prices. For example, between October 1972 and October 1973, the wholesale cost of cotton ranged from a low of 27 cents to a high of 90 cents per pound. Comparable increases occurred for plastic film to wrap the products, cartons to ship them, and fuel to run the mills.

While strong consumer demand produced a sellers' market for manufacturers (a very rare situation for the textile industry), maintaining desired profitability levels was still extremely difficult because government price controls did not allow manufacturers to pass through many of their increased costs.

Bed and bath fashions were sold primarily through department stores, specialty shops, and mass merchandiser outlets, including discount houses, chains, variety stores, and other outlets. Since the mid-1950s, operations of traditional department stores had become increasingly complex as they opened branches in suburban shopping centers, and competition had become more intense with the rise of mass merchandisers. By 1973, most large retailers used computerized inventory systems to calculate turnover rates for individual items and dropped slow-moving items at the earliest sign of weakness. This meant that retailers were placing smaller, more frequent orders than in the past.

FIELDCREST OPERATIONS, DECEMBER 1973

Fieldcrest clearly delineated its target markets, and it had different product lines and channels of distribution for each. Fieldcrest brand products were targeted at well-educated, fashion-conscious, affluent consumers. (While only 22 percent of all consumers were in the $15,000 plus income group, 48 percent of Fieldcrest brand consumers were there.) They tended to be young suburban homemakers with young children and to shop in department stores which offered fashion, wide selection, quality, and service. Fieldcrest sold through 1,780 department stores and bed and bath specialty shops.[3] In 28 of the top 40 marketing areas, Fieldcrest had exclusive distribution[4] through what company management considered to be the top-quality store in the area. Company policy was to increase Fieldcrest brand volume by better account management rather than by opening new accounts. Working with an account in areas such as advertising and merchandising, Fieldcrest tried to increase the account's total volume and simultaneously increase Fieldcrest's share of that volume. New accounts had to be reviewed and recommended by a Fieldcrest regional manager and approved through company headquarters.

The St. Mary's brand was positioned for younger, price-conscious consumers who shopped primarily in mass merchandiser outlets. St. Mary's was sold to 420 customers, including discount houses, chains, variety stores, and other outlets. As in many other businesses, a small number of customers accounted for a large share of the sales.

In addition, Fieldcrest sold both brands to a small number of wholesalers and to over 300 other customers, including premium accounts, stamp plans, the military, and various institutional customers. It also had several private-label customers.

In October 1973, sales of Fieldcrest brand products were running about 16 percent and St. Mary's about 36 percent ahead of 1972. Total division sales showed an overall increase of 12 percent over 1972.

David Tracy, Fieldcrest president, commented on the fashion home textile industry and his organization as follows:

> This is essentially a fashion business. Our concepts and designs will be accepted only if we stay on top of what consumers are talking about, what changes are occurring in their ideas and interests and activities, and then design to meet those consumer interests.
>
> Our company's strength, our ability to cope with this fashion business, is due in large part to our "people orientation." We feel strongly that this

---

[3]These numbers refer to corporate entities, not to individual retail outlets. For example, a department store with ten branches would be counted as only one department store.

[4]Exclusive distribution was the policy of selling through only one retail store (and its branches, if any) in a given trading area.

same "people orientation" permeates the atmosphere of our company, our recruiting programs, and our compensation plans.

(See Exhibit 2 for organization chart and Exhibit 3 for sales data.)

The Merchandising Organization

Fieldcrest's merchandising organization was headed by Herb Bergen, vice president and director of merchandising. It consisted of a design department and five product departments—blankets, bedspreads, sheets, automatic blankets, and bath fashions (that is, towels, rugs, and shower curtains). Each department was headed by a division vice president located in New York, who had a counterpart located at the mill which manufactured his products. Together, they were responsible for the profitability of the total department, including mill operations. Working with top sales executives, the department heads in New York selected and priced the product line, determined quantities to be produced, and assigned customer priorities. They ranged in age from 37 to 47, and most had come up through the Fieldcrest sales organization. They received an annual base salary of $27,000 to $49,000, plus a bonus of up to 35 percent of their base salary (25 percent of which was related to the profitability of their specific departments and 10 percent to the profitability of the Fieldcrest Marketing Division). In addition, a new incentive program had been inaugurated whereby they could aspire to certain stock incentives.

325

Under the blanket, bedspread, automatic blanket, and sheet department heads were one or two product managers. In the bath fashions department, three managers (two for towels and one for rugs and shower curtains) were in between the department head and product managers. A product manager had essentially the same responsibilities as a department head, except that his focus was usually limited to either the Fieldcrest or the St. Mary's line. Most product managers had previously worked in the sales organization. They ranged in age from 26 to 35. Their base salaries ranged from $15,000 to $32,000. They could earn a bonus of up to 20 percent of their base salary (15 percent of which was based on the profitability of their department and 5 percent on the profitability of the division).

One department head commented as follows on the structure of the Fieldcrest merchandising organization:

It's almost as if we have six or seven different companies strung together sharing the same sales force. Each has different products, different competitors, different opportunities and challenges, and often different buyers to sell to.

In 1973 the major concern of department heads and product manag-

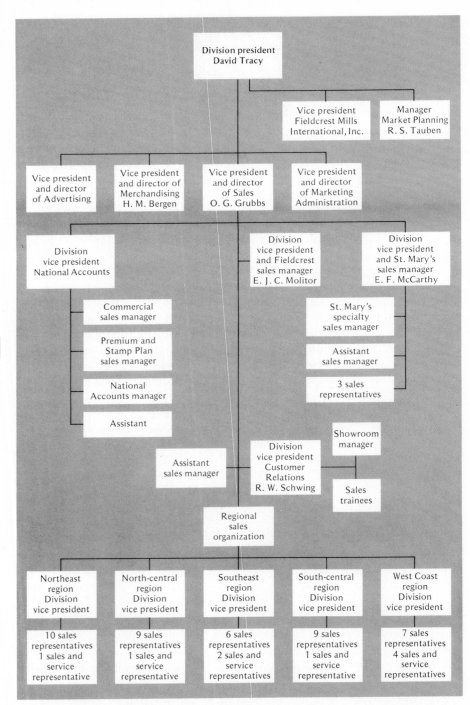

Exhibit 2 Abbreviated organization chart (the complete sales organization is included).

Exhibit 3   BUDGETED AND ACTUAL SALES (000 omitted)

	January-September			Total year	
	1972 actual	1973 budget	1973 actual	1972 actual	1973 budget
Fieldcrest					
Blankets	$ 4,158	$ 4,515	$ 5,054	$ 6,264	$ 7,592
Bedspreads	3,070	4,159	3,411	4,530	5,426
Sheets	13,790	15,329	14,882	19,971	23,065
Towels	18,955	20,158	22,643	26,877	31,572
Bathroom rugs	1,727	2,130	2,718	2,701	4,599
Automatic blankets	2,758	2,909	2,758	5,158	5,423
Total Fieldcrest	**$ 44,741**	**$ 49,539**	**$ 51,783**	**$ 65,927**	**$ 78,237**
St. Mary's					
Blankets	$ 2,270	$ 2,774	$ 3,730	$ 3,568	$ 5,167
Bedspreads	1,466	1,713	1,677	1,865	1,956
Sheets	4,418	4,869	4,363	6,721	7,255
Towels	6,502	7,193	10,461	9,352	13,485
Bathroom rugs	53	312	390	101	628
Shower curtains	—	—	—	—	—
Automatic blankets	2,185	2,127	2,393	3,727	4,397
Total St. Mary's	**$ 16,894**	**$ 18,988**	**$ 23,014**	**$ 25,334**	**$ 32,888**
Private label					
Blankets	$ 2,896	$ 2,836	$ 3,170	$ 5,090	$ 5,158
Bedspreads	10,357	10,924	10,251	14,416	15,275
Sheets	1,264	1,708	1,065	1,718	1,701
Towels	11,011	13,369	11,667	14,831	17,148
Bathroom rugs	583	754	774	778	1,012
Shower curtains	—	—	—	—	—
Automatic blankets	2,982	3,658	3,503	5,512	6,198
Total private label	**$ 29,111**	**$ 33,229**	**$ 30,430**	**$ 42,345**	**$ 46,492**
Military and institutional[a]	**$ 18,321**	**$ 16,752**	**$ 15,900**	**$ 26,175**	**$ 21,201**
Seconds and drops	6,921	8,376	8,283	7,329	11,045
Total	**$115,988**	**$126,884**	**$129,410**	**$167,110**	**$189,863**

[a]While these products normally carried the Fieldcrest or St. Mary's label, company accounting practice was to consider them separate from regular branded sales.

Source: Fieldcrest Division of Fieldcrest Mills, Inc., records.

ers was not volume so much as profit. In five of the seven product areas, sales had shown significant increases over 1972. However, raw material shortages and skyrocketing costs had cut deeply into profits. The need to eliminate marginally profitable items and to emphasize the more profitable items in each line had become increasingly apparent.

The two areas in which sales were weakest were sheets and bedspreads. Since 1971, the sheet department had suffered from a growing retailer and consumer trend away from percale blends toward less costly muslin blends.[5] Muslin blends were especially important in the mass merchandiser market, and even department stores were becoming increasingly interested in muslin as skyrocketing raw materials costs

[5]Percale blends were made of thinner yarns woven more tightly than muslin blends. Their fibers were generally costlier and the resultant products softer than muslin blends.

threatened to price percales out of the market. Through most of 1972, Fieldcrest's muslin production capabilities were insufficient for it to take an aggressive sales posture. By 1973, however, almost half of its looms had been shifted from percale to muslin. Most Fieldcrest brand sheets still were percale, and they were selling well. If the department store market did shift to muslin, Fieldcrest would either have to change over more looms or increase its total capacity. It was already involved in one muslin capacity expansion program, but that had been designated for the St. Mary's brand. Sales of Fieldcrest brand sheets were up 8 percent over the first three-quarters of 1972, but this was 3 percent below target. Furthermore, St. Mary's brand sales were down 1 percent, and private-label sales were down 16 percent from 1972.

Sheet department personnel thought that sales of other products were strongly affected by sheet sales because sheets represented the cornerstone of a coordinated program in retail domestics departments. Sheets were extremely important, they argued, because they accounted for a high percentage of domestics departments' sales, were style coordinated, and were packaged to expose the Fieldcrest and St. Mary's names and build brand awareness. Special sales incentives on sheets might be in order, they thought, because other manufacturers were becoming increasingly competitive in styling and were aggressively seeking the business of the better department stores and stronger mass merchandisers.

In the bedspread department, St. Mary's branded sales were thought to be doing well, as sales were up 14 percent over the previous year and 98 percent of budget had been attained. However, Fieldcrest branded sales had fallen 18 percent short of target, and though overall sales had increased 11 percent over 1972, sales to traditional department stores had decreased 5 percent. Private-brand volume was down 1 percent, but it still accounted for about 70 percent of total bedspread sales, and it was concentrated in a few very large accounts. Bedspread department management felt very strongly that they should decrease their dependence on so few customers. Furthermore, they felt that they had to increase total volume considerably in order to run their mill at capacity, a condition almost essential to profitable operation.

The Sales Organization

The Fieldcrest sales organization was headed by O. G. Grubbs, vice president and director of sales. It consisted of five major divisions—national accounts, customer relations, Fieldcrest sales, St. Mary's sales, and regional sales. The first four divisions were headed by division vice presidents (ages 37 to 49). They received base salaries ranging from $33,000 to $47,000, plus a bonus of up to 35 percent of the base salary. The bonus was based on the profitability of the Fieldcrest Marketing Division.

They also received the same stock options as division vice presidents in merchandising.

National Accounts Division

The National Accounts Division had three sales managers. They ranged in age from 35 to 49. They received a base salary of from $20,000 to $29,000, plus discretionary bonus determined by the Fieldcrest Marketing Division president. It usually amounted to about 10 percent of their base salary.

The manager of commercial and military sales worked with product departments to determine the products and prices to be offered to hospitals, hotels, and other institutional customers. He had sole responsibility for selling to a few accounts, but he made most of his contacts with customers with the Fieldcrest sales representative who normally handled the account. The manager of premium and stamp plan sales had essentially the same tasks as the manager of commercial and military sales, except that his customers used the products as promotional devices. For example, a bank might offer a free Fieldcrest blanket to every customer who opened a savings account; a company might request specially printed towel sets to use as incentives with its sales force; or Fieldcrest products might be a regular part of a stamp redemption company's program. The national accounts manager handled Fieldcrest's private-label business with large chains such as Grants, J C Penney, Korvettes, and Sears. He also supervised the private-label business which field sales representatives did with small accounts.

329

Customer Relations Division

The vice president for customer relations was responsible for recruiting and initial training of sales personnel and for supervising the Fieldcrest and St. Mary's showrooms. In addition, Fieldcrest's market-week activities were channeled through his office. (Market week was held in New York three times a year. Sponsored by a trade association, it afforded buyers the opportunity of viewing manufacturers' new lines and was an important part of industry sales efforts.) In December 1973, his major activity was the creation of a personnel development program both for trainees and established employees.

FIELDCREST SALES DIVISION
AND ST. MARY'S SALES DIVISION

The Fieldcrest sales manager and St. Mary's sales manager (both of whom were also division vice presidents) worked with merchandising executives to determine product lines and volume. They also supervised and directed regional managers and sales representatives, collected market information, and maintained close contact with major customers.

Because headquarters of many major St. Mary's customers were located in the Northeast, three sales representatives who sold only St. Mary's products operated out of the New York office and reported directly to the St. Mary's assistant sales manager. Also located in New York was a St. Mary's specialty sales manager who handled large accounts in all areas, except where there were special St. Mary's sales representatives. For compensation purposes, these three sales representatives and the specialty sales manager were considered regular regional sales representatives.

Regional Sales

At the top of the regional sales organization were five division vice presidents who served as regional managers. In reality, they were not on the same level with other division vice presidents, but had been given the title largely to increase their prestige in dealing with customers. They were all college graduates, ages 35 to 52, who had considerable experience in Fieldcrest sales and/or merchandising. Each was responsible for infield training, directing, and evaluating 6 to 10 sales representatives (42 in all) and 1 to 4 sales-service representatives (9 in all). One regional manager estimated that he spent 40 percent of his time on the road with his salespeople. Regional managers maintained strong relationships with the management of key accounts in their regions. While a region might contain as many as 500 customers, the regional manager would probably visit only 80 or 90. Regional managers received base salaries ranging from $23,000 to $37,000, plus bonuses of up to 45 percent of their base salaries. One-half of the bonus was based on the total volume of the region, one-fourth on target account volume[6] within the region, and one-fourth on top management's evaluation of the regional manager's performance.

Fieldcrest's 42 sales representatives were responsible for anywhere from 16 to 120 accounts; most had 50 to 60. While some sold only St. Mary's brand products and others only Fieldcrest brand products, most were responsible for both lines and for calling on a wide variety of customers—department stores, specialty stores, mass merchandisers, institutional and premium customers, and wholesalers. About 90 percent of the sales representatives were college graduates. They received base salaries ranging from $10,000 to $28,000, plus bonuses of up to 35 percent of their base.[7]

330

[6]See "Fieldcrest Division of Fieldcrest Mills, Incorporated (C)" for more on the target account program.

[7]See "Fieldcrest Division of Fieldcrest Mills, Incorporated (C)" for more on the sales compensation plan.

Sales territories ranged in volume from $1.4 million to $3 million. In geographical areas, the smallest territory covered New York City alone, while the largest covered Wyoming, Utah, Colorado, and half of New Mexico. Call frequency varied considerably, according to the sales representative's location, territory, and account size. A sales representative in New York City might visit a major Manhattan customer four times a week, while another might visit a minor account in a remote area of his territory only once every 6 weeks. His normal contacts were with buyers and merchandise managers. He usually made one to three calls a day, depending on the size and complexity of the customers visited. Occasionally, a single person could make purchase decisions for all products. More frequently, however, the sales representative had to contact at least two buyers and/or merchandise managers, and sometimes as many as six within a single account.

Fieldcrest's account dominance program which was initiated in 1970 brought multilevel executives of both Fieldcrest and the client company into the selling situation. This was a comprehensive program of advertising, sales promotion, and product mix designed to help the retailer improve penetration over a 3-year period and to enable Fieldcrest to attain a larger share of the retailer's business. Fieldcrest management thought that, on the whole, this program had been successful, especially in strengthening relationships with customers from the top down. However, a few sales representatives had reported that the program generated negative feelings among some buyers. "If we sell in at a high level, we take away much of the buyer's prerogative," said one executive. "If he gets angry enough, he can do a lot to make our products flop. It's up to our salesmen to maintain a good relationship with that buyer, and that isn't always easy."

331

Fieldcrest's nine sales-service representatives went into retail outlets, counted stock, and took orders on items which were included in the basic inventory the account maintained. They were paid a salary of $8,000 to $13,000.

In addition to salaries and various incentive programs, Fieldcrest paid its salespeople's travel and selling expenses. It supplied cars to all regional managers, sales representatives, and sales-service representatives. In 1972, the average sales representative's travel and selling expense, car included, was $6,891. Other fringe benefits included comprehensive medical and retirement plans.

THIRTY-SEVEN Fieldcrest Division
of Fieldcrest Mills, Incorporated (B)

In December 1973, O. G. Grubbs, vice president and director of sales, was reviewing the methods used to motivate the Fieldcrest sales force. He thought that sales meetings at resort areas, videotape sales aids, luxurious showrooms and offices, and séveral other factors contributed greatly to the exciting atmosphere associated with the fashion home-textile industry and made Fieldcrest a very enjoyable place to work. However, many of these were very costly, and in recent years, though Fieldcrest sales had made healthy increases, expenses had soared. Mr. Grubbs felt that he should look very carefully at how Fieldcrest was spending money and eliminate unnecessary expenses whenever possible.

NONFINANCIAL MOTIVATION

Mr. Grubbs isolated five major nonfinancial factors which he felt contributed to the motivation of the Fieldcrest sales force—sales contests, sales meetings, videotape sales aids, a sales force newsletter, and a newly created personnel development program. To deal with several less tangible factors, he created a "method of doing business" category.

Sales Contests

Historically, Fieldcrest had run sales contests on a very limited basis. The prevalent opinion among top management had been that Fieldcrest salespeople were very well paid and that the company should not have to provide special contests to get them to do their jobs.

In 1972 it became obvious that, for the recently acquired mill that manufactured bathroom rugs to operate profitably, bathroom rug sales would have to be very substantial. (In the past, Fieldcrest had sold only a very limited line of bathroom rugs manufactured by another company.) Therefore, Fieldcrest management decided that during the first three-quarters of 1973, in addition to offering monetary incentives amounting to 30 percent of a sales representative's bonus on bathroom rug sales, they would run a contest. The four salespeople who achieved the highest percentage over sales quota on bathroom rugs received a so-called president's award, an original Picasso lithograph. The cost of the four lithographs was about $700.[1]

During this time, the company's bathroom rug distribution was

[1]By December 1973, the market price of the lithographs had doubled.

greatly expanded and branded bathroom rugs sales increased about 75 percent over the previous year. Opinion among Fieldcrest management differed as to the contest's importance in generating the increase. Some executives felt that the type of prize and the label, "president's award," were very powerful motivators. "An art object is the kind of thing an average guy would like to own but wouldn't buy for himself," one executive said. "The contest gave him a chance to own one by just doing his job very well. Furthermore, calling this the 'president's award' greatly increased its prestige." Some argued that the financial incentive was far more important, and others said the greatly improved and expanded product line was the key. Some even felt that the rug contest actually had negative effects in that it "bribed salespeople to spend too much time on rugs and not enough on the line as a whole."

Sales Meetings

Fieldcrest's New York headquarters traditionally sponsored a national sales meeting and a set of regional meetings one year and two sets of regional meetings the following year. These meetings were held for about 3 days at exclusive resort areas and were widely considered an excellent means of generating excitement for new product lines and building company morale. Meetings were scheduled only during the daytime. Evenings and one afternoon were left free for various recreational activities. (See Exhibit 1 for sample schedule of a regional meeting.)

333

National meetings were attended by 110 to 150 people, including corporate officers, the division president, division vice presidents of sales, merchandising, advertising, and marketing administration, several other sales executives, department heads, product managers, and plant managers. National sales meetings were considered especially useful for making major merchandising presentations. However, they took longer to prepare and were more expensive than regional meetings, primarily because of the cost of transporting people from all parts of the United States.

If regional meetings were held, salespeople from the region plus about eight sales executives and four department heads from the New York office usually attended. Occasionally, two regions held meetings together. Regional meetings were usually structured as workshops, and much individual involvement was encouraged. However, they were not thought to be as valuable as national meetings in strengthening overall company morale.

To help make decisions for 1974 sales meetings, Fieldcrest management had gathered data from previous meetings. The cost figures included travel, hotels, meals, special entertainment and activities, and audiovisual aids. (See table at top of page 334.)

Concerned with the rising cost of sales meetings, Mr. Grubbs had isolated five major alternatives for cutting cost.

Date	Type and place of meeting	No. of days	Approximate no. attending each meeting	Total cost
May 1972	National meeting, Disneyworld, Orlando, Florida	3	150	$130,000
November 1972	Five regional meetings	$2\frac{1}{2}$ days each	35	34,000
May 1973	Five regional meetings	$2\frac{1}{2}$ days each	35	30,000
November 1973	Three regional meetings Phoenix, Arizona (West and South Central regions)	$2\frac{1}{2}$ days each	35	45,000
	Hot Springs, Virginia (Southeast and North Central regions)		35	
	Southbury, Connecticut (Northeast region and numerous New York management personnel)		50	

1 Eliminate one meeting per year and delegate responsibility for introducing that season's new line to regional managers.

2 Have only regional meetings.

334

3 Shorten meetings by eliminating recreational periods.

4 Hold meetings at more modest locations.

5 Send fewer New York personnel but have them make videotapes to be shown at the meetings.

The Fieldcrest–St. Mary's Salesletter

In June 1973, Reg Tauben, manager of market planning, put out the first Fieldcrest–St. Mary's Salesletter. (See Exhibit 2 for sample.) Mr. Tauben commented on the Salesletter as follows:

> A newsletter oriented toward salespeople is a good way to convey information, acknowledge accomplishments, inspire salespeople to do a better job, and mold the competitive spirit. The letter, however, should deal only with factual sales information.

In December 1973, Mr. Tauben was sending two salesletters each month to field salespeople; sales, merchandising, advertising, and marketing administration personnel in the New York office; and executives at corporate headquarters in Eden, North Carolina. Mr. Tauben estimated that once he had collected news items, by far the most frustrating and time-consuming part of the task, he spent about 2 hours writing each salesletter. "The only additional cost is the paper," Mr. Tauben stated, "and that's negligible."

Videotape Program

During the summer of 1972, Fieldcrest management decided to institute a limited videotape program. The theory was that it would sharply reduce sales costs, since many executives who usually attended sales meetings could simply tape a presentation to be shown at the meetings. Moreover, it could improve communication between the home office and the field, and it could be used for sales training. Fieldcrest then purchased about $20,000 worth of videotape equipment and asked Cynthia Stewart, an advertising department employee, to run the program. The initial $20,000 purchase consisted of a black and white camera, one recorder, a tape eraser, five players and monitors, and a supply of videotape cassettes. A 30-minute tape cassette cost about $25, and could be recorded over an unlimited number of times.

Videotapes were first used at the sales meetings in November 1972. One executive later commented as follows:

> Cynthia was the only one who knew anything about making tapes, and unfortunately she had no control over the content. Our first presentations were too long, we tried to show new merchandise on black and white films, and we either read our speeches or paused and stammered a lot. We've gotten a little better, but our tapes still could hardly be called "polished."

335

In 1973 the decision was made to expand the videotape program to include sales aids. To do this, Fieldcrest purchased 14 Fairchild projectors at $370 each. These were portable, self-contained units which played super 8 mm film. They were distributed among regional offices for sales representatives to use in making presentations to customers. To convert videotape for use in the Fairchild projector cost about $25 per minute for the first film and about $25 for each additional film.

In addition to tapes made by Fieldcrest personnel, professionally made films could also be converted for use on the regular video equipment and the Fairchild projectors. To introduce the 1974 spring line, a professional film-making company produced "Fieldcrest Presents Freestyle," an 8-minute film about Rosita and Octavio Missoni, the Italian designers who created the Freestyle line. The cost of the film was $30,000. (This was charged to the advertising department.) Fourteen copies for the Fairchild projectors were made and distributed among Fieldcrest's five regions, and sales representatives were encouraged to use them in their selling activities.

While none of Fieldcrest's major competitors had equipment comparable to this, one executive called it "paltry compared to what retailers like Marshall Field and JC Penney use for sales training and internal communications." He went on to say that many of the audiovisual department's expenses were covered by either advertising or sales meeting budgets and that the total audiovisual budget was only about

$5,000 a year. Ms. Stewart's salary came out of the advertising budget.

In December 1973, the advertising department was considering an additional $15,000 expenditure for new lighting, a color camera, editing equipment, audio equipment, microphones, and additional wiring. (They were currently renting a color camera and lights.) It was thought that this equipment would result in more professional, higher-quality tape presentations. However, many felt that this expenditure was not justified at the present time because Fieldcrest already had excellent internal communication, the equipment had not decreased sales meeting costs as they had hoped it would, and the sales training program was not yet sophisticated enough to make good use of the equipment.

Personnel Development Program

In December 1973, Bob Schwing, vice president of customer relations, began working on a personnel development program. "Our objective is to utilize our employees more effectively," said Mr. Schwing. "We feel that as we become a better managed company, that will be a motivational factor in itself." The program consisted of four parts:

1 *Job descriptions* According to Mr. Schwing, Fieldcrest's existing job descriptions "bear very little relationship to what people actually do." In rewriting the job descriptions, Mr. Schwing was attempting to reflect the reality of what people were doing without overlapping their responsibilities. He felt strongly that management should be precise about responsibilities associated with specific positions and should evaluate employees on how well they handled those responsibilities.

2 *Evaluation* To aid managers in evaluating employees, Mr. Schwing created a lengthy questionnaire (see Exhibit 3). This as yet had nothing to do with compensation but was a tool to facilitate communication.

3 *Training* In the past, training of new salespeople was not tightly structured. Before a salesperson went into the field, he received a good deal of instruction about each line from product managers. However, since salespeople joined the company one at a time, numerous meetings had to be arranged and product managers had to repeat the information about their products each time a new salesperson came on board. These meetings were often second-priority items for product managers, and new salespeople reported that they spent "an inordinate amount of time folding towels in the showroom."

The training program Mr. Schwing was developing would utilize videotapes for product managers' presentations so that a trainee could proceed through the program at his own pace. Mr. Schwing was also working on training programs for current employees. He thought these would probably be administered in workshops at regional meetings.

4 *Projection* The final element of the program involved projecting long-range personnel needs. Since the sales organization frequently served as a pool for the advertising and merchandising departments, expansion in one area would necessitate expansion in the other areas.

Method of Doing Business

Under the "method of doing business" classification, Mr. Grubbs grouped miscellaneous factors which contributed to the overall atmosphere and image of the company. He commented as follows:

> Our basic products—sheets, towels, and so forth—are commodity items. We have merely embellished them with design and quality. We want the management of retail stores to look at our products in a new way—not as basic commodities but as fashion home textiles. Presentation is very important in getting them to do this.

An important element of Fieldcrest's "presentation" was the setting in which it entertained customers and displayed merchandise. Throughout the company, offices were tastefully decorated with textured wall coverings, carpets, artwork, wooden desks, and at the higher levels, expensive contemporary furniture. The showrooms through which guests entered the building were equally elaborate. The initial cost of the Fieldcrest showroom had been about $500,000. Early in 1973 it was remodeled at a cost of $150,000. This included new lighting (about $60,000 alone), a huge white shag carpet, glass-top tables, and display racks and shelves. Mr. Schwing commented on the showroom.

> We're pleased with the results—the showroom is indeed a beautiful place to display merchandise. But we thought the costs were never going to end. The new lighting produced so much heat that a new air-conditioning system was necessary, and this in turn required major changes in the electrical wiring. We haven't calculated the maintenance costs, but keeping fingerprints off glass tables and stains off a white carpet requires an incredible amount of upkeep.

The St. Mary's showroom was only slightly less elaborate. Its initial cost had been about $300,000. Each showroom had a receptionist. One manager and her assistant supervised both showrooms. In addition, one or two trainees were in the showrooms most of the time. While all of Fieldcrest's competitors had showrooms, none were thought to be as distinctive as Fieldcrest's.

Another element of Fieldcrest's presentation was the flair which often surrounded the selling situation. This was created partly by inexpensive, creative "sales aids" such as dotted Missoni bow ties for salesmen and umbrellas for saleswomen. The more important and costly element, however, was customer entertainment. This was especially obvious during the three annual market weeks sponsored by the industry trade association. These were weeks in February, May, and November, when retailers came to New York to view manufacturers' new lines. During at least one market week every year, Fieldcrest threw a formal party, centered around the theme set forth by the new merchandise line, for about 100 press representatives and about 400 Fieldcrest customers. The November 1973 party, held at the Plaza Hotel, was an Italian festival inspired by the Missoni Freestyle line.

In addition to New York area salespeople and executives, about 20 key salespeople from across the United States attended market week. Most of their expenses came out of their regular travel and entertainment budgets. However, there was a fund for extraordinary expenses such as lunches, dinners, or theater tickets for a large number of customers. One executive estimated that, in addition to costs absorbed by regular travel and entertainment budgets, Fieldcrest spent $25,000 to $30,000 annually on market week activities.

Fieldcrest salespeople had complete freedom to decide how their travel and entertainment allocations would be spent. "Of course, we encourage our salespeople to hold down costs, but to a large extent, they are their own boss," Mr. Grubbs said. "We've always believed that allowing them considerable discretion increases their opinions of their job and hopefully makes them more concerned about the overall performance of the company, not just about their own sales volume. We think that they feel pressure to control selling costs just as we do."

As Mr. Grubbs considered the various nonfinancial motivators, he was aware of the difficulty of measuring the return generated by any specific investment. While many executives argued that it was foolish to continue expenditures on so-called frills, Mr. Grubbs felt that, in the fashion home-textile business, a manufacturer's image was extremely important. He knew, furthermore, that his salespeople were especially restless now because demand was high, raw materials were in short supply, and Fieldcrest was frequently unable to deliver orders as promised. These factors, Mr. Grubbs reasoned, actually increased the importance of nonfinancial motivators as a means of keeping salespeople happy and enthusiastic. He wondered if perhaps now was the time to invest more in them rather than cutting back.

Exhibit 1

1973 November Sales Meeting Agenda

First Evening

7:00	Cocktails
8:30	Dinner
	Welcome by D. M. Tracy, president of Fieldcrest Marketing Division

Exhibit 1 *(Continued)*

First Day

8:30– 8:45 A.M.	Welcome
	Corporate report W. C. Battle (VTR),[2] president of Fieldcrest Mills, Inc.
8:45– 9:00	*Sail into '74* O. G. Grubbs (VTR), vice president and director of Sales
9:00–10:00	*Fieldcrest programs* H. M. Bergen (VTR), vice president and director of Merchandising
	J. P. Robertson, vice president and director of Advertising
10:00–10:15	*How to sell Fieldcrest programs* E. J. C. Molitor (VTR), Division vice president and Fieldcrest sales manager.
10:15–10:45	Discussion
10:45–11:00	Coffee break
11:00–11:10	*Fieldcrest sheets* R. R. McGill (VTR), Division vice president, Sheet Department
11:10–11:30	Discussion
11:30–11:45	*Design concept to finished products* S. K. Babiss (VTR), manager and Product Development coordinator
11:45–11:55	*Fieldcrest automatics* J. J. O'Grady (VTR), Division vice president, Automatic Blanket Department
11:55–12:10 P.M.	Discussion
12:10–12:25	Smithfield tour (VTR)
12:25– 1:30	Lunch
1:30– 1:40	*Fieldcrest blankets* A. S. Thompson, Jr. (VTR), Division vice president, Blanket Department
1:40– 1:55	Discussion
1:55– 2:05	*Fieldcrest bedspreads* J. M. Foster (VTR), Division vice president, Bedspread Department
2:05– 2:20	*How to sell Fieldcrest bedspreads* J. M. Foster (VTR)
2:20– 2:40	Discussion
2:40– 2:55	Coffee break
2:55– 3:05	*Fieldcrest towels and bath fashions* F. X. Larkin (VTR), Division vice president and Merchandise manager, Towels
3:05– 3:15	*Fieldcrest rugs* G. D. Stewart (VTR), manager, Bath Fashions Department
3:15– 3:35	Discussion
3:35– 3:50	*How to manufacture rugs* G. D. Stewart (VTR)
3:50– 4:00	*Fieldcrest towels* D. J. Taylor (VTR), Division vice president, Fieldale Towel Department
4:00– 4:20	Discussion

339

[2]Videotape recording.

Exhibit 1 *(Continued)*
Second Day

8:00– 8:45 A.M.	*St. Mary's programs* H. M. Bergen (VTR), J. P. Robertson
8:45– 9:00	*How to sell St. Mary's programs* E. F. McCarthy (VTR), Division vice president and St. Mary's sales manager
9:00– 9:30	Discussion
9:30– 9:40	*St. Mary's sheets* R. R. McGill (VTR)
9:40–10:00	Discussion
10:00–10:10	*St. Mary's automatics* J. J. O'Grady (VTR)
10:10–10:30	Discussion
10:30–10:45	Coffee break
10:45–10:55	*St. Mary's blankets* A. S. Thompson, Jr. (VTR)
10:55–11:05	*How to sell blankets* A. S. Thompson, Jr. (VTR)
11:05–11:20	Discussion
11:20–11:30	*St. Mary's bedspreads* J. M. Foster (VTR)
11:30–11:45	Discussion
11:45–11:55	*St. Mary's rugs* G. D. Stewart (VTR)
11:55–12:10 P.M.	Discussion
12:10–12:20	*St. Mary's towels* D. S. Ness (VTR), manager, Columbus Towel Department
12:20–12:40	Discussion
Afternoon	Lunch and recreation (golf, tennis, swimming, etc.)

Third Day

9:00– 9:30 A.M.	Fieldcrest standards S. Ellington (VTR)
9:30–10:00	Advertising J. P. Robertson (VTR)
10:00–10:20	Discussion
10:20–10:35	*Premium and commercial sales* C. B. Arnold (VTR), Division National Accounts J. H. Staak, manager, Commercial Sales J. J. Bedell, manager, Premium and Stamp Plan Sales
10:35–10:55	Discussion
10:55–11:15	Coffee break
11:15–11:30	*Fieldcrest wrap-up* E. J. C. Molitor (VTR)
11:30–11:45	*St. Mary's wrap-up* E. F. McCarthy (VTR)
11:45–12:00 P.M.	*Fast start '74* O. G. Grubbs (VTR)
12:00– 1:00	Lunch
1:00– 2:30	Regional meeting (attended by regional managers, sales representatives, and sales-service representatives)

340

Exhibit 2
Fieldcrest–St. Mary's Salesletter of June 15, 1973

Alan Green is due a well-deserved pat on the back for a great job in placing the St. Mary's Monaco rug program in the Merrimack Stores, Glencone, Indiana. Despite the price competition that we are all faced with, Alan has the wall-to-wall, scatter rugs, lids and tank sets on a basic stock reorder basis in all of Merrimack's 14 stores. He already had the Happiness and Square Dance rugs on basic. If we had eight more styles, he would probably have them placed, too.

We all knew that Fieldcrest was the number one towel brand in major department stores. Now, we're number one in sheets also. Market Research Corporation of America, based on their panel of 7,500 families, reported that during the first quarter of 1973 major department store shoppers spent more dollars on Fieldcrest sheets than on any other single brand. You can tell this to your accounts because we've got the numbers to prove it.

At the Allenwood minimarket, sales people voted for the best vendor presentation. Jim Upton, Glenda Trains, and Marty Kelly gave an award-winning performance, while our two friendly competitors did not even receive mention.

And it was a great May Market Week in Dallas covering 200 accounts for August White Sale, plus a record market two weeks earlier at the Gibson show. These markets were worked by Bill Hall, Tim Leary, Bert Flowers, Frank Laughton, Betty Dalton, Dennis Rawkins, and Sheila Edwards.

Nat Turner has been able to get his foot in the door with Good Deal Food Stores. They have 4,200 stores.

This should be quite a year for Ben Dole. He just sold the Gifts Galore Contract Company of Columbus some 26,000 Century 21 and 4,000 Castle blankets for fall delivery. Will be used as "New Account Openers" at the Community Banks. This order was made possible through the able help of Jake Rollins. To date, Ben has also shipped $131,000 of Velvet Touch bedspreads to Leonlynes in Columbus. Ben is estimating 1973 sales of $250,000 on this one bedspread alone.

341

Paul Foulkes just placed our new Daybreak with Crowley Stores, Inc. The initial order was for $17,000. Won't that look nice in his bonus check at the end of the year?

Exhibit 3
Management Evaluation Form
Implementation: Suggested Format for Use

March   The supervisor and the person being evaluated would each be given a copy of the "Evaluation System."

April   A definite date will be set to develop performance objectives for the coming year. Prior to this meeting, the person being evaluated and his supervisor would write these objectives. At this meeting, the objectives would be *jointly* determined . . . written on the appropriate page of the attached form.

July-August   Follow-up session between the supervisor and the person being evaluated to review performance on the interim basis pointing out progress and/or problem areas.

January-February   Formal evaluation filled out and signed by both the supervisor and the person being evaluated and sent to the division office. [This is the last form on the attached material.]

It should be clearly understood that this form is intended as a guide "checklist" . . . obviously many of the things listed in the form are not appropriate to the person being evaluated. The determination of what is relevant to the person's performance would be the decision of the person doing the evaluating.

Exhibit 3 *(Continued)*
Evaluation

The following evaluation form has been prepared to improve the total business effectiveness of the Fieldcrest Division. We believe that professional growth is dependent upon continuous self-evaluation. This evaluation is an attempt to help our people focus on their behavior and to take appropriate action to bring about positive change.

It must be remembered that this device can only assist an individual in identifying areas of needed improvement. In the final analysis, the individual must be willing to make a commitment to act upon the specific information that is derived from the evaluation if improvement is to take place.

This form is intended to be used as a guide and outline since many things listed are not appropriate to the person being evaluated. It is recommended for use in self-evaluation and administrative evaluation.

Encircling the number "1" denotes an answer of "never"; encircling "2" means "occasionally"; encircling "3" denotes "usually"; encircling "4" means "always."

I Information and Background

The person:

( ) ( ) ( ) ( )   **A** Has appropriate knowledge of company policy, direction, and background

1   2   3   4   1. Company history
1   2   3   4   2. Key factors in Fieldcrest growth
1   2   3   4   3. Legal requirements to comply with government regulations
1   2   3   4   4. Five-year plan projections

( ) ( ) ( ) ( )   **B** Has necessary knowledge of manufacturing processes

1   2   3   4   1. Quality control standards
1   2   3   4   2. Research and development projects
1   2   3   4   3. Knowledge of mill personnel and their functions
1   2   3   4   4. Familiarity with cost accounting systems
1   2   3   4   5. Working knowledge of mill reports
1   2   3   3   6. Inventory control systems
1   2   3   4   7. Order-service operations

( ) ( ) ( ) ( )   **C** Has appropriate knowledge of division marketing philosophy and direction

1   2   3   4   1. Retail distribution policy of Fieldcrest brand
1   2   3   4   2. Retail distribution policy of St. Mary's brand
1   2   3   4   3. Knowledge of private-brand customers
1   2   3   4   4. Knowledge of co-op advertising policies by brand
1   2   3   4   5. Knowledge of important retail customers by brand

( ) ( ) ( ) ( )   **D** Has appropriate working knowledge of departments within the division

1   2   3   4   1. Automatic blankets
1   2   3   4   2. Bath fashions
1   2   3   4   3. Bedspreads

Exhibit 3 *(Continued)*

1	2	3	4	4. Blankets
1	2	3	4	5. Sheets
1	2	3	4	6. Towels

II Planning

The person:

( ) ( ) ( ) ( ) **A** Works cooperatively with other people in a professionally responsible manner to provide for the individual differences that exist within a group

1	2	3	4	1. Gives and takes in verbal interaction
1	2	3	4	2. Submits original ideas and approaches
1	2	3	4	3. Considers a variety of alternatives
1	2	3	4	4. Selects jointly the most appropriate solutions or procedures
1	2	3	4	5. Follows selected procedures of the group
1	2	3	4	6. Supports consensual decisions

( ) ( ) ( ) ( ) **B** States performance objectives aimed at meeting the needs of the company upon request of staff members or customers

( ) ( ) ( ) ( ) **C** Formulates specific plans for reaching stated objectives

1	2	3	4	1. Selects content pertinent to the needs of individual projects
1	2	3	4	2. Plans a variety of appropriate material to be used
1	2	3	4	a. Research reports
1	2	3	4	b. Sales reports
1	2	3	4	c. Customer analysis reports
1	2	3	4	d. Exposure reports
1	2	3	4	e. Production schedules
1	2	3	4	f. Inventory reports
1	2	3	4	g. Market information, reports, letters
1	2	3	4	h. Trade publications
1	2	3	4	i. Customer contacts
1	2	3	4	j. White sale catalogs
1	2	3	4	k. Other _____
1	2	3	4	3. Determines the appropriate method and materials to be used to communicate action
1	2	3	4	a. Telephone
1	2	3	4	b. Memo
1	2	3	4	c. Formal report
1	2	3	4	d. Sales bulletins
1	2	3	4	e. Letters
1	2	3	4	f. Workshop
1	2	3	4	g. Maps and charts
1	2	3	4	h. Pictorial materials
1	2	3	4	i. Personal meeting
1	2	3	4	j. Audiovisual equipment

Exhibit 3 *(Continued)*

1	2	3	4	(1) Overhead projector
1	2	3	4	(2) Record player
1	2	3	4	(3) Tape recorder
1	2	3	4	(4) Filmstrip projector
1	2	3	4	(5) 8mm projector
1	2	3	4	(6) 16mm projector
1	2	3	4	(7) Opaque projector
1	2	3	4	(8) Videotape
1	2	3	4	4. Structures the content, methods, and materials in order to evoke a variety of responses
1	2	3	4	a. Evaluating
1	2	3	4	b. Outlining
1	2	3	4	c. Classifying
1	2	3	4	d. Comparing
1	2	3	4	e. Defining problems
1	2	3	4	f. Solving problems
1	2	3	4	g. Interpreting
1	2	3	4	h. Hypothesizing

III Implementation

The person:

( )	( )	( )	( )	**A** Works cooperatively with others, sharing in:
1	2	3	4	1. Verbal communication
1	2	3	4	2. Responsibility for action
1	2	3	4	3. Adaptation of plan based on change as determined by on-going evaluation
( )	( )	( )	( )	**B** Carries out specific plans outlined under IIC (formulating plans)
1	2	3	4	1. Selects appropriate content (C1)
1	2	3	4	2. Uses a variety of appropriate materials and communication methods (C2, C3)
1	2	3	4	3. Evokes a variety of responses (C4)
( )	( )	( )	( )	**C** Assumes roles consistent with the stated objectives
1	2	3	4	1. Initiator—gets the ball rolling
1	2	3	4	2. Supporter—assists, verifies, and comforts
1	2	3	4	3. Clarifier—restates a concept in order to make it clear
1	2	3	4	4. Questioner—elicits information
1	2	3	4	5. Challenger—questions the validity of opinions, ideas, and concepts
1	2	3	4	6. Information supplier—supplies facts
1	2	3	4	7. Summarizer—brings together and states material previously discussed
1	2	3	4	8. Harmonizer—reconciles personality and viewpoint differences
1	2	3	4	9. Coordinator—organizes personnel and material for problem solving

Exhibit 3 *(Continued)*

1	2	3	4		10. Observer—objectively perceives and takes note of behavior for evaluation and planning behavior changes
1	2	3	4		11. Blocker—impedes progress of the group
1	2	3	4		12. Subversive—undermines group movement
1	2	3	4		13. Monopolizer—usurps the attention of the group
1	2	3	4		14. Digressor—diverts group discussion
1	2	3	4		15. Passive participator—observes without overt interaction
( )	( )	( )	( )	D	Demonstrates the use of behavioral variables in order to promote positive action
1	2	3	4		1. Increases or decreases tension for optimum action
1	2	3	4		2. Promotes pleasant feeling tone
1	2	3	4		3. Conveys enthusiasm and interest
( )	( )	( )	( )	E	*Self-acceptance:* Accepts and discusses objectively the following qualities in himself and his fellow staff members without overwhelming embarrassment, defensiveness, or guilt
1	2	3	4		1. Virtues
1	2	3	4		2. Impulses
1	2	3	4		3. Personal feelings
1	2	3	4		4. Capacities
1	2	3	4		5. Goals
1	2	3	4		6. Shortcomings
1	2	3	4		7. Background experiences
( )	( )	( )	( )	F	*Self-actualization*
1	2	3	4		1. Discusses and provides for meeting the immediate needs of himself and fellow staff members without losing sight of long-range effects
1	2	3	4		2. Postpones immediate personal pleasure and reward to facilitate progress toward long-range objectives
1	2	3	4		3. Feels that personal contribution to the company is worthwhile
( )	( )	( )	( )	G	*Coherence of personality*
1	2	3	4		1. Maintains a stable balance between unconscious impulses, intellectual functioning, and concern for others
1	2	3	4		2. Adjusts to a variety of viewpoints and unfamiliar situations
1	2	3	4		3. Maintains a personal unifying life philosophy which provides a framework for decision making
( )	( )	( )	( )	H	*Autonomy*
1	2	3	4		1. Makes decisions based on both socially accepted norms and personal convictions
1	2	3	4		2. Accepts the authority of others without yielding his own beliefs
1	2	3	4		3. Challenges policy which appears harmful to individuals or groups within the company
1	2	3	4		a. Requests confrontation

345

Exhibit 3 *(Continued)*

1   2   3   4   b. Organizes opposing concepts and person

1   2   3   4   c. Plans effectively for activating changes

1   2   3   4   d. Discusses rationally

( ) ( ) ( ) ( )   **I** *Perception of reality*

1   2   3   4   1. Considers and is tolerant of the perceptions, ideas, and beliefs of others

1   2   3   4   2. Distinguishes personal perceptions, ideas, and beliefs from those of others

1   2   3   4   3. Acts in accordance with objective accumulated information

( ) ( ) ( ) ( )   **J** *Problem solving*

1   2   3   4   1. Relates to others in a personally satisfying and socially acceptable manner

1   2   3   4   2. Adapts and adjusts personal behavior to meet situational requirements

1   2   3   4   3. Solves problems in an organized and consistent manner

1   2   3   4   a. Defines the problem

1   2   3   4   b. Considers a variety of alternatives

1   2   3   4   c. Determines the most appropriate alternative

1   2   3   4   d. Implements a plan of action

1   2   3   4   e. Evaluates results

1   2   3   4   f. Adjusts behavior accordingly

1   2   3   4   4. Maintains appropriate feeling and directness of approach in the problem-solving process

( ) ( ) ( ) ( )   **K** *Sense of humor*

1   2   3   4   1. Sees incongruity in life situations and daily events

1   2   3   4   2. Utilizes humor to allay anxiety temporarily

1   2   3   4   3. Utilizes humor without letting it interfere with responsible action

IV Mutually Determined Performance Goals

A _____

B _____

C _____

D _____

E _____

F _____

G _____

H _____

I _____

J _____

K _____

_____   _____

(Supervisor)   (Person evaluated)

(To be filled out by supervisor and signed by both parties)

Exhibit 3 (Continued)
Formal Evaluation Report

Introduction   The basic purpose of our evaluation program is to improve the quality of performance. This purpose is served by using evaluation to define staff growth opportunities and to make sound administrative decisions affecting staff assignments. In this process, we need to recognize that:

1 A performance evaluation based on your job descriptions is usually an important but not an exclusive source of evaluation data. Casual everyday contacts, products of office activity, staff meetings, conferences, and cooperative projects are among the other important sources of information.

2 Evaluation is primarily a helping process—a process calculated to identify strengths on which a person can build as well as weaknesses that need to be corrected or minimized. Thus, the process works only if judgments and suggestions are communicated to the person whose activities are being evaluated.

3 Everyone concerned with the evaluation process needs to be thoroughly familiar with criteria for evaluation. In our division these criteria are established in handbooks available from your supervisor: this checklist can be especially helpful for self evaluation.

Sample considerations   Familiarity and compatibility with division philosophy, objectives, programs, and resources; familiarity with job descriptions and basic business techniques; use of well defined performance objectives; creation of a variety of business activities or alternatives; sensitivity to the needs of individual customers, creation of an interesting and positive business environment; use of modern business tools; appearance and behavior; cooperation with other staff members; enthusiasm; quality of communication with other staff members, the general public, and customers; completeness and accuracy of reporting procedures; involvement with division activities, curricular and extracurricular; proper use and conservation of physical resources; professional growth activities (conferences, workshops, travel, etc.); planning for budgets, new programs, use of staff; use of self evaluation programs; punctuality; dedication to hard work; fulfillment of special division responsibilities.

Evaluator's comments

_____

_____

_____

Position or title of evaluator _____   Signature of evaluator _____   Date _____

Person Evaluated

Position _____

Department _____

Date _____

Directions

Supervisors are to complete reports on the following timetable:

1 By March 1—Initial meeting with each person supervised

2 By July 1—A second meeting with each person for a discussion and interim discussion of progress and problems

3 By December 15—A formal written report

Note: In all cases, a formal report is to be forwarded to the office *only* if a copy signed by the evaluator has also been forwarded to the person evaluated.

Overall Rating (Check One)

In comparison with others whom I have observed, I classify this person's performance

☐ Superior   ☐ Good   ☐ Average

☐ Poor   ☐ Completely Unacceptable

Recommendation (Check One)

☐ Retain   ☐ Reevaluate

☐ Release

THIRTY-EIGHT Fieldcrest Division of Fieldcrest Mills, Incorporated (C)

In December 1973, Fieldcrest top management was reviewing the compensation system for field sales representatives. Complaints about the system had been relatively minor. While most felt this was because the plan was a fair one under which sales representatives were very well compensated, others argued that the system was too complex for anyone to know what to complain about. "Ideally, we would have a separate system tailored to each salesman," said O. G. Grubbs, vice president and director of sales. "As a practical matter, however, the more simple and uniform the system, the easier it is to understand and administer."

In addition to making decisions about the overall plan, the group had to make specific decisions about how to structure the system for 1974 so as to direct the sales representatives' efforts among the products or accounts, or both, in a manner that would be most beneficial to the company.

348

THE COMPENSATION PLAN FOR FIELD SALES REPRESENTATIVES

The basic system under which Fieldcrest field sales representatives were compensated was developed in the 1960s to replace a system of discretionary bonuses determined by the Fieldcrest president. The aims were to create a system which would motivate salespeople to accomplish company objectives for each item in a multiproduct line and yet retain as much of the "human element" of the former system as possible. In 1970 the president, general sales manager, and manager of operations revised the system so as to encourage the sales force to concentrate on target accounts which they felt offered Fieldcrest the best opportunities for increased sales.

The sales representatives received a salary plus a bonus based partly on sales above quota and partly on overall account management. The base salary of a new trainee who had not had previous selling experience was $10,000. The base salaries of experienced salespeople ranged from $15,000 to $28,000 with the midpoint being $21,300. Theoretically, a salesperson could earn a bonus up to 35 percent of his salary. In reality, however, it was impossible to reach that level because doing so would require a perfect score in a very complex rating system. In 1972, the average bonus was 18.6 percent of base salary, and in December 1973, company sources estimated that it would "be 20 percent or better" in 1973. (See Exhibit 1 for information on various salaries and bonus levels.)

Several steps were involved in the computation of a bonus. At the

Exhibit 1   SALARY AND BONUS DATA FOR FIELDCREST SALES
REPRESENTATIVE, 1972

Salary ranges		
At least	**But less than**	**No. of sales representatives**
$10,000	$15,000	12
15,000	20,000	21
20,000	25,000	8
25,000	30,000	1
		42

Bonus ranges	
Lowest bonus paid	$ 1,352
Highest bonus paid	4,888
Average bonus paid	2,887
Lowest % to base paid	11.3
Highest % to base paid	26.6
Average % to base paid	18.6

beginning of the year, each sales representative's target accounts were
identified. After lengthy discussions with sales representatives about
various accounts, company executives selected target accounts for the
Fieldcrest line and for the St. Mary's line. Occasionally, a sales representative would have only one or two accounts of sufficient size to be
considered target accounts. The sales representative and his regional
manager together assigned percentage values to each of his target
accounts and to "all other" of his accounts. For example, the following
evaluations might be made:

Target account A is worth	30 percent
Target account B is worth	25 percent
Target account C is worth	20 percent
Target account D is worth	15 percent
All other accounts are worth	10 percent
	100 percent = total potential bonus, or
	35 percent of base salary

Assuming that the sales representative's gross income was $20,000,
the bonus that he or she could earn on each account would be as follows:

On target account A, the sales rep could earn	30 percent of total potential bonus or $2,100
On target account B, the sales rep could earn	25 percent of total potential bonus or 1,750
On target account C, the sales rep could earn	20 percent of total potential bonus or 1,400
On target account D, the sales rep could earn	15 percent of total potential bonus or 1,050
On all other accounts the sales rep could earn	10 percent of total potential bonus or 700
	100 percent **$7,000**

The target accounts and their values were then typed onto a Salesperson's Compensation Plan Summary Sheet.

The next step was to establish volume quotas for each target account.
From headquarters, a regional manager received regional sales quotas for
each category of Fieldcrest and St. Mary's brand products, total private-
label products, and total promotional products. Each of the manager's

sales representatives then gave him quotas which the sales representative himself had set, both by product category and by target account. Regional managers had repeatedly found that sales representatives tended to set unrealistically high quotas, so that the quotas which they eventually sent to the Fieldcrest and St. Mary's sales managers for final approval were usually arrived at only after much discussion with the sales representatives. The Fieldcrest and St. Mary's sales managers said they tried to agree to quotas which were "challenging and obtainable but not requiring windfall or a lot of luck."

Different procedures and evaluation forms were used for Fieldcrest accounts and for St. Mary's accounts. Performance on a Fieldcrest target account was evaluated in five different areas—volume, product mix, establishment of a constructive and complete merchandising plan, effectiveness and utilization of plan, and cooperative advertising control. Performance on a St. Mary's target account was evaluated in two areas—volume and the achievement of special tasks.

Computation of Bonus on Fieldcrest Target Accounts

At the beginning of the year, actual sales for the preceding year and targeted sales for the current year were typed onto Part I of a form entitled Salesperson's Compensation Plan, Fieldcrest Account. At the end of the year, actual sales figures and percent of quota achieved were filled in (these data are rendered in italic type). Part I of a sample form is given below for salesperson A. L. Powell. The target account was Martin's Department Store in Louisiana, and the value was 30 percent of the plan.

I VOLUME (75 POINTS)

	Actual prior year	This year quota	This year actual	Quota % achieved
Fieldcrest brand				
Blankets	30.2	35.0	11.3[a]	32
Bedspreads	28.1	33.5	23.9	71
Sheets	78.4	88.5	109.7	124
Towels	52.7	62.9	56.6	90
Bath products	15.3	19.9	13.1	66
Automatics	4.5	6.2	5.2	84
Total brand	209.2	246.0	219.8	89
Private and St. Mary's	0.1	0.1	2.1	2100
Promotional	20.4	20.4	22.7	111
Total volume	**229.7**	**266.5**	**238.3**	89 = 19 points

[a]The italic numbers here and on later charts indicate sales results and calculations filled in at the end of the year.

The percent of quota achieved was converted into points using the Salespeople's Compensation Rating Chart (see Exhibit 2). This chart had been constructed by a group of management consultants in the 1960s.

Part II centered on the mix of Fieldcrest brand products sold to the particular account.

II PRODUCT MIX (5 POINTS ON BRAND)

		Points earned
No line	less than 5 points below the average	5
1 line	less than 5 points below the average	4
2 lines	less than 5 points below the average	3
3 lines	less than 5 points below the average	②
4 lines	less than 5 points below the average	1
5 lines	less than 5 points below the average	0

Rating: *2* points

This meant that if none of the first six lines in the Quota % Achieved column of Part I was less than five points below the percent of quota achieved by the total brand, the sales representative earned five points. If one line was less, he earned only four points, and so on. For example, in

Exhibit 2   SALESPEOPLE'S COMPENSATION RATING CHART

% of quota attained		Points earned		
At least	But less than	Fieldcrest target accounts	St. Mary's target accounts	All other account responsibility
0–80		—	—	—
80–82		5	5	6
82–84		9	10	12
84–86		12	13	16
86–88		16	17	21
88–90		19	20	25
90–92		21	22	28
92–94		23	25	31
94–96		25	27	33
96–98		26	28	35
98–100		27	29	36
100–102		28	30	38
102–104		30	32	40
104–106		32	34	43
106–108		35	37	46
108–110		37	40	50
110–112		40	43	54
112–114		44	47	58
114–116		47	51	63
116–118		51	54	68
118–120		54	58	72
120–122		57	61	76
122–124		59	63	79
124–126		62	66	82
126–128		64	68	85
128–130		65	70	87
130–132		67	71	89
132–134		68	73	91
134–136		70	74	93
136–138		71	76	94
138–140		72	77	96
140–142		73	78	97
142–144		74	78	98
144–146		74	79	99
146–148		75	80	100
148–150		75	80	100

the sample part I above, three lines are less than five points below the average, 89 percent. Therefore, the sales representative would earn two points on Part II.

Parts III, IV, and V consisted of the regional manager's evaluation of certain elements of the sales representative's performance. Part III focused on the quality and completeness of the merchandising plan which he constructed for each of his target accounts:

III ESTABLISHMENT OF A CONSTRUCTIVE AND
COMPLETE PLAN (5 POINTS)

Rating	Points earned
Outstanding	5
Excellent	4
Above average	③
Average	2
Fair	1
Inadequate	0
	Rating: 3 points

The fourth part dealt with how well the sales representative executed the merchandising plan and accomplished goals set forth in it:

352

IV EFFECTIVENESS AND UTILIZATION OF PLANS
(5 POINTS)

Rating	Points earned
Outstanding	5
Highly effective	④
Very effective	3
Effective	2
Somewhat effective	1
Inadequate	0
	Rating: 4 points

Finally, Part V was essentially a yes or no response to whether the sales rep had effectively controlled the account's cooperative advertising program:

V COOPERATIVE ADVERTISING CONTROL (10 POINTS)

Rating	Points earned
Effective	⑩
Ineffective	0
Rating:	10 points
Total points:	**38**

After the sales representative's performance was scored in each of these areas, the points were tallied. The total became the percentage of the total bonus on that particular account which the sales representative received. In the above example, the sales representative received a total of 38 points on the Martin's Department Store account. This meant that the bonus from this particular account was 38 percent of $2,100, or $798.

Computation of Bonus on St. Mary's Target Accounts

Part I of the bonus plan for St. Mary's target accounts was very similar to that of Fieldcrest target accounts. The salesperson was A. L. Powell, and the account was Redford's 5 & 10 in Mississippi. The value was 20 percent of the plan.

I VOLUME (80 POINTS)

	Actual prior year	This year quota	This year actual	Quota % achieved
St. Mary's brand				
Blankets	18.3	25.0	8.4	34
Bedspreads	—	5.0	3.2	64
Sheets	—	10.0	14.7	147
Towels	126.6	149.3	81.9	55
Bath products	—	—	—	—
Automatics	58.3	61.3	61.9	101
Total brand	203.2	250.6	170.1	68
Private and Fieldcrest	10.4	15.0	(1.0)	0
Promotional	387.5	387.8	422.5	109
Total volume	**601.1**	**653.4**	**592.5**	**91** = 22 points

Part II, which in the past had also been used for Fieldcrest target accounts, was structured to enable sales management to focus on whatever specific problems arose from time to time. The regional manager assigned the tasks and rated the sales representatives on how well they accomplished them. (In the past, sales representatives had rated themselves, but it was found that the better the salesperson, the greater the tendency to give himself a low rating.) Part II looked like this:

II SPECIAL TASKS (20 POINTS) REDFORD

1 Task: In 1972 place at lease one coordinated One Look in better stores consisting of at least three classifications.
   Weight 50% Rating[a] 5 points

2 Task: Place a promotional package for towels consisting of a jacquard, print, or solid in a chainwide promotion. This must be an ensemble promotion (bath, hand, wash).
   Weight 50% Rating[a] 5 points

3 Task: _____
   Weight _____ Rating[a] _____ points

4 Task: _____
   Weight _____ Rating[a] _____ points

Total weight 100%

353

II   SPECIAL TASKS (20 POINTS) REDFORD (*Continued*)

Rating schedule [a]

Accomplishment of task	Points earned
Outstanding	5
Excellent	4
Above average	3
Average	2
Fair	1
Inadequate	0

$$50 \times 5 = 250$$
$$50 \times 5 = 250$$

Total rating part II $500 \div 25 =$	20 points [a]
Total target account	**42 points**

[a] To determine the total points earned on Part II, multiply the weights by the rating points earned, and divide by 25.

Completing the Salesperson's Compensation Plan Summary Sheet

When the bonus for each target account had been calculated, the Salesperson's Compensation Plan Summary Sheet was completed as follows:

Maximum potential bonus per account [a]	Target accounts [b]	% of plan	% of maximum potential bonus earned [a]	Bonus
$2,100	Martin's Dept. Store	30	38	$ 798
1,750	Redford's 5 & 10	25	42	735
1,400	Cobb's Dry Goods	20	21	294
1,050	Morton Dept. Store	15	61	640
700	All other [c]	10	79	553
$7,000	Total	100		$3,020

Volume (100 points)		Value 10% of plan
Quota	$643.5	
Actual	$791.5	
% of quota	123%	
Points earned	79	

[a] These columns were placed here by the casewriter to help clarify the calculations.
[b] In 1973 a special incentive was placed on bathroom rug sales. Bathroom rug sales were worth 30% of a sales representative's bonus. On the Summary Sheet, the special rug program was listed as a target account.
[c] All other account responsibility (excluding target accounts).

The gross income of the sales representative in the above example would be:

Salary	20,000
Bonus	3,020
	23,020

Management and Sales Force Reaction to the Compensation System

Mr. Grubbs stated that there had been "some criticism but no major complaints" about the compensation system. He felt that sales representatives definitely preferred it to some competitive systems which offered a straight $1\frac{1}{2}$ percent commission. Other competitors had salary and bonus systems comparable to Fieldcrest's, but Mr. Grubbs was sure that Fieldcrest's compensation level and fringe benefits were better than any of its competitors.

Mr. Grubbs admitted, however, that Fieldcrest's system had some readily identifiable weaknesses. One regional manager commented on these weaknesses as follows:

> The beauty and the horror of our compensation system is that it gives me the opportunity to treat each of my salespeople as individuals. It's really difficult to evaluate your people fairly because personalities get involved. You naturally like some people better than others, so that remaining impartial is like fighting yourself.

Another regional manager stated that setting tasks for his sales representatives to accomplish with their St. Mary's accounts, a job which normally took about 3 full working days, had caused some problems. He elaborated as follows:

> I try to set tasks that are meaningful, reasonable, attainable, and challenging, but it's difficult to repeatedly meet those criteria. It's especially hard to set tasks for the few salespeople who sell primarily to small stores. You have to focus on his sales of a particular product line to a group of small accounts in the "all other" classification rather than on the mix sold to any single account, and very often a total dollar volume goal just won't accomplish what you want it to. For example, one of my men had been having trouble selling a particular bedspread, so I assigned him the task of increasing his total sales of that bedspread by a certain percent. Early in the year, he stumbled across a premium account and got all the dollar volume increase he needed right there.

355

One executive stated that regional managers had come to spend much less time identifying problems and setting tasks than they did in the early days of the system.

Another problem this regional manager identified was that situations beyond a salesperson's control sometimes prevented the accomplishment of tasks. For example, the regional manager had instructed a salesperson to sell a certain amount of St. Mary's sheets. Two months later, because of labor problems, the mill could not deliver the sheets. The salesperson was unable to sell the sheets and accomplish the assigned task. The regional manager was then forced to devise a new task even though the selling season was well under way. A similar situation occurred when a leading target account encountered unexpected financial difficulty and was unable to purchase the amount of merchandise projected. Because the Fieldcrest sales representative would have been unable to make quota in any area of this account, the regional manager selected a new target account and assigned new tasks.

A frequent criticism levied at the compensation system was that it might place too much emphasis on the target accounts. "That really stifles sales because it encourages us to concentrate on four to six big customers and limit our efforts among our smaller customers," said one sales representative. "The weight given to the 'all other' category is so small that it's meaningless for us to go after those accounts."

Additional criticism centered around the method by which target accounts were selected. Though sales representatives made considerable input into the decision, a few top executives had the final say about which customers would be considered target accounts. One sales representative said that there had been "a couple of times" when top management had inadequately appraised the target accounts and selected accounts with very limited growth potential.

Numerous pros and cons were voiced about using the compensation system to encourage sales of one particular product line. "In 1973, 30 percent of a sales representative's bonus was determined by his total sales of bathroom rugs, and we ran a special sales contest on bathroom rugs," said one executive. "During this time, sales increased dramatically—75 percent in total and 635 percent in the St. Mary's line. That suggests to me that the strategy works pretty well." "I maintain that the increase was due more to the expanded and strengthened product line than to the special incentives," one sales representative replied.

Some executives felt that special incentives for one line meant that salespeople often placed too much effort on that line and neglected their other products. Others felt that a nationwide special incentive program for one line was of limited value because there were many regional variations in demand. "Demand for higher priced towels is generally greater on the West Coast," said one regional manager. "Therefore, if we decide to offer special incentives on the sale of towels, the sales representatives in the West will have an advantage over those in other areas. Similarly, heirloom bedspreads are strong in the Northeast and South Central states but hardly sold at all in Western states."

Even when regional variations were taken into account by regional managers directing their sales representatives to emphasize certain products, there were still problems. For example, one regional manager mentioned the tendency of salespeople to overload customers in the particular line being emphasized. "One year I instructed one of my salespeople to increase his sales of automatic blankets hand over fist. For the next 2 years, however, automatic blanket sales to those accounts were severely depressed." Other regional managers stated, however, that this was "really an oddball situation" which almost never occurred.

Yet another criticism of the compensation system was simply that the sales force could outguess it. Said one sales representative:

We know our accounts better than anyone else, so when we work out product quotas with our regional managers, we make sure we agree to figures we can attain. Furthermore, when we assign different values to our accounts, we give the most weight to those accounts we think we have the best chance with. There's no way that Ed Molitor and Gene McCarthy [Fieldcrest and St. Mary's sales managers who gave final approval to quotas] can know minute details like the buyer's idiosyncrasies or the potential for muslin sheets or Temptation towels in every one of our target accounts.

Mr. McCarthy stated that the runaway inflation and price increases which the country was experiencing in 1973 made setting quotas more difficult than ever.

Other sales representatives took issue with the assertion that they agreed to figures they could attain. "I almost never achieve the mix the quotas call for," one person stated. "If I do all right with a target account, it's usually because I've sold it a lot more of one or two products than I expected to. Those extra sales then compensate for my failure to make quota in other areas."

Another sales representative mentioned that focusing only on existing accounts meant that there was no incentive to force new distribution. "That's what the company is after with the Fieldcrest line," he said.

> With the St. Mary's line, however, we want mass distribution, but we really don't get paid for opening new accounts. Of course, our position with some of our present St. Mary's customers needs to be strengthened, and that's what our compensation system is structured to do. But I still think we should be encouraged more to find new customers.

Top executives stated that using the compensation system to help develop major accounts had worked well as growth with those accounts had been "phenomenal." They wondered, however, if continuing this focus might now be counterproductive.

A different kind of complaint was voiced by a former sales representative who had recently been promoted to product manager in the merchandising department. "I was really happy about my promotion until I realized what was about to happen to my bonus," he said.

> As a salesman, I could earn up to 35 percent of my base salary in bonus, and how much I earned was largely dependent on how hard I worked. Now my bonus is limited to 20 percent of my base salary—15 percent is based on the profitability of my mill and 5 percent on the profitability of the whole Fieldcrest Marketing Division. We have control over too few of the factors that determine profitability for this to be a fair system. I was better off as a salesman. Not only did I have more control over my income, but I also got a company car.

Additional Considerations for Structuring the 1974 Compensation System

As Fieldcrest executives considered how the compensation system should be structured for 1974, they were keenly aware of certain situations which might call for special sales force incentives. During 1973, the Fieldcrest brand had experienced no growth with half of its top 20 accounts. The reasons for this were that the total volume of these accounts was increasing very slowly, competitors had become extremely aggressive, and some of the accounts had not been cooperating with Fieldcrest's advertising and promotional programs as completely as in the past. To reverse this situation, management felt it should help solve problems related to merchandising, inadequate buyers, and inadequate inventories. They wondered if special incentives should be offered to encourage salespeople to assist in tackling these more complex problems.

Fieldcrest executives were also considering placing special incentives on problem products. The success of the bathroom rug incentive plan in 1973 was seen as evidence for such a program. The two areas which needed sales increases most were sheets and bedspreads. The possibility of a capacity shortage in sheets made the executives reluctant to initiate an aggressive sales program there. In bedspreads, however, though Fieldcrest ranked first in the market, its position was a function of private-label volume. Sales to traditional department stores had actually decreased by 5 percent, and well over half of the company's bedspread sales were to chain stores. At the November sales meetings, the sales force was told that company management was considering revising the compensation program so that bonuses would be tied more closely to bedspread sales. Reaction was immediate and negative. One salesman commented:

> What you are saying is that we haven't been doing our job, haven't been pushing bedspreads as hard as we should. That just isn't the case. I've showed that line so many times that my buyers have gotten really bored with it. Let's face it. We need new merchandise and a whole new program like we had with the rugs. Simply tacking a bonus on to the old merchandise isn't going to help at all.

THIRTY-NINE   Clairol, Incorporated

APPLIANCE DIVISION

In April 1974, Tom Comstock, recently named director of sales for the Clairol Appliance Division, was trying to decide what his sales organization could do to better motivate distributor[1] salespeople, the division's

---

[1]Distributors, often referred to as wholesalers, purchased merchandise from manufacturers and resold it to retailers. They took title to the merchandise, paid the manufacturer upon receiving it, provided local warehousing and delivery, and handled the receivables of the retailers to whom they sold products.

primary link with many retail outlets. The problem was that distributor salespeople were far removed from Clairol headquarters—Clairol's small sales management staff supervised reps[2] who sold products to distributors whose salespeople in turn sold them to retailers. Therefore, it was very difficult for Clairol management to get the distributor salespeople to push Clairol appliance products and service Clairol shelves in retail outlets. Failure to perform the latter task had resulted in severe retail "stockouts" and haphazard displays of some appliance products.

DIVISION HISTORY

The Clairol Appliance Division was a part of Clairol, Inc., a company best known for quality haircoloring products. Clairol, Inc., in turn was a subsidiary of Bristol-Myers Company whose ten autonomous divisions marketed a wide range of prescription pharmaceuticals, orthopedic implants, health and beauty aids, over-the-counter medicines, and household care products.

The Appliance Division was established in 1967 to market electric hairsetters and any other personal care appliances which Clairol might develop or acquire. It experienced immediate success with its wide line of Kindness hairsetters which were sold by Clairol's Haircoloring and Toiletry Division sales force primarily to drug wholesalers. In 1968 the Appliance Division added a lighted makeup mirror. Moreover, in order to sell better to mass merchandisers[3] and department stores, it contracted with several manufacturers' representatives agencies, whose salespeople were referred to as "reps." (Hereafter, the name "Clairol" refers to the Clairol Appliance Division, not to the total corporation.)

Gradually, the haircoloring and toiletries sales force was relieved of responsibility for appliances as more reps were hired. However, some of the newer reps proved to be unenthusiastic about Clairol's line. In 1969 they were replaced by about 35 salespeople, employed directly by Clairol. Sales increased steadily through 1970, but by early 1971, it had become apparent that the trade had been oversold as large quantities of merchandise were returned to Clairol.

In the summer of 1971, Donald Crenshaw became division president and began tightening the organization and paring the product line. By 1974 in all its departments, the division employed only about 50 people directly. Primary selling responsibility was in the hands of 65 reps. The

[2]Reps were independent salespeople who sold Clairol appliances and complementary but noncompeting products manufactured by other companies. They did not warehouse or take title to the merchandise, but rather functioned as a field sales force for different manufacturers.

[3]Mass merchandisers consisted primarily of discount houses, such as Zayre and K-Mart, and variety stores, such as Kress and Woolworth.

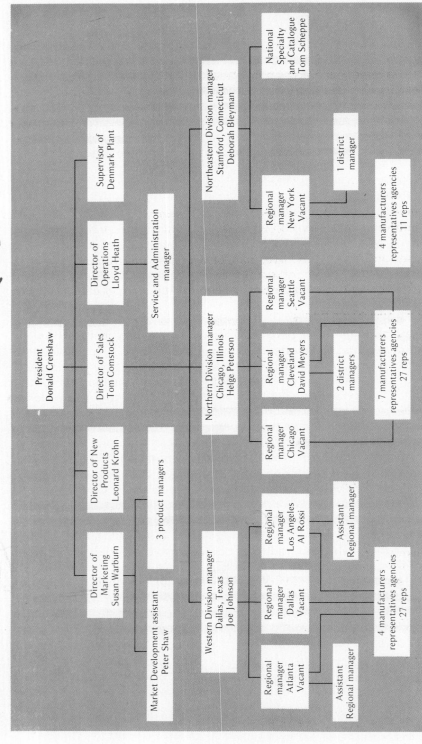

Exhibit 1 Abbreviated organization chart of the Appliance Division.

reps sold to some direct buying chains and cooperatives and to a large number of distributors who in turn sold to a wide variety of retail outlets. Clairol marketed five electric hairsetters, three lighted mirrors, a battery-powered facial brush known as a skin machine, three hand-held dryers, and a steam curling iron. 1973 sales were $35 million, with after-tax profits of $1.75 million. (See Exhibit 1 for an organization chart and Exhibit 2 for an operating statement.)

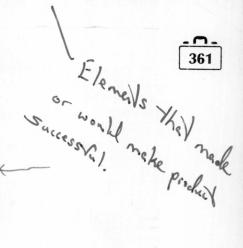

THE PERSONAL CARE APPLIANCES INDUSTRY

The personal care appliance industry was characterized as "highly volatile, faddish, and fashion conscious, somewhere between consumer package goods and durable appliances." The products were heavily advertised impulse items, over half of which were given as gifts. Merchandising factors, such as creative packaging, special displays, and good shelf space, were considered key elements in a product's success.

Exhibit 2 APPLIANCE DIVISION OPERATING STATEMENT, FISCAL 1973 (January 1, 1973 – December 31, 1973)

	$ in millions	%
Sales	$35.00	100.0
Cost of goods, warehousing, and distribution	17.50	50.0
Gross profit	17.50	50.0
Advertising	5.25	15.0
Product promotion, service, and warranty	3.50	10.0
Product contribution	8.75	25.0
Selling expenses	0.70	2.0
Reps' commissions	1.225	3.5
Marketing administration	0.70	2.0
Other overhead[a]	2.625	7.5
Pretax earnings	3.50	10.0
Net earnings after taxes	1.75	5.0

Annual selling expenses (Field force only)

Salaries	$225,000
Travel and entertainment	80,000
Bonus	45,000
Payroll taxes	15,000
Car rentals	10,000

[a]Includes cost of money on assets employed in business, financial, personnel, and other services, R & D expense, public relations.
Notes: (1) Each district, regional, and divisional manager can earn up to 20% of base salary if quotas are met and exceeded (paid quarterly). (2) Each field person has a company car. (3) All are covered by company medical insurance plan, life insurance, and participation in pension and savings plan.

Exhibit 3 MANUFACTURER SALES OF PERSONAL CARE ELECTRIC
APPLIANCES, 1962–1973 (Thousands of Units Shipped)

	1962	1963	1964	1965	1966	1967	1968
Hair dryers	7,000	9,700	5,150	4,325	3,800	4,300	4,600
Hairsetters	—	—	—	—	—	—	2,700
Heating pads	2,900	3,050	2,715	3,000	3,200	3,200	3,540
Makeup mirrors	—	—	—	—	—	—	—
Oral hygiene devices							
Water pulsating units	—	—	—	—	475	875	1,450
Toothbrushes		2,200	3,100	3,300	3,000	2,600	2,400
Total	**9,900**	**14,950**	**10,965**	**10,625**	**10,475**	**10,975**	**14,690**

Source: 1974 Statistical and Marketing Report, *Merchandising Week,* February 25, 1974,
pp. 28–29.

Repurchases generally occurred 3 to 5 years after the initial sale, if at all.
Test marketing was almost impossible, because research and development (R & D) and tooling were too costly to justify producing a limited
number of items, and because the industry was such that success often
depended on being the first out with a "really hot item." The business
tended to be highly seasonal, with half the retail volume being done
between September and December. Manufacturers' gross margins for
small appliances generally ranged from 45 to 60 percent, as compared to
75 to 90 percent for package goods. Manufacturers in the business often
experienced very rapid growth and equally rapid decline. In 1974, Clairol,
Gillette, Schick, General Electric, Sunbeam, Remington, Continental, and
Norelco were considered the major manufacturers. (See Exhibit 3 for
record of total industry sales of personal care appliances and Exhibit 4 for
market share data.)

The manufacturers' selling task consisted of two basic parts—

362

Exhibit 4 PERCENTAGE OF MARKET SHARE DATA, 1973

Electric hairsetters		**Hand-held hair dryers**	
Clairol	49	Gillette	32
Shick	14	Schick	26
General Electric	12	Remington	10
Sumbeam	10	Clairol	9
All others	15	General Electric	4
	100	Continental	3
Lighted makeup mirrors		Sunbeam	3
Clairol	45	Norelco	2
General Electric	22	All American	2
Northern Electric	5	Braun	1
Sunbeam	4	All others	8
All others	24		**100**
	100	**Skin machine**	
Curling iron		Clairol	100
Clairol	45		
Sunbeam	45		
All others	10		
	100		

Source: Internal company reports

Exhibit 3
(Continued)

1969	1970	1971	1972	1973
4,725	4,100	4,350	5,000	5,500
6,700	5,500	3,800	3,400	3,250
3,600	3,900	3,900	4,200	4,375
2,100	2,700	1,975	1,750	1,625
1,325	1,050	900	1,080	1,100
2,500	1,800	1,350	1,200	1,100
20,950	**19,050**	**16,275**	**16,630**	**16,950**

headquarters selling and retail selling. Headquarters selling involved contacting buyers and/or merchandise managers of various distributors, department stores, and chain or cooperative drugstores, mass merchandisers, hardware stores, jewelry stores, appliance stores, and so forth. With some chains or cooperatives,[4] all decisions about product line, shelf space and position, and advertising and promotion policies were made at company headquarters. With others, headquarters "approved" products for the stores to carry, but each individual outlet had the flexibility to choose its own products from among those approved by headquarters.

Retail selling tasks sometimes involved convincing store managers to order products the headquarters had approved, and it often involved convincing the retailer to take advantage of cooperative advertising programs. It almost always involved basic merchandising tasks—checking shelf and backroom inventories, straightening merchandise, and setting up special displays.

The majority of manufacturers' sales were made to a wide variety of distributors—drug wholesalers and appliance, electrical houseware, and hardware distributors.[5] While the details of distributor operations varied greatly from one company to the next, most distributor organizations were headed by two or three principals. Normally, one to three buyers or merchandise managers purchased products from a wide range of manufacturers, although very often purchasing was done by the principals. Distributor organizations also had sales forces of varying sizes which sold products to retail outlets, as well as extensive billing, warehousing, and delivery operations.

In recent years, as distributors' product lines broadened and as they

[4]Cooperatives were independent stores joined together under a wide variety of arrangements, usually for such purposes as joint purchasing and advertising.

[5]Within the industry, wholesalers traditionally received a margin of 17 percent of their selling price to retailers. Retailers traditionally received a margin of about 35 to 38 percent of the suggested retail price if the product were sold at the suggested retail price. Price-cutting and promotions were prevalent, especially among larger retailers. Volume discounts and other trade promotions were typical. Credit terms were also often generous.

363

Manufact. became increasingly responsible for retail selling

began to carry more and more competing products, the task of actually selling to retailers fell increasingly to the manufacturers themselves. Nevertheless, manufacturers still considered distributors essential participants in the distribution process because of their wide-scale warehousing services and their contacts with numerous small retailers. Manufacturers sometimes sold products at distributor prices directly to large retailers who had centralized warehousing and distribution facilities. However, in order to avoid carrying large inventories, many large retailers preferred to make smaller, more frequent purchases at higher prices from distributors.

Dist- Valuable

Reliable data on total industry sales of personal care appliances by category of trade were not available. It was thought, however, that major chains, including department stores, mass merchandisers, and drugstores, as well as some large independent retailers, accounted for about 60 percent of retail sales. About 15 percent went through catalog showroom retailers and "pure" catalog retailers.[6] The remaining 25 percent was spread among smaller department store, mass merchandiser, and drug chains and thousands of very small drugstores, hardware stores, jewelry stores, appliance stores, stamp redemption stores, customers who used the products as premiums,[7] home improvement centers, and food stores. In larger retail outlets, personal care appliances were often sold in both housewares and drug departments and were purchased by two different buyers. (See Exhibit 5 for Clairol's sales by category of trade.)

Size and Allotment

364

Because retailers had frequently used personal care appliances as promotional items, retailer margins throughout the industry had deteriorated to the point that retailers had very little incentive to display the products well or even to try to maintain a fairly profitable selling price. The result was that, unless manufacturer or distributor salespeople checked retail shelves regularly, "stockouts," inadequate displays, and extremely inconsistent pricing occurred repeatedly. Some retailers objected to having manufacturer or distributor detail people in their stores, and manufacturers stated that they resented having to do retailers' tasks

---

[6]Catalog showroom retailers presented their merchandise in catalogs and also had showrooms in which one item of each product carried was displayed. Additional items were warehoused on the premises. Very often catalog showroom retailers offered their products at discount prices. "Pure" catalog retailers did not display products in showrooms. Rather, their products were presented only in catalogs, and sales were handled through the mail. They generally did not discount their prices. Catalog retailers often belonged to associations which had "coordinating committees" to screen products for their members.

[7]So-called premium customers used products as special incentives for their customers or their sales forces. For example, a bank might offer a hand-held hairdryer to anyone who opened a savings account during a certain time period, or a company might offer a similar premium to salespeople who sold a stipulated amount of merchandise during a given time period.

Exhibit 5 CLAIROL SALES BY
CATEGORY OF TRADE, 1973
(Millions of dollars)

Drug trade	
Drug wholesalers	4.0
Drug chain	2.0
Other drug	1.0
Total drug	**7.0**
Appliance trade	
Housewares electric distributors	17.0
Jewelry distributors	0.8
Hardware distributors	0.4
Hardware cooperatives	0.6
Catalog retailers	3.0
Stamp incentive	0.6
Private label	0.9
Direct retailer	0.7
Total appliance trade	**24.0**
Other (direct accounts) [a]	
Mass merchandisers	2.5
Food trade	0.1
Department stores	0.1
Variety stores	0.3
Miscellaneous	1.0
Total other	**4.0**
Gross total	
(all categories)	**35.0**

64%

[a] All chain accounts were not direct accounts. Many purchased from wholesalers.

for them. Manufacturers also often participated in retail operations by
hiring so-called demonstrators to work as salespeople in major retail
outlets, especially during the Christmas selling season.

THE APPLIANCE DIVISION'S MARKETING DEPARTMENT

Sales/Marketing Coordination

The division's marketing activities were headed by Susan Warburn,
director of marketing. Under her were three product managers and a
market development assistant, each of whom spent about one week a
month making calls with reps at both customer headquarters and retail
outlets. They also met with reps, distributor buyers, and retail store
buyers at two or three houseware shows each year. Ms. Warburn stressed
that the marketing department worked very closely with the sales
department. "Our offices are located right next to theirs," she said, "so
we're in daily contact with sales management. Also, we attend the two
meetings they hold each year for reps and Clairol salespeople. These plus
our field trips with reps keep us informed about their objectives and
concerns and keep them informed about ours."

In mid-1973, the marketing managers decided that more information
about Clairol's position at the retail level was needed than was currently

Stockouts

supplied by independent research companies.[8] They decided, therefore, to do their own informal survey. While doing this survey, they noted that retail shelves frequently were out of stock on Clairol products, even though the products often were in backroom inventories. Moreover, Clairol seldom had prime shelf space, and its displays were often in disarray. Pricing varied from one outlet to another, but on the whole retail prices were substantially lower than Clairol management thought they should be. Retailers frequently complained that they could not make any money from Clairol products.

Small Margins

Clairol traditionally had done more national advertising than local cooperative advertising, and more national and local cooperative advertising than most of its competitors. Its total advertising budget for 1974 was about $5 million. Though data on the effectiveness of most of its ads were not available, some data did exist on television advertising of the skin machine. Ms. Warburn called the response of the skin machine to television advertising "very dramatic."

National vs. Local Coop Advertising

THE APPLIANCE DIVISION'S SALES DEPARTMENT

Sales Director & the Division Mgrs.

In March 1974, Mr. Comstock left the Clairol Cosmetics Division to become director of sales for the Appliance Division. Reporting to him were three division managers (average age, 35), all of whom had wide sales experience with either Clairol or other appliance or package-goods companies. Their salaries ranged from $28,000 to $32,000, and they received bonuses based on quarterly quotas. For every 1 percent over quota their respective divisions attained, they received 1 percent of their base salary up to 10 percent. The division managers' job consisted primarily of supervising regional managers, but they also often went with reps when the reps called on major accounts' headquarters. Ms. Bleyman, Northeast division manager, was also responsible for selling major programs to headquarters of national accounts, stamp plans, catalog accounts, and premium accounts. These programs were then disseminated to the accounts' branches and to reps, and the reps then did the daily servicing of the accounts. On sales to all but one of these accounts, reps received their regular commission.

Clairol's national accounts consisted of one major distributor and

---

[8]In order to get concrete data on retail sales of its products, Clairol, like many other manufacturers, contracted with companies whose primary business was gathering such data. Some companies did distribution audits by sending people into a certain number of stores to identify which products were on the shelves and, if possible, which were in backroom inventories. Others did movement audits in which they reviewed retailers' purchase and sales records of various products. Others did consumer audits by telephoning a number of consumers and asking questions about recent purchases. Still other companies did all these types of audits.

Call Frequency

eleven direct-buying drugstore chains and mass-merchandiser chains, which were composed of some of the largest retail accounts, such as K-Mart and J C Penney. Ms. Bleyman visited each of these accounts' buyers or merchandise managers once every 4 to 6 weeks, and contacted them by telephone weekly. She visited buyers or merchandise managers of Clairol's ten stamp plan accounts (S&H, Top Value, Gold Bond, etc.) only once a year, since reps had primary responsibility for these accounts. She made annual presentations of the Clairol line to about five major catalog-retailer coordinating committees which approved or rejected products for their members. Once the committees approved Clairol products, however, reps had the task of selling to the makers of the individual catalogs (about 40 in all). Clairol had not yet established a strong foothold in the premium business, though in recent months it had received several calls from what Ms. Bleyman termed "good prospects." The premium business was markedly different from the rest of Clairol's business, partly because it tended to be characterized by nonrecurring sales. The better rep agencies usually had a salesperson who specialized only in premium accounts.

Regional Managers

Under the division managers were seven regional manager positions, but in April 1974, only two of these positions were filled. These two regional managers were in their early thirties. Their salaries were between $20,000 and $25,000 plus expenses. They also received bonuses based on regional quotas and computed in the same manner as division managers' bonuses. The regional managers' primary job was to supervise the activities of sales reps and Clairol district managers (described below) and to call on major retail and distributor accounts in their areas.

Reps

In all, Clairol contracted with 15 manufacturers representatives agencies, with a total of 65 reps. The agencies served as a field sales force for from four to ten different manufacturers. They were responsible for selling to a wide variety of wholesalers and direct-buying retailers and for performing merchandising tasks in retail outlets. They accounted for about 92 percent of Clairol's sales. Each agency carried a different line of products, most of which were small electrical appliances, housewares, or small personal care appliances. One Clairol executive estimated that the total gross revenue of individual Clairol rep agencies ranged from $5 million to $25 million. Clairol was thought to represent 20 to 60 percent of its agencies' gross revenue. The agencies received 4 percent commission on sales of Clairol appliances. This was said to be "about average" for products whose volume was comparable to Clairol's. On products of lower volume, a rep agency generally received 5 to 10 percent commission. The agencies were then responsible for compensating their reps. While some paid a straight commission out of which the reps covered all their own selling expenses, others paid any combination of salaries, commissions, bonuses, and expenses.

Reps' Commissions

Perhaps not enough time spent in retail outlets. ↓

Mr. Comstock estimated that reps spent about 40 percent of their time at distributor headquarters, 40 percent at headquarters of drug chains, mass merchandisers, and department stores, and 20 percent in retail outlets. He emphasized that this varied greatly, however, according to the number and importance of distributors in various regions. He stated that, on the whole, Clairol's reps were highly motivated entrepreneurs who were well aware that the only way they made money was by selling. They were often career salespeople whose contacts and experience were considered very valuable. On the other hand, Mr. Comstock felt that, since reps were responsible to several other manufacturers, they did not push Clairol's products as effectively as a direct Clairol sales force would, and since paying reps by commission meant that Clairol's selling expenses followed sales, those selling expenses could be far higher than they would be if salespeople working on fixed salaries and bonuses were doing the selling.

Conflict; reps didn't push Clairol

C. A. Connor Associates, Inc., which one Clairol executive described as "our best agency," sold Polinex home medical equipment (footbaths, massagers, etc.), International Silver, Galloping Gourmet housewares, and Clairol Appliances. It employed five reps, all of whom were college graduates, under age 40, with at least 5 years as buyers or salespeople in the appliance or housewares industry. Each received a salary, commission, and bonus, which together ranged from $20,000 to $30,000. Connor Associates covered metropolitan New York, southern New York State, northern New Jersey, and southern Connecticut. One rep handled only premium and specialty accounts. Each of the other four had about 50 direct-buying retail or distributor headquarters accounts, plus about 4,000 retail outlets. They visited customer headquarters anywhere from once a week to once every 3 months. In addition, "regular" telephone contact was maintained with customers by the agency's office manager who coordinated the activities of the reps, the manufacturers, and the customers.

Mr. Connor, agency president, said he normally contacted principals, often the owners or general managers, of distributor firms because they usually purchased the higher-dollar product lines—such as the products he sold. At large direct-buying retail headquarters, he usually met with buyers and merchandise managers. He said his chief headquarters task was to convince principals to include his products in "basic," the standard inventory which they maintained throughout the year. Such sales, he said, generally amounted to from $250,000 to $1 million. "For those kinds of sales, you can't take in a list and check off what the customer wants," Mr. Connor said. "We get pretty deeply involved with their operations to the point of discussing their credit problems and how they handle their salespeople and buyers."

Mr. Connor stated that his primary concerns were merchandising tasks, such as making sure customers used manufacturers' cooperative advertising and promotion allowances properly and seeing that all

Rep's responsibility

products which chain headquarters purchased were displayed well in the chain's retail outlets. If the retail tasks were done well, Mr. Connor stated, his products generally moved so rapidly that headquarters selling was easy. He emphasized, however, that doing those tasks well in all retail outlets was virtually impossible because of the multitude of retail outlets that carried personal care appliances. He stated that each of his reps generally called on only about 400 of the 4,000 retail outlets in his territory, and much fewer than that, with any degree of regularity. The company objective was one visit per month to the major retail outlets. Most of the retail outlets Mr. Connor's reps contacted were department stores, mass merchandisers, chain drugstores, and some very large independent drugstores. They usually only contacted headquarters of hardware, jewelry, and appliance chains, distributors, or cooperatives. Servicing the retail outlets of these companies was left to distributor sales people.

In three districts, Clairol employed its own salespeople, known as district managers, to perform the same tasks which reps performed in other districts. The districts chosen were Detroit and Pittsburgh, where volume was sufficiently concentrated to be handled by one salesperson, and Washington, D.C., where the large number of chain drug headquarters and the headquarters of Best Products, the largest catalog retailer in the United States, called for the extra push which, it was thought, the company's own salesperson would provide. While some Clairol executives viewed district managers as the first step toward a direct sales force, most felt that a sufficiently large, well-motivated sales force would be prohibitively expensive and that the district manager position was actually a training slot for future managerial positions. Clairol's three district managers (average age, 28) were all college educated and each received a salary of $15,000 plus expenses.

Clairol products were sold to approximately 450 drug wholesalers and appliance, electrical, jewelry, houseware, and hardware distributors. Clairol management stated that, in theory, distributor salespeople should visit major retail outlets weekly, should know their products well enough to make good sales presentations, and should discuss manufacturers' promotion and advertising programs with the retailers. What actually happened, however, according to Clairol management, was that distributor salespeople functioned mainly as order takers, and retail selling and servicing were either done by reps or not done at all. Mr. Connor stated that the product lines and details of operation varied greatly from one distributor to the next. For example, he said, drug wholesalers typically sold to smaller retailers more than did appliance distributors, and drug wholesaler salespeople often provided more selling and less merchandising for the manufacturers they represented. He said, however, that there was "little difference in the way they handled Clairol appliances." He identified three distributors whom he considered "more or less typical of their different areas."

Distributor of Appliances and Hardware

Finegold Distributors, one of Clairol's largest customers, distributed appliances, hardware, and household chemicals such as cleaners, waxes, and room deodorants. In all, it carried about 10,000 items manufactured by about 300 companies. Its appliance line consisted of about 1,000 items from 40 manufacturers. Richard Finegold, company president, described the appliance business as "a very small, fragmented industry which is very difficult to coordinate." He stated that he and one other principal handled most of the selling to larger chains, while selling to smaller chains and independents was done by regular salespeople. He expected salespeople to also straighten racks, keep inventories current, and perform other retail merchandising tasks. Each of the company's 25 salespeople was responsible for 200 to 300 retail outlets. Retail call frequency varied from twice a week to once a month, with the average being about once every 2 weeks. The average age of the salespeople was 40. All were high school educated, and a few had college degrees.They were paid a commission which varied according to product of from $1/2$ to $5^{1}/2$ percent. (Appliance products were said to be "on the low end of the commission structure.") Their gross incomes, out of which they paid all selling expenses, ranged from $15,000 to $80,000. The latter figure was considered "very rare" for the industry.

Mr. Finegold stated that manufacturers offered everything from trips to tennis balls to his salespeople to get them to push their products. "Spiffs[9] work very well here," he continued.

> Manufacturers seem reluctant to believe that whatever is best for our total company is best for our salespeople. For example, if a manufacturer grants us the exclusive right to distribute his products in our trading area, we can maintain a good wholesale margin, our people make more money from the products, and they're more interested in selling them. But if several distributors are competing with us for the same retailers, we have to keep prices low to remain competitive, our people don't make much money, and they become apathetic about those products.

Electrical Distributor

One of Clairol's major electrical distributors was Vitrielli Electric. Vitrielli had five salespeople, four of whom handled both headquarters and retail tasks while the fifth had only headquarters accounts. Those who handled both had 4 or 5 major headquarters, 20 to 35 retail stores, plus anywhere

---

[9]A spiff, also referred to as "push money," was a sum of money given to a salesperson in addition to his usual compensation for each unit of a product he sold. The money was usually given by a manufacturer to distributor or retail salespeople over whom the manufacturer exercised virtually no direct control. Its purpose was to encourage the salespeople to push that manufacturer's products rather than those of his competitors.

370

Comp. from other distributors.

from 5 to 30 smaller independent accounts. The other salesperson had 15 headquarters accounts. The company guideline was that headquarters should be contacted weekly, retail outlets about once every 3 weeks, and independent accounts about once every 2 weeks. Vitrielli executives seldom got involved in actual selling tasks, but this was considered atypical of the industry which consisted mainly of family-owned distributorships in which principals were the main headquarters salespeople. (There was one national electrical distributorship which had approximately 30 branches and which accounted for about 20 percent of Clairol's total sales.) Vitrielli carried about 1,000 electrical appliances for 30 different manufacturers. Jack Raymond, Vitrielli president, estimated that, throughout the industry, the average age of electrical distributor salespeople was about 50, and all were at least high school educated. He stated further that some distributor salespeople received salaries, while others received commissions based on the percentage of profit the distributor made on the manufacturer's product lines. Commissions generally ranged from 1 to 3 percent. Commissions on Appliance products were said to be "low to middle." Mr. Raymond estimated that the gross income for most electrical distributor salespeople was from $15,000 to $25,000. Salespeople paid all their own selling expenses. As Mr. Raymond said,

371

> The best way to motivate distributor salespeople is to provide a good profit for the distributor house itself. If the house is getting a good profit, top management will want to sell more and will get salespeople to push the products by giving them better commissions. Special incentive programs are also fairly useful motivators. One manufacturer runs trips to Europe, another gives away steaks, one gives the salesperson 25 cents per unit sold, while another has started giving away gasoline. About a third of our manufacturers have some special incentive program going all the time.

Clairol had no such programs.

Incentive Programs to motivate distributor salespeople.

Drug Wholesaler

Morton Wholesale Drug Company was a full-service drug wholesaler that could supply the total needs of a drugstore, from health and beauty aids to prescription drugs. It carried about 24,000 items produced by about 1,500 manufacturers. Roger Holland, Morton's sales manager, stated that there were numerous "short-line" wholesalers who specialized in one particular type of item such as health and beauty aids. There was one national full-line drug wholesaler and about eight others who had several branches and were considered strong in particular regions.

Selling to headquarters of chain drug and department stores was usually done by Morton's principals. According to Mr. Holland, during peak selling seasons, headquarters buyers would often buy a quantity of merchandise and designate how much went to each of their retail outlets. At other times, the buyers would purchase and warehouse merchandise and let retail store managers order what they needed from the company warehouse. To reach the store managers, Morton had eight salespeople (ages 21 to 65), each of whom was responsible for 50 to 75 retail outlets. Their retail-call frequency varied from once a week to once a month. Though they might be in an outlet for an hour, they usually had 8 to 12 minutes to talk to the store manager about specific products. All of Morton's salespeople had high school educations and many were college graduates. A few received commissions only, while others received a salary and bonus. Their gross income ranged from $10,000 to $25,000. They paid their own selling expenses.

Automating selling process to cut costs

"Personal selling in this business is a dying art," said Mr. Holland. "The average profit after tax for drug wholesalers is about 1 percent. With so small a margin, we have to look for ways to cut distribution costs, and one way is by automating the selling process. For many products, a customer simply telephones the order to our computer." Mr. Holland stated that, to motivate his salespeople, manufacturers tried a wide variety of incentives. He said further that Morton often allowed some manufacturers to come to sales meetings. "Obviously, we encourage our men to push the products we make the most money from," he continued. "The problem with Clairol appliances is that, if we sell them at full list price, our competitors will undersell us. Therefore, it's very difficult for us to make any money from them, and our men don't get very excited about selling them." *Pricing structure too high. To be competitive Morton sells Clairol products below list price, thereby reducing its margins.*

372

→ CLAIROL'S RETAIL PROBLEMS, APRIL 1974

Retail Problems

In recent months, checks by Clairol personnel had increasingly indicated that appliance products were not being displayed or promoted well and often were not even available in retail outlets.[10] In theory, reps were responsible for retail tasks for all Clairol customers. Certainly, the retail outlets of direct-buying chains were solely the reps' responsibility, since distributors had no role in selling to these customers. Furthermore, most large retail outlets might be covered both by reps and distributor salespeople. "Our position in major outlets should be really strong since theoretically both reps and distributor salespeople call on a lot of them," said Mr. Comstock. "In reality, however, each group seems to leave the retail tasks for the other group, and consequently they don't get done."

At smaller, independent outlets, retail tasks usually were left to distributor salespeople. Small retailers generally inventoried a very

[10]Appliance Division executives estimated that Clairol appliances were sold by between 13,000 and 14,000 retail outlets.

Issue of motivation of dist. salespeople.

CLAIROL, INCORPORATED

limited number of personal care appliances and carried only a few of each item. They often chose products that were pushed by manufacturer salespeople, reps, or distributor salespeople. It was imperative, therefore, that Clairol find some way of motivating its distributor salespeople to sell its products well and service small retail outlets frequently if it were to get a significant share of the small retailer business.

In April 1974, Mr. Comstock met with other top sales managers to discuss what could be done to improve Clairol's retail position. Since distributor salespeople were responsible for the majority of Clairol's retail contacts, it was decided that the primary topic of the discussion would be how to motivate them to do a better job for Clairol.

Virtually all of Clairol's sales managers repeatedly characterized distributor salespeople as order takers. Mr. Comstock commented as follows:

Clairol's sales managers thought distri salespeople were "order takers."

Alternatives

Distributor salespeople go into a retail outlet with a checklist and merely mark off whatever the retailer says he needs. They do a mediocre job of selling our products and checking our stock at retail outlets, and they do nothing to improve our retail shelf position. Their time allocation problem is really serious. They have too many products to know them all well and to do a balanced selling job. The result is that they push the items most profitable for them, and unfortunately our gross margins are too narrow for our products to be among them. *Distr. salespeople push most profitable prod. line.*

373

Helge Peterson, Northern division manager, felt that the best way to motivate distributor salespeople was through reps.

Except for our three district managers, those of us hired directly by Clairol deal mainly with distributor principals and have very little contact with their salespeople. The reps' job is to see that necessary retail selling is done. They themselves usually do retail tasks in as many outlets as they can manage, and it's up to them to see that distributor salespeople do them in the rest. If our market surveys and personal observations indicate that the retail situation is deteriorating in a particular area, we can sit down with the rep and tell him he has a certain length of time—say 30 days—to pull the area together. If he doesn't do it, we look for another rep. I suspect that's how Norelco, Remington, and Gillette deal with their reps, and it seems to work well for them.

Mr. Peterson stated further that he thought Clairol's position with distributor salespeople would improve considerably once all Clairol's regional manager positions were filled, because the regional managers could work with the reps to plan special local incentive programs for distributor salespeople. He continued as follows:

Fill 3 Reg. Mgr. Positions

A few years ago, we tried a lot of incentives—spiffs, trips, premiums—all on a nationwide basis, and they weren't successful. We finally decided that unless incentive programs were handled on a local basis, they wouldn't work.

Possibility of hiring direct sales force.

We could exert even more influence if we replaced our reps with a direct sales force as Schick, Sunbeam, and GE have. Our salespeople could meet regularly with distributor salespeople and plan incentive programs for them. Most importantly, they could personally do retail tasks at more retail outlets themselves than reps can currently handle, so that we would not be so dependent upon distributor salespeople. Realistically speaking, however, recruiting, training, and maintaining a sufficiently large sales force would be a monumental task which very few of us are willing to undertake.

Different Strategies That Perhaps Might Work.

Options #1 #2

Some executives thought Clairol should do "whatever possible" to make its products more profitable for distributors and retailers and thereby get them to push the products. One way of doing this was by cutting Clairol's margins, but this idea was summarily rejected. Another way was by granting exclusive distribution to some distributors. This would mean that Appliance products would go through fewer distributors and probably fewer retailers than at present, but that these distributors and retailers should be more enthusiastic about Clairol's appliances.

Net effect It would mean, furthermore, that Clairol would have to do more local cooperative advertising than at present, in order to direct consumers to the outlets which carried its products.

374

#3

Ms. Bleyman strongly opposed granting exclusive distribution to any distributors, arguing that doing so would not balance Clairol's business well, that it was to Clairol's advantage for the retailer to be able to call different distributors when he needed products, and that relying on only one distributor within a trading area concentrated Clairol's risk and granted the distributor too much control over the manufacturer. She went on to say that Clairol should concentrate on a pull strategy by increasing its already heavy national advertising. She concluded as follows:

If consumer demand is high, the trade will be forced to carry Clairol products and we'll get very wide distribution. Our products will continue to sell no matter how low wholesaler and retailer margins fall. Let's face it—distributor salespeople don't get excited about anything. We'd have to luck upon the most creative incentive program in the world just to get their attention!

Distr. salespeople most not aggressive.

#4

David Meyers, regional manager in Cleveland, said that the only way he had found to motivate distributor salespeople was to work with them personally on a one-to-one basis. "Even then, it's impossible for us to motivate a lot of them," he said. "Of the 80 or 90 distributor salespeople in my region, about 5 are aggressive salespeople who would respond fairly well to coaching or special incentives. Most sell products by accident." Mr. Meyers stated that he had once run a contest in which distributor salespeople could accumulate points which were then exchanged for various premiums. He continued as follows:

That no doubt stimulated some sales, but I'm sure those incremental sales were very small. We gave away a lot of expensive prizes for sales we would have gotten anyway. Another time, we offered a 25-cent spiff for every hand-held hairdryer a distributor sold. Gillette came out with an identical offer, and since the Gillette product was a "hotter" item and easier to sell anyway, that's what the distributor salespeople pushed.

#4 — "Special promotions for distributor salespeople must work sometimes, since some manufacturers run them perpetually," said Mr. Comstock. "From what I can gather, their offers haven't been any more attractive than ours, so there must be some other factors that have made them willing to keep running the programs." Mr. Comstock stated that costs and revenues associated with various incentive programs had not been properly measured.

One factor might be manufacturer's image in the trade industry.

375

costs and revenues associated with various incentive programs hadn't been properly measured.

Section
NINE

Organizing
the Sales Effort

FORTY   Organizing the Sales Effort

Sales organization is perhaps the most neglected part of sales force management. It certainly receives less attention than motivation programs or compensation, but often has more impact.

There are several key organization decisions which top-level sales managers must confront. These are:

1   How many different sales forces should the company (or division) have and how should they be arranged? That is, should different products, customer categories, or sales functions have different sales forces?

2   Should sales-related functions be integrated into the sales organization? If so, at what level?

3   How will the selling effort for key accounts and national accounts be structured? How will the selling effort for multiunit accounts (multiplant manufacturers or multistore retailers) be organized?

4   How will the sales organization be managed? How many levels of sales management are appropriate? Where will sales managers be located? What span of control is best?

5   What role will each sales manager play? Will there be staff specialists to handle certain functions? At what level will the staff reside, and where will various functions be carried out?

Each of these decisions will be the subject of one of the following sections of this note.

HORIZONTAL ORGANIZATION OF THE SALES EFFORT
Geographical Organization

The traditional form of sales organization has been geographical. In such a structure, each salesperson is responsible for performing all selling tasks for all products for all customers and prospects within the territory. This form of organizational structure has several advantages. First, it generally minimizes costs because it minimizes travel distance and time. If there were more than one salesperson covering the same territory, travel cost and time would be higher. Second, it minimizes confusion. There is no question (or almost no question) in the customer's mind concerning who is responsible for what. In addition, there is less confusion and overlap in the company's own organization because there is only one sales force and only one sales management.

The prime disadvantage of this organization is that it requires each salesperson to be able to sell all products to all customers, and to perform all of the selling functions. It also inherently gives the salesperson more freedom of choice over which functions to perform, which products to emphasize, and which customers and prospects to call on. In such a situation, salespeople often do those things which are easiest or most comfortable. This tendency can be alleviated with close management, carefully developed evaluation plans, and good sales information systems; but the basic problem still remains. The salesperson in such an organization generally makes, for example, key deployment decisions at the lowest level in the organization.

Product Organization

Some companies have specialized their sales force by product line. Sometimes this happened by historical accident. Often when one company acquired another, it seemed most appropriate and was certainly most expedient to maintain two separate sales forces, each responsible for different product lines. If the surviving company was organized by divisions and the acquired company became a division, the separate sales force continued as a separate division's sales force. This general type of process apparently helped develop General Foods' separate divisional sales forces.

Companies often choose a sales organization by product if the total product line is large or diverse, or both, or if different products require different sales approaches or different knowledge. A large or diverse product line is difficult for a salesperson to master. In addition, presentations of many products and their associated promotions become very long, probably so long that both buyer and seller become bored.

Industrial firms in which the products demand specialized technical or applications knowledge often use product-oriented sales forces. In that way each product receives the expert knowledge it requires.

When manufacturing facilities are organized by product type (for example, each factory produces one product line), a product-oriented sales organization encourages close sales-manufacturing coordination. This is clearly more important in some situations than in others. Generally, it would be most important when delivery is a key sales variable, when production scheduling and sales forecasting must be coordinated on a day-to-day basis, or when the product line includes many custom or semicustom products. Sometimes, in fact, the sales force and branch manufacturing facilities will report to the same manager, or the local sales force will report to a local manufacturing manager.

An added benefit of the product-specialized sales force is that the decision regarding deployment by product line can be made at policy levels and implemented by varying the number of salespeople assigned to each product sales force. In this way the salespeople are partially removed from the deployment decision.

Organization by Market

Recently, it has become increasingly popular to organize by customer and prospect type. This has several advantages. First, the decision concerning the deployment of the sales force across markets is made at the policy level, not in the field by salespeople.

Second, each customer type or category obtains the expertise it requires. The sales forces learn a great deal about the customer's business and can more fully service customer needs. This type of organization is becoming popular in banks, where it is believed loan or calling officer (actually a salesperson!) can be of more value to customers when he has specialized, customer-oriented knowledge.

In addition, the sales force can be used to implement specialized marketing or promotional programs, or both, and to approach the customers and prospects in a particular fashion.

When divisions or the top-level marketing structure is organized by customer industry, a sales force organized the same way encourages close cooperation and integration. It can be argued that the customer-oriented sales organization encourages the flow of new product ideas and new marketing approaches back to research and development and marketing management. This has definite advantages in rapidly changing, highly competitive markets.

Sometimes, sales forces which are separated on a product basis are automatically separated on a customer basis. Thus, when an apparel firm separates its dress and sportswear sales forces, it also partially separates its sales force by customer, in that in larger retailers dresses and sportwear are chosen by different buyers.

Organization by product and/or customer entails added costs and confusion. Since two or more salespeople cover the same geography, travel time and cost are higher. Some salespeople resent the added travel, especially if it means additional nights away from home. The apparel firm which has separate dress and sportswear sales forces has two salespeople calling on the same buyer in small stores. This confuses and irritates some buyers. In product-oriented sales forces, a customer with a complaint against one salesperson's service or product is often annoyed when another salesperson from the same company, but a different sales force, refuses to offer help.

The book by DeVoe provides a relatively complex analysis of the pros and cons of a customer-oriented and to some extent a product-oriented sales force. He makes the strong point that a sales force organized by customer type is a natural culmination of the "marketing concept" and market segmentation.

Organization by Function

Kahn and Shuchman have made a strong argument for separating a sales force by function into one for development (creating new accounts) and one for maintenance (servicing existing accounts). Because these func- tion differ substantially in some situations, they could benefit from separation.

Implementation is difficult, however. New accounts can be expected to object to being "turned over" from the development salesperson with high talent to the maintenance salesperson who is better suited to mundane tasks. Transitions like these are always hard to make, especially when the account is new or large, or both.

It would also be very difficult to manage such a sales force, since one crucial objective would be close coordination between the development and maintenance functions. It is likely, however, that jealousy and irritation would limit the efforts to provide coordination.

Another form of functional separation involves that often found in consumer package-goods sales forces. There, one group of salespeople sometimes makes the headquarters sales calls while other salespeople make the store visits to service the shelves and "sell" the store manager. Separation of this same general form occurs in the national account function described later.

General Issues of Separate Sales Forces

All of the separations described above (by product, customer, and function) can occur at any level in the sales force. At one extreme, salespeople responsible for different products, customers, or functions can report to the same first-level field sales manager. At the other extreme, the sales forces can report to different national sales managers who in turn could report to different autonomous divisions.

If the different salespeople must be well coordinated it usually makes good sense to make the separation as low as possible in the organization, usually at the first-level sales manager. This would be, I believe, a necessity in the development-maintenance separation. On the other hand, if coordination between the sales forces and their respective marketing, manufacturing, or other functional managements is most important, high-level separation is called for.

In some sales forces some separation occurs in a de facto manner. Industrial sales forces often have product managers whose prime functions are product policy, pricing, and sales. The product managers will make calls on large customers with, or instead of, the geographical salesperson, thus acting as a specialized, product-oriented sales force. Industry sales managers, marketing managers, or specialists often play the role of specialized industry salespeople who reinforce the geographical sales force.

Many industrial-goods firms also have developmental salespeople who are responsible for the early sales of new products. These are often very experienced and capable salespeople who are organizationally in the research and development (R & D) arm of the company or division. Their function involves a combination of market research and personal selling. They often need to have a great deal of knowledge about customer technology and operations, as well as company capabilities and resources. Their input should be carefully integrated into decisions concerning new products. This selling function is one of the most difficult, as well as one of the most important. Its management sometimes involves very subtle and complex policy decisions, involving the basic strategy of the firm, as well as marketing, manufacturing, and R & D policies.

Sometimes, these de facto forms of separate sales forces work well, while at other times, they are dismal failures. The key seems to be the ability of higher level management to coordinate the efforts of the specialists and the line sales force and to engender cooperation among the groups.

ORGANIZATION OF SALES-RELATED FUNCTIONS

Many companies are faced with markets which require some high level of service. It might be maintenance and repair of the product (for example, capital equipment), rapid delivery (for example, fashion apparel), specialized product design or applications engineering (for example, electronic components), or unusual credit terms (for example, toys). In such companies, the organizational location of the departments providing the services will have a profound effect on the ability of the firm to compete.

Order entry is usually a sales-related service which reports in some fashion to the top-level sales manager. Sometimes, however, it reports to manufacturing management, perhaps through a warehousing and/or inventory control function, or to a separate data-processing function. Usually, the more important rapid customer response is, the more appropriate it is for the function to report to the sales organization. On the other hand, the more important manufacturing-inventory control coordination with shipping, the more appropriate it is for the order entry and processing function to report into the operations organization. Such distinctions are important. While order entry is a nonglamorous, mundane function with no strategic attraction, its malfunction can ruin the finest marketing strategy and sales program.

The credit function is usually at the opposite extreme. It almost never reports to the sales operation. Instead, it is usually viewed as a function of the controller or treasurer. This is probably appropriate, since salespeople and managers with sales experience are usually too generous with credit arrangements.

Maintenance and repair, as well as functions such as applications engineering, usually report through the sales force only when they must be well coordinated with the sales effort. Both are sometimes functions which are geographically decentralized and thus can best be managed by the geographically decentralized sales function. Both of these functions and similar functions are subject to the same type of issues as the sales force in terms of horizontal organization; that is, they may be organized by geography, product, customer type, or function. Usually, the same factors which influence the sales force decision also influence this decision. In fact, considerable improvement in coordination results from a direct relationship between these service functions and the sales function. That encourages the development of a team made up of sales, applications engineering, and repair and maintenance personnel. If the team can be coordinated at the field level (salesperson or first-level sales manager), the customer or prospect usually receives better service and the company greater sales effectiveness. Of course, such low-level coordination leads to dotted-line responsibilities between the applications engineers, for example, and their functional superiors at headquarters. This can cause problems of intrafunctional coordination and personnel development. These problems, although vexing, are often less damaging to the company's profits and sales than poor interfunctional coordination, which soon becomes apparent to the customer.

In all of these decisions, careful analysis of conflicting needs and requirements is necessary. Usually, those decisions made with customer goodwill as the prime objective will be the best. Such an approach, however, can be carried too far. If the internal operations of the company do not move smoothly and efficiently, the customer does not gain.

NATIONAL AND KEY ACCOUNTS

Usually, a disproportionately large percentage of a company's sales arise from national and key accounts. This is true in both the industrial and consumer-goods fields.

382

There are a variety of approaches to these large and important accounts. In cases where there are only a few key or national accounts, and in which all selling and servicing activities are directed at customer headquarters, most firms take one of three approaches:

1 They set up a separate integrated division to deal with the key or national accounts. This is most appropriate where sales, marketing, and manufacturing decisions must be closely integrated. Some apparel companies who sell to the three large private-level general merchandise chains (Sears, Montgomery Ward, and Penney) use this approach.

2 They set up a separate national or key-account sales force staffed by experienced, able salespeople. This works best where the sales to key accounts have relatively little effect on manufacturing operations. Thus, the salespeople do not have to be concerned with setting production schedules, allocating scarce resources, etc.

3 They use top sales, marketing, and/or general management to call on the national or key accounts. This approach is most normal in smaller firms which cannot afford separate management, sales forces, or production facilities. In selling to the accounts, the managers implicitly make decisions regarding the allocation of manufacturing capacity, inventory backup, and pricing. This approach enables the company to provide top-drawer service to its largest accounts. On the other hand, the top managers who call on the national or key accounts sometimes develop a warped view of their own firm and devote too much of its capabilities to their accounts. One symptom of this problem is the desire to "get all the business we can" from the large customers with no concern for the sales, operating, or profit impact of such business. This approach also obviously takes top management time away from the more management-oriented functions.

These three approaches are usually the ones used in industrial firms which sell to original-equipment manufacturers, as well as to end users.

The situation grows more complex when (1) the number of national or key accounts increases and/or (2) the amount of servicing which must be done by the field sales force increases. The number of options also increases.

One obvious option is to allow the salespeople in the field to sell to national and key accounts. One concern here is that the large account may require more experience, expertise, and organizational prerogative than the typical salesperson possesses. In addition, if the sales force is on commission, there are sticky questions concerning who gets the commission when one salesperson does the headquarters selling and another the in-store or in-plant servicing.

Another approach is to use field sales managers for key-account selling. If the key accounts are numerous and not national in nature, this approach is often used. Sometimes it is combined with the approach mentioned above in a program in which the salesperson has primary responsibility but receives much support from the sales manager.

Still another approach is a national or key-account sales force. This ensures that the accounts receive experienced, expert sales attention. Sometimes the key-account salespeople report to the field sales managers, but at other times they report through a separate organization. In some companies the account managers, as they are often called, do their own in-store or in-plant servicing of the account. In others, they manage assistants who work only on that account. In still other situations, the field salespeople perform the service function. If the field salespeople are on commission, they will usually receive some portion, perhaps one-half, of their normal commission rate for such sales. When the product is shipped to a central distribution point and then distributed by the customer to its own plants or stores in several different sales territories, it is often difficult to ascertain what was sold in which territory. Good customer relations clearly help alleviate the problem.

Sometimes, key-account salespeople are used as "blockbusters" or "openers." Once the key account becomes an established account, it is turned over to the field salesperson for regular maintenance. This is a variation of the Kahn and Shuchman approach mentioned earlier.

384

A key-account organization has another advantage. Positions such as key-account managers provide a useful way for salespeople who are capable and hard working, but either not suited for or not interested in sales management, to develop. Pearson describes this approach quite completely. Its importance should not be neglected.

Because of their disproportionate effect on sales, operations, and profits and their unusual service needs, national and key accounts need special treatment. The books by Kaven and Pegram provide more information on their care and development.

VERTICAL ORGANIZATION

The sales force must be organized horizontally by geography, product, market, or function. It must also be organized vertically. The three key decisions here are (1) the number of vertical levels, (2) the span of control, and (3) the geographical location of the sales managers.

The span of control and the number of levels are related to each other. For a given number of salespeople, the greater the span of control (that is, number of subordinates reporting to one manager) the fewer the levels of management and the fewer the managers that will be needed. Thus let us consider span of control first.

Most first-level sales managers have between 5 and 15 salespeople reporting to them. In general, the shorter span occurs when (1) the sales task is complex, (2) the profit impact of each salesperson is high, and (3) the salespeople are well paid and professional. The shorter the span, the more top management can expect in terms of the amount of supervision provided to each salesperson. As the notes "Field Sales Management" and "Compensation, Evaluation, and Motivation" point out, if the sales management philosophy is based upon close supervision, the span of control should be limited. As a rule, it seems appropriate to expect a first-level sales manager to spend between 1 and 2 days per month on an individual basis in the field with each of his subordinates. This and the amount of selling assigned to the field sales manager are the prime determinants of the appropriate span of control.

Usually, but not always, the span of control decreases at higher levels in the sales management organization. Thus it would not be unusual to find the following type of relationship:

No. of people	Title	Span of control
1	Marketing vice president[1]	
1	National sales manager	4
4	Regional sales manager	5
20	Zone sales manager	8
160	District sales manager	10
1,600	Salespersons	

Some companies feel that they get greater responsiveness if the sales force has a "flat" organization, that is, few levels of management. The argument is that, if there are few levels between the national sales manager and the salespeople, he can be "close to them," thus improving two-way communication. Others argue that such a flat organization limits two-way communication because it necessitates large spans of control.

The flat organization with a large span of control is, of course, cheaper in terms of direct cost because of the smaller number of sales managers involved. Some argue that the saving is illusory, since it is lost many times over because of the lower quantity and quality of management it provides.

One of the discouraging things concerning this argument is that few, if any, of the large sales forces for whom it is most relevant carry on well-designed, validated experiments to determine optimum span and number of levels. The saving grace here is that these variables can be gradually changed in an evolutionary fashion, and the results can be determined experientially if not statistically. The large opportunity loss from poor organization, however, is seldom considered.

An important and sometimes overlooked decision involves the location of the sales managers. First-level sales managers are almost

---

[1]The marketing vice president would also have nonsales personnel reporting to him. Other managers might have staff managers reporting to them in addition to the line managers shown.

always out in the field with the salespeople. This is appropriate since their prime concerns should be the salespeople and their territories.

The location of the sales managers just below the national sales manager is an interesting variable. If they are at headquarters with him, they tend to get involved in policy decisions and to act as his staff. They, in essence, become assistant national sales managers. If they are in the field, on the other hand, they tend to view themselves and to be viewed as top-level field sales managers. They tend to have less impact on, and interest in, policy-level matters.

For the large sales force, it seems clear that it is best to have them at headquarters. It aids their development as well as improves the policy decisions because of more careful and broader consideration. Usually, the quality of field management suffers little if at all. One can argue, in fact, that it is improved because the next level of management has more autonomy with which to develop. For the smaller sales force, on the other hand, the added level of sales management in the field is sometimes necessary.

MANAGEMENT ROLES AND STAFF SUPPORT

The definition of management roles is an important part of the development of the organization structure. For example, as the span of control of the field sales manager increases, the time available for each subordinate decreases. In addition, the amount of time available for staff-oriented work decreases because of the press of line responsibilities. Thus, management roles must be developed in concert with the total sales organization.

One crucial question is where the authority to hire, fire, and evaluate lies. In some sales forces, the first-level sales manager hires his subordinates, while in others, he has some input to a decision made by higher-level managers. Usually, the more important the decision, the higher up in the organization it is made. Thus, in sales forces which hire many low-paid salespeople, the decisions are made by the first-level sales manager. In sales forces which hire few highly paid salespeople, the decisions are made at higher levels. This is especially true if the sales force is seen as a training ground for management (sales, marketing, and general) positions.

In almost every sales force, there is a crucial level of management in which resides most of the "real" field management authority. This is usually a level with a short enough span of control so that the manager can closely supervise his subordinates, and the managers at that level usually have a great deal of freedom. Sometimes they are first-level managers, sometimes the highest level stationed in the field. This level is often viewed as a "keystone" level in implementing sales-force management programs.

Most larger sales forces include some staff personnel—that is, managers responsible for certain activities but without the general responsibility of the line managers. The most common functions for staff specialists are recruiting, training, and sales analysis.

It is useful to separate staff positions into those which are primarily used for training of the incumbent, and those in which the incumbent is primarily there to perform the function. Many sales forces use staff positions to train prospective sales managers. In smaller sales forces they are used to train first-level managers, while in larger ones, they are often used to train higher-level managers. One common pitfall of the training position is to make it a position with little work. This decreases the incentive of the incumbent, gives him a poor view of the organization, and gives the organization little basis upon which to judge him. The best training positions are challenging in addition to being way stations on the road to better things.

Sometimes, staff specialists are used as a way to remove onerous but important tasks from sales managers. At other times, they provide useful input. This will occur only if they are at the appropriate level in the organization. Thus, the sales analyst who is concerned with individual territories can do little if he does not interact with the first-level manager. By the same token, the developer of sales force–wide training programs should reside high enough to have an impact on the whole sales force.

387

Staff specialists should be considered when deciding the optimum span of control and number of levels. The creative use of staff people can enable a sales force to function with fewer managers. This can improve responsiveness while cutting costs.

Many sales managers are responsible for managing nonsales functions such as warehouse, repair and maintenance, and clerical personnel. In some cases, this is efficient as well as a means of improving the interfunctional coordination of the firm for the benefit of customer and company. Such tasks do, however, detract from the sales manager's other duties and thus must be considered in developing job descriptions and planning organizational structures. Many branch bank managers, for example, who view themselves as salespeople and sales managers feel constrained by their administrative functions, which they claim are not shared by loan officers of insurance companies who are competing for the same business.

BIBLIOGRAPHY

Business Week: "NCR's Radical Shift in Marketing Tactics," December 8, 1973, pp. 102–109.

————: "Specialist Selling Makes New Converts," July 28, 1973, pp. 44–45.

Corey, E. Raymond, and Steven H. Star: *Organization Strategy: A Marketing Approach*, Boston, Mass.: Graduate School of Business Administration, Harvard University, 1971.

DeVoe, Merrill: *How to Tailor Your Sales Organization to Your Markets*, Englewood Cliffs, N.J.: Prentice-Hall, 1964.

Doody, Alton F., and William G. Nickels: "Structuring Organizations for Strategic Selling," *MSU Business Topics*, Autumn 1972, pp. 27–34.

Kahn, George N., and Abraham Shuchman: "Specialize Your Salesmen!" *Harvard Business Review*, vol. 39, no. 1, January-February 1961, pp. 90–98.

Kaven, William H.: *Managing the Major Sale*, Research Study 105, New York: American Management Association, 1971.

Pearson, Andrall E.: "Sales Power Through Planned Careers," *Harvard Business Review*, vol. 44, no. 1, January-February 1966, pp. 105–116.

Pegram, Roger M.: *Selling and Servicing the National Account*, New York: The Conference Board, 1972.

388

FORTY-ONE   Homewood Furniture Company

In December 1972, the top executives of the Homewood Furniture Company were in the midst of considering how to organize the firm's sales force. The decision was perceived to be so important to the firm that the president, Arthur Martinez; the marketing vice president, Paul Daley; and the national sales manager, Harold Cohen were devoting a great deal of time to the decision (see Exhibit 1 for an organization chart). Four years earlier, the firm had introduced its Burlington line of convertible sofas[1] as the finest, most expensive convertible sofas in volume production. While the line had gained some sales volume, its performance had been disappointing. Meanwhile, the firm's Omaha line of medium-priced convertible sofas had exhibited moderate growth, while its Stoneville line of upholstered porch furniture had shown rapid growth. As of 1972, all the lines were being sold by one sales force. The company was considering using a separate sales force either for the Burlington line of high-priced convertible sofas or for the Stoneville line of porch furniture.

---

[1] A convertible sofa is one which opens to a full-size bed for two people. When closed, it appears to be a conventional sofa.

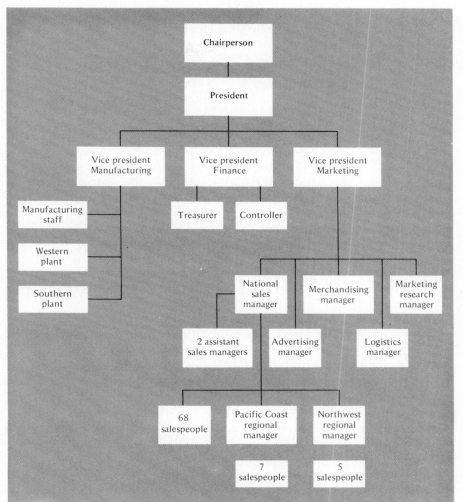

Exhibit 1 Organization chart.

THE BURLINGTON LINE

In 1968, Homewood introduced the Burlington line with a great deal of advertising and promotion. According to management, the line was of unique quality. The mechanical device for opening and closing the unit had been carefully designed, so that even a small child could operate it. Competitive designs, it was stated, did not operate so easily and smoothly and required a substantial amount of tugging and pulling. More important, however, to the marketing vice president was the comfort he believed was built into the unit.

It's the first convertible sofa that is both a comfortable sofa and a comfortable bed. Our unique patented design allows us to use a full-thickness, comfortable mattress, effective springing under the mattress, and a comfortable seat cushion and springing under the seat cushion. Furthermore, the design enables us to style the sofa as a conventional sofa is styled. Quality control is carefully maintained. No expense is spared. The labor input in one of these units is about 70 percent greater than in that of one of our regular units. It's a fantastic product.

The Burlington line had been introduced for two reasons, one competitive and one based upon projected changes in demand. The company's Omaha line was designed and manufactured to sell at high-volume price points which were in the medium-price range, about $200 to $400 at retail [equivalent with the typical 50 percent retail gross margin to $100 to $200 at wholesale (Homewood) prices]. The company's outlets were primarily furniture stores, including a large number of small stores as well as some major regional chains of furniture stores. A primary competitor with a profitability substantially higher than Homewood, the Elgin Corporation, had a product line which was sold primarily through department stores at retail prices in the $330 to $600 price range, with most of the volume in the $350 to $500 range. Homewood's management reasoned that the Burlington line (to be priced from $450 to $700 at retail) would be effective in opening department store distribution. People in the furniture trade believed that department stores typically carried higher-priced merchandise than furniture stores.

The second reason for introducing the line involved management's belief that average per capita income and the percentage of professional and managerial people in the population would grow. These people, and people with higher incomes in general, it was reasoned, would be willing to spend more for home furnishings. The Burlington line was designed to appeal to them. The emphasis was on quality tailoring and upholstering, fine fabrics, and traditional designs.

The introduction of the line was accompanied by relatively heavy consumer advertising and strong incentives for the trade to order and display the line and for the salespeople to push the line. The media budget for consumer advertising was $500,000, the highest in Homewood's history and, according to Homewood management, considerably higher than other furniture firms of comparable size. Sales contests and extra-high commission rates were used to encourage the sales force to push the line. Retailers were offered large price cuts, especially for accounts willing to display several styles of the line. Special point-of-purchase displays were designed and provided free to interested retailers.

Early sales were encouraging. In 1968, shipments were almost $500,000, and in 1969, they exceeded $2 million. Some salespeople and some retailers seemed to do better with the lines than others. Sales management and top corporate management constantly congratulated the salespeople who did well with Burlington and cajoled those who did not sell the line. During late 1969 and early 1970, management began receiving reports that the line was not selling off the retail floor. Retailers complained about price and styling. Although management thought that part of the problem might be the generally slow introduction of a new concept, they were concerned.

At the annual sales meeting in June 1970, an attempt was made to reeducate the salespeople in the "concept of Burlington." Management stressed (1) the uniqueness of the product, (2) the importance of obtaining quality stores as Burlington accounts, and (3) the importance of training retail sales help in the Burlington concept. According to management, retail sales clerks were used to selling Omaha and other similar convertible sofas in the fabric color and pattern available in the store's own inventory. In contrast, it was expected that the Burlington line, with its high prices and more demanding customers, would be ordered in the customer's choice of the many fabric colors and patterns offered by Homewood.

Management suspected that many of Homewood's salespeople and current accounts could not sell sofas of the quality, fine design, or price of the Burlington line.

Sales in 1970, 1971, and 1972 had been disappointingly in the $3 million range (see Exhibit 2).

Exhibit 2 OPERATING DATA

	Sales (millions of dollars)		
	1970	1971	1972
Omaha	$18.3	$18.8	$19.3
Burlington	3.2	3.1	3.2
Stoneville	8.7	13.6	18.2
Total	**$30.2**	**$35.5**	**$40.7**
	Profit contribution[a] (thousands of dollars)		
Omaha	$4,850	$4,900	$ 4,830
Burlington	810	710	740
Stoneville	2,380	3,950	5,100
Total	**$8,040**	**$9,560**	**$10,670**

[a]Defined as net sales minus salespersons' commissions and manufacturing expenses, including materials, labor, and factory overhead.

The abbreviated 1972 income statement is as follows:

Net sales	$40,700,000
Cost of goods sold	25,600,000
Gross profit	15,100,000
Selling, administrative, and general expense	12,000,000
Net profit before tax	3,100,000
Tax	1,500,000
Net profit after tax	1,600,000

THE OMAHA LINE

The Omaha line had been the initial product line of the firm in the late 1940s, when it had been founded. It was considered in the industry to be one of the top convertible sofa lines. In 1972 the line was offered in 60 styles, 21 of which were new that year. These had replaced other styles which had been discontinued. The number of styles offered had been about the same since the mid-1960s, when the line had been considerably pared down from what management considered was an overly long and inefficient product line.

The line and the other two Homewood lines were produced in relatively modern and automated facilities. The firm offered its merchandise in approximately 100 different fabric patterns available in three to eight different colors.

New items were introduced into the Omaha line and into the other Homewood lines at the High Point, North Carolina, furniture markets in April and October. Most major furniture retailers had representatives at these markets, and almost all major furniture manufacturers displayed their wares there. Since most of the firm's salespeople attended the market, they could service their customers there.

THE STONEVILLE LINE

The Stoneville line of upholstered porch furniture had been introduced in 1966, and sales had grown quite rapidly. The firm, in fact, had consistently underforecast its sales. In the 1970 5-year plan, management had forecast Stoneville 1972 sales of $11 million. Actual sales were over $18 million. This phenomenon had happened every year since the 5-year planning process had been introduced in 1969.

The line consisted of about twelve groupings. Each grouping contained about five upholstered items including sofas (both convertible and nonconvertible), loveseats,[2] and chairs. Management attributed the success of the line to two things: (1) a general lack of competition in the upholstered porch furniture business, and (2) the almost unique idea of including a convertible sofa as part of each group. Only one other manufacturer, the Bedford Sofa Company, also sold upholstered porch furniture with a convertible sofa in the group. Bedford Sofa, Elgin, and Homewood were the major factors in the standard (non-porch) convertible sofa business.

Homewood management felt confident that their Stoneville line was the largest-selling upholstered porch furniture line in the industry.

---

[2]A loveseat is a small sofa, sufficient in size to seat two people comfortably instead of the three to four typical with a sofa.

Competitors consisted of Bedford and a few smaller manufacturers who specialized in upholstered porch furniture. Management estimated that in 1972 only one sold more than $5 million but that it sold less than $8 million.

COMPETITION

There were two major competitors in the convertible sofa market. One of these was the Elgin Corporation which sold a heavily advertised, relatively high-priced product line, primarily through department stores. Elgin was the largest manufacturer of convertible sofas in the nation, with sales of close to $50 million, all in convertible sofas. Elgin sold a separate line through a separate sales force to furniture stores.

The other large competitor was the Bedford Sofa Company. Bedford sold a lower-priced line than Elgin, with prices going from about $175 to $400 at retail. Bedford had a relatively limited line. Its distribution was almost solely through large department stores in metropolitan areas. It had a policy of selective distribution, choosing one or two stores per metropolitan area to carry its line. According to Homewood executives, Bedford was both an intensely price-competitive firm and a highly profitable firm. They attributed this to the long production runs possible because of its large accounts and narrow product line. Many department stores used both Bedford and Elgin merchandise—Bedford for the low-price merchandise and Elgin for the high-priced.

A variety of smaller firms also competed in this market. One had substantial strength in the West Coast metropolitan areas because it designed its products for the "California taste," according to Homewood management. Even though its total volume was below $15 million, it had a large market share in its strong territories. The other manufacturers were substantially smaller (under $5 million), and competed on the basis of low price made possible, according to Paul Daley, by their low overhead and marginal quality.

Distribution[3]

There were four major kinds of furniture retailers: department stores, furniture stores, mail-order chain stores, and warehouse showrooms.

Large department stores typically devoted one or two entire floors to furniture display. They offered a variety of services, including decorator assistance, special order fabrics on upholstered items, free delivery, and credit. Lower-priced stores often promoted sales of matched sets, while

[3]Much of the initial part of this section is condensed from Jeanne Deschamps, "Industry Note on Wood and Upholstered Household Furniture," Harvard Business School, Boston, Mass., 1972.

expensive specialty shops and furniture stores sold many single items. Department stores varied from those which offered primarily high-priced merchandise (for example, Bloomingdale's) to highly promotional stores in the volume price points. In general, however, industry experts believed that department stores carried higher-priced merchandise than most other types of outlets.

Furniture stores varied by size and price line. A few operated several stores as a chain, but most furniture stores were small family-owned businesses which offered relatively low-priced merchandise. W&J Sloane which operated separately owned stores in New York, Washington, D.C., and San Francisco was considered by many to be the epitome of the expensive specialty furniture stores. Most metropolitan areas had several furniture stores which specialized primarily in expensive furniture.

The three large mail-order chain stores, Sears, Penney, and Montgomery Ward, sold large volumes of furniture in the medium to medium-low price range. It had been estimated that Sears alone did 3 percent of the total retail furniture sales.

The furniture warehouse showrooms spread rapidly in the very late 1960s and early 1970s. They were introduced by the Levitz family and often were known as *Levitz-type stores*. They offered a wide selection of medium-priced, brand name merchandise in very large buildings which combined a warehouse and showroom. The furniture was presented in relatively attractive room settings, with up to 350 settings per showroom. All furniture was available from warehouse stock (except when the store oversold its inventory), and no special orders were accepted. The warehouse showrooms operated on 38 percent markup instead of the typical furniture and department store markups of 45 to 46 percent, since (1) they had lower occupancy costs because the showrooms were built as free-standing stores in the suburbs rather than downtown; (2) they received quantity discounts because they purchased large volumes in carload lots from a limited number of resources; and (3) they charged extra for delivery and uncrating in the consumer's home. The showrooms advertised heavily and had substantially higher sales per square foot than traditional outlets. In the 1970s these outlets proliferated as existing retailers and new ones attempted to enter the market. Industry experts had described the growth as "explosive."

Several variations on the warehouse-showroom concept developed. Mangurians developed the concept of a high-priced, full-service store using the same display, assortment, and location strategy as the lower-priced stores. Mangurians units were opening in New York State, Florida, and Texas. Several traditional retailers, including Macy's New York and Sloane's, opened "clearance centers" which were low-overhead stores to sell regular markdown and clearance merchandise. Bloomingdale's was in the process of opening full-service "home furnishings centers" which would sell expensive, stylish merchandise. These were planned for locations along the East Coast both within and beyond its traditional New York metropolitan trading area.

Homewood had almost 8,000 accounts ranging from very small ones to very large ones. It sold a substantial amount of its output ($5.2 million) to a large mail-order chain store. Other large accounts included two chains of warehouse showrooms. Net sales to one were about $1.2 million and to the other $1.1 million. No other account represented more than $300,000 in net sales. (See Exhibit 3 for more data on distribution.)

The top 25 accounts in terms of net sales included 4 department stores, 3 mail-order chains, and 5 warehouse-showroom organizations. The remaining 13 accounts were furniture stores or hard goods retailers who sold large volumes of furniture.

According to the 1967 *Census of Business*, there were 33,274 furniture stores in the United States (compared with 37,216 in 1963). Homewood management, however, estimated that at the very most, only 23,000 of these were in any way worthwhile accounts in terms of credit, volume potential, or merchandising capability. Total furniture-store sales volume had been $6,564,388,000 in 1967 versus $5,316,739,000 in 1963.

Homewood's information system did not enable management to find out who the largest Burlington accounts were. The managers were also not willing to guess as to the nature of those stores.

395

The Sales Force

Homewood had a sales force of 80 exclusive[4] salespersons. They were assigned geographic territories, ranging from less than one state to several sparsely populated states. According to industry sources, Homewood had an unusually aggressive sales force with high morale and loyalty. Many of the older salespeople had been with the firm for 15 to 20 years. Younger people had been hired from other furniture manufacturer

[4]An *exclusive* salesperson was one who represented only one manufacturer.

Exhibit 3 1972 DISTRIBUTION OF ACCOUNTS

Account size	% of accounts	Cumulative % of accounts	% of sales dollars	Cumulative % of sales dollars
0–$100	4.2	4.2	0.1	0.1
$100–$500	20.0	24.2	1.5	1.6
$500–$1000	15.9	40.1	3.3	4.9
$1000–$2000	20.1	60.2	8.2	13.1
$2000–$3000	11.3	71.5	7.8	20.9
$3000–$4000	8.2	79.7	8.2	29.1
$4000–$5000	4.9	84.6	6.2	35.3
Greater than $5000	15.4	100.0	64.7	100.0

Notes: Total number of accounts was 7,953. Total sales were $40.7 million.
Source: Homewood Furniture Company records

sales forces or had entered the firm's sales training program. The program lasted from 2 to 6 months, depending upon the needs of the trainee. During the first part of the training period, trainees learned the product line and worked in the order-processing department, entering and expediting orders. Later, they assisted the headquarters sales management team in handling customer problems and in working on special projects. Toward the end of the training period they were placed in territories where they traveled with a regional sales manager or one of the assistant sales managers for a period of about 2 weeks. The regional sales manager or assistant sales manager would usually visit the new salesperson frequently (for example, once every 2 weeks) for several months.

The sales force worked relatively independently. Sales management became involved in traveling with the salespeople only when a problem arose (for example, threat of losing a large account) or when major accounts were being called upon. The salespeople were paid on a straight commission basis with the commission ranging from 4.5 to 7.0 percent, depending on the gross margin percentage of the item. In 1972, the average commission rate for individual salespeople ranged from 4.8 to 6.2 percent. The salespeople paid their own expenses. Median gross compensation for them was about $28,000 and ranged from about $16,000 to $62,000 in 1972. Because 1972 had been a very good year in the furniture industry, these figures were higher than they would have been during the industry recession of the late 1960s. The low end of the range, however, varied little over the business cycles, while the high end varied substantially. New salespeople were typically guaranteed a minimum salary until their commissions became large enough to support them.

Sales force turnover was very low, especially among the established salespeople. In the past 4 years, only 4 of the 52 or so veteran salespeople left, one to form his own business. The others were fired with a generous severance pay because of continued poor performance. Exhibit 4 gives data on the top 10 salespersons.

Exhibit 4 THE TOP TEN SALESPERSONS

Rank in dollar sales	Approximate age	Territory
1	Early fifties	Rural Southeast
2	Late forties	Rural and urban Midwest
3	Early fifties	Rural Southeast
4	Early thirties	Rural and urban Southwest
5	Early thirties	Rural Southeast
6	Mid-fifties	Urban Northeast
7	Early forties	Urban Northeast
8	Early thirties	Urban Southeast
9	Mid-forties	Rural Northeast
10	Late thirties	Rural South Central

Note: The rural territories often contained one metropolitan area of several hundred thousand people, as well as the rural areas.

According to a Homewood Market Research Department survey of the sales force, made in early 1970, the salespeople made from four to ten calls per day with a median of six to seven. The same survey concluded that they drove between 50 and 250 miles per day, with an average of about 100 miles per day. Because this was a mail survey, line sales management doubted the accuracy of the figures for any one salesperson, but thought that the median figures were probably true.

The sales force carried all three lines. In 1972, the percentage of unit sales accounted for by the Burlington line for each salesperson ranged from just over 3 to almost 19. The unit percentage for the top ten salespersons (in dollar volume) is given below (in order of decreasing volume of salesperson):

1	4.4%[5]	6	3.3%
2	8.0	7	6.8
3	5.0	8	3.8
4	11.5	9	6.9
5	4.6	10	8.4

The Current Situation

The section devoted to highlights in the 1970 5-year plan (drawn up in late 1970) stated:

> The sales of the Burlington line were disappointing. We did not meet our goals even though much effort was expended. We are not satisfied with our activities and are planning to emphasize this line by the following means:
>
> 1 Hiring a Burlington sales manager
> 2 Separating the sales force
> 3 Remerchandising the line with an accompanying broadening of its price category
>
> Stoneville is our fastest growing product line. We plan to continue expanding this line and establishing ourselves as the recognized leader in this specialized field.
>
> It is our opinion that the warehouse showrooms will be the fastest growing retail furniture outlet for the next 5 years and will take top priority in our key account program. During the next 3 to 5 years most of the increase in industry dollar sales will come from the warehouse showrooms.
>
> In order to strengthen the Burlington sales effort at the same time we grow in other product categories, we are planning to split the sales force so that one sales force will be devoted to Burlington and the other will carry the remainder of our line.

The body of the plan continued:

[5]To be read: 4.4 percent of the top salesperson's unit sales were accounted for by the Burlington line.

After careful analysis, it was decided that the Homewood sales force should be separated into two segments, one carrying Burlington and one carrying the balance of the line. The decision was made for a variety of reasons, including:

1 Often the stores most appropriate to carry Burlington are not also appropriate for the remainder of the line. Therefore, the salesperson currently does not have enough incentive to search out and open accounts which will sell only Burlington.

2 Some salespeople are more capable of selling and merchandising the Burlington line and more interested in its development than others.

3 Past experience shows that the Burlington line needs selling attention which it can obtain only from its own sales force. A sales force devoted to Burlington will result in salespeople who are more knowledgeable about and more interested in that line. In addition, the Burlington salesperson will be able to make a shorter, more forceful presentation because it will include only Burlington rather than the whole Homewood line.

Distribution is a key aspect of Homewood's marketing effort. It is also an area in which rapid change outside Homewood is forcing change within Homewood. The major change is the emergence of the warehouse showrooms as a powerful retail force in the furniture business. These will account for a large portion of the growth in the retail furniture industry and, by 1976, a large portion of the retail sales. This is especially significant for Homewood because of our relatively weak position in current large outlets, particularly department stores, and our strong record in selling warehouse showrooms. Thus, warehouse showrooms present a great opportunity for Homewood although they may in some cases compete with established Homewood accounts.

398

Accordingly, Homewood will emphasize the development of warehouse showroom accounts during the coming 5 years. These outlets will have top priority in the key account program and will be prime targets for the Omaha and Stoneville lines and, in some cases, for the Burlington line. We are prepared to develop a special brand or product line for warehouse showrooms because two or more of these accounts will be in some of the same cities. It is also felt that by having a different brand line we can maintain good relations with existing retailers.

The 1971 Burlington results were very disappointing. Implementation of the previously developed plan had been tabled because Homewood management was not sure what action to take. The highlights section of the 1971 plan included the following comments:

We believe there is substantial potential in the higher priced convertible sofa market but are disappointed that Burlington has not as yet fulfilled earlier expectations. In order to exploit the potential in this market, we are recommending an aggressive revitalization of the Burlington line.

The section on the Burlington line was extensive:

> There seem to be three possible alternatives for the Burlington line. First, it could be dropped. This alternative was considered but rejected because of the substantial profit potential in that product line and because the current profit contribution is considerable (about $700,000 before advertising and product development). The second alternative would be to not make any major change in the line or its method of sale. This does not appear to be the right way to tap the profit potential available in that area of the market. The third approach is to obtain maximum profits from that area of the market through a revitalization of the line as proposed here. The revitalization involves remerchandising the line and creating a separate Burlington sales force to develop the retailer support and high quality distribution needed by the line.
>
> The Burlington sales force will be managed by a Burlington sales manager reporting to the national sales manager. The Burlington sales manager will also have prime direct responsibility for merchandising the line.
>
> At the same time Burlington receives added sales effort, it will receive an added boost through remerchandising. Studies of the Omaha-Burlington product lines have shown a weakness in the $180–$250 (wholesale) price category. Remerchandising of the line will strengthen this price category. Burlington will appeal to these consumers who desire a well-made, well-designed convertible sofa and who are willing to pay for it. Because it is a quality product of a complex nature, it will require intensive sales support at the retail level. It will also require the reputation of a store known for quality products and styling.
>
> The Burlington salespeople will have to be able to obtain high quality distribution and strong retailer support. They must be capable of helping the retailer to effectively merchandise the line and of training retail sales personnel to sell the line.
>
> A policy of selective distribution is most appropriate for Burlington. This would consist of about 1,200–1,500 accounts soon after the revitalization of the line and might grow to 2,000. This can be translated into a maximum of 100 stores per salesperson.
>
> This degree of exclusivity is necessitated both by the nature of the product line and by the demands which will be placed on the retailer in the selling of this line. The retailer will have to support the Burlington marketing program by providing display, advertising, and sales assistance. If it is appropriate to the nature of his business, the retailer will also be expected to inventory a selection of Burlington sofas.
>
> The ideal outlets for Burlington will be full-service stores. Either department or furniture stores will be appropriate. The desired stores will not present a "discount-store image." The policy with regard to Burlington and the warehouse showrooms has not been defined.
>
> A sales force of 20 salespersons, which would cover all the current sales territories except a few in the Mountain and Plain states, is recommended. The average guaranteed compensation for the sales force is estimated at $22,000 and commission rates are estimated at 7%. The program includes no

special plans for compensating current Burlington salespeople during the transition.

It will be necessary to have two different sales training programs before the revitalization of Burlington. One will be for experienced salespeople and will last about 2 weeks; the other for trainees will last between 6 and 26 weeks, depending on the trainees' needs. It is expected that there will be about 10 people in each program.

Table 4 [reproduced as Exhibit 5] attempts to gather the relevant financial data together. The program will probably cause a decrease in attention paid to the non-Burlington items during the transition.

The section on distribution stated:

One reason we have been as successful as we have in selling the warehouse showrooms is the attitude of our competitors. Elgin has been unwilling to sell them and has only entered the field through one new local warehouse showroom this past spring. Bedford has been willing to sell the warehouse showroom a counterpart[6] line, but only under a separate name.

Homewood's strength with the warehouse showroom is primarily in its porch groupings that have done so well in this type of operation and, secondarily, in its strong medium and medium-high price range of convertible sofas.

400

Department stores have not kept up with the growing awareness of furniture selling in today's market. It is our feeling that the percentage of the furniture volume done by the department stores decreased during this past year and will go down even more so, even though their dollar volume will be up. In the next 3 years, we can look for a number of national and/or local department stores with strong furniture departments to open free-standing home furnishings complexes. Some of them will be along the lines of the present warehouse showrooms but others will be large traditional type furniture stores. We can also look for a number of department stores presently selling furniture to discontinue furniture sales as they find it increasingly difficult to obtain high dollar sales per square foot against the faster turnover of other items. Also, the difficulties encountered in service, delivery, and return policies seem to plague these operations.

Management was also concerned because the line did not seem to be reaching its targeted market. Exhibit 6 provides some data from a 1972 guarantee card survey of Burlington buyers.

By the fall of 1972, the firm had still not implemented the plans put forth. Arthur Martinez, the president, did not feel that the proposal concerning a separate sales force for the Burlington line was attractive enough to implement, especially in view of the large amounts of capital needed to increase production capacity because the plants were operating at capacity.

[6]A counterpart line is one which contains items that are counterparts to the regular line. The counterparts are similar but not exactly the same as the regular line, usually differing in cover fabric and tailoring.

Exhibit 5 PROPOSED BURLINGTON PROGRAM

Year[a]	0	1	2	3	4
Number of Burlington salespersons	0	20	20	20	22
Burlington sales of non-Burlington salespersons	$3,500,000	$ 350,000	$ 450,000	$ 550,000	$ 0
Burlington sales of Burlington salespersons	0	4,150,000	6,550,000	8,450,000	12,000,000
Total Burlington sales	**$3,500,000**	**$4,500,000**	**$7,000,000**	**$9,000,000**	**$12,000,000**
Total profit contribution	**$ 812,000**	**$ 938,000**	**$1,542,000**	**$2,064,000**	**$ 2,880,000**
Commissions for Burlington salespersons (assumes 7% commission rate)	$ 0	$ 290,000	$ 458,000[b]	$ 0	$ 0
Guarantee (assumes each salesperson will be guaranteed an average of $22,000)	0	440,000	440,000[b]	0	0
Guarantee less commissions	0	150,000	0[b]	0	0
Show space (high point)	25,000	10,000	10,000	10,000	10,000
Advertising & promotion (above regular budget)	50,000	150,000	250,000	350,000	450,000
Product development (above regular budget)	35,000	25,000	40,000	30,000	40,000
Direct overhead (includes sales manager and support)	15,000[c]	40,000	50,000	65,000[d]	70,000
Sales training	37,000[e]	0	0	0	0
Total expenses not including commissions	**$ 162,000**	**$ 375,000**	**$ 350,000**	**$ 455,000**	**$ 570,000**
Net profit contribution	$ 650,000	$ 563,000	$1,192,000	$1,609,000	$ 2,310,000

[a] Assumes that year 1 begins three months after announcement of revitalization and that year 0 includes preselling costs of the changes.

[b] In year 2, commissions exceed the amount of guarantees; therefore, the guarantee becomes irrelevant in calculating selling costs.

[c] One man one-half time @ $30,000.

[d] Assistant sales manager added.

[e] Ten trainees × 16 weeks × $175 per week + 10 salesmen × 2 weeks × $450 per week.

Exhibit 6 GUARANTEE CARD SURVEY

Occupation of respondent	
Blue collar	37%
Professional and technical	10
Managerial	10
Retired	13
Sales	7
Teacher	7
Clerical	2
Homemaker	1
Other	7
No response	6
Age of respondent	
Under 25	5%
25-34	19
35-44	18
45-54	22
55-64	20
65 or over	14
No response	2

Note: Based on over 10,000 guarantee cards which were attached to Burlington sofa beds and returned by purchasers.

402

Messrs. Martinez, Daley, and Cohen were still willing to consider the alternative of a separate Stoneville sales force and leaving the Burlington and Omaha lines for the existing sales force. But they feared the great disruption they thought that change would cause.

The situation was of such concern to them that by mid-December they had not developed a 1972 5-year plan. Traditionally, this effort commenced in September and was completed in early December. The 1972 plan, they agreed, should not be put together until the dilemma of the sales force had been resolved.

FORTY-TWO Heinz U.S.A. *Major issues*

In August 1973, Joe Kaeser, recently named general manager of grocery sales for Heinz U.S.A., was formulating plans to improve sales force morale and organization. The morale problem could be solved, he thought, through better direction from and communication with headquarters sales personnel and through better merchandising and advertising which other new managers were providing. The organization issue, however, posed major problems, because in recent years, while the sales force increased in size and complexity, almost no useful data on how individuals spent their time were generated. A recent independent survey of Heinz customers revealed that the trade perceived Heinz salespeople as being loosely managed, poorly trained, less aggressive in their coverage of accounts, and lacking in sales aids when compared with other leading package-goods companies. Though several Heinz people supposedly covered retail outlets, many customers reported that retail service was the company's weakest area.

BACKGROUND OF HEINZ U.S.A.

The H. J. Heinz Company was founded in 1869 in Pittsburgh, Pennsylvania, and by 1973, its operations consisted of 24 companies in 16 countries. Total corporate net sales for fiscal 1973 (April 30, 1972–May 1, 1973) were $1.2 billion, with net income of $21.5 million after taxes.

In the early 1960s, Heinz experienced considerable difficulty with its U.S. operations. Top management changed frequently, and for 4 consecutive years, sales decreased. In 1965, a new president began turning the division around, but in 1967 he left to become chief executive officer of the entire corporation. Under his first two successors, sales increased but profits were lackluster and erratic. In fiscal 1972, the division generated about a third of total corporate sales, but it accounted for only a very small portion of total corporate profits.

In September 1972, Raymond F. Good was named president of Heinz U.S.A. Mr. Good immediately began improving the division's profitability by cutting operational and administrative costs and by spending sales dollars more efficiently. By the end of fiscal 1973, he had reduced office personnel by 100 and factory personnel by 200, for a net savings of about $6 million. He had also "cleaned house" so far as top management was concerned. Of the seven people reporting directly to him, four were new to their positions and three were new to the company. For fiscal 1973, total division sales, including grocery, institutional, and private label, were $360 million, and after-tax return on sales was 1 percent.

The area which Mr. Good felt needed most attention was cost control. The grocery business concerned him because its profitability was among the lowest in the food industry, well below the industry average of 3.7 percent profit after tax. In fiscal 1973, grocery sales had been slightly over $200 million, with after-tax return on sales of about 1 percent. (Grocery sales included both sales to the regular grocery trade and to military commissaries.) Early in fiscal 1974, Mr. Good hired Dick Patton, then president of Cunard Lines, as vice president of grocery marketing and sales. Mr. Patton then promoted Joe Kaeser, East Central zone manager, to the position of general manager of grocery sales, and hired two new marketing managers, Robb Bell and Jim Nault. The new team planned to increase grocery sales modestly while doubling after-tax return on sales in 1974 by phasing out unprofitable products and controlling sales and administrative costs, among other things. For future years, it planned to continue primary emphasis on profitability as well as sales increases. (See Exhibit 1 for an abbreviated organization chart of Heinz U.S.A.)

Review

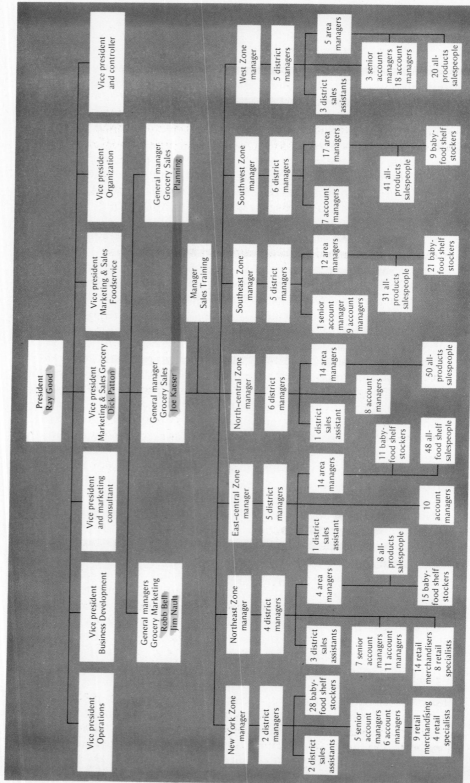

Exhibit 1 Abbreviated organization chart, August 1973.

THE RETAIL GROCERY BUSINESS

In 1972 total retail grocery sales exceeded $100 billion for the first time in history. However, grocery department margins averaged 12 to 14 percent, down from their traditional range of 16 to 18 percent, primarily because of wholesale price increases and excessive retail promotional activities. In recent years, retailers had demanded more and more services from manufacturers. For example, they increasingly encouraged manufacturer representatives to visit individual stores to pick up damaged goods, rotate merchandise, build displays, announce new products, and check shelf allocations.

While no hard and fast classifications existed within the industry, Heinz generally grouped its customers into five categories:

1 *Chains* Ten or more stores owned by a corporation. Examples included A & P, Kroger, and Stop and Shop.

2 *Cooperatives* Independent stores joined together under a wide variety of arrangements, usually for purposes such as joint purchasing and advertising.

3 *Independents* Stores free of both corporate and cooperative control. An independent owner normally operated one to ten stores.

405

4 *Commissaries* Retail outlets operated by the military.

5 *Distributors* Wholesalers who sold to any grocery store.

Heinz also classified retail stores according to their weekly volume:

	Weekly retail volume	Total no. stores in U.S.
Class I	Over $75,000	1,046
Class II	$50,000–$75,000	5,941
Class III	25,000– 50,000	18,512
Class IV	10,000– 25,000	10,061
		35,560

These 35,560 stores accounted for about 85 percent of the all commodity volume in the United States. (Commissaries were not included in these numbers.)

The Selling Task

Heinz's selling task consisted of two basic parts: *direct* selling at the headquarters level and *indirect* selling at the retail level.

Direct selling consisted of actually securing orders for products to be shipped to the customer's warehouse. There were no established benchmarks as to the time and contacts involved in headquarters selling. The

Heinz salesperson first contacted one or more buyers or merchandise managers, or both, who might or might not be able to make final purchasing decisions. He or his supervisor often also contacted vice presidents of operations and purchasing and other higher-level management. One Heinz district manager stated that he visited about 20 different people at his largest chain account each year. Several multilevel calls and follow-ups, either in person or by telephone, were usually necessary before final decisions were made.

The degree of control exercised by headquarters varied considerably. Some decreed the products, volume, facings, promotions, and so forth, for their retail outlets. Others mainly warehoused products and let retail outlets make their own purchasing and merchandising decisions. In the latter case, input from field supervisors[1] and retail people was often gathered before final decisions were made at headquarters. Generally speaking, fewer contacts with headquarters were required in selling to wholesalers and independents. Wholesalers wanted to know that Heinz had secured firm commitments from the stores they supplied, while buyers (who were often store owners) at independent stores could usually make purchase decisions relatively quickly.

In making headquarters calls, a Heinz salesperson virtually always asked for a 15- to 30-minute appointment. One salesperson emphasized that clear, concise presentations were necessary, since buyers for larger stores often saw 100 salespeople and purchased 7,000 to 8,000 different items each week. Some buyers kept appointments promptly, while others sometimes required salespeople to wait for up to an hour. Sometimes they asked salespeople to speak with other headquarters personnel that same day. During headquarters calls, Heinz salespeople first talked about special promotions and then discussed varieties and sizes which the account did not purchase or purchased only in small quantities. Geographic area played a key role in determining how many headquarters contacts could be made. In Los Angeles where headquarters were widely spread out, two headquarters calls per day were the norm, whereas in Philadelphia the average was about four.

Indirect selling involved generating demand among retail personnel. It covered four major operational areas—distribution, departments, display, and pricing. *Selling distribution* meant getting an outlet to carry a product it had not been carrying. Heinz salespeople contacted individual store managers to get them to order from the warehouse all varieties which their headquarters or their wholesalers warehoused. *Selling departments* consisted of getting store managers to improve Heinz product groupings,[2] shelf space, and positions within individual departments.

406

---

[1]Field supervisors were managers in charge of about 10 to 20 stores in a particular area. They were considered to be extremely important elements of the decision-making process.

[2]Improving product groupings meant placing all varieties and sizes of a brand together within a given department.

Selling display involved convincing the store manager to participate in promotional features approved by company headquarers. And the final task was to encourage the stores to sell at Heinz's recommended retail prices.

Some basic "housekeeping" chores were associated with each of these selling tasks. To maintain desired distribution, inventory checks were frequently necessary. To properly keep up departments, Heinz salespeople had to put up point-of-purchase materials and check shelf positions, percentage of space, and variety distribution. Sometimes they even had to dust the products and remove broken stock, although these were normally the responsibility of the retailer. They had to set up special displays and to make periodic checks to maintain correct retail pricing.

In the West zone,[3] Heinz contracted with different companies who performed retail tasks for several manufacturers. In the New York and Northeast zones, Heinz employed its own retail merchandisers and retail specialists to cover the outlets. In other areas, the Heinz persons responsible for selling to headquarters also covered their customers' retail stores.

HEINZ U.S.A.'S GROCERY OPERATIONS, AUGUST 1973
Marketing Strategy

In August 1973, Heinz marketed 14 products, all sizes and varieties of which totaled 115 items. Mr. Bell was responsible for marketing plans for ketchup, chili sauce, barbecue sauce, vinegar, HELP (fruit drinks), pickles, relish, 57 sauce, Worcestershire sauce, and salad dressing. Mr. Nault handled soup, mustard, baby food, beans, and miscellaneous entrees such as beef stew.

When allocating marketing funds in the past, Heinz marketing staff had differentiated very little between high and low profit items and had stressed trade promotions rather than consumer advertising and promotions. In fiscal 1973, total marketing expenditures had been $27 million, only 20 percent of which had been used for consumer advertising and promotion as compared to some major competitors whose ratio of consumer spending to trade spending was 55:45. (The ratio for major soap companies was thought to be about 60:40.) The marketing strategy which Mr. Bell and Mr. Nault developed for fiscal 1974 called for total marketing expenditures of $26 million and a consumer spending to trade spending ratio of 40:60. They planned to increase advertising even more in the future. Their objectives were (1) to spend more marketing funds on high-growth, high-profit varieties and less on limited-growth, limited-profit varieties; (2) to spend more money on better advertising and less

[3]Heinz divided the U.S. into seven zones.

on inefficient trade allowances; and (3) to maximize the effectiveness and efficiency of whatever trade spending they continued to do.

Competitive Position

Heinz U.S.A. competed with 18 national manufacturers and numerous local and regional manufacturers. Division management stated that ketchup, pickles, and vinegar offered them the most opportunities for increased sales and profits and that soup and baby food were their most problematic products. (See Exhibit 2 for market share data.)

In the ketchup business, while Heinz still enjoyed a strong consumer franchise, Hunt had recently increased its consumer advertising and had begun aggressively promoting its 32-ounce size in the Southeast, Heinz's weakest area. Mr. Bell's objective for ketchup was to increase Heinz's market share from 43 percent to 47 percent over the next 5 years, primarily by transferring trade promotion funds to consumer advertising. (Since 1968 Heinz ketchup's ratio of advertising to promotion had been 30:70.) He also planned to test market a 40-ounce bottle of ketchup.

Exhibit 2 RETAIL MARKET SHARE DATA[a]

	Market share, %		Market share, %
Baby food		**Pickles**	
Gerber	65.3	Vlasic	15.0
Heinz	16.0	Heinz	11.3
Beechnut	15.9	All other	73.7
All other	2.8		**100.0**
	100.0		
Barbecue sauce		**Relish**	
Open Pit	23.3	Heinz	15.8
Kraft	35.1	Vlasic	10.1
Heinz	15.9	Private label	29.5
All other	25.7	All other	44.6
	100.0		**100.0**
Canned soup (14 markets)		**Steak sauce**	
Campbell Condensed	67.7	A-1	49.2
Chunky (Campbell)	13.3	57 (Heinz)	23.7
Heinz	3.9	Prime Choice	11.7
All other (including		Steak Supreme	7.1
private label)	15.1	All other	8.3
	100.0		**100.0**
Fruit drinks (10 markets)		**Vinegar**	
Hi-C	23.8	Heinz	34.5
Hawaiian Punch	15.6	Private label	36.3
HELP (Heinz)	2.4	All other	29.2
All other	58.2		**100.0**
	100.0		
Ketchup		**Worcestershire sauce**	
Heinz	42.9	Lea & Perrin	44.8
Del Monte	17.2	French	44.2
Hunt	16.3	Heinz	6.6
All other	23.6	All other	4.4
	100.0		**100.0**

[a]Market share data were not available for mustard, canned beans, and miscellaneous "main courses."

The pickle business was highly fragmented, with numerous manufacturers providing strong competition within limited market areas. Heinz's major national competitor, Vlasic, had been aggressively building its business through a combination of trade dealing and consumer advertising. Mr. Bell wanted to increase substantially Heinz's return on pickle sales and to establish Heinz as the leading national brand. He had pinpointed operational areas where he thought savings could be made. Furthermore, he was testing an increased advertising program where Heinz had good distribution and a distribution-generating program where distribution was weak. He stated that chief emphasis would be placed on selling pickles better where Heinz already had good distribution before it undertook costly wide-scale distribution-building programs.

In the regular vinegar business, though private-label products were very strong, Heinz competed with them successfully at substantially higher prices. In specialty vinegars, Heinz and Regina dominated the market. Mr. Bell felt these products offered tremendous possibilities and only 25 percent of U.S. households currently used them.

Heinz's two problem products, soup and baby food, both operated at a loss in 1973. While there was some talk of phasing out these products entirely, it was necessary to keep them in the short term because of their contribution to overhead. Launched in 1968, Heinz's Great American Soups had never become a significant force in the soup market, partly because they had received only limited marketing support and partly because of the tremendous strength of Campbell who controlled over 80 percent of the canned soup market. Campbell traditionally had invested large amounts in consumer advertising and promotion, while Heinz had run trade deals only. Furthermore, Campbell had kept its prices and margins low, forced competitors to do likewise, and thereby tightly squeezed competitors' margins.

The baby food business was characterized by fierce competitive pricing and high service costs. Traditionally, Heinz and Beechnut had priced their baby foods at the same level as Gerber, by far the market leader. About 1968, in an attempt to increase market penetration, Heinz lowered its prices and Beechnut soon followed suit. While Beechnut and Heinz sometimes sold baby food for as little as $1.80 per case, Gerber had never been forced below $2.69 per case. High service costs were generated by the traditional practice of manufacturers' employing people to stock retail shelves with their baby food. So long as margins were good, manufacturers could absorb these costs and still maintain desired profits. However, in recent years, rapidly escalating raw materials costs, intense trade dealing, and lack of meaningful price increases had depressed earnings throughout the industry, and all manufacturers were anxious to phase out the shelf stockers. They thought that consumer advertising and promotion would become increasingly important competitive factors in the future.

The Sales Organization

Earlier in his business career, Mr. Patton had been a product manager at Heinz. When he rejoined Heinz, he found an extremely demoralized grocery marketing team, as well as a somewhat demoralized sales force, and executives who were frequently at odds, partly because of personality clashes and partly because their jobs conflicted. The general managers of sales and sales planning were on the same level, reporting directly to the vice president of grocery sales and marketing. According to his job description, the general manager of sales was "accountable for assuring sales growth and profitability by managing the grocery sales function to meet sales targets." He supervised seven zone managers. The job description elaborated on his position as follows:

> The primary requirements of the position are the achievement of annual, semiannual, and periodic sales targets; the regular review of the size and coverage of the grocery sales force; the training and development of sales personnel; the development of effective relationships with major grocery accounts; and the reduction of sales cost and dollar expense.
>
> The incumbent works closely with the vice president, grocery sales, in developing sales targets. He works closely with his zone managers in developing plans for achievement and in implementing controls to monitor progress. Being responsible for achieving the results planned by marketing, he is deeply involved with the general manager–grocery marketing and the general manager–grocery sales planning in implementing joint strategies that push a product volume mix providing optimum profit results. . . . He maintains firsthand knowledge of each district's operations. He frequently contacts key-account personnel at high levels to build Heinz as a valuable supplier.
>
> The incumbent must see that sales costs are kept within budgets for which he has received approval. He oversees the operation of the sales incentive plan. He keeps the vice president–marketing and sales, grocery, informed on progress as revealed by reporting systems that he develops, and takes appropriate action to correct deficiencies. As business development creates new product lines for grocery, he works closely with that division in introducing them to the trade.

The general manager of sales planning was "accountable for continuous improvement in profitability and volume through the development of effective sales programs and merchandising plans." His responsibilities were further described as follows:

> The incumbent has primary accountability for integrative management of trade promotion programs through the zones. He transmits those plans to the grocery zones and sees that they are carried into effect. He works closely and directly with the zones to schedule and inform them of trade promotions, evaluate results, detect the need for special activity, and develop additional appropriate action as necessary. . . . He acts as the coordination point between the marketing and sales departments. . . . The incumbent

must synthesize this wealth of sales and marketing data and decide on the timing and type of promotional programs and merchandising plans that will attain the volume and profit objectives for the grocery division at minimum cost. . . . The incumbent must make regular trips into the field to assess the effectiveness of Heinz promotional plans with major accounts in the market. He is also responsible for planning successful introductions and expansions of new Heinz grocery products and coordinating the sales and marketing activities associated with the execution of these programs to ensure that satisfactory distribution is achieved. He also acts as the focal point for analyzing the results attained.

Shortly after Mr. Patton's arrival, the general manager of sales left the company, and Mr. Patton promoted Mr. Kaeser to the position. The general manager of sales planning was placed under the general manager of sales. Mr. Kaeser was given authority to do virtually whatever was necessary to restructure the sales organization so as to improve its efficiency, effectiveness, and morale. He realized that he should reduce the $10.5 million (5.1 percent of sales) spent in fiscal 1973 in spite of an inflation rate of 5 to 8 percent. Thus, he believed that to meet his goal he would have to cut 5 to 8 percent of the cost out of the sales force.

One of Mr. Kaeser's first actions was designed to improve the personnel development program. The existing position of manager of

411

Objectives: reduce $10.5mm sales expense
2. Improve personnel development program

Exhibit 3 TOTAL GROCERY SALES EXPENSES, FISCAL 1973

Salaries and bonuses—sales representatives[a]	$ 4,597,500
Salaries and bonuses—supervision[b]	1,827,000
Campaign awards and prizes	900
Separation allowances	93,400
Termination vacation pay	53,800
Total payroll	**$ 6,572,600**
Payroll expenses (insurance, social security, and other benefits)	$ 1,149,100
Samples and allowance for spoilage	186,300
Traveling expense, auto rental and maintenance, entertainment	2,061,700
Employee moving expense	85,900
Purchased services	35,700
Commissions—agents and brokers[c]	193,800
Merchandising service fee[d]	268,200
Miscellaneous[e]	18,600
Total sales expense (this fiscal year)	**$10,571,900**

[a]Included senior account managers, account managers, all-products salespeople, retail merchandisers, retail specialists, and baby-food shelf stockers.

[b]Included zone managers, district managers, district sales assistants, area managers, and three assistants at corporate headquarters who made $11,000 each.

[c]Included commissions paid to agents and brokers who performed retail functions for Heinz in the West zone and for a few months in the New York and Northeast zones.

[d]In some areas where Heinz did not provide baby-food shelf stockers, they gave their accounts a 10-cent per case allowance to cover their costs of stocking baby food shelves.

[e]Included supplies, sales accessssories, moving expense adjustments, and export labeling and packing.

sales training had been used primarily to give the manager himself experience for other managerial positions. No one in a long series of managers had created a comprehensive, useful program. The current manager, an extremely competent individual but one who had no sales training credentials, was named general manager of sales planning. Mr. Kaeser thought a new person with professional experience in personnel development should be hired. To attract such a person, Mr. Kaeser thought the salary would have to be increased from $20,000 to $26,000 plus expenses. Mr. Kaeser also felt that the pool of highly promotable lower-level employees at Heinz U.S.A. was so small that each zone needed a full-time sales trainer[4] who would also be responsible for college recruiting. He defined the purpose of this job as follows:

Goals →

(1) To improve the quality and skills of field sales personnel by executing approved sales manpower development programs in the field; (2) to develop primary recruiting sources for sales personnel, particularly at colleges and universities; (3) to implement training projects at zone and national level; and (4) to prepare the incumbent for promotion to a district manager position through observation of methods, training, and skills development.

412

The zone sales trainers would report directly to the manager of personnel development with functional reporting to zone managers. Mr. Kaeser estimated the salary for zone sales trainers would be about $12,000 to $13,000, plus expenses, and that they would be recruited from existing area managers.

Mr. Kaeser also recruited a new military sales manager at a salary of $25,000, plus expenses.

FIELD SALES

By August, Mr. Kaeser had gathered considerable information on the structure and activities of the field sales force.

Seven Zone Managers

Reporting directly to Mr. Kaeser were seven zone managers, ages 30 to 46. Some had come up through the Heinz sales organization. A zone manager's salary and incentive together amounted to about $35,000, plus expenses. The incentive, based 40 percent on target volume attainment, 50 percent on the zone's gross return, and 10 percent on management evaluation, accounted for about 15 percent of the gross income. Each

[4]Ten districts had district sales assistants who supposedly handled recruiting and training tasks. Mr. Kaeser found, however, that they spent most of their time doing miscellaneous administrative tasks and actually devoted little time to recruiting and training.

zone manager was responsible for attaining "zone sales targets in the variety mix most contributory to profit. This he must do within budget limitations by assuring effective use of personnel resources for which he is responsible." The zone manager's job description further defined the nature and scope of the position as follows:

> He must keep the customer informed of promotions, advertising, and other consumer-oriented marketing devices. He must facilitate the consumer's ability to take advantage of these by assuring that the customer provides displays, positioning, inventory, and pricing to move the goods. . . . He has a deep trade involvement in marketing programs. Though primarily involved in selling, he also assists in market tests and surveys and provides feedback for program evaluation.
>
> He works with the general manager–field sales to establish sales targets and budgets, and with the district managers to plan and follow up on implementations. . . . He maintains intimate knowledge of each district's operations. He frequently contacts key-account personnel at high levels to build Heinz as a valuable supplier. He exercises judgment in devising and modifying sales tactics to take advantage of continually changing sales developments. . . . He oversees the selection, training, and development of the zone's district managers and other personnel and evaluates performance through systems of control and follow-up.

Each zone manager supervised two to six district managers. He supposedly visited customers "as needed," often in conjunction with the salesperson who normally contaced the account, in which case he usually dealt with merchandise managers and buyers. He was also expected to maintain contact with top management of key accounts. The frequency with which zone managers visited customers varied considerably from one zone to another, but Mr. Kaeser felt that none spent enough time with his customers. He also thought the number of zone managers could be reduced without seriously overloading the zone managers by merging the New York and Northeast zones.

Reduce Zone Mgrs.

Thirty-three District Managers

District managers' incomes ranged from $15,000 to $26,000, plus bonus and expenses. Their incentive plan was comparable to that of zone managers, and incentive accounted for about 15 percent of their gross income. Their average age was 38, and 80 percent had college educations.

Each district manager was responsible for volume and profit of his district. He managed up to six account managers and either one to three senior account managers or one to six area managers. (Except in Jacksonville, Florida, a district did not have both area managers and senior account managers.) Ten district managers had district sales assistants reporting to them.

The typical duties of a district manager were defined as follows:

1 Responsible for achieving planned sales goals and for keeping sales management informed of results and sales requirements in his district
   (a) Implements sales plans and personally participates in the improvement of selling effectiveness through:
      (1) Development of business with key accounts
      (2) Analyses of sales opportunities in each account and of planning programs to take advantage of such opportunities

2 Personally exercises control over key accounts, supplementing activities of area managers,[5] especially at the higher levels of these accounts (also personally becomes involved in the business of larger accounts handled by sales representatives)
   (a) Develops intimate knowledge of each customer's facilities, policies, and operations
   (b) Makes policy-level presentations through operations reports
   (c) Maintains contact with other account personnel (buyers, merchandise managers, etc.) to evaluate progress, to contribute selling ideas, and to act as management contact

414

3 Works with area managers to evaluate their effectiveness in carrying out approved programs
   (a) Studies performance records of each key account and meets with area managers individually to develop plans for sales improvement
   (b) Guides area managers in the development of specific sales programs for major accounts
   (c) Through constant contact with area managers, determines that key objectives are met
   (d) Assists, makes suggestions for, and counsels area managers in making presentations

4 Responsible for obtaining the greatest possible volume of business with the fewest possible sales personnel through effective deployment and utilization of personnel
   (a) Determines that all sales personnel are strategically located to provide maximum sales effort
   (b) Provides overall direction of sales representatives' time (with assistance of area manager)
   (c) Approves all changes in retail-store assignments of prescribed call frequency
   (d) Personally directs area managers to ensure their time is spent productively and that agreed-upon goals are accomplished

---

[5]For "area managers," account managers or senior account managers could be substituted throughout this job description.

5   Exercises close control over training, development, and supervision of area managers and sales reprsentatives
   (*a*) Maintains close contact with sales representatives to ensure firsthand evaluations of selling effectiveness
   (*b*) Schedules frequent work sessions with sales representatives in the field to communicate objectives directly

6   Responsible for communicating appraisals of all personnel under his direction to sales management
   (*a*) Develops specific improvement and development programs for each individual
   (*b*) Takes action, where and when required, on terminations, promotions, transfers, reassignments, and the like

7   Evaluates overall performance against objectives of the district on sales by district, by product, by major accounts, on retail objectives and achievements, on headquarters' objectives and achievements, distribution by accounts, departments by accounts, campaign performance, training, and expense control

8   Organizes, develops, and directs district staff meetings to communicate sales plans, ideas, and promotions, and for the personnel development of the district field sales organization

9   Keeps informed and reports on competitive pricing, sales, and promotion activity

10 Makes recommendations on such matters as quality, packaging, new varieties, product improvement and deletion, and the like

11 Cooperates with home office personnel in market tests of new or improved varieties

12 Sees that the district office operates efficiently in providing necessary warehouse, delivery, and office services

Mr. Kaeser was told that district managers called on customer headquarters "as needed," but specific data on their call frequencies were not available. They usually visited customers in conjunction with salespersons who normally handled the accounts. Occasionally, a district manager assumed primary responsibility for selling to headquarters of one major account. One district manager said he spent 40 percent of his time visiting customers, but he thought he was in the field a good deal more than other district managers. He visited about 30 of the 62 headquarters' accounts (chains, independents, and wholesalers) in his district in the course of a year. There were about 1,500 retail outlets in his district, but he did not visit them with any regularity.

Mr. Kaeser felt he could reduce the number of district managers to 30 without hampering their effectiveness by merging the Miami and the

Jacksonville districts, the Oklahoma City and Dallas districts, and the two districts in Los Angeles.

Mr. Kaeser was also concerned that several district managers had become lax in training and supervising their people. Though they received reports, few combined them into meaningful summaries to help in managing their business. Those who did compile useful reports for zone managers or corporate headquarters seldom got feedback from their superiors. Mr. Kaeser thought the district managers should be made to feel more confident and more a part of the Pittsburgh operation.

Ten District Sales Assistants

District sales assistants tended to be young (25 to 30 years old) college graduates who, as lower-level sales personnel, had demonstrated some managerial capabilities. Their salaries averaged about $9,000, and Heinz paid their sales expense. They were "responsible for initial and continued training of all-products salespeople, baby-food shelf stockers, and where applicable, retail merchandisers and retail specialists in all grocery activities and for sales management functions as assigned by the district manager." Their typical duties included:

1 Responsibility for recruiting sales personnel
   (a) Developing sources of sales applicants, such as colleges and universities, military, employment agencies, newspaper ads, and other companies in related fields
   (b) Performing special prerecruiting activities at colleges and universities
   (c) Participating in screening, interviewing, testing, and checking references of all sales applicants

2 Responsibility for initial and continued training of sales personnel
   (a) Providing initial training for all new sales representatives as scheduled in the "Training Guide"
   (b) Maintaining and personally following the continuous training of field sales personnel, as directed by the district manager and as scheduled in the "Training Guide"
   (c) Working on special training assignments with individuals of sales force, concentrating on areas of personal weaknesses, special objectives, or any outside training courses, such as communications and education in industry

3 Performance of sales management functions, as assigned
   (a) Aiding in developing sales presentations, implementing their use, and following up with the area manager, all-products salespeople, baby-food shelf stockers, retail merchandisers and specialists

(b) Planning and moderating all district sales meetings; also aiding in planning area meetings and other meetings, such as new product introductions or special training sessions

(c) Developing and administering, under direction of district manager, motivational programs such as sales contests, sales bulletins, etc.

(d) Periodic reviews of staff and sales representative sales reports and records, with special attention to accuracy, accomplishments, and allotment of time

(e) Aiding in preparation of the weekly district sales calendar

(f) Accompanying the district manager and the district staff personnel on headquarters calls and while working wih people in the field (minimum 3 days per week)

4 Gathering and communicating marketing information

(a) Working with staff and sales representatives in developing sources for obtaining accurate up-to-date competitive information

(b) Reporting all competitive activity (allowance, advertising, new-product introductions) to district, zone, and home-office personnel

(c) Gathering information to complete all reports requested by the district manager, zone manager, or divisional headquarters personnel

(d) Aiding district manager in maintaining up-to-date market information and in keeping the field sales personnel abreast of this information

(e) Maintaining up-to-date knowledge and the recapping of district store volumes

(f) Gathering and maintaining records on current retail pricing by individual accounts

Mr. Kaeser found that district sales assistants were doing very little recruiting and training but were spending most of their time doing jobs district managers did not want to do. He thought that in theory an assistant to a district manager could be a very useful position. If kept, however, he felt that its responsibilities should be made clear so that its occupants would not become, in essence, "assistant district managers." Moreover, if the district sales assistants retained recruiting and training responsibilities, their positions should be closely coordinated with zone sales trainers.

Sixteen Senior Account Managers

To qualify as a senior account manager, a salesperson had to be responsible for more than his proportionate share of district volume. For example, if a district had five people, each proportionate share of the volume was 20 percent. Anyone with over 20 percent share qualified as a senior account manager. Senior account managers (average age, 55) were usually more experienced salespeople who were responsible for one to seven key accounts. They received a salary plus a bonus which together amounted to $12,000 to $16,000, and Heinz paid their selling expenses. Most were located in the New York and Northeast zones.

The job description for senior account managers stated that they were "responsible for contacting key accounts to sell products and programs and also for the long-term improvement of business in these accounts by national and local sales building programs." It listed their typical duties as follows:

1 Contacting and maintaining good working relationships with key accounts to improve sales

2 Selling distribution, departments, displays, and retail pricing to key accounts and their retail affiliates

3 Contacting field supervision of key accounts in order to develop understanding of where major decisions are made and to provide a basis for getting agreement on important recommendations

4 Contacting various retail stores of their accounts for the purpose of department resets, pricing checks, handling spoils, and reviewing accomplishments of retail specialists and retail merchandiser[6]

5 Working with district manager to develop for each account specific business building programs

6 Developing effective brand presentations, making use of the information services the company supplies (SAMI, Nielsen, etc.)

7 Gathering and reporting data on competitive pricing, sales, and promotional activity

8 Maintaining panel store figures on assigned products

9 Making recommendations on such matters as quality, packaging, new varieties, and product improvement within the scope of their experiences

No hard data existed on exactly how much time senior account managers spent at headquarters and how much working with retail specialists and retail merchandisers. Mr. Kaeser was convinced, however, that they were failing to manage their people well because the retail tasks were not being performed satisfactorily.

---

[6]Retail specialists and retail merchandisers handled basic retail functions in the New York and Northeast zones only. The one senior account manager located in Jacksonville handled retail functions himself, while the three senior account managers in the West zone supervised employees of an independent company Heinz had contracted with to do the retail tasks.

Sixty-nine Account Managers

Account managers (average age, 50) had essentially the same responsibilities and duties as senior account managers. They sold merchandise at corporate headquarters of one to six key accounts. In the New York, Northeast, and West zones, they supervised some retail people. In other zones, they did the retail tasks themselves. Their base salaries and bonuses together ranged from $8,000 to $13,000, plus selling expenses.

Mr. Kaeser had no hard data on how the account managers spent their time, but he thought some were spending far too much time servicing their customers. Many actually did the day-to-day work of stocking shelves. In the New York and Northeast zones, they often sold promotions at retail and performed other tasks assigned to retail specialists and retail merchandisers. Mr. Kaeser felt this was an extremely inefficient use of their time and actually compromised their ability to sell.

Sixty-six Area Managers

About 85 percent of the area managers (average age, 35) were college graduates. Their salary and incentives together ranged from $8,000 to $13,000; Heinz covered selling expenses. Their general responsibilities were:

> Supervise day-to-day activities of all-products salespeople. Direct planning of area's headquarters and retail objectives to ensure meeting of sales targets. Take responsibility for seeing that all-products salespeople are trained and economically and productively developed. Work closely with account managers to determine that retail store objectives are carried out. Be responsible for realization of sales objectives for personal accounts (as assigned).

Typical duties included:

1 Supervision of activities of all-products salespeople as follows:
   (a) Responsibility for the performance of all-products salespeople, both retail and headquarters levels
   (b) Directing the planning of retail and headquarters' objectives and evaluation of performance attained
   (c) Seeing that sales personnel operate efficiently and economically
   (d) Working with all-products salespeople on a regular basis to evaluate their performance

2 Administering the deployment and utilization of sales personnel based on class of store and recommending changes in depth of coverage accordingly

3 Serving as the major link between account managers and sales personnel to ensure that retail store objectives reflect the needs and opportunities of key accounts

(a) Meeting with district manager and account managers, as necessary, to provide effective follow-up of key-account service

4 Responsibility for the selection, training, and appraisal of all-products salespeople

(a) Applying the recruiting and selection techniques as outlined in the *Salesman Selection Manual*

(b) Working regularly with all-products salespeople to develop effective performance in a working atmosphere

(1) Providing guidance in making presentations that secure desired results

(2) Demonstrating the efficient use of time in planning retail calls and coverage

(c) Evaluating continuously the overall performance of all-products salespeople

(1) Identifying outstanding individuals and recommending salary recognition, promotion, and/or transfer to more responsible activity

(2) Recommending separation of marginal or inadequate individuals

(d) Seeing that employees are familiar with and participate in such benefit programs as insurance, retirement, tuition aid, etc.

5 Developing and implementing plans to ensure satisfactory results for personal accounts

420

Area managers also supervised baby-food shelf stockers (except in the New York and Northeast zones where the stockers were supervised by senior account managers and account managers). Each area manager had two or three accounts whose headquarters he sold to. He seldom made regular visits to retail outlets, but he trained his people to do these retail tasks.

Area managers were expected to spend 2 days per month with each of their all-products salespeople. Mr. Kaeser found, however, that this benchmark was seldom met. He estimated that 50 percent of their time was spent planning, 40 percent with personal accounts, 10 percent doing administrative tasks, and 10 percent on miscellaneous tasks. He felt strongly that they spent too much time in their offices and, except for their own accounts, were not at all close to the trade.

One Hundred and Ninety-eight All-Products Salespeople

All-products salespeople (ages 21 to 62) generally called on headquarters and retail outlets of smaller chains and on independent grocery stores which made purchasing decisions at the retail outlet. In addition, some handled retail tasks for area managers' accounts. Each covered about 100 retail outlets. Their salaries and bonuses ranged from $8,000 to $11,000, plus selling expenses. Almost all were college graduates, and most had joined Heinz immediately after college.

The general responsibilities of all-products salespeople were defined as follows:

> Responsible for selling and merchandising all Heinz products and promotions. Responsible for departments, distribution, displays, and proper prices in all retail stores and headquarters' accounts (where applicable) within a prescribed territory.

Mr. Kaeser felt that, on the whole, these people were untrained and very loosely managed. The best retail coverage he found was one person who regularly visited 48 percent of his assigned stores. Most were extremely demoralized, because in recent months Heinz had eliminated about 100 baby-food shelf stockers, and many supermarkets expected them to pick up this task. Many in the New York and the Northeast zones were upset because they had heard that the company was about to eliminate retail merchandisers and retail specialists and that they would have to cover those jobs.

Eighty-four Baby-Food Shelf Stockers

By August 1973, Heinz had reduced its staff of baby-food shelf stockers to 84, down from almost 200 in 1972. Each made weekly 45-minute visits to 30 to 50 retail grocery stores and put up about 200 cases of baby food a day. Their normal contacts were with aisle clerks. Most were under age 30, and few had college educations. They received salaries ranging from $7,000 to $10,000, plus expenses.

According to their job description, their general responsibilities were as follows:

> Responsible for performing service and promotion work for baby food departments of retail stores assigned; selling new or improved distribution, improved departments, in-store special displays, use of POP [point of purchase] material; placing orders for baby foods; maintaining competitive and accurate pricing in accordance with chain or distributor policy.

Their typical duties were defined as follows:

1 Placing major emphasis in performing merchandising activities to increase sales volume of baby foods through retail stores

2 Planning effectively work objectives through identification of important opportunities in each account

Like other Heinz executives and other baby food manufacturers, Mr. Kaeser felt the grocery stores should be performing these tasks. While the baby-food shelf stockers generally covered their outlets well, turnover among them was high, and very few turned in accurate call records or data regarding competitive practices. All manufacturers were trying to phase them out, but the trade had become accustomed to the service and reacted very negatively to its being stopped. Mr. Kaeser thought it would be especially difficult to remove Heinz's baby-food shelf stockers from the New York and Northeast zones because Heinz's baby food controlled so little of those markets that customers would drop the line entirely if Heinz did not provide requested services.

Fourteen Retail Merchandisers

Retail merchandisers were located only in the New York and Northeast zones. According to their job description, they were "responsible for the maintenance and overall condition of all Heinz varieties and departments at retail store level." Their duties included all the basic retail functions that were discussed earlier. Each had about 170 stores which were supposedly contacted once every 3 weeks. It was thought, however, that the average call frequency was closer to once every 5 weeks. Their normal contacts were store managers, owners, and/or the persons in charge of ordering stock. Most retail merchandisers were under 25, high school educated, and received salaries of from $6,000 to $8,000, plus expenses.

Eight Retail Specialists

Retail specialists, also located only in the New York and Northeast zones performed essentially the same functions as retail merchandisers, except that they also did setups whenever necessary. Occasionally stores rearranged all their departments and called in retail specialists to move all the Heinz products. Such major setups often took a full day. Each retail specialist covered about 100 stores. Like the retail merchandisers, most were under 25, high school educated, and received salaries of from $6,000 to $8,000, plus expenses.

Mr. Kaeser felt strongly that Heinz was wasting a tremendous amount of money on the retail merchandisers and retail specialists. Account managers did not manage them well, their performance was marginal, and turnover was high. Mr. Kaeser wondered if the salespeople who did headquarters selling could and should perform retail tasks as well. He thought, however, that many of these salespeople would oppose taking on retail tasks on the grounds that it would greatly increase their work load and that such housekeeping chores were not a part of a professional salesperson's tasks.

MR. KAESER'S THOUGHTS ABOUT REORGANIZATION

Mr. Kaeser thought that the sales organization should be streamlined considerably. There were, he felt, too many poorly defined and poorly coordinated positions and too little control and direction of salespeople's daily activities.

In the past, the basic assumption of Heinz sales management had been that the company's primary job was to sell products into headquarters. Customers themselves, they thought, would see that the products were displayed well at retail. Mr. Kaeser felt that this assumption was becoming less and less valid as customers became more accustomed to the excellent retail services provided by some manufacturers, and he was sure that Heinz retail coverage was poor. He thought an all-products salesperson should average 170 retail calls per month. (Ten calls per day times 17 days equal 170 per month. He thought the remaining days would be taken up with miscellaneous activities—meetings, headquarters calls, commissary calls, illness, paper work, and so forth.) He wanted class I and II stores to be visited twice a month and class III and IV stores once a month. To help determine how many retail people were needed in each district, he had stores broken out by class by district. (See Exhibit 4 for number of stores by class by district and Exhibit 5 for details of sales personnel in each district.)

Exhibit 4 RETAIL GROCERY STORES BY SALES VOLUME CLASS PER WEEK BY DISTRICT

	Class I over $75,000	Class II $50,000 – $75,000	Class III $25,000 – $50,000	Class IV $10,000 – $25,000	Total grocery stores	Military commissaries	Total retail outlets
New York	9	221	851	493	1,574	0	1,574
New Jersey	110	352	625	110	1,197	0	1,197
Total New York zone	**119**	**573**	**1,476**	**603**	**2,771**	**0**	**2,771**
Baltimore	7	208	433	267	915	0	915
Boston	47	324	726	364	1,461	12	1,473
Buffalo	2	127	717	468	1,314	7	1,321
Philadelphia	66	373	466	260	1,165	0	1,165
Total Northeast zone	**122**	**1,032**	**2,342**	**1,359**	**4,855**	**19**	**4,874**
Cincinnati	40	111	451	363	965	3	968
Cleveland	35	141	458	276	910	1	911
Columbus	20	179	340	206	745	4	749
Detroit	68	366	757	400	1,591	5	1,596
Pittsburgh	9	118	529	226	882	1	883
Total East-central zone	**172**	**915**	**2,535**	**1,471**	**5,093**	**14**	**5,107**
Chicago	127	550	897	568	2,142	5	2,147
Indianapolis	8	33	435	317	793	7	800
Milwaukee	4	60	432	246	742	7	749
Omaha	5	76	320	402	803	3	806
St. Louis	29	143	306	562	1,040	7	1,047
St. Paul	20	114	355	398	887	7	894
Total North-central zone	**193**	**976**	**2,745**	**2,493**	**6,407**	**36**	**6,443**
Atlanta	45	251	699	—	995	11	1,006
Birmingham	14	99	858	178	1,149	14	1,163
Charlotte	20	195	1,412	217	1,844	42	1,886
Jacksonville	45	216	393	79	733	23	756
Miami	50	200	394	79	723	3	726
Total Southeast zone	**174**	**961**	**3,756**	**553**	**5,444**	**93**	**5,537**
Dallas	12	110	1,000	400	1,522	22	1,544
Houston	13	147	525	455	1,140	16	1,156
Kansas City	17	120	415	424	976	12	988
Memphis	13	55	248	384	700	5	705
New Orleans	15	31	519	184	749	11	760
Oklahoma City	6	60	217	175	458	5	463
Total Southwest zone	**76**	**523**	**2,924**	**2,022**	**5,545**	**71**	**5,616**
Denver	11	167	398	319	895	22	917
Los Angeles chain	64	467	396	4	931	20	951
Los Angeles distributor	45	190	676	494	1,405	15	1,420
San Francisco	57	67	932	256	1,312	28	1,340
Seattle	13	70	332	487	902	10	912
Total West zone	**190**	**961**	**2,734**	**1,560**	**5,445**	**95**	**5,540**
Total U.S. grocery	**1,046**	**5,941**	**18,512**	**10,061**	**35,560**	**328**	**35,888**

423

Review

Exhibit 5   SALES PERSONNEL, SEPTEMBER 1973

Districts	Zone managers	District managers	District sales assistants	Senior account managers	Account managers	Area managers	All-products salespeople	Baby-food shelf stockers	Retail merchandisers	Retail specialists	Total
New York		1	1	2	4	—	—	14	5	2	29"
New Jersey		1	1	3	2	—	—	14	4	2	27
Total New York zone	1	2	2	5	6	—	—	28	9	4	57
Baltimore		1	1	3	2	—	—	—	4	4	15
Boston		1	1	2	6	—	1	5	5	1	22
Buffalo		1	—	—	—	4	7	10	—	—	22
Philadelphia		1	1	2	3	—	—	—	5	3	15
Total Northeast zone	1	4	3	7	11	4	8	15	14	8	75
Cincinnati		1	—	—	2	2	6	—	—	—	11
Cleveland		1	—	—	2	3	7	2	—	—	15
Columbus		1	—	—	1	2	10	1	—	—	15
Pittsburgh		1	—	—	3	3	10	8	—	—	25
Detroit		1	—	—	2	4	15	—	—	—	22
Total East-central zone	1	5	—	—	10	14	48	11	—	—	89
Chicago		1	—	—	1	4	18	—	—	—	24
St. Louis		1	—	—	—	3	10	—	—	—	14
Indianapolis		1	—	—	1	2	4	—	—	—	8
Milwaukee		1	1	—	1	1	5	—	—	—	9
Omaha		1	—	—	2	1	6	—	—	—	10
St. Paul		1	—	—	3	3	7	—	—	—	14
Total North-central zone	1	6	1	—	8	14	50	—	—	—	80
Atlanta		1	—	—	1	3	5	5	—	—	15
Birmingham		1	—	—	3	2	3	7	—	—	16
Charlotte		1	—	—	1	4	14	1	—	—	21
Jacksonville		1	—	1	1	3	9	3	—	—	18
Miami		1	—	—	3	—	—	5	—	—	9
Total Southeast zone	1	5	—	1	9	12	31	21	—	—	80
Dallas		1	—	—	1	6	10	1	—	—	19
Houston		1	—	—	2	3	11	—	—	—	17
Kansas City		1	—	—	2	1	7	—	—	—	11
Memphis		1	—	—	1	2	7	—	—	—	11
New Orleans		1	—	—	1	3	3	8	—	—	16
Oklahoma City		1	—	—	—	2	3	—	—	—	6
Total Southwest zone	1	6	—	—	7	17	41	9	—	—	81
Denver		1	—	—	5	1	3	—	—	—	10
Los Angeles chain		1	1	—	4	1	3	—	—	—	10
Los Angeles distributor		1	1	1	4	—	3	—	—	—	10
San Francisco		1	—	2	3	—	2	—	—	—	16
Seattle		1	1	—	2	3	9	—	—	—	16
Total West zone	1	5	3	3	18	5	20	—	—	—	55
Total U.S. grocery	7	33	10	16	69	66	198	84	23	12	518

"Numbers in this column do not add up to subtotals because zone managers are not included.

Headquarters' calls, Mr. Kaeser reasoned, required an indefinite amount of time. He felt that, since field management often got involved in headquarters calls anyway, they should assume primary responsibility for them. Some all-products salespeople should continue to contact headquarters of small chains and independents, he thought, but the number of people and headquarters involved in this was so small that he felt it was not necessary to consider it when calculating the number of salespeople he needed.

FORTY-THREE General Foods Corporation: 1973 Sales Reorganization

On February 9, 1973, James L. Ferguson, president of General Foods Corporation, was considering alternative plans for restructuring the General Foods sales organization. During the past year, numerous plans had been proposed, but in recent months there had been a tendency to focus on two proposals. Mr. Ferguson had to decide whether to accept one of the two proposals, or whether more data should be gathered so that he could better evaluate the various approaches.

GENERAL FOODS CORPORATION

General Foods Corporation was one of the largest manufacturers of packaged food products in the world. In fiscal 1972 (April 1, 1971–March 31, 1972), it had net sales of $2,424 billion with earnings of $221 million before taxes and extraordinary items. Sales were divided as follows:

U.S. grocery	34%
U.S. coffee	29
Overseas	17
Canada	8
Institutional food service, fast food restaurants, and nonfood enterprises	12
	100%

The U.S. grocery business also accounted for about 34 percent net profits.

General Foods traced its origins to the Post Cereal Company which was founded in 1926. Over the years as new acquisitions were made, five relatively independent operating divisions—Birds Eye, Jell-O, Kool-Aid, Post, and Maxwell House—evolved to handle the U.S. business. While all divisions shared some corporate services, each had its own manufacturing, product management, and sales organizations. New products were assigned to the divisions more or less by historical accident, though channels of distribution and variations in selling tasks for different products were major considerations. The result was that each division came to be responsible for products which had very little apparent relationship to each other as products. For example, the Post Division handled cereal, syrup, pet food and Tang (a powdered breakfast drink mix). Products whose relationships were more obvious, beverages other than coffee, for example, were scattered among several divisions. Company management felt that this structure prevented them from seeing the interaction of General Foods brands with each other and with competi-

425

tive products and made them shortsighted and vulnerable to missing opportunities for new products. In fiscal 1972, the sales of these divisions were:

	$ sales (millions)
Post	331
Kool-Aid	102
Jell-O	211
Birds Eye	173
Maxwell House	703

In the spring of 1972, acting on the advice of outside consultants and an in-house task force, top management decided to restructure the product management organization according to six so-called strategic business units (SBUs)—coffee, beverages, breakfast, main meals, desserts, and pet food. An SBU was a group of brands held together by their natural interrelationship on the consumer's menu, rather than by manufacturing technology or distribution mode. For example, instead of having frozen vegetables in the Birds Eye Division, Minute Rice in the Jell-O Division, and Shake'n Bake and Good Seasons salad dressing in the Kool-Aid Division, all these products were brought togther in the main meal SBU.

426

Once the SBU concept had been accepted, several questions arose about how the SBU would relate to top management, whether and/or how they would be grouped together, and whether functions such as research and development should be centralized in one large corporate department or decentralized according to SBU or some divisional structure. By December 1972, it was decided that the five grocery SBUs would be grouped into three divisions, and the coffee SBU would make up the Maxwell House Division. The main meal and dessert SBUs would be combined into the Food Products Division, and the breakfast and beverage SBUs would comprise the Beverage and Breakfast Foods Division. Pet foods would be an entirely separate division because they represented the company's major growth opportunity if adequately serviced and merchandised to perform well in an intensely competitive, rapidly expanding market. Using 1972 figures, sales of the grocery divisions would be as follows:

	$ sales (millions)
Food Products Division	397
Beverage and Breakfast Foods Division	290
Pet Foods Division	130

(See Exhibit 1 for old and new grocery organizations and Exhibit 2 for product lines of former divisions and new SBUs.)

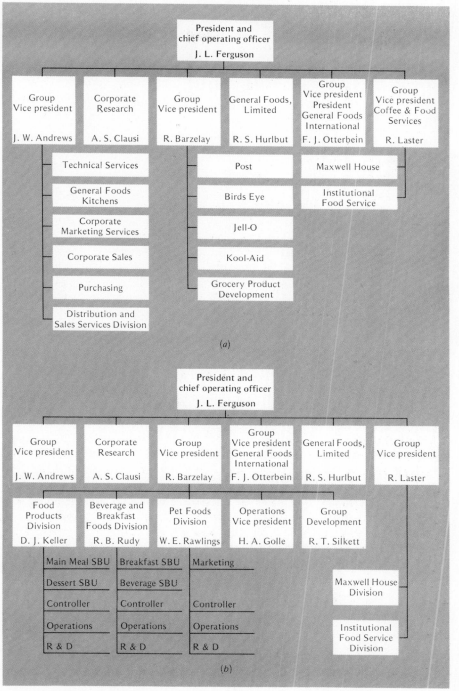

Exhibit 1 Sales reorganization, 1973. (*a*) Former grocery organization chart; (*b*) new grocery organization chart.

Exhibit 2 FORMER AND NEW DIVISIONS, SBUs, AND THEIR PRODUCT LINES, EXCLUDING MAXWELL HOUSE

Former divisions

Post Division	Jell-O Division	Birds Eye Division	Kool-Aid Division
Pet foods	**Desserts**	Birds Eye quick-frozen vegetables, prepared vegetables, International Vegetables	Kool-Aid soft drink mixes
Gaines Meal	Jell-O Brand gelatin dessert		Kool-Pops pop bars
Gaines Biscuits & Bits	Jell-O pudding & pie filling		Stove Top Brand stuffing mix
Gravy Train	Jell-O instant pudding	Awake & Orange-Plus frozen breakfast drink concentrates	Shake'n Bake seasoned coating mixes
Gaines-burgers	Jell-O tapioca pudding		Roast'n Boast oven cooking bags & sauce mixes
Prime	Jell-O golden egg custard mix	Birds Eye frozen concentrated orange juice	Good Seasons salad dressing mixes
Prime Variety	Jell-O Whip'n Chill	Birds Eye quick thaw fruits	Open Pit barbecue sauces
Top Choice	Jell-O Soft Swirl	Cool Whip nondairy whipped topping	
	Jell-O Cheesecake	Cool'n Creamy frozen puddings	
Syrup	Jell-O Lemon Meringue Pie Mix		
Log Cabin regular, buttered, and maple-honey syrups	D-Zerta low calorie desserts		
Country Kitchen syrup	D-Zerta low calorie topping mix		
	Dream Whip whipped topping mix		
	Minute tapioca		
Cereals			
Post Toasties	**Baking and canning products**		
Grape-Nuts	Calumet baking powder		
Grape-Nuts Flakes	Baker's chocolate		
Post Raisin Bran	Baker's coconut		
Post 40% Bran Flakes	Swans Down cake flour and mixes		
Fortified Oat Flakes	Certo and Sure-Jell fruit pectins		
Alpha-Bits	Minute rice & Deluxe rice mixes		
Super Sugar Crisp			
Frosted Rice Krinkles			
Crispy Critters			
Pebbles			
Pink Panther Flakes			
Tang and Start instant breakfast drinks			
Instant Postum cereal beverage			

Exhibit 2 (Continued)

New divisions and strategic business units

Pet Foods Division	Beverage and Breakfast Foods Division		Food Products Division	
Pet foods SBU	Beverage SBU	Breakfast SBU	Main meal SBU	Dessert SBU
Gaines Meal	Kool-Aid soft	**Syrup**	Birds Eye quick-frozen	Jell-O Brand gelatin
Gaines Biscuits	drink mixes	Log Cabin regular,	vegetables, prepared	dessert
& Bits	Kool-Pops pop bars	buttered, and maple-	vegetables, interna-	Jell-O pudding and pie filling
Gravy Train	Awake and Orange Plus	honey syrups	tional vegetables	Jell-O instant pudding
Gaines-burgers	frozen breakfast	Country Kitchen syrup	Minute rice and Deluxe	Jell-O tapioca pudding
Prime	drink concentrates		rice mixes	Jell-O golden egg custard mix
Prime Variety	Tang and Start instant	**Cereals**		Jell-O Whip'n Chill
Top Choice	breakfast drinks	Post Toasties	**Seasonings and condiments**	Jell-O Soft Swirl
	Birds Eye frozen	Grape-Nuts	Shake'n Bake seasoned	Jell-O Cheesecake
	concentrated	Grape-Nuts Flakes	coating mixes	Jell-O Lemon Meringue Pie
	orange juice	Post Raisin Bran	Roast'n Boast oven cooking	Mix
	Instant Postum	Post 40% Bran Flakes	bags and sauce mixes	D-Zerta low calorie desserts
	cereal beverage	Fortified Oat Flakes	Good Seasons salad	D-Zerta low calorie topping
		Alpha-Bits	dressing mixes	mix
		Super Sugar Crisp	Open Pit barbecue sauces	Cool Whip nondairy whipped
		Frosted Rice Krinkles		topping
		Crispy Critters		Cool'n Creamy frozen
		Pebbles		puddings
		Pink Panther Flakes		Dream Whip whipped topping
				mix
				Minute tapioca
				Birds Eye quick thaw fruits
				Baking and canning products
				Calumet baking powder
				Baker's chocolate
				Baker's coconut
				Swans Down cake flour and
				mixes
				Certo and Sure-Jell fruit
				pectins

THE SALES ORGANIZATIONS, FEBRUARY 1973

Through the years, the divisional sales forces had operated independently of each other. In February 1973, the Post, Jell-O, and Maxwell House Divisions all had completely direct-sales organizations, while the Kool-Aid Division used only brokers.[1] The Birds Eye Division was half brokered and half direct, depending upon the geographic area. While one division's regions and districts seldom coincided with those of another division, job titles generally did mean about the same thing from one division to another.

Each division was headed by a national sales manager, each of whom supervised regional managers. The regional managers were located at division headquarters, and their primary responsibility was supervising district managers. Even though regional managers maintaind contact with major accounts, they seldom had sole responsibility for selling and servicing any accounts. Their salaries ranged from $26,700 to $44,100. District managers handled headquarters selling tasks for a few major accounts, but their primary responsibility was to meet district volume and profit objectives by effectively managing area managers. Their salaries ranged from $23,000 to $36,800.

430

Area managers usually had a wide variety of tasks, including selling to headquarters of major accounts, occasionally doing some retail merchandising tasks, and supervising account managers and sales supervisors. Their salaries ranged from $15,400 to $25,500. Account managers were primarily headquarters salespeople, though some, especially those in the Post Division, also often performed retail tasks. Occasionally, an account manager in a large, sparsely populated geographic area would have a sales representative reporting to him, but such supervisory responsibility was rare. Primary responsibility for seeing that retail tasks were performed well was delegated to sales supervisors (salary range, $9,300 to $15,300). They occasionally performed retail tasks themselves, but they primarily trained and directed sales representatives who did the retail merchandising and shelf maintenance. In some sparsely populated areas, sales representatives sometimes also did some headquarters selling. Sales represesnatives' salaries ranged from $8,900 to $14,700. (See Exhibit 3 for personnel data by division.)

---

[1]Brokers were independent business people who handled both headquarters and retail selling tasks for a wide variety of noncompeting products manufactured by different companies. They received commissions of from $1\frac{1}{2}$ to 10 percent of net sales, depending on the products sold. They tended to concentrate on relatively small marketing areas and to develop strong long-standing relationships with the grocery trade in their specific localities. Some of them, however, covered large regions and employed hundreds of salespeople. They frequently handled products with high retail maintenance requirements and therefore had a larger retail force in any given marketing area than did most manufacturers. Brokers employed by the Kool-Aid Division received 4 percent commission on net sales, while Birds Eye Division brokers received $2\frac{1}{2}$ percent. On the average, these brokers represented 22 manufacturers.

Exhibit 3 DIVISIONAL SALES PERSONNEL DATA, FEBRUARY 1973

Title	Post Division	Maxwell House Division	Jell-O Division	Birds Eye Division		Kool-Aid Division	Total
				Direct	Broker		
Headquarters							
National sales manager	1	1	1	1		1	5
Regional managers	5	5	5	4		4	23
Headquarters staff	15	15	11	9		8	58
Statistical clerks and secretaries	15	15	13	11		11	65
Field							
District managers	26	25	22	20		17	110
Assistants to district managers	1	1	2	1		1	6
Area managers	4	6	4	0		0	14
Account managers	100	95	42	32		0	269
Sales supervisors	30	46	55	12		0	143
Sales representatives	211	269	232	90		0	802
Secretaries	26	25	22	20		17	110
Total	**434**	**503**	**409**	**200**		**59**	**1,605**
Broker organizations					46	63	109
Broker sales supervisors					81	103	184
Broker account managers					131	208	339
Broker sales representatives					452	529	981
Broker combination personnel[a]						167	167

[a]Combination personnel included part-time sales representatives plus some sales representatives who had both retail and headquarters responsibility.

The targeted *retail*[2] call frequency for all divisions depended on the size of the store:

	Weekly retail volume	Total no. stores in U.S.	General Foods call frequency
Class I	Over $75,000	1,000	Once a week
Class II	$50,000–$75,000	5,000	Every 2 weeks
Class III	$25,000–$50,000	18,000	Once a month
Class IV	$10,000–$25,000	10,000	Once a quarter
		34,000	

The average number of *retail* calls per day for each division was:

Post Division	5.7
Jell-O Division	6.3
Birds Eye Division	6.9
Kool-Aid Division	n.a.
Maxwell House Division	6.8

Comparable data for headquarters calls were not available.

It was estimated that, without restructuring, sales costs would be $36,211,000.

RESTRUCTURING THE SALES ORGANIZATION

It was widely held among top General Foods management that the product realignment by SBUs called for some restructuring of the sales

[2]Did not include headquarters calls.

organizations. It was decided, however, that the Maxwell House Division would not be included in the reorganization, because it had always been regarded as an efficient SBU and because its operations differed markedly from those of other General Foods divisions since coffee was very heavily promoted to the trade and sales were more heavily concentrated at the end of selling periods than in other divisions. Moreover, it was felt that tampering with so large and profitable an organization involved unjustifiable risks.

Process of Analysis

When top management originally discussed changing the merchandising organization to the SBU structure, the idea was that the sales and operations organizations would be centralized. All SBUs would share the same sales force and each salesperson would be responsible for all General Foods products. By autumn of 1972, management thought that one sales force was not necessarily the best and by no means the only approach. In September 1972, Leo Shepherd, vice president of corporate sales, was placed in charge of a five-man in-house task force that would work with an outside consulting firm to research various sales force reorganization plans. On November 9, 1972, the task force presented its findings on four major reorganization plans to a steering committee consisting of James Ferguson, General Foods president; Richard Laster, group vice president of coffee and food services; Ross Barzelay, group vice president of food products; James Andrews, group vice president of staff areas; and Magnus Bohm, senior executive vice president. The major alternatives discussed at this meeting were (1) one large centralized sales organization which would handle products for all SBUs;[3] (2) five separate sales organizations, one for each SBU; (3) four separate sales organizations which retained the structure of the existing divisional sales organizations, but to which products were assigned according to SBU groupings; and (4) a "high-frequency" and a "low-frequency" sales force to which products were assigned according to their retail merchandising needs.

During the course of the meeting, a fifth alternative gradually emerged. This plan was for two separate sales organizations to be made by combining the four existing divisional sales organizations into two and assigning products to them according to SBU groupings. By the time the meeting concluded, it was decided that the task force would further study and evaluate two sales organizations. The first would consist of two sales forces made by combining the existing Post and Kool-Aid forces into one and making it responsible to the pet foods, breakfast, and beverage SBUs and by combining the Birds Eye and Jell-O forces and assigning

[3]In this context and hereafter, "all SBUs" means *all but Maxwell House.*

them the main meal and dessert SBUs. The second organization to be studied consisted of two sales forces organized by high-frequency and low-frequency retail needs. Detailed national requirements for district managers, account managers, sales supervisors, and sales representatives were to be determined for two conditions: (1) if General Foods retained its current brokers and (2) if it went to a completely direct force.

The criteria by which alternative sales structures would be evaluated were:

Resource utilization Does the organization provide opportunities to leverage limited resources of skill and experience?

Manageability Does the structure facilitate control and coordination?

Accountability How clearly can results be attributed to individuals?

Flexibility Can local opportunities and trade differences be communicated and accommodated within the structure?

Responsiveness To what degree does the structure relate to different product needs identified by SBUs?

Efficiency Which alternative meets General Foods' need for cost effectiveness?

433

By February 1, 1973, the field evaluation of the two plans had been completed, and the task force presented its findings to the steering committee. On February 2, 1973, the consulting firm which had been working with the General Foods task force sent top General Foods management a memorandum which supported the direction in which the task force was proceeding, but did not go as far as the task force had gone. (See Exhibit 4 for consultants' memorandum.) On February 6, 1973, in response to the consultants' memorandum, Mr. Barzelay and Mr. Andrews circulated a memorandum supporting their position. (See Exhibit 5 for executives' memorandum.)

EXHIBIT 4
Memorandum from Consultants, February 2, 1973

Re: *U.S. grocery sales reorganization*

We do not feel that a clear-cut case has been made for either the main meal-dessert and beverage-breakfast-pet foods or the high-frequency–low-frequency sales forces. We therefore urge that an additional study be undertaken before committing to a target structure.

Specifically:

1 There is mounting evidence that a high-frequency–low-frequency sales force is not only feasible but offers GF significant long-term benefits at the retail level.

(a) Possible competitive advantage of high maintenance for products needing it (including current "stars" like dog food and new entries).
(b) Potential reduced sales costs for products with low maintenance needs.
(c) Potential for further cost savings by building a viable alternative to brokers (for example, enough personnel) in suitable areas.
(d) Allows extra push for top priority efforts (for example, introduction of pet foods).

2 Additionally, the task force report has indicated that there are major problems in the concept of sales forces controlled directly by two strategic business divisions (SBDs).
(a) Significant (+ 50%) coselling[a] for the SBDs by a sales force controlled by another SBD.
   (1) Even if pet foods is excluded, coselling is over 30% of group volume.
   (2) Given broker contracts, it is likely GF is locked into Kool-Aid brokers for 6 months.
   (3) Therefore, there will be a continuing need for coordinating processes between the three SBDs.
(b) No clear and adequate substitute for brokers which can offer high-frequency maintenance is available.
(c) Management responsibility for broker supervision is split and will require dual frozen contacts (retail and headquarters in both sales forces).
(d) Disparity of merchandising needs of products in each sales force could lead to individual priority assessments by each salesperson.
(e) There is a compromise in coverage frequency which could hurt some products (for example, frozen).
(f) There is no opportunity to give pet foods highest frequency maintenance.

3 Implementation of separate sales forces for each division could close off option of moving to high/low frequency model for at least 2 years.
(a) Separates low-maintenance products and sales forces (for example, Jell-O and Post, cereals and desserts).
(b) Separates high-frequency products (for example, envelope salad dressings and envelope soft drinks, frozen citrus and frozen vegetables).
(c) Moving to high-low frequency would require another total restructuring of the sales force at both retail and headquarters level.

4 Before any decision is reached, some fundamental issues may have to be resolved: specifically, in addition to those outlined in the 2/1/73 task force report.
(a) Are there viable alternatives to the Kool-Aid and Post and Birds Eye and Jell-O models that offer greater efficiency or effectiveness?
(b) Is there an opportunity to test the dimension and reality of hypothesized benefits from a high-low frequency force?
(c) What minimum retail call frequencies and coverage are required to maintain effective support of existing categories? What kind of personnel will be needed to provide this?
(d) What headquarters organization and planning processes are needed? How

---

[a]Coselling referred to having the main meal/dessert sales force sell frozen juice and drink concentrates in addition to all the products in the main meal and dessert SBUs.

will coordination of coselling needs be handled? What processes are needed? Who will make priority decisions?

(e) How can the group vice president ensure that sales resources are deployed optimally for implementation of category strategies? What mechanism will allow concentration of sales effort behind high priority needs (for example, introduction of new pet foods)?

(f) How many districts should there be to meet both trade and control needs? How should district organizations be structured to cope with increased spans of control and to be effective in accenting brand marketing programs?

(g) How many region managers are required to supervise effectively the district level and provide a responsive link with the headquarters organization?

(h) What revision in sales administration and communication systems will be needed to drive the organization and to account for and allocate fairly its expenses?

(i) How should existing ordering, distribution, and billing systems be adapted to service the new organization at least costs?

5 Therefore, the following course of action seems indicated:

(a) Do not "lock-in" on an organization structure for sales at this time; do not change assignments or consolidate the sales force by April.

(b) Assign all four sales forces to one person and charge him with responsibility for sorting out all the sales issues.

(c) Continue to resolve issues outlined in original study plan of November 9.

EXHIBIT 5

Messrs. Andrews and Barzelay's Memorandum, February 6, 1973

1 Our consultants disagree with our plan to consolidate our four sales organizations into two.

(a) They feel that the possibility of a centralized sales force—enabling a high-frequency/low-frequency coverage—is so appealing that we should continue to study this possibility for at least another 3 months. They suggest we delay any sales decision—allowing our four sales departments to operate as is but under the direction of one man—presumable reporting to Barzelay.

(b) They feel the delay is necessary as they're assuming that our present plan of merging Birds Eye and Jell-O, and Post and Kool-Aid would preclude another move—going to a centralized organization—for at least 2 years.

2 We believe that our present proposal—merging the four sales forces into two—is still sound.

(a) We continue to feel that a move from four separate organizations *directly* to a centralized structure is too risky. We could risk a complete breakdown in communications, budgeting, sales direction, and control during the transitory period.

Probably the greatest risk is setting up a communications and control system between each of the five SBUs and the two sales organizations in the centralized structure.

(b) The cost savings of our proposal are virtually equal to any centralized structure.

3 Our proposal recognizes that experience with our new two-force approach may turn up more problems than anticipated. If so, we can move to a centralized structure if that seems to be the best answer. Within 6 months to a year, our two new sales organizations should be working well.

If at that time we want to move to a high-frequency/low-frequency retail force, we can do so by reassigning products.

On the other hand, if we want to move to a retail organization that covers *all* GF products, we can do so.

EVALUATION OF ALTERNATIVES

1 One Centralized Sales Organization

The first plan was to have one centralized sales organization. Some executives felt that this plan was especially strong because sales territories could be organized geographically and costly overlapping of salespeople would be avoided. This was especially important in the so-called white area, the sparsely populated North and Central Western states which accounted for only 5 percent of total U.S. food volume. It would also enable each salesperson to call on and become very familiar with only a limited number of accounts. Finally, it would eliminate any customer confusion about which General Foods salesperson sold what.

However, other executives pointed to negative features. They felt that it would be extremely difficult to open communication channels between SBUs and the sales organization and that dissension would occur among SBU managers as they vied for the time and efforts of a single sales force. Moreover, they said it would be hard to hold an SBU manager accountable for the total performance of his unit, since he had no direct control over the salespeople.

Another argument against one centralized force was that the change was huge. Most salespeople would be assigned new territories, and all would have new products. Many believed that such a move might endanger one of General Foods apparent competitive strengths: strong experienced sales forces with good customer relationships. These relationships had been strained, some argued, by a restructuring of the Jell-O Division sales organization in selected districts. This restructuring had begun in fiscal 1971 and had not yet been completed. There was, furthermore, considerable doubt that a single salesperson could handle all General Foods products. A final negative factor was that the four existing divisional vice presidents then had far more power and responsibility than they would have as SBU managers. It was felt that, without being able to control operations, sales, and consequently, profits, they might become disenchanted and leave the company.

2   A Separate Sales Organization for Each SBU

Under the second plan, five new sales organizations would be created out of the four existing divisional sales organizations, and each SBU would have its own sales organization. A very strong argument in favor of this scheme was that each SBU manager would control his SBU's sales function, and could therefore better control the SBU's success or failure. Moreover, several SBUs would not be competing for the attention of a single sales force; rather, the salespeople could focus on the limited product line of a single SBU. Also, coordinating merchandising and sales programs would be easier than if several merchandising departments were drawing on a single sales force, and there would be a direct line of communication between customers and SBU managers.

Several negative features were cited, however. As with the first plan, this scheme would necessitate massive reshuffling of salespeople's territories and products. Many felt that salespeople would react negatively to such drastic changes and that important customer relationships would be endangered. Secondly, matching salespeople with SBU product groupings created numerous inefficiencies, because the beverage, main meal, and dessert SBUs all contained both frozen and dry groceries. Since there were different distributors and retail store buyers for frozen foods than for dry groceries, more customer contacts at headquarters would be required. At the retail level a person from each of these SBUs would have to service the same frozen food cases. Moreover, these three SBUs had some products which were being sold by General Foods' own direct salespeople and others which were being sold by brokers. If brokers were retained, responsibility for supervising them would be divided among the three SBUs. If they were eliminated, retail tasks for the SBU forces would increase considerably. An early analysis revealed that this alternative would require 1,590 salespeople (including managers) and would cost about $34,986,000.

437

3   Retention of the Four Existing Divisional Sales Organizations

The third alternative involved simply assigning products according to SBUs to the current four divisional sales forces. This plan would keep the existing structure intact, and the only change would be in individual salespeople's product lines. The idea was to assign the pet foods and breakfast SBUs to the Post Division sales force, the beverage SBU to the Kool-Aid Division sales force, the main meal SBU to the Birds Eye Division sales force, and the dessert SBU to the Jell-O Division sales force. While many people approved of the minimal change involved in this plan, they thought that it shared with alternative 2 the inefficiency of having more than one salesperson calling on each buying unit and shared with alternative 1 some of the problems of SBU—sales force coordination.

4 Two Sales Organizations Structured according to Merchandising Needs

In the course of researching various plans, members of the task force did time studies of headquarters and retail tasks of different products and held interviews with divisional sales managers and product group managers. They concluded that General Foods products fell into two categories according to their retail merchandising needs. The high-frequecy category included new products, frozen products, pet foods, and products packaged in envelopes and displayed in racks (Kool-Aid and dry salad dressing mixes), which required repetitive shelf maintenance by General Foods personnel in order to avoid "stockouts." Moreover, the number of outlets which had to be serviced was very high (approximately 34,000 outlets), because large volumes of the products, especially Kool-Aid, were sold through "mom-and-pop" and convenience stores which normally did not receive as much retail servicing as did supermarkets. General Foods currently employed brokers to handle most of these products. In fiscal 1972, high-frequency products generated sales of $373 million. The low-frequency category consisted of products such as cereals, Jell-O desserts, and cake mixes which required less retail maintenance in fewer stores (only about 29,000 outlets). In fiscal 1972, low-frequency products generated sales of $444 million. (See Exhibit 6 for products included in each category.)

438

The fourth plan called for the sales organization to be structured according to products' retail needs rather than according to SBU or geographic considerations. Products from all five SBUs would be assigned to either the high-frequency or low-frequency sales force, and different retail call frequencies would be established for each.

The task force felt strongly that the high-frequency–low-frequency forces had several advantages. First, they argued, the General Foods product mix was ideally suited to the high-frequency–low-frequency categories. Assuming they went to full direct forces, the wide product line of the low-frequency force coupled with the lean product line of the high-frequency force would create a fairly balanced personnel distribution (1.5:1) and make it easier to create uniform management responsibility across the organization. Second, driving-time efficiencies would result from the reduction of the number of salespeople calling on both headquarters and retail outlets, and only the high-frequency force would have to cover both frozen and dry products. Third, if brokers were retained for the present, this structure would allow better broker supervision, and if in the future General Foods decided to eliminate brokers, the transition to a direct sales organization would be easier because brokers would be in the high-frequency force only. Fourth, with the low-frequency force, there was a potential opportunity to reduce the

Exhibit 6 PRODUCT LINES OF HIGH-FREQUENCY AND LOW-FREQUENCY SALES FORCES

High frequency	Low frequency
Kool-Aid soft drink mixes	Tang and Start instant breakfast drinks
Kool-Pops pop bars	Instant Postum cereal beverage
Awake and Orange Plus frozen breakfast drink concentrates	*Syrups*
Birds Eye frozen concentrated orange juice	Log Cabin regular, buttered, and maple-honey syrups
Good Seasons salad dressing mixes	Country Kitchen syrup
Birds Eye quick-frozen vegetables, prepared vegetables, international vegetables	*Cereals*
Birds Eye quick thaw fruits	Post Toasties
Cool Whip nondairy whipped topping	Grape-Nuts
Cool'n Creamy frozen puddings	Grape-Nuts Flakes
	Post Raisin Bran
Pet foods	Post 40% Bran Flakes
Gaines Meal	Fortified Oat Flakes
Gaines Biscuits & Bits	Alpha-Bits
Gravy Train	Super Sugar Crisp
Gaines-burgers	Frosted Rice Krinkles
Prime	Crispy Critters
Prime Variety	Pebbles
Top Choice	Pink Panther Flakes
	Seasonings and condiments
	Shake'n Bake seasoned coating mixes
	Roast'n Boast oven cooking bags and sauce mixes
	Open Pit barbecue sauces
	Minute rice & Deluxe rice mixes
	Stove Top Brand stuffing mix
	Jell-O Brand gelatin dessert
	Jell-O pudding and pie filling
	Jell-O instant pudding
	Jell-O tapioca pudding
	Jell-O golden egg custard mix
	Jell-O Whip'n Chill
	Jell-O Soft Swirl
	Jell-O Cheesecake
	Jell-O Lemon Meringue Pie Mix
	D-Zerta low calorie desserts
	D-Zerta low calorie topping mix
	Dream Whip whipped topping mix
	Minute tapioca
	Baking and canning products
	Calumet baking powder
	Baker's chocolate
	Baker's coconut
	Swans Down cake flour and mixes
	Certo and Sure-Jell fruit pectins

439

number of stores covered or to make fewer calls on each store. Fifth, new products could initially be assigned to the high-frequency force for the introductory cycle, then reassiged if needs changed. Sixth, having fewer General Foods salespeople, each of whom would spend longer periods of time in stores, would facilitate the development of productive relationships at the store level. And finally, this structure would provide attractive careers and reduce turnover for professional merchandisers. On the negative side, the task force admitted that the high- and low-frequency forces represented a very significant short-term change.

To handle headquarters calls under a high-frequency–low-frequency plan, the task force offered three possible models. In model A, each SBU would have its own headquarters sales force, while the retail tasks would be handled by the separate high-frequency and low-frequency merchandising forces. This model had essentially the same advantages and disadvantages for headquarters calls as alternative 2 (a separate sales organization for each SBU) had for all calls. One advocate of the plan stressed the motivation and accountability benefits derived from having each SBU manager control at least the salespeople who sold his products into headquarters. He admitted, however, that coordination of headquarters and retail efforts could be extremely difficult. This plan would require about 1,555 salespeople (including managers) and would cost about $33,471,000.

In model B, a single separate sales force would handle all headquarters tasks, while the high-frequency and low-frequency merchandising forces would handle retail tasks. This model had many of the same strengths and weaknesses for headquarters selling as alternative 1 (one large centralized sales force) had for all selling. Its opponents stressed that, as in model A, it would be difficult to coordinate SBUs, headquarters salespeople, and retail merchandising people. Furthermore, they argued, structurally it was not directly responsive to the needs of SBUs, and it dispersed SBU group identification. Personnel and cost requirements were not calculated for this model.

Model C called for two sales organizations. One would have some people who handled headquarters tasks for high-frequency products and others who handled retail tasks for those products. The other sales organization would have some people to handle headquarters tasks for low-frequency products and others to handle retail tasks for those products. A major strength of this plan was that coordination problems between retail and headquarters salespeople would not be as difficult as in other models. Moreover, only one General Foods salesperson would contact any given frozen food distributor or buyer, and if the decision to retain brokers was made, they would be easier to accommodate and supervise since they would all be included in the high-frequency force. Accountability for success or failure with any given customer could be assigned directly to the headquarters and retail salespeople responsible for that customer. The major weakness of model C was that, since the sales force structurally were not directly responsive to the SBUs, coordination and communication problems between SBUs and salespeople would exist. One result might be that information about local field activities, which would aid greatly in planning promotions and performing market tests, would not be readily communicated to SBU headquarters where those plans were formulated.

5 Combining the Four Existing Divisional Sales Organizations into Two and Assigning Products according to SBU Groupings

Members of the task force concluded that the option to combine the four existing divisional sales organization into a main meal-dessert sales force and a breakfast-beverage-pet foods sales force would save considerable travel time and money, as it would decrease the number of salespeople calling on any single account. Moreover, since it could be implemented with the current direct forces, it would not require the drastic upheavals in the sales organization that alternatives 1, 2, and 4 would cause. It also lacked, of course, some of their advantages.

The problem of how to sell frozen products since some would be in each divisions had to be solved. Dealing with the frozen food problem could, they thought, help answer the question of how brokers should be handled in any reorganization, an issue which was of great concern. This particular reorganization plan would allow them to use the districts where frozen products were currently brokered to see what divisional-broker communication problems would develop if brokers continued to handle all frozen products. If the decision was made to go to completely direct sales forces, the problem of whether to have each sales force handle its own frozen products had to be resolved. Many felt strongly that the main meal-dessert sales force should sell the frozen juice and drink concentrates, even though they were in the breakfast SBU, because doing so would avoid dual frozen food contacts at both headquarters and retail levels and, therefore, would be much more economical. Others felt, however, that the decision could not be made on the basis of initial cost alone because, they argued, considerably better sales and servicing would result if each divisional sales force had direct control over all products in its division.

441

A major negative feature of the main meal-dessert–breakfast-beverage-pet foods option was that it did not provide for the separation of products by merchandising need and frequency. For example, in the main meal-dessert division, either the requirements of frozen food coverage would cause overcoverage of Jell-O products, or frozen foods would suffer from undercoverage if Jell-O call patterns were set appropriately. Moreover, since the main meal-dessert force would be about three times larger than the other force and, if brokers were retained, control over them could be divided between both forces, various management problems would be created. (See Exhibit 7 for task-time summary for headquarters and retail calls of various options, Exhibit 8 for sample calculations by which personnel and cost requirements were determined for the main meal-dessert–breakfast-beverage-pet food option and the high-frequency–low-frequency option, Exhibit 9 for total personnel and cost requirements of these options, and Exhibit 10 for a cost summary.)

Exhibit 7 TASK-TIME SUMMARIES

Task-time summary for headquarters calls (average minutes per call)

Sales organization	Talking with buyer	Merchandising	Waiting	Administrative tasks	Other	Driving	Average total time per call
Former Post Division	32.3	3.5	21.3	15.3	3.5	25.0	100.9
Former Jell-O Division	19.4	2.8	31.9	15.0	7.2	30.3	106.6
Former Birds Eye Division	31.1	13.0	32.0	6.5	7.4	20.1	110.1
Former Kool-Aid Division	Not available, but thought to be similar to Birds Eye						
High-frequency force	50.7	14.8	67.5	13.9	5.0	20.7	172.6
Low-frequency force	45.3	14.2	42.8	24.7	8.7	28.9	164.6
Main meal-dessert force	Not available						
Beverage-breakfast-pet food force	Not available						

Task-time summary for retail calls (average minutes per call)

Sales organization	Presentation	Merchandising	Shelving and other	Administrative	Driving	Contact of more than one buyer	Average total time per call
Former Post Division	4.8	1.3	24.9	6.0	8.5	0	45.5
Former Jell-O Division	7.0	1.0	22.8	6.0	8.5	0	45.3
Former Birds Eye Division	6.0	1.7	21.1	6.0	8.5	0	43.4
Former Kool-Aid Division	Not available						
High-frequency force	9.7	2.6	42.0	6.8	8.5	5.0	74.6
Low-frequency force	10.7	2.0	42.6	5.3	8.5	0	69.1
Main meal-dessert force	13.6	2.6	51.7	6.0	8.5	5.0	87.4
Beverage-breakfast-pet food force	6.8	2.0	31.5	6.0	8.5	5.0	59.8

Exhibit 8 SAMPLE CALCULATIONS FOR DETERMINING SALES REPRESENTATIVES REQUIREMENTS FOR THE HIGH-FREQUENCY/LOW-FREQUENCY SALES FORCES

Including Kool-Aid brokers and Birds Eye brokers where in force

	Total stores	×	Min. per store	=	Total time	=	Retail worker days	×	Contacts per quarter	=	Retail days required per quarter	÷	Retail worker days available	=	Retail personnel needed
High frequency															
Retail sales force current Birds Eye broker areas	18,705		29.8		557,409		1,327		3		3,981		49.5		80
Birds Eye direct personnel market areas	10,295		68.4		704,178		1,677		5		8,383		41.75		201
Total	29,000				1,261,587		3,004				12,364				281 256[a]
Low frequency (no Birds Eye products are in this product group)															
Retail sales force current Birds Eye broker areas	18,705		69.1		1,292,515		3,077		3		9,232		41.75		221
Birds Eye direct personnel market areas	10,295		69.1		711,384		1,694		3		5,081		41.75		122
Total	29,000				2,003,899		4,771				14,313				343 312[a]

Direct personnel situation

	Total stores	×	Min. per store	=	Total time	=	Retail worker days	×	Contacts per quarter	=	Retail days required per quarter	÷	Retail worker days available	=	Retail personnel needed
High frequency															
Total Birds Eye + Kool-Aid, dog food, GSSD	29,000		74.6		2,163,400		5,151		5		27,754		41.75		617
Low frequency															
Total Jell-O + Post (– dog food) + Shake'n Bake, Open Pit	29,000		69.1		2,003,900		4,771		3		14,314		41.75		343
Total															960

[a]Adjustment for Shake'n Bake, Good Seasons salad dressing, and Open Pit Bar-B-Que sauce remaining brokered.

Exhibit 9 PROJECTIONS FOR TOTAL PERSONNEL AND COST OF MAIN MEAL/DESSERTS–BREAKFAST/BEVERAGE OPTION AND HIGH-FREQUENCY/LOW-FREQUENCY OPTION, CURRENT BROKER SITUATION, AND TOTAL DIRECT FORCE

	Current broker situation					Total personnel and costs
	Sales representatives required[a]	Sales supervisors required[a]	Account managers required[a]	District managers required[a]	Total	
Main meal-desserts						
Personnel	377	54	87	18	536	
Compensation and benefits	$ 16,000	$ 23,000	$ 23,000	$ 31,000		
Total cost of GF salespeople	$ 6,050,000	$1,250,000	$2,000,000	$600,000	$ 9,900,000	
Birds Eye brokers					3,250,000	
Total main meal-dessert cost					**$13,150,000**	
Breakfast-beverage						834
Personnel	189	27	64	18	298	
Compensation and benefits	$ 16,000	$ 23,000	$ 23,000	$ 31,000		
Total cost of GF salespeople	$ 3,050,000	$ 650,000	$1,500,000	$600,000	$ 5,800,000	
Kool-Aid brokers					6,300,000	
Total breakfast-beverage cost					**$12,100,000**	**$25,250,000**
Total direct force						
Main meal-desserts						
Personnel	764	109	127	18	1,018	
Compensation and benefits	$ 16,000	$ 23,000	$ 23,000	$ 31,000		
Total cost	$12,250,000	$2,500,000	$2,950,000	$600,000	$18,300,000	
Breakfast-beverage						1,383[b]
Personnel	224	32	91	18	365	
Compensation and benefits	$ 16,000	$ 23,000	$ 23,000	$ 31,000		
Total cost	$ 3,600,000	$ 750,000	$2,100,000	$600,000	$ 7,050,000	**$25,350,000**

Current broker situation

	Sales representatives required[a]	Sales supervisors required[a]	Account manager required[a]	District manager required[a]	Total	Total personnel and costs
High frequency						
Personnel	256	37	60	18	371	
Compensation and benefits	$ 16,000	$ 23,000	$ 23,000	$ 31,000		
Total cost of GF salespeople	$ 4,100,000	$ 850,000	$1,400,000	$600,000	$ 6,950,000	
Birds Eye brokers					3,250,000	
Total high-frequency cost					**$10,200,000**	
Low frequency						875
Personnel	312	45	129	18	504	
Compensation and benefits	$ 16,000	$ 23,000	$ 23,000	$ 31,000		
Total cost of GF salespeople	$ 5,000,000	$1,050,000	$3,000,000	$600,000	$ 9,650,000	
Kool-Aid brokers					6,300,000	
Total low-frequency cost					**$15,950,000**	**$26,150,000**
Total direct force						
High frequency						
Personnel	617	88	116	18	839	
Compensation and benefits	$ 16,000	$ 23,000	$ 23,000	$ 31,000		
Total cost	**$ 9,900,000**	**$2,050,000**	**$2,700,000**	**$600,000**	**$15,250,000**	
Low frequency						
Personnel	343	49	129	18	539	1,378
Compensation and benefits	$ 16,000	$ 23,000	$ 23,000	$ 31,000		
Total cost	**$ 5,500,000**	**$1,150,000**	**$3,000,000**	**$600,000**	**$10,250,000**	**$25,500,000**

[a]In calculating the personnel needed, members of the task force did not attempt to adhere strictly to existing job classifications and responsibilities. Rather, they simplified the functions of each position considerably. For the calculations in this chart, they assumed that sales representatives would have only retail responsibilities, sales supervisors would only supervise sales representatives, account managers would only handle headquarters selling, and district managers would have only supervisory responsibility. Area managers were not listed separately because the functions they performed were included in the calculations of the sales supervisors and account managers needed.

[b]These numbers assume that frozen juice and drink concentrates would be sold by the main meal/dessert sales force.

445

Exhibit 10 TOTAL COST COMPARISON (000's omitted)

Broker	Cost	Direct	Cost
Main meal/dessert direct	$ 9,900	Main meal/dessert	$18,300
Birds Eye brokerage	3,250		
Total main meal/dessert cost	$13,150		
Breakfast-beverage direct	$ 5,800	Breakfast-beverage	7,050
Kool-Aid brokerage	6,300		
Total breakfast/beverage cost	$12,100		
Total strategic business division forces	**$25,250**	**Total direct forces**	**$25,350**
High-frequency direct	$ 6,950	High frequency	$15,250
Birds Eye brokerage	3,250		
Total high-frequency cost	$10,200		
Low-frequency direct	$ 9,650	Low frequency	10,250
Kool-Aid brokerage	6,300		
Total low-frequency cost	$15,950		
Total high-frequency – low-frequency forces	**$26,150**	**Total direct forces**	**$25,500**

Section
TEN
Recruiting and Selection

FORTY-FOUR   Recruiting and Selection

INTRODUCTION

This note and the one which follows on training are concerned with the process of building the sales force, one of the major tasks facing sales managers. This can be accomplished in an evolutionary way in which the sales force is constantly changed to keep pace with a changing marketing strategy and sales program. It can also happen, although less typically, in a revolutionary way in the creation of a new sales force because of (1) creation of a new company or division, (2) a switch from independent representatives or "piggybacking"[1] to a company sales force, and (3) a shift in organization. In the third case, a firm may choose to use a different sales force for a particular product line or for calls on a particular type of an account.

The process of building a sales force consists of recruiting, selecting, and training the salespeople and field sales managers. If the sales force is totally new, the program will be on a large scale, but it will not differ substantially from the evolutionary process. It is important to plan meticulously the creation of a new sales force, since the effort is great and there is no existing organizaion or procedure for the task. Because evolutionary changes are gradual, on the other hand, they can be programmed through the existing organization and procedures.

This note is concerned with both recruiting and selection. Recruiting refers to the generation of applicants and selection to the choice of "hirees" from among the applicants. Much of the note will be devoted to consideration of the recruiting and selection process, and the criteria upon which salespeople are hired. The final section of the note discusses the recruiting and selection of sales managers.

---

[1]"Piggybacking" is the process by which one company uses the sales force of another to sell its merchandise.

Before confronting these topics, it may be useful to place recruiting and selection in perspective by considering which needs the process and criteria must meet and the relationship of recruiting and selection to other aspects of sales force management.

THE ROLE OF THE SALES FORCE

Probably the most critical part of the recruiting and selection process is the *detailed* definition of the role of the sales force. The role of the sales force determines the attributes, qualities, and nature of the salespeople who are needed, and that, in turn, sets the process and the selection criteria.

Among the determinants of the role of the sales force are (1) the importance of personal selling within the marketing strategy of the company, (2) the complexity of the selling task, and (3) the profit impact of each salesperson.[2] The specific tasks of the salesperson must be carefully determined. In some situations, for example, the major task is meticulous servicing, involving, perhaps, inventory control, setting up displays, etc. In other situations, the primary task is a complex selling one, involving detailed cost justifications and lengthy executive presentations.

450

Once the role of the sales force is determined, a complete job description and a detailed set of salesperson specifications should be developed. This will ensure that the end product of the process—the new sales recruit—is appropriate for the position as it actually exists and that the position is appropriate for that person. Often, recruiters are shortsighted in attempting to hire "the best qualified salespeople possible." Although this sounds good, it can lead to the hiring of overqualified people who leave once the realities of their role become apparent. The rapid turnover generated by such a situation is expensive to the company, wasteful for the recruit, and preventable.

Careful role consideration will not ensure effective recruiting and selection, but haphazard or no role consideration will almost certainly ensure ineffective recruiting and selection.

RECRUITING AND SELECTION AS A PART OF SALES FORCE MANAGEMENT

Recruiting and selection are an important part of the total sales force management program and should be considered in relation to the other aspects of the program.

[2]For a more detailed discussion of the importance of the complexity of the selling task and the profit impact of each salesperson, see the note "Sales Costs and Budgets."

Turnover

As alluded to earlier, overqualified hiring can lead to high turnover. The hiring of underqualified applicants can also lead to high turnover. Poor performance either frustrates new persons and they leave of their own accord, or it frustrates management and the ineffective salespeople are fired.

The relationship is often circular. High turnover necessitates a great deal of hiring. Open territories with their attendant lost sales, account servicing problems, and lost accounts generate strong pressure for rapid hiring. The rapid hiring of a large number of salespeople almost invariably leads to a shortened selection process and less stringent criteria—the tendency to fill the open territories with "warm bodies." This, in turn, leads to a poor match of the recruit and the job, and thus continued high turnover which leads to another iteration of the process.

High turnover is not always bad. If the cost of hiring and training a recruit is low, termination cost is low, initial sales are reasonable, and the job is such that it is hard to hire people for it, then high turnover may be a more cost-effective approach than careful screening. This, apparently, is the philosophy used by many large insurance sales forces. Hiring is rapid and initial training cost is kept low by minimizing the training provided and by making it part time, and in the field. Termination costs are low because the account does not need regular servicing. Initial sales are reasonable through sale to relatives and friends. So, the process is as follows: (1) many are hired and briefly trained; (2) all attempt to sell to relatives and friends, and some who are more aggressive attempt to sell to others, too; and (3) some are successful and decide to stay, but the unsuccessful leave or are fired. Thus, the real selection takes place after hiring.

Many low-powered,[3] mundane selling tasks are carried out in such a rapid turnover, posthiring selection mode. It is common in most retail selling situations.[4] Most high-powered, complex selling tasks, on the other hand, require a more stable sales force with more careful recruiting and screening.

Training

One decision here can be described as "make or buy." Some sales forces, particularly large, sophisticated ones, hire young recruits and provide relatively extensive training. Other firms, usually smaller ones, hire experienced sales personnel. In the first instance, the company is

---

[3]See the note "Sales Costs and Budgets" for a definition of this term.

[4]These are positions in which salespeople sell merchandise to the ultimate consumer, often in a retail store.

spending training dollars but hiring a lower-priced recruit. The situation is reversed in the second instance.

Another decision involves the relationship between training and recruiting-selection through turnover. Some sales managers argue that good training provides confidence and improves sales performance, thus decreasing turnover. The decreased turnover then cuts recruiting and selection costs. Thus, in a sense one is trading training costs for hiring costs.

The Size of the Sales Force

This is a decision of "better versus more." Some sales forces work on the basis of hiring fewer but better salespeople who can effectively cover more accounts and obtain higher sales. Others work on the other concept of hiring more but of expecting less from each. Here again, recruiting and selection dollars are being traded against other dollars.

Clearly, the specification of the role of the salesperson and the formulation of the sales program as a part of the marketing strategy will be the primary determinants of the more-versus-better decision. The situation grows more complicated, however, when one considers the alternatives of various sales organization structures.[5] There are a variety of ways to divide selling tasks so that less qualified people can be used for less demanding tasks.

Supervision

This is similar to the training issue raised above. Some firms hire inexperienced people and supervise them closely. Others give free rein to more experienced sales recruits. The tradeoffs are again dollars versus dollars and can best be resolved by considering marketing and sales policies.

General Relationships

The task of sales force management is to allocate funds efficiently and effectively so that the optimum level of compensation, training, supervision, etc., is present. This is indeed a difficult task.

Perhaps of even more concern than its inherent difficulty is the propensity of many sales managers to disregard the tradeoffs which are present. Each aspect of sales force management cannot be considered by itself. They must be combined into a coherent focused program with due regard for many objctives (some of which conflict) and many sales force management approaches.

[5]See the note "Organizing the Sales Effort" for more on these alternatives.

SELECTION CRITERIA

For many years this has been perhaps the most talked about subject in sales force management. Researchers constantly looked for the "ideal sales personality." While there may be no magic formula, it is possible to shed considerable light on the criteria relevant to choosing salespeople.

Empathy and Ego Drive

Empathy and ego drive seem to be the two traits most important for many typical selling situations. Mayer and Greenberg have discussed their relevancy in detail.

Empathy is the ability to understand the other person's position and feelings. It is important to make clear that empathy does *not* involve liking the other person. Empathy is needed so that the salesperson can understand the needs of the prospective buyer and can predict the buyer's response to various approaches the salesperson uses.

Ego drive provides the need to make the sale. Mayer and Greenberg view it as a desire for conquest and state, "A subtle balance must be found between (a) an ego partially weakened in precisely the right way to need a great deal of enhancement (the sale) and (b) an ego sufficiently strong to be motivated by failure but not shattered by it."[6]

453

In essence, the ego drive provides the horsepower to make the sale and the empathy provides the rudder. Empathy without ego drive leads to the "nice person" who cannot close the sale while ego drive without empathy leads to a "bulldozer" who closes some sales but who is often a disaster in a continuing relationship.

Other Personality Attributes

The human personality is a wonderfully complex thing, with many relationships among a person's attributes. There are many theories of personality, many of which conflict with each other. Psychologists and other investigators find it difficult to even agree on definitions of attributes, so that this section as well as the preceding one should be viewed with caution. *They are clear oversimplifications* but, hopefully, are operationally useful.

Empathy and ego drive seem to be the two necessary basic attributes for all selling jobs involving any degree of persuasion, as opposed to "sales" jobs which are purely service oriented.

The definition of balanced ego drive put forth above clearly implies the importance of self-confidence. The salesperson needs confidence to stand up to frequent refusals to buy. The self-confidence also helps the

[6]See in the bibliography Mayer and Greenberg, "What Makes a Good Salesman," p. 121.

salesperson develop within the buyer a feeling of confidence in the seller. It may even help to raise the buyer's self-confidence, thus making it possible for the prospective buyer to make a decision to buy.

"Likability," whatever that means, is another useful quality but it clearly is not at all necessary. In fact sometimes being too likable indicates that there is too much empathy and too little ego drive—the salesperson cannot close the sales. Many fine salespeople are just not likable. They understand their customers and prospects, but they do not put forth the "hale fellow well met" stereotype of the fictional salesperson. On the other hand, it is clearly easier, under most conditions, to do business with someone you like.

Ego drive often involves other related attributes such as aggressiveness, need achievement, etc. It is hard for the layman to separate these, and the expert often cannot do it either.

Self-discipline is important in some sales situations, typically those in which the salesperson must work independently, that is, covering territories as opposed to inside sales. Without self-discipline the salesperson can become sloppy about call strategy and territory management (scheduling calls, preparing itineraries, etc.). High ego drive alone can probably keep him out on the road making calls. Self-discipline improves the efficiency of the process.

Physical attractiveness can help open the door, but it probably is not very useful after that. In fact, it might engender jealousy on the part of the prospect or customer.

Intelligence is an interesting variable. Its importance varies with (1) the complexity of the product and selling task and (2) the intelligence of the buyer. Complex products and tasks probably require enough intelligence to understand them well. The seller usually has to be intelligent enough to function at the buyer's intelligence level if there is a need for rapport. Too much intelligence on the seller's part, on the other hand, might frighten the buyer.

Other similarities have been found to be important.[7] While obvious similarities (or perceptions of similarities), such as education, earnings, political party, religion, etc., may have some effect in simpler selling situations and possibly even in more complex selling situations, in those selling situations requiring intimate contact and rapport, similarity in life outlook, life-style, and basic values is probably more important. Clearly those basic similarities may be influenced by the more obvious similarities.

Honesty is clearly important in any situation involving repeated contact with the same prospects or customers. The salesperson who blatantly lies or takes advantage of the customers will, over time, be

[7]F. B. Evans, "Selling as a Dyadic Relationship: A New Approach," *American Behavioral Scientist*, vol. 6, no. 9, May 1963, pp. 76–79.

discovered by the customers. People may forgive an occasional lack of competence (for example, I don't know which product to use in that situation), but will not forgive a lack of integrity. It undermines the organizational as well as the personal relationship.

Experience

Experience can be classified in one or more of five categories:

1 With the customer or specific customers and prospects (for example, an exbanker hired by a computer firm to call on banks).

2 With the product (for example, an applications engineer hired to sell computers).

3 With the company (for example, an expediter moved to selling)

4 With the geography of the territory (for example, an inexperienced salesperson to sell in his hometown)

5 In selling (for example, an insurance salesperson hired to sell computers)

The importance of each of these types of experience varies with the selling situation and the amount of training (formalized and on the job) which the company can offer.

If the company can offer no training, it clearly is necessary either to hire an experienced salesperson or to pay for an inexperienced one to learn for himself on the job, if that is possible. Experience is also clearly more important when a company is expanding into an area it does not know well and where it is not known. For example, the first salesperson hired to sell an existing product to a new customer-industry category should probably have knowledge of that industry.

If the product is complex and must be sold to technically complex buyers, a person experienced with the product has a clear advantage. If, on the other hand, the selling job requires in-depth customer knowledge but not a great degree of product knowledge, a customer-experienced salesperson is appropriate. Often, of course, the product and customer knowledge come together. Many apparel and consumer durable goods manufacturers hire people with retail experience because they know retailing and the product category.

If the salesperson's prime task is to relate one's company to the customers (for example, obtaining bids on custom products, managing complex delivery or installation situations, etc.), "inside" experience with the company can be very useful. Some firms, in fact, use inside jobs (for example, expediting, sales order processing, inventory control, estimating, etc.) for training salespeople.

Selling experience is usually meaningful only if the selling situation is similar, at least in complexity. On the other hand, selling experience does enable the prospective recruit to understand the job being described better.

General Note on Criteria

It is relatively easy to develop a set of criteria for the "perfect salesperson" in a particular situation. It is often difficult to evaluate a particular person on these criteria. Perhaps even harder is the job of finding an appropriate person with an acceptable set of attributes and experience.

Almost always, hiring is a series of tradeoffs—tradeoffs between looking more, on the one hand, and hiring one of the prospective salespeople on the other, and tradeoffs among prospects. Perfection is not often attained. Realism and objectivity in setting criteria add immeasurably to the efficiency and effectiveness of the process.

THE RECRUITING AND SELECTION PROCESS
The Primary Responsibility of Whom?

456

One of the most important questions facing sales managers is who has the primary responsibility for recruiting and selection. In a small sales force the decision is usually clearer than in a large, multilevel one.

In large sales forces the responsibility often lies with the first-level sales manager who usually receives assistance of an immediate superior. In high turnover, active hiring situations, the first-level sales manager often has exclusive responsibility. When the sales force is seen as a training ground for sales, marketing, or general managers, headquarters people, either professional personnel executives or top-level managers, often become involved.

One of the intriguing aspects of the situation is the small number of companies which use professional personnel people to recruit salespeople. It is usually an internal sales force decision. This is apparently contrary to most hiring decisions. Some sales forces have recruiting specialists who are either staff managers or a special level of line management. This position is normally used as a development slot for a sales manager who is passing into higher responsibilities.

The Recruiting Process

There are three main ways to find recruits: (1) personal contacts; (2) outside personnel agencies, including college placement offices; and (3) advertisements.

There are three major sources of recruits: (1) people within the company; (2) people within the industry, either working for a competitor or a current or prospective customer; and (3) others.

People within the company are usually found through personal contact or possibly through the internal "advertising" of the opening by "posting" or the "grapevine." Hiring from within has several advantages: (1) the person knows the company; (2) the company knows the person and has a better chance of obtaining an objective or at least an honest assessment of his past performance; (3) it builds morale within the firm; (4) the applicant is likely to have greater company loyalty, especially if he perceives the sales job as a good opportunity. Often, however, such people are not available.

People within the industry can be approached in all three ways. When a particular person is desired, it is often possible to approach him directly or through an intermediary such as a supplier or customer. If a lower profile is desired, a personnel agency is sometimes asked to approach the person, or an advertisement specifically directed to the individual may be placed in a trade journal. When the approach is personal, it can be open (for example, we have an open territory in California and would like to discuss it with you) or less direct (for example, we have an open territory in California and were wondering if you knew of anyone who would be good for the job).

457

Sometimes the desire is not for a particular person. Then, "asking around," hiring an agency, and advertising in a trade journal are the typical approaches. Sometimes, industry associations will have placement services. Particularly good sources of leads are customers. Asking a customer to whom the company is close, "Who are the best salespeople calling on you?" is excellent. Another source is the company's purchasing department, because many supplier salespeople are knowledgeable about the total industry. Another source is the sales force. Many companies provide a bonus to salespeople who suggest applicants who are accepted. Such applicants usually have a better-than-average understanding of the job and the company.

When the recruiting goes beyond the industry, the usual sources are agencies and advertisements in more general publications. Here again company personnel are sometimes used as sources of leads as are important community leaders such as merchants and clergymen. Again the company's own purchasing department is a useful source.

There are important tradeoffs to be made in the recruiting process. The most important involves the quality versus quantity issue. Many sales managers believe that the more recruits they have to select from the better their selection will be. This is not at all true. First, large numbers of recruits tend to hurt the selection process because they overload it. It is a much easier task to find the best candidate among 5 than among 500. Finally, numbers do not ensure quality. The question is not how many recruits but how many good recruits. In fact, it could be argued that the ideal recruiting process would produce but one recruit per opening—a fully qualified one.

This implies that the recruiting process should be the first step in the selection process. Self-selection is in many ways the most effective and efficient means of selection. Thus, the recruiting screen should be adjusted so that inappropriate candidates are screened out at this stage. To do this, communication with prospective recruits should not point out only the good points of the job; the disadvantages should be reported also. The necessary qualifications should be spelled out in detail. Compensation should be clearly stated, so that only those with appropriate aspirations are recruited.

The Selection Process

Before considering the selection process proper, it should be clear that in some situations the recruiting process is the first step, and in others the initial employment period is the last. If training is expensive or time consuming, or both, or termination difficult or expensive, using the initial employment period as the last part of the screening process is poor policy. Careful maintenance of records will allow sales managers to ascertain whether or not posthiring turnover is higher than desired.

The selection process can be viewed as a screen whose mesh size can be adjusted. If the process is long and detailed, few recruits make it through. If it is short and crude, many may get through, but some who should have been rejected will pass. This analogy forces sales managers to consider one of the key questions in selection. Is it better to allow unqualified people to be hired or to allow qualified people to be rejected? Clearly, the ideal process makes neither error, but realistically, errors can be expected. The traditional bias has been to reject good applicants rather than accept poor ones. In some complex selling situations, that may be shortsighted. Unfortunately, just as it is difficult to estimate sales which were not made, it is difficult to identify good performers who were rejected.

The typical selection process usually includes all or most of the following:

1 An initial screening, either over the telephone or by a résumé or application letter

2 A review of an employment application

3 A first face-to-face interview

4 A reference check

5 A test of some sort

6 An in-depth interview with the applicant and often the spouse

7 Interviews by higher management

8 An interview by a staff or consulting psychologist or by a personnel professional

A candidate may be rejected at any step in the process.

The initial screening is designed to cut down the number of people entering the core of the selection process. It is usually based on a series of "knock-out" questions often intended to determine a prospect's stability and responsibility. Among others, it might include, "How many jobs have you held in the past three years?" Recent laws regarding equal employment opportunities have limited the nature of allowable questions.[8]

Many personnel experts believe that a standard application form makes assessment much easier. People reviewing many such forms can easily find the information they are looking for. Professional-level salespeople also use résumés, but are often asked to supplement them by filling out an application form. Good forms facilitate communication between interviewer and interviewee.

There are many types of face-to-face interviews. Some interviewers prefer a more structured approach, while others use a free-form style with such questions as, "Tell me about yourself." The stress interview is preferred by some interviewers. It can take many forms, ranging from rudeness and inattention on the part of the interviewer to constant aggressive probing and questioning. The interviewer should be attempting to ascertain ego drive, empathy, honesty, sincerity of interest, presentation ability, etc. Sometimes interviewers lose sight of their purpose in an effort to "get inside the recruit's gut." Gimmicks often get in the way of open two-way communication.

One purpose of the interview is for the interviewer to present a picture of the company and the job. If the interviewer will be the new salesperson's immediate supervisor, another purpose should be to determine if their mutual "chemistry" is right. Gimmicky interviews usually preclude the accomplishment of either objective.

One approach often used by sales managers is to ask the applicant to sell something: " . . . hand the prospect a stapler, a pencil, or any other object that's handy and ask him to 'sell' it to them." A pro should be able to sell anything," McElveen says. "The one thing he's got to do is to ask for the order. Seven of ten, he's discovered, fail to do so."[9] While this may be useful for determining certain qualities, such as quickness and general approach, it can only be one of many parts of the interview. Too many

[8]For some indication of allowable questions, see *Business Week*, May 26, 1975, p. 77, "How to Keep Biases Out of Job Interviews."

[9]"How Friedrich's McElveen Finds Super Salesmen," *Sales Management*, August 5, 1974, p. 4.

sales managers look for the "one way" to assess selling skills. The "make him sell something" may be part of the way, but it is certainly not *the* way. Many good applicants, in fact, might fail the test or be "turned off' by it.

If the applicant passes the face-to-face interview, a reference check is usually the next step. It is, of course, important to respect the applicant's desire not to prejudice his position with his current employer. Much can be learned by checking references. Often, casual recruiters do not understand the importance of the reference check. "They always say nice things" does not mean that references are not valuable sources in the data-gathering operation. It just means that the interviewer must be resourceful.

Usually two kinds of data can be ascertained from reference checks. First are factual data, such as dates of employment. Falsification of such data can indicate an honesty problem in general, as well as a need for something to be hidden. The importance of checking such factual data cannot be overemphasized. One has to be terribly naïve to expect that all of the data on all of the applications are true. Such naïveté is dangerous.

460

Second, the reference check can provide subjective and objective material on performance and behavior. Clearly the interviewer's goal is to separate the subjective from the objective. It is important to remember that biases can be both against and for an individual. Usually, the applicant will try to provide only "good" references, but by finding out the applicant's immediate superiors at previous employers and checking with them, the interviewer can gather useful data. If the reference is clearly biased toward the applicant in general, questions such as, "If you were hiring this individual today, what qualities would you think it most important to develop?" are useful.[10] Such in-depth probing and follow-up is time-consuming but very worthwhile.

Many firms use some form of testing, such as tests for intelligence, similarity in tastes to successful salespeople, personality traits, and a wide variety of other attributes.[11] As might be expected, some recruiters swear by these tests and others at them. Some find them a useful crutch to ease the difficulty of making a complex decision. Others will not use them at all. Both extremes seem wrong. The tests are another tool in an exceedingly complex task. The way to use them well is:

1 Use them as only one input of the decision and do not depend upon them to do the work of other parts of the process (for example, reference checking).

[10]This example was provided by Russell Taylor of Taylor Associates.

[11]The use of tests has been recently changed by equal employment opportunity considerations. In general, testing which results in discrimination is illegal even if the intent is without malice. It is the burden of the employer to prove the relevance of the tests to the job.

2 Set the objectives for each test. Know why it is used and what it should provide. For example, if there is no reason to believe that intelligence is a determinant of success in the selling task, do not test for it.

3 Carefully check the validity of the test and the testers. Ensure that they are competent professionals.

The next steps usually involve a series of in-depth interviews with the recruiter who has the prime responsibility, a staff or consulting psychologist, or higher management. Some recruiters like to interview the candidate on "his turf," often with the spouse present. There are several reasons to involve the wife (or husband, if the applicant is female). First, if travel is involved, the spouse should know and concur. Second, a problem-filled home life often spills onto the job. Thus a good marriage helps to indicate some degree of stability. Finally, a good interviewer can often learn a great deal from watching the two people interact. It also relieves tension and allows for a more natural communication to take place.

Other recruiters prefer to take the prospective recruit back to headquarters to "see him respond to a new environment." This also enables the interviewee to see the company in depth and to meet other executives. Probably, this is particularly important in small company situations where the salespeople must work intimately with headquarters personnel.

The interview can be with a single interviewer or with more than one. Double or triple teaming of the applicants can be used to increase stress or encourage meaningful discussion. It also allows the interviewers to observe the candidate as he or she responds to the other interviewers' comments and questions. This is a luxury not afforded by one-on-one interviews.

If the sales force is used as a training ground for sales, marketing, and general managers, higher-level executives are often involved in the interviews. Their insight as well as their ability to provide applicants with a policy-level view of the firm can be very valuable.

One of the most controversial parts of the selection process is the use of a psychologist or psychologically oriented personnel professional. This usually brings out even stronger feelings than the testing issue. Many sales managers seem insulted at the thought that someone without "experience on the road" can be as insightful about people as they are. The well-trained competent psychologist does seem to have something to offer precisely because the stock-in-trade of the profession is analysis and not persuasion. But, as with other selection tools, the role of the psychologist should be clearly spelled out. The psychologist should not make the hiring decision either implicitly or explicitly. A psychologist is a staff expert who recommends and counsels but does not decide.

Clearly, any psychologist chosen should be competent and should understand the selling task as well as the organization. The psychologist will be much more useful if he or she interviews the candidate rather than just reviews test results, although some sales managers are very impressed with the results of test interpreters.

If the selection process is to work well, each part must function effectively. Even more importantly, the total process must fit well together. Haphazard or quick recruiting will not produce appropriate selections.

WOMEN AND MINORITY GROUP MEMBERS

Of late there has been greater government and public pressure to hire women and minority group members. In addition, and of more long-term importance, the need for good salespeople requires that prospective talent not be turned away because of ill-founded tradition.

The sales manager who goes out specifically to hire a woman or minority group member is probably doomed. The approach should be to hire a competent salesperson who might (preferably) be a woman or minority group member. Competence is a requirement. In the past, it may have been a requirement that would be hard to meet, but increasingly there clearly are women and minority group members with the relevant experience and training.

Those companies which have made an effort to do such hiring seem to be pleased, and somewhat surprised, by the good results. There have been few if any problems integrating women and minority group members into the sales force, and adverse customer reaction has not been present. On the contrary, the reception generally has been good, and this goes all the way to such untraditional instances as a mother-daughter team selling welding supplies and equipment.

Any sales manager who attempts to avoid hiring women and minority members is shortsightedly passing up a good pool of prospective talent as well as courting government and public censure and sanctions.

462

RECRUITING MANAGERS

The general topic of management recruiting is beyond the scope of this note. Two points should be made briefly here, however. First, the sales force is a fine hunting ground for managers. The salesperson is exposed to the market in a very intimate fashion and learns how to cope with people and disappointment. Selling is good training for management.

Second, good salespeople do not necessarily make good sales managers. It is a poor decision to make a good salesperson into a mediocre sales manager. The ego drive necessary for good selling sometimes makes it impossible for a salesperson who is used to doing it himself to learn to do through other people. In addition the inbred independence of many salespeople precludes the team play necessary for many management activities.[12]

BIBLIOGRAPHY

A reading list is appended. Its purpose is not to be exhaustive but to be selective and representative. Many pieces have been written on recruiting and selection, and particularly on "important sales personality traits."

Dartnell Corporation: *How to Recruit, Select and Place Salesmen*, Chicago (various dates since it is revised regularly and classified usually as a serial publication).

Greenberg, Herbert, and David Mayer: "A New Approach to the Scientific Selection of Successful Salesmen," *Journal of Psychology*, vol. 57, 1964, pp. 113–123.

Lavin, Henry: "Not Wanted: 'Aggressive' Industrial Salesman," *Management Review*, May 1972, pp. 2–11.

Mayer, David, and Herbert M. Greenberg: "What Makes a Good Salesman," *Harvard Business Review*, vol. 42, July-August 1964, pp. 119–125.

Miner, John B.: "Personality and Ability Factors in Sales Performance," *Journal of Applied Psychology*, vol. 46, no. 1, 1962, pp. 6–13.

Newgarden, Albert (ed.): "Recruitment and Selection" in *The Field Sales Manager*, New York: American Management Association, 1960, pp. 251–311.

Sales Management: "Everything You Always Wanted to Know about Hiring," February 21, 1972, pp. 17–24, 29–31, 33–36, 38, 40, 42, 44, 46.

---

[12] The note "Field Sales Management" provides additional comments on recruiting managers.

FORTY-FIVE Paper Distributors, Incorporated (C)

In early February 1975, Bill Hogarth was in the process of hiring a new salesperson to handle the general line of printing customers with some possibility over time of specializing in large accounts.

The three prospective employees were Harry Scott, an older experienced ink salesperson; Robert Nordstrom, a dynamic young man with an impressive sales record; and Leon Okarowski, an experienced paper mill representative. Mr. Scott had been recommended to Bill Hogarth by Fred Harvey, his second highest-paid salesperson. Mr. Harvey was a close personal friend of Mr. Scott and he spoke highly of him. Bill Hogarth had a letter from Mr. Scott (Exhibit 1) and his own comments from the initial screening interview (Exhibit 2). Mr. Hogarth believed it unnecessary to ask Mr. Scott for a completed employment application. It seemed inappropriate in view of Mr. Scott's relationship and background. Bill Hogarth's brother Dean had been unable to interview Mr. Scott.

Mr. Nordstrom had been referred to PDI by a local employment agency who had previously referred people (both sales and nonsales) to PDI. The agency received 10 percent of the annual wages of anyone placed with PDI. Bill Hogarth had his own interview notes (Exhibit 3), those of his brother Dean (Exhibit 4), and Mr. Nordstrom's application (Exhibit 5).

Bill Hogarth had learned of Mr. Okarowski from Barry Shaughnessy, sales manager of a St. Louis paper merchant at a paper merchants' convention. Mr. Okarowski was employed by Parker Paper Mills which owned the distributorship for whom Mr. Shaughnessy worked. Mr. Okarowski had been briefly interviewed in St. Louis by Dean Hogarth who was there for other business-related matters. Bill Hogarth had Dean Hogarth's memo on Mr. Okarowski (Exhibit 6) as well as Mr. Okarowski's application (Exhibit 7).

Bill Hogarth had to decide whether to bring Mr. Okarowski to Pittsburgh for an interview and whether or not to hire one of the three.

Issue — Hire one of three.

EXHIBIT 1
Harry Scott's Letter to William Hogarth

January 21, 1975

Dear Mr. Hogarth:

My friend Fred Harvey has informed me of a sales opening with your company that I would like to pursue. As a matter of fact, Mr. Hogarth, I believe we met, however briefly, at the opening kickoff dinner for the United Fund drive held at the Duquesne Club. As Fred has probably mentioned to you, I have been very close to the printing industry in this city for almost thirty years. Having supplied them with printing ink through thick and thin, shortages and whatever for these many years, I feel that if you were to make a few phone calls, you would find my credentials well in order and my reputation in this industry well respected. Candidly, I know nothing about paper, but I understand printers and lithographers, their pressures and their requirements.

As you probably know, we have sold Allegheny Ink Co., and I have chosen not to stay with the current owners.

I feel that I can offer your company my sales skills, well-established reputation and the very highest level contacts with every major printer within one hundred miles of Pittsburgh.

I'm looking forward to an opportunity to have lunch with you to explore further the promise of the possibilities that lie ahead for both of us. I will call you early next week to arrange a meeting.

Very truly yours,
Harry A. Scott

EXHIBIT 2
Interview Notes on Harry Scott by Bill Hogarth

465

February 4, 1975

Comments

Handsome appearance

Tremendous prestige

Articulate and cultivated

Well-established contacts

Personable

Knows everyone in this industry well, including many of our best customers and those prospects we want the most

Impressive, warm, friendly

Does not know paper well (would we have trouble teaching him?)

Extremely smooth and confident

Made in the $50,000 to $60,000 range for the last 10 years; seems impressed by money but doesn't seem hungry

Seems satisfied with his position in Pittsburgh

Great community contacts

Age, 54

EXHIBIT 3
Interview Notes on Robert Nordstrom by Bill Hogarth

January 30, 1975

Comments

Good dresser

Articulate

Strong manner

Probably a high-pressure salesman

Challenging attitude during interview—comes right after me

Moves in quickly for a close on the job

Hobbies: skydiving

Good war record

Excellent grasp of selling techniques (can he master the detailed nature of our business?)

Has 2 years of college—probably sufficient for our business

Considers himself an accomplished salesman, not a trainee

EXHIBIT 4
Interview Notes on Robert Nordstrom by Dean Hogarth

Comments

Bright

Aggressive

Enthusiastic

Seems to have a good grasp of selling fundamentals

Knows nothing about paper but probably could learn

Gutsy

Money-motivated

Opportunistic

References need checking?—probably all good

Dresses well

Good talker

A bit cocky

Immature?

1. IDENTIFYING DATA

PRINT NAME	LAST
	Nordstrom
	FIRST
	Robert

MIDDLE: S.

SOCIAL SECURITY NUMBER: 039-15-9887

DATE (today): April 29, 1975

PRESENT STREET ADDRESS: 321 South Street

HOW LONG: one year

CITY: Turtle Creek

STATE & ZIP: Pennsylvania 19115

TELEPHONE NUMBER	AREA	*AGE	*BIRTH DATE
765-8990	412	27	February 14, 1948

PREVIOUS ADDRESS

STREET	CITY	STATE
5055 Windham Street, Turtle Creek, Pennsylvania		

WEIGHT	HEIGHT	*CITIZEN
172 lbs.	6' 1"	☒ YES ☐ NO

APPLICATION FORM FOR SALESMEN

To The Applicant: This application for employment by sales candidates has been suggested by the National Paper Trade Association as a specially designed form for the paper industry. All information will be treated confidentially. No attempt will be made to check or verify any information without prior approval from you. Complete this form in your own handwriting.

2. PERSONAL DATA

Number of children: 0

List their ages: _____ _____

Date available for work: at once

PRESENT MARITAL STATUS (CHECK ONLY ONE)

☒ Single never married ☐ Married (Date) _____ ☐ Separated (Date) _____
☐ Divorced (Date) _____ ☐ Widowed (Date) _____ ☐ Engaged

If presently married or engaged, were you married before? ☐ Yes ☐ No
Do you support anyone other than your wife and children? ☐ Yes ☒ No

Who should be notified in case of accident or illness? NAME Mrs. A.A. Stutler
ADDRESS 345 South Street, Turtle Creek   TEL. NO. 765-3355

3. EDUCATION

Encircle highest grade or number of years completed ➤

	GRADE SCHOOL	HIGH SCHOOL	JR. COLLEGE	COLLEGE
	4 5 6 7 8	1 2 3 4	1 2 3	1 ② 3 4 5 6 7

Names and locations of schools attended (full time attendance during days only)			Years attended from to	Did you graduate?	Course of study or degree earned
HIGH SCHOOL(S)	CITY	STATE			
Turtle Creek High	Turtle Creek	Pa.	1963-1966	yes	diploma
COLLEGE(S)	CITY	STATE			
University of Pittsburgh	Pittsburgh, Pa.		1967	no	psychology
University of Pittsburgh	Pittsburgh, Pa.		1969	no	psychology

Are you presently enrolled in any course or program of education? ☐ Yes ☒ No

If so, elaborate _____

4. PHYSICAL STATUS

What is your present health? ☒ Excellent ☐ Good ☐ Fair

How is your hearing? excellent   How is your vision? excellent

Date of last physical exam April, 1969   Conducted by Major Franzen

Date of last hospitalization Nov.'69-Apr.'69   Name of hospital General McCord Hospital

Reason for hospitalization Wounded - shrapnel and small arms fire - multiple wounds

Which of the ailments or diseases listed below have you ever had?

☐ Diabetes   ☐ Tuberculosis   ☐ Migraine   ☐ Malignancy
☐ Asthma   ☐ Alcoholism   ☐ Kidney trouble   ☐ High blood pressure
☐ Hernia   ☐ Arthritis   ☐ Heart trouble   ☐ Nervous breakdown
☐ Allergies   ☐ Epilepsy   ☐ Fainting spells ☐ Stomach trouble
☐ Backaches   ☐ Foot trouble   ☐ Drug addiction   ☐ Other (specify)

If you now have any of the above, then encircle the box you checked.

Name and address of your family physician none

Are you willing to take a physical exam for employment? ☒ Yes ☐ No

*It is recommended that the employer check local and state laws. If local or state laws prohibit employers from requesting this information, omit.

Exhibit 5 Mr. Nordstrom's application.

5. EMPLOYMENT HISTORY

Begin with your last position or present position if you are now employed (omit military duties).

JOB NO.	NAME OF EMPLOYER	STREET ADDRESS, CITY AND PHONE NUMBER	YOUR JOB	MONTH — YEAR FROM — TO	EARNINGS
1 ☐	Universal Encyclopedia Name of Immed. Supervisor Mr. Poppe	Pittsburgh, Pa. Reason for Leaving --	book sales man	9/74 - Present	18,000
2 ☐	Timberline Recreation Properties Name of Immed. Supervisor Bob Amster	Wheeling, West Va. Reason for Leaving business bad	salesman recreation land	8/72-4/74	28,000
3 ☐	World Book Encyclopedia Name of Immed. Supervisor J.H. Linghren	Pittsburgh, Penn Reason for Leaving to make more money	book salesman	9/70-8/72	22,000
4 ☐	Name of Immed. Supervisor	Reason for Leaving			
5 ☐	Name of Immed. Supervisor	Reason for Leaving			

(Check (X) the box opposite any job we will **not** be able to contact for references.) DID YOU HAVE AN INVESTMENT IN OR WERE YOU AN OWNER OR PART OWNER OF ANY OF THE ABOVE FIRMS? ☐ Yes ☒ No   Indicate which ones by job number_____
Are you related to any of the above employers? ☐ Yes ☒ No.
Which of the above jobs did you like best? Job No. 2_____ Why? Fast moving, high dollar volume_____

Do you wish to be in business for yourself someday? ☒ Yes ☐ No   When?__unknown_____
In what line or industry?_____unknown____

6. ECONOMIC AND FINANCIAL STATUS

(Check all the boxes that apply to you.)

☐ Own your home ☐ Condominium or coop	☒ Rent home or apt. ☐ Rent a furnished room	☐ Live in a transient hotel ☐ Own your furniture

Living with: ☐ Spouse   ☒ Alone   ☐ Parents   ☐ Roommate(s)   ☐ Friends or Relatives

☒ Own your car(s)   ☐ Rent your car   Make 'cuda   Year 1974   Car Payments $ 210 Mo.

Monthly payments: (Check all that apply)
☐ Home mortgage   ☐ Bank loan   ☐ Medical-Dental
☐ Air line acct.   ☐ Bank card acct.   ☐ Finance Co.
☐ Furniture Co.   ☐ Insurance Co.   ☐ Other (specify)

Where do you have bank accounts?
First National Bank of Pittsburgh
TC Branch

☐ Wife is employed   ☐ Part time   ☐ Full time   ☐ Temporarily   Type of work_____

Are you bondable?
☒ Yes
☐ No

Insurance you carry:
☐ Ordinary life   ☐ Term life   ☐ Hospitalization
☒ Auto   ☐ Major medical   ☐ Income protection
☐ Insurance on wife   ☐ Insurance on children   ☐ Tenant's-homeowner's
☐ Other (specify)_____

Do you receive more than $3,000 annually from outside sources? ☐ Yes ☒ No

Exhibit 5 *(Continued)*

7. MILITARY SERVICE IN THE ARMED FORCES OF THE UNITED STATES ONLY

[x] Veteran   Date entered service June, 1967   Type of work performed Infantryman

Type of discharge Honorable   Date discharged April 1969   Branch of service Army

Do you get a disability pension? [x] Yes   [ ] No

Highest rank achieved   Sergeant

If deferred from military service, state reason

Training received in military service   none

*Present draft classification	Draft board number and location
discharged veteran	not applicable

Are you now a member of a military reserve organization? [ ] Yes   [x] No

Name and location of group   Rank

8. THIS SECTION FOR SALES TRAINEES ONLY

Scholastic standing while in

High school   College

College majors and minors

Clubs and organizations in college. (Including varsity sports and omit religious, racial, or foreign national groups.)

Principal source of your spending money while in college	% of expenses earned

Different jobs (part time and summer) you held while in high school and college

What sales experience have you had?

Why do you believe you are interested in a sales career?

What is your long-term ambition in life?

469

9. THIS SECTION FOR APPLICANTS WITH PREVIOUS OUTSIDE SELLING EXPERIENCE WHO ARE NOT IN THE "TRAINEE" CLASSIFICATION.

What do you realistically expect to earn: After one year? $ 20,000   After five years? $ 50,000   After ten years? $?

If you were to summarize your total sales experience, what would you say are your strong points and weak points? Print your answer below.

Strong points: strong presentation and strong closing; artistic and creative; total domination of the sales interview.

Weak points: I don't wish to sound like a braggart, but I really don't feel I have any.

My selling background required the ultimate in selling skills, because of the emotional appeal of the product line and also because it's one on one selling.

List the names and addresses of two customers who know you well and whom we can contact, pending this application.

Mr. John Winters, 15 Edgewater Hillside, Pittsburgh, Pennsylvania

Mr. Shane S. Kennedy, 15 Wakeman Place, Pittsburgh, Pennsylvania

Have you any other business interests or activities which will continue if you come to work for us? Elaborate.

no

What are your aims or ambitions for the future? To express myself with the utmost candor, I'm really interested in making a lot of money.

*It is recommended that the employer check local and state laws. If local or state laws prohibit employers from requesting this information, omit.

Exhibit 5 *(Continued)*

10. BACKGROUND FACTORS: (To be answered by all applicants.)

What is or was your father's occupation? ___sold lingerie___

What is or was your mother's occupation? ___Housewife___

Occupations of your brothers and sisters ___Priest who runs a halfway house; Sister - whereabouts unknown___

Where did you spend most of your life when you were growing up? (Omit foreign countries.) ___Pittsburgh___

What are your interests, hobbies, amusements, leisure time activities? ___Skydiving. Racing sport cars - own Formula 1___ Member of Western Pennsylvania Automobile Club.

Do you like to read? ___yes___ What have you read recently? ___sports pages, automobile books___

What clubs and organizations do you take an active part in? (Omit religious, racial, or foreign national.)___ Skydivers of America. Plus above-named automobile club.

Are you willing to relocate? ___yes___ Area preferred ___anywhere - southwest of Florida___

Have you ever been arrested for other than traffic violations? ___no___

Explain___

In signing this application form, I clearly understand and agree: (1) that all the statements are true to the best of my knowledge; (2) no attempt has been made to conceal or withhold pertinent information; (3) I authorize investigation of all statements with no liability; (4) I will abide by all company rules and regulations; (5) any falsification or misrepresentation may be considered cause for termination; and (6) I agree to take physical exams at the Company's request to determine my suitability for continued employment.

Copyright N.P.T.A.

Signed *Robert Nordstrom*

470

Exhibit 5 *(Continued)*

EXHIBIT 6
Memo to Bill Hogarth from Dean Hogarth concerning Leon Okarowski

January 22, 1975

To: Bill Hogarth

From: Dean Hogarth

Subject: Interview of Leon Okarowski, prospective salesperson

I met Leon for about 30 minutes at the St. Louis Airport. I asked, "How are you related to Barry Shaughnessy?" Barry Shaughnessy, Sr., is Okarowski's wife's father-in-law from her first marriage. Young Shaughnessy was killed in Viet Nam. Knows the paper business very well; could identify competitive merchants and their strengths and weaknesses; has good grasp of the business; comes across honest, very sincere, and likeable; would require very little training except for our methods; is a good talker, not overly dressed, a little nervous with interview; willing to transfer to Pittsburgh to earn more money; seems like a very nice guy; would fit in well with our organization—probably no problems; might be useful for Polish customers and prospects.

1. IDENTIFYING DATA

PRINT NAME
LAST: Okarowski
FIRST: Leon
MIDDLE: S.

SOCIAL SECURITY NUMBER: 021-55-6784
DATE (today): April 29, 1975

PRESENT STREET ADDRESS: 21 East End Boulevard
HOW LONG: 9 years

CITY: St. Louis
STATE & ZIP: Missouri 33013

TELEPHONE NUMBER: 544-9723
AREA: 314
*AGE: 32
*BIRTH DATE: September 8, 1942
CITY / STATE:

PREVIOUS ADDRESS: Military Service
STREET:

WEIGHT: 180 lbs.
HEIGHT: 6' 1"
*CITIZEN: ☒ YES ☐ NO

APPLICATION FORM FOR SALESMEN

To The Applicant: This application for employment by sales candidates has been suggested by the National Paper Trade Association as a specially designed form for the paper industry. All information will be treated confidentially. No attempt will be made to check or verify any information without prior approval from you. Complete this form in your own handwriting.

2. PERSONAL DATA

Number of children: 2
List their ages: 9 7 (boys)
Date available for work: one months notice

PRESENT MARITAL STATUS (CHECK ONLY ONE)
☐ Single never married   ☒ Married (Date) 1967   ☐ Separated (Date)
☐ Divorced (Date)   ☐ Widowed (Date)   ☐ Engaged

If presently married or engaged, were you married before? ☐ Yes ☒ No
Do you support anyone other than your wife and children? ☐ Yes ☒ No

Who should be notified in case of accident or illness? NAME: Mary Okarowski
ADDRESS: 21 East End Boulevard, St. Louis, Missouri   TEL. NO. 314-544-9723

3. EDUCATION

Encircle highest grade or number of years completed →

	GRADE SCHOOL	HIGH SCHOOL	JR. COLLEGE	COLLEGE
	4 5 6 7 8	1 2 3 4	1 2 3	1 2 ③ 4 5 6 7

Names and locations of schools attended (full time attendance during days only)	CITY	STATE	Years attended from to	Did you graduate?	Course of study or degree earned
HIGH SCHOOL(S) St. Francis High School	St. Louis	Mo.	1956–1960	yes	business
COLLEGE(S) Washington University	St. Louis	Mo.	1960–1963	no	business
Washington University	St. Louis	Mo.	1966	no	business

Are you presently enrolled in any course or program of education? ☐ Yes ☒ No
If so, elaborate

4. PHYSICAL STATUS

What is your present health? ☒ Excellent   ☐ Good   ☐ Fair
How is your hearing?   How is your vision?
Date of last physical exam   Conducted by
Date of last hospitalization   Name of hospital
Reason for hospitalization

Which of the ailments or diseases listed below have you ever had?
☐ Diabetes   ☐ Tuberculosis   ☐ Migraine   ☐ Malignancy
☐ Asthma   ☐ Alcoholism   ☐ Kidney trouble   ☐ High blood pressure
☐ Hernia   ☐ Arthritis   ☐ Heart trouble   ☐ Nervous breakdown
☐ Allergies   ☐ Epilepsy   ☐ Fainting spells   ☐ Stomach trouble
☐ Backaches   ☐ Foot trouble   ☐ Drug addiction   ☐ Other (specify)

If you now have any of the above, then encircle the box you checked.

Name and address of your family physician: Dr. Lesley Rudolph, St. Louis, Missouri
Are you willing to take a physical exam for employment? ☒ Yes ☐ No

*It is recommended that the employer check local and state laws. If local or state laws prohibit employers from requesting this information, omit.

Exhibit 7 Mr. Okarowski's application.

471

5. EMPLOYMENT HISTORY

Begin with your last position or present position if you are now employed (omit military duties).

JOB NO.	NAME OF EMPLOYER	STREET ADDRESS, CITY AND PHONE NUMBER	YOUR JOB	MONTH — YEAR FROM — TO	EARNINGS
1 ☐	Parker Paper Company Name of Immed. Supervisor Fred Hansen	555 West 14th Street St. Louis 544-0800 Reason for Leaving	paper salesman	2-71 - present	14,000
2 ☐	St. Louis General Envelope Name of Immed. Supervisor Fred Almond	211 15th Street St. Louis 542-7878 Reason for Leaving more income	envelope salesman	1-67 - 2-71	12,800
3 ☐	Name of Immed. Supervisor	Reason for Leaving			
4 ☐	Name of Immed. Supervisor	Reason for Leaving			
5 ☐	Name of Immed. Supervisor	Reason for Leaving			

(Check (X) the box opposite any job we will **not** be able to contact for references.) DID YOU HAVE AN INVESTMENT IN OR WERE YOU AN OWNER OR PART OWNER OF ANY OF THE ABOVE FIRMS? ☐ Yes ☒ No   Indicate which ones by job number____
Are you related to any of the above employers? ☐ Yes ☒ No.
Which of the above jobs did you like best? Job No. 1____ Why? I liked the people____

Do you wish to be in business for yourself someday? ☐ Yes ☒ No   When?____
In what line or industry?____

6. ECONOMIC AND FINANCIAL STATUS

(Check all the boxes that apply to you.)

☒ Own your home   ☐ Rent home or apt.   ☐ Live in a transient hotel
☐ Condominium or coop ☐ Rent a furnished room   ☒ Own your furniture

Living with: ☒ Spouse   ☐ Alone   ☐ Parents   ☐ Roommate(s)   ☐ Friends or Relatives

☒ Own your car(s)   ☐ Rent your car   Make Dodge   Year 1972   Car Payments $ paid Mo.

Monthly payments: (Check all that apply)
☒ Home mortgage   ☐ Bank loan   ☐ Medical-Dental
☐ Air line acct. ☐ Bank card acct. ☐ Finance Co.
☐ Furniture Co.   ☐ Insurance Co.   ☐ Other (specify)____

Where do you have bank accounts?
St. Louis Savings & Loan
Second National Bank of St. Louis

☐ Wife is employed   ☐ Part time   ☐ Full time   ☐ Temporarily   Type of work____

Are you bondable?
☒ Yes
☐ No

Insurance you carry:
☒ Ordinary life   ☐ Term life   ☐ Hospitalization
☒ Auto   ☐ Major medical   ☐ Income protection
☐ Insurance on wife ☐ Insurance on children ☒ Tenant's-homeowner's
☐ Other (specify)____

Do you receive more than $3,000 annually from outside sources? ☐ Yes ☒ No

Exhibit 7 *(Continued)*

7. MILITARY SERVICE IN THE ARMED FORCES OF THE UNITED STATES ONLY

[x] Veteran   Date entered service June, 1963   Type of work performed Medic

Type of discharge Honorable   Date discharged June, 1966 Branch of service Navy

Do you get a disability pension? [ ] Yes [x] No

Highest rank achieved Seaman - second class

If deferred from military service, state reason

Training received in military service first aid, medical technique

*Present draft classification	Draft board number and location
not applicable	not applicable

Are you now a member of a military reserve organization? [ ] Yes [x] No

Name and location of group _____ Rank _____

8. THIS SECTION FOR SALES TRAINEES ONLY

Scholastic standing while in

High school good   College adequate

College majors and minors business

Clubs and organizations in college. (Including varsity sports and omit religious, racial, or foreign national groups.)
track team, baseball team, fraternity, business club

Principal source of your spending money while in college	% of expenses earned
working for my father in his bakery	80%

Different jobs (part time and summer) you held while in high school and college
baker and baker's helper

What sales experience have you had?
selling envelopes and paper

Why do you believe you are interested in a sales career?
I like people

What is your long-term ambition in life?
to become a really professional salesman

473

9. THIS SECTION FOR APPLICANTS WITH PREVIOUS OUTSIDE SELLING EXPERIENCE WHO ARE NOT IN THE "TRAINEE" CLASSIFICATION.

What do you realistically expect to earn: After one year? $ 15-17K   After five years? $ 20,000   After ten years? $ 25,000

If you were to summarize your total sales experience, what would you say are your strong points and weak points? Print your answer below.

I sincerely like to call on people and serve their needs. I feel that sincerity and honesty are the salesman's biggest assets in calling on customers, particularly when you call on them over and over again.

My weak point is that I do not have a college diploma and I would like to finish up my education at night.   I feel I am a very good salesman, loyal to customers, and I represent Parker Paper Company fairly and effectively.   I won the summer sales contest in 1973.

List the names and addresses of two customers who know you well and whom we can contact, pending this application.
AAA Printers & Lithographers, St. Louis, Missouri
Bear Printing, St. Louis, Missouri

Have you any other business interests or activities which will continue if you come to work for us? Elaborate.

What are your aims or ambitions for the future? I look forward to getting into management as a sales manager. My present employer has no plans for expansion and the present positions are all occupied.

*It is recommended that the employer check local and state laws. If local or state laws prohibit employers from requesting this information, omit.

Exhibit 7 *(Continued)*

10. BACKGROUND FACTORS: (To be answered by all applicants.)

What is or was your father's occupation? Owned a bakery

What is or was your mother's occupation? Housewife

Occupations of your brothers and sisters Brother – military service. Two sisters – housewives

Where did you spend most of your life when you were growing up? (Omit foreign countries.) St. Louis

What are your interests, hobbies, amusements, leisure time activities? Bowl in St. Francis Alumni League; Baseball coach – St. Francis Junior High School (Little League)

Do you like to read? yes What have you read recently? Readers Digest, Time Magazine, World War II history books.

What clubs and organizations do you take an active part in? (Omit religious, racial, or foreign national.) Polish-American Social Club (I speak Polish fluently)

Are you willing to relocate? yes Area preferred Atlantic Coast

Have you ever been arrested for other than traffic violations? no

Explain

Signed *Leon S. Okasowski*

Copyright N.P.T.A.

Exhibit 7 *(Continued)*

FORTY-SIX Norton Company

In June 1975 William Howard, vice president and head of the Abrasives Marketing Group (AMG) of Norton Company, was in the midst of reviewing AMG hiring practices. Mr. Howard had two concerns. First, he wondered whether the process AMG used, including psychological testing, was the best way to recruit and select sales trainees. Second, he was concerned about the use of his sales force as a source of management talent by other Norton operating units.

THE NORTON COMPANY

The Norton Company, established in 1885, was the world's largest manufacturer of abrasive products, including bonded abrasives (that is, grinding wheels) and coated abrasives (that is, the commonly called "sand paper"). Norton sales had grown from $201 million in 1963 to $558 million in 1974, and profits from $14.7 million to $21.1 million. Although Norton was a manufacturer of many products, including refractories, biomedical equipment, and plastic products, abrasives remained its primary product. The Abrasives Marketing Group had been established in 1973 to consolidate bonded and coated abrasive sales and marketing operations. Mr. Howard was the first manager of the group.

THE ABRASIVES MARKETING GROUP

Norton's 1973 Annual Report explained the thinking behind the formation of the group.

> The study of the marketing of abrasives has long been in the forefront of Norton's continuing search to gain the maximum return from its major product line. The completely separate marketing of grinding wheels and coated abrasives made sense historically because of their different end uses. However, with the new sophisticated communications systems and modern management techniques, unification offers improved effectiveness and substantial economies.
>
> Norton's plan to integrate the marketing of its two major domestic abrasive lines envisages a long range program to combine all functions, eventually even to field salesmen. A complex program, it will be carried out in phases over a three to five year period. Initially top personnel have been aligned into a single organization known as the Abrasives Marketing Group with many sales support functions already combined.

By 1975 the group's sales force consisted of approximately 240 sales representatives. The assignment of salespeople in 1975 was primarily geographic with some specialization by products (that is, grinding wheels or coated abrasives) still present. Certain salespeople also specialized by type of account such as steel mills or foundries. The goal of the "synergy move," as it was called within AMG, was to have the best of both product specialization and geographic allocation. This required the salespeople in low density areas to be familiar with all products while allowing salespeople in higher density areas to specialize by product or market.

The Selling Task

The Norton salesperson was principally a technical representative of the company. Historically, Norton had had an industry-wide reputation as the company best able to solve difficult technical problems. In recent years, this clear leadership had been challenged by other large abrasives companies. Norton management felt that the sales force had to take a more aggressive role when selling. To accomplish this, more training in selling was introduced into the training program.

The salesperson's job, whether sales were handled directly or through distributors, was to develop new business. These opportunities most often arose when the customer had a problem. Usually the customer called in technical representatives of three to four companies to present their recommendations. Customers valued (1) speed of response and (2) capability of the product recommended. The Norton representative attempted to write a specification for a standard Norton product. (According to Norton management most industry specifications were written in terms of equivalency to Norton.) This enabled the company to respond quickly by supplying test wheels out of stock. If a special wheel were required, samples would be produced and sent to the customer for testing, a process which required 2 to 4 weeks, depending on the difficulty of the problem and the work load in the lab.

After the customer was satisfied that a product accomplished the task in a cost-effective manner, he often requested bids on the product. If all represented companies had the capability to produce the product, they submitted bids, and the customer chose the supplier or suppliers. Thus, the salesperson's job was threefold: (1) to convince the customer that Norton should be the supplier, (2) to recommend the most effective design, and (3) to supply marketing management with data so that they could properly evaluate the bidding situation.

Recruiting of Salespeople

Norton's personnel policies demanded that all job listings be posted for general review by Norton employees prior to the seeking of outside applicants. Historically, this had not resulted in a large number of qualified applicants for the sales jobs, however, and most sales trainees were recruited from colleges. Norton contacted many of the best schools in the country. To inform the students of the jobs available, the job description (Exhibit 1) was posted.

The first Norton representative the recruits met was the college recruiter, Steve Dewey. Mr. Dewey had joined Norton approximately 18 months earlier as the result of an interview at his undergraduate institution, Williams College. His original interest was in the sales job, but in his interview at Norton, management felt that his interpersonal skills would suit him well for the recruiter's position. When the psychological tests confirmed this, Mr. Dewey was approached and accepted the position as recruiter. He was then made responsible for all college recruiting.

Mr. Dewey stated that during the interviews (usually $\frac{1}{2}$ hour in length) he attempted to have the applicant speak about 50 percent of the time, while he spent the other half talking about Norton and the job. Management felt that the sales task did not require an engineering graduate, but that familiarity with technical terminology was useful. In addition to testing for this ability, Mr. Dewey assessed the interest of the applicant by seeing how much research had been done on the Norton Company and its products. He also tried to evaluate the motivation or energy level of the applicant by probing into past accomplishments and future goals.

During the interview, Mr. Dewey encouragd the applicant to relax. He felt that the two things which most adversely affected an interview were tension and the school-imposed time constraints. When pressed on whether he felt he was capable, after only 18 months, of evaluating

PERSONNEL REQUIREMENT
NORTON COMPANY · WORCESTER, MASSACHUSETTS

METALLURGICAL ENGINEERING

Grinding wheels, particularly those with diamond as the abrasive, are metal bonded. Grinding causes surface reactions to metals and alloys that are not fully understood, and many of Norton Company's newer developments are in the metallurgical field. Opportunities are open for metallurgical engineers in research and sales.

JOB DESCRIPTIONS

Research and Development

Norton Company has a Research and Development Department of about 300 people, of whom one-third are located at the plant in Worcester, Massachusetts. This department is concerned with development of grinding wheels, high temperature refractories and a wide range of other products in the ceramic, chemical and metallurgical fields. Positions are available for metallurgical engineers who have a basic interest in research and are capable of doing original and creative work.

Grinding Wheel Sales

Grinding wheel sales require a general background in engineering or a strong mechanical aptitude. Men are given a nine month's training program covering the manufacture and application of grinding wheels and Company operations. At its conclusion, they are assigned to a territory anywhere in the U.SA. The initial selection of the assignments depends upon the man's preference and the requirements at the time.

Refractories Sales

The technical aspects of high temperature refractories and products for nuclear and jet applications require well-trained engineers in selling activities. After a training period of nearly a year, sales engineers are assigned either to positions at the Worcester plant, or given a territory in some other section of the country. This initial assignment depends both on the engineer's preference and the requirements at the time.

QUALIFICATIONS

B.S., M.S., or Ph.D. in Metallurgical Engineering, with or without experience.

GENERAL

The positions are in Worcester, Massachusetts, Troy, N.Y., Akron, Ohio, or Kansas City, Missouri.

Men with military commitments ahead of them are given equal consideration with veterans, providing they have a few months to start on the job.

Exhibit 1 Personnel requirements.

candidates, he seemed confident that he could eliminate those who were poorly suited. He felt he tended, if anything, to be occasionally overly critical in his evaluation, since he was conscious of the cost to the company of the second phase of the interview process.

Based on the interview, Mr. Dewey filled out his evaluation form

EXHIBIT 2

Application Form

Applicant's name _____ Date of interview _____

College _____ Degree _____ Major _____

Interviewer _____ Date available _____

Ratings: (Check appropriate line along scale)

	Poor	Fair	Average	Good	Very good	Out-standing
Appearance	___	___	___			
Ability to get along with others	___	___	___	___	___	___
Academic record	___	___	___	___	___	___
Maturity	___	___	___	___	___	___
Aggressiveness	___	___	___	___	___	___
Poise	___	___	___	___	___	___
Leadership ability	___	___	___	___	___	___
Motivation drive	___	___	___	___	___	___
Verbal expression	___	___	___	___	___	___
Alertness	___	___	___	___	___	___
Decisiveness	___	___	___	___	___	___
Interest in Norton	___	___	___	___	___	___
Overall impression	___	___	___	___	___	___

Application given: yes ____ no ____   (Follow-up if not returned in two weeks?
yes ____ no ____)

Recommend: Invite ____ Close out ____ Refer ____ Location ____

Specific job _____ General area _____ Division(s) _____

Geographic preference: _____

Military status: _____

Graduate school plans: _____

Comments: _____

(Exhibit 2). Upon returning to Worcester he reviewed the forms and generally invited 10 to 20 percent of the applicants to Norton for the next step in the process. This percentage varied according to the quality of the applicants and the needs of Norton at the time. No other member of management reviewed the forms, since it was the company's view that only the person who personally had contact should evaluate the applicant. All applicants were notified of their status within 2 weeks. Those who were to continue in the interviewing process were asked to arrange for a trip to Worcester at Norton's expense. Included in the response to these people was a Norton employment application which they were asked to fill out and bring with them on their visit (Exhibit 3).

LAST NAME		FIRST NAME		MIDDLE NAME		SOCIAL SECURITY NO.		DATE
						— —		

CURRENT ADDRESS – STREET		CITY		STATE	ZIP CODE	COUNTRY	PHONE
							AC Number
PERMANENT ADDRESS – STREET		CITY		STATE	ZIP CODE	COUNTRY	
							AC Number

FOR WHAT TYPE OF POSITION ARE YOU APPLYING?	APPROXIMATE SALARY REQUIREMENTS	DATE AVAILABLE

NORTON

Norton Company, an equal opportunity employer, is a diversified multi-national manufacturer of consumable supplies, advanced materials and related capital equipment with corporate offices located in Worcester, Massachusetts.

Check Division location for which application is being completed –

☐ Akron, OH 44309 Chemical Process Products and Plastics & Synthetics

☐ Newton, MA 02161 Vacuum Equipment and Metals

☐ Troy, N.Y. 12181 Coated Abrasive and Tape

☐ Worcester, MA 01606 Corporate, Abrasive Materials, Grinding Wheel, Machine Tool, Protective Products and Refractories

☐ Other U.S.A. ————————— Location

☐ Norton International Inc. ————————— Country

EDUCATIONAL RECORD

COLLEGE, UNIVERSITY AND GRADUATE SCHOOL (most recent first)

SCHOOL		LOCATION		FROM	TO	GRADUATED? Yes ☐ No ☐	DEGREE
MAJOR	MINOR		SCHOLASTIC AVERAGE	SCHOLASTIC STANDING		1st Qtr. ☐ 3rd Qtr. ☐ 2nd Qtr. ☐ 4th Qtr. ☐	
SCHOOL		LOCATION		FROM	TO	GRADUATED? Yes ☐ No ☐	DEGREE
MAJOR	MINOR		SCHOLASTIC AVERAGE	SCHOLASTIC STANDING		1st Qtr. ☐ 3rd Qtr. ☐ 2nd Qtr. ☐ 4th Qtr. ☐	
SCHOOL		LOCATION		FROM	TO	GRADUATED? Yes ☐ No ☐	DEGREE
MAJOR	MINOR		SCHOLASTIC AVERAGE	SCHOLASTIC STANDING		1st Qtr. ☐ 3rd Qtr. ☐ 2nd Qtr. ☐ 4th Qtr. ☐	

LIST THESIS SUBJECT, PUBLISHED ARTICLES AND PATENTS, IF ANY

COLLEGE HONORS AND ACTIVITIES

SCHOLARSHIP? Yes ☐ No ☐	IF YES, WHAT KIND OR TYPE?

479

Exhibit 3 Job application form.

The Worcester Visit

Upon arriving at the Norton headquarters, the applicants were introduced to Dr. Jones who explained that he would administer a series of psychological tests to them for the duration of the morning and would

PERCENT OF COLLEGE EXPENSES EARNED _____ %	HOW EARNED?					
CURRENT COURSES AND/OR FUTURE EDUCATIONAL GOALS						

HIGH SCHOOL, PREPARATORY, TECHNICAL AND BUSINESS SCHOOLS (most recent first)

SCHOOL	LOCATION	FROM	TO	DEGREE	MAJOR
SCHOOL	LOCATION	FROM	TO	DEGREE	MAJOR
SCHOOL	LOCATION	FROM	TO	DEGREE	MAJOR

HONORS AND ACTIVITIES

U.S. MILITARY RECORD

SELECTIVE SERVICE CLASSIFICATION	BRANCH	ACTIVE DUTY	
		☐ COMPLETED	From _____ To _____
WAS YOUR DISCHARGE OTHER THAN HONORABLE?		☐ PRESENTLY SERVING From _____ To _____	
		☐ ANTICIPATED From _____ To _____	
		☐ DEFERRED Reason	

SPECIAL SCHOOLS ATTENDED	DUTIES

RESERVE STATUS	CAMP OR CRUISE REQUIREMENTS	EXPIRATION DATE

EMPLOYMENT RECORD (most recent first)

EMPLOYER	COMPLETE ADDRESS	YOUR POSITION

FROM Mo. Yr.	TO Mo. Yr.	NAME OF SUPERVISOR	TITLE OF SUPERVISOR	LAST SALARY

DESCRIBE DUTIES AND SCOPE OF RESPONSIBILITIES (These comments may be supplemented by attached resume)

May we contact present employer? Yes ☐ No ☐

REASON FOR LEAVING OR CONSIDERING POSITION CHANGE

EMPLOYER	COMPLETE ADDRESS	YOUR POSITION

FROM Mo. Yr.	TO Mo. Yr.	NAME OF SUPERVISOR	TITLE OF SUPERVISOR	LAST SALARY

DESCRIBE DUTIES AND SCOPE OF RESPONSIBILITIES

REASON FOR LEAVING

Exhibit 3 *(Continued)*

collect the applications so that they could be reviewed by the manager of staffing. If, at this point, an applicant stated that he did not want to take the tests, the testing was skipped and he proceeded to the next step. It was uncommon for this to happen, however, and Dr. Jones felt that less than 1 percent refused.

Dr. Jones had originally joined Norton during World War II, when he

EMPLOYER	COMPLETE ADDRESS		YOUR POSITION

FROM Mo. Yr.	TO Mo. Yr.	NAME OF SUPERVISOR	TITLE OF SUPERVISOR	LAST SALARY

DESCRIBE DUTIES AND SCOPE OF RESPONSIBILITIES

REASON FOR LEAVING

PERSONAL DATA

IN CASE OF AN EMERGENCY WHOM SHOULD WE NOTIFY?	NAME	RELATIONSHIP

STREET ADDRESS	CITY AND STATE	PHONE (Include Area Code)

U. S. CITIZEN Yes ☐ No ☐	If not, give citizenship if applying for position outside U.S.A.	VISA STATUS, if applicable	DO YOU INTEND TO BECOME A U.S. CITIZEN? Yes ☐ No ☐

ARE YOU WILLING TO RELOCATE ANYWHERE IN U.S.A.? Yes ☐ No ☐	IF NOT, GIVE RESTRICTIONS	WHAT IS YOUR GEOGRAPHIC PREFERENCE

ARE YOU WILLING TO RELOCATE OVERSEAS? Yes ☐ No ☐	ARE YOU INTERESTED IN AN OVERSEAS ASSIGNMENT? Yes ☐ No ☐	IF SO, GIVE PREFERENCE

LANGUAGES – LIST LANGUAGES WITH WHICH YOU HAVE SOME DEGREE OF FLUENCY.

ON SCALE OF 1 THRU 4 WITH 1 REPRESENTING NATIVE TONGUE FAMILIARITY OR EQUIVALENT, CIRCLE THE NUMBER CORRESPONDING TO YOUR LEVEL OF COMPREHENSION AND FLUENCY.

LANGUAGE																				
SPEAK	1	2	3	4	1	2	3	4	1	2	3	4	1	2	3	4	1	2	3	4
READ	1	2	3	4	1	2	3	4	1	2	3	4	1	2	3	4	1	2	3	4
WRITE	1	2	3	4	1	2	3	4	1	2	3	4	1	2	3	4	1	2	3	4

DESCRIBE SPECIAL INTERESTS, HOBBIES, AND COMMUNITY ACTIVITIES IN WHICH YOU ARE ACTIVE, EXCLUDING ORGANIZATIONS THE NAME OR CHARACTER OF WHICH INDICATES THE RACE, CREED, COLOR, OR NATIONAL ORIGIN OF ITS MEMBERS.

NEW EMPLOYEES ARE REQUIRED TO PASS A PHYSICAL EXAMINATION. DO YOU HAVE ANY KNOWN PHYSICAL IMPAIRMENTS?
YES ☐   NO ☐   IF SO, LIST

HEALTH STATUS

HAVE YOU EVER FILED A CLAIM OR COLLECTED FOR ANY INJURY OR ILLNESS ARISING OUT OF AND DURING THE COURSE OF YOUR EMPLOYMENT?
Yes ☐   No ☐   IF SO, LIST

481

Exhibit 3 *(Continued)*

had approached the company offering his assistance as a consultant for the summer. He was originally asked to develop a training program for the many new supervisors who were needed due to expansion to meet the needs of the war. In light of his background, B.A. and M.A. from the University of Virginia in educational psychology and English and an M.A. and Ph.D. from Columbia University in educational psychology, he was

HAVE YOU EVER BEEN CONVICTED OF A FELONY?
Yes ☐   No ☐   IF SO, EXPLAIN

LIST ANY RELATIVES EMPLOYED BY ANY DIVISION OF NORTON COMPANY

NAME	DEPARTMENT	DIVISION AND LOCATION
NAME	DEPARTMENT	DIVISION AND LOCATION

HAVE YOU EVER PREVIOUSLY BEEN EMPLOYED BY ANY DIVISION OF NORTON COMPANY ?
Yes ☐   No ☐   IF SO, GIVE WHERE, WHEN AND FOR WHOM.

HAVE YOU PREVIOUSLY FILED AN APPLICATION WITH NORTON COMPANY?
Yes ☐   No ☐   IF SO, WHERE AND WHEN.

THROUGH WHAT MEANS DID YOU APPLY FOR A POSITION WITH US ?

COLLEGE INTERVIEW ☐	ADVERTISEMENT ☐	EMPLOYMENT AGENCY ☐	PERSONAL REFERRAL BY NORTON EMPLOYEE ☐	OTHER MEANS ☐
Name of School	Where Appearing?	Name of Agency	OTHER PERSONAL REFERRAL ☐	

REFERENCES

REFERENCES WHOM WE MAY CONTACT OTHER THAN FRIENDS OR RELATIVES

NAME		TITLE	HOW ACQUAINTED?
PRESENT ORGANIZATION	ADDRESS		PHONE
			Area Code Number Ext.
NAME		TITLE	HOW ACQUAINTED ?
PRESENT ORGANIZATION	ADDRESS		PHONE
			Area Code Number Ext.
NAME		TITLE	HOW ACQUAINTED?
PRESENT ORGANIZATION	ADDRESS		PHONE
			Area Code Number Ext.

I am in agreement with Norton Company's policy of hiring and promoting on the basis of ability without regard to race, creed, color, sex, age, or national origin. I certify that my statements are true and complete to the best of my knowledge and belief. I understand that any misrepresentation of facts on my part may be cause for dismissal.

APPLICANT'S SIGNATURE   DATE

Norton Company follows the usual practice of requiring new technically-trained, professional and other employees with access to confidential information to sign an agreement at the time of employment covering   a) non-disclosure and non-use of information,   b) assignment of inventions and, in the case of certain divisions,   c) restrictions on employment by others in the same fields for not more than three years after termination of the employment.

NOTE: Consistent with Public Law 91-508, we advise you that a routine inquiry may be made in connection with the processing of your application for employment which will provide applicable information concerning character, general reputation, personal characteristics and mode of living. Upon written request, additional information as to the nature and scope of the inquiry, if one is made, will be provided.

Exhibit 3   *(Continued)*

later asked if he could develop a series of tests which, combined with his completed training program, would improve the development of managers.

Dr. Jones was aware of the problem of nervousness adversely affecting test results and, therefore, explained to the applicants that the tests were only a small part of the total evaluation process. Having reassured the applicants, generally two to four people at one time, he proceeded with the tests. Dr. Jones tested to measure the following variables:

1 *Verbal abstract*   A 20-minute test similar in style to the verbal part of the college entrance tests designed to test for language skills on an objective basis.

2 *Quantitative abstract*   A 25-minute test similar in style to the quantitative section of the college entrance tests designed to test for facility with numbers.

3 *Mechanical aptitude*   In two parts designed to test, first common sense evaluation of mechanical relationships by evaluation of diagrams and, second, knowledge of tools and processes used in mechanical operations.

4 *Interests*   A test to match the interests of the applicant with those of persons in various occupational groups. Emphasis was on engineering and production management, salesperson, office management, and management sections since these were the areas Dr. Jones felt best reflected the type of work done by Norton's salespeople.

5 *Personality tests*   To determine:
Dominance (ego drive)
Introversion versus extroversion
Self-sufficiency (self-confidence)
Sociability (empathy)
Energy and drive (with emphasis on consistency)
Self-restraint (control)
Ascendency (leadership)
Friendliness
Thoughtfulness
Cooperativeness

Evaluation of Testing

Dr. Jones was aware of Mr. Howard's concerns on the issue of testing. In 1970 a report was prepared in which the validity of the tests as a predictor of performance was checked. To check validity, Dr. Jones rated past applicants on a scale of 1 to 5, based on test results, and compared this with the supervisors' evaluations of these same people on the job. A summary of the results of this study as prepared by Dr. Jones is Exhibit 4.

Norton was also aware of the importance of privacy in handling the test material. Only one person, the manager of staffing, was allowed to view Dr. Jones's summary and only after being instructed in its proper interpretation. The forms themselves were stored in a special, locked cabinet with access limited to the manager of staffing. Should a supervisor want information on the tests, specific questions were posed and a qualified person conveyed, very selectively, the information that was appropriate.

EXHIBIT 4
Excerpts from Summary of Dr. Jones's Study

The purpose of this study has been to follow up the applicants who were tested and hired in the Company between January 1963 and July 1969. During this period, 1,753 individuals were tested. Of that number 1,607 were applicants for positions in the home organization. Of these approximately 40% received offers, and 298 accepted and were hired.

The records of 261 of these 298 were sufficiently complete to form the base of this investigation. 169 of these were in technical lines in the Company and 92 in sales.

The first goal of the study was to determine the degree to which the test results predicted, or agreed with, subsequent performance of hirees on the job. Test results and job performance were each rated on a five-point scale, ranging from unsatisfactory to distinguished. The ratings on the tests were made by the writer by reading each test report carefully and assigning a predictive rating (1 to 5) for each hiree. After this was completed, the ratings of the job performance were taken directly from the official appraisals of the supervisors of these same employees.

484

The supervisors' ratings were taken as the criterion or target, and the predictions or ratings from the tests were measured in terms of the degree to which they agreed. An exact hit was scored as a 0 miss, and misses were measured in $\frac{1}{2}$ points on the rating scale.

The results for the 261 cases were 49% exact hits, 33% misses by $\frac{1}{2}$ a point, 15% by 1.0, 2% by 1.5, and 0.8% by 2.0. The hits and misses for technical and for sales were almost identical.

In the process of studying our tests we discovered that a sizeable number of new employees had left the Company. It was found that 95 of the 261 hirees had left the Company, and that 73% of these had left during their first 3 years. Indeed, 25 men or 27% had left in less than $1\frac{1}{2}$ years.

Of course some of those who left did so on Company initiative because of poor work or adjustment on the job, but these were few, that is, 13% for technical and 20% for sales, as judged by exit interviews, supervisor ratings, and the like. The main "reasons" given by the employees themselves in exit interviews were: going to better job, 27%; not satisfied with job or inadequate challenge in the Company, 20%; not satisfied with salary, 10%; to return to home state or community to live, 6%; to return to college, 5%; to form own business, 5%; for family considerations (housing, wife discontented, etc.), 3%.

In the writer's test reports the main clues as to the likelihood of short tenure were such expressions as:

1 Not suitable for area of his application, difficult to match abilities with interests and aspiration level, 20%

2 Changeable, in big hurry, likes adventure, may not stay, 16%

3 Personality not suitable, doubt if he will be happy with work, 22%

Finally we were interested in the abilities, aptitudes, and performance on the job of the hirees who left compared with those who stayed in the Company. This led to the most disheartening result in the study. It is that we are losing too many promising people. From the objective test results on abilities and aptitudes, the weighted average for those who left was 60.3 while that for those who stayed was 54.0. The fact that both of these scores are significantly above the norm of 50 is encouraging, but the finding that we are losing many very promising young employees is sufficiently serious to deserve special attention and study. These ability-test results are supported by supervisors' appraisals. Of all hirees of 1963 to mid-1969 who left the company, 31% had been rated as *above* the acceptable level. Our conclusion from all the evidence we were able to gather is that between $\frac{1}{3}$ and $\frac{1}{2}$ of the hirees who have left the Company during the period under review were promising people whom it was a pity to lose.

We are not sure that it is proper in this report to try to make any recommendations, and we cannot claim any expertness in this direction; however, amid all the encouraging results found in this investigation, there is this one last result which we definitely think should be studied with a view to some organized effort toward satisfying the professional aspirations of all the people we get.

485

We believe that the assets of the Norton Company as a stable, friendly, developing business, where satisfying careers can be achieved, should be maximized early in the career of promising young men. One line of approach might be to work imaginatively toward greater involvement and challenge of each hiree who shows real promise. This involvement might range all the way from (1) assisting new hirees and their families with housing and social acceptance, to (2) special provisions for the very promising to participate as early as feasible in regular or special meetings, or in certain projects, with management in research, development, or planning.

Lunch

Following the testing, which took most of the morning, the applicant was taken to lunch by a sales trainee. Although the trainee as well as all interviewers filled out an evaluation form (Exhibit 5), the primary purpose of the lunch was to give the applicant the opportunity to meet a trainee and learn about the program. Honesty and frankness were encouraged, since Norton wanted the applicant to realize that much of the training and work was hands-on operation of grinding equipment. This point was emphasized by the trainee to encourage anyone not wanting this type of assignment to drop out.

Afternoon Interviews

The afternoon consisted of a series of $\frac{1}{2}$-hour interviews. Generally an applicant spoke to 4 to 6 people. The manager of staffing was responsible

TO: _____   RETURN TO: _____

Personnel Department

**IMPRESSION RATING
NORTON COMPANY
WORCESTER 6, MASS.**

You are scheduled to see _____ on _____.

For the position of _____.

Would you please list your impressions below and return this form to my attention?

	Below Ave. − +	Average	Above Ave. − +
APPEARANCE			
General Physical Appearance			
Carriage and Neatness			
Appropriateness of Dress and Manner			
Size and Physique			
BACKGROUND			
Formal Education As It Applies To Us			
Practical Education As It Applies To Us			
EXPERIENCE			
Work as It Applies To Us			
Other Work Experience			
PERSONALITY			
Interest In Job			
Energy and Drive			
Poise and Self Confidence			
Voice and Speech			
Mental Alertness			
Sociability and Friendliness			
Enthusiasm for Norton Company			
Ability to Lead Conversation			
Ability to Listen			
Aggressiveness			
Ability to Inspire Confidence			
Tactfulness and Judgment			
Flexibility			

OVERALL INTERVIEW RATING

Do you rate this applicant Poor_____ Average_____ Outstanding_____.

Would you hire him for your section?   Yes _____   No _____

Would you recommend him for another department: _____ ; if so which _____.

GENERAL COMMENTS

Signed _____

Exhibit 5 Impression rating form.

for arranging these interviews. If they were available on the day of the interview, management felt it was important for the recruit to speak to a variety of people, including peers, supervisors, managers, and heads of

486

areas with which a salesperson would have contact in the normal course of the job. The list of those who might be asked to interview recruits included the following job titles:

Field salespeople and field sales managers

General sales manager
Manager sales training
Manager product engineering
AMG director of marketing development
Marketing managers

Manager sales administration and manager of staffing
Director of personnel
Vice president and head of AMG

During these interviews the interviewer had a copy of the application but not the test data. Each interviewer handled the meeting in his own way, but the company had published guidelines which many of the people used (Exhibit 6). Following the interview the interviewer complet-

EXHIBIT 6
Interview Guideline

1 *Introduction and welcome* Establish a cordial atmosphere.   5 minutes
2 *Small talk* Continue to put the candidate at ease.
3 *Ask questions* The *most important* part of the interview, see
   comments below.   15 minutes
4 Describe the company, your department, the job.   5 minutes
5 Give and take.   5 minutes
6 *End interview* on time.
7 *Complete rating form* Make your decision and recommendations.

Comments (Step 3)

Questioning is the most important part of the interview and often the most difficult to keep going. Here are some suggestions.

Ask "broad brush" open-ended questions. Do not ask questions that can be answered with a yes or no.

Always give the candidate time to complete his answer before asking another question.

Ask questions which require the candidate to evaluate himself.

Avoid leading questions. This type of question almost always telegraphs the answer.

Probe for complete answers when you believe that the candidate has given only a partial answer.

When interviewing a candidate, remember that past "track records" have proved to be the most effective barometer for selection for future success. A well-planned "patterned" interview will enable you to gain insight into this.

ed the evaluation form (Exhibit 5) and forwarded it to the manager of staffing.

The Application Form

It was the responsibility of the manager of staffing, Stephen Anderson, to review the application form. To Mr. Anderson there were only four items on the application that immediately disqualified an applicant from further consideration:

1 A strong geographic preference, since the applicant must be willing to accept an assignment wherever an opening developed at the end of the training period

2 Conviction for certain criminal offenses, because this was taken as indicative of a potential customer relations problem

3 A major physical disability—if and only if it prevented the recruit from doing the sales job as designed

4 A lack of a permanent visa

488

If none of these items was a consideration, Mr. Anderson reviewed the application, looking primarily at past accomplishments. He also contacted the last employer and confirmed the data concerning the time spent on the job to verify the accuracy of the information. During the telephone interview, Mr. Anderson attempted to elicit at least one negative comment about the recruit. If he were unable to do this, he felt that the employer was probably attempting to cover-up something, and he pursued the next employer.

Mr. Anderson did not feel it was worthwhile contacting the personal references. Only as a last resort would he do this, and again he would attempt to elicit some negative comment before he ended the conversation.

Decision

Using the test results as summarized by Dr. Jones, the application, the comments of previous employers and the interviewer's evaluation forms, it was the responsibility of the manager of staffing to coordinate the hiring decision. If there was a consensus, it was simple. If, however, a minority felt strongly one way or the other (as expressed in the comments section of the evaluation form), Mr. Anderson talked with them on a one-to-one basis to resolve the conflict. If this failed, a meeting of those who had interviewed the applicant was called. Tradition dictated that the decision must be made by consensus. Regardless of how long this process might take, the applicant was notified of the current status within 2 weeks.

Although he had been generally pleased with the outcome of this decision-making process, some of the data concerning the hiring results bothered Mr. Anderson. Despite the fact that the applicants were told that they were expected to cover a territory volume twice as large as the industry average and that the job was unglamorous, of 111 offers made by Norton in the last 5 years, 83 had accepted. To Mr. Anderson this seemed high given the nature of the job. His feeling was that if Norton had a higher-quality applicant, the turndown rate would go up.

To the end of improving the recruiting process Norton was considering certain changes:

1 The modification of the psychological testing program to include different tests more specifically related to selling.

2 A change in the schools to which Norton went to recruit. In recent years, the market for certain types of technical graduates had softened and thus might allow Norton to get better applicants.

3 Improvement in interviewing skills.

"Raiding"

In considering the refinement of the sales force recruiting function, Mr. Howard felt a reassessment of the goals of recruiting was essential. Historically, the sales force had been a primary source of management talent. While Mr. Howard agreed with this (he had started as a field sales engineer), he knew that the process was being biased in favor of potential managers. He wondered if better salespeople could be recruited and held in the sales position if the system were focused on hiring the best possible salesperson without regard to management potential.

Also disturbing Mr. Howard was the news that he had just lost three of his best salespeople on lateral transfers to other divisions of the company. According to the company-wide job classification system, the salespeople had not changed classifications when changing divisions. Since each division was responsible for the control of recruiting costs, and this was not the first incident of such "raiding" of his sales force, Mr. Howard was considering bringing "raiding" to the attention of higher management while submitting his changes in the recruiting process.

In reviewing the turnover statistics, Mr. Howard was surprised to find that AMG typically trained 25 new salespeople per year. A significant percentage of these were to replace people who had been transferred within the company. He was determined to figure out a way to convince top management to reduce this practice before his sales force was completely "cherry-picked" of its best people.

Section
ELEVEN
Training

FORTY-SEVEN Training for Selling and Sales Management

In the past, training was a generally neglected part of sales force management. Recently, however, it has received new emphasis. It has also benefited greatly from the emergence of new technology, particularly videotaping.

Still, training is not very well understood, partly because so little is known about learning and teaching, especially of complex and subtle skills such as selling and sales management. Before discussing each aspect of the training, including content, participants, teachers, and methods, it is useful to consider the relationship between training and motivation. Sales management training will be considered at the end.

TRAINING AND MOTIVATION

Most practioners are well aware of the close relationship between training and motivation. When the journal *Sales Management*, for example, devoted a complete issue to training in May 1972, it was entitled "Man and Motivation '72: Training and Re-Training." This relationship has at least two aspects.

First, good training is a powerful motivator. Selling requires confidence. Training helps to build confidence, thus providing positive motivation. Salespeople seem also to be motivated by the attention shown to them in the training process. Thus, both the process of training and its content apparently provide motivation.

Second, one important aspect of motivation is the motivation to use the approaches provided by the training. One of the trainer's main complaints is, "The salespeople know the technique, they just won't use it."

This dual relationship produces a cycle—motivation improves the use of training, and training improves motivation. The two thus nearly become opposite sides of the same coin.

CONTENT

There are four standard categories of knowledge provided in sales training: (1) product, (2) company, (3) customer, and (4) selling. In addition, it will be useful to consider briefly inspirational content after discussing the four standard categories.

Product Knowledge

Most sales training efforts have focused on providing product knowledge. Since the salesperson is called upon to explain the product line to the prospect and customer, he must completely understand the product.
Product knowledge includes subjects such as the following:

1 *A list of the products being offered* Many salespeople are responsible for selling a large array of products and must be aware of the total product line. This is especially true of salespeople who are employed by wholesalers and distributors. Many of them have more than 10,000 individual items in their lines.

492

2 *Product characteristics* The salesperson should know the physical attributes of the product, including such internal factors as construction and durability.

3 *Available options* What colors do the products come in? Are there special accessories, etc.? Can I buy custom alternatives?

4 *Characteristics in use* What benefit does it provide the user?

5 *Availability and delivery* Is it carried in stock? What is the standard delivery time?

6 *Terms of sale* What guarantees are offered? What credit is provided?

7 *Adjunct services* Are installation, techical service, maintenance, etc., offered?

8 *If it is to be sold to a reseller* How will this product improve the profitability of my business? Will it improve the saleability of my product (OEM)? Will it generate traffic? What's the markup? What merchandising services are provided, such as display aids, cooperative advertising, etc.?

In the ideal situation, product knowledge would include comparison data for all relevant competitive products and would be customer oriented.

Company Knowledge

A close adjunct to product knowledge is company knowledge, including both the formal policies and procedures, such as how to write an order and where to submit the order [sometimes a nontrivial question when many products at different prices (volume discounts, promotions, etc.) are available from different company manufacturing units], and informal approaches, such as how to get the shipping clerk to expedite an order. Such knowledge is so important that it deserves to be classified in a category separate from product knowledge. If salespersons cannot manage their company's resources for the benefit of their customers, it is unlikely that they will be able to adequately serve the customers or sell for the company.

Customer Knowledge

If salespersons are to be successful, they must understand their prospects and customers well. Most important are the basic nature of the business and the ability to talk about it. Thus, the salesperson must understand the jargon not only of the industry but of the customer. The basic nature of the business includes how the customer makes his money and the risks involved in his purchase decisions.

493

If salespeople are to be useful adjuncts to their customers' businesses they must understand that business. For example, if a customer is a retailer, the salesperson should know the retailer's business well enough to show the retailer how the product will generate profits and turnover and fit into the appropriate merchandise category. They should be able to explain how cooperative advertising and display aids will help the retailer. In the case of a manufacturer, the content of the information might be different, but the use of it would be the same.

Selling Skills

This subject is a comparatively new area of knowledge. The focus is on the sales process and on the salesperson's ability to make an impact on the prospect and customer.

Because this is a skill-oriented and not a knowledge-oriented area, it is the most difficult form of training. This apparently prevented its early development. It will be discussed in detail below.

Inspiration

In the past, a good deal of "sales training" consisted of inspirational material. This was especially true for low-powered sales forces.[1] Such

---

[1]See the note "Sales Costs and Budgets" for a detailed definition of this term.

programs usually emphasized the importance of "knowing your inner power" and "convincing yourself that you can do it."

As salespeople have grown more sophisticated, the popularity of inspirational programs has faded. They are still in general use in low-powered sales forces, and remnants of this approach still appear in sales meetings and sales training sessions.

Perhaps their greatest value for the high-powered sales force is their use as a method of transferring the other types of knowledge. An inspirational delivery of product knowledge is a useful way to obtain both motivation and training. It is difficult, however, to keep such an approach from degenerating into a "pat me on the back and I'll pat you on the back" session or into a low-level, "corny" session which will be resented by professional-level salespeople.

PARTICIPANTS: WHO GETS TRAINED?

The issue here usually is between training only new recruits and training both recruits and experienced salespeople.

It is clear that new recruits need training. Often this training, which is sometimes more orientation than training, has focused on product and company knowledge. Recently, it has improved considerably in many companies, with more emphasis on customer knowledge and selling skills.

Initial training usually took one of two forms: (1) brief orientation or (2) more extended work as a sales trainee. The orientations were 1- to 2-week sessions of acquiring knowledge and meeting people. If the salesperson were experienced or the industry particularly simple, the orientation might be even shorter.

The sales trainee route was considerably longer, lasting from a few months to several years. Usually the orientation on product and company knowledge remained. Then, in an industrial firm, the program might include 6 months as a technician in a technical service laboratory to 1 year as an application engineer. In an apparel firm, the training might consist of a few months acting as an administrative assistant in the sales and sales order departments to several months as a showroom salesperson. At a wholesaler, such as a mill supply house, a salesperson might pick orders[2] for a year, do inside sales work for 2 years, and then become an outside salesperson.

The final part of this program usually includes on-the-job training, sometimes traveling an open territory, and sometimes traveling with a field sales manager. This type of training will be discussd below.

The primary problem with past training efforts was that it usually

[2]To "pick orders" is to select and ready for shipment individual items in an order from inventory.

included a large share of "busy work" and a small portion of training. In a sense, the time allowed the salesperson to become acquainted with the company and vice versa, but sometimes little else took place. Recently, the trend has shifted toward more substance in training.

Another recent trend has been toward training for experienced salespeople. This is most significant. It means that increasingly a salesperson will be encouraged to grow and develop instead of just perform at the same level year after year. Some of these programs are designed for better-than-average salespeople while others are remedial. The best programs are usually modularized and include specific segments applicable to salespeople with different needs. These will be discussed below.

TRAINERS: WHO DOES IT?

There are two sharply divided schools of thought on training—one is that it is a field-oriented activity and should be done primarily, if not exclusively, out in the field; the other is that it should consist of both centralized training and field training.

495

Most of the proponents of a purely field-oriented program fear that if the training is centralized, the field managers will lose control over it. It will become, they argue, staff oriented and of little relevance to people in the field.

The proponents of centralized training argue that it is more efficient (more training per dollar spent) because of the use of professional materials and people. They also believe that such a program provides a standardized approach—each trainee getting the total package without "editing" by idiosyncratic field managers. The field managers, of course, view that process as "customizing." Perhaps the most important argument advanced by the "centralists" is that training is, by and large, a forgotten activity in the field. They feel that, in spite of all the materials provided and all the emphasis placed on it, it is still neglected.

Most centralists desire a combination of field and centralized training. This appears generally to be the best approach. In fact, one could posit the following general program as being a good format for a large, professionally oriented sales force:

1 Orientation or a period of product, company, customer, and selling training, including formal programs at headquarters, attendance at trade shows and sales meetings, and travel with expert salespeople.

2 Initial field work with a heavy dose of field management supervision.

3 Continuing training, including formal programs at headquarters and/ or the region, sales-meeting programs, and on-the-job coaching. The formal programs should be modularized, if possible.

Such a program strives to provide the salesperson with the best aspects of sales approaches. Because selling is a skill and not a collection of knowledge, it must be learned through experience (can one learn to swim without getting into the water?). The field experience is limited, however, because it cannot provide the facilities, material, or breadth of the centralized facilities.

Sales meetings are a useful opportunity for providing advanced training in skills as well as exposure to new products, programs, and techniques. The meetings can be held at the district, region or zone, or national level. Each has its own advantages in terms of cost, impact, and orientation. The important point is that the general attendance makes formalized training at sales meetings very efficient.

Another key issue concerning the trainers is the choice between in-house and outside capabilities. Some companies prefer to develop in-house trainers and programs, because they believe that it is cheaper and more customized. This is not an easy task, even for a large sales force. Training positions are often used as developmental assignments— way stations to higher positions. In such a situation, the trainer has the job for only 1 or 2 years and finds it almost impossible to (1) learn the job, (2) develop some professional competence in training, (3) develop a program, and (4) implement it. If the training position is a full-time one, it is often filled with a manager who is "a nice person" but who "didn't have what it takes to manage." In that situation, the trainer lacks capability and loses credibility.

496

Some firms are willing to make the investment to hire top-quality training professionals and to provide them with the support they need. In these situations, the in-house training programs are very effective.

Some companies prefer to use outside talent. Available programs range from large national organizations such as Xerox Learning Systems, with its well-known Professional Selling Skills program, to small firms such as Sales Development, Inc., of Ridgefield, Conn., and Taylor Associates, of Wellesley, Mass. Both of these are essentially one-man companies run by experienced sales managers. In between is a wide range of firms, including the Professional Salesmanship Center of McGraw-Hill, Dale Carnegie Sales Course, American Management Association, Lacy Sales Institute, and the Lee DuBois Company. Some offer material such as videotapes, records, audio tapes and/or workbooks for in-house administration. Some sales training firms specialize by industry. National Training Systems, Inc., and Tratec, Inc., have specialized, respectively, in broker and distributor sales forces (for example, tobacco and food) and capital equipment and computer sales forces. Some universities, including the University of Massachusetts and Northeastern University, also offer sales courses. Industry trade associations and local sales and marketing executives organizations also tend to offer courses.

Some of the programs offered are highly standardized, while others are customized to the client company. Some companies will accept a few people from a sales force and offer generalized training; others prefer to work with a total sales force. Xerox Learning Systems, for example, holds general, open classes and offers three degrees of customization for in-house programs.

Some of the outside programs are clearly better than others. Most do at least one thing well. It is important for the client company to determine its educational objectives and then to find the best organization to meet that objective. Unfortunately, the sales training industry has, especially in the past, contained both incompetent and unethical firms. This has hurt the industry in general.

HOW IS IT DONE?

Training can be carried out in a variety of ways, including:

1 Readings
2 Lectures
3 Workbooks
4 Discussion
5 Role playing
6 On-the-job training
7 Field bulletins and newsletters

497

Readings and lectures are relatively passive methods of transferring knowledge. They are passive in the sense that the participant's involvement is generally low. They are useful for transmitting knowledge on products, customers, company policies, etc.

Because salespeople are a restless breed, it is important for lectures and readings to be as stimulating, exciting, and enjoyable as possible. Although good showmanship will not ensure the efficient transmittal of information, a dull, droning lecture is unlikely to transmit anything but yawns. Interest is a necessary but not sufficient condition for learning to take place.

Readings and lectures are often most useful when interspersed with other media. They definitely can and should play an important role in the training program because of their efficiency and ease of operation.

Workbooks are useful for encouraging participants to become involved in learning, to internalize rather than intellectualize. A workbook is a reading with some space for participants' responses, preferably from their own experience and responsibilities. Workbooks are harder to develop and administer than straight readings, but the involvement definitely offers an opportunity for improving the transmittal of skills as well as knowledge.

In a sense, discussions are to lectures what workbooks are to readings. They generate excitement and involvement and are likely to produce internalization. Again, they are harder to work with than lectures.

There exists a continuum between lectures and discussions, and workbooks and readings. That is, one can picture a line with a total one-way lecture at one end and a totally nondirective discussion at the other end. In between would be a lecture supplemented by a question-and-answer period, a lecture supplemented by short directed discussions, a directed discussion supplemented by short lectures, and a nondirective discussion supplemented by short lectures. All have their place.

The discussion can be built around a reading, lecture, case study, or personal experience (for example, "What is the best way to close a large sale?"). Again all have their place.

Role playing is a most useful pedagogical technique for developing skills. In a sense, a good case study discussion is a role playing situation. Role playing is by far the hardest medium to administer. Many companies have had terrible luck with situations in which they ask two salespeople to play roles in a manner such as, "Charlie you play the salesman, Susan you be the customer." That approach is doomed to disaster. Successful role playing requires the careful development of roles and situations. Each role playing situation should provide enough latitude for personal expression but also enough background for reasonable understanding of the situation and people. The emphasis should be on realism.

498

Technology has made important changes in several of these media. Workbooks have been developed into programmed learning texts. Lectures can be delivered by audiotape or videotape. Most dramatic and useful is the ability to videotape role playing situations. This enables the participants to go back and meticulously review the action. Videotape is much more powerful than audiotape because it holds the discussants closer to the discussion, and because it enables consideration of nonverbal communication.

Videotaped role playing is by far the most effective nonfield approach to selling skills training. Although it is expensive, time-consuming, and requires meticulous preparation, in the long run, it is clearly cost efficient and most effective. The learning is internalized and the skills used. The impact is very high. It is important that the replay and review of videotape role playing be carefully administered. The player's self-confidence and self-respect can be significantly damaged if the discussion leader does not cushion criticism. Videotape role playing is a powerful technique which must be used with care.

The five techniques mentioned so far are nonfield approaches. They are useful in the orientation program, in advanced training situations, and at sales meetings. Each has its particular advantages and limitations.

The necessary task is to combine the appropriate media into a coherent program with focus and a central theme.

The next technique to be discussed is field training, sometimes called *curbside counseling*. This is the field sales manager's responsibility. A variety of techniques can be used here. One is demonstration, in which the manager shows the salesperson an approach or technique in action. This method has its place, but sometimes it leads to frustration and embarrassment on the part of the salesperson. It is relatively passive unless followed by a discussion. Thus, involvement is limited.

Another approach is evaluation and discussion of the salesperson's methods. If done properly, this can be very useful.

Often, the sales manager can use a Socratic approach to encourage the salesperson to set goals, manage the territory, develop account plans, and implement the plans. This approach is especially useful in conjunction with the field evaluation. For example, before the call, questions such as the following are most useful. "What do you expect to accomplish on this particular call? Who is your primary competition here? How much can they buy and what share can you reasonably expect to obtain?"

Field training must be integrated into the total training program. It should reinforce classroom training and concentrate on the application of skills and techniques.

The final medium to be considered is written communications to the salesperson in the field. These include product-related bulletins as well as more general sales newsletters which provide information about the company, customers, and selling techniques. It is an inexpensive way to provide continuing reinforcement for more expensive media.

The most important part of the choosing of media is the setting of training objectives. The objectives determine the content and media. Without carefully set objectives, the training program will be a failure.

EVALUATING THE PROGRAM

It is very difficult to evaluate sales training programs. Ideally one would like to evaluate them on the basis of a comparison between their cost and their profit generation. This is sometimes tried, but it is indeed a difficult task because other variables are changing simultaneously. A large sales force can attempt to compare two different training programs by testing them in perhaps three pairs of districts, in much the same way as the more elaborate advertising effectiveness tests are run. This is expensive, difficult, and seldom done.

That leaves two alternatives. One way is to say that sales training at a certain budget level, perhaps 5 percent of the total sales expense budget, is a necessary cost of doing business. This is easy but not very effecive because it provides no feel for cost versus benefits.

The final alternative is to measure the effectiveness of the program against specific objectives developed for it. These objectives might include (1) improvement in particular aspects of product knowledge, (2) improvement in customer knowledge, (3) improvement in knowledge of company policy and procedures, and (4) improvement in specific selling skills. More broadly, the objectives might include (1) increased sales of particular products, (2) increased sales to a particular customer category, and (3) increased use of a particular approach or technique.

The first set of objectives can be measured by tests if appropriate. The selling skills can be assessed either in the field or by comparison of before-and-after videotapes. Such a videotape comparison, in fact, can be a strong motivator for increased and continued use of the approach. The salesperson can "see" the improvement and understand its value. Clearly, the evaluation of selling skills acquisition in this way is subjective, but that is a "flaw" in almost all management.

The measurement of the accomplishment of the broader objective gets difficult because of the simultaneous changing of other variables such as the product, advertising, etc. If a product is to gain additional sales support, for example, it is often because market demand is growing or because the product has been redesigned, repriced, etc. Still, good field sales managers can often develop good, useful estimates of the impact of training on such programs.

500

Clearly, the evaluation problem is a serious one. The better the definition of objectives, the easier and more accurate the evaluation will be. However, even with clearly stated and explicit objectives, the evalation will not be a clean, clear-cut process. This is especially true for small sales forces without the ability to test in large numbers and for complex selling situations where many variables are simultaneously active.

TRAINING SALES MANAGERS

Sales managers need training, too. They need an initial orientation type of training as well as continuing training to aid in their growth and development.

Because there are fewer sales managers, and the turnover is usually lower than among salespeople, considerably more resources can be applied per person. The issues are much the same as for salespeople:

1 Who does the training?
2 Where is it done?
3 How is it done?

Again, there is a variety of outside programs available to sales managers, including those offered by Sales and Marketing Executives

International, universities such as the University of Virginia, and companies including several of those listed earlier. Sales management is also an important subject in many marketing management training programs including that given at Harvard Business School.

Larger sales forces often have extensive in-house sales management training programs, sometimes combined with other management training activities. Multilevel sales management teams also assign some training responsibilities to each supervisor.

The same media are available as in sales training, and again, a coherent, focused program is necessary.

The greatest difficulty in sales management training is in setting objectives. There are two general objectives: (1) to improve performance in the current job and (2) to facilitate devlopment for higher positions. Both are important and both can be accomplished in a well-planned program. A good program would include training in all primary sales management tasks, such as recruiting, training, evaluation, and motivation, as well as training in broader marketing-type areas. The latter is important because sales management is a part of marketing management, and a source of top-level marketing managers.

Career paths also offer good training opportunities. Exposure to headquarters sales and marketing positions is useful and in many cases necessary. Exposure to other functions (for example, manufacturing, finance, etc.) is generally an excellent way to develop breadth and a mutuality of understanding among functional areas. All of this must be planned meticulously.

BIBLIOGRAPHY

Christian, Richard C.: "Have We Forgotten How to Train?" *Journal of Marketing*, vol. 26, no. 4, October 1962, pp. 81–82.

Dartnell Corporation: *How to Plan and Conduct Successful Sales Meetings*, Chicago (various dates because it is in looseleaf form and updated frequently).

Frey, John M.: "Missing Ingredient in Sales Training," *Harvard Business Review*, vol. 33, November-December 1955.

Korn, Don: "Don't Call Inland's Salesmen Just Run-of-the-Mill," *Sales Management*, November 13, 1972, pp. 23–27.

McLaughlin, Ian E.: "Training Salesmen on the Job," in Albert Newgarden (ed.), *The Field Sales Manager*, New York: American Management Association, pp. 327–332.

Sales Management: "Man and Motivation '72: Training and Re-Training," May 1, 1972 (entire issue).

Thompson, Joseph W., and William W. Evans: "Behavioral Approach to Industrial Selling," *Harvard Business Review*, vol. 47, March-April 1969, pp. 137–151.

FORTY-EIGHT   Cole National Corporation (C)
Consumer Products Division

SALES TRAINING PROGRAM

In January 1975, Boake Sells, executive vice president of Cole National Corporation, was reviewing the recently announced promotion of Joe Long, former national sales trainer, to the position of district manager. Because Mr. Long's district encompassed the region around the corporate headquarters in Cleveland, and because he would continue to use the headquarters as his district office, Mr. Long would be readily available to fall back upon should any experimental program fail. This convinced Mr. Sells that spring 1975 was an appropriate time for a reevaluation, redirection, or both of the sales force training program.

Mr. Sells thought that the sales training program at the Consumer Products Division (CPD) had been in a state of flux for quite some time, and that it had not received the attention it deserved or needed because of other seemingly more pressing problems. He was concerned about the nature of the sales training program at CPD for the next few years and about convincing the field management team, many of whom were former trainers, that changes were necessary.

Training Prior to Formal Training[1]

Regardless of their previous experience, all new salespeople followed the same schedule for the first few months as Cole National employees. Before being sent to Cleveland for a week of group training, each person worked in the field with an experienced salesperson, observing all facets of the job. Mr. Sells explained the basis for this common experience.

> If you look at the hiring situation in the field, the district manager, who does most of the preliminary interviewing and, in most cases, goes all the way through the process, has a number of other priorities on his mind. The major one is to translate his district's potential into sales dollars. And here he is sitting in some motel, probably in a very dull town, for at least a week,

[1]For background on the company and its marketing strategy and sales force, see Cole National Corporation (A) and (B).

interviewing a bunch of "yokels" who have responded to our ad. Remember, on an ad placed in a Sunday paper with a phone response, this person could get from 90 to 100 calls very easily. The calls can come in seemingly without end. And the district manager must go through a very tedious interviewing experience. The district manager is a salesperson, and the easiest thing for one salesperson to crack is another salesperson. Not only that, but the district manager *wants* to be sold, because the faster he "buys" one of those bodies that walk through the door, the faster he can get back to his serious work of getting out in his district and getting in the sales dollars. So the district manager generally tends to grab at the first person who agrees with him and looks good. The district manager will rarely say, "Nobody I spoke to appealed to me. I'm going back for a second week." A zone manager might make that statement, but not a district manager.

During this interaction in the interview process, there is a high probability for miscommunication: for the district manager to say one thing and for the person who is being hired to hear another thing. One of the reasons for spending that week with an experienced salesperson is to guarantee that the person really understands what the job entails. The new salesperson must reassure himself that the job he sees being done in a territory is really the same job he thought he heard the district manager talking about in the motel room.

In several cases, that week in the field produces a different perception of the job and as a result people have dropped out during this time. Reasons have included: it takes more travel than they thought, or they don't like getting their hands dirty, or there's not enough selling, or there's too much selling, or the customers don't like them, or vice versa.

The second reason for the week in the field is to provide the new hire with a solid orientation to the realities in the field. In the home office he sees his tasks in a very favorable environment—the key machines are clean, and the displays are neat. In real life the machine may be filthy, the display damaged and stuck in a corner, and just a million different things wrong. We want him to have a feel for what he might encounter.

Surprisingly, the new hires do pick up a lot of things during that week, both from the salesperson they're working with and from the store managers. They begin to form an opinion about the job and the company. We always try to put them with good salespeople who convey a positive image. On the other hand, there are trainees who come in with a somewhat worse attitude because the week has revealed the difficulties associated with being a salesperson, but really hasn't emphasized the positive benefits of mastering the job.

So what we end up with is an "unloading" period where all the new people from different parts of the country and with different experiences meet for the first time before the formal training classes begin and exchange much of what they know. The group will usually compare starting salaries and perceptions of the district managers and will trade "horror stories" of their first weeks in the field. Since these sessions tend to highlight the negative aspects of the job and the problems these people are facing, we have a problem in responding quickly to these negative feelings very early in the training class.

503

The national sales manager had devoted a portion of a recent sales management meeting to proving that it was more productive to spend extra time interviewing in order to ensure that the district manager had made a good hire since, the probability of repeating the experience in the near future was reduced. The zone and district managers agreed in principle, but their counterarguments indicated that they felt that no amount of screening was going to significantly change the present success rate. As one district manager put it, "There are just too many variables that are going to affect whether the person stays with Cole, and I can't cover them all if I interviewed everybody for a month! The best I can do is pick the best of what I see and keep my fingers crossed."

Training in Cleveland

New hires were generally scheduled into Cleveland in groups of four to eight. They were all lodged at a nearby motel and remained very close to one another throughout the entire week. Friendships usually developed and were encouraged by CPD management, because it was felt that, after salespersons were out on their own, the greatest loss of morale resulted from feelings of isolation and loneliness. In any job which required extensive travel away from home, it was felt that the salesperson began to believe that no one cared or understood what he was going through. The knowledge that there were other people just like him experiencing the same problems and that these people were personal friends had been shown to provide many new salespeople with the will to continue and to solve their initial problems.

504

In the recent past, a substantial amount of time had been spent in exposing the new hires to a great deal of information about the corporation. Meetings with corporate executives, including the president, were conducted, as well as lengthy discussions on the corporation's views of the future, prospects for advancement, and a multitude of other nonjob-related topics. This area had received less attention lately, because the coordination problems involved appeared to the sales managers to be greater than benefits derived.

Of more lasting benefit, according to several managers, was the opportunity for new people to meet and develop personal contacts with division staff personnel they would be contacting after they were in the field. Knowing whom to call when a paycheck was late or how to get help for an account's credit problems was seen by management as a major goal of the training week.

Knowing the home office people made it much easier to explain the reasons for a number of the division's policies and also to ensure that questions relating to the procedure manual were answered quickly. Each person was given a policy manual and a chain store procedure manual and it was explained that these policies and procedures must be followed exactly.

Many new people arrived in Cleveland lacking all the completed administrative forms. Time was taken in the training class to complete benefit statements, personnel files, and whatever other paper work might be incomplete.

The remainder of the week was spent learning the mechanics of servicing the division's product lines. Emphasis was placed on key-machine maintenance, instruction of clerks, inventory balancing, and order-taking procedures. Throughout all these discussions, relatively little time was devoted to improving the salesperson's selling techniques, except to explain the steps involved in a complete sales call and some hints on how to close a sale effectively. Product knowledge had become the primary focus of the Cleveland training week, and members of the field management team were satisfied that techniques of salesmanship were best learned through on-the-job experience.

The present philosophy of the division's management seemed to be summed up as, "The objective is to get the person on board and moving as quickly as possible."

The week's schedule for a recent training class is reproduced in Exhibit 1.

Training Techniques Used by CPD

CPD had always prided itself on its willingness to adopt new and innovative training techniques. This desire to experiment had often been accompanied by a great deal of discussion among the field management team as to the usefulness and applicability of these techniques to CPD's needs. There were distinct differences between home office personnel and field management as to which techniques had proved most effective in the past. Home office managers tended toward techniques which had a "carry-over" effect that the salesperson could continue to apply and learn from after leaving the training class. District managers had traditionally

Exhibit 1 TRAINING PROGRAM: TYPICAL WEEK'S TRAINING SCHEDULE

Sunday P.M.	Arrive in Cleveland
Sunday evening	Cocktail party and dinner with sales trainer and NSM
Monday A.M.	Introduction to CPD; tour of facilities
Monday P.M.	Required reports; administration in the field
Monday evening	Read self-teaching manual on keys
Tuesday A.M.	Selling and servicing of key-product line
Tuesday P.M.	Maintenance and repair of key machines
Tuesday evening	Read self-teaching manual on knives
Wednesday A.M.	Practice presentations on key-product line
Wednesday P.M.	Selling and servicing of knife-product line
Wednesday evening	Read self-teaching manual on LNS
Thursday A.M.	Selling and servicing LNS-product line
Thursday P.M.	Practice presentations on knives and LNS
Thursday evening	Dinner with home office management personnel
Friday A.M.	Review and discussion of territories
Friday P.M.	Depart Cleveland

supported programs that permitted them a great deal of leeway in directing salespersons after they finished the home office course. Field sales managers had opposed the more costly training programs, indicating that they felt the money could be better spent on increased support of the salespeople in the form of product promotions, better catalog sheets, or more sales contests.

The division was one of the early adopters of programmed instruction booklets for use by the new employees. Workbooks were developed for each product line, as well as for policies and procedures, and given to the salespeople upon their arrival in Cleveland. Every person was expected to work through the books during his free time in the evenings and to ask questions concerning the material the following day in class. It was felt that this concept could also be applied to people in the field, since workbooks covering areas of specific product knowledge in greater detail could be sent to the salespeople to complete during their evenings away from home. The entire concept was viewed with disdain by the district managers who felt that the entire process was slow and clumsy and would be resented by the salespeople as an invasion of their free time.

As a result, no attempt was made to develop workbooks for use outside the training class. By late 1974, in fact, the product line workbooks were still being distributed to new employes even though some sections had become obsolete, but no requirement was made that they be completed outside of class.

Lectures or "canned presentations" were almost universally disliked because it was felt that the most productive learning occurred when the trainees were involved in the activity rather than sitting back absorbing information. Nonetheless, since the programmed learning had fallen into disuse, most product line information was being presented in the form of lectures interspersed with practical demonstrations of the material being covered. This was particularly true in the area of key-machine servicing, where the trainer was lecturing on all the problem areas on the machine and then demonstrating the correct solution on an actual machine. Afterward, the trainees were presented with defective machines and were required to diagnose and repair the malfunctions.

In 1968, CPD began to experiment with the use of closed circuit television (CCTV) and videotape recording (VTR) equipment for in-house production of training tapes. Initially, the equipment was used to produce demonstration tapes which were staged situations designed to show the proper solution to many of the common problems encountered during a typical sales call. These tapes were produced using in-house personnel in the roles of salesperson and store manager. They were shown to the training classes and then analyzed during a group discussion.

CCTV and VTR were later used for in-class situations with the sales trainer playing the part of the store manager and one of the trainees attempting to make a product line presentation. Immediately after the participants finished the scenario, their presentation would be played back and discussed by the group. The instant feedback, stop action, and capability of viewing a scene over and over facilitated the discussion and enabled the trainer to highlight the strong and weak points in the presentation. The level of trainee involvement was always extremely high during these sessions, and discussions were animated. Home office personnel felt that VTR was a valuable training tool, because individuals were able to see themselves making a presentation and diagnose their faults right on the spot, which indicated a more complete understanding of what was required of them. Attempts were also made to teach sales skills through the use of videotaped situations, but not much effort was expended, and the results were not considered worth further development.

Even though CCTV and VTR had many appealing qualities, they had their drawbacks and detractors. CCTV and VTR involved a fairly sizeable investment, over $12,000 for any training program budget, and the equipment was delicate and required special handling. Further, a trained operator was required for the camera and recording equipment, which meant the additional cost of a second person in the training class at least part of the time.

507

The district managers tended to view CCTV and VTR as expensive toys that had a high level of immediate impact but were of little long-term value in teaching any of the skills necessary to succeed in the field. They felt that the staged presentations tended to be unrealistic and the trainee simulations were extremely time-consuming and prone to be useless if the trainee chosen decided to ham it up rather than approach the role seriously.

CPD had even used a commercially developed audio-programmed instruction package which was designed to increase the ability of a salesperson "to influence another person's way of thinking." The bulk of the program was comprised of tape-recorded dramatizations of typical selling situations; however, it also included programmed instruction booklets and coaching guides to instruct the management team on how to use the package in teaching. The entire approach was viewed as extremely mechanistic and not at all suited to CPD's style of selling. As one district manager put it, "It had all the drawbacks of other techniques, very few of the benefits, and was boring as hell."

The function of role playing as a training technique was discussed at great length by one sales executive.

Role playing is particularly susceptible to not being liked by managers in general because 95% of it is handled poorly. In a good role-playing situation, each person has a well-defined role, not some vague generality such as, "You're the store manager and he's going to try to sell you something."

Rather, the role is clearly defined and a particular problem is posed. For example, the person playing the store manager might be told that Joe Jones is coming to see him and that Joe wants to sell him a key program. Joe has tried to sell him this plan twice before but he has turned him down. The store manager is very concerned with increasing traffic in the store and has doubts about what service he will receive with the Cole National program, but he is convinced that keys could be a viable product in his store. Now what all this does is limit the possibility that a person will ruin the role-playing situation because he is required to remain within the conditions set forth in the outline.

In a similar manner, the person who is to play the salesperson is provided with enough information, such as the fact that the customer's competitors all have key programs and are satisfied with the results, in order that he might realistically respond to any comments made by the store manager. The purpose here is to determine what a person will do in a rapidly changing, well-defined situation, not how well he can create a fantasy in front of an audience.

The greatest problem preventing a more widespread adoption of role playing is the high level of skill which the trainer must possess in order to make the technique productive. He must be able to lead a critique of the role-playing situation, and that requires a complete understanding of the teaching points which were trying to be made, plus an ability to draw meaningful comments from the members of the class. Further, it takes a special skill to develop the background material in order that it be sufficiently descriptive without being confining and that it contain all the necessary elements to bring the scenario to a close. This last point is really vital and, if handled properly, practically guarantees that the role playing will be successful. For example, the store manager's "script" could say, "Refuse the first offer to close, but if salesperson continues to probe indicate that you are concerned with the program's price and you would like some payment terms. If the salesperson provides you with complete payment terms, accept."

508

I think many people, trainers included, regard role playing as a funny game and don't realize its potential for learning or its danger of embarrassment. Of major importance in any training situation is the infusion of a sense of confidence in the trainee. You want the new hire to leave the training class after you have given him positive feedback and a confirmation of his ability to sell in any situation. Fail to provide either, and chances are you have wasted the training week. Role playing can provide both, but only under the most careful of controls.

MEASURING A SUCCESSFUL TRAINING PROGRAM

When asked how he would evaluate the success or failure of a training program, a division executive replied, "I don't know how you measure success in a training program. Your most important question is, 'Was a particular person successful when he went into the field?' You hardly, if ever, ask the question of what contribution did the training program make toward that success or failure because you lack the tools to measure that contribution."

Mr. Sells felt that one of the major failings of the training program was that its objectives were never set and no criteria were esablished to measure the success of the entire program over time or of any particular technique. Programs were always defined in terms of what the management wanted the trainees to know and never in any manner that related to the success of each group. Individual sales trainers had attempted to maintain sales performance records of each of their classes but collection of the information usually ceased about 4 or 5 months after the class left Cleveland or whenever the sales trainer moved to another position.

One of the formal mechanisms used was a trainer evaluation report which was sent to the district manager after one of his salespeople had completed training. This report was a completely subjective analysis of the salesperson's performance during the week in Cleveland and was concerned with attitude, enthusiasm, willingness to cooperate, and ability to get along with others. Most managers viewed this report as worthless because no provable correlation had ever been made between a new hire's performance in the training class and his subsequent performance out in a territory.

509

The only other attempt to measure the effectiveness of the training program involved a pretraining and posttraining test given to trainees to determine the changes in the level of their product knowledge after the week in Cleveland. The very same test was given on both occasions and the measures of success were the total net gain per person for the class in their test scores. A typical page of this test is reproduced in Exhibit 2. As with the trainer evaluation report, no perceivable correlation existed between pretest scores, posttest scores, net change in scores, or any other statistic and a salesperson's actual success. The test was still used in 1975 in order to provide a class with an insight into what should be their focus of attention during the week.

ALTERNATIVE TRAINING PROGRAMS

During the past few years, a great deal of discussion had been going on concerning alternatives to the present system of training. One proposal had recommended that the new hires ride with experienced salespeople for at least 2 weeks and then come to Cleveland for only 3 days to be thoroughly briefed on administrative procedures. District managers would then take a more active role in coaching the new hire during his first few weeks in his own territory. This plan would eliminate the need for a sales trainer and the savings could be applied elsewhere.

Another plan involved changing the sequence in which aspects of

Exhibit 2   PAGE FROM CPD PRODUCT KNOWLEDGE TEST

9   Compared to brass, color keys have: (a) equal tensile strength _____
     (b) less tensile strength   _____
     (c) more tensile strength _____

   Compared to brass, color keys are: (a) equal in weight _____
     (b) heavier   _____
     (c) lighter   _____

10   How many key styles are on the: Quik Key display   _____
     3K display   _____
     Available from Cleveland _____

11   Match:
   (1) Duplicate blank _____   (a) Stamped numbers
   (2) Original blank   _____   (b) Embossed numbers

12   The 3K display has _____ panels.

13   The Quik Key display has _____ panels.

14   Our new key machines are the _____ and the _____.

15   List the types of cutters on the machines.
   (a) _____
   (b) _____
   (c) _____

16   List the types of repairs you should be able to make on the key machines.
   (a) _____
   (b) _____
   (c) _____
   (d) _____
   (e) _____

510

17   Eight steps will become second nature to you in servicing national key accounts. List them briefly.
   (a) _____   (e) _____
   (b) _____   (f) _____
   (c) _____   (g) _____
   (d) _____   (h) _____

training were presently handled. A new hire would ride with a salesperson for 10 days to 2 weeks and then the district manager would ride with the new salesperson for a week helping him set up the territory. The new salesperson would then be left on his own for approximately 2 months to manage the territory and then would come to Cleveland for a week of training which would be concentrated on helping the salesperson solve particular problems found in his territory. The training would be more individualized and more time could be spent on the sales techniques. However, most members of headquarters management believed that letting an untrained person operate alone in the field for 2 months would result in an explosion of procedure violations.

   Mr. Sells had been investigating the possibility of a two-phase training process whereby new employees would come to Cleveland twice. The first class would occur after the new person had spent a week in the field with a salesperson and would concentrate on administrative procedures and simple servicing of an account. Approximately 6 months later those salespeople who were still with the sales force would return to Cleveland for a week of advanced training in new product introduction, account upgrading, and sales skills. While this approach would result in increased training costs and the need for a better training staff, it was felt that the potential benefits in terms of a more professional sales force were quite large. Most district managers felt that a second training session would be a waste of time and would reduce sales by removing people from the field just as they were reaching an acceptable performance level and beginning to earn a bonus.

Determining Training Costs

The decision as to whether or not to undertake any changes in the training program was clouded by the inability of CPD to define the cost parameters of any of the alternatives. The major question dealt with whether it was possible to establish a causal relationship between training and turnover. Mr. Sells commented on the general attitude held by the home office personnel.

> The problems within the training area are a function of the turnover because it is both the "cause" of the turnover and the "cure" to which you turn for relief. So now, if you train them better, you should decrease your turnover. There's no proof of that, but somehow it seems logical. More often than not, and this is my own opinion, turnover is more a function of a "bad hire" than anything else. When CPD can do a better job of hiring, I believe our turnover problem will be drastically reduced.

It was felt that training probably made better salespeople out of the new employees more quickly, but that anyone who remained with the sales force would eventually learn everything necessary to perform adequately. The problem with this laissez faire approach, according to some managers, was that the reason for "sticking with the program" was lacking and that training provided the incentive to stick with it. The desire to succeed, to impress your peer group, to do better than the other people was never greater than at the end of the training class, they argued, and it was felt that this motivation was at least as important as any knowledge imparted to the new employee.

CPD had been collecting data on turnover rates and the direct costs of the sales force for a number of years. Exhibit 2 of "Cole National Corporation (B)" shows the composition of CPD's sales force in terms of length of employment.

In July 1966, only slightly over 8 percent (6 out of 73) field salespeople had been with the division for more than 5 years. By January 1973, this number had risen to slightly over 24 percent (22 out of 90) and it was felt that this group formed the nucleus of any future efforts to improve the quality of the sales force.

Many members of CPD management were still concerned by what they considered to be an excessively high turnover rate. One member of the Cleveland staff remarked, "Things aren't as bad as they were a few years ago, but we still hire and fire salespeople faster than I can keep track of them!" Exhibit 3 of "Cole National Corporation (B)" contains a breakdown by month of all the new employees, terminations, and resignations in the field sales force for a 40-month period. In every discussion of turnover problems, someone mentioned that more time should be spent in prehire screening in order to select only the best candidates. This opinion was almost always countered by someone responding that if the new people were given more thorough training they would not become disheartened by their initial problems and leave.

As the composition of the field sales force became more stable, some members of the management team in Cleveland remarked that an analysis of bonus data seemed to indicate that the longer a salesperson remained with the company the more expensive he became in terms of bonus and salary, and therefore it might not be such a bad idea to keep the turnover high and the compensation low. Exhibit 3 presents an analysis of average bonus earnings by length of service.

As a result of these comments a study was made of the actual direct costs related to a sample of salespeople who had from 2 to 18 years of service with CPD. A summary of the results of the sample survey based on 1971 data is shown in Exhibit 4.

Mr. Sells commented,

> If I knew what the learning curve for a new person versus an established person in a territory looked like, I might have a better answer to what turnover costs in sales dollars. I don't know how to quantify what improper or incomplete training costs in terms of turnover. I mean, I could answer the question in the conventional manner by describing all the overhead costs and then add and multiply and divide and probably come up with a price tag of $3,000 or $4,000 per person, but that doesn't mean anything. The real cost is at the field level, in lost customer relations.

THE TRAINING PROGRAM IN THE DIVISION STRUCTURE

The responsibility for the training program in CPD had always been part of the national sales manager's functions. Recently the alternative of a separate training department reporting to the division president had been put forth, in part to highlight the increased attention most executives felt this area should receive in the future. Mr. Sells commented,

> One problem that exists when a national sales manager retains control of the training program is that the division loses many of the interplay situations which are always productive for improving the program. If the national sales manager and the training section find themselves interacting as equals, I believe that better formulated programs may result. The training section can

Exhibit 3   SUMMARY OF AVERAGE BONUS EARNINGS (per length of service)

		Less than 1 year	1-2 years	2-3 years	3-4 years	4-5 years	5 years and over	Total
TMs who finished fiscal year with CPD and earned some bonus	Average per person	$ 1,678	$ 3,798	$ 3,902	$ 2,444	$ 3,668	$ 4,848	$ 3,626
	No. of persons	15	13	11	5	9	22	75
	Total	$25,166	$49,368	$42,920	$12,219	$33,014	$106,651	$269,338
	% of total dollars	9.3	18.3	15.9	4.6	12.3	39.6	100.0
	Cumulative % of total dollars	9.3	27.6	43.5	48.1	60.4	100.0	—
	% of TM's	20.0	17.3	14.7	6.7	12.0	29.3	100.0
	Cumulative % of TM's	20.0	37.3	52.0	58.7	70.7	100.0	—
TMs who finished fiscal year with CPD and were eligible to earn bonus	Average per person	$ 1,144	$ 3,526	$ 3,902	$ 2,444	$ 3,310	$ 4,848	$ 3,206
	No. of persons	22	14	11	5	10	22	84
	Total	$25,166	$49,368	$42,920	$12,219	$33,014	$106,651	$269,338
	% of total dollars	9.3	18.3	15.9	4.6	12.3	39.6	100.0
	Cumulative % of total dollars	9.3	27.6	43.5	48.1	60.4	100.0	—
	% of TM's	26.2	16.7	13.1	5.9	11.9	26.2	100.0
	Cumulative % of TMs	26.2	49.9	56.0	61.9	73.8	100.00	—

Source: Report prepared in early 1973.

Exhibit 4 RESULTS OF SAMPLE SURVEY, 1971

Salesperson	Years of service	Total sales	Salary	Bonus	Reimbursable expenses	Fringe benefits (est.)	Auto costs (est.)	Total salesperson-related costs
Marmon	8	$195,492	$ 8,840.00	$ 7,799.10	$2,203.63	$ 884.00	$1,320.00	$21,146.73
			4.5%	4.0%	1.2%	0.4%	0.7%	10.8%
Hudson	18	210,695	8,060.00	7,408.10	622.09	806.00	1,320.00	18,216.19
			3.8	3.5	0.3	0.4	0.6	8.6
Talbot	6	199,328	8,320.00	450.35	2,264.42	832.00	1,320.00	13,186.77
			4.2	0.2	1.1	0.4	0.7	6.6
Rio	4	130,634	8,320.00	361.17	1,069.08	832.00	1,320.00	11,902.25
			6.4	0.3	0.8	0.6	1.0	9.1
Mercer	16	150,478	8,700.00	382.58	873.11	870.00	1,320.00	12,145.69
			5.8	0.3	0.6	0.6	0.9	8.1
Kaiser	14	165,889	9,100.00	783.76	1,565.39	910.00	1,320.00	13,679.15
			5.5	0.5	0.9	0.5	0.8	8.2
Pierce	2	129,320	7,280.00	5,421.75	3,153.19	728.00	1,320.00	17,902.94
			5.6	4.2	2.4	0.6	1.0	13.8
Nash	6	149,721	7,880.00	220.74	2,177.22	788.00	1,320.00	12,385.96
			5.3	0.1	1.5	0.5	0.9	8.3
Dusenberg	8	240,987	10,920.00	10,336.80	3,535.62	1,092.00	1,320.00	27,204.42
			4.5	4.3	1.5	0.4	0.6	11.3
Apperson	4	250,994	7,800.00	9,289.16	3,838.86	780.00	1,320.00	23,028.02
			3.1	3.7	1.5	0.3	0.5	9.2
Stutz	3	250,576	7,540.00	10,714.25	3,184.81	754.00	1,320.00	23,513.06
			3.0	4.3	1.3	0.3	0.5	9.4
Delange	8	184,169	8,060.00	5,183.35	2,521.67	806.00	1,320.00	17,891.02
			4.4	2.8	1.4	0.4	0.7	9.7
Bugatti	5	164,593	8,580.00	480.44	2,399.84	858.00	1,320.00	13,638.28
			5.2	0.3	1.5	0.5	0.8	8.3
Packard	7	172,813	8,580.00	6,130.60	2,451.07	858.00	1,320.00	19,339.67
			5.0	3.5	1.4	0.5	0.8	11.2

pick up and indicate the shortcomings in the field operation as they conduct follow-up studies at each training class. At the same time, the field management team will act as a check to prevent the training section from developing any programs which they don't believe will have real benefits in terms of increased sales.

The national sales manager was convinced that the sales trainer should report to him because the results of the trainer's efforts directly affected the outcome of his operation. Further, the national sales manager felt that he could more effectively utilize the trainer's services when he was not conducting a class. The present practice was to send the trainer into any district having a problem in order to provide temporary relief. Thus the sales trainer filled in for salespeople on vacation, in critical open territories, and even functioned as a district manager where necessary. He was also used to staff the CPD booth at trade shows and to help set up the quarterly sales management meetings.

The national sales manager put it this way:

> You must understand that the person in the trainer's position was probably a salesperson before he became a trainer and will probably be a district manager sometime in the future. It's silly to pull him out of the organization and then plug him back in. Besides not all training is controlled by the sales trainer. Remember a substantial portion of the training a new person receives takes place in the field under the direction of a district or zone manager. On-the-job training is probably superior to any other technique such as videotape or role playing.

515

Selecting a Sales Trainer

In the late 1960s the management of CPD recognized that advances in training techniques were occurring rapidly and that CPD should be a participant in this development. A three-person personnel training and development department was organized and given responsibility not only for the sales force training program, but for all in-house training, plus consulting on executive development programs. During 1968 to 1970, this department produced and developed most of the training programs and techniques in use in 1975.

In 1970 the division sustained a number of operating setbacks coupled with the national economic recession and rising expenses in the field sales force. Other divisions of Cole National were experiencing similar difficulties and the only short-term solution was to cut expenses wherever possible. With the extremely high turnover in the sales force it was felt that most of the department's efforts were being wasted. The decision was made to eliminate it. At the same time, an increasingly large number of managers came from the ranks of the experienced field salespeople and showed less commitment to the concept of a professional sales training department.

The previous three sales trainers had moved on to positions in field management.

The national sales manager indicated that the position of sales trainer provided an excellent opportunity to take an experienced salesperson who had demonstrated the potential to become a manager, bring him into the home office, and round out his education. It also gave the corporate staff a chance to observe the person over a reasonable period of time and make an accurate assessment of his long-range potential.

While agreeing that all these benefits existed, Mr. Sells felt that CPD was developing a set of expectations about the job which were not related to the job. "If every trainer believes that he will only hold the position temporarily, there is no incentive to devote any time to improving the program. Also, because of this attitude, members of management are reluctant to spend any money training the sales trainer."

In 1975, a new sales trainer observed the old sales trainer for a few weeks while at least one training class was conducted. The first training class that a new sales trainer handled was usually observed by the national sales manager, who would then make a critique of the trainer's presentation.

516

As Mr. Sells saw it, the next sales trainer could be one of three general types. One of the salespeople could be brought into Cleveland and the program could continue as it was presently functioning. A second alternative would be to go outside the corporation and hire a professional sales trainer who would be responsible for updating and improving the material presently being used. Finally, CPD could recruit a recent business school graduate to set up and staff another personnel training and development department and then perhaps move into a personnel or sales management position. A decision had to be made soon because a new training class was scheduled for early March.

FORTY-NINE Metropolitan Life Insurance Company (B)

DISTRICT SALES MANAGER TRAINING

In March 1973, Stephen London, of Metropolitan Life Insurance Company, was developing a training program for its district sales managers. There was some disagreement about the nature of the program and much concern over its content and method of presentation. There was total agreement, however, that a good training program was necessary because of the key role played by the district sales manager in the company's sales program.

METROPOLITAN LIFE AND THE LIFE INSURANCE INDUSTRY

Metropolitan had the largest amount of insurance in force and the largest premium income of any life insurance company in the world. Management estimated that it had 7 percent of the personal life insurance market.

The company sold life insurance; annuity contracts, which paid a certain amount of money per month to the retired beneficiary; health insurance, which paid for medical bills when the beneficiary was sick or injured; and disability insurance, which paid an income when the insured was disabled. It sold these policies either to individuals or to groups. The groups would usually be either an employer or professional organization which would contract for the insurance for its employees or members. Group insurance was sold by a different sales force than personal insurance and reported through a completely separate executive organization. In 1971 the amount of Metropolitan group life insurance in force exceeded the amount of personal life insurance for the first time.

Metropolitan's personal life insurance business could be divided into two parts: ordinary insurance and account insurance referred to as "debit insurance" in other companies. Ordinary insurance included the larger policies which were paid for in person or by mail on an annual, semiannual, quarterly, or monthly basis. Account insurance consisted of small policies (often called "burial insurance") which were paid for only on a weekly[1] or monthly basis through a program of home collection. Metropolitan had both account and ordinary salespeople or agents. The account agents had routes or territories upon which they collected the small amounts of money for the insurance policies. The account agents were paid a "servicing commission" for the collection function and commissions for selling. They were free, however, to sell all of the company's insurance policies. The ordinary agents, on the other hand, sold only ordinary insurance and would not sell account policies. They were paid on a straight commission basis and did no collecting.

Prudential and several other of the largest life insurance firms had both account and ordinary agents. Many smaller firms were more specialized. Some of them were growing substantially faster than the industry. While the larger firms generally had sales forces which sold only their insurance contracts, smaller firms often used independent agents or salespeople who sold for several firms (brokers).

During the 1950s and 1960s, there had been a trend toward ordinary insurance and away from account insurance, and toward more complex contracts necessitating more sophisticated and personalized selling. Throughout this period Metropolitan and other firms introduced new contracts.

517

[1]Metropolitan had discontinued the sale of weekly policies in 1965.

In the early 1970s, Metropolitan made two major changes in its product line. In late 1971 it announced the sale of variable annuity contracts in which the payment to the insured or his beneficiary was based upon the value of common stocks and other equity securities in which the company had invested the premiums. These contracts typically guaranteed a minimum amount as a death benefit. Industry experts viewed the moves into variable annuities as a way to protect policyholders against inflation, to allow policyholders to obtain better returns on their money, and as a way for the insurance firms to enter the market for equity investments. This new product was designed primarily to provide retirement benefits.

In September 1972, the firm announced that it would enter the property liability insurance business in early 1974. Such insurance included contracts protecting homes and automobiles from loss through burglary, fire, and other hazards.

On January 1, 1973, Metropolitan announced another major change: it would add no more account salespeople, and with time, the practice of household collection would gradually cease. Whenever an account agent left the firm, his collection customers would be converted to mail payment. Thus, all agents who were to be hired would be ordinary agents. At the time, account agents were generating 62 percent of sales, ordinary agents 33 percent, and management (unit sales manager and above) 5 percent.

THE METROPOLITAN SALES FORCE

The personal insurance marketing and sales organization numbered over 35,000 people at the end of 1972. It included 7 agency vice presidents to whom reported 39 regional sales manager. The regional sales managers supervised 815 district sales managers to whom reported over 3,500 unit sales managers. The unit sales managers had direct supervisory responsibility for the salespeople. The company had 16,800 account agents at the end of 1972 and 6,100 ordinary agents. It also had about 1,400 unfilled account openings. At the top of the sales force organization was a vice president for line operations to whom reported the 7 agency vice presidents. Another vice president was responsible for the staff operations, including marketing planning and development, marketing and training services, field sales administration, and performance and expense control. Both vice presidents reported to Jason Atlas, one of three executive vice presidents in the firm. Exhibit 1 is an organization chart of the marketing and field sales management department.

A typical district office had a district sales manager and four unit sales managers, one of whom supervised only ordinary insurance salespeople, three of whom supervised account salespeople or a combination of

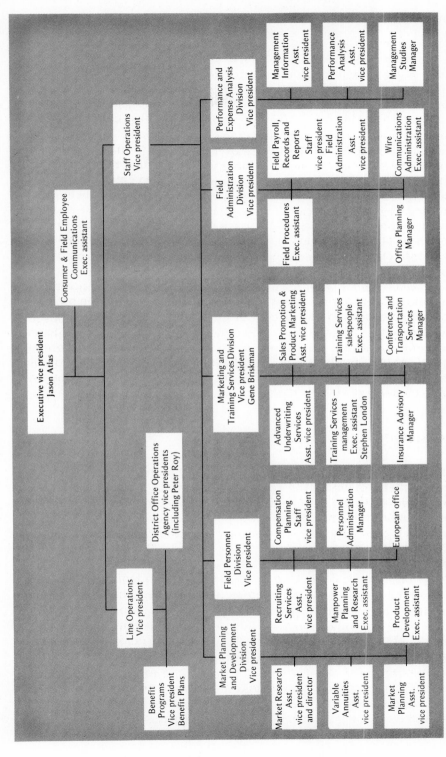

Exhibit 1 Organization chart of marketing and field sales management.

account and ordinary agents. Each unit sales manager would ideally supervise eight salespeople. A clerical force of about six people reported to an office supervisor who reported to the district sales manager. The clerical group provided secretarial services to the managers and salespeople, processed incoming premiums and outgoing benefits, and handled other routine clerical matters.

The company had a good deal of turnover in its sales force although it was somewhat lower than the industry average. In 1972, 4,172 account salespeople and 2,765 ordinary insurance agents had been hired. As was true of the whole industry, many of the salespeople left before the end of the first year. The turnover rate for more experienced salespeople was considerably lower.

In 1973, the firm was attempting to use a nominator method of recruiting, in which the district sales manager or the unit sales manager would ask various people active in the community (for example, ministers, businessmen, etc.) to suggest potential recruits. Because the company was interested in upgrading the size of its contracts and the average income of its policyholders, and in developing ordinary as opposed to account salespeople, it was attempting to hire a "better grade of salesperson" which usually meant a salesperson with better academic qualifications and higher aspirations with regard to status and income. In many cases the district and unit sales managers were being asked to recruit salespeople with better qualifications than they had possessed when they were hired.

520

Training Salespeople

As of 1973, the salespeople were trained in the district by the unit sales managers. Before 1970, the company had several training centers which presented 2-week training programs for them. The training centers were discontinued because exhaustive statistical analysis had failed to show that the salespeople trained in the centers performed better than those trained in the districts.

In 1973, some salespeople underwent a precontract training program lasting from several weeks to a month. During this period, they spent time after their current jobs or studies during weekdays and on weekends with the unit sales manager learning the rudiments of product knowledge. The company advocated this program, but due to pressures for personnel, many managers did not practice it. After officially joining the firm, the salespeople had a 14-week training period during which they were supposed to receive intensive coaching from the unit sales manager. During this time, they received a training salary. After this period they were supposed to receive frequent coaching during the first year and some coaching afterward. The home office training staff provided the sales training aids.

Compensation

Salespeople received commissions on the policies they sold. In the year the policy was sold, the agent received a percentage of the premium, depending upon the type of policy and the age of the policyholder (first-year commissions). Additional commissions were paid during the second through the fourth year if the policy remained in force (renewal commissions). These renewal commission rates were considerably lower than the first-year commission rates, but were a substantial source of revenue for the agent. The agent also received a bonus based on renewals. A small additional commission was paid after the fourth year and for the life of the policy.

Unit sales managers were paid on a relatively complex basis as follows:

A salary of $100 per week or more, depending upon longevity

A percentage override of the first-year commissions credited to their salespeople (additional payments being made on commissions earned by *newer* salespeople)

A percentage override of the renewal commissions credited to their salespeople

Bonus awards for salespeople promoted to unit sales manager from their unit

Commissions on policies they personally sold

District sales managers were compensated in a manner similar to unit sales managers. They received a salary of between $135 and $200 per week with increases based on an annual performance appraisal. They received override commissions on their salespeople's commissions in the same manner as unit sales managers and also could earn commissions by selling insurance. They, too, received bonuses for salespeople and sales managers who were promoted from their district. These bonuses were in the $1,000 range.

The table below provides information on average compensation:

	1970	1971	1972	1972 range
Account salesperson[2]	$ 8,967	$ 9,345	$10,036	
Ordinary insurance salesperson	9,712	10,796	11,648	$ 5,000–$75,000[3]
Unit sales manager (accounts)	12,968	13,718	[4]	10,000– 35,000
Unit sales manager (ordinary)	15,874	16,658	[4]	
District sales manager	25,688	27,401	29,380	16,000– 75,000

[2]Account salespeople averaged $4,000 salary for their collection duties although some earned as much as $5,000–$6,000.

[3]A few salespeople earned in excess of $100,000 per year.

[4]The 1972 average for all unit sales managers was $14,996.

Recognition

The company had conventions for the leading salespeople and managers. Trophies, plaques, and certificates were awarded for outstanding performance. The lobby of its headquarters building in New York City contained the pictures of the firm's very top salespeople and managers.

Each region also had conventions for the leading salespeople and managers within that region. These programs were attended by salespeople who met certain performance standards but did not qualify for the company recognition programs.

THE UNIT SALES MANAGER

The unit sales manager, the first level of sales management, was typically promoted from among the better salespeople. Often highly productive salespeople would have to take a pay cut when they moved up to unit sales manager.

One high-level executive described the unit sales manager's job as primarily one of training. He saw a typical unit sales manager as spending his 52 weeks per year in the following fashion:

522

1 Two introductions of new salespeople per year with 6 weeks devoted to each (12 weeks in total)

2 Continued training of eight persons with two 2-week assignments with each (32 weeks in total)

3 Meetings including 1 week at the Leaders Conference and 2 weeks at training sessions (3 weeks in total)

4 Vacation averaging 3 weeks

5 Two weeks for miscellaneous

Unit sales managers were also responsible for helping in the recruiting of new salespeople. Often they helped salespeople close large sales in which their positions and status and/or experience and skill were needed.

Each unit sales manager was expected to have a 1-hour conference each week with each of his salespeople and to have a 1-hour meeting with his unit once each week. Some meetings would be sales training meetings and others would be to introduce the salespeople to new products, laws, regulations, or procedures. The sales promotion, training, and other staff groups provided materials and packaged programs for many of these meetings.

One high-level manager stated that the unit sales manager's function as described above was an objective and "not necessarily the way that it's been done." He went on to say that "many unit sales managers *help* the agents by going out with them to 'beat the bushes' for prospects or by going along as the 'major sale closer.' When the sales manager consistently goes with the salesman to close the sale, the salesman becomes a eunuch. Too many unit sales managers are nothing more than good salesmen. They have the great ego drive of the good salesman which gets in their way in accomplishing things through others. They must be taught to manage the salesmen, not to do the salesmen's work."

The turnover among unit sales managers was quite high. One executive estimated that 750 unit sales managers had either been promoted or demoted, or had left the firm in 1972. It was not viewed by some as a permanent position. One executive commented, "The unit sales manager moves up if he likes management and turns out to be willing and able to manage. Otherwise, he moves back to being a salesman." The company, however, had been taking steps to enhance the position by giving the unit sales manager full responsibility for his salespeople and by adding a longevity factor to his salary.

Until 1963, the function of each sales manager was determined by the district sales manager to meet the short-term needs of the district sales office. Thus, while a unit sales manager was responsible for supervising a staff of salespeople, he might be assigned duties, such as recruiting, training, detail work, etc., by the district sales manager for the district office as a whole. These functional assignments tended to change from time to time. The compensation of the unit sales manager depended on the performance of the district office as a whole and on the production of his salespeople. This practice was changed in 1963 to a more line-oriented organization, in which each unit sales manager was responsible for all functions for his salespeople. The previous practice, according to one agency vice president who favored the new approach, led to a unit sales manager who "was sterile in areas other than his specialty and who was lopsided in his outlook when he was promoted to district sales manager."

THE DISTRICT SALES MANAGER

Metropolitan sales management viewed the district sales manager as the key management level in their organization. One commented, "The unit sales manager has his boss right there with him. But it's different with the district manager. His boss [the regional sales manager] is in a separate location in the region. That location can be close, as in the densely populated New York area, or very remote, as in the mountain states."[5]

---

[5]The agency vice presidents were located in the home office in New York. Regional sales managers had offices in their regions. District and unit sales managers had offices with the salespeople in the district offices.

Another executive commented, "Not only is he remote from his boss, but he is the ranking manager in the field. He has the ultimate responsibility for the salesmen and their results. He is the highest level executive that the salesmen and the community see on a regular basis."

Because of the perceived importance of the position to the company, it had devoted a great deal of effort to defining the position and improving the performance of the district sales managers. In 1959, a 25-page detailed job description had been developed. (See Appendix A for excerpts.) It had been revised in 1969 and was about to be revised in 1973. It stressed the district sales manager's responsibilities in six areas: (1) develop and maintain a sales program, (2) recruit and select district personnel, (3) train and develop district personnel, (4) motivate district personnel, (5) direct administrative activities, and (6) develop and maintain good public relations.

The company had also developed a procedure for evaluating the district sales manager's performance. The directions were 15 pages long, and the evaluation form 8 pages long [Metropolitan Life Insurance Company (A)].

The company had also conducted studies of district sales manager attitudes and opinions in 1968 and 1971. The report on the 1971 study was 165 pages long. (See Appendix B.)

524

The average age of the district sales managers in 1973 was in the early forties, although they ranged from the early thirties to mid-sixties. Traditionally, there had been three routes to appointment as a district sales manager. The district sales managers for large districts had usually been district sales managers of smaller districts. This practice had been almost discontinued. The second mode of promotion had been direct appointment of a unit sales manager to the district sales manager position. This approach was frequently used with very experienced and/or older candidates for the district sales manager position. The preferred route was through the use of two training positions. In such a procedure the chosen unit sales manager was promoted to the position of field training consultant, reporting directly to the regional sales manager. A field training consultant was paid a straight salary of between $14,000 and $20,000 per year. This was often less than the candidate had made as a unit sales manager. The field training consultant was supposed to help the regional sales manager in setting up training meetings and seminars. In addition, he helped teach the unit sales managers in the region how to train and supervise the salespeople. When a district sales manager was disabled, the field training consultant would often manage his district under the close supervision of the regional sales manager.

After a period of time (1 to 4 years) as a field training consultant, the candidate usually became an advanced underwriting adviser. In this position he conducted clinics or coaching sessions for sales managers and salespeople on advanced sales procedures, taxation, pensions, estate planning, etc. Again, he reported to the regional sales manager. After 1 to 3 years in this position, the advanced underwriting adviser was promoted to district sales manager. The length of time spent in both the field training consultant and advanced underwriting adviser positions was determined by the district sales manager openings in each region.

The new district sales manager did not attend a formal training program. The regional sales manager was expected to spend between several days and 2 working weeks on the job with the new district sales manager.

During this period it was expected that the regional sales manager would "work in tandem" with the new district sales manager, checking his knowledge and working on each key area of responsibility. As the district sales manager became acclimated, the regional sales manager would spend less time with him.

The regional sales manager was also responsible for the continuing training and coaching of district sales managers. The frequency of regional training sessions varied with the density of the district offices. The Brooklyn regional manager, for example, met with his district sales managers as a group once each month and often met with small groups of district sales managers. The Denver regional sales manager, on the other hand, met with all of his district sales managers only four times each year and with smaller groups only four times each year. The regional sales managers also spent a great deal of time meeting individually with their district sales managers for coaching and/or evaluation sessions.

The headquarters training staff provided the material for meetings and sometimes participated in the sessions. One "packaged" session, for example, was a $4\frac{1}{2}$-day program on compensation, recruiting, and training called the *management of change*. It used filmstrips supplemented by recordings, lectures, role playing, and videotape. Some parts of the material for the session could be used by district managers in training unit sales managers or in explaining the new compensation program to salespeople.

The production of this particular training session was done partly by internal personnel and partly by outside firms specializing in that field. The direct cost for the material and outside production assistance was estimated at $120,000. In addition, 25 members of the training staff spent $2\frac{1}{2}$ months full time on the project.

In March 1973, management had to make several decisions regarding district sales manager training. One controversial key decision involved the location and general nature of the training program. Other decisions involved the content, timing, length, and mode of presentation of the program.

Peter Roy, an agency vice president, was opposed to a centralized training program because he believed that the one-on-one tutoring by the line managers at each level in the organization was the key to training.

525

He felt that the existence of a line management organization stressed the importance of having each sales manager responsible for the total management of his subordinates. This line orientation led to the 1963 change in the nature of the unit sales manager's job in which each unit sales manager became responsible for all of the functions of his subordinates. After line management was adopted in 1963, the method of management training had been changed.

Prior to line management, district sales managers were brought together for centralized training. According to Mr. Roy, "The schools were a waste of time. The faculty was made up of staff people and junior-level management who taught theory. They had no experience on which to draw." The schools were closed after an intensive study by a committee which included Mr. Roy and Mr. Atlas, executive vice president. Mr. Roy strongly believed that training was a crucial management function and that each manager should have the responsibility for training his subordinates:

> Because we now have direct line responsibility for other sales management functions, we should have it for training. Training should travel down the organization. The agency vice presidents should train the regional sales managers for whom they are responsible, and the regional sales managers should in turn train the district sales managers all the way down to the unit sales managers who should train the salesmen. In the best of all worlds, every salesman would end up with the same philosophy and learning through this process. This, of course, won't happen. But the results are still much better than with staff training.

Mr. Roy also believed that each manager was responsible for training his direct subordinates to train their subordinates. Under such a system the district sales manager would provide intensive coaching to teach his unit sales managers how to train salespeople. Such a coaching system would be built around the company's PEDOS concept of training which stood for Preparation, Explanation, Demonstration, Observation, and Supervision.

The district sales manager, employing this concept to teach a unit sales manager how to train a salesperson in a specific selling technique, would first prepare himself to train the unit sales manager by gathering relevant materials and developing a training plan. He would then explain to the unit sales manager the purpose of the technique and the manner in which to teach it. The district sales manager would then demonstrate the use of the selling technique to the unit sales manager. Next, the unit sales manager would train a salesperson in the use of the technique in front of the district sales manager. The final step was the district sales manager's provision of feedback based on his observation and continuing follow-up and supervision. Mr. Roy thought that this same procedure could be used by regional sales managers in training district sales managers.

Both Gene Briskman, vice president for marketing and training services, and Stephen London, executive assistant for marketing and training services, believed in a more centralized training program for newly appointed district sales managers. Before becoming involved in staff activities, Mr. Briskman had been an agency vice president and Mr. London had been a district sales manager who had come to that position through the company's program for M.B.A.s. Mr. London believed that "ongoing training and development must be performed by the regional sales managers but the new district sales manager needs a centralized program soon after appointment." He had proposed a 2-week program which would take place at least 3 months after appointment so that the new district sales manager would have an opportunity "to appraise his own strengths and weaknesses on the job" but no more than 6 months after appointment so that he "would not develop bad habits and can keep his problems in hand."

Mr. London favored centralized training because "the regional sales managers don't allocate sufficient time to do the early, intensive training which the newly appointed district sales managers need. They need to be given a mixture of management philosophy and management skills such as how to assign priorities among their different activities, how to manage their time, and how to delegate administrative matters."

He saw substantial advantages in gathering the newly appointed district sales managers in groups of about fifteen. He favored a training program in which they could

527

> tackle key issues so that they can develop their own management guidelines, helped in the process by high powered teachers. Since we plan to appoint about eighty district sales managers per year we can hold one session in each territory with some combining of territories to facilitate scheduling. An agency vice president could be in charge of each session so that it would maintain its line orientation. He would, of course, be supplemented by other faculty.

Mr. London felt emphatically that "the line organization will never do this type of intensive training in a decentralized form."

Mr. Briskman stressed the importance of relating the training a district sales manager received after appointment to the training he received before.

> We should stress the importance of beginning training early with preappointment training as a field training consultant or advanced underwriting adviser. In those positions, the district sales manager candidate has two jobs: (1) to get trained and (2) to perform the tasks which he is currently assigned. To do this we must alert the regional sales manager to his training function. As the advanced underwriting adviser nears appointment to district sales manager, we should help him to get variety in his job assignments so

that he has some good experience for the district sales manager job. It's especially useful if he can get some "hands-on" experience running a district. That is better than any training program. Throughout this consideration of training we must keep two things in mind: first, all we can do is to reshape the man a bit because of his previous experience in the business, and second, the regional sales manager has total discretion in these matters.

Mr. Briskman had a four-phase view of district sales manager training. The four phases were:

1 Preappointment training as field training consultant and advanced underwriting adviser

2 Intensive coaching by the regional sales manager right after appointment

3 A school after some period on the job

4 Continued regional sales manager coaching

> In the third phase it is important for the district manager to obtain exposure to regional sales managers other than his own. The training for the jobs below district sales manager can be structured because the jobs are highly structured. The district sales manager's job, however, requires a great deal of flexibility, imagination, and creativity. To have those qualities he needs broad exposure in training. He must learn about different managerial styles and different ways of managing people and analyzing situations.

528

Mr. London had been asked to develop a prototype for a centralized training program. He thought that a highly concentrated 2-week program which included 95 hours of planned activity, supplemented by informal contact with participants and faculty, was reasonable. He wanted to include material on management philosophy, and the management of four areas: time (personal), results, salespeople, and managers.

He knew that he had a variety of training methods available, including lectures, case studies (highly structured or unstructured), in-basket exercises, role playing, game-like simulations, highly structured models, programmed learning, and regular books. Costs of some of these materials are estimated in Exhibit 2. He also had a staff made up of training specialists and former line managers, including a person with a doctorate in psychology who specialized in buyer-seller behavior, three former district sales managers, and a certified public accountant who specialized in product knowledge. The total budget for the group had been $220,000 in 1972, with an additional $763,000 for printing and reproduction services. Each regional office had a videotape monitor for playing videotapes (it was not capable of recording), and every district office had an audio-cassette player.

As Mr. London pondered the nature of an appropriate program he

Exhibit 2 COST OF TRAINING MATERIAL (ESTIMATED BY MR. LONDON)

Videotape (30–40 minute black-and-white tape)	
Produced internally	$1,000
Produced by an outside supplier	$4,000–$5,000
Reproduction for 39 regional offices	1,000
Filmstrip combined with record (30–40 minutes)	
Produced internally	$4,000–$5,000
Produced internally with outside actors	$7,000–$8,000
Reproduction for 39 regional offices	$1,000
Reproduction for all district offices	$2,000
Cassettes (audio only, 30–40 minutes)	
Production by an outside supplier	$400–$500
Reproduction per unit	3.00
Workbook per unit	1.00
Videotape equipment	
Cost of monitor for display only	$1,200 per unit
Cost of unit for recording and playback	2,000 per unit

was concerned, because he knew that the stronger regional sales managers, whose regions were often also the company's leading producers of sales, preferred to train their own district sales managers.

APPENDIX A: EXCERPTS FROM "DETAILED JOB DESCRIPTION BOOK"

The District Objectives

Each district, regardless of location or size, contributes to the successful operation of the company by discharging its responsibilities to the people it serves and by achieving certain objectives. These objectives are:

To provide each policyholder with prompt, courteous, and efficient service

To produce an increasing amount of new business and economically maintain existing business

To keep operating expenses at optimum levels

The District Manager's Role

Although metropolitan districts vary considerably in locality, in size, in market potential, and in the share of the market obtained, each district's accomplishments are determined primarily by one key element—the district sales manager. The company's continued success depends heavily upon the extent to which each district sales manager recognizes the significance of his role and provides the necessary leadership.

The district sales manager is responsible for maximizing his district's performance. This embraces a wide range of duties and responsibilities, including sales and conservation performance,[6] service to policyholders, control of costs, personnel development, and public relations.

The district sales manager's job is to achieve the desired results through the efforts of other people—not to do it himself. Therefore, the company's organizational pattern provides for the delegating of part of these duties and responsibilities to others. Thus, the unit sales managers have the responsibility for the first-line management and guidance of field representatives. The office supervisor has a similar responsibility for clerks. Each of these has authority commensurate with his responsibility, and each is accountable to the district sales manager for the results obtained.

At the same time, the district sales manager is the primary tutor in developing managerial skills. In this role he operates as a "director of managers." Conversely, the time he spends with individual field representatives or clerks should be primarily for the purpose of appraising the effectiveness of their performance and the training they have received.

In his role as director of managers, the district sales manager is responsible for the total results of his district, as well as for the guidance and supervision of each member of his management team. In carrying out this responsibility, he must be the chief architect in developing plans for the total district operation—on both a short-range and long-range basis.

530

This includes the following:

Developing and maintaining a sales program
Recruiting and selecting district personnel
Training and developing district personnel
Motivating district personnel
Directing administrative activities
Developing and maintaining good public relations

No two district sales managers will, or should, operate in exactly the same manner. Nevertheless, there are four basic functions that every district manager must perform well in order to satisfactorily discharge the six managerial responsibilities outlined above.

These basic functions are planning—determining the objectives and courses of action to be followed; organizing—providing the necessary personnel within the framework of authority and responsibility; leading—motivating personnel to carry out the planned action; and controlling—following up to ensure that activities are carried out according to plan and that the planned end results are attained. Each of these basic functions is discussed below.

[6]*Casewriter's note*: Conservation was the process of keeping existing contracts in force (re-sold).

Planning

Since every district sales manager is accountable for achieving his objectives, he cannot afford to leave attainment of these objectives to chance. Whenever possible, his objectives should be set down in measurable terms of "when" and "how much," so as to provide a mutual understanding among those involved with the expected accomplishments. Once objectives have been established, action plans must be developed that are based on the conditions and assumptions under which the work will be done.

Organizing

To implement his plans successfully, the district sales manager must organize in a way that provides an orderly utilization of both human and material resources. This includes selecting the right people for specific assignments. Then it involves making certain that they have an understanding of what is to be done by them, the end result expected, and the length of time they have to perform these assignments.

Leading

As district leader, the district sales manager's primary function is to get all members to strive to achieve the objectives that *he* wants them to achieve because *they* also want to achieve them. He must recognize that the district's goals are quite different from individual goals. Accordingly, he must lead his people in a way that will achieve the goals of the district and at the same time satisfy personal goals.

Controlling

In controlling performance, it is the district sales manager's responsibility to make certain that everything is being carried out in accordance with the plans that have been adopted. This involves periodic comparison of actual results to preestablished objectives, and initiating corrective action when planned results are not being attained.

The District Manager's Six Major Areas of Responsibility

1 *Develop and maintain a sales program* Develop sales objectives based on capabilities of district personnel and market potentials; follow up performance and modify programs to meet changing conditions, including the development of new markets.

2 *Recruit and select district personnel* Employ people with a high potential for success.

3 *Train and develop district personnel* Develop and maintain an environment that will enable district personnel to acquire the knowledge and skills needed to perform their jobs well.

4 *Motivate district personnel* Build and maintain good human relations; create a climate in which all district personnel will strive for excellence in performance.

5 *Direct administrative activities* Direct the supervision of clerical detail; maintain adequate sales and performance records; ensure proper handling of funds; maintain effective communications; control district expense.

6 *Develop and maintain good public relations* Build and maintain an organization of dedicated, courteous, professionally competent people who will be recognized as good citizens in the community they serve.

Developing and maintaining a sales program involves:

1 Acquiring a comprehensive knowledge of the market potential in the area and matching this with individual representatives

2 Keeping abreast of changing market opportunities and recommending the establishment of additional field representatives' positions or the consolidation of agencies

3 Establishing long-term objectives for the district within the framework of regional plans by working closely with the regional manager

4 Working with unit sales managers in setting individual objectives for field representatives to ensure realistic district objectives

5 Pricing out the cost of annual objectives to ensure that they can be attained economically

6 Guiding and counseling unit sales managers in formulating training and supervisory plans for their agents

7 Keeping sales promotional approaches and materials current in light of changing conditions from year to year

Recruiting and selecting district personnel involves:

1 Establishing standards relating to background, history of prior success, and personality characteristics required for openings in the various district positions

2 Establishing an on-going recruiting program designed to furnish an

adequate number of qualified candidates to meet anticipated and unexpected personnel needs

3 Developing a selection procedure that will provide intimate knowledge of each candidate and ensure the appointment of an appropriate person to fill each vacancy

4 Training, guiding, and counseling his management associates in their use of standards, programs, and procedures to maximize the effectiveness of the district program

Training and developing district personnel involves:

1 Developing training patterns that maximize effectiveness of company programs by relating them to the needs of the individual district

2 Guiding the unit sales managers in identifying specific markets in which their agents can sell most effectively and in selecting appropriate training methods for the individuals, so as to develop sales specialists

3 Developing the managerial skills of the unit sales managers and the office supervisor so they can effectively carry out their own training responsibilities

533

4 Assessing the effectiveness of training efforts periodically and taking corrective action when needed

5 Being alert to changes in the life and health insurance and annuities environment and adjusting training patterns to meet these changes

6 Leading district personnel in engaging in self-development programs

7 Recognizing and developing individuals with management potential and keeping the regional manager advised of their progress

Motivating district personnel involves:

1 Developing and maintaining good human relations with the district staff by applying the basic principles of thoughtfulness, consideration, respect, and sincere interest in their welfare

2 Ensuring that his management associates also practice good human relations in the same manner

3 Acquiring an intimate knowledge of the personality differences of each staff member, their personal ambitions, and the motivational approach to which each responds best

4 Taking advantage of opportunities to build a spirit of unity and pride in the organization

Directing administrative activities involves:

1 Ensuring that all administrative activities required by the company are properly performed in the district

2 Establishing administrative practices that ensure prompt and efficient handling of new business and subsequent servicing of existing policies

3 Directing the proper use of district conservation control procedures

4 Ensuring the proper handling of funds

5 Reviewing and analyzing records and reports to determine how the district is progressing and to take corrective action as needed

6 Controlling district expense

Developing and maintaining good public relations involves:

1 Maintaining an orderly office with a courteous and efficient clerical staff; encouraging all district personnel to maintain a favorable appearance

534

2 Training sales personnel to give prompt, courteous, and efficient service and competent insurance advice

3 Gaining a high degree of professionalism through a continuing program of self-development; actively participating in local insurance organizations

4 Participating in activities of organizations devoted to serving the community, with proper consideration for maintaining a balance between this and other responsibilities

5 Assuring that health and welfare material is used to the best advantage

6 Making use of publicity and advertising which will promote a favorable public image

Organizational Status

The district sales manager has authority commensurate with the responsibilities of his position. He is responsible for total district operations and exercises direct authority over all activities of his management associates. In general, this authority provides him with latitude for independent judgment and action.

The district sales manager is under the direct supervision of his regional sales manager and is accountable to him for the district's performance. The district sales manager does, however, receive direction and advice regarding certain technical and special areas from appropriate staff groups.

APPENDIX B: EXCERPTS FROM "A STUDY OF DISTRICT SALES MANAGERS"[7]

Excerpts from the Summary of the Report

The District Sales Manager's Position

Overall, there is a high degree of satisfaction with the district manager position and the opportunities it provides for personal fulfillment. This is particularly true of the younger, newer, more successful managers, i.e., those who will be with us for a long period of time. However, the managers do believe that their status and prestige have deteriorated, and there are widespread feelings of being worried, tense, and insecure about their positions. As a result, the level of satisfaction with the district sales manager position is lower than it was in 1968.

Training is a major problem in the view of the managers. In this context, they, especially the younger and newer managers, do not particularly feel that they have been sufficiently well trained in their own jobs to function effectively. (This also is lower than 1968.) In fact they would be willing to pay their own expenses to attend advanced seminars conducted by marketing and training services.

535

They are well satisfied with and clearly understand the amount of job responsibility they are given, and they are satisfied with the scope of their work. These feelings are particularly strong among younger managers.

They still feel they have to spend too much time on paper work, but this has improved somewhat since 1968.

The managers, especially the younger and more successful ones, want more authority. (A concrete example would be the authority to make the decision on terminating poor producers.)

The managers believe in setting objectives and believe that appropriate ones have been set for their districts. This represents an improvement over 1968.

The managers like the line management concept. This is particularly true of newer and more successful managers.

The Unit Sales Manager's Position

The managers agree almost unanimously that training the salespeople should be the basic function of the unit sales manager. They do not feel he has time enough to accomplish this, let alone any of his other

[7]Prepared in December 1971 by the Market Research Department of the company.

responsibilities. As a result, they do not believe the position is attractive to the person with the greatest management potential. These negative feelings are stronger than they were in 1968.

The managers further say that they themselves have not been able to train unit sales managers successfully in their own districts, and they want these people (who are in turn to be primarily trainers and motivators of the salespeople) to be trained by the home office. (This confession of failure may account for a substantial amount of the feelings of failure and inadequacy that many managers express, both concerning their jobs and their ability to train.)

Home office support The company training programs and materials are evaluated highly. What the managers really want, however, is to have the home office take over some of their functions in training unit sales managers and salespeople.

Excerpts from the Body of the Report
The District Sales Manager's Position

Satisfaction and opportunity Managers report feeling a great deal of pleasure in and enjoyment of their work and experiencing a genuine sense of accomplishment while developing their talents and abilities. Not only do they like their jobs, but also their job progress.

Young managers, newer managers, better-paid managers, and those whose income is increasing are much more satisfied than are older managers, those in the job and company for longer periods, those with lower incomes, and managers whose income is decreasing or static.

In general, the level of satisfaction with the district sales manager's position is lower than it was in 1968.

Training Only slightly more than half the managers feel that they have been sufficiently well trained in their jobs to work effectively, representing a drop from 1968. Younger and newer district sales managers are much less likely than older and established managers to feel they have received enough training. Managers in some territories feel they have received sufficient training, while those in others are less likely to feel so.

Almost two-thirds of the managers would be willing to pay some or all of the costs to attend advanced training seminars conducted by marketing and training services. And most of those who are unwilling say they want the additional training, but that the company should pay for it (See Exhibit B-1).

The Unit Manager's Position

Training District sales managers emphatically do not believe that the in-district training of new unit sales managers is more effective than the

Exhibit B-1 TRAINING FOR THE DISTRICT SALES MANAGER'S POSITION

	Agreement index	Strongly agree, %	Tend to agree, %	Tend to disagree, %	Strongly disagree, %	Not ascertainable, %
I receive sufficient training in my job to discharge these responsibilities effectively. (1971)	7	14	41	34	11	1
(1968)	15	15	46	30	8	
Completing CLU studies contributes significantly to an individual's effectiveness as a district sales manager. (1971)	31	35	33	22	10	—
(1968)	15	23	37	28	12	

Would you be willing to pay or share the costs (e.g., paying travel expenses) of your attending training seminars on a centralized basis conducted by Marketing and Training Services on such topics as advanced underwriting, management techniques, etc.?

Yes	62%
No	38

Why do you say that?

Would be willing to pay (N = 451)

	39%
Would be paid back by improved performance	24
Training is the backbone of the business	23
They would be worth it	7
Would gain understanding of advanced topics	6
If I could choose courses I wanted	3
Not ascertainable	

Would not be willing to pay (N = 278)

	48%
Company should pay; it's company responsibility	31
Already pay for too much that is not reimbursed	24
Not worth it	5
Not needed; know enough; nothing more to learn	2
Other reasons	3
Not ascertainable	

training formerly given. Almost two-fifths of all the district sales managers believe that their unit sales managers (and even salesmen) would be willing to pay all or some of the costs of centralized home office training courses and seminars and most of the remainder think the company should foot the bill. Once again they say that they and their people in the districts cannot train effectively.

Recruitment   Recruitment is seen as very much less of a problem than was· the case in 1968. The district sales managers feel that they can hire people of good potential.

The managers still feel, as they did in 1968, that selection standards are too low, that we should upgrade the quality of those already hired rather than worrying about filling open territories and that they cannot successfully recruit on college campuses. Not only are they unsuccessful at recruiting college graduates, but the district managers are not at all certain that they should even try. They are still more negative about the view that college graduates make more effective ordinary agents than they were in the previous survey.

Regional Management

Relationship and communications   The district sales managers see both their relationship with their regional managers and their communications with these superiors as being very good. There has thus been no change in this area since the 1968 survey was taken. They believe that the regional sales manager encourages them to discuss their problems and, to almost the same extent, their opportunities with him.

Method of operations   The regional sales manager is usually seen as being a strong leader and providing effective help and support to the district. There is also agreement that there is a real sense of management teamwork throughout the region (less strong than that expressed above, perhaps because the regional sales manager may be seen sometimes as being too strong a leader). The district sales managers believe that their regions operate on a planned basis rather than jumping from one crisis to another. The examples of "crises" given by the district sales managers usually consist of operating on the basis of a large number of one-shot sales campaigns and programs, stressed one at a time.

Company

Performance   The major factors that determine company success were considered to be salesmen's compensation (listed by 86 percent of the district sales managers), training of salesmen (84 percent), recruiting salesmen (76 percent), management compensation (75 percent), training sales management people (64 percent), and motivating the sales force (55 percent).

The company was thought to be doing the best job on policies, e.g., products (65 percent), advanced underwriting assistance (35 percent), net cost (30 percent), advertising (22 percent), recognition programs (20 percent), forward planning activities and salesmen's compensation (19 percent of the district sales managers).

There was some need for improvement, according to the district sales managers, in management compensation (48 percent), salesmen's compensation (42 percent), underwriting services (39 percent), other policyholder services (38 percent), training sales management people (38 percent), recruiting salesmen (36 percent) and training salesmen (35 percent).

Training materials and programs   The assistance received from training services is seen as somewhat effective. The company's programs and materials for training new salesmen are seen as quite useful but less so than in 1968. The district sales managers clearly want formal programs with definite outlines and objectives in the training area, perhaps because of their own feelings of frustration and inadequacy in this sphere, as noted above several times.

Almost two-thirds of the managers believe there are areas in the training programs produced by the home office that could be strengthened (64 percent). As we would expect by now, what they want is more training for both unit managers and salesmen—to be conducted by the home office rather than by them.

The major advantages of the company's training programs and materials are that the materials are well prepared and organized (39 percent), that the programs are effective (28 percent), and that they provide a guide that can be followed (11 percent). The disadvantages are seen as poor presentation (29 percent), too much material to be assimilated (22 percent), not responsive to geographic differences (11 percent), and requiring too much time (10 percent).

As used in the training and promotion programs, audiovisual mechanisms are thought to be effective; the managers want to see more use made of these techniques, but they themselves are much more likely to use the "personal touch" rather than audiovisual materials.

Problem markets   Only 2 percent of the district sales managers say that they have no problem markets, i.e., markets that their salesmen have been comparatively unsuccessful in selling to.

The main problems are with professionals (cited by 67 percent of the managers), small business (33 percent), teachers (22 percent), farmers (21 percent), and corporate heads (22 percent).

The managers say that the causes of the problem markets are most often lack of proper training (again!) and (therefore, presumably) not being comfortable with these people.

Section
TWELVE
Legal and Ethical Considerations

FIFTY   Legal and Ethical Considerations

This note does not pretend to have been written to make students legal experts. It is designed to alert them to some of the important legal aspects of sales management and to raise important ethical issues.

In any dealing which appears to present legal considerations, it is wise to contact an expert. Many parts of the law concerning matters related to sales management are exceedingly complex. It is unduly risky to operate without appropriate guidance.

The discussion of ethical issues in a separate section should not indicate that ethics is a special subject not to be integrated into the mainstream of sales management. To the contrary, the issues are so important that they need to be integrated into all aspects of sales management *and* to receive special attention as well.

This note is divided into sections focusing on dealings with customers and on dealings with salespeople.

DEALING WITH CUSTOMERS AND PROSPECTS
Commercial Bribery

Commercial bribery is in general the act of influencing or attempting to influence the actions of an employee, such as a purchasing agent or buyer, by giving the employee a gift of some sort without knowledge of the employer. It is important to note that the attempt to bribe is itself a crime.

There is no general federal statute against commercial bribery although it is considered an unfair method of competition under the

Federal Trade Commission (FTC) Act. Thus, it is generally controlled by state law. In addition, there are special state laws which make it illegal to bribe government officials. There are also federal laws which make it illegal to attempt to bribe federal employees and employees of federal contractors. Commercial bribery has also been attacked on the basis of conspiracy and tax evasion laws.

Jules Kroll, a purchasing consultant, claims that "$1 in every $5 spent on raw materials is 'tainted'—that is 'the purchasing agent is getting more than a free lunch or baseball and theater tickets.'"[1]

Commercial bribery is usually a considerable distance beyond the normal lunch or entertainment typically given to purchasing personnel by salespeople. That difference, however, raises some important ethical questions.

In most situations where the salesperson and buyer come into regular contact, the salesperson will often provide some special attention to the personal needs of the prospect or customer. It may vary from a cup of coffee to an evening's entertainment for the buyer and his or her spouse. Often the salesperson and buyer develop a warm personal relationship in addition to their business dealings. After all, they usually share personal attributes as well as industry interests and frequent contact.

542

Most sales managers would not consider traditional gifts, such as lunch, dinner, a sporting event, or a "regular" entertainment event, as unethical. The standards will vary by industry, but those types of consideration tend to be accepted. Usually considered beyond the bounds of propriety are gifts, any amount of cash or near cash, and "elaborate" entertainment such as vacations. Companies sometimes offer customers participation in "industry meetings," which are little more than paid vacations. Many sales managers would consider those to be beyond the limits of propriety, especially if they are promoted as working meetings to the superiors of the purchasing people. The provision of major personal services, such as prostitutes, is also considered beyond the bounds of propriety, partially because prostitution itself is illegal.

An important distinction here seems to be between consideration given to the owner of a company and that secretly given to an employee. The owner cannot be put into a conflict-of-interest situation whereas the employee can. On the other hand, if the owner takes items of substantial value, it becomes unreported income and makes him liable for income tax evasion.

Some people argue over whether it is the seller or the buyer who is at fault in commercial bribery. It seems to me that that is an irrelevant discussion. Both are at fault. The act cannot take place without coopera-

[1]*Business Week*, "Marketing Observer," July 13, 1974, p. 50.

tion. Some buyers will not accept even token gifts. When a furniture company sent its customers turkeys at Christmas, one sent a check back for the value of the turkey, $7.38. On the other hand, some buyers aggressively solicit improper gifts or bribes, or both. Some observers think that this is especially prevalent among state and local government purchasing agents.

A good rule on commercial bribery seems to be to provide limited entertainment at most. It is a sorry salesperson and company who have to resort to bribes to make a sale. It is not only poor ethics to bribe, it is poor business. Companies and salespeople can become known as "easy marks," liable to frequent blackmail for orders. When considering the propriety of a specific gift or form of entertainment there seem to be two good rules: (1) when in doubt, do not provide it; and (2) let the company executives know that is being provided.

Price Fixing

Price fixing is the act of setting prices in concert with competitors and is per se illegal. Agreements to allocate markets among suppliers are illegal.

Price fixing is a particularly insidious form of treachery, because it undermines the essence of the competitive capitalistic society. Any business person who fixes prices has no reason to complain about government interference in his business.

543

Price fixing and allocating markets with competitors is usually a subtle affair. Most price fixers probably do not decide explicitly to set prices. Instead, at a trade association meeting, several competitors discuss industry conditions. One common subject is price erosion and the low prices in the industry. The discussion turns to "wouldn't it be nice if prices were 'more fair' to us?" The next step is price fixing.

It most often occurs in industries that are concentrated enough to allow enforcement and coordination. It is very difficult for suppliers in a market with many competitors to control prices—someone is always breaking ranks. It is not unusual for price fixing to take place on a regional basis. Often, the price fixers are sales managers, not headquarters marketing executives.

There is not much more to say about price fixing. It is just plain illegal and unethical, and enforcement is becoming stricter and more determined. Jail sentences, as well as fines, are increasingly being meted out.

Robinson-Patman Act

The Robinson-Patman Act forbids a supplier from discriminating in price or services among competing buyers. Thus, a housewares manufacturer must provide the merchandise at the same price and with proportionally good services to each retailer it sells in a market. The Act does allow a marketer to grant discounts based upon savings in the cost of manufacture or distribution. Some volume discounts are thus allowed.

The major purpose of the Act is to protect small customers from being unfairly discriminated against by key account programs which offer special incentives to larger buyers.

Any promotional or pricing program must be carefully reviewed to ensure that it conforms to the Act. It is necessary, for example, for display, advertising, and merchandising services to be offered on a proportional basis to competing customers. It is also necessary for all customers to be informed of the availability of such services.

The Act is generally considered to be among the most ambiguous and complex in the marketing area. Many current promotional and pricing policies violate it. Enforcement here is growing more aggressive and is not limited to large companies.

Other Legal Considerations

There are a variety of other legal considerations in selling. The Federal Trade Commission Act forbids "unfair methods of competition in commerce." Thus, it is illegal to interfere with competitors. Disparaging the products or services of a competitor is not legal.

544

Door-to-door selling and other consumer selling practices including, for example, credit extension are covered by federal and state legislation. The sale of some specific products, such as alcoholic beverages and securities, is covered by special state and/or federal regulations.

Tying arrangements, in which a seller forces a buyer to purchase one product to obtain the right to purchase another, are illegal under the Clayton and Sherman antitrust legislation. Thus, a supplier could not, for example, force a customer to purchase supplies for a machine it sold.

It is also illegal to arrange for reciprocal dealing—the "I'll buy from you if you'll buy from me" type of deal. This practice is coming under increasing pressure from enforcement agencies. For one thing, it gives large companies a big advantage, because they are large buyers as well as large suppliers. Reciprocal dealings are especially easy in industries such as the chemical industry, where companies which are generally competitors are also suppliers and customers for each other. In high volume inorganic chemicals which are too cheap to ship very far, for example, competitors may operate so that one supplies a product to the other in one regional market, and in another region the transaction is reversed. It is important for purchasing and sales personnel in a company to limit their contact with each other to prevent the appearance of reciprocal dealings.

Other state and local statutes cover other aspects of selling to dealers, business users, and consumers.

General Dealings

It seems important to me that a company not only abide by the letter of the law but that in its dealings with its customers and prospects, as well as in its other business dealings, it act in an ethical as well as a legal manner. In fact, it seems important for a company not only to be ethical but for it to *appear to be* ethical.

As the note "Account Management" stressed, the same buyers are constantly meeting the same sellers in the marketplace. The unethical company or salesperson is sooner or later found out. Sometimes, the prosecution for illegal and/or unethical behavior in the marketplace is more severe than in the courtroom. Purchasers generally desire to trust in the integrity and competence of their suppliers, especially when the amount of goods and/or services being purchased is large.

It is becoming increasingly clear also that the public as well as the government is going to be demanding a higher level of business ethics. The causes are not clear. The effect is that those people and businesses which do not conform to higher standards will be under great legal and ethical pressure. It seems that people in general desire a higher level of ethics in their dealings and that they will obtain it one way or another.

545

DEALING WITH SALESPEOPLE

The major area of legal impact in dealing with salespeople is the equal employment opportunity legislations. As the note "Recruiting and Selection" indicated, it is illegal to discriminate against a person in either selection or promotion because of race, religion, nationality, sex, or age. The trend here is also clear. Enforcement is getting tougher. Certain forms of testing, for example, have had to be discontinued. Some financial settlements running into the tens of millions of dollars have been made.

Perhaps even more important to the astute sales manager is the fact that good salespeople are hard to find and should be recuited and promoted only on the basis of expected performance. Sales managers cannot afford to miss the opportunity to hire someone because of inappropriate biases.

A much broader issue, however, is the general tone of dealings with the sales force. Salespeople and their managers expect to be dealt with in an ethical and forthright manner. Increasingly they will demand that their employer function and appear to function in such a manner. For example, performance appraisals will have to become more performance related and less based on bias or friendships. Compensation schemes which take advantage of the salesperson or which appear to take advantage will be verboten.

The company which wants its salespeople to deal ethically with its customers will have to set the example by dealing ethically with its salespeople.

Perhaps at an even more basic level, managers are beginning to appreciate better the responsibility which accompanies their power. Because they have the power to hire, fire, promote, reward, and punish their employees, they have the responsibility to do it fairly. This same attitude is beginning to pervade the public's view of managers. RHIP, rank hath its privilege, has been a stock phrase for some time. Now it seems the companion phrase is privilege implies responsibility.

BIBLIOGRAPHY

Buggie, Frederick D.: "Lawful Discrimination in Marketing," *Journal of Marketing*, vol. 26, no. 2, April 1962, pp. 1–8.

Business Week: "Price-Fixing: Crackdown Under Way," June 2, 1975, pp. 42–48.

Corley, Robert N., and William J. Robert: *Principles of Business Law*, 10th ed., Englewood Cliffs, N. J.: Prentice-Hall, 1975.

Garrett, Thomas: *Business Ethics*, New York: Appleton-Century-Crofts, 1966.

Howard, Marshall C.: *Legal Aspects of Marketing*, New York: McGraw-Hill, 1964.

Kotler, Philip: "Social, Legal, and Ethical Issues in Marketing," in *Marketing Management: Analysis, Planning, and Control*, 2d ed., Englewood Cliffs, N. J.: Prentice Hall, 1972, pp. 803–841.

Selekman, Sylvia K., and Benjamin M. Selekman: *Power and Morality in a Business Society*, New York: McGraw-Hill, 1956.

FIFTY-ONE Petite Playthings, Incorporated

When Harold Cassady received his M.B.A. in June 1975, he joined Petite Playthings, Inc., of New York City, as a management trainee. He expected to work for 6 to 9 months as a trainee and then to be assigned to a sales territory for 1 to 2 years. Following that, he would return to New York in a sales or marketing management position.

By industry standards, Petite Playthings was a large children's wear manufacturer, with sales of $20 million. It employed 25 salespeople who were paid a straight commission of 6 percent of sales. As was typical in the industry, all salespeople reported to the national sales manager, Bob Rodgers.

In early September 1975, Ed Autry, the salesman who covered Texas, died suddenly. During the fiscal year July 1974 to June 1975, the territory had shipped slightly over $700,000. Ed was a long-term employee of Petite Playthings and had a good reputation for sales skill and servicing ability among the sales force.

When news of Mr. Autry's death reached headquarters, Mr. Rodgers asked Mr. Cassady to take the territory. Hal Cassady perceived this as a real opportunity. First, it shortened his training period. Second, it gave him a territory considerably better than most trainees, since the commissions for the past year had been almost $43,000. Third, it was a territory with good potential for growth.

Mr. Rodgers went on to explain that since he was about to leave for a 2-week trip to Europe, Mr. Cassady would have to introduce himself to the territory. This was unfortunate, since he preferred to introduce Mr. Cassady to the major accounts.

On Sunday, September 7, Mr. Cassady flew to Texas to begin to cover the territory and get settled. On Monday and Tuesday he traveled the suburban and exurban areas around a large city. He had arranged to meet his second largest customer, the children's wear buyer for a large department store, for dinner on Tuesday evening. In reviewing his orientation to the territory on his way to dinner, Mr. Cassady was pleased with his approach. He had begun to learn the accounts and had been successful in the early stages of developing rapport with some smaller accounts. After that experience he felt confident about meeting Mr. Carson, the buyer, who had purchased over $80,000 from Petite in the 1974 fiscal year, accounting for $4,800 in commissions to Mr. Autry.

Mr. Cassady was anxious to discuss the upcoming winter line as well as to find out how the fall line was selling. While he wanted to discuss business, he did not want the dinner conversation to become too "weighty."

The dinner meeting seemed to go well to Mr. Cassady. Mr. Carson appeared to be a shrewd and knowledgeable merchant with over 20 years of retailing experience. Conversation covered general topics as well as the children's wear business in Texas. As they were enjoying brandy after dinner, Mr. Cassady decided that it was an appropriate time to discuss the upcoming winter line. He explained the general concept of the line to Mr. Carson and showed a few color pictures of the most striking items in the line. After a bit of banter about the line, Mr. Cassady asked what Mr. Carson thought about it. The following conversation then ensued:

Carson   The line looks good but so do those of several of your competitors including [Mr. Carson mentioned two aggressive competitors represented in Texas by high-powered salespeople].

Cassady   Our line is better styled than the other two, offers more value to the consumer, and we provide the kind of service you need to operate effectively.

Carson   Old Ed Autry did provide excellent service, but others offer the same good service.

Cassady   I'll provide you with service and help at least as good as Ed did. And I realize how good he was.

Carson   I really hope that you'll take care of my needs the way good old Ed did.

Cassady   I certainly will help with merchandising, delivery, and inventory control in every way I can. You are an important customer for me.

Carson   I meant beyond that. You are aware of Ed's arrangement with me, aren't you?

Cassady   Arrangement? No, I don't think so.

Carson   Before each season Ed took special care of my needs.

Cassady   Special care?

Carson   Yes, he gave me a little bonus at the beginning of each season.

Cassady   A bonus?

Carson   Five hundred dollars.

Cassady   I didn't know that.

Carson   I hope that we can continue to work together the way Ed and I did. Of course, there are a lot of good competitive lines and a lot of good salespeople. But Ed—he was special.

An uneasy silence followed.

Section
THIRTEEN
Review

FIFTY-TWO   Review and Integration

This note provides additional thoughts on sales management and its role as a marketing and corporate function.

SALES MANAGEMENT AS RESOURCE MANAGEMENT

Broadly speaking, sales management is the management of three types of resources: (1) customers or accounts, (2) salespeople, and (3) sales managers. Each of these resources can be divided into prospective and current categories. This conceptual scheme leads to the following matrix:

	Prospective	Current
Accounts	Prospects	Customers
Salespeople	Prospective recruits	Employed salespeople
Sales managers	Prospective recruits	Employed sales managers

Sales management can thus be considered the management of a pool of prospective accounts such that the profitable ones become customers who in turn are appropriately managed; management of a pool of potential salespeople such that the most appropriate are recruited, trained, motivated, evaluated, compensated, and organized for maximum profitability; and management of a pool of potential sales managers such that it too maximizes the firm's profitability.

By virtue of being in business, the firm has some access to potential accounts, salespeople, and sales managers. But just as a hunting license does not ensure a successful hunt, a pool of prospects does not ensure a sale. The sales manager's job is to turn the hunting licenses into profits.

It is useful to divide sales management into two parts. The first part involves managing the pool of potential and current accounts. This is formulating the sales program. The second part involves managing the pools of potential salespeople and sales managers.

THE SALES FORCE AND ITS ACCOUNTS AS A CORPORATE ASSET

A major part of strategic planning in a company is an analysis of the company's competitive strengths and weaknesses. For example, a strong balance sheet might be viewed as a competitive asset, while lack of a particular technical capability might be a weakness.

The sales force can be a definite corporate strength or weakness. The same is true of account relationships. In fact, an exceptional sales force with excellent account relationships is a particularly good competitive asset because it is so hard to duplicate. Account relationships develop slowly. It usually takes several years for a supplier to generate deep-seated credibility and respect among its major accounts. In many industries, for example, it takes at least one business cycle for an account to believe that it will be effectively serviced in times of both overwhelming demand and poor business. In fashion-related industries, it takes several fashion cycles to show the long-term track record in serving accounts as well as identifying important style trends.

The sales force itself develops slowly. It takes time to find good managers and several years to train a truly effective sales manager. In addition, it takes time for the managers, no matter how capable, to learn to work together as a team. It takes time to develop and implement good programs.

In terms of responsiveness to time and resource commitments, the sales force is different from advertising. The advertising budget can be changed quickly. One telephone call, for example, can double, triple, or change in any way the media budget. While it may take time to gain a prime space or time position, the changes can by and large be made quickly. This is not true of the sales force. It takes about as much time to build and organize an effective sales force as it takes to build, equip, and start up a major plant. In some cases it takes even more time to get the sales force up and running.

This situation is aggravated because part of the value of a sales force resides in its account and company relationships. If a sales force, or part of it, is pirated by a competitor, it may take several years for it to regain the effectiveness it had under its previous owner. During that time, the sales force must develop new operating relationships within the company.

Finally, good sales and sales management talent, like most valuable commodities, is scarce.

Just as strong sales force with good account relationships is a powerful asset, a weak or nonexistent sales force without good relationships is a pronounced liability. The sales force, account trust, and industry reputation take time to develop. Thus, major sales force changes must be carefully planned like other major changes in important productive assets.

THE SALES FORCE AS A PRODUCTIVE CAPACITY

Many companies view excess manufacturing capacity as both a resource and a wasted corporate asset. For example, when excess capacity is available, many firms rush to introduce new products, promote existing products, and enter new markets.

The previous section viewed the sales force as a corporate asset. It is an asset with capacity which can be used for the good of the company. Once a sales force is in place and operating it is in the best interest of the company to use it to its capacity. It may, for example, have the capacity to handle more products. Then it is appropriate to develop more products or to take on products from other companies in a sales agency relationship. This is analogous to selling excess manufacturing capacity when the plant is underutilized. Another approach is to assign the sales force to generating more accounts in the same markets or to opening new markets.

If the sales force with its account relationships is a productive capacity, it can be overloaded, too. It is long-range folly to attempt to push too many products, accounts, market segments, and functions on to a sales force. Its effectiveness and efficiency go down, and if the process is continued for too long, its capacity fades. It is like a misused or overused piece of machinery. It should be used to its capacity and needs preventative maintenance.

553

THE SALES PROGRAM AND THE SALES FORCE

The sales force exists to implement the sales program. The sales program exists to implement the marketing strategy. It is important for that hierarchy not to be reversed. The manufacturing plant is designed around its mission. The sales force should be designed around its sales program.

The sales program can usually be viewed as including the following functions: (1) generating sales volume, (2) developing account relationships, and (3) providing market intelligence. In addition, the sales force must maintain its productive capacity. That is a prime part of sales management.

BEYOND THE SALES PROGRAM

The sales force also has two implicit missions in most companies. Advertising and the sales force are usually the two most visible parts of the company. It is important for them to project an image consistent with the goals, values, and nature of the company.

Second, the sales force serves as a prime training ground for general managers. Because capable top-level managers are important and scarce, it is important for sales managers to be cognizant of this responsibility.

FIFTY-THREE   Gilbert Printing Company

In August 1972, Bob Peterson, executive vice president of the Gilbert Printing Company, was seeking an approach to increasing sales $500,000 in the next 2 years. In the past few years he had participated actively in two programs—the move of Gilbert Printing Company into a new plant in a suburb of Baltimore, and major acquisitions of new printing equipment. The move and expansion had been quite successful, but Mr. Peterson was concerned about the performance in his primary area of responsibility—sales. For the past 5 years, sales volume had remained essentially stable, slightly above an annual level of $3,500,000 (see Exhibits 1 and 2). Mr. Peterson wondered if he could increase the sales output of his present sales force of four persons and how he should go about recruiting new salespeople.

INDUSTRY BACKGROUND
Printing Processes

In 1972 the major printing processes in commercial application were letterpress, offset lithography, gravure, flexography, and screen. Gilbert Printing Company had concentrated on quality letterpress work until the mid-1960s when it began a shift to offset lithography (see Exhibit 1).

Offset presses were of two types, sheet-fed and web-fed. Sheet-fed presses received paper one sheet at a time, while web-fed presses printed from continuous roles. Most web-fed presses, printed on both sides of the paper at the same time. Sheet-fed offset printing applications included general commercial printing, such as annual reports and brochures, direct mail advertising, catalogs, calendars, labels, letterheads, business forms, greeting cards, posters, packaging, folding boxes, coupons, trading stamps, and art reproduction. Web offset was used in printing business forms, newspapers, preprinted newspaper inserts, catalogs, books, encyclopedias, and magazines. It was fairly widely believed that web offset, with its faster feeds and greater output volume, could not quite match the quality of printing obtained from sheet-fed offset, but this question was subject to some dispute. A large 4-color sheet-fed offset press might cost $250,000, while a large 4-color web-fed offset press would cost approximately $2,000,000.

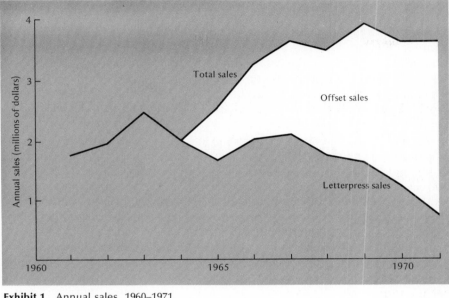

Exhibit 1 Annual sales, 1960–1971.

Exhibit 2 INCOME STATEMENT, 1971
(000 omitted)

Net sales		$3,640
Cost of sales:		
Materials	$1,353	
Direct labor	1,132	
Variable factory expense	160	
Fixed factory expense	220	
Total		2,865
Gross profit		775
Selling and administrative expenses		625
Net profit (before taxes)		$ 150

Industry Characteristics

Printing and publishing was the seventh largest industry in the Baltimore metropolitan area according to "value added," and the largest according to number of plants employing more than 10 persons, roughly 800 compared to a total of 5,000 plants listed in the directory. Approximately 70 percent of all commercial printing firms in Maryland employed 9 or fewer persons, only 15 commercial printing plants in Maryland employed 100 or more persons, and only 3 of these employed 250 or more. Printing was the industry with the largest number of individual firms in the United States.

A 1966 study commissioned by the printers' trade association,

Printing Industries of America, Inc., found that the printing industry was healthy and growing. Growth of printing and publishing had roughly paralleled the growth of all manufacturing. The study also found that the printing industry was more profitable than three-quarters of American industries, with an average return on investment of 10 percent. However, the study found a highly uneven distribution of profits among printing firms—out of every five printing firms, one lost money, three averaged about 6 percent return on assets, and one earned three times more (return on assets) than all the rest.

COMPANY BACKGROUND

Production

In 1968 Gilbert moved from an old three-story plant to a new single-level facility in a suburb convenient to downtown Baltimore. Gilbert personnel designed the plant and oversaw every detail of the construction and moving efforts. They continued to operate the old plant while moving equipment—some old and some new—into the new plant. According to trade sources, the move went smoothly and customer service continued satisfactorily throughout the move.

In 1972 total company employment was approximately 150. Production equipment was geared to the product mix in 1972—85 percent offset and 15 percent letterpress. Two modern 4-color sheet-fed offset presses, two 2-color offset presses and two single-color offset presses were operated on two shifts during most of the year. Older letterpress equipment, including 17 presses of various sizes, handled the declining portion of letterpress jobs.

The first step in preparing a printing job to be run on an offset press was workup of a "board," or layout of the art work in full color. A full-time artist was retained on Gilbert's staff to prepare layouts or consult with customers and salespeople on art problems.

After a job was printed, it was usually further processed. Stitching machines were available to bind sheets into pamphlets or books. Cutting, folding, and packaging were also standard operations often performed after printing. Gilbert maintained its own delivery fleet. To ensure that jobs could be processed promptly, an extensive inventory of paper was maintained in a warehouse adjacent to the pressrooms. A typical job could be shipped within 2 weeks after a final specification was received, and faster if desired. Roughly 2,500 printing jobs per year were processed during the 1970–1971 period.

The specifications for each order were transmitted by the individual salesperson to the production supervisor. An estimator assisted during the initial workup of specifications and estimation of price and delivery time for the salesperson to submit to the customer, especially on those jobs requiring competitive bidding. Gilbert's estimator was able to handle the estimating function by devoting only half of his time to it. Thus he was also able to handle a large portion of the company's purchasing activity. Four "customer men" worked in the production department and acted as liaison between the salespeople and customers, and the production department. These people received customer phone calls and handled the customer's request or problem when that customer's salesperson was not in the office. The duties of these people also included expediting orders, making sure that the jobs were processed exactly according to specifications, and in general following through to satisfy the customer after the salesperson had obtained the original order. According to Mr. Peterson, this back-up capability was a unique strength of the Gilbert Printing Company, since many competitive printing companies required the salespeople themselves to perform the duties handled by these customer men. The customer men ranged in age from 40 to 50 and earned between $12,000 and $16,000 per year. All had substantial printing production experience. Each tended to work with a particular salesperson and a particular group of customers.

The process for preparing bids on jobs requiring competitive bidding consisted of the following steps, with average time estimated for each step:

Step		Time required (minutes)
1	Salesperson records initial customer specifications	15–30
2	Salesperson completes specification form	5
3	Salesperson transmits form to estimator	5
4	Estimator prepares bid from standard rates	30–45
5	Salesperson reviews bid	5
6	Salesperson decides on the price quotation	15
7	Salesperson submits and explains bid to potential customer	10
8	Salesperson prepares written confirmation of bid	5
9	Written confirmation typed and mailed by secretary	5

557

Organization and Management

Steve Gilbert, president, was a grandson of the founder, Abraham D. Gilbert, who started out as his own salesman and pressman in 1890 in Baltimore. Steve had been president since 1965 when his father, David Gilbert, retired as president at the age of 80. Bob Peterson, executive vice president, had started out as a printing salesperson with no background in the industry after a stint in the service in World War II. He had been so successful as a salesperson that in 1958 he was offered status as a principal stockholder, which he accepted. In 1972 Messrs. Gilbert and Peterson controlled all of the stock.

Mr. Gilbert and Mr. Peterson were joint decision makers on all management questions. Mr. Gilbert concentrated on the operations end of the business, while Mr. Peterson concentrated on sales, but both principals conferred frequently and preferred to reach concurrence before making management decisions. Alex Petroski, sales manager, assisted in managing the sales effort.

Steve Gilbert gave his views on the present status and on the future of the Gilbert Printing Company (as paraphrased by the casewriter):

> We are a very tightly run company. I personally review internal operating and financial data every day. Our production crew is young and well trained. Our craftsmen and supervisors are very company-minded, and they really care about doing good work. There is no union.[1] We pay very good wages and we have liberal fringe benefits—group hospital and medical plans, dental insurance, a profit-sharing retirement plan, free flu shots, free eye exams, and even a tax expert who comes in to help employees with their income tax returns. We are a quality-minded company, and the main element in quality is our top production crew—they give us a real competitive advantage. Our approach has paid off in the past—we have been in the top 20 percent of printing companies as far as profitability is concerned, except for one or two of the past 5 years. Right now, unfortunately, sales volume is static.
>
> As for the future, I am enough of a realist to admit that we cannot succeed by remaining static. If we could be assured of maintaining a static, profitable level it would be ideal. But we cannot—we have to grow just to stay even. Right now we are not as profitable as we should be. Our existing plant could produce an added $2 to $3 million of work, and we have allowed room for expansion to handle more. Expanding our production capacity is absolutely no problem.
>
> We do not use so-called sophisticated management techniques. We do not set our sights on future targets and push to make them. As to how we grow, it is somewhat "in the clouds"—we follow the market and respond to it rather than trying to anticipate where the market is headed and get there first. I would not say we have the inventive kind of management that could develop new techniques—we stay with the stable, established technology. This is because we have a sound company and good strategy right now—naturally we avoid risks we do not have to take. We have a lot to lose if we make mistakes.
>
> Our main problem for the future is to increase sales. But we do not want to increase sales volume unless it can be done profitably. The trouble with a lot of the high volume work is that it is low margin. We are profit oriented, not sales-volume oriented. What we need is to hire some proven, experienced salespeople who have some accounts to bring along, and who would appreciate our company for the excellent production support we can give them. If we could hire an entire four-man trained sales force from outside and have them bring their business along, it would be Utopia.

MARKETING PRINT IN THE BALTIMORE AREA

The major characteristics of print marketing—huge primary demand, intense competition, wide diversity of demand, and long-established customer-vendor relationships—were both the keys to success and the barriers to expansion of Gilbert's marketing efforts, in Mr. Peterson's opinion.

[1] *Casewriter's note:* Few competitors were unionized either.

To a considerable extent the market for print in Baltimore followed the trends and practices in the major customer groups served—retailers, manufacturers, advertising agencies, publishers, financial companies, educational institutions, etc. For example, in the late 1960s the trend was away from "showpiece" annual reports, coveted business for reasons of both prestige and profit, because companies had become more frugal in response to the recession and the sagging stock market. Another recent trend among many print buyers was toward requests for competitive bidding for printing jobs. In the past, many buyers had done business primarily on the basis of past service and quality rendered by the printer, or on the basis of the printer's reputation. One Gilbert salesperson estimated that 60 percent of his jobs were sold on a bid basis 4 years ago, but that 90 percent of his jobs were sold on a bid basis in 1972.

The casewriter accompanied a Gilbert salesman during a call on a typical customer, a publisher. During the call the buyer commented to the casewriter that he had an average of six print salespeople calling on him every day. Following the call, the Gilbert salesperson commented that he would estimate that ten print salespersons per day called on major buyers of print, such as the publisher. The salesperson commented that, while the list of companies competing for business from such a buyer was too long to list, he believed that his serious competition came from seven of the larger and more highly regarded printing firms in the area (see Exhibit 3).

MARKETING STRATEGY

Bob Peterson's description of Gilbert's marketing strategy was paraphrased by the casewriter as follows:

> Our product is the best there is in the area for the kind of work our customers want. We provide the highest quality work, absolutely on-time delivery, strict adherence to customer's special instructions or changes, and expert professional consulting and personal service from our salesperson.

Exhibit 3 PRIMARY COMPETITORS

Competitor	Estimated sales 1971 ($ millions)	Comments[a]
Foremost Printing Company	3.5	Quality closest to Gilbert in 4-color work
Wood Printing Company	4.0	Recently purchased large web offset press
Quality Press	2.0	
A. T. Berg Company	3.5	Lower prices, lower quality
Morris Printing Company	1.5	Lower prices; no 4-color capability
AAA Lithographers	2.0	
Robinson Printing Company	1.0	Has one top-notch salesperson

[a]Comments based on opinions expressed by Gilbert salespeople.

Exhibit 4 SALES DATA ($000 OMITTED)

	1967	1968	1969	1970	1971
Accounts over $100					
House Accounts					
Old Ironside Distiller					
& Bottler	162	201	219	188	142
XYZ Paper Company	204	169	153	199	99
Industrial Valve Company	75	54	79	85	126
Consumer Package Goods Co.	1,790	1,582	1,528	1,083	1,607
Sterling Silver Company	233	195	206	228	125
Subtotal	2,464	2,201	2,185	1,783	2,099
Alex Petroski					
ABC Mutual Fund	88	78	123	107	100
Dave Shea					
TVW Paper Company	7	44	44	116	73
Educational Associates	167	30	9	30	37
Over $100 total	**2,726**	**2,353**	**2,361**	**2,036**	**2,309**
% of total company sales	74	68	60	56	64
Accounts $30 to $100					
House accounts					
Clothing Mfg., Inc.	37	21	27	26	18
White Paper Company	43	55	6	10	0
Black Paper Company	26	29	35	34	14
Subtotal	106	105	68	70	32
Alex Petroski					
Misc. Indust. Inc.	0	0	4	62	1
AA Publishing Company	96	7	73	34	12
BB Publishing Company	55	65	50	49	87
AA Mutual Fund	78	62	67	36	20
CC Publishing Company	34	17	3	2	6
Top Food Company	0	46	35	29	34
Church Press	17	38	5	16	*a*
Indust. Goods, Inc.	0	2	52	52	5
BB Mutual Fund	21	42	49	91	51
Subtotal	301	279	338	371	216
Dave Shea					
Ace Consumer Manufacturing	0	5	12	79	6
Ideal Advertising Agency	39	42	49	37	50
Industrial Manufacturing Company	0	4	98	10	1
Plastics Manufacturing Company	0	0	0	37	0

We do have a reputation for being higher priced than most of our competitors. Our prices are up to 10 percent higher than the low bid on many jobs. As a result, we have to hire the best salespeople we can get, because it is entirely up to them to carry out our strategy and make sure that our customers are satisfied that they get the service they are paying for.

Our profits for the past 5 years have been somewhat erratic, and we have been unable to increase our sales volume, but we are confident that our strategy is sound. Our problem has been implementation.

SALES FORCE

All customer accounts were classified either as "house" accounts or as "salesmen's" accounts. House accounts were handled directly by Mr.

Exhibit 4 (Continued)

	1967	1968	1969	1970	1971
Home Products, Inc.	0	3	8	19	90
DD Publishing Company	0	0	0	2	31
Creative Advertising Agency	36	54	60	61	8
Subtotal	75	108	227	245	186
Harry Cohen					
Admirable Ad Agency	11	31	20	0	20
CC Mutual Fund	0	4	25	57	53
Industrial Electronics Co.	0	1	41	28	26
DD Mutual Fund	0	20	54	37	0
Subtotal	11	56	140	122	99
Dick Peterson					
Eastern University	54	80	60	38	63
Andrew Ad Agency	0	11	32	41	40
Consumer Electronics Mfg.	38	36	81	18	5
EE Mutual Fund	0	0	0	0	35
Subtotal	92	127	173	97	143
Frank Barr[b]					
Arnold Ad Agency	0	0	0	44	1[a]
Albert Ad Agency	31	20	26	15	5[a]
Subtotal	31	20	26	59	6
Robert Darman[b]					
$30–$100 total	**616**	**695**	**972**	**964**	**682**
% of total company sales	17	20	25	26	19
Accounts under $30[c]					
% of total company sales	9	12	15	18	16
Total company sales	**3,689**	**3,458**	**3,910**	**3,664**	**3,597**
"House" sales, $	2,570	2,306	2,253	1,853	2,131
"House" sales, %[d]	70	67	58	51	59

[a] Gone out of business.

[b] Some of Frank Barr's and Robert Darman's sales are included in sales of persons to whom their accounts were reassigned.

[c] There were 150 accounts in this category in 1971.

[d] For first 6 months of 1972 "house" sales were 57 percent of total.

Gilbert or Mr. Peterson, and often involved long-standing "understandings" or relationships that required minimal efforts to maintain. Many of these understandings had existed for as long as 25 years. Almost all printers, according to Mr. Peterson, had a few such accounts. It was standard practice in the industry for owners of the companies to handle their own house accounts. Other accounts were handled by a sales force of four people, including Alex Petroski, who was the sales manager. A breakdown of major accounts for the past 5 years, by salesperson, is given in Exhibit 4. Further information on the salespeople is given in Exhibit 5.

Mr. Peterson described the Gilbert philosophy of managing salespeople as laissez faire. He commented that the salespeople had to be "creative" and adapt themselves to each unique situation. This required, according to Mr. Peterson, that each salesperson be allowed to work

Exhibit 5   SELLING PERSONNEL

Name	Age	Years of service	Background	Sales volume ($000)			
				1972 1st 6 mo.	1971 1st 6 mo.	1971 total	1970 total
Steve Gilbert (president)	42	20	Administrative				
Bob Peterson (executive vice president)	53	25	Sales			2,324 (house sales)	2,054 (house sales)
Alex Petroski Sales manager– salesperson)	39	13	Sales; qualified as stockbroker	320	192	507	498
Dave Shea (salesperson)	34	15	Sales, 5 years; estimating & production, 10 years	234	212	450	324
Harry Cohen (salesperson)	32	7	Sales, 5 years; art director, 2 years; extensive art education	195	115	200	363
Dick Peterson (salesperson)	25	4	M.B.A. '71; extensive part-time printing experience prior to 1971	98	—	—	—
Frank Barr[a]	28	2	Sales; industrial	24	—	11	—
Robert Darman[b]	30	4	Sales; art education	—	48	105 (through Sept.)	425

[a]Dismissed June 1972.
[b]Quit September 1971.

independently, develop his own style, and learn for himself the kinds of customers he could succeed with.

Salespeople were paid a commission of $7\frac{1}{2}$ percent of sales.[2] In the event that salespeople cut prices to obtain a sale, however, their commissions were reduced for that sale. The amount of reduction was negotiated with Bob Peterson and varied according to company need for business and other factors. In no case, however, was the commission reduced below 5 percent. During sales slumps, a salesperson's draw could be continued even if it was not covered by commission, but he was then expected to make it up during following months so that his annual salary worked out to $7\frac{1}{2}$ percent of his sales. In addition to commission, each salesperson was furnished a company car and expense account.

Exhibit 5 includes two salespersons who were no longer employed with Gilbert. Frank Barr was considered a high potential salesperson when he was hired, and he had been highly successful selling locks in quantity to motels, hotels, and office buildings. The locks were purchased in large quantities by a few buyers. However, he was unable to sell print and he was fired. Bob Peterson commented on Frank's failure:

> He was the stereotype of a good salesman—if he walked in here tomorrow, unknown, I would hire him immediately. He was well-groomed, well-spoken, smooth, and likable. But selling print is unlike selling anything else, and it is almost impossible to tell beforehand who will be able to sell print. Frank's problem may have been a failure to learn the technical aspects of printing or possibly that he was simply calling on the wrong customers. We do not really know why he failed. There was no attempt to diagnose the reasons he could not close sales.

563

Robert Darman, on the other hand, had been highly successful. He had some art talent and could sell well to ad agencies. He was selling $400,000 of print per year when ad agency business was booming, then, when their business turned down, his sales fell off, and he got behind in his ability to "make up" the salary he was drawing. Also, he encountered some problems in his personal life. He quit actually "owing" back salary. As of August 1972, he was working as a print salesperson for another company.

Selling Approaches

The casewriter interviewed Bob Peterson and each of the Gilbert salespeople. All of the following comments are paraphrased.

---

[2]New salespeople were paid salaries of between $10,000 and $15,000 (plus automobile) until they had developed enough sales so that their commissions were equal to their salaries.

Bob Peterson

Bob continued to sell in addition to his management responsibilities:

A big problem in selling print is that it is like selling "blue sky." There is nothing tangible to sell—the product is just press time, along with some attendant services. Of course, we offer premium service and strict attention to quality, but these are intangibles and it is often difficult to find a customer who appreciates these factors, let alone convince him that we are better than the competition. Of course, after getting an initial order we have to live up to our claims in order to get repeat business.

Selling blue sky requires salesmanship at its creative best. A good print salesperson has to have all the usual qualities—good appearance, charm, and empathy with the buyer. Also, a print salesperson has to use all the other influences expected of him—tickets to athletic events or the theater, holiday presents, and wining and dining. But a top salesperson has to do these things plus something else—the extra variable that clinches the sale.

When I first began selling after the service, I had no printing background at all. Nor did I have much knowledge of practices or terminology in the industries I was selling to. But I was extremely successful because I relied on my intuition and tried to do something extra besides the things all the competitors were doing. Probably the most effective thing I did was to make sure that I invited the buyer's wife and my wife to the occasion or event where he was my guest. I made him feel comfortable and welcome as a friend, not just a business prospect. Getting the buyer's wife to like my wife and me was a major breakthrough. Many of the people my wife and I have met through this process have remained good friends, above business considerations. Because I had a good deal of charm and taste in this type of "social selling," many buyers were willing to overlook some of my shortcomings in the technical areas. One factor about selling print in the Gilbert company that allows this "social selling" to succeed is that a salesman needs only 10 good accounts to be earning a good income for himself and the company. He has ample time to concentrate on each one of his top customers.

In cultivating customer relationships, of course, it is vital to know who really influences the purchase decision. Most buyers in purchasing departments base decisions on price and delivery—only a few really care about quality and special service. It is usually the creative people—the ones in the advertising department—who are willing to pay a higher price to get exactly the quality they want. So we concentrate on the people in the advertising departments of companies. In some companies, though, the purchasing department will not take suggestions from the advertising people, or there is a purchasing director with set ideas, a lot of power, and little sympathy with the "creative types" who care more about quality than price. We have a great deal of trouble with such companies. Fortunately, most companies do have creative people in influential positions, and many of these persons like their work and stay in their positions for a long time. This has been the case with some of my best customers, whom I have served for up to 25 years.

One tendency many young salespeople have is to withhold information about their customers from their company. Our salespeople do not do this—they cannot and still be successful. The opposite is true. They can help themselves by bringing their customers in to see our plant and meet our people in production and customer service. Then if a customer calls when a salesperson is not in the office, one of our production people or "customer men" can handle this call. If the call had to be turned away, the first thing the customer would do would be to call another printer who could help him right away. Another reason our salespeople must be open with our inside customer men is that they can help immensely by handling many of the details of customer orders. To earn a really good salary of, say, $50,000, a salesperson would have to do $670,000 of business a year. Servicing even one-half that much business would be next to impossible without relying on our inside people to handle a good deal of customer work. This adds another dimension to the talents required of our salespeople—they have to be able to coordinate their work with our inside people, keep them informed, and maintain excellent working relations with them.

The four inside customer people we have are very important in providing the high-quality service we promise our customers. Few of our competitors use such inside people to beef up their service capability.

In a small company like ours, we don't have time to do market analysis. We just get out and call on as many customers as possible. I don't really even have time to be talking to you—I have six phone calls I should be making right now.

565

We do not have the time or money to "train" salespeople. They have to be top people who can make it on their own. Most salespeople prefer it that way, in fact.

Alex Petroski

The casewriter traveled with Alex Petroski, the salesperson-sales manager, for one day.

9:00 A.M. The first half hour of the day was spent in the office on paper work. Along with other work, Alex dictated a letter inviting a high potential company buyer and his wife to spend a weekend in September at the Petroski's summer home at a nearby resort area. Alex indicated that the buyer had expressed interest in the resort area during his last sales call. Alex spent a few minutes with the estimator.

Alex then explained his first sales call. He had obtained an order for 10,000 copies of a 4-color direct mail flyer. He indicated that he had shaved the price to $1,200 from $1,260 to get the order, but that the standard price for a volume of 15,000 copies was only $1,600 due to economy of scale. He said he would convince the buyer to take 15,000 copies, and this would allow Alex to earn his full commission.

9:30 A.M. Left the office for first call, a publishing company. While driving to the call in a suburban location, Alex commented that he would make $120 for the morning's work.

10:00 A.M.   Arrived in the customer's lobby. The receptionist admitted Alex to see the buyer.

10:10 A.M.   Alex introduced the casewriter to the buyer, then began small talk. When the talk turned to details of the printing job, Alex said to the casewriter that he would now see a "professional" buyer dealing with a professional salesman—and he requested the buyer to act out his usual professionalism as well as he would. After several details were taken care of, Alex suggested that what he would do, if he were the buyer, would be to order 15,000 copies instead of 10,000 because of the great price break, which Alex then explained. The buyer became noticeably tense and commented that he would like to order the higher volume, but that he was already in trouble with his budget. Alex did not comment further and left the conversational initiative with the buyer for the next major portion of the visit. The conversation turned to small talk, and the buyer asked if Alex had heard of another printing firm that was about to go out of business. Alex expressed interest and ignorance on the matter. Later in the discussion, Alex agreed to take the "boards" to the buyer's artist in downtown Baltimore later in the day. Toward the end of the call the buyer appeared more relaxed and said he would purchase 15,000 units instead of 10,000.

10:40 A.M.   First call was completed, and Alex headed back to the office to set up two sales calls in downtown Baltimore. During the return trip, Alex answered questions about Gilbert's sales program, and selling print in general.

> No, our salespeople have no way of knowing the actual profit to the company of various kinds of orders. This is somewhat of a problem to management, but we have not had time to solve it.
>
> I am recognized as one of the three or four best nonowner print salespeople in the Baltimore area, and I have been in the business 14 years. The only generalization I can make about how to sell print is that each sale is different.
>
> I have toyed with a possible sales idea—a new marketing outlet for the Gilbert company. Students on many university campuses would be our sales representatives at their schools. They ought to be in a better position to find out who buys the print, and on what basis, than our regular salespeople. And the $7\frac{1}{2}$ percent commission should look quite attractive to them.
>
> A print salesperson could probably make at most five meaningful sales calls in a single day.
>
> I did, at one time, request our salespeople to fill out call records so we could begin to establish some data on numbers of calls, where the calls were, etc. But the salespeople lost interest after the first few weeks, and started "fudging" the data. So we dropped the program.

11:10 A.M.   Back at the office, Alex promptly set up two calls in Baltimore.

11:25 A.M.   Left office for second call.

11:35 A.M.   Arrived at customer's store, an old-line specialty retail outlet catering to the "carriage" trade. The objective was a repeat order for a color catalog. Throughout the call, Alex acted as if it were a forgone conclusion that Gilbert would get the repeat order. He said that in situations like this the objective was to make it as easy as possible for the potential customer to give him the order. During the call Alex obtained a "dummy" of the catalog from the advertising manager. After the call Alex mentioned that last year was the first time he had obtained the order for the catalog. He then commented that he had called on the advertising manager for 3 years before getting the order and that his problem had been in thinking that the advertising manager himself had responsibility for the catalog. Alex finally learned that it was actually the president of the company who made the decision about the design and printing of the catalog. With this knowledge, Alex said, it was easy to get the order because he talked directly to the president, who had been somewhat displeased with the service rendered by printers who had done the last catalog.

12:00 P.M.   The next stop was to drop off the material at the studio of the artist who did the work for the publisher called on earlier in the day. The studio was two doors away from the previous call. Alex made small talk and expressed a great deal of interest in an old nickelodeon that the artist, a young fully bearded man dressed in an open pullover shirt, old jeans, and sandals, was playing full blast. Alex told a story of how he barely missed purchasing an old nickelodeon from a boardwalk arcade that had gone out of business a few years ago.

12:20 P.M.   After the call, Alex asked the casewriter if he had noticed the layout that the artist had been doing. Alex said it was obviously a big printing job and that he would keep in touch with the publisher to find out when selection of a printer was to begin. He said that keeping in touch with a customer's artist was a good way to learn of potential printing jobs.

12:40 P.M.   Arrived at the office of the next call, a recently founded, four-man investment banking firm. Gilbert would be printing an advertising brochure, and a principal of the firm was making the selection of paper from samples Alex had brought. The customer was quite hesitant about choice of paper, and Alex expressed confidence in his choice. Alex then turned the discussion to some ocean-front real estate the firm was developing, and Alex got the principal to talk about the project. Alex then mentioned that he had a chance to buy a sizeable piece of land in a particular resort area and the customer said no one had ever lost money buying land in that area. Alex said his problem was coming up with the cash, and the principal said that was what banks were for. Following the call, Alex stopped in at his bank, located a few doors away, and confirmed that financing was indeed available for this type of investment. The bank visit took approximately 5 minutes.

1:15 P.M.   During lunch Alex asked if the casewriter thought that a job selling print would have an appeal for an M.B.A. graduate from a top-rated business school. Alex asked about aspirations of M.B.A. graduates, and how they might view working for a family-owned and managed company. He commented that if he had held an M.B.A. degree when he first started working, he would have expected his business efforts to earn some equity, since that was the only way to really make money. The discussion then turned to the problems and opportunities of owning one's own business.

2:00 P.M.   On the return trip to his office, Alex talked further about his role as sales manager:

> It is frequently difficult to get a salesman to give up an account he has cultivated without success. For example, one of our salespeople had called on an account for years without success, but refused to give it to another salesperson because the buyer had become such a good personal friend and golfing partner.

Dave Shea

Dave had the strongest technical background of the Gilbert salespeople. He had worked for Gilbert in production and estimating for 10 years and subsequently moved to the sales position which he had held for the past 5 years. Dave talked about himself, his work, and other aspects of printing sales:

> In my job in estimating and production I became interested in sales because I could see the potential earnings that were available. Before that I had never wanted to be a salesman, and at times I still question my interest in a sales career. I was convinced by others that I could succeed in sales, so I tried it with the knowledge that I could always fall back on my production knowledge if I could not succeed in selling.
>
> I am not a strong "stand-up" salesperson like Alex Petroski, and I have no design talent or artistic taste. That is a serious flaw for a print salesperson. But I have been successful because of my strong technical background. I sell best to two types of buyers—the ones who are true professionals and demand a true technical salesman, and the ones who know little or nothing about print and need the education I can give them. My part-time job as a professor, teaching graphic arts cost estimating, helps my image as a competent technical man and educator.
>
> A salesman would probably make six "hello" calls in a day, but four calls per day to active accounts is the maximum. After the two calls in the morning, it is invariably necessary to return to the office to do some paper work in support of the sales calls.

During a sales call I spend a good deal of time working with the technical aspects of the job itself. Frequently, I am in two- or three-on-one situations, trying to solve problems, looking at details of preliminary proofs. Frequently, I will have to refer back to the preliminary proof book or the original outline to solve the problem. Also, during a sales call to an active account, there is a checklist of technical information that has to be obtained and this takes time.

The customers I prefer the most are the ones with a good deal of technical expertise, for example, paper companies or consumer manufacturers who are large enough to have a competent professional purchasing department. I have thought about ranking print buyers on the basis of expertise, and I would give the following rankings on a 1 to 10 basis: paper companies, 10; publishers, 9; mutual funds, 7 to 8; miscellaneous media to large industrials, 3 to 7; and advertising agencies, 1. All small buyers I would rank 1. The reason funds are sophisticated is that they buy so much print and can afford to have good buyers. But I cannot sell to funds because I do not "talk the language" of investments, stock market, etc. I should probably make more of a study of the mutual fund industry and learn their terminology.

One of my best customers is a large consumer-goods manufacturer. They have one purchasing department that does all of the purchasing for other departments in the company. It took me 3 years to get a sizeable order from them. The way they operate is to investigate vendors and classify them on their ability to handle certain types of work. Then when a job comes along, they will ask the qualifying print vendors to bid—usually I am competing against five or six other vendors—and they generally give the business to the low bidder. However, they make sure to cultivate their vendors by spreading the work around—if they didn't, a printer would probably stop bidding. For this reason the potential of this business is limited on the upside, but there is also some minimum amount of business a vendor can count on as long as he continues to deliver good service and quality at reasonable prices.

569

When I started selling I quoted strictly list price, even with padding in some cases. But lately I have been negotiating more closely, and I will cut my commission if I feel it is desirable to do so on a particular job. Another technique I have been using more lately is quoting alternatives to the specifications that a purchaser has submitted for bids. By altering the paper, the largest single cost component of most printing jobs, I can sometimes meet the intent of the specifications at a lower cost. Of course, a danger in this technique is that the buyer may adopt my standard the next time he requests bids and my advantage disappears.

One of the things I dislike about selling is making cold calls. I do have somewhat of a lack of confidence, and the thing you have to do on a first call is to sell *yourself*. It takes a strong "stand-up" salesman to do that. I am more of a "service" man than a stand-up salesman such as some of our other men.

When I deliver a speech, people frequently say they think I must be a strong stand-up man. I once trained 4 weeks to sell pharmaceuticals. Their method was to memorize a canned sales pitch to deliver to the pharmacist on the first call, but I found that I was extremely averse to the approach. The first Monday morning after the training program, I sat in the car with the district manager outside my first drugstore and argued about the canned approach. I resigned on the spot.

Dick Peterson

Dick (Bob Peterson's son) had joined the firm in 1971 after receiving an M.B.A. from Columbia:

> The key to selling print is having a personality that will win over the buyer. It helps to have something in common with the buyer—age, for example. I can usually sell better to younger buyers than older ones.
>
> Eight calls in one day are probably the most a salesman could make. I average four or five every day. We try to spend as much time as possible making calls. I may spend more time in the office—$1\frac{1}{2}$ hours per day—than the other salespeople, because I spend a lot of time on the phone.
>
> It is not possible to predict how a customer will react ahead of time. The only way to find prospects is to keep your eyes open. I use the classified section of the newspaper to get leads, since companies hiring personnel frequently will also have more activity in other areas of their business—and make a lot of calls.
>
> It might take 3 months of making calls before a buyer will even trust you enough to ask you to quote on a job. Then he will be suspicious if your first bid is low, but he may still give you a chance if he has any desire at all to do business with you. This is largely a function of how well his other printers are serving him.
>
> I bid on six different jobs at an insurance company, which I initially considered a good prospect. I finally concluded that they always took the lowest bid and that quality of work did not enter into the purchase decision. As soon as I discovered that fact, I dropped them as a prospect.
>
> Our company's image is that we have no late deliveries and consistently high quality. We have to live up to it because we also have a reputation for being more expensive than our competitors.
>
> The recent trend toward competitive bidding may be hurting our sales prospects. We did a study a couple of years ago showing that we obtained roughly one job for every three bids submitted. Now the ratio is probably worse—I would guess one sale is closed for every four jobs we bid on. The problem is that many buyers have the idea that they should be able to get the high-quality service we offer for the lower prices they paid during the recent recession or for the lower prices our competitors quote. I would guess that prices for printing sales in this area have risen 10 percent in the last 15 months.
>
> Many purchase decisions by print buyers are based on politics or social connections. For example, a buyer may throw business to a printer if he represents a company with a service that the printer uses—accounting, legal, etc. A salesperson always has to be careful not to waste time on buyers with established ties that cannot be broken on the basis of a better printing service.
>
> Most of our salespeople have not intentionally tried to match their customers to their special talents. But through the process of making many sales calls, that fit is usually established naturally.

570

Harry Cohen

Harry had the most design talent of the salespeople. He held undergraduate and graduate degrees in graphic arts designing. Harry was hired as
art director at the Gilbert Printing Company, a position he held for 2 years
before he became a salesman:

> When I first started selling, I had no background in sales at all. I would have
> liked more training and guidance than I received, but it is company policy
> that a salesperson learns mostly on his own.
>
> Of course, with my background, I go after the accounts that can use my
> talent. What I do is to give away a design service to obtain the printing order.
> The trouble with this approach is that it limits the volume of business I can
> handle, since it takes time to produce good designs.
>
> When I began selling, I got leads on prospective customers any way I
> could—I even wrote down names from trucks I passed on the road. One of
> my best customers today I read about in the Sunday paper when the
> company first moved to Baltimore. I got in touch with the advertising
> manager and gave him a lot of good advice about art services in Baltimore. I
> set him up with an agency and helped on initial designs. I was able to make
> sure that the design specifications fit our printing capability best, so I
> naturally got the printing business.
>
> I accumulated more than 600 entries in a notebook on potential
> customers. I don't use it any more, however. I really spend less time
> prospecting for new customers than I should. It is much easier to concen-
> trate on my present customers.
>
> I become deeply involved in all phases of processing an order for my
> customers. I follow it all the way through the production sequence. This
> ensures that the job is done exactly the way I know the customer wants it.
>
> In a sales situation, I sell myself—all aspects. For example, I have a farm
> and I bring it into conversations. At Christmas I do not give my customers the
> usual gift certificate or liquor that most salespeople do—my wife puts up
> jams and pickles and I give those. They mean a lot more; they're something
> personal.
>
> I stay away from purchasing agents because all they know is the unit
> cost at the bottom of the line. They do not see the total package. Also, I
> cannot relate to most purchasing agent types. I also stay away from most ad
> agency production managers for the same reason. The last thing ad agencies
> need is my design talent. Some of my best customers are mutual funds, who
> can really use my design talent. If I design a piece it saves them a fee. I am
> really selling on the basis of economics when I give away free design work.
>
> Every printer tells his potential buyers that he has high quality. That is all
> right for getting the first order, but you do have to provide acceptable quality
> to get repeat business. A print jobber[3] once won a competitive bid from me,
> and the job he delivered looked like an out-of-tune color television picture. I
> had no trouble with competition from the jobber after that.

571

---

[3]A print jobber was an independent salesperson who obtained orders from his customers
and then selected a printer to do the work. The jobber earned his profit from the difference
between the price charged the customer and the price paid the printer to do the work.

Exhibit 6 MARKET INFORMATION: PRINT BUYERS WITH POTENTIAL OF $25,000 AND UP PER YEAR

Customer group	No. of accounts potential	No. of accounts sold	Purchase decision maker
1 Mutual funds	20	10	Advertising manager,[a] purchasing agent
2 Advertising agencies	15	6	Production manager
3 Paper companies	12	6	Advertising manager
4 Universities, colleges	75	6	Special print buyers, public relations directors, others
5 Consumer and industrial manufacturers	100+	20	Product managers, advertising managers, purchasing agents, art directors
6 Insurance companies	4	0	Purchasing agents
7 Banks	6	1	Advertising manager, purchasing agent
8 Publishers	3	3	Advertising manager, others
9 Financial report buyers[b]			
(a) Annual reports	200	20	Vice presidents of finance, advertising managers, treasurers, attorney who works on documents
(b) Proxies; prospectuses	100–200[c]	5	

[a]The title "advertising manager" was used as a proxy for any marketing executive with influence over printer selection.

[b]While many other customer groups included financial report buyers, this segment was important enough to form a special group.

[c]If the firm were to enter this market in a major way, it would need $75,000–$100,000 worth of new equipment, most of it for typesetting. The company presently had no typesetting equipment and relied on outside contractors for that function. This market segment demanded fast delivery. Prospectuses would often be delivered early in the evening with delivery required at the start of the following working day.

THE SITUATION IN AUGUST 1972

Bob Peterson had several courses of action in mind for increasing Gilbert's sales. He was actively trying to recruit salespeople from other printers, but it was always difficult to lure away a good salesperson. Another possibility was to promote an employee with good technical knowledge of printing production, but no sales background, to a sales position. Such a salesperson could certainly service existing accounts, freeing more experienced salespeople to call on potential new accounts.

The success of his son, Dick, had led Mr. Peterson to consider recruiting a salesperson from an M.B.A. program. He was confident that such a person would have the talent, general knowledge of business, and personal drive required of the high-caliber salesperson he was seeking. However, he was still unsure how to select a person who had the particular qualities that would make a good print salesperson. Mr. Peterson knew there was a considerable element of chance involved in hiring an unproven salesperson. Also, he wondered what it would take to attract and motivate a high-caliber M.B.A. to a career in printing sales. He thought that the monetary incentive was a strong lure to potential printing salespeople and that the broad range of customers should interest and challenge an M.B.A. graduate.

Mr. Peterson had compiled some data on potential customers (see Exhibit 6). He wanted to have a new salesperson to call on these customers. He knew that some printing companies had succeeded by hiring persons with knowledge of certain customer groups and then training them to sell to those customers. But any training effort would have to take time away from present sales efforts and could cause a net loss to the company, especially in the short run.

Mr. Peterson believed that the sales plateau of the Gilbert Printing Company would result in decreases in profit as costs in general rose faster than revenues. He wanted a plan to increase the sales in the short run and to build a foundation for longer-term growth at a good profit level.

CASE INDEX

SUBJECT INDEX

577